Business Research Methods and Statistics Using SPSS

Business Research Methods and Statistics Using SPSS

Robert B. Burns and Richard A. Burns

Los Angeles • London • New Delhi • Singapore • Washington DC

SAGE Publications Ltd
1 Oliver's Yard
55 City Road
London EC1Y 1SP

SAGE Publications Inc.
2455 Teller Road
Thousand Oaks, California 91320

SAGE Publications India Pvt Ltd
B 1/I 1 Mohan Cooperative Industrial Area
Mathura Road
New Delhi 110 044

SAGE Publications Asia-Pacific Pte Ltd
33 Pekin Street #02-01
Far East Square
Singapore 048763

Library of Congress Control Number: 2008920625

British Library Cataloguing in Publication data

A catalogue record for this book is available from the British Library

ISBN 978-1-4129-4529-5
ISBN 978-1-4129-4530-1 (pbk)

Typeset by **Keyword Group Ltd**
Printed in Great Britain by TJ International Ltd, Padstow, Cornwall
Printed on paper from sustainable resources

Mixed Sources
Product group from well-managed
forests and other controlled sources
www.fsc.org Cert no. SGS-COC-2482
© 1996 Forest Stewardship Council

Contents

Preface

This text aims to enable students to:

- understand the importance and application of statistics and research in the business world;
- design effective research studies;
- interpret statistical results;
- use statistical information meaningfully;
- use a statistical package on a computer.

We have set ourselves the daunting task of writing about statistics and research methods for those studying statistics and research methods on business courses at degree and diploma levels. Most students believe they have trouble coping with numbers. So the book is addressed predominantly to non-mathematicians who do not consider themselves to be mathematically minded. These people will constitute part of the next generation of managers and executives, and thus the health of the organizations for whom they will work and carry responsibility will benefit from studying this book.

What business persons need

Our experience as teachers of research methods and statistics has taught us that business people need:

- Reassurance that they are not being 'blinded by science' or bamboozled by the number providers.
- The ability to judge the validity, reliability and true worth of the data provided to them and, if necessary, to be able to challenge the data and the way they have been displayed, summarized and statistically manipulated.
- Sufficient understanding of the basic principles of data collection and processing and some working knowledge of the more important quantitative techniques in common use, including their uses and limitations.

- Enough knowledge to be able to formulate problems and to discriminate between and select the most appropriate techniques for finding the solution to a given problem.
- The confidence to take decisions and to act on the basis of the data provided.

We are all receivers and users of other people's data. Numbers are all-pervasive in our lives, as business people, as consumers, as voters for political parties and as readers, listeners and viewers of the media. We have to live, work and survive in an increasingly complex world, force-fed on a diet of often incomprehensible, indigestible and, frequently, spurious statistical gobbets from the computer kitchens of government, stock exchanges, banks, market research organizations, and professional and educational institutions. As business people, we are frequently called upon to 'do something' with the figures, to regurgitate them for other people's use, probably in a different form, write a report, give an oral presentation, and make decisions based on them. We are often required to produce data of our own to submit to others (e.g. tax returns, sales analyses and forecasts, membership statistics, consumer surveys and the like).

With a minimum of mathematical and statistical knowledge, most people can reduce the data to more manageable proportions and make their own valid interpretation. A few simple statistical techniques and test procedures can be applied by most business people to the numbers they are normally presented with; all you need is to know enough about a particular technique or mathematical tool to be able to judge its value and validity in a particular situation and what significance to attach to the figures presented to you. What can be done with the information? Is it actionable? What conclusions can safely be drawn from it? How reliable and valid is it?

You do not need any special aptitudes, mathematical or otherwise, to get to grips with the contents of this book. All you need is (a) the ability to add, subtract, multiply, divide, square and square root, and (b) the willingness to work through the book with an open mind. Being fairly simple fellows, mathematically speaking, the authors are not clever enough to engage in other than the most simple arguments and explanations which they themselves can understand. This should benefit the reader.

The goals of the book

In writing this book, we have tried to achieve several important goals:

1 We wanted a book that really explained statistical concepts and their application in the field of business rather than one focusing on the mathematics and derivation of formulas. What is important is not that the students learn to calculate a correlation coefficient with a large set of numbers, because now computers can do that for them. But what is really important is that students become aware of the underlying logic of the procedure. This text emphasizes the logic behind statistical operations rather than the mathematics. In practice, nearly all the procedures described in the text are inevitably performed by computer, so learning to use them in practice requires learning to perform them by computer and this is provided for in the text. There is comprehensive introduction to data analysis and interpretation using the SPSS (Statistical Package for the Social Sciences)

statistical programme with numerous screen shots and 32 SPSS data files for teaching purposes and student activities.

2 The second goal was to write a book that is rooted in the business world. We carefully chose problems and examples from business situations, covering marketing research, finance, management, transportation, tourism, accounting, public administration, economics, production, advertising, and other areas.

3 The third goal was to present a wide range of statistical topics and write as complete a book as is possible at an introductory level. We have included several important topics that are not usually included by other authors, such as *meta-analysis, the role of effect size and power as alternatives to significance testing, factor analysis, logistic regression, cluster analysis* and *discriminant analysis*. Some of these chapters form extension material on the text's associated website www.sagepub.co.uk/burns

In summary, the emphasis throughout the text is on the common-sense rationale underlying the research methods and statistical methods described. Mathematical explanatory techniques are reduced to an absolute minimum. This book is designed to help you get the feel of statistics and some research methods used in business activities.

Organization of the book

We have tried to maintain a fairly thematic approach to development of this text since there is a logical structure to understanding statistics and research methods. A good deal of material in this book gets carried over from one chapter into another, as many procedures are based on procedures and concepts introduced earlier.

In Part 1 introductory chapters explain the need for knowledge of statistics and research methods in the business field, and introduce some basic concepts such as ethical considerations, literature reviewing and developing a research study.

The material moves into Part 2, which focuses on an introduction to SPSS, data presentation, descriptive statistics, and some very basic concepts of probability theory – the basis for statistical inference. The student is provided with a detailed explanation of normal distribution. Once the student is comfortable with probability and normal distribution, the ideas of sampling and standard error are carefully explained, followed by estimation and confidence intervals with a very thorough discussion of statistical hypothesis testing.

Then we show in Part 3 how to use some standard statistical tests for testing hypotheses of difference and relationships, both parametric and non-parametric, as well as introducing the concept of regression and prediction. Factor analysis completes this introduction to statistical analysis. All these techniques are illustrated with SPSS examples.

In Part 4 we tackle the major methods deployed to obtain data used by managers to analyze such issues as consumer behaviour, advertising effectiveness, employee motivation, namely survey research, interviewing and attitude questionnaire techniques.

To conclude the text in Part 5 we present the culmination of conducting research, that is how to report and present the research we have designed and analyzed.

Part 6 on the website deals with more advanced extension topics such as meta-analysis, cluster analysis, discriment analysis and logistic regression.

Questions and activities in the text and on the website
www.sagepub.co.uk/burns

Students are strongly encouraged to undertake the questions and activities within each chapter and on the associated website. These activities and exercises vary in nature, as some are of the multiple choice mode, while others involve group discussion. Some activities require the student to use the SPSS programme to practise some of the analytic techniques taught. The chapter material completely prepares the student for these kinds of exercises and test questions. The reader's knowledge of the topic under discussion should be increased by completion of these exercises.

Answers to the multiple choice and other activities where necessary are provided on the website, where the teacher will also find Powerpoint slides to support their lectures on the chapter topics. The teacher should go through the questions and activities with the students after they have completed them. This will really ensure an even firmer grasp of the material.

To the student

Why learn research methods and statistics?
(Besides it being required)

Understanding statistics is crucial to being able to understand the results of investigations and studies, carry out simple investigations and surveys, making sense of it for yourself and others so that you can prepare readable reports or summaries. In most of the social and behavioural sciences, nearly every course you will take emphasizes the results of research studies, and these are usually expressed in statistical terms. If you do not understand the basic logic of statistics – if you cannot make sense of the jargon, the tables, and the graphs that are at the heart of any research report or business report – your reading, understanding and your ability to make a clear and succinct presentation for others will be impossible – or superficial at best.

On entering the business world you will be amazed to discover that many of your daily tasks will involve assembling numbers or data such as sales or production figures, writing reports on the data that provide some degree of analysis about what the information implies for the organization. This text gives you a solid foundation in the basic elements of statistics you need for collecting, displaying and analyzing data as part of any research activity in an organization. It may not be called research in your organization; it will simply be a task you have been asked to do, such as provide a report on the characteristics of persons (age, sex, income level, etc.) forming the client base of the company you work for, or an analysis of a recent market research on a proposed new product, or a projection of sales based on different levels of advertising expenditure. Further, by mastering the basic logic and ways of thinking about statistics, you will be unusually well prepared to take on more advanced courses, which focus far more on the nitty-gritty of analyzing research results.

Understanding statistics develops your analytic and critical thinking. Of all the courses you are likely to take in the social and behavioural sciences, this course will probably do the most to help you learn to think precisely, to evaluate information, and to apply logical analysis at a very high level, rather than employing subjective impressions, stereotypic thinking and unfounded assertions as the basis of your daily decision making.

The few mathematical symbols introduced are simple and explained. As you thumb through this book and compare it with other basic business statistics textbooks, you will notice a minimum of mathematical notation. Thus there is no need to feel intimidated or wrongly believe you are not intellectually capable of understanding the concepts and content of the text.

How to gain the most from this course

There are six things we can advise:

1   Keep your attention on the concepts. When you read a section of a chapter, your attention should be on grasping the principles. When working through the activities and questions, think about why you are doing each step. If you simply try to memorize how to come up with the right answer, you will have learned very little of use in your future studies.
2   Understand each concept and key idea before you go on to the next chapter. Statistics is cumulative. Each new concept is built on the last one. Even within a chapter, if you have read a section and you do not understand it – **stop. Reread it, rethink it, ask for help**. Do whatever you need to do to grasp it.

    Having to read the material in this book over and over does not mean that you are stupid. Most students have to read each chapter several times. Each reading is much slower than reading an ordinary textbook. This academic area has to be pored over with clear, calm attention for it to sink in. Allow plenty of time for this kind of reading and rereading.
3   Keep up with the work of the class. Again, statistics is cumulative. If you fall behind in your reading or miss lectures, the lectures you then attend can be almost meaningless. It will get harder and harder to catch up.
4   Study especially intensely in the first half of the course. It is particularly important to master the material thoroughly at the start of the course since everything else in statistics is built on what you learn at the start. Yet the beginning of the semester is often when students study least seriously. If you have mastered the first part of the course, the second half will be easier than the first. If you have not mastered the first half, the second half will be far more difficult.
5   It is essential that you undertake the questions and activities in each chapter and associated website to consolidate your learning. The website is at www.sagepub.co.uk/burns
6   Help each other. There is no better way to solidify and deepen your understanding than to try to explain it to someone who is having a harder time. (Of course, this explaining has to be with patience and respect.) For those of you who are having a harder time, there is no better way to work through the difficult parts than by learning from another student who has just learned it and discussing it with them. Form study teams with one to three other students. It is best if your team includes some members who expect this material to come easy and some who do not. Those who learn statistics easily will really get the very most from helping others who have to struggle with it – the latter will tax the former's supposed understanding enormously. It is amazing how it aids understanding to try and explain a difficult point to someone else in simple terms. Pick team mates who live near you so that it is easy for you to get together. Meet often – between each class, if possible.

The role of the computer

As computers and software packages for statistical analysis are so prevalent, it has become more important than ever before to teach business practitioners and others the correct use of statistics. Using computing power should go hand-in-hand with – not replace – statistical reasoning, the correct selection of a statistical test, careful evaluation of the underlying assumptions, and cautious interpretation of the printout of results. This book stresses these aspects.

The book therefore shows how to use a computer program to undertake most of the statistical tests discussed and how to interpret the printout of results. There are many widely used packages of statistical software available today. Almost any one of them will be able to perform all the operations discussed in this text. In particular, we have given examples of how to use SPSS for the statistical procedures as this program is perhaps the one in most common use. Each chapter where data analysis is conducted contains a section on the use of the computer for that particular test.

We offer you our best wishes with this course and in your future careers.

Dr Robert Burns Dr Richard Burns
Buderim, Queensland, *Canberra,*
Australia *Australia*

Part 1
General Orientation to Research in Business and Management

Chapter 1
Research, Statistics and Business Decisions

'If there is a 50-50 chance that something can go wrong then 9 times out of 10 it will'
(Source unknown – a classic Murphy's Law)

'39% of unemployed persons wear glasses; 80% of employed persons wear glasses; therefore working stuffs up your eyesight'
(Source unknown)

'Gambling is a tax on those who know nothing about statistics'
(Source unknown)

Content list

By the end of this chapter you will understand:

1 Why knowledge of statistics and research is useful in the world of business.
2 How knowledge of research and statistics would help reduce uncertainty in business decisions.
3 The relative merits of in-house and external consultants.
4 The different roles of descriptive and inferential statistics.
5 The distinction between basic and applied research.

Introduction

This chapter will provide a general introduction about how statistics and research methods can help to reduce uncertainty and lead to more effective planning and decision making for businesses and their managers.

The relevance of research and statistics to management and business

As our world grows in complexity, it becomes increasingly difficult to make informed and intelligent decisions. Often decisions essential to our well-being must be made with less than perfect knowledge and in the presence of considerable uncertainty. We are continually pressured by economic problems such as inflation, cumbersome taxation systems, fluctuations in exchange and interest rates, excessive demands for scarce and costly power and water resources, and swings in the business cycle. Management structures, employment conditions, and advertising issues continually present changing business environments. Our entire social and economic fabric is threatened by environmental issues such as climate change, pollution, power and water resource problems, by burdensome public and private debt, unemployment, the need for two-income families, unpredictable government interference, and global effects that swamp non-involved countries.

No responsible corporate executive would consider making important business decisions and recommending policy changes without first consulting others and trying to obtain and interpret the facts or data. Sometimes these facts can inform; at other times, they may mislead or deceive. Business people who are illiterate in statistics face a two-edged sword – they are deprived of a powerful tool that may provide a competitive edge, and they are unable to distinguish intelligently between useful and useless statistical information.

> *Statistics and research methods can help to reduce uncertainty and lead to more effective planning and decision making in the business and management fields.*

Let us look at a few specific examples and see how intelligent business decision makers research for relevant data and apply statistics to plan, control, and reduce the uncertainty involved in business decisions.

- An investment advisor calculates the rate of return on a specific kind of investment for the most recent year. He compares this with rates obtained on the same investment in other years. He also compares this rate with the current rates on other investments in order to provide reliable advice.
- The personnel manager uses data on the proportion of handicapped persons in various job categories to determine compliance with affirmative action legislation and what recommendations need to be made to the CEO on this issue.
- The national marketing manager of a large supermarket chain locates and reviews statistics on income distribution in each region of the country to set prices for a new product. Based on obtained data, decisions may be made to set prices differently for different areas.
- An ammunition manufacturer must be sure that there are very few dud rounds. The only perfect indication would be to fire every round but this is not very practical. What percentage should be fired in order to have a very good indication of what the remainder are like? How safe is this indication? An indication will not be perfect – only probable – so what level of probability is acceptable.
- Given the increasing demand for water supplies in the country over the last 10 years what is the best estimate the National Water Board can make of the likely demand over the next 20 years so that new supplies can be planned.
- The Community National Credit Union Bank has learned from hard experience that there are four factors that largely determine whether a borrower will repay their personal loan on time or default. These factors are (1) the number of years at the present address, (2) the number of years in the present job, (3) whether the applicant owns their own home, and (4) whether the applicant has a cheque or savings account with the bank. It has computer files of information on applicants and on how each granted loan turned out. John Smith applies for a loan. He has lived at his present address four years, owns his own home, has been in his current job only three months, and is not a Community National Bank depositor. Using statistics, the bank can calculate the probability of John repaying his loan on time if it is granted.

All of the above examples have one thing in common. Facilitating decision making under uncertainty is the main purpose of the use of research and statistics. Through the application of precise statistical procedures, it is possible to predict the future with some degree of accuracy. Any business firm faced with competitive pressures can benefit considerably from the ability to anticipate business conditions before they occur. If a firm knows what its sales are going to be at some time in the near future, management can devise more accurate and effective plans regarding current operations and take important decisions regarding inventory levels, raw material orders, employment requirements, and virtually every other aspect of business operations.

What is research?

We have a stereotype of research being something conducted by people in white coats in science labs. But research can be carried out in many contexts. Research is a process of systematic enquiry or investigation into a specific problem or issue that leads to new or improved knowledge. There are many approaches and methods that this systematic investigation can follow from the stereotypic scientific quantitative, objective, replicable experimentation based on hypothesis testing to more subjective and qualitative face-to-face depth interviewing and participant observation modes. But whatever the general approach or method of investigation in the business field, the aim is to enable managers and consultants to deliver informed decisions that generate successful outcomes. A range of different research approaches and methods are briefly introduced in Chapter Two, although succeeding chapters give emphatic focus to the quantitative approach to business research

What are statistics?

Most people associate the term statistics with masses of numbers or, perhaps, with the tables and graphs that display them and with the averages or similar measures that summarize them. This mental image is reinforced daily by the abundance of numerical and graphical information in newspapers, magazines, and on television screens: on the prices of bonds and stocks, on the performance of businesses and sports teams, on the movements of exchange rates and commodity futures, on the rates of unemployment, on the incidence of poverty and disease, on accidents, crime, water supply, and climate change – the list goes on. It is not surprising, therefore, that people imagine statistics as being concerned with the collection and presentation of numbers.

In reality, the term statistics has four meanings. Depending on context it can imply:

(a)   the actual data;
(b)   characteristics of data such as an average or percentage;
(c)   techniques for the collection, presentation, analysis and interpretation of data for decision making; and
(d)   the science of developing and applying such techniques.

All these meanings are repeatedly illustrated in this text. But overall, the term statistics is a guide to the unknown and best defined **as a branch of mathematics that is concerned with facilitating wise decision making in the face of uncertainty.** It develops and utilizes techniques for the careful collection and effective presentation of data to highlight patterns otherwise buried in unorganized data (**descriptive statistics**), and proper analysis of such numerical information (**inferential or analytic statistics**).

Only in a world of standardization and cloning in which everything is the same – a bit like *'The Stepford Wives'* – you would not need any statistics. Unfortunately, our world is far more complex than this. You see, if nothing varies, then everything that is to be known about people could be obtained from information from a single person. Generalizing would be perfect since what is true of Jane Smith is true of everyone else. Fortunately, we are not all cloned – yet! Variability is an essential characteristic of life and the world in which we exist. This sheer quantity of variability has to be tamed when trying to make statements about the real world. **Statistics helps us to make sense out of variability.**

Statistics is concerned with the collection, organization, presentation, analysis, and interpretation of data. It enables data to be parsimoniously described and more precisely and objectively analyzed than by merely 'eyeballing the columns', or following a hunch. But statistical results should not be equated with the final conclusions of scientific judgement.

Even with a skilfully designed study and the judicious use of statistical methods, the wise decision maker must weigh other factors, such as legal constraints, ethical issues, political realities and costs, with the statistical results in reaching a conclusion and making a wise management decision.

In sum, statistics and research methods are used to conduct systematic investigations to find answers to problems.

Descriptive and inferential statistics

There are two primary types of statistics as applied to business, each with their own purpose. Statistical techniques which are used to describe data are referred to as **descriptive statistics** which summarize sets of numerical data such as production levels, sales by district, and years of employment.

The term descriptive statistics relates to:

- the process of collecting, organizing, and presenting data in some manner that quickly and easily describes these data; and
- the numbers that reduce a mass of data to one or two relatively easily understood values, such as averages, percentages and counts.

Given a mass of numerical data to interpret, it is first necessary to organize and summarize these data in such a way that they can be meaningfully understood and communicated. A computer printout of all the employees of a large organization providing a host of details such as age, sex, length of service, current salary, etc. is unwieldy and with patterns difficult to discern. However, reducing the data to such as average salary for males and females, percentages of employees in different age groups or salary levels, makes the data more understandable. Counts and percentages, such as the count of the number of people now residing in Mexico City and the percentage of those people who possess a mobile phone in the People's Republic of China, the average age of persons making insurance claims for car accident repairs, and the average weekly household expenditure for retired persons are examples of descriptive statistics. Other descriptive statistics involve the collection of data on exports, imports, incomes, and expenditures in order to facilitate the collection of taxes. A look at present-day government publications suggests that the tradition of descriptive statistics aiding government has certainly not died out.

The principles of descriptive statistics give us a pathway for getting from raw scores to a usable summary of data.

Presenting descriptive statistics

Frequently the most useful first step in understanding what patterns and trends exist is to arrange the data in some logical order. The effective presentation of data can lead a production engineer to discover the pattern behind recent breakdowns of motors produced by a firm, or can help a sales manager unravel variations in sales by month, district and type of goods. Output from various assembly lines on a daily basis could be displayed in a table in which the assembly lines were listed across and days down. Inspection of the data can then provide information about the general pattern of the performance of the particular group. Daily changes and variations in performance between different assembly lines can be detected. In particular, visual presentation with graphs and charts add to the discerning of patterns. In our example, we might wish to know whether or not there is a relationship between performance and day (does performance decrease on the last working day of the week?) using a histogram. We will consider descriptive statistics and methods of presentation in Chapter 7.

> **Descriptive statistics** *involves the collection, presentation, summarization and description of data so the data can be more easily comprehended.*

Inferential statistics

The second principal use of statistics in business is to allow the manager **to draw better inferences** as to whether a phenomenon such as work satisfaction, or relative demand among competing brands, measured in a sample, can be legitimately generalized to a population. This second use of statistical methods is usually termed **inferential statistics**.

Information about particular small groups is often of little intrinsic interest. If you want to draw meaningful conclusions with implications extending beyond your limited data, statistical inference is the way to do it. The business enterprise is often more interested in determining if the findings from a small finite group are likely to be true for larger groups or for all the potential observations that could be made, as in the case of marketing and advertising studies. For example:

- In marketing research, we are often interested in the relationship between advertising and sales. A sample of randomly chosen sales and advertising figures for a company over a given period may be of some interest in itself, but the information in it is much more useful if it leads to implications and inferences about the underlying process – the general relationship between the firm's level of advertising and the resulting level of sales. An understanding of the true relationship between advertising and sales derived from our sample data would allow us to predict sales for any level of advertising and thus to set advertising at a level that maximizes profits. (This involves the concept of regression – see Chapter 16).
- A pharmaceutical manufacturer interested in marketing a new drug may be required by law to demonstrate conclusively that the drug does not cause serious side effects. The results of tests of the drug on a random sample of a defined population may then be used in a statistical inference about the effects of the drug on that entire population who may use the drug if it is introduced.
- A bank may be interested in assessing the potential use and popularity of banking from home using computer links. The system can be tried on a randomly chosen sample of bank customers. The conclusions of the study could then be generalized by statistical inference to the entire population of the bank's customers.

- A quality control engineer at a plant making brake discs for cars needs to be sure that no more than 3% of the discs produced are defective. The engineer will routinely collect random samples of discs and check their quality. Based on the random samples, the engineer may then draw a conclusion about the proportion of defective items in the entire population of discs.

These are just a few examples illustrating the use of statistical inference in business situations.

> **Inferential statistics** *are used to infer or predict population parameters from sample measures.*

The principles of inferential statistics provide a bridge across the chasm that looms between having data about a sample and having a description of a population. Crossing that chasm to tender a description of a population based on an observation of a sample drawn from that population is called *generalization*.

Inferential statistics comprise the middle section of this book.

Who should conduct research into business organizations and activities?

There are two major options here: in-house versus the external consultant.

1 **In-house.** The research can be conducted in-house by a member of, or team from, the organization. The advantages of in-house research include existing in-depth knowledge of the organization so the researcher can hit the ground running. Provided the in-house researcher is personable and able to build positive relations, they can gain collaboration faster than an external consultant can as trust already exists. Conversely, because the internal researcher is known, employees may be wary of giving too much information or speaking the truth if it is unpalatable. Pressure can also be brought to bear on an in-house researcher by more senior staff if they want a particular view/proposal promoted. However, the study can be conducted at minimal cost as the person is already an employee, and since an in-house researcher will remain in the organization, they are on hand to prompt follow-up on the recommendations and findings preventing the report simply being filed.

2 **External consultant.** The hire of outside expertise (university academic or business expert from a specialist consultant company) can be costly but if there is no one capable in the company then it is the only way. However, it can take an outsider some time to get to grips with the company's organization, culture and gain employee trust, but the external consultant can be more objective and subject to less bias and pressure than an internal researcher. Once the consultant has finished and left, there is unfortunately less chance of implementation or follow-up.

Business research is the objective and systematic process of obtaining, recording, analysing and interpreting data to discover new information or relationships or expand existing knowledge to remove uncertainty for business decision making.

Basic and applied research

A way of classifying research is based on the reasons for undertaking the research: either to extend knowledge, or to solve practical problems.

Basic research

This type of research aims to extend the frontiers of knowledge. It may lack practical application in the short term. It is often concerned with developing a theory, further confirmation of an existing theory, providing more knowledge about an existing concept, or developing new perspectives. For example, does the amount of time available to reach a decision affect the balance between task oriented behaviours and socio-emotional behaviours in a group?

Applied research

This focuses on solving a particular business problem. This could be as mundane as *'is mail drop advertising more cost effective than newspaper advertising for pizza sales'*, or *'what sort of offers stimulate demand for our product?'*

Most business research tends to fall into the applied category. Basic research is associated more with longer-term university projects.

It must be emphasized that research is only a tool to assist management to make better decisions. It will rarely eliminate all uncertainty but it will certainly reduce it and form a vital input into the decision-making process.

What you have learned from this chapter

Statistics serve the useful purpose of reducing uncertainty in decision making and facilitates the use of systematic research in the business world to improve the effectiveness and efficiency of business. Statistical procedures help us reduce vast quantities of information to manageable form and to reach reasonable decisions with limited information.

Descriptive statistics summarize data, as you will discover from Chapter 7, while inferential statistics enable researchers to reach an understanding of characteristics of the population from sample statistics without having to measure the whole population – an issue more comprehensively explained in Chapter 9.

There are advantages and disadvantages associated with who conducts business research. Most business research is applied research rather than basic research.

Review questions (Check answers where necessary by referring back to the material above)

Qu. 1.1
Which of the following best describes what descriptive statistics does:

(a) explain what is

(b) interpret economic policy

(c) evaluate what is

(d) find out what is

Qu. 1.2
Compare the main purposes and uses of descriptive and inferential statistics.

Qu. 1.3
Discuss in groups and comment on the statement that if managers learned how to conduct research by taking a course such as this there would no need to seek outside consultant help to solve their problems.

Qu. 1.4
In class discuss and compose a list of some situations or issues where you believe research will help you as a manager make more effective decisions.

Now visit the Web page for Chapter 1 and attempt the additional questions, problems and activities located there.

Chapter 2
Contrasting Philosophies and Approaches to Research

'I didn't think; I experimented'

(Wilhelm Roentgen)

'Why think? Try an experiment'

(John Hunter, in a letter to Edward Jenner)

'Qualitative research reaches the parts quantitative research cannot'

(Source unknown)

'Experimental results must be reproducible; they should fail in the same way each time'

(Source unknown)

Content list

> ## By the end of this chapter you will understand:
>
> 1 The characteristics of and differences between the positivist and interpretivist philosophies or paradigms that underlie different approaches to research.
> 2 The characteristics of and differences between the scientific objective quantitative method of research that stems from the positivist paradigm and those of the more subjective qualitative approach that is supported by the naturalistic interpretivist paradigm.
> 3 The differences between inductive and deductive approaches to research.
> 4 How the reaction of subjects can affect the outcomes of research.

The philosophy of research methods and statistics

Introduction

This chapter introduces two major approaches to research, each of which is based on a particular philosophy or world view and demonstrates that while they seem to be in direct opposition to each other, they are each vital parts of the research cycle sequence.

Two paradigms

A paradigm is a particular way of viewing the world, a framework of assumptions that reflect a shared set of philosophic beliefs about the world which places strict guidelines and principles on how research should be conducted. The two major paradigms are the positivist paradigm (called positivism) and the interpretivist (or constructivist) paradigm (called interpretivism). In some texts this latter paradigm may also be referred to as a naturalistic or phenomenological paradigm.

Research in the field of business and commerce, like research in other subjects, has generally followed the traditional objective scientific method, particularly in aspects such as quality control and productivity management, index numbers and trend analysis, consumer attitudes, structured interviewing, psychometric approaches to employee selection, etc. Since the middle of the 20th century, however, strong moves towards more qualitative, naturalistic and subjective research methodologies, employing techniques such as participant observation, case study, unstructured individual depth interviews and focus groups when studying human activities and events, has left research divided between two seemingly competing and diametrically opposed research methods:

- **the scientific quantitative research method** reflects the **positivist paradigm**, and
- **the qualitative research method** reflects the **interpretivist paradigm** (also sometimes referred to as the **constructivist paradigm**).

The main elements of the **positivist paradigm** include:

- An objective world with universal laws and causality.
- Value free contexts.
- The use of precise, objective measures usually associated with quantitative data.
- Researcher remains separate from the subjects.
- Research is rigorous, linear and rigid, based on hypothesis testing.
- Methods include experimental studies, re-analysis of secondary data, structured questionnaires, structured interviews.
- The implication of a scientific research method with deductive reasoning.

The main elements of the **interpretivist paradigm** include:

- A subjective world where people experience physical and social reality in different ways.
- A socially constructed reality with subjective evaluation and meaningfulness of experience for the individual.
- Researcher becomes fully involved with individual subjects.
- Explicit values.
- Flexible research process which flows from the material provided by participants.
- Methods include ethnography, participant observation, focus groups, depth interviews – generally inductive.

Thus, research methods are underlain by two major paradigms. In a common-sense example, the interpretist paradigm claims the same game of football can be viewed and interpreted by different people in different ways: the referee has a particular interpretation of what has occurred, the players may see it differently from the referee, and the spectators always interpret events and actions within the game differently from the referee. Yet, from the perspective of the positivist paradigm, it is the same game, on the same pitch between the same two teams with an objective sequence of actions from start to finish such as Brown kicks the ball which is caught by Smith who then …

There exists a third research paradigm not covered in this text that of **critical science**, or the critical approach, which explores the social world, critiques it, and seeks to empower the individual to overcome problems in their social world. It enables people to understand how society functions and methods by which unsatisfactory aspects can be changed.

The quantitative scientific research method

The positivist paradigm assumes that the environment or the social reality in which we all operate is objective and external to the individual. Quantitative scientific research methods are employed to establish general laws or principles through rigorously controlled experimentation. Employee selection techniques used by human resource personnel involve standardized tests such as aptitude tests; production and sales managers are vitally interested in trend analysis and business forecasting; economists engage in the calculation of index numbers to chart changes in the costs of goods and the effects of price rises on demand, while the organizational psychologist is interested in objective measurements of stress levels and absenteeism in the work force as a response to real and objective changing technologies.

Scientists hold that data must yield proof or strong confirmation, in probability terms, of a theory or hypothesis in a research setting, and ultimately aim to formulate laws to account for the happenings in the world around them, thus providing a firm basis for prediction and control. The assumptions built into this scientific approach incorporate objectivity, reliability, and generalizability. 'Truth' within this paradigm tends to be fixed, reflecting a causal and factual view of reality.

Science is not just a body of knowledge but a logic of inquiry, for generating, replenishing and correcting knowledge. So, ideas, beliefs, opinions, and personal judgements must be tested and not simply accepted. The scientific method has one essential characteristic over ideas, opinions and personal beliefs, and that is self-correction, by determining the facts, measuring accurately and conducting experiments in controlled situations. **Positivism** ensures that the methods and principles of science are applied to the study of human behaviour and human events.

Human beings unfortunately function on a folklore of unjustified assumptions about behaviour and woolly armchair philosophizing, with many of our everyday observations and opinions distorted through subjective bias and prejudice. Managers, employees, accountants, lawyers, human resource officers, public servants, politicians and media celebrities often are guilty of making unjustified generalized assertions on important issues. For example:

- 'Female employees always have more days of absence than male employees'.
- 'Compulsory conscription for all unemployed young people would develop their character and national spirit'.
- 'Immigrant labour causes a reduction in wage rates'.
- 'All managers are self-seeking autocrats at heart'.
- 'All trade union leaders are covert communists', and so on.

Such claims, believed and accepted, even though unsubstantiated, can have important consequences at work, home and in daily living. Those who can evaluate such claims through research and statistical analysis of evidence are better able to distinguish valid and reliable evidence from current fads and old wives' tales. Thus, the difference between the layperson and the 'scientific' business researcher is that the latter employs objective, systematic research with statistical analysis of data in order to discern **what actually is the case** rather than a patchwork of likes and dislikes, rules of thumb, analogy and prejudice, and half-truths.

Characteristics of the scientific research method

The scientific method has four important and specific characteristics. These are: **control, operational definitions, replication** and **hypothesis testing.**

Control

Perhaps the single most important element in scientific methodology, control enables the investigator to identify the causes of their observations. To answer questions in business and commerce, such as 'what new skills do my employees need?', 'what variations in stock do I need to meet changing demands of summer and winter?', 'what are the personal characteristics of effective sales people and can they be developed in others?', and 'which type of advertising is most effective for my products?', we have to eliminate the simultaneous influence of many environmental and human variables to isolate the cause of an effect. Controlled inquiry is an absolutely essential process because without it the cause of an effect cannot be isolated, and the observed effect could be due to any one or combination of uncontrolled variables.

Here is an example:

> In order to test the hypothesis that shoppers prefer tins of peas in green labelling rather than blue, yellow or red, tins of peas in all these colours must be equally available in the same shelf area, be the same can size, shape, brand and price, etc. If any of these other variables differ then variations in choice may be due to these other variations rather than colour, e.g. if blue tins are cheaper than green tins this may bias the choice. Of course, this could be another investigation: i.e. exploring which is the most important factor, the can colour, the labelling, or the price, but the design of the study would exert control of other variables so that it could be determined on which basis the purchasing decision was made.

Operational definitions

Operational definition means that variables are defined in a way that they can be measured. This eliminates confusion in meaning and communication. Consider the statement, *'Anxiety causes employees to make mistakes in their work'*. One might ask, 'What is meant by *"anxiety"* and by *"making mistakes"*?' Stating that anxiety refers to being tense, worried or some other such term only adds to the confusion. However, stating that anxiety refers to a score over a stated criterion level on an anxiety scale enables others to realize what you mean by anxiety, and how you would actually classify each employee into the 'anxious' or 'not anxious' categories. Similarly, you need to define the particular categories of 'mistakes' or 'errors' you are concerned with. In this manner, ambiguity is minimized. Again, in a study of industrial accidents, accident prone might be defined by the number of industrial accidents a person has suffered in the last year which required an official report to management, while social class in most studies is defined by occupation. Operational definitions will be considered again in Chapter 10 when we discuss hypothesis testing.

Replication

Only if the results of a study can be found again if other researchers repeat the study can we be fairly certain that our obtained results are reliable. That science has such a requirement is quite obvious, since it is attempting to obtain knowledge about the world.

If observations are not repeatable, with results that vary considerably, then our descriptions and explanations are unreliable – how do we know which one is correct?

Hypothesis testing

The layperson uses theories and concepts in a loose fashion, often accepting ludicrous explanations for human behaviour. For instance, *'Being ill is a punishment for being sinful'* or *'current economic problems are the result of the manipulation of free trade practices'*. On the other hand, the scientific researcher would systematically create a hypothesis with very specific operational variables and subject it to empirical testing.

Laypeople may also 'test' their beliefs but usually in a selective fashion, choosing evidence to fit the hypothesis. They may believe that job applicants with long hair will be sloppy in their work. The layperson will verify this belief by noting a single instance, and turn the stereotype into a general rule. Blinded by selective perception, exceptions will fail to be noticed. The more sophisticated researcher, aware of this tendency, will test the relationship systematically. The logic of hypothesis testing will form the focus of Chapter 10.

Limitations of the scientific research method

Humans can think

However, the rigid application of methods of scientific inquiry derived from the philosophy of positivism may only be truly valid for the natural sciences. They are less valid and less easily applied in the human behavioural sciences **due to the ability of humans to reflect on their own behaviour and to seek meaning and purpose in their own and others' behaviour**, i.e. humans can think. Subjects are likely to respond idiosyncratically to elements in their environment as a function of their own past experience and expectations, needs and moods of the moment.

The human environment is complex

Significant problems are faced by the researcher in business and behavioural science as human beings, business conditions and events are far more complex than the inert matter studied in physical sciences. This arises because a huge range of environmental forces impact on the human, with the individual interpreting and responding to these in an active way. Although we might try to determine what colour of packaging appeals to shoppers, some shoppers will always react differently from others because of their past experiences, their own colour preferences, and all sorts of idiosyncratic factors (some males may be colour blind!). We can never predict how a particular shopper will respond although we may develop a good idea how shoppers in general will respond. Similarly, a particular workplace, while physically the same environment for all those working in it, can be interpreted in a variety of ways by each employee. For some it is a boring context, others see it as a source of personal satisfaction as they develop and use increased skills, others perceive it as a focus of comradeship and social life, while many may simply regard it as a source of money to fund other things in their lives. Business research cannot operate in the sort of controlled environment available to the physical scientist with formal laboratory techniques and rigid control of conditions. Too strict experimental laboratory controls would prevent any result being meaningful in the complex real world of human activities.

Ethical considerations

The scientific research method, with its heavy emphasis on objective measurement, control and ignoring of thinking, may denigrate human individuality and exclude notions of choice freedom and personal responsibility. Quantification can become an end in itself rather than a humane endeavour seeking to explore the relationships between behaviour and the context in which it occurs. Behind all the numbers lie human experiences, meanings and personal interpretation of what each interprets 'real' life to be.

The qualitative research method

Studying human behaviour in a qualitative non-experimental way

The interpretivist paradigm on which the qualitative approach to research is based reflects a much lower degree of control over the research context and subjects involved. Its basic assumption is that the world is socially constructed and subjective. Experimentation in the scientific sense is not acceptable since the aim is to study and document authentic behaviour in a real situation, not contrived behaviour in a controlled context. Thus field studies rather than laboratory studies dominate the qualitative approach. Qualitative research stresses the validity of multiple meanings of events with 'reality' not a fixed stable entity but a variable that can only be discerned through an analysis of multiple understandings and meanings held by different persons. For example, qualitative research has made managers realize they must become more sensitive to individual needs and motivations of employees in order to have more productive and satisfied staff.

Every consumer and employee carries around a kitbag of unique experiences, feelings, and beliefs which they bring to bear in research studies. As Epictitus declared in AD 1 *'people are not disturbed by things but by the views which they take of them'*. One apocryphal story recounts how two hat salesmen arriving in an overseas country found everyone wore hats. One returned home immediately perceiving a saturated market. The other stayed, excited by the market size and possibilities for introducing new types of headgear. Effective studies in the business world must take account of human individuality and the interpretation of experience.

Imagine you have recently taken on senior administrative responsibilities and become responsible for improving customer relations and the organizational efficiency of human resources. You are familiar with your company's general objectives for change but you want to optimize the transitions for all involved parties.

In this situation, immediate action – such as announcing a new quality review programme – would directly address the challenges you face but might cause resentment and loss of goodwill from employees and customers. However, more information might help you more effectively meet your professional responsibilities. You might want to learn what systems already work well and better understand what services would be valued by both employees and customers. You might also want to learn about employees' perceptions of their mission and service to identify strategies that could motivate them for change. The information to help you meet these objectives will come primarily from the people involved in your questions and plans – your clients and employees. One can use qualitative research techniques for this purpose, particularly in new situations and environments.

Qualitative research enables researchers to gather and analyze information conveyed through language and behaviour exhibited in natural settings. It captures expressive information not conveyed in quantitative data about perceptions, values, needs, feelings, and motivations that underlie behaviours at an individual level. Qualitative methods are used to learn directly from employees and customers what is important to them, to provide the context necessary to understand quantitative findings, and to identify variables important for future quantitative studies.

Qualitative approaches tend to use thoughtful reflection and analysis of verbal/written content. With specific questions in mind, qualitative researchers immerse themselves in an environment to discover the meanings, conventions of behaviour, and ways of thinking important to individuals of a group as they emerge in unrehearsed encounters.

The essential task is to observe study subjects in their natural settings. They can do so as silent background observers or as 'participant-observers' who ask questions as they accompany study subjects in their activities. In either role they collect data in both unstructured and structured ways. They can write spontaneous 'field' notes that detail what they see and hear, or organize their observations around categories, checklists, or rating scales that they bring to the setting. Beyond observing, they conduct in-depth open-ended interviews and learn from well-positioned individuals who can provide useful information (also called 'key informant' interviews); to understand experiences especially important to shaping perceptions and decisions ('critical incident' reports); or to generate new information from groups of employees and customers in focus groups. Audiotaping or videotaping these interactions helps guarantee that expressive data are captured accurately and completely as they emerge. Taping also permits the researcher to carry the data to more controlled settings, where they can be transcribed, coded, analyzed for important themes and meanings, and verified using trained evaluators (aided by computer software where appropriate). The use of more than one evaluator helps ensure the reliability of qualitative data, as does a detailed accounting of how a study analysis is performed. Researchers can be reasonably assured of the validity of their findings by collecting data from independent sources, presenting preliminary findings to study participants for their feedback, and fully examining unusual information. These strategies are likely to become increasingly standardized as consensus emerges around the need for greater methodological rigour in qualitative research, and the methods are appropriate for practical situations in which a fuller understanding of behaviour, the meanings and contexts of events, and the influence of values on choices might be useful for managers and businesses.

So, while science provides an approach that offers reliable and valid conclusions when dealing with humans, the answer to every problem cannot always be found through the application of standardized tests and the use of experimental and control groups.

Limitations of the qualitative research method

Problems of generalization

Qualitative studies are valuable tools to understand and describe the world of human experience. However, this world is often dismissed as 'subjective' and regarded with suspicion by scientifically inclined researchers. It is difficult to apply conventional standards of reliability and validity, yet subjective qualitative studies have the redeeming quality in the depth to which explorations are conducted and descriptions written. Contexts, situations, events, conditions and interactions cannot be replicated to any extent nor can generalizations be made to a wider context than the one studied with any confidence. This difficulty of applying the usual scientific criteria does not, however, make such understandings any less real or valid for that participant, and the explanatory function of such understandings for that person's behaviour is highly predictive.

Time commitment

Perhaps one of the major limitations of qualitative research and evaluation is the time required for data collection, analysis and interpretation. There is a critical need for the researcher to spend a considerable amount of time on the factory floor, at company meetings, or in the employees' cafeteria in order to observe, holistically and individually, the interactions, reactions and minute-by-minute activities, or conduct unstructured interviews (conversations) with numerous subjects.

Strengths of qualitative research methods

Awareness of complexity

Because qualitative investigation is like the net of a deep-sea explorer, trawling up unexpected and striking things on which to gaze with the investigator maintaining close association with both participants and activities within the business setting, an insider's view of the field can be obtained. This proximity to the field often allows the evaluator to see (and document) the qualities of human motivation, needs and pressures too often missed by scientific, more positivistic inquiries. Such propinquity can reveal subtleties and complexities that could go undetected using more standardized measures.

As a preliminary to a quantitative study

Qualitative open-ended surveys, focus groups, in-depth interviews and observational techniques can play the important role of suggesting possible relationships, causes, effects, and dynamic processes in business settings, and provide the bases for possible hypotheses that can be subjected to more detailed and controlled quantitative scientific scrutiny on large representative samples using reliable and valid measuring instruments. Qualitative methods can highlight, for example, subtleties in employee behaviour in response to variations in managers' management and leadership styles that could then be subject to more formal investigation.

This link between the two approaches will be raised again in discussing inductive and deductive methods later.

More in-depth study of qualitative findings

After determining from a large-scale controlled investigation that there are considerable differences between individuals on a particular behaviour, the selection of a few subjects from each end of the spectrum for detailed qualitative study, say using open-ended interviews, can tease out some of the important but rather subtle reasons for the differences in the range of responses from the large-scale scientific study.

Rapprochement

In summary, both scientific quantitative and interpretivist qualitative methods are needed to provide the information required for sound and effective decision making in the business world. Each approach can inform the other with a study of an issue following a circular course through a qualitative-quantitative or quantitative-qualitative sequence. Human variability does not imply that the scientific approach to studying human activity should be abandoned. Within the limits imposed by having human subjects, we must try to apply the basic attributes of scientific method so that findings are as objective, reliable, replicable and quantifiable as possible.

Even though a strong contrast has deliberately been made in the preceding pages to emphasize the different approaches and philosophical rationales, the practice of dichotomizing and polarizing research into quantitative and qualitative modes is overdone and misleading. It suggests only serious and rigorous researchers will use quantitative methods and that only such designs are capable of producing legitimate research. In practice, many researchers will use both approaches as appropriate within one investigation (see Table 2.1).

The comparative strengths and weaknesses of qualitative and quantitative research are a perennial, hot debate, in the social sciences. The issues invoke a classic 'paradigm war'. The personality/thinking style of the researcher and/or the culture of the organization are under-recognized as key factors in preferred choice of approach and methods. Overly focusing on the debate of 'qualitative *versus* quantitative' places the methods in opposition. It is important to focus also on how the techniques can be integrated or used to support each other. Many researchers now concede that neither method is superior but each has relevance for particular issues and contexts. The sequence, depicted in Figure 2.1, provides a link.

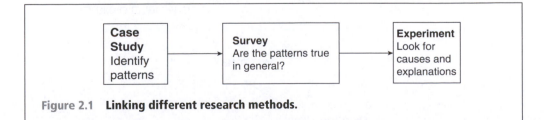

Figure 2.1 Linking different research methods.

Table 2.1 **Comparison of qualitative and quantitative methods**

Qualitative	Quantitative
The aim of **qualitative** analysis is a complete, detailed description.	In the **quantitative** approach, researchers classify and count features, and construct statistical models in an attempt to explain what is observed.
Recommended during earlier phases of research projects.	Recommended during latter phases of research projects.
Researcher may only know roughly in advance what they are looking for. Theory developing.	Researcher knows clearly in advance what they are investigating. Usually testing a theory or elements of a theory.
The design emerges as the study unfolds.	All aspects of the study are carefully designed before data is collected.
Researcher is the data gathering instrument.	Researcher uses questionnaires, attitudes scales, tests or equipment to collect numerical data.
Data are usually words, pictures (e.g. videos) or objects (artefacts).	Data are always numbers and statistics.
Qualitative data are more 'rich', time consuming, and less able to be generalized.	Quantitative data are more efficient, able to test hypotheses, but may miss contextual detail.
Researcher tends to become subjectively immersed in the subject matter.	Researcher tends to remain objectively separated from the subject matter.

Deduction and induction

Induction

Research involves both description and explanation. If the research starts with specific observations/descriptions followed by analysis that produces explanation of the observations/ explanations we have an **inductive process**. This develops theory from initial data – a bottom-up approach. This is open-ended and exploratory, major characteristics of the qualitative interpretive approach (see Figure 2.2).

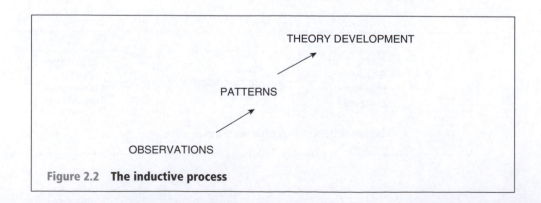

Figure 2.2 **The inductive process**

Deduction

If, however, the sequence is reversed, starting with a theory or hypothesis from which certain other things should logically follow, these implications can be tested and on the basis of the results the initial theory/hypothesis can be supported or rejected. This process is the **deductive process** – a top-down strategy, working from the general to the specific (see Figure 2.3).

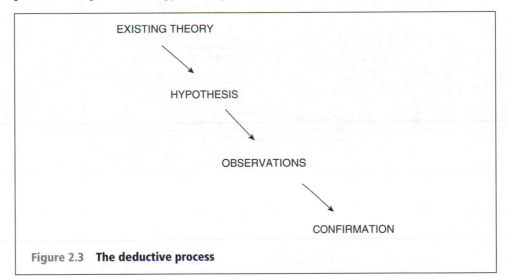

Figure 2.3   **The deductive process**

Positivist researchers, by the very nature of their approach, tend to be deductive rather than inductive while interpretive researchers generally emphasize induction. You can see a link between the scientific approach and the qualitative method here, since the conclusions of an inductive approach (a developing theory) can be further evaluated with a view to confirming it by the deductive approach. Conversely, a quantitative deductive study may unearth some unexpected and hard to explain result which could be explored using an inductive approach. For example, a study might be investigating the problems of being a single parent who can only find part-time work. This is an inductive qualitative study as it employs one-to-one interviews to tease out the issues. These issues form patterns and themes which lead to two different general propositions about single male and single female parents. Then a more controlled study can be designed to test these two propositions or theories among a properly selected sample to seek confirmation that significant differences are substantial between the two gender groups over particular part-time work issues. Much research, as indicated earlier, will involve both inductive and deductive stages as investigators cycle and recycle observations up to theories and down again to observations and back up to revamped theories (Fig. 2.4). This is often termed the **Research Cycle.**

The problem of reactive subjects

Both quantitative and qualitative studies are plagued by subjects' reactions to being involved in a study. We know only too well that subjects try to meet the perceived expectancies of the investigator. For example, the 'Hawthorne Effect' was discovered in early studies of the industrial context when, no matter what experimental manipulation was

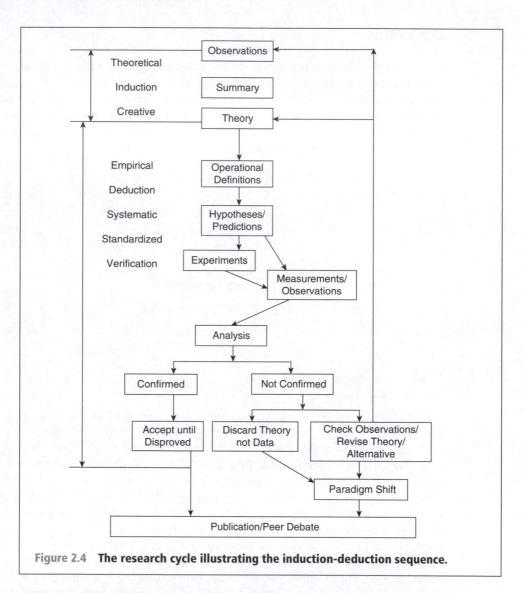

Figure 2.4 **The research cycle illustrating the induction-deduction sequence.**

tried, worker productivity improved. This apparently occurred because the workers 'knew' that they were in a 'special' group and therefore tried to do their best at all times. Thus, the workers' perception of being in an experiment was as important in determining the workers' productivity as the actual experimental manipulations. We are in no doubt now that the presence of an investigator will have profound reactive effects on the subjects in any study.

For example, interview or survey responses may not be very valid or reliable as respondents may lie, employ defence mechanisms, lack self-insight, or give socially approved answers. However, when a person says something about themselves such as *'I do not feel able to succeed on this training course'* they have the right to be believed. Validation of what a person says is effected by observing what they do, but unfortunately, as the Hawthorne studies showed the very act of observing can alter their behaviour in unknown ways.

Being involved in a study is similar to being on stage or in front of a television camera. While in front of a television camera most people do not act as they normally would but produce behaviour that ranges from silly to stilted. Likewise, involvement in a study may generate behaviour that is more socially desirable, restrained, subdued, or defiant than normal. When such a tendency is coupled with the behaviour that may be produced by deliberate attempts to either 'cooperate' or 'outwit' the experimenter, it is easy to see how results can be produced that are invalid and cannot therefore be generalized to the 'population'. Some qualitative researchers resort to participant observation to gain their data so that they appear to be part of the group or the ritual, and the other participants, not knowing there is an 'intruder' in their midst, present more authentic behaviour.

Cooperation in studies conducted for commerce and industry are only infrequently a result of the subject's desire to contribute to knowledge. Instead, cooperation is often attained because subjects are paid to participate, or pressured by friends or, as frequently occurs, compulsory participation is required by the business organization or educational establishment. Most subjects resent this last requirement, and may express their pent-up feelings by 'beating the investigator' in such a way that the researcher can never find out. All subjects enter a study with a variety of positive and negative attitudes, expectations, and suspicions, any of which can distort performance. Replication of studies often reveal variations in results due to human variability, different samples, subtle differences in the conditions under which the study was conducted. In other words a host of variables can intrude in unknown ways and change results from one occasion to another.

What you have learned from this chapter

The Positivist and Interpretivist paradigms underlie two contrasting approaches to conducting research. Quantitative scientific methods reflect the positivist paradigm; qualitative subjective approaches derive from the interpretivist philosophy. The former adopts a scientific rigour emphasizing objectivity, reliability and generalizability to establish general laws/principles, while the latter accepts that humans behave in individually meaningful ways which are not susceptible to generalization.

Although the two research approaches, the quantitative and the qualitative, appear opposed to each other they are actually complementary, and valuable in understanding business events, activities and human behaviour in the business setting.

Inductive approaches are bottom-up, working from data to look for pattern and eventually propose theories or principles. Induction is a central feature of qualitative studies and reflects the interpretivist paradigm. Deductive approaches start from theory and establish testable hypotheses to determine if the theory holds in particular contexts or with specific samples. This approach is consonant with the scientific method which reflects the positivist paradigm.

The reaction of subjects when involved in studies can seriously affect the outcome.

Review questions and tasks

Qu. 2.1
Explain the advantages of a scientific approach to research. Check your answer by referring back to material above.

Qu. 2.2
Briefly indicate and explain the major characteristics of the scientific method. Check your answer with the information above.

Qu. 2.3
Outline what you believe are the main disadvantages or problems with the scientific approach to research. Check your answer with the material above.

Qu. 2.4
What are the main advantages and disadvantages of the interpretivist approach to research? Check your response with the material above.

Qu. 2.5
If research in the business/management area cannot be 100% scientific is there any use in doing it?
Discuss this statement in class or in groups.

Qu. 2.6
The following are characteristics of the scientific method except for:

(a) the definition of the problem in specific terms
(b) development of hypotheses
(c) analysis of data
(d) verification of hypotheses using expert judgement

Qu. 2.7
If a researcher starts with a theory, is this indicative of:

(a) an inductive approach?
(b) a deductive approach?
(c) an interpretist approach?
(d) a descriptive approach?

Qu. 2.8
If a researcher wants to understand the multiple realities of individual employees' perceptions of their workplace they are following:

(a) a positivist philosophy
(b) an applied philosophy
(c) an interpretivist philosophy
(d) the process of generalization

Qu. 2.9
Which major paradigm includes the view that people experience reality in different ways:

(a) political
(b) positivist
(c) interpretivist
(d) critical

Qu. 2.10
The setting for quantitative research studies is:

(a) natural
(b) social
(c) artificial and controlled
(d) real and uncontrolled

Qu. 2.11
The aim of qualitative research is to:

(a) richly describe the data in-depth
(b) rank the data in terms of importance
(c) make quantitative measurement
(d) understand objective meanings

Qu. 2.12
Induction is a reasoning process moving from:

(a) analysis to hypothesis to data testing
(b) data collection to hypothesis
(c) data collection to pattern seeking to theory building
(d) hypothesis to data collection

Further reading

Perry, C., Reige, A. & Brown, L. 1999. Realism's role among scientific paradigms in marketing research. *Irish Marketing Review,* 12, 16–23. A good overview of research paradigms.

Now visit the web page for Chapter 2 and check your answers to the multiple choice review questions as well as attempting the additional questions, problems and activities located there.

Chapter 3
Ethical Issues in Research

'I haven't eaten for three days', said the beggar to the statistician. 'Ah, said the statistician, how does that compare with the same period last year?'

(Russell Lewis)

'There are lies, damned lies and statistics'

(Attributed by Mark Twain to Benjamin Disraeli)

Content list

By the end of this chapter you will:

1 Be aware of the major ethical issues and obligations that impact on the research process and understand why they are important.
2 Be aware of guidelines for conducting ethical research.

Introduction

This chapter aims to raise awareness of ethical issues and dilemmas that are embedded in the research process. Most research in business involves studying the behaviour of people in their roles as employees, managers, customers, clients, etc. Ethical issues therefore come into play. Ethical issues have no easy answer; none of the issues are black or white but rather various shades of grey. Hence we are trying to make you aware of the issues so that you have a basis on which to develop your own choice of appropriate behaviour in the various situations you may meet when conducting research.

There is a an erroneous tendency to limit our perception of ethical issues to those stemming from the researcher–subject relationship. But other reciprocal rights and responsibilities, involving researcher, sponsoring client (end user of the results) and society in general exist, increasing the number of potential ethical interactions.

> **Ethics.** *The application of moral principles and/or ethical standards that guide our behaviour in human relationships.*

Development of the concern for ethical behaviour in human research

Human participation in research has a long and sometimes unpleasant history. Aulus Cornelius Celsus, a 1st century Roman physicist, cruelly experimented on prisoners of war, yet this work, detailed in his famous treatise *De medicina*, became a major source of knowledge of early medicine. It emphasized the importance of cleanliness and the use of antiseptics, it described facial skin grafting, and stated the four cardinal signs of inflammation. Much later, the advent of vaccination trials in the 18th and 19th centuries saw physicians use themselves, their family members and others as test subjects, often conducting experiments without informing subjects of the dangers associated with the procedures. One famous case included Jenner's experimentation on his son and neighbourhood children in the development of smallpox vaccines.

Even during the 20th century, incidences of unethical research continued. For example, in the United States, from 1932 until the mid-1970s, members of the public participated in the Tuskegee Syphilis Study, whereby many thousands of syphilis sufferers were not treated, despite the known effectiveness of penicillin as a treatment by early 1947. The US Public Health Service's desire to document the effects of the disease on the body meant that treatment was withheld for many decades.

But perhaps there are no more famous cases of ethical impropriety than those undertaken by social psychologists Milgram, Zimbardo and Asch.

Asch's conformity experiment

In the early 1950s, following the atrocities committed by Nazi Germany in the previous decade, Soloman Asch studied the power of individual integrity to determine whether most people could withstand group pressure to conform. Asch invited groups of eight subjects, all university students, to compare the lengths of black lines drawn on cards. In reality only one of the subjects was a 'bona fide' volunteer. The others were stooges and had been instructed to say that lines of obviously different lengths were the same length. Most subjects initially resisted the peer pressure to conform, but contrary to Asch's expectation, one-third eventually ignored the evidence of their own eyes and agreed with the rest of the group, claiming the lines were of the same length when they obviously were not, demonstrating the power of group conformity.

Although you may think Asch's experiment as not being of a serious breach of ethical propriety, his participants were deceived about the true nature of the experiment. Each subject thought they were one of eight subjects involved in a simple cognitive experiment, yet had they known the true nature of the study, what would Asch's results have been? The ethical dilemma is that while deception should not be practised, in some experiments like Asch's there is no option, and we would know far less about group pressure to conform that translates into employee work groups, union meetings, and directors' meetings. However, the long-term effects of being deceived can include a growing mistrust of researchers and the research they are doing. Participants may be less likely to participate again if they had felt embarrassed and ridiculed by previous involvement.

Milgram's obedience studies

Stanley Milgram's investigations into obedience perhaps more clearly delineate the ethical considerations of performing human research. In a similar vein to Asch, Milgram attempted to test the influence of authority figures in demanding obedience and to assess just how far people would be willing to adhere to an authority figure. In one experiment, the authority, a stern-looking experimenter in a white lab coat, would inform the test subject – the 'teacher' – that the experiment was investigating the effect of punishment on the performance of a memory word-matching test. The punishment consisted of implementing an electric shock to another subject – the 'learner' – whenever the 'learner' made a mistake on the test. As the strength of the electric shock increased with each error, up to a potentially lethal 450 volts, many 'learners' cried and shouted to be let free, until eventually all were rendered quiet by unconsciousness. Although many of the 'teachers' protested and showed obvious signs of stress and worry, Milgram found that 65% of his 'teachers' eventually gave the maximum 450 volts. All of the teachers administered at least some level of pain, and the first 'teacher' to revolt did so only when the 'learner's' cries silenced. In reality, the 'learner' was a stooge and accomplice of Milgram's and no electric shocks were actually given. However, Milgram's conclusion at the time (1961) was so alarming that it received widespread publicity. Most people would obey and even hurt human beings simply because someone in authority told them to.

Zimbardo's prison study

Philip Zimbardo's 1971 'prison' experiment brought more condemnation about the types of research being undertaken with human participants. In attempting to demonstrate that authority figures did not even need to be present to exert influence and that individuals live according to the roles they think society expects of them, Zimbardo recruited a number of college students to replicate prison life in a two-week experiment. The students were divided into one of two conditions – 'prisoners' and 'guard' – and were then placed into a simulated prison in the basement of the Stanford University psychology building.

Prisoners were 'picked up' by official policemen, before being transported to the make-shift prison. Their personal effects were confiscated, they were given prison clothes, and referred to by their prisoner identification numbers.

The guards were informed that they were responsible for the running of the jail and were told to do whatever they thought necessary to maintain order. From the outset, guards began to treat the prisoners in cruel manner, stripping them naked for misbehaviour, requiring the cleaning out of toilets with bare hands, spraying them with fire extinguishers, even simulating acts of sodomy. Although only some of the guards performed so cruelly, the rest of the guards merely turned a blind eye. Furthermore, guards became more violent when they thought they were not being supervised by Zimbardo, who acted as prison warden, although they were in fact being recorded by video camera. Eventually, Zimbardo had to halt the two-week experiment after six days. It may be unethical but it certainly does predict real human behaviour like Abu Ghraib prison in Iraq.

More detailed information about these studies can be found:

Asch:
o   http://www.bbc.co.uk/radio4/science/mindchangers1.shtml
o   http://www.psych.upenn.edu/sacsec/about/solomon.htm
Milgram:
o   http://www.stanleymilgram.com/
o   http://www.bbc.co.uk/radio4/science/allinthemind_20041130.shtml
Zimbardo:
o   http://www.prisonexp.org/
o   http://www.zimbardo.com/zimbardo.html

Development of codes of conduct

The development of current official country and professional codes of practice has its foundation in the Nuremburg war trials following the conclusion of the Second World War. Twenty-three Nazi doctors and scientists were tried for the murder of concentration camp inmates who were used as research subjects in human experimentation studies. Of the 23 charged, 15 were convicted, of which seven were condemned to death by hanging and eight received prison sentences from 10 years to life. The Nuremberg Code was developed as a consequence of these proceedings.

The Nuremberg Code consisted of the following guidelines:

- ○ Informed consent is essential.
- ○ Research should be based on prior animal work.
- ○ The risks should be justified by the anticipated benefits.
- ○ Research must be conducted by qualified scientists.
- ○ Physical and mental suffering must be avoided.
- ○ Research in which death or disabling injury is expected should not be conducted.

Twenty years later, in 1964, the World Medical Association developed a code of research ethics, the Declaration of Helsinki, that was a re-interpretation of the Nuremberg Code. Subsequently, in accordance with the Declaration, numerous professional codes of ethical research practices have been developed by national professional associations who have been at the forefront of research with human subjects, such the American Psychological Association (APA) and the British Psychological Association (BPS), which reflect the need to maintain professional and scientific credibility in the public eye. Examples of both their guidelines are summarized in Figures 3.1 and 3.2.

Psychological associations have taken a lead in the development of ethical principles as their research is essentially about human behaviour, and many business research areas such

---

American Psychological Association

ETHICAL PRINCIPLES OF PSYCHOLOGISTS AND CODE OF CONDUCT

Guided by six principles:

Principle A: Beneficence and Nonmaleficence
This principle requires psychologists to do no harm and to safeguard the welfare and rights of those they provide professional services for.

Principle B: Fidelity and Responsibility
Psychologists must establish a relationship of trust with those they work with cooperating with other professionals to ensure all parties adhere to the highest level of ethical propriety.

Principle C: Integrity
Psychologists must work with accuracy, and be honest and truthful by not misrepresenting facts. They must also consider the consequences of their actions on perception of the profession.

Principle D: Justice
Psychologists must adhere to a principle of justice and fairness for all.

Principle E: Respect for People's Rights and Dignity
Psychologists must respect the dignity and worth of all people, and the rights of individuals to privacy, confidentiality, and self-determination.

The complete details of the ethical principles of the APA can be found at the following website: http://www.apa.org/ethics

Figure 3.1   Summary of APA Code of Ethics.

British Psychological Society

Charter, Rules, Ethics and Code of Conduct

GENERAL PRINCIPLES

I Responsibility
Members remain personally responsible for the professional decisions they make.
(a)   Members are expected to be cognisant of the reasonably foreseeable consequences of their actions and to endeavour to ensure that their services are used appropriately.
(b)   Members shall have ultimate regard for the highest standards of their profession.

II Competence
Members shall bring and maintain appropriate skills and learning in their areas of professional practice.
(a)   Members must not misrepresent their competence, qualifications, training or experience.
(b)   Members must refrain from offering advice or undertaking work beyond their professional competence.

III Propriety
The welfare of clients and the public, and the integrity of the profession, shall take precedence over a member's self interest and over the interests of the member's employer and colleagues.
(a)   Members must respect the confidentiality of information obtained from clients in the course of their professional work. They may reveal such information to others only with the consent of the person or the person's legal representative. However in those unusual circumstances where failure to disclose may result in clear risk to the client or to others, the member may disclose minimal information necessary to avert risk. Members must inform their clients of the legal and other limits of confidentiality.
(b)   Members must be sensitive to cultural, contextual, gender and role differences and the impact of those on their professional practice on clients. Members must not act in a discriminatory manner nor condone discriminatory practices against clients on the basis of those differences.
(c)   Members must refrain from any act which would tend to bring the profession into public disrepute.
(d)   Members must be mindful of the legal context in which they work, their obligations towards clients and employers, and their duties towards clients.
(e)   Where the demands of an organization require members to violate this Code, members must clarify the nature of the conflict between the demands and these principles. They must inform all parties of members' ethical responsibilities and seek a constructive resolution of the conflict.

Figure 3.2   **Summary of the ethical principles of the British Psychological Society.**

as marketing, consumer behaviour, organizational climate, personnel selection, employee motivation, etc. are studied from a psychological perspective. Other professional based codes are listed with the website material. In addition, many countries have legislated on Privacy and Disclosure. Universities have Ethics Committees which evaluate research proposals to ensure they comply with ethical standards.

So, if ethical constraints restrict the range of methodologies available to researchers, and as results are likely to be a consequence of the methodologies used, ethical procedures may produce results less congruent with what would happen in real life. This is a major dilemma in studying human behaviour. Of course, the researcher's own personal values will tend to prohibit or encourage certain unethical behaviours and attitudes too. But relying on personal judgement is problematic. Yet government laws and professional rules demanding strict adherence may be over-restrictive. Clearly, with codes that guide, and ethical review bodies that help researchers design and plan research, ethical problems can be mitigated although perhaps not eliminated.

Common ethical issues: Guidelines and codes of conduct

There are a number of key components in the system of ethical protections that the contemporary business and social research establishments have created to better protect their research participants, and manage rights and responsibilities of researchers, sponsors, participants and society in general.

Societal rights

Researchers are obligated to be objective in their research, maintain scientific rigour, and report results, fully informing society of important results whether positive or negative. For example, in 2000 and 2001, the Ford car-production company and Bridgestone-Firestone tyre manufacturer were responsible for the recall of 13 million tyres, costing Ford $2.1 billion as research discovered that the tyres in question had been seriously damaged during the manufacturing process. In order to ensure passenger safety, the car manufacturer recalled its products at a tremendous cost. On a more positive note, Dr Jonas Salk (1914–1995), discoverer of the Polio vaccine, refused to patent his vaccine, declaring that the discovery belonged to the people of the world, for their own benefit.

Further information about the tyre recall can be found at:

o http://news.bbc.co.uk/2/hi/business/1345087.stm

Society can expect that research should be objective, unbiased and scientifically sound. In recent years, however, several highly publicized cases have failed to live up to this expectation. In 2005, Sudbo of the Norwegian Radium Hospital in Oslo published a report in the highly reputable British medical journal *Lancet*, reporting on the results of a study into the success of common pain medication in reducing the incidence of certain types of cancers such as oral cancer. Within six months, Sudbo's research was found to have been falsified, and that over 900 of the participants shared the same birth date, i.e. they didn't exist. This occurred at the same time that South Korea's Dr Woo-Suk claimed to have successfully cloned a human embryo and produced stem cells from it, a technique that could one day provide cures for a range of diseases. These findings were also found to be falsified. Such behaviour is highly unethical and is not in line with adhering to society's rights to be informed about objective and scientifically valid research.

Further information about Woo-Suk's research can be found at:

o http://news.bbc.co.uk/2/hi/health/4617372.stm
o http://news.bbc.co.uk/2/hi/asia-pacific/4554704.stm

Participants' rights

Participants' rights revolve around many important issues, including *the right to voluntary participation, the right of safety and freedom from harm, the right to be informed, the right to privacy and confidentiality*.

Voluntary participation and informed consent

Voluntary participation requires that people not be coerced into participating. This is especially relevant where researchers generally rely on 'captive audiences' for their subjects – universities, work places, prisons, etc. Researchers should ensure that participants are given sufficient details of the study so they can make an informed decision whether or not to participate. This is the concept of **informed consent**. Participants must also be informed of the right to end their participation at any time during the research process, and to even have their responses excluded from the final report.

However, while participation should be voluntary, there are consistent reports that people who volunteer to participate are usually of a higher social class, are more intelligent, more extroverted, less conforming and have a higher need for approval. So ethical requirements for volunteering can act in direct opposition to the methodological requirements of the research design, where proper sampling techniques should be employed (Chapter 9) to obtain a representative subset of the population. Through drop out and selective willingness to be involved the sample can become biased. However, the advancement of knowledge and the pursuit of information are not in themselves sufficient justifications for overriding ethical values and ignoring the interests of those studied and those who do not wish to be studied.

Informed consent forms

Consent forms can vary in content depending on the type of research project. However, the following list provides examples of the type of information that most informed consent forms include:

- information about the nature and purpose of the research;
- a statement that participation is voluntary including the choice to opt out at any time;
- information about data collection methods and the option to agree/refuse to being recorded (if applicable);
- a description of the extent to which confidentiality will be maintained and an option to choose anonymity;
- a description of any possible risks or discomforts to participants;
- a description of any possible benefits to participants or others;
- contact addresses, emails and/or telephone numbers for any questions about the research;
- a description of the intended uses, and disposal/storage and documentation procedures for data, including an option to agree/disagree with these procedures;
- finally, an option to agree or refuse to participate (signature of participant, date, signature of witness/researcher).

Sensitive data

Information about a research participant that falls into any of the following categories is regarded as sensitive personal data and should be strictly confidential:

- ethnic origin of the participant;
- political opinions of the participant;
- religious beliefs or beliefs of a similar nature held by the participant;
- physical or mental health of the participant;
- the sexual life of the participant;
- commission or alleged commission by the participant of any offence.

The right to be informed

The dissemination of research findings is a way to inform participants of the results of their participation in a study, providing them with a sense that their participation was of value.

The right to be safe and not harmed

Participant safety generally relates to issues of subject anonymity, and the freedom from undue stress and deception. By being informed of the nature of the research, participants are able to determine for themselves if their participation is likely to be of threat to their mental or physical state. However, researchers are still responsible to ensure that participants are safe from harm both during and after the research process. In those instances where hurt, discomfort or stress is likely, researchers may need to consider alternative methods. In other words, use dummies rather than real people in testing a new type of car seat belt in simulated accident conditions or ensure no allergic person is used when testing consumer perceptions of a new scent. Good research practice often requires the use of a no-treatment control group – a group of participants who do not get the treatment or programme that is being studied. But when that treatment or programme may have beneficial effects, persons assigned to the no-treatment control may feel their rights of equal access to services are being curtailed. Unfortunately, good design does require a control group as a base line to measure the effects of the treatment on the experimental group. To get round this requirement the researcher can offer the beneficial treatment to the control group after the study has finished.

Harm may not be physical danger but something just as insidious – emotional stress. A study to compare two methods of learning for a new industrial technique may be stressful to a few older employee participants who feel threatened by innovation. Researchers need to take special care where research participants are vulnerable by virtue of age, social status and powerlessness; i.e. attitude studies of unemployed disabled youth or studies on the effectiveness of management of care homes for the aged. Researchers should be aware of cultural, religious, gendered and other significant differences within the research populations in the planning, conducting and reporting of their research. The best judge of whether an investigation will cause offence may be members of the population from which the research participants will be drawn.

The right to anonymity and confidentiality

Confidentiality and anonymity are two standards that are applied in order to help protect the privacy of research participants.

- Anonymity refers to concealing the identity of the participants in all documents resulting from the research.
- Confidentiality is concerned with who has the right of access to the data provided by the participants.

Almost all research guarantees participant *confidentiality* – they are assured that identifying information will not be made available to anyone who is not directly involved in the study. The stricter standard is the principle of *anonymity,* which essentially means that the participant will remain anonymous throughout the study – even to the researchers themselves. Clearly, the anonymity standard is a stronger guarantee of privacy, but it is difficult to accomplish, especially in situations where participants have to be measured at multiple time points (e.g. a pre-post study).

Privacy and confidentiality can be protected by:

- restricting access to completed original data survey forms or test answer sheets;
- restricting access to data on computer files;
- revealing information only with participant consent;
- ensuring case numbers on the original data forms are always kept separate from the coding keys.

Another privacy and confidentiality issue involves videoing respondents without their knowledge, say behind a one-way mirror. In fact, if respondents are asked whether they mind being observed, most are quite happy to take part and after a few minutes begin to act normally.

The issue of deception

The primary justification for deception is that knowledge of the real purpose of the study might well contaminate results. Deception therefore is an element in the experimental design in many cases. In a study to see how investors work the stock market, some false information might be spread to one group to see how they respond in terms of stock purchase or sales. If they were told in advance of the deception then the study would be pointless. Placebo is another common form of deception and involves administering a participant with a dummy condition of the Independent Variable.

In some studies you may not want anyone to know a study is even going on. For example, pretending to be a customer in a large supermarket and observing the purchasing choices of other customers. Or it may be observations and field notes of the frustrations and comments of people waiting in queues at a bank or rail station.

Debriefing after the study has ended is a way of mitigating most deceptions and usually is quite acceptable to the participants when revealed in this way with the purpose explained.

Researchers should never use participation in a study as a ploy for gaining other ends, such as adding the participant to a prospect list if they fit certain criteria. Researchers must stand back from anything that smacks of any taint of marketing or selling.

Legitimate and illegitimate data

Not all data is ethically legitimate. Ethical codes of practice stress that researchers should only collect data:

*   for which consent has been obtained;
*   which is relevant to the research.

'Illegitimate' data gathered deliberately by eavesdropping, fudging one's purpose, simulating friendship, surreptitiously reading documents on desks, is collected with the intent to deceive participants in order to obtain data that can be used for research purposes. It is ethically questionable because it violates both the principle of informed consent and the participant's right to privacy.

Debriefing

For informed participants, debriefing mainly involves informing them of the study's results and the conclusions reached. For 'deceived' participants, this is an opportunity to disclose the true nature of the study. To offset any negative feeling, such debriefing is usually most effective in one-on-one or small group settings, and when sufficient time is provided for participants to discuss their experiences and behaviour during the study. In many circumstances, participants will find participation a form of self-discovery, as some in the Zimbardo and Milgram experiments reportedly experienced. Debriefing therefore usually involves:

*   explanation of any deception;
*   description of goals or purpose of study;
*   sharing of results.

The issue of rewarding participation

Many participants are offered a small incentive to take part – a book voucher, a sample of company product, or even money. But generally it should be inconsequential and be related to the time and effort the participants have donated to the research. The dilemma is balancing incentive against implicit coercion, as by not taking part no incentive is available. The incentive should never be something that would jeopardize the participant if they refused to take part, such as lower marks at university or removing the annual bonus. Research subjects should not be offered any form of inducement that is disproportionately large so that they are encouraged to act against their interests by taking part in the investigations.

In summary the researcher's responsibilities include:

- to develop proposals that are ethical and seek approval from the Research Ethics Committee, where such a committee exists;
- to conduct research to the agreed protocol (i.e. of the Research Ethics Committee) and in accordance with legal requirements and guidance (e.g. codes of practice provided by the professional association; national privacy of information laws);
- to ensure the honest and respectful treatment of research participants, informing them of the purpose of the study and adhering to the guidance requirements (e.g. on consent and confidentiality), and at all times ensuring safety and well-being *vis-à-vis* the research procedure, equipment and premises;
- to ensure that data collected is accurate, relevant and valid;
- to ensure that data is suitably stored and archived and that attention is paid to issues of confidentiality;
- to manage resources such as finances, time and intellectual property efficiently;
- to report any project-related problems, failures, adverse incidents or suspected misconduct to the appropriate body;
- to provide feedback of the research results to participants, or at least the intended use of the results, including any intention to publish;
- to provide accurate, truthful and complete reports, and disseminate the research outcomes through authorized and agreed channels, ensuring that the work is available for critical review.

Participants' responsibilities

Once a participant has agreed to take part, they also accept certain responsibilities and must try to be honest and conscientious in responding, and not try to 'beat' the researcher. They should follow research instructions to the best of their ability and cooperate. They should turn up on time at the required place (this aspect of the contract should be emphasized).

Sponsors' clients' rights

Undertaking research for a client requires a consideration of the rights and needs of the client.

Competency

Ethical issues in a sponsored study commence before the research project starts. The researcher needs to assess their own competency to carry out the envisioned study and if they lack the skills or resources then must decline and not attempt a half-hearted or incomplete job. The client is paying for competence and a report of value. The researcher must also indicate exactly what the research can achieve (the deliverables) and be able to present results in an understandable fashion. Researchers therefore must:

- recognize the boundaries of their professional competence and not accept work they are not qualified to carry out;
- ensure all aspects of research are reported in enough detail to allow sponsors and other researchers to understand and interpret them.

Access to privileged information

Generally, in the interest of effectiveness and efficiency, researchers will be informed of client information that is both privileged and confidential. This requires ethical responsibility by the researcher, who must balance the rights of a client to confidentiality in research findings with the rights of society to be informed about those factors which may have an impact on them. Popularized by the movie *The Insider*, the case of Dr Jeffrey Wigand, who was fired and subsequently sued by his former employee, the tobacco manufacturer Brown & Williamson, demonstrates the sort of ethical considerations faced by those working in business and marketing. Wigand, as Head of Research and Development, made public the various ethical issues that the tobacco industry chose not to disclose to the general public, information relating to the carcinogenic properties of cigarettes and the use of 'impact boosting' – the means by which to increase the delivery of nicotine, the addictive ingredient. Researchers have to decide their position on such ethical issues.

> ## More information about the Wigand case can be found at:
>
> ○   http://www.jeffreywigand.com/

Such decisions will need to take account of your own personal values, the values of employees and employers, current social sensitivities, as well as the law. But sometimes these issues, as in the case of Wigand vs. Brown & Williamson, can have serious economic and personal consequences.

Conflict of interest

A conflict of interest can arise when the result and information derived from one study paid for by a company can be used or adapted for a study commissioned by a second company. Many companies are interested in the same things, such as effectiveness of different advertising media, effectiveness of in-house training, etc. The ethical researcher would in fact decline the second job as the information belongs to the first company who paid for it.

Sponsor responsibilities

A sponsor must be fully open with the researcher about the specific research question they want answered, the resources available, the access that will be permitted and the time frame. The sponsor should not attempt to influence the results by requesting the omitting of some result or that a particular result be promoted in the research report. Researchers should refuse to undertake research under these conditions. Researchers should attempt to ensure that sponsors and/or funders appreciate the obligations that the researcher has, not only to them but also to society at large. Researchers should be careful not to promise or imply acceptance of conditions which are contrary to their professional ethics or competing commitments.

There should be no contractual conditions that are contingent upon a particular outcome. Researchers should clarify in advance the respective obligations of funders and researchers, where possible, in the form of a written contract.

Impact of technology on research ethics

New technology has not only made plagiarism far easier but also increased the likelihood that participants' privacy can be violated. This is particularly applicable to employee data and company financial data. Research in cyberspace should provide no special dispensation from the general ethical obligations already noted. The World Wide Web provides a unique research environment because:

- the distinction between private and public space is unclear;
- data can be collected without consent;
- participants and the researcher may never meet or speak to each other and the identities they may choose to assume may be 'virtual', bearing little resemblance to their 'real' self.

Not only does this create ethical implications for the collection of data in terms of privacy, anonymity and confidentiality, but it also points to the need to raise awareness about concerns regarding the mistaken inclusion of vulnerable or unsuitable populations (e.g. children) in a research project, who are not identifiable because of pseudonyms.

The perceptions people have of what constitutes public and private domains on the Web may not correspond with their actions when they come to log on. People often use public domains in cyberspace for private conversations. The use of the terms 'private' and 'public' refer to the accessibility of information, not the individual's own perception of the privacy of their actions. The individual's perception of privacy may well be determined by who they believe to be looking at their work and what they believe is being done with it.

It is recommended that the participant supplying the data, whether an individual author or a site owner, is consulted personally. Researchers must NOT assume that where access to the Web is 'public', that the information available in such domains is also 'public' and 'up for grabs'. Extracting data in such a manner from the Web contravenes some basic ethical principles:

- the author's privacy has been invaded;
- informed consent has not been obtained from the author;
- the anonymity of the author is at risk.

There are currently very few guidelines for ethical codes of conduct regarding Web-based social research. Getting consent from participants in an online location can be very difficult, largely because of the 'faceless' nature of Web participants and the possibility that they may also be assuming a pseudo-identity. Kraut *et al.* (2004) provide a responsible and authoritative discussion of the issues of online research.

The ultimate dilemma: Ethical principles or reliable and valid research?

Although criticism of the unethical methodology undertaken in the Milgram and Zimbardo studies is fairly unanimous, the value of their work in informing on human behaviour is without question. There clearly exists a need to balance the rights of the individual and protection of their health and sense of well-being during research participation with the value of advancing knowledge about individual and group behaviour in the realm of business.

There is some concern that the imposition of strict guidelines, in relation to human research, has detrimental effects on the quality of research undertaken. To test this hypothesis, Resnick and Schwartz (1973) investigated the effect of full disclosure on a verbal conditioning task. Two groups, an *ethical* group who were fully informed about the true nature of the study, and an *unethical* group who were deceived about the true nature of the study, were conditioned or rewarded for using the pronouns 'I' and 'We'. Subjects in the *unethical* condition showed a considerable conditioning effect, in line with previous findings. Results from the *ethical* group actually indicated a decline in the use of these pronouns. Clearly, disclosure reduced a well-established effect, which was replicated as expected in the *unethical* condition.

What do participants think?

Interestingly, whereas most would agree that some studies may be of a questionable ethical nature, there is also an acceptance of the important role for studies which inform on individual and social behaviour. In fact, survey evidence exists which suggests that ethical propriety is more important to professionals than the public themselves. Within business management, marketing and psychological research, a common source of research participants are undergraduate students themselves. They participate for extra course credit, and in some instances even as a requisite for fulfilling course requirements, far from the voluntary nature of participation that is prescribed to by many professional organizations. However, the surveying of thousands of undergraduate students in a number of institutions around the world suggests that students are not concerned about having to participate to fulfil course credit requirements, are less concerned about deception (Collins *et al.*, 1979), and reported that harm and negative effects that arose through deception was eliminated through adequate debriefing (Soliday and Stanton, 1995; Kemmelmeier *et al.*, 2003). Despite the fears for the welfare of participants (Baumrind, 1964; Hertwig and Ortmann, 2001), only a handful of participants in the Milgram, Asch and Zimbardo experiments reported negative effects from participation.

What you have learned from this chapter

Ethics are norms of behaviour that guide moral behaviour in human relationships. Because research into management and business activities generally involves people, ethical issues and dilemmas are unavoidable.

Two events stand out (among many others) as major elements of the drive to develop ethical standards in research: The Nuremberg War Crimes Trial following World War II and the 1950s/1960s' Tuskegee Syphilis Study. These events led to the re-examination of ethical standards and resulted in the development by professional associations of Codes of Conduct for ethical research, and national legislation on privacy and disclosure.

Researchers enter into a personal and moral relationship with those they study and should strive to protect their rights, and ensure that the physical, social and psychological well-being of research participants is not adversely affected by the research and that no participant is harmed, loses privacy, feels compelled to take part or is uninformed about what their part in the research involves. The use of deceit is questionable and when used to maintain valid research design purposes, full debriefing must be provided. The advancement of knowledge does not provide a right to override the rights of others.

Sponsors of research have the right to receive reliable and competent service. Sponsor demands for a particular slant to the results must not be acceded to.

Adhering to Codes of Conduct and national guidelines will enable the general public to develop a sense of trust in researchers and to believe that involvement is worthwhile.

Review questions and activities

Qu. 3.1
Obtain a copy of the ethics code for your university and a copy of the form researchers have to complete to apply for approval. Study both carefully.

Qu. 3.2
Access the Web page of this chapter for a list of the Internet sites for the ethics codes of major professional organizations concerned with business and human behaviour research. Select several and review their major principles.

Qu. 3.3
Design a simple yet thorough consent letter and acceptance form for a survey on a topic of your choice. Include the following information/items.

- Introduce yourself and your organization.
- Describe the topic and purpose of the research.
- Describe in simple terms how it will be done.
- Estimate the time required.
- Emphasize privacy and confidentiality and how these will be achieved.
- Emphasize that participation is voluntary and declining is acceptable.
- Ask for a decision and that it be signed and returned in the stamped addressed envelope.

Qu. 3.4
What ethical issues are raised in the following:

(a) Prisoners volunteer in anticipation of more favourable treatment.
(b) Students participate in the lecturer's research in case non-participation has some negative implications.
(c) Unemployed persons are offered some financial reward.

Discuss in groups.

Qu. 3.5
Imagine if you were researching sales techniques directed at vulnerable or unaware populations with regard to the sale or promotion of new pop alcohol drinks that emphasized the pop ignoring the alcohol, or of products and magazines relating to deviant sex behaviour, or of Halal meat that wasn't really Halal. What position would you take? Is it simply buyer beware or have you a social responsibility in view of your knowledge of what is happening? Discuss in class.

References

Baumrind, D. 1964. Some thoughts on ethics of research: After reading Milgram's 'Behavioural Study of Obedience'. *American Psychologist*, 19, 421–423.

Collins, F.L., Jr., Kuhn, I.F., Jr. & King, G.D. 1979. Variables affecting subjects' ethical ratings of proposed experiments. *Psychological* Reports, 44, 155–164.

Hertwig, R. & Ortmann, A. 2001. Experimental methods in economics: A challenge for psychologists? *Behavioral and Brain Sciences,* 24 (3), 383–403.

Kemmelmeier, M., Davis, D. & Follette, W.C. 2003. Seven sins of misdirection? Ethical controversies surrounding the use of deception in research. In W.T. O'Donohue and K. Ferguson (eds), *Handbook of Professional Ethics for Psychologists*. Beverly Hills, CA: Sage.

Kraut, R., Olsen, J., Banaji, M., Bruckman, A., Cohen, J. & Couper, M. 2004. Psychological research online. Report of Board of Scientific Affairs' Advisory Group on the Conduct of Research on the Internet. *American Psychologist, Feb/Mar*. (This is a report into many of the ethical and research issues arising from online research undertaken by the American Psychological Association.)

Resnick, J.H. & Schwartz, T. 1973. Ethical standards as an independent variable in psychological research. *American Psychologist*, 28 (2), 134–139.

Soliday, E. & Stanton, A. 1995. Deceived versus nondeceived participants' perceptions of scientific and applied psychology. *Ethics and Behaviour,* 5, 87–104.

> **Now access Chapter 3 website and undertake the questions and activities there. Study the additional material there.**

Chapter 4
Selecting the Topic and Conducting a Literature Review

'When you steal from one author it's considered plagiarism, but if you steal from many it's a literature review!'

(W. Mizner – USA screenwriter)

'Keep on the outlook for ideas that others have used successfully. Your choice has only to be original in its adaption to the problem you are working on'

(Thomas Edison)

Content list

By the end of this chapter you will:

1 Know how to locate a problem to investigate.
2 Understand how to source primary and secondary information and documents.
3 Be able to conduct a library and Internet search, locating appropriate databases.
4 Know how to write up a collated review of relevant information and document.
5 Be able to cite references in the appropriate form.

Introduction

This chapter introduces you to a preliminary but crucial element of a research study. Before you can undertake any research study you have to obtain some in-depth knowledge of the field and what has already been done. This information will guide your thinking about what aspects you should study, offer insight into the design of the study and how it could be analysed and reported. 'Literature - What's this about?' For most of you this term initially conjures up novels and poetry, Shakespeare, Wordsworth and Henry James. In research, the meaning is more specific. 'Literature' means the documents, reports, journal articles and the like you consult (a) to gain understanding of your topic area and proposed problem, and (b) to develop a critical review of previous work.

Locating a problem to investigate

This provides the first hurdle for the would-be researcher. In the next chapter, we will demonstrate how we proceed from a hazy but interesting problem, to a clear precise testable hypothesis. Here we are only concerned with how we locate a problem in the first place. The success of research depends largely on the care taken with the preliminary preparations to identify what has been done in that direction already. Considerable thought needs to be given to choosing the problem, much of which involves searching the literature to determine whether it has already been solved and, if not, whether it is feasible. Once we have performed a literature search and refined our problem, then the study can be designed. This initial stage often takes up a considerable amount of the total time invested in the research study.

There are no set rules for finding a problem, but frequent sources of ideas are:

1. **Experience:** Topic choice must be very personal so that it engenders your deep interest or considerable curiosity. There is little merit in choosing something that doesn't engage you as boredom and declining motivation will impede completion. So your own business and marketing experiences, either as an employee, or on work placement, or simply through observation when in a shop, or involved with the delivery of some service, often will generate ideas. For example, you may notice that customers enter a shop and usually turn right rather than left; or you may wonder what particular messages do viewers of different demographic characteristics perceive in a TV address by the Prime Minister or President; or which penalties reduce the rate of employees turning up late for work? We are sure you can generate many such issues and problems like these for which answers would be very useful.

2. **Theory:** There are numerous theories in the management sciences and many of their implications need to be specified more clearly. We often find that theories and models are really only abstractions from reality and therefore need a bit of massaging to fit specific situations – one size does not fit all. For example, many theories have been developed in the Western world (predominantly in the USA) and may have limited applicability in Asian or African business contexts where norms and values differ tremendously. For example:

   • Do the Belbin/Foy team role inventories and the Jehn-Mannix conflict model hold in Asian cultures where deference to authority and group conformity are very important?

- Do successful managers have higher levels of Emotional Intelligence than unsuccessful managers, and are there contextual factors affecting this relationship such as type of business, age of manager, culture, etc.?
- Under what conditions does price increase not result in demand decrease?
- Do work values really differ between Boomer and X generations?
- Do different behaviourist schedules of reinforcement lead to variations in task performance levels and under what conditions?

3. **Journal articles:** Papers in reputable academic peer reviewed journals are stimulating sources of ideas. Most researchers will include in their Discussion/Conclusion section some thoughts about further research in the topic. For example, many studies are conducted in specific industries; do the findings hold in a range of other industries and contexts?
4. **Discussion with colleagues and peers:** Tutorial groups, staff room coffee chats and brainstorming sessions are all useful ways of turning up ideas.

Developing a focused research topic is an important first step in order to undertake an effective literature review, leading to a well-planned and successful research project. Selecting a good topic can be hard as the topic must be narrow and focused enough to be interesting, yet broad enough so that relevant information can be found.

Once the topic is selected you then need to explore it and move towards the research itself. The following steps, from seeking a research topic to commencing the study, will help act as a guide:

1. Read the general background information to gain an overview and identify useful keywords for the literature search.
2. Conduct a preliminary literature search. This can be an evolving process – as the literature review will locate relevant research articles that may offer other keywords.
3. Refine the topic following an initial literature review and define the topic as a research question within a conceptual and theoretical framework (Chapter 5).
4. Research the literature on the narrowed research question/framework.
5. Formulate testable hypotheses (Chapter 10).

Conducting the search – reviewing the literature

Why undertake a literature review?

This is a key stage in the research process so as to obtain in-depth information and evaluate existing material related to your chosen area of study, providing a theoretical base for your research. A literature review is more than a descriptive annotated bibliography, summarizing and listing each relevant finding. It is a **critical review** of what has been done, pulling disparate strands together, and identifying relationships and contradictions between previous research findings. From this you can then establish your hypotheses to investigate. This initial step, prior to conducting any research, generally requires a great amount of time in order to gather, collate and evaluate necessary information so that a thorough review of the relevant literature can be written.

The end product should be a critical analysis of collated and integrated information, not a chronological sequence of uncoordinated fragments of material.

Reasons for spending time and effort in developing a full review of the literature include:

- identifying aspects of your topic that have received little focus in past research;
- preventing you from 'reinventing the wheel';
- identifying what previous research has found, so that you can incorporate and develop existing knowledge and ideas;
- providing a perspective on which to develop your own work;
- identifying researchers with similar research interests;
- increasing your knowledge of the area, discovering important findings and which variables are important;
- providing a context for your own work, enabling you to position your project relative to other work;
- identifying appropriate research methods, instruments and statistical analysis techniques;
- identifying opposing views and contradiction in previous studies.

It is common practice to modify your topic and research questions during the literature review as you consult more resources. Be prepared to be flexible on this as you will often find yourself in one of the following situations:

- too much information and a need to narrow your focus;
- too little information and a need to broaden your focus; or
- an understanding that you have found other areas that are more important than the area you initially sought to investigate.

Changing the focus of your research is quite normal and shouldn't be seen as a failure to identify an appropriate topic from the outset. For instance, you may be interested in the importance of leadership in organizational performance. This is such a wide topic that you will need to narrow this study to a more manageable area, perhaps comparing two different leadership styles, transformational versus transactional leadership, on organizational performance in a particular industry. Restricting your topic to a smaller area of interest will make the literature search and subsequent study easier to conduct.

Delimiting some search boundaries

Before the search begins consider the following points:

1 What indexes/sources should you search? You need to consider the depth of the subject coverage provided by an index (i.e. whether it indexes the main journals for your profession or subject interest) and what types of literature are included (i.e. are articles alone covered or do they include book chapters?) Indexes do not generally suggest the level of the information contained in an article. Abstracting indexes can be more helpful in this respect as they briefly describe the content of an article.

2   Decide which libraries are able to help you, check what resources they have and ask about your rights of access to them. Some libraries allow reference access to their collections but you may find other services are not provided, e.g. database access.

3   Time allotted to complete the project will affect the depth to which you can pursue a topic.

4   How many years do you search back? For popular topics, five years may be adequate but for subjects with less material it could be necessary to search back over 20 years or more. Often very early references on a subject are of key importance.

5   Will you set geographic boundaries? Are sources from Paraguay relevant enough to the investigation you are doing in outback Australia, or are you only interested in publications from the UK; or are you interested in all publications irrespective of from where they come?

6   Should you expand your search to foreign material? But have you a working knowledge of the language?

7   Are specialized topics of information relevant? Apart from journals and books, you may need parliamentary sources, corporate reports, dissertations, audio-visual material, etc.

Primary and secondary data/sources

Primary data is that collected by the researcher for analysis; it is new data. Secondary data is the important type for literature reviews as it is information that already exists, for example, company data on sales, trade associations, government records such as census data and previous research studies located through database and library searches. Secondary sources are consulted before any research design is considered as they shed light on the research topic, relevant methodologies and existing knowledge. Secondary data can also be the initial trigger for the recognition of a research problem or opportunity as indicated above.

> *The literature review. This is essentially a secondary data search in which the researcher locates relevant literature and evaluates it.*

Sources of information

Journal articles

Effective literature searching needs a methodical approach and some advanced planning. There is heavy emphasis in this text on searching the journal literature as this is the most complex and crucial literature area to access. Journal articles provide the most up-to-date source of published research and often cover subjects not readily found in book format. Some articles, known as review articles, provide overviews of a subject with extensive reference lists and make excellent starting places for research. You may frequently have to search beyond the confines of your subject area to find relevant literature, so consider journals in related subject areas such as psychology, sociology, politics, economics, education, etc. to locate relevant business related material.

Peer-reviewed journal articles

Peer-reviewed articles are the most credible of all documents to peruse as they are subjected to numerous evaluations and revisions prior to publication. A reputable journal editor will ensure the article has been scrutinized by several knowledgeable researchers familiar with the field of investigation and acknowledged as worthy of publication, before actual publication – though as the Sudbo example in Chapter 3 showed, these publications are not above being fraudulent.

Journals on the Web

Increasingly, journals provide the full text of the journal on the Web, although you often need a subscription before accessing though abstracts are generally always available. Most journal websites also list the contents of recent issues. Even where an institution has online access to the full text of journals, access may only be possible while on site. Licence arrangements may preclude off site access to the full text of journals.

Indexes

Major indexes to the literature normally have a highly structured arrangement, usually an alphabetical list by topic and/or author indicating the source either in printed format or as a database. Obviously, many journals have their own annual indexes to their content but, for a more extensive search, you will need to use more comprehensive indexes that locate relevant literature in journals, books and a variety of other sources. The main method of search is based on the selection of a keyword, often your topic name or an important author in the area. Different forms of indexes exist.

(a) **Abstracting indexes:** These provide the normal details of any bibliographical index but also give you an abstract that summarizes the content of the article. This information can be crucial in deciding whether the article is valuable to read in entirety. Useful ones include:

Applied Social Science Abstracts	Human Resources Abstracts
ABI/INFORM – ProQuest	Psychological Abstracts
Business Source – Ebsco	Sociological Abstracts
Business Source Elite	Vocational Search
Business Source Premier	Wilson Business Periodicals Index/Wilson
BusinessLink	Business Abstracts
Emerald Management Reviews	

(b) **Citation indexes:** These can be used for normal subject or author searches but also have a unique function. Having found a key author and paper it is possible to find out subsequent authors who have referred to this original work, possibly building on it or even criticizing it. One major citation index is the Social Science Citation Index

Most of the printed indexes are also available as databases, accessible either via the Internet or through CD-ROM based systems. Clearly, being able to search for information using a computer has many advantages. For instance, search terms can be combined for more complex topics, something that printed indexes cannot easily provide and thousands of records can be scanned very rapidly.

Textbooks

Textbooks can be valuable in providing an overview of a subject and a distillation of knowledge on a subject. The major drawbacks are that books date very rapidly and there may be nothing specifically published on your topic. Books can be searched for in individual library catalogues, most of which are now computer-based or through a range of bibliographies, either general or subject specific. Some key examples are:

- British Books in Print: This has no subject section but lists books by title and author.
- British Library: Access to the British Library catalogue which lists all the books, etc. held by the national UK library.
- Amazon: Useful source of online information and ordering of books, etc.
- US Library of Congress: Online catalogue
- Australian Books in Print: Published by Thorpe-Bowker. Over 110,000 books listed.

Grey literature

This includes a diverse range of material not usually available off the shelves of your local bookshop because it is not published through normal channels. Examples of this type of literature are university theses, conference proceedings, government, and business reports. The information from these sources can be valuable and indeed it may be the only (or often the first) place where the results of research work or new economic, demographic and other data are published.

Examples of grey literature are:

- Zetoc: Table of contents database for journal and conference papers. Athens registration needed.
- Index of Conference Proceedings: Lists the proceedings of conferences from around the world and is based on the collections held by the British Library.
- Index to theses: This index lists theses produced at universities and colleges in the UK.
- British reports, translations and theses: This British Library publication lists a varied collection of grey literature.
- Dissertation abstracts: American database of dissertations – only available on subscription.

Directories

Directories provide useful information on organizations or individuals and are useful guides to other sources of information. There are a number of directories that list ongoing research and it is wise to check that your research is not going to duplicate an existing research project. A few examples are:

- Current Research in Britain: This is a national register of research in progress at British Universities and Colleges.
- Professional Bodies research lists: The professional organizations may keep their own registers of ongoing research.

The Internet

The World Wide Web provides a multimedia interface to the Internet and Web pages provide links to information and documents. The Internet can access library catalogues, online databases and to browse through publications, such as journals, in electronic format. The major problem with using the Internet has been locating relevant information and at times it can feel like being left in a jungle without a guide and a compass! Increasingly organizations are developing Web pages that provide information plus hypertext links to other sites of interest.

Using a database

Having identified the topic and keywords you must carefully choose a database(s) to search. Databases, usually either abstract or full text, are an important source of background information, containing millions of articles and citations on numerous subjects. In the past, databases were published, often monthly or annually, as a collation of abstracts in book form with all the necessary publication details which would allow a researcher to locate the citation. The advent of CD-ROM meant that thousands of abstract periodicals could take up far less space on one CD-ROM. Although the CD-ROM still exists, most databases are now on servers, accessible online. Universities, government departments and businesses all vary in the extent to which they provide access to these facilities, and you should acquaint yourself with whatever resources you have at your disposal. Currently, many publishing houses that produce various journals and academic textbooks allow individuals to purchase single articles over the Internet. Articles, chapters from a book, and even books themselves can be downloaded as a .html or .pdf document. Abstract databases are useful for the first searches, as by reading the abstracts you can decide which are pertinent and then print out only these selected articles in full.

Subject directories

Subject directories are catalogues of different subject material, created by a number of different Internet users, including universities, libraries, professional organizations, and individuals. You should use these for general, research oriented queries, and when you want to view sites often recommended by experts. Most directories are searchable. There are commercial directories and academic/professional subject directories.

The commercial directory: An example is Yahoo. Here you will find subjects ordered under headings like Finance, Management, Social Science, Tourism and Recreation. There is very little or no evaluation of content – commercial interests pay to be included in the directory. You must evaluate very carefully any information obtained and it is unlikely to be an important source for academic research.

The academic/professional directory: These directories contain carefully chosen and annotated lists of quality Internet sites. Many may not be available via a crawler search engine, as explained below. Good examples include Omni, Bubl, and Infomine. The last, compiled by the University of California (infomine.ucr.edu), selects only sources considered relevant to the academic and research community for inclusion in the database.

The crawler

This is the programme we generally think of as a search engine, e.g. Google and AltaVista for targeted, specific searches. Each is a searchable database of Internet files collected by a computer program (called a wanderer, crawler, robot, worm, spider). Indexing is created from the collected files, e.g. title, full text, size, URL, etc. There is no selection criteria for the collection of files, though evaluation can be applied to the ranking of results. Crawlers work best for clearly targeted and specific queries.

First generation search services: These often rank order to what they produce in attempting to put what they think will be the most useful hits at the top of your list. Altavista is basically a first generation service.

Second generation search services: These rank 'hits' by 'off-page' criteria. For example, Google ranks by the number of links to a page from other sites which it rates highly.

The Deep Web

The Deep Web consists of information stored in searchable databases mounted on the Web which crawlers are unable or not programmed to enter. These include multimedia and image files, and files created in non-standard file types such as Portable Document Format (.pdf). Many commercial directories offer an option to search databases offering specific content such as news, business, shopping, multimedia files, and so on. These databases constitute a small subset of the Deep Web. Academic directories or gateways (Omni, Bubl, Tripdatabase, Virtual Library, etc.) would be your usual access to information on the Deep Web for research purposes. Other sites that collect databases on the invisible web include:

- http://dir.lycos.com/Reference/Searchable Databases/
- http://www.invisibleweb.com/
- http://www.webdata.com

The extent of your resource availability will determine how effective your review of the literature can be, and the subsequent relevance of your research project. Obviously, the more sources accessed, the more likely you will find relevant citations, and develop a clear

Table 4.1   **Summary of Internet sources**

Subject directory	Web search engine	Deep Web
When researching a broad topic.	When researching a narrow or obscure topic.	When you want dynamically changing content such as the latest news, job postings, etc.
To identify sites annotated by experts.	When identifying a specific site.	When you want to find information that is normally stored in a database, such as a phone book listing, listings of lawyers, doctors, bank branches, etc., searchable collections of laws, company data, and so on.
To access moderated sites.	To search the full text of millions of pages.	
To retrieve a list of relevant sites, rather than numerous individual pages.	To retrieve a large number of documents on your topic.	
To avoid low-content documents.	To search according to the types of documents, file types, source locations, languages, date last modified, etc.	

in-depth knowledge of the topic you propose to investigate. On the other hand, access to a wide range of resources can backfire, resulting in numerous irrelevant search results. If a keyword search is too general, you may end up with thousands of search results that will have to be sifted through to find the information wanted.

Using a database: Keyword search

There are some simple techniques that will reduce the number of superfluous citations, but hopefully not remove the important and relevant documents. Boolean operators '*and*', '*or*', and '*not*' allow researchers to combine search terms and limit the scope of the search. These operators will help save research time by focusing the search to what you're looking for.

For instance, assume I am interested in identifying the role personal employee characteristics, such as personality and motivation, have within successful project management outcomes. Searching for citations with these terms are represented in the Venn diagrams (Fig 4.1). Using the Boolean operator '*OR*', searching for the terms 'personality' *or* 'motivation' *or* 'project management' produces a large number of results, which in Figure 4.1 are represented by three circles. Circle 1 contains all the search results for the term 'personality'; Circle 2 contains all the search results for the term 'motivation'; and Circle 3 contains all the search results for 'project management'. As Table 4.2 demonstrates, the use of the Boolean operator '*OR*' will produce over 673,700,000 (Google) and 90,837 (Academic Search Premier) articles by searching for citations that include any of these terms. By using the Boolean operator '*AND*' to pair the variables, we are able to reduce the number of results returned. When all three are linked by '*AND*', the search demonstrates a consequence of limiting search criteria, as exemplified by Academic Search Premier, which now reports no results.

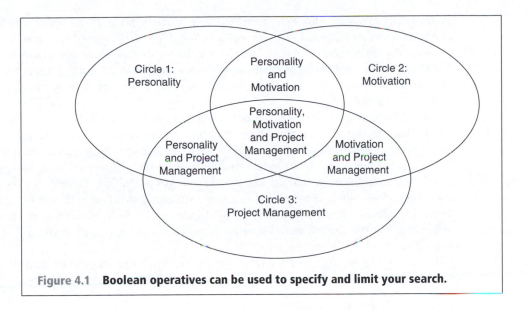

Figure 4.1 Boolean operatives can be used to specify and limit your search.

Such a response requires rethinking a number of steps to the literature review process. Firstly, the term 'project management' could be too narrow a term to use. Using an alternative term or simply using 'management' may increase the number of results generated. Another factor that could determine your response rate is the database engine you have used to search. As you can see from Table 4.2, Google clearly reports more search results than Academic Search Premier, simply because of the differences in the number of data records each search engine compares your search criteria against. But citations from Academic Search Premier are from peer-reviewed journals and are generally more

Table 4.2 The results from searching with Google, Academic Search Premier and Business Source Premier

Boolean Operator	Term	Google	Academic Search Premier	Business Source Premier
Or	Personality	93,300,000	59,575	0
	Motivation	94,400,000	27,487	0
	Project Management	486,000,000	3,775	0
	TOTAL	673,700,000	90,837	0
AND	Personality and Motivation	1,990,000	1643	0
	Personality and Project Management	3,230,000	11	0
	Motivation and Project Management	25,600,000	19	0
	Personality, Motivation and Project Management	1,130,000	0	3

academically credible. Although 'googling' will certainly bring up reputable articles by reputable researchers, there is far more information of dubious authorship, a reality which one should keep in mind. In this instance, it may be worthwhile using other more relevant academic search databases. For example, when running the same search criteria for these three terms, with the '*AND*' operator, using the alternative Business Source Premier, three citations were reported.

A third Boolean operator '*NOT*', allows researchers to more precisely distinguish within a term that may incorporate more than what they are interested in. Continuing with the example of the role of Personality and Motivation in successful Project Management, you become aware that motivation can be classified as intrinsic or extrinsic. Whereas intrinsic motivation comes from within the individual (you do something because it is personally rewarding; gives you a sense of self-esteem), extrinsic motivation is driven by external forces (pay, fear of being sacked). You may decide that intrinsic motivation is a form of motivation that you think is most important in your topic of study, and so you include this in your keyword search criteria.

This can be accomplished in two ways. Firstly, the '*AND*' operator can be used to simply search for 'Intrinsic motivation'. For example, the terms to be inputted would read:

'Project Management' *AND* 'Intrinsic Motivation'

Alternatively, the '*NOT*' operator would include the following commands:

'Project Management' *AND* 'Motivation' *NOT* 'Extrinsic Motivation'

Whilst '*NOT*' excludes records from your search results, one should take care not to lose important citations that also contain the words you are searching for.

You will note the use of quotation marks in the above examples. They are referred to as **forcing the order of processing**. By surrounding a word or words the search engine will process these first. Next, the search engine will combine this result with the last part of the search with the other search terms. This method ensures that semantically related OR terms are kept together as a unit.

As an alternative to Boolean operators, **Implied Boolean logic** refers to a search in which symbols are used to represent the Boolean logical operators. '**+**' replaces the '*AND*' operator, and the '**−**' replaces the '*NOT*'. The *absence* of a symbol is also significant, as the space between keywords usually defaults to '*AND*' logic.

Boolean Logic Operators:

AND *narrows the search*   **OR** *broadens the search*   **NOT** *excludes concepts*

Accessing citations

The procedures for accessing the citations reported in your results will vary according to whether you have used the Internet, online databases, abstract periodicals, or CD-ROMs. CD-ROMs and abstract periodicals will provide enough bibliographic information, relating to the author, publishers, journal, book or article title, and date of publication, so that you may locate a printed copy of the article you want. However, you may have limited availability to the actual journal or report in your local resource centre, though inter-library loan allows users to borrow from other libraries.

The results from Internet and online database searches are perhaps much easier in accessing the primary material. Both the Internet and database searches will contain links either directly to the material, or to a site whereby you can download the material. Documents usually kept on the Internet are available in a number of formats including html, .doc, .ppt or .pdf. In some instances, payment will be required to download these files.

Searching the Internet

As demonstrated in the keyword search and Boolean operator section of this chapter, the use of the Internet can be a very effective medium for obtaining a high response rate to a literature search. However, there are serious weaknesses to using the Internet for academic purposes. Firstly, the Internet is a self-publishing medium and searches will include content with a wide range of quality from a variety of sources. Evaluation of Internet sources is critical. There is little or no peer evaluation on some sites. To guard against this, it is highly recommended to access multiple sites when undertaking an Internet literature search as subject directories and search engines vary in contents features, and accuracy of information.

In summary, literature searching, while a vital process at the start of a research project, is very much a practical activity and to appreciate how to do it requires hands-on experience using the sources. Only then will some of the methods outlined above begin to make sense to you, particularly as each index and database has its own unique layout and idiosyncrasies. Internet search engines are valuable and enable you to enter keywords and retrieve citations to Internet sites that contain the keywords. Whilst their advantage lies in offering access to a vast range of information resources many of the results may be outdated, inaccurate, and/or incomplete.

> *You will find a selection of relevant and useful journals and databases on this book's Website.*

Critically reviewing the literature

Evaluating research reports

Once you have found your essential literature then you must evaluate it critically to decide its worth as a piece of research, and its relevance to your topic. There are five key processes:

1 Identifying the source of the research, including the provider of financial support for the study.
2 Analyzing the foundations on which the research question is based.
3 Examining the research methodology.

4   Evaluating the results, including the appropriateness of the statistical tests used.
5   An objective analysis of the conclusions in the light of the results, and the appropriateness of the implications of these findings.

To some extent your ability to review academic papers, review articles and the like, located from your search, is something that requires practice and experience. However, the process can be aided by following a checklist of things to look out for and by comparing the paper under review to the criteria. The basic following key questions should be asked:

- Introduction........................... Why did they undertake the research?
- Methods............................... What did they do?
- Results................................ What did they find?
- Discussion............................ What do the results mean?

To expand the four questions above, you can follow the questions in Table 4.3 as a guide to analyse documents for your literature critically. You will need to learn more about research methods and statistical issues in later chapters before some of these questions make sense.

Evaluating Internet resources

Special consideration needs to be given when evaluating Internet resources. As Internet information can vary in type, quality, presentation and format it is difficult to advise on a process by which you can critically evaluate all web resources. Instead, questions relating to the following themes need to be considered.

Purpose

It is important to identify the audience for whom the Web resource was aimed at. It is common for Web pages to be biased to appeal to a certain readership, or to express the author's personal opinion. Hence, it is important to identify whether the source is a personal expression of an opinion or a scholarly document.

Source

The identity of the author(s) or their organization should be clearly identifiable. It should also be possible for you to assess their level of expertise on the subject of discussion. Often the URL address can indicate the degree of certainty that any information, for example, the website www.bps.org.uk (the homepage to the British Psychological Society), is perhaps more reputable as the provider of information about psychology than http://www.psychosrus.com.

Table 4.3   Tips for for analysing research papers critically

Title	Catchy titles may not inform on what the article is about. However, a poor title does not necessarily indicate a poor paper.
Author(s)	Consider author(s) academic background, job title, qualifications, and their place of work as these indicate the writer's level of competency to conduct research. Experts in the subject area should produce work of a high standard.
Source	Where the article was published should indicate its potential value. The key issue is whether it is a peer reviewed journal or simply a posting on the net.
Abstract	This should be a concise description of the background, methodology and report findings.
Introduction	The introduction should introduce the topic of investigation, adequately reviewing relevant literature, identifying key concepts and landmark findings with a clear link to the aims of the research.
Purpose/ Justification	Is the report logical and convincing? Do author(s) show how the results have important implications for theory and/or practice?
Definitions	Are major terms operationally defined?
Previous research	Has this been adequately covered? Is it clearly connected with the present study?
Research Questions/ Hypotheses	Are the hypotheses clear, feasible, operational? Do they follow from the literature review?
Method	The procedures used to collect data should be detailed enough to allow for full and precise replication.
Design and validity	What threats to the validity of the study are evident? Were they controlled or even discussed?
Sampling	What sample was used and was sample and sampling technique adequate? Can generalization to a population be made?
Instrumentation	Were the test instruments adequately described? Is there evidence of their reliability and validity?
Data analysis	Is data summarized and presented appropriately? Are descriptive and inferential statistics used appropriately and interpreted corrected? Are imitations and assumptions discussed?
Results	Are results clearly presented and summarized in tabular and/or graphical format, explaining what the data is meant to show, relating to the hypothesis being tested. Are the statistical results in the tables correctly interpreted?
Discussion and conclusion	Should clearly identify whether or not the research question has been answered. Do the authors place the results into a larger context and do they recognize the limitations of the study? Are the implications for theory, research and practice related to the findings?
Supplementary material	A references list should identify all work cited. Appendices should include copies of the measures used, unless they are standardized instruments or where the protection of copyright necessitates its exclusion. Additional tabulated data can also be presented, which could include details of the scale's reliability, and full descriptions of means and standard deviations which are too numerous to be included in the results section.

As well, the URL will also indicate the type of site. The following conventions of URL's exist:

- .edu or .ac for educational or research material;
- .gov for government resources;
- .com for commercial products or commercially sponsored sites;
- .org for organizations, both non and for-profit.

Content

Whilst important for all sources, it is especially important not to take Web information at face value. Websites are rarely the subject of peer-review. Possible exceptions include databases like Wikipedia (www.wikipedia.org), which allow all Internet users to add, edit and modify information. Unfortunately, the accuracy of such information is victim to the expertise of users who choose to add and monitor listed information. It is important then to identify not only possible content errors, but also statements that are simply personal points of view and evidence of bias. Clearly, the identification and citation of other sources is important in determining a critical evaluation of the Web resource.

Style and functionality

Whether dressing up for a job interview or meeting the 'in-laws' for the first time, first impressions do count. The same can be said for assessing the accuracy of a website. Websites that are well designed and logically structured, easily navigable with links that are working and up-to-date, and are written in an appropriate scholarly style, are more likely to consist of accurate and reliable information, though this is not always an appropriate safeguard.

Despite its flaws, it is clear that the Internet is a valuable source that enables the quick dissemination of ideas and information, and is an appropriate starting point to the initial literature review process.

Collating the information and writing the research review

As you read through your collection of reports, abstracts and full articles, if the abstract looks promising, you should summarize the important elements on the basis of the four key questions above and Table 4.3. Taking notes on your readings is as important as the searching and reading because you will soon forget what you have read. Or, even worse, you will be unable to find something that you have read when putting together your reference section of your literature review. The traditional way of keeping notes on literature is using index cards. The cards should include all the information you are likely to need for drawing up the references or bibliography for your project. In addition to the reference details, it is also important to include notes relating to the content of the article relating to the tips above. Include memorable quotations, always remembering to note the author, page and text title.

Now, computer copy and paste procedures enable you to make up a file of abstracts, which can be re-ordered and elaborated, as well as linked in various ways by your own argument and comment. As your reading of the literature becomes more extensive, you should start to notice themes and patterns emerging. There may be obvious themes and there may be subtle themes which require you to probe further into the literature. Use these developing themes and patterns to structure your literature review rather than writing a chronological progression of summaries of research studies. Remember to summarize and evaluate the material, emphasizing relationships and inconsistencies, relating it all to what you propose to do.

Do not write a literature review that is either disorganized ramblings or a chain of pointless isolated summaries of each document with each sentence beginning '*Brown (2001) says …*', '*Burns (2005) says …*', '*Green (2003) says …*' etc. Create a coherent argument that paraphrases and evaluates the literature and shows its relevance to what your problem or topic is. Review the literature, don't reproduce it, and avoid long quotes. It is more important to indicate what you think about the study rather than what the author says. Remember that the *raison d'être* for the literature review is to provide a background to the proposed research problem.

Tips for writing a literature review

1   Arrange your written or computer file notes in a logical order. If you are having difficulty seeing an order, look for clues in the sequence of your ideas or try concept mapping the topic.
2   Identify the major themes – these can be used as draft major headings.
3   Sort your abstracts, reviewed articles and notes to fit under the headings. Revise the headings, order, or both, as necessary.
4   Look for relationships among ideas and group them as subtopics. Build a step-by-step, hierarchical list of the points you plan to cover, e.g.:
    - 1st main idea
        - 1st supporting point
            - evidence, argument, or examples
        - 2nd supporting point
            - evidence, argument, or examples
        - brief summary
    - 2nd main idea, etc.…
        - 1st support point
            - evidence, argument, or examples
        etc.…
5   Try to avoid long lists of subtopics. Consider combining these into related ideas. In nearly all cases, your literature review will be better if you link related ideas.
6   If you can't decide where to put something, put it in two or more places in the outline. As you write, you can decide which place is the most appropriate.

The second method requires providing the author's name and date following a phrase or paragraph expressing an idea or concept proposed or identified by another author which supports an argument that you are discussing. For example:

It is the perception of many managers that they are often under pressure to compromise personal ethical standards to meet company goals (Cavanaugh, 1980).

If two or more authors have authored a reference all their surnames are provided. When citing a reference with three or more authors on further occasions, every subsequent citation after the first need only list the first author's surname followed by the term 'et al.' – Latin for 'and others' – and then the publication date. For example, the initial citation of (Burns, Bakken, Holmen and Parker 2006) can be replaced with (Burns *et al*. 2006) for all future citations, except in the final reference list.

When multiple references are used, list in chronological order with the earliest publication date first. For example,

There are clear implications for researchers of workplace health in research that links elevated uric acid to the development of coronary arteriosclerosis and coronary heart disease (Brand et al., 1985; Frohlich, 1993; and Lee et al., 1995).

If two or more references for the same author or authors are used, list in chronological order. For example:

Ryff and Singer (1998, 2000) describe well-being not simply as the attaining of pleasure, but as a striving for perfection, the realization of one's true potential.

Increasingly, citations involve referencing sources from the Internet, radio and television. Generally, references from the Internet involve citing the author's name and publication, if available, in the same way as for print material. Citing television or radio sources usually involves citing the title of the programme or feature with the date of airing. For example:

A spokesman for the finance department stated that continuing economic pressures would lead to a recession of the nation's economy (Lateline, Channel 7, 26 November 2006).

Reference lists

All cited references must be included in an alphabetically sorted collation of references, and when two citations from the same author are to be referenced, these are placed in chronological order with the earliest citation first. There are also different formats for listing books, journal articles and electronic sources, which are described below.

Citing books

The general format for citing a book includes the following details in the stated order:

- The name/s of author/s, editor/s, compiler/s. (Names are provided in the order of surname first, followed by their initials). There may be instances where publications do not identify individual authors, such as government reports, in which case the author details would be the institution or department responsible.
- The year of publication.
- The title of publication and subtitle, if any. Titles must be either underlined or italicized.
- The series title and individual volume, if any.
- The edition number, if other than the first.
- The publisher.
- The place of publication.
- The page numbers in the instance of a chapter of a book.

Examples of writing references for books follow the following format for single or multiple authors.

One author

Goleman, D. 1998, *Working With Emotional Intelligence*, Bloomsbury, London.

Two or more authors

Parkin, D. & Bourke, P. 2004. *What Makes Teams Work: How to Create and Maintain a Winning Team in Business and Sport,* Pan Macmillan Australia Pty Limited, Sydney.

Edited books

Edited books involve one or more editors, editing the work of several authors who will be tasked with writing a specialized chapter within a book on a specific topic. Reference to the edited text is as follows:

Silberman, M. (ed.), 2002. *The 2002 Team and Organization Development Sourcebook*, McGraw-Hill, New York.

Reference to a chapter in an edited text would follow this pattern:

Hart, S.J. 1991. A first time users guide to the collection and analysis of interview data. In N. Smith and P. Dainty (eds), *The Management Research Handbook*. Routledge, London. 190–204.

Institution, corporation or other organization

Australian Bureau of Statistics 2002. Projections for the Population of Australia, States and Territories: 1999–2061 (Cat. No. 3222.0) ABS, Canberra.

Edition

A popular and well-used text can come out in successive editions over a period of years often revised and extended in each new edition. In this instance the publication date relates to the year of the current edition and the edition number is included after the title of the text.

Burns, R.B. 2000. *Introduction to Research Methods*, 4th edn, Pearson Education, Australia, Frenchs Forrest, NSW.

Citing an article

The general format for citing an article is similar to that for texts and includes the following details in the stated order:

1 name/s of author/s of the article
2 year of publication
3 title of article (normal font type)
4 title of periodical (underlined or italicized)
5 volume number and/or the issue number
6 page number(s)

Journal article

Hormozi, A.M. & Giles, S. 2004 Data mining: a competitive weapon for banking and retail industries. *Information Systems Management*, 21(2), 62–71.

Conference paper

Burns, R. 2003. Personal Growth: An essential element in professional training. *8th European Congress of Psychology, Vienna, July.*

For electronic resources

This could include sources from CD ROMs, electronic journals or other sources from the Internet. The basic form of the citations follow the principles listed for print sources (see above):

1 name/s of author/s
2 date of publication
3 title of publication
4 publisher/organization
5 edition, if other than first

6   type of medium
7   date item retrieved
8   name or site address on Internet (if applicable)

However, in some circumstances it is not always possible to provide all of these details. Frequently details of the author, or date of publication are not always available. Whilst in those societies with freedom of speech the lack of authorship suggests dubious accuracy of the source, in some societies it is necessary for authors to protect their identity. But even within 'free' societies, it may be necessary for authors to not declare ownership for a number of privacy reasons.

World Wide Web

Curtin University Library and Information Service, *Harvard Referencing 2006*. http://library.curtin.edu.au/referencing/harvard.pdf Retrieved 26 December, 2006.

Singh, P. L. (2001) Developing knowledge capital. *Journal of Organisational Assets*. (Web document, 8, (21), 9 pages). Available; http://www.orgassets.edu/knowledge/fremt/821 Retrieved 17 June 2006.

A note of caution

Unfortunately, the advent of subsequent citation systems, based on the Harvard citation system, such as the American Psychological Association (APA) citation style, has seen a profusion of different citation styles. In trying to present the 'correct' version of the Harvard citation system, the author has attempted to describe the most correct and original. Try an Internet search for the Harvard citation system and you will find a plethora of university and education sites purportedly describing the Harvard citation system. Whichever sites you choose, you will find that they all differ in some miniscule way. When citing books, some versions will suggest including parenthesis around the year of publication, whilst other say not to. Some versions include a '.' following a book's title whilst others use a ','. And when it comes to listing the publishers and place of publication, different versions place these in different orders, sometimes separated by a ':' and sometimes separated by a ','.

If you suffer by having your reports or essays marked down because of following a 'version' of the Harvard citation system that your lecturer does not approve, then you are advised to check with each of your lecturers as to the 'correct' version they want you to follow. You may be interested to know that even within, let alone between, some faculties at the same university institution, there are marked differences of opinion.

What you have learned from this chapter

It is essential that you select a research topic in which you are interested. Gain a broad summary of your area first to develop an overview of the topic and then identify a specific focus. From this glean keywords usable for a databased literature search, using secondary data, particularly online abstracts, indexes and citations.

(Continued)

The literature review should be written in an integrated format using major themes and not be a sequential summary of each piece of research. Learn how to use the Harvard system for referencing your sources.

Supplementary reading

Curtin University. http://library.curtin.edu.au/referencing/harvard.pdf

Denison, T. & Stewart, J. 1998. *Electronic Sources of Information for Business in Australia and N. Zealand*. Melbourne, RMIT Publishing.

Hart, C. 2001. *Doing a Literature Search*. London, Sage.

Leedy, P. 1997. *Practical Research Planning and Design*. 5th edn. Macmillan, London.

University of Queensland. http://www.library.uq.edu.au/training/citation/harvard.html

Review questions and activities

Qu. 4.1

In groups, think up some interesting issues and problems that you might like to research. These may arise from experiences or from other lecture courses in Business and Management.

Qu. 4.2

Can you list some of the main sources of literature other than journals that you might want to use? Can you describe the type of information they can provide?

Qu. 4.3

You have now learnt some issues of literature searching. From your earlier reading can you recall the main reasons why a literature review is an important part of research work?

Activity 4.1

Locate five journal articles or a combination of five journal articles and reviews on a topic of interest to you in the business field.

Activity 4.2

Select a topic of interest to you, and choose three or four keywords. Conduct a database search and select four or five of the hits. Write a brief collated summary of what you have discovered about the topic. Integrate your material; do not simply produce a paragraph on each.

Access Chapter 4 Web page on the book website for more materials that may help in your searches.

Chapter 5
Theory, Problem Definition, Frameworks, and Research Design

'The great tragedy of science is the slaying of a beautiful hypothesis by an ugly fact'
(T. H. Huxley)

'Enough research will tend to support your theory'

(One of Murphy's laws)

Content list

> ## By the end of this chapter you will:
>
> 1 Understand the value of theory as a basis for research.
> 2 Be able to state a research question that defines predicted relationships between your abstract concepts.
> 3 Be able to define a management problem.
> 4 Be able to develop conceptual and theoretical frameworks
> 5 Understand why we operationalize variables.
> 6 Be able to differentiate between Independent, Dependent and Moderating variables
> 7 Understand the uses and purposes of different research designs.

Introduction

This chapter will assist you in designing relevant and focused research, whether starting from theory, as most quantitative research does, or from observations and local problems, as much qualitative research does. Research is based on the empirical testing of ideas. These ideas come from any number of sources. They might start with an existing theory found through a literature search. Or a researcher might notice in the literature that a series of findings are conceptually related. From these observations they might devise a theory to explain the findings. Or, more simply, the researcher might just be curious. Perhaps they have seen a particular behaviour occur in a particular circumstance, and wonder why, e.g. they have noticed that '*customers will pay more for organic vegetables*'. Finally, a company manager may have a local issue he wants investigating, such as why cannot he find well-qualified IT staff; there is no theory as yet and the researcher has to start from scratch with observations, individual interviews and the like. In all these circumstances there is an attempt to gain some feel of the theories and local issues in order to generate some specific research questions that can be turned into hypotheses by clarifying relationships in conceptual and theoretical frameworks.

Starting from theory

The starting point of Quantitative Research is Theory. Most theories are complex and well established (coming from the academic literature as we explored in the previous chapter). There are many well-known theories, such as *Einstein's theory of relativity; Darwin's theory of natural selection; Newton's theory of universal gravitation*; and *Pythagoras' Theory*. In the business world, the theory of competition predicts that firms within an industry that are able to differentiate themselves gain a competitive advantage, Herzberg's theory offers motivational proposals, and Tuckman provides a theoretical model of stages in team development. A theory or model proposes relationships between abstract concepts and allows for generalizations based on individual situations and facts.

Thus the first stage of research is:

- to evaluate critically a collation of previous research (Chapter 4) and develop a model or theory using relationships between abstract concepts or use existing theory.
- If no previous research has been performed or is of meagre quality, or if no relevant theory exists, then defining your problem, such as '*why has the Japanese tourist influx reduced by 25% this year?*' is the equivalent stage. Chapter 1 introduced the inductive process as a means of theory generation, whereby from many specific observations a general principle can be proposed that underlies the observed phenomena. In business research, this inductive process usually comprises the qualitative research element.

From either of these approaches, the theory is derived and expressed as a **conceptual framework**, followed by its expression in measurable variable terms as a **theoretical framework**. This then leads into a statement of **hypotheses** that are tested to find support for the theory or lead to its rejection. We will work our way through this sequence, from theory to hypothesis.

How do we express a theory or model?

With a verbal statement: We can state Pythagoras' famous theory as 'the square on the hypotenuse is equal to the sum of the squares of the other two sides in a right angled triangle'. Similarly, we could have a theory which states that 'leadership style influences employee retention rates, a relationship that is mediated through employee stress level'.

As a set of equations: We can express Pythagoras' theory as $A^2 + B^2 = C^2$ or $C = \sqrt{(A^2 + B^2)}$. Our theory of leadership style affecting retention rates, influenced by individual stress level, could be given a pseudo-formula:

ERR = LS(ST) + other unknown variables

Where: ERR = Employee Retention Rate
        LS   = Leadership Style
        ST   = Stress
        Other = all other influences on retention levels (may be unidentified as yet)

Graphically: Visual representation enables the theory's essential elements and relationships to stand out better than in a verbose explanation.

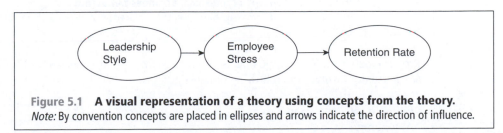

Figure 5.1 A visual representation of a theory using concepts from the theory.
Note: By convention concepts are placed in ellipses and arrows indicate the direction of influence.

Concepts – the building blocks of theory

We live in a complex world and simplify it by interpreting it in terms of general principles or abstract concepts, e.g.:

Brand loyalty	Leverage
Quality	Customer satisfaction
Emotional intelligence	Transformational leadership
Empathy	Demand

> **Concepts:** *Concepts are abstractions of reality*

These abstract concepts are not things that we can directly see. An abstract concept is used to summarize and describe behaviours that share certain attributes. The abstract concept of **ethical business behaviour** is manifest in a multitude of specific behaviours and events, such as advertising offers/discounts which are not what they seem, inflating mileage business travel claims, taking waste materials home from work without permission, taking longer lunch breaks than permitted, etc. A businessperson or employee with a high level of ethical standards would not indulge in these specific behaviours, whereas one with a lower level of ethical values would be more likely to display behaviour like this. We could put these objective and measurable specific behaviours that reflect the concept of ethical business behaviour into a diagram (see Fig. 5.2).

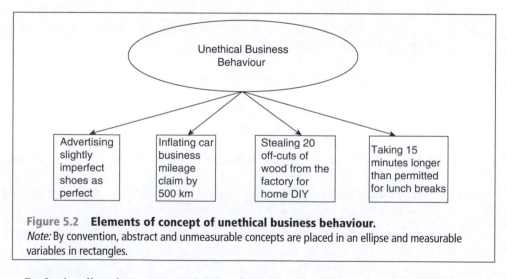

Figure 5.2 **Elements of concept of unethical business behaviour.**
Note: By convention, abstract and unmeasurable concepts are placed in an ellipse and measurable variables in rectangles.

Professionalism is a concept that is often used in business research. This complex concept usually involves the following dimensions:

- Belief in self-regulation.
- Autonomy.

- A sense of calling.
- A belief in service to the public.
- The use of the professional organization as a major reference.

Each of these dimensions could be measured by responses to questionnaire statements measured on a five-point scale. For example, '*I am a member of my professional organisation*'; '*I make my own decisions in regard to what needs to be done in my work tasks*'. Then, by taking the average score of the responses over all the questionnaire statements, a single score or composite variable is created representing respondents' perceptions of the concept 'professionalism'. Another concept frequently met is that of customer satisfaction. Specific behaviours that demonstrate this involve amongst others, revisiting for further purchases, recommending the company to relatives/friends, writing a letter of thanks to manager, smiling and praising employees personally (Fig. 5.3).

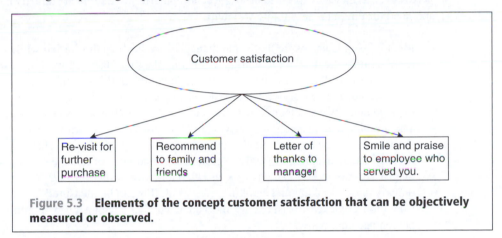

Figure 5.3   Elements of the concept customer satisfaction that can be objectively measured or observed.

Figures 5.2 and 5.3 propose that there are specific and measurable behaviours that indicate the degree to which particular persons or groups behave ethically in their work or differ in their customer satisfaction with a particular company. By specifying concepts in the form of specific behaviours that are measurable, as in these two examples, it is possible to subject them to hypothesis testing. We do this by constructing conceptual and theoretical frameworks.

Conceptual and theoretical frameworks

Once the literature survey is completed and the theory clearly delineated with relationships between factors identified, frameworks must be developed enabling the researcher to make sense of the relationships and identify the relevant variables. These frameworks aid our understanding of the relationships because they are graphic displays. Brief verbal material can be added to explain why we suggest these relationships and believe the variables are relevant.

The conceptual framework

This is the starting point for much quantitative research (such as questionnaire surveys). Our Theory or Model specifying proposed relationships between theoretical concepts can be drawn graphically as a flow diagram. The example in Figure 5.1 of the Leadership Style, Stress, Retention Rates link above is a conceptual framework, proposing that the management style (degree of authoritarian or democratic style) under which employees work affects their stress levels which, in turn, influences their likelihood to remain with the organization.

> **A conceptual framework** – this links abstract concepts as a first stage in designing a piece of research.

However, as they are expressed in abstract conceptual terms they are not directly measurable and need turning into measurable variables.

- Most laypeople are aware that some managers are fairly authoritarian while others are more democratic, leading to workplaces being pleasant places to work in while others are unpleasant. But how do we as researchers quantify all this – perhaps with a questionnaire on management style? This would enable us to categorize workplaces in terms of management style and then look at the retention rates in the various categories of style.
- The individual employee's stress level could be assessed in a number of ways – which? Well we might use physiological measurements (e.g. blood pressure change over a time period), changes in health status (e.g. increasing number of headaches/tummy upsets over a six-month period), changes in behaviour over a period (e.g. roused to anger quickly, more drinking and smoking, etc.) as all this can be measured.
- Retention could be measured by the actual number leaving on a monthly basis or percentage changes.

So, for each theoretical concept, we need to be able to agree upon at least one measurable variable which we can use to represent each concept. The process of doing this is called operationalizing the concepts as variables. A variable is any measurable aspect of behaviour that can vary.

Operationalizing variables

Your ability to obtain evidence for research questions will remain at a stand-still until you are able to translate abstract, vague, squishy constructs like *charismatic leadership* into something specific, concrete, and ultimately, observable and therefore measurable. For example, the conceptual definition of *workaholic* could be operationalized as '*someone who works more than x hours per week*'. It could also be defined through seeking the employee's degree of agreement/disagreement to attitude statements such as '*I hate not being able to go to work on public holidays*'.

The concept '*purchasing intent*' could be operationalized by indicating on a scale of 1 to 5 the likelihood of purchasing the item in the next seven days. We could define '*career success*' either from the perspective of the profession or from the individual's perspective.

The former would define it in terms of the prestige of the profession, the position and status held and by salary. The more individually subjective perspective would focus on definitions that express how one feels about where one aspired to be at this point in time with where one actually is, using questionnaire items such as '*to what extent do you feel you have achieved whatever you had hoped to achieve at this stage of your career?*'

Operational definitions of '*Job Satisfaction*' would involve questionnaire items tapping various dimensions of satisfaction to do with pay, supervision, promotion, etc. Such questions rated on a five-point scale might include:

'*To what extent would you agree with the following:*

- Opportunities for advancement are good here.
- My work gives me a sense of accomplishment.'

There is no single acceptable way to operationalize a concept. Suppose we want to measure how depressed an employee is in a work stress study. A variety of options exist:

- We could ask the person if they are depressed (yes or no) or to rate their depression on a 1 to 7 scale.
- We could ask the person's parents or friends if he or she could be characterized as depressed.
- We could have the person evaluated by a clinical psychologist to see if there are clinical signs of depression.
- We could have the person take a test such as the Beck Depression Inventory (a standardized self-report questionnaire designed to measure depression).
- We could ask the person how many serious life events he or she recently experienced that we know often precede depression (such as job loss, death of a spouse, failing an exam).
- We could examine how much of a neurotransmitter called *serotonin* the person has (depressed people tend to have deficiencies in this neurotransmitter).
- We could evaluate glucose metabolism with a technique called Positron Emission Tomography (depressed people often don't metabolize glucose very actively).

The important thing you should realize is that operational definitions turn the vague construct into something that can be measured and quantified.

Choosing an operational definition

As illustrated above, there are often many different ways of operationalizing a construct. But which one is best? There are three broad answers.

1   Use the definition or definitions that work for you, depending on the resources you have or to which you have access. Some operational definitions, such as self-reports, produce data easily. It is fairly easy to get someone to fill out a questionnaire. Other operationalizations might be more difficult. For example, you may not have the money to hire

clinical psychologists to evaluate every participant in your depression study, with several hours of clinical interview required per subject. Similarly, access to medical equipment required to measure physiological markers of depression is not easy.

2   Use the operational definition or definitions that will be convincing to those who will be reading and evaluating your research. Use operationalizations that have been employed by other people before, then if someone criticizes your methodology invoke precedent. (Of course, the previous study may have been less than ideal and subject to criticism as well!).

3   Use more than one operationalization. Each operational definition is likely to be incomplete, capturing only one part of the meaning of your construct. By using more than one operational definition, you are better able to cover the richness and complexity of your construct. You will also be able to calculate the *reliability* and *validity* of your measurement, which would indicate that you are obtaining the same result on several different operationalizations of the construct (Chapter 17). This would provide converging evidence of your construct. You could also aggregate your measurements on the different operationalizations (adding them up).

Remember that one of the philosophies underlying research is that we can disprove but not prove. Instead, each study gives us one small piece of evidence in a large and complex puzzle. It is now easier to see why this is true. Because there are many ways of operationalizing constructs being studied, it is always possible that any results found may be specific only to that single operationalization, and that had a different operationalization been used, a different result may have been found.

> **Operationalization** – *turning concepts into measurable variables by defining the variable in terms of the procedure used to measure it.*

The theoretical framework

When we present the measurable variables in a diagram that defines the expected relationships between them and specifies the direction of such relationships, we have a **theoretical framework**, a base for developing testable hypotheses. It is the stage where the structure of the design is refined. But in terms of design we can label variables in different ways.

Independent, dependent, moderating and mediating variables

In many studies, we manipulate one variable and note the effects of the manipulation on another variable. For example, you could manipulate the amount of overtime to be worked and measure the effect on employee motivation, or vary the price of a product and assess the change in demand. The variable that is varied such as management style, overtime or price is termed the **independent variable** or **IV**. These variations are often termed different conditions of the variable.

> *The independent variable. Is the variable that is manipulated.*

The variable that is measured or observed to chart the effect of the manipulation, e.g. retention rate in the above examples, is the **dependent variable** or **DV**. Changes in the dependent variable depend on variations in the independent variable.

> *The dependent variable. Is measured or observed to detect changes due to the variation of the independent variable.*

A third type of variable is the **moderating variable** which affects the nature of the relationship between the independent and dependent variables. For example, the effect of varying levels of stress in different employees acts to influence the relationship between the management style and retention in that it is likely that the more stressed an employee is by the management style the more likely they are to leave. *Gender* and *Age* are often moderating variables.

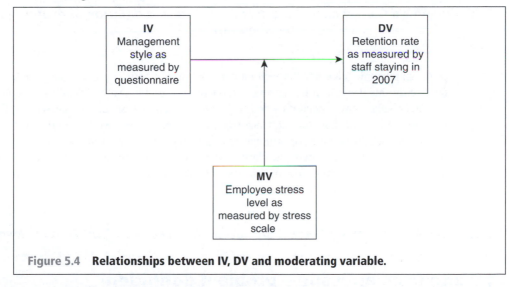

Figure 5.4   Relationships between IV, DV and moderating variable.

> *The moderating variable. Affects the nature of the relationship between IV and DV.*

The mediating variable is one that lies between the effect of the IV on the DV. Whereas the moderating variable affects the IV-DV relationship through the different levels of the moderating variable, it is the variations in the IV's that influence the effect of the mediating variable on the DV (see Fig 5.5). Here staff turnover and availability of training both

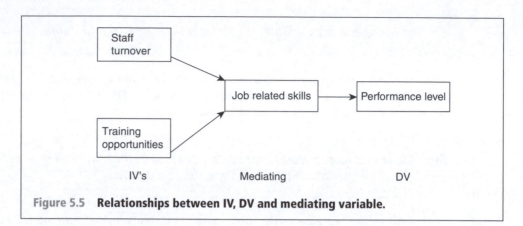

Figure 5.5   Relationships between IV, DV and mediating variable.

influence the level of job related skills, which in turn affect the performance of the employees. The moderating variable is almost a DV for the original IV's and then converts into another IV in its effect on the DV.

> **The theoretical framework** – *this offers the nature and direction of relationships between variables.*

As an example, consider the well-known relationship between price change and demand change. In this theoretical framework, a moderating variable can be added as the amount of demand change may depend on whether the type of item is essential or unessential. The two diagrams (Fig. 5.6) show the sequence from a conceptual framework to derive a theoretical framework which provides operationalized variables. This diagrammatic process is exactly what we need for measurement, clarifies the research design, and enables us to develop specific hypotheses, using these operational variables and postulated relationships, that can be subjected to testing (see Chapter 10).

> **Variables** – *these are a reflection of concepts at an empirical, measurable level.*

Starting from an issue – problem definition

Many researched issues do not stem from theory and may only reflect a local 'problem'. In this case, we must define the problem carefully to ensure the right questions are asked and answered. If this stage is not done correctly, the remainder of the research effort may be flawed. If we can state the problem or goal precisely and accurately then we can design a strategy to solve the problem or achieve the goal. Defining a problem can be done by following a series of steps.

1   The management problem

The first step is to make a broad statement of the problem as the management see it. While we use the word 'problem' this does not necessarily mean something serious but more usually

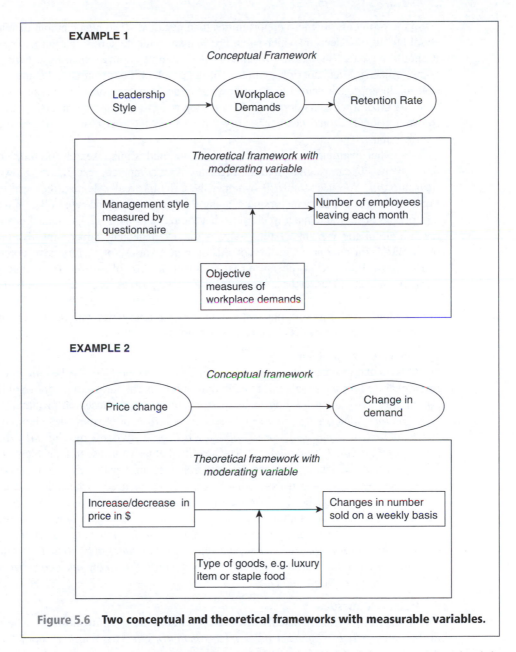

Figure 5.6   Two conceptual and theoretical frameworks with measurable variables.

that management is faced with a decision or uncertainty and feel that some research might clarify the issue better. For example:

- Can we identify another gap in the market that we can exploit?
- Can we determine which media outlets are best for advertising different types of our products?
- How can we attract better qualified IT staff?
- How can we increase productivity?

So the problems are more opportunities than negatives. The management problem then should focus on a decision which should be in management's terms, not in the researcher's. It should be stated in question form as in the examples above, ensuring a focus on outcome or decision and not on a symptom of the problem. For example, a business association might approach you to find out how they can 'educate' local businesspersons about their organization and its purposes. In fact they want to increase membership and simply informing locals would not necessarily have solved the real issue – that of increasing membership.

As another example, imagine a CEO visits you and wants research to come up with a new advertising campaign to stem falling sales. As a competent researcher, you would not rush into this. You need to clarify whether the CEO has really defined the right problem. For instance, could other factors be causing the sales slump, and what other information and people need you contact to clarify what the real problem is? The manager may have taken a simplistic view that falling sales is due to inadequate advertising. By talking to other staff, you may arrive at the conclusion that a variety of factors have combined to cause the decline, such as cheap import competition, loss of sales staff, inventory shortages. You need to focus on these problems. Where the problem is unclear or ambiguous you will need to conduct some preliminary exploratory research using more qualitative techniques such as focus groups, observation, or in-depth interviews with relevant people, and in some cases secondary data analysis like company reports.

2   The research problem

Next, the management problem is translated into a research problem, i.e. becomes potentially researchable. This too should be stated in question form. In our example above of the local community association wanting to increase membership, the research problem might be '*what factors influence a person to join this association*', or for our sales slump example, '*what factors are causing reduced sales levels?*' or '*why don't our job advertisements attract well qualified IT applicants?*' The test of whether your research problem is spot on is, 'if you had the answer to it, would you be able to answer the management problem?' Thus, the research problem asks what information you need to be able to answer the management problem, because frequently managers describe a symptom and not the causes. Low sales are a symptom and the research must focus on the causes or antecedents. Other research problem examples include, '*does expansion into international operations enhance the firm's image*', '*does new packaging affect the sales of a product*', '*what factors constitute a corporate culture as perceived by managers*' or '*how does corporate culture influence employee performance?*'

3   Research questions

The research problem can usually be developed into more specific questions. The research problem '*what factors influence a person to join this business association?*' could be broken down into several questions such as '*are there restrictions on who can join; what is the financial commitment in joining; what benefits are there in joining; what are the relative importance of factors that affect the decision to join?*' The issue of low productivity may involve a range of antecedent factors from low pay to low morale and low motivation, inviting such research questions as '*does increasing pay increase productivity?*' These specific research questions can be turned into testable hypotheses.

Using the above sequence a rather local problem can be brought into a structure that will allow it to be investigated in a rigorous way, just as we did with testing a theory.

Here is an example of identifying the problem and then expressing it as a conceptual then theoretical framework:

Stop-Go Wagons take a smaller share of the truck market in China than Premier Trucks, Great Wall Movers and Mass Movement Motors. They are aware they have quality issues with such problems as oil seal leaks and faulty electric window winders.

What is the broad problem and can we define it more specifically?

- The management problem is 'market share'.
- The research problem is: 'How can the quality of Stop-Go Wagons be improved so as to increase its market share?'.

In this problem statement, we have two concepts: namely, quality of Stop-Go Wagons and market share. To develop our theoretical framework we might provide measurable variables for the first concept by referring to the number of oil seal leaks per 100 trucks, or number of complaints about window winders per month. The second concept could be defined by the percentage of the national total supplied by Stop-Go Wagons in 2007. Thus, the conceptual and theoretical frameworks combined might look like that in Figure 5.7, with the latter the basis for the research questions hypotheses.

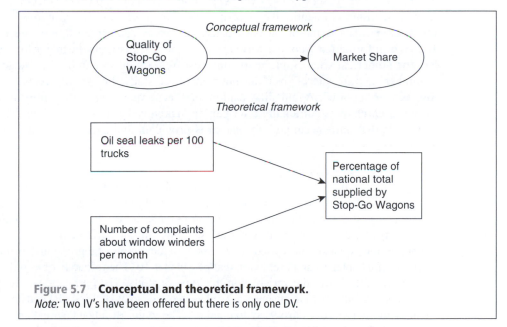

Figure 5.7 Conceptual and theoretical framework.
Note: Two IV's have been offered but there is only one DV.

4 Hypotheses

Finally, testable hypotheses can be formulated for each of the specific research questions. From some of the research questions above we may hypothesize that '*increased productivity is positively related to increased pay*' and '*high level of membership fees influence the decision to join the business association*'. The way hypotheses are formulated will be developed in the next chapter.

Types of research studies

1 Exploratory studies

When the study area is new or vague some initial exploration is needed before a conceptual and theoretical framework can be devised. It is like a fishing expedition which will give insights and suggested directions but not conducted with sufficient rigour for decision making and hypothesis testing. The goal is to improve the final research design by becoming familiar with basic facts and concerns, developing a picture of what is occurring, generating tentative conjectures and determining the feasibility and sense of direction for more rigorous follow-up. Exploratory designs therefore tend to be mainly qualitative, using in-depth interviews, observation, focus groups, and pilot studies as a preliminary step in the research process. Refer back to the discussion in Chapter 1, which argues for a link between qualitative and quantitative approaches, with the former informing the latter.

Their advantage is that they are quick and cheap and clarify the direction the research should take, however, they lack experimental control, adequate sampling, so interpretation of results tends to be judgemental.

2 Descriptive studies

Here the researcher attempts to document what is actually occurring. The study may be either qualitative (descriptions in words) such as records of a business meeting, or shop floor interactions, or quantitative (descriptions in numbers) such as variations in sales by month or changes in the client base. Surveys, census data, trade figures are common sources of information. Summarization by descriptive statistics is the major form of analysis for numerical data. Some marketing research would fall into this category. The researcher has no control over the phenomena of study, but simply records what is observed or reported. Again, like exploratory techniques, they offer information for further research, but additionally offer help in making very simple decisions. The major strength is that quite accurate information is provided although causal links cannot be established.

3 Correlational studies

A correlational study leads only to interpretations about the degree to which certain things tend to co-occur or are related to each other. For example, does an increase in the sales force increase the number of items sold? The purpose is to measure the strength of the association between variables. It is not to use values in one variable to predict values in another. Prediction takes us beyond correlation into the realms of regression. Correlation is the focus of Chapter 15 and prediction that of Chapter 16. The researcher has only moderate, if any, control over the variables in this type of study. The correlational study is the most often used approach in business as well as in many areas of the social and behavioural sciences and is typically fairly easy to conduct. The major disadvantage is that the actual reason for the associations found remains quite unclear *as correlation does not imply causality*. This is because no independent variables are being manipulated and the researcher therefore has no control over variables. The cause of a relationship may be a third unmeasured variable. For example, there is a close relationship between the number of umbrellas raised and the number of people putting on rain coats and the like – the cause is wet weather.

4   Experimental studies

Here, the researcher manipulates the level of the independent variable and observes any corresponding change in the dependent variable. The purpose is to determine if there is a causal relationship between the two variables. Experimental studies require strict control of all variables and are sometimes called laboratory studies, in contrast to field studies that occur in natural uncontrolled situations like observing a management meeting or shop floor interactions. The goal is to advance knowledge, extend a theory into a new area, provide evidence to support or refute a hypothesis/theory. However, they are costly in time and money with control often difficult to achieve.

Research design

What is experimental design all about?

Experimental design is a planned interference in the natural order of events. Researchers are rarely satisfied simply to describe the events they observe. They want to make inferences about what produced, contributed to, or caused events. To gain such information without ambiguity, some form of experimental design is ordinarily required to *rule out* the possibility of alternative relationships, consequences or causes, leaving only the actual factor of interest as the measured effect and provide clear unambiguous results.

Selected conditions or changes (treatments) are introduced. Observations or measurements are taken to assess any change in conditions. Emphasis on experimentation reflects the higher regard given to information derived from a design that is sound. Most gains in knowledge come from actively manipulating or interfering with the stream of events.

Considerations in design selection

The selection of a specific design depends primarily on both the nature and the extent of the information we want to obtain. Complex designs, usually involving a number of 'control groups' offer more information than a simple group design. There are constraints on this. Collecting information is costly. The money, time and staff resources available have limits. Subjects are usually found in finite quantities only. Thus, there has to be a sensible balance between aiming for a perfect design and collection cost. A research design itself entails:

- a clear operational statement of the theoretical framework or the actual problem or issue to be investigated;
- unambiguous and operationally stated hypothesis(es);
- random selection or assignment of subjects into groups;
- random selection or assignment of groups for specific treatments or conditions of the experiment (experimental manipulation), e.g. into experimental and control groups;
- specifying the order or arrangement of giving the treatment or treatments to the groups;
- specifying the sequence and types of observations or measurements to be taken;
- specifying how the observations/measurements will be obtained and analysed.

The whole process aims to obtain reliable, valid measures/observations/data for which measurement error is reduced to the minimum. This chapter will consider experimental design in a broad sense.

Research Design: *a framework for the collection and analysis of data.*

Research Method: *a technique for collecting data.*

Cross-sectional and longitudinal designs

Many studies gather data just once and are called **one-shot** or **cross-sectional**. Much survey and descriptive research is like this, such as determining the relative popularity of brands of soap powder. **Longitudinal studies**, in contrast, allow data to be gathered at several time points to chart changes. Cross-sectional studies are obviously less resource intensive in time and cost than longitudinal studies, though the latter are essential for cause and effect studies. For example, to demonstrate the effect of an intensive TV advertising campaign on sales levels, or of a new training programme for hotel receptionists or of a counselling programme for stressed air traffic control officers, we would want to assess before and after treatment.

Experimental design

What makes a true experiment is:

(a) The degree of control that the researcher has over the subjects and conditions in the study. An experiment is an investigation in which some Independent Variable (IV), the presumed cause, is manipulated to determine whether it has some effect on the Dependent Variable (DV). Some IV's, often subject variables, cannot be manipulated as they are already given as fixed categories, e.g. gender, departments in a company. You have to take them as they come.

(b) Random assignment of people or groups to treatments. Human judgement should play no role in who gets into which experimental condition. The strength of randomization is that it creates two or more groups that are equivalent at the very beginning of the study.

Therefore, an experiment consists of assigning participants to at least two groups, **experimental** and **control**, and administering or manipulating an **independent variable** in the **experimental group** (sometimes called treatment group) while holding conditions constant and equivalent for the **control group**. The performance of the control group usually serves as a baseline against which to measure the treatment effect on the experimental group.

The groups (assumed to be equivalent in all respects initially) are then compared on the DV (performance or change in behaviour) to determine the probability that the IV caused these changes in the experimental group. **Probability** is used since the experimenter is *never* absolutely certain that the independent variable was the actual '*cause*' of the observed changes. Alternative explanations may exist. Among the most obvious is the possibility that the two groups differed prior to the administration of the treatment, for example interest in the task or intelligence. There are four ways of ruling out this.

1 Random assignment of subjects to groups tends to spread out differences between subjects in random ways so that there is no tendency to give an edge to any group, and increases the likelihood that there are no important initial differences between the experimental and control groups. Without random assignment, some other interfering factor might intrude to bias the results, as when a group of very intelligent friends all volunteer for the same group, making it brighter on average than the other group. Random assignment usually ensures that important extraneous factors are randomly distributed in both groups. This design is often called the **between groups** or **independent groups** design. For example, as a production manager, you may wish to determine the effects of different types of background music on defective items produced. You randomly select two production teams and fit each up with ipods heard through ear pieces. One group has loud rock music, the other has soft romantic music. Neither knows that each is listening to different music. The DV of mean defective items produced per day are measured before and after the two-week treatment.

2 Subjects may also be assigned to each group in pairs on the basis of matching on important factors such as age, ability, gender, income, SES and other relevant variables. Which member of the pair goes into which group is done randomly. The pairing is an attempt to create two similar groups at the outset with individual differences balanced across the groups. This is the **paired groups** or **matched samples design**. For example, in our music type–defect production study above we could eliminate some individual variation between the groups by ensuring members in each group were paired on the basis of age, length of experience, gender, and existing defect production rate.

3 The third method of equating groups consists of **pre-testing** for initial group differences on the DV. If they are found to be different prior to applying the independent variable, then analysis of covariance (ANCOVA Chapter 13) will provide a statistical adjustment in the final results based upon initial group differences. Such a procedure is superior to examining gain scores and is most often used where random assignment of subjects to groups is not possible because the groups are intact already, e.g. educational or employee groupings. For example, in our background music–defect production study we could measure individual defect rates and then insert this difference into an ANCOVA to ensure statistical adjustment in the final results.

4 A fourth way to avoid initial group differences is achieved by controlling or eliminating them through using the same group twice in a **repeated measures** design. However, when individuals are used twice, exposure to either condition initially, i.e. order of conditions, could change the results. For example, practice or training by undertaking the first task could improve performance on the second. Other confounding order effect variables are boredom and fatigue. Therefore, the experimental design provides for counterbalancing the order so that half the subjects receive the control condition first, followed by the experimental condition, while the other half receive the experimental condition and then the control. Whatever the potential effect of having a particular

order of conditions has on the outcome is cancelled or offset by combining the results for both experimental subgroups and both control subgroups. For example, in our music type–defect production half the group would experience rock music for the first week, then the soft sentimental music for the second week, while the other half would reverse the procedure.

> **Between groups design.** Two independent samples are selected randomly, one for each treatment condition and compared often in a control and experimental contrast.

> **Repeated Measures Design.** One sample is measured in both treatment conditions – a before and after approach.

> **Paired or Matched Samples Design.** Individuals, units or observations are matched as pairs on one or more variables and allocated at random one of each pair to each sample.

Between groups vs. repeated measures designs

The distinction between **Between groups** and the **Repeated measures** designs is a very important one. The design decision has major ramifications for how participants are selected and allocated, how data is entered into SPSS, and what analyses are conducted (see Chapter 12).

Several basic research designs will be introduced and more complex designs left to more advanced courses.

Random independent group design

Similarity of the groups before treatment begins is attempted by assigning subjects to groups at random then groups are allocated to the experimental and control conditions randomly (Fig. 5.8).

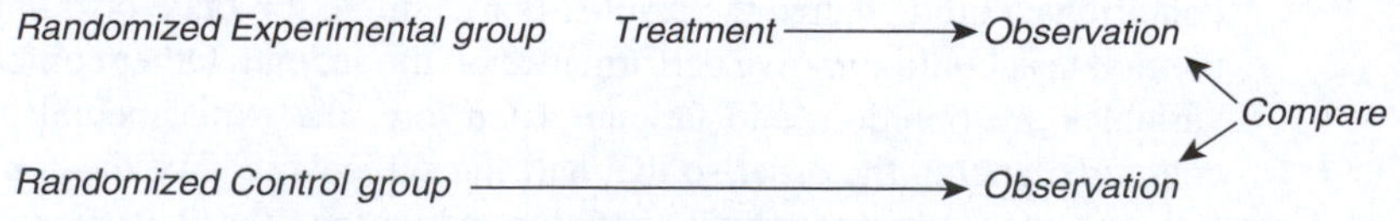

Figure 5.8   Random independent groups design.

This independent groups design is economical. It provides fairly clear-cut information as to the relationship between treatment and post-treatment measurement or behaviours. Since this is often the sole reason for the research, the randomized group design is frequently the appropriate selection.

Uncontrolled variables are assumed to affect both groups equally so that a comparison of the post-treatment behaviour should reveal any differential effects of the treatment using analysis of variance or a 't' test.

Pre-post random group design

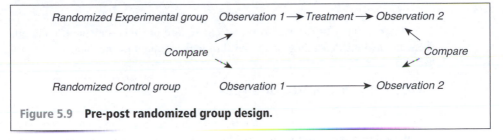

Figure 5.9 **Pre-post randomized group design.**

This design strengthens the previous design by adding a pre-test as a check on the degree of comparability of the control and experimental groups before the treatment is given (Fig. 5.9).

For example, we may wish to test the effectiveness of a new brand of acne cream for adolescents. We would allocate adolescents who are using an existing cream and are medically assessed as having approximately the same degree of acne (observation 1) randomly into two groups; one group receives the new cream to apply twice each day for two months, the other group, the control, continues with the existing cream (treatment). Neither group knows which treatment group they are in as no labels appear on the tubes. Two months later the effects are compared. So we have created two similar groups. They were 'blind' as to whether they were in the experimental or control group and post tests could be compared to determine whether the new cream produced the better results (observation 2).

Factorial designs

Sometimes we may wish to assign subjects to different groups on the basis of some of their own characteristics such as age, weight, employment status and also assign different variations of the treatment as well. For example, we may wish to compare effects on response time for two different levels of alcohol consumption split by gender (this would be a 2×2 factorial design). Factor A is gender (A1 and A2) and factor B is alcohol level (B1 and B2). Using four groups we can combine every possibility. These variations are the treatment and the measurement of the response time is the observation. A diagram of a 2×2 factorial design would look like Figure 5.10.

In a single 2×2 factorial design similar to the one above, information can be gained about the effects of each of the two treatments and the effect of the two levels within each treatment, and the interaction of the treatments, i.e does response time depend on alcohol level, or on gender, or on an interaction between gender and alcohol level. If all these are questions of interest, the factorial design is much more economical than running separate

Randomized group male(A1)/drink(B1)	Treatment	⟶	Observation
Randomized group male(A1)/drink(B2)	Treatment	⟶	Observation
Randomized group female(A2)/drink(B1)	Treatment	⟶	Observation
Randomized group female(A2)/drink(B2)	Treatment	⟶	Observation

Figure 5.10 **Factorial designs.**

experiments. Analysis of variance and chi square are the statistical techniques used for factorial designs depending on the level of measurement of the data.

Quasi-experimental designs

When a design does not meet randomization and control requirements necessary for controlling the influence of extraneous variables, a quasi-experiment is the second-best choice – a fallback position. Randomization just isn't always possible. Some treatment groups are initially formed on the basis of performance (high, medium, low, for example), some variables on which people differ (e.g. shoplifters and non-shoplifters) cannot be experimentally induced.

Thus comparisons between treatment and non-treatment conditions are made with non-equivalent groups. You can still *observe* what happens, when, and to whom. But you forfeit control when you do not use random assignment. Many of the types of quasi-experimental designs are very similar to experimental designs except that initial randomization never takes place.

One-group, pre-post designs

One group is given a pre-treatment measurement or observation, the experimental treatment, and a post-treatment measurement or observation. The post-treatment measures are compared with their pre-treatment measures (Fig. 5.11).

For example, you want to evaluate whether a special window display in your shop will increase sales. You could measure average daily sales for a week before installing the display (observation 1) then install the display (treatment) and measure average daily sales for the next week (observation 2). The assumption is that all other variables remain the same. But suppose you are selling swim suits and there is a sudden cold snap; sales would decline. The impact of an extraneous confounding variable has been strong. Control is lacking.

Group	*Observation 1* ⟶ *Treatment* ⟶ *Observation 2*
(non-random)	

Figure 5.11 **One-group, pre-post design.**

We need a comparable store that does not have the special display to compare sales on the two occasions. But even then there are still uncontrolled variables in that each store has a different location, different clientele, size, management, etc. It is not a very effective design but sometimes the only one available for the situation. This design is typically analysed with a repeated measures t-test.

Non-equivalent group comparison designs

Here we add a control group to the previous design (Fig. 5.12). This design with no random assignment is common with intact groups such as educational classes or employee groups. Some groups receive the treatment while the control groups do not but we still have no way of knowing to what extent post-treatment differences may be attributed to: (i) differences in the characteristics of the subjects in each group, and (ii) the treatment. How does one know how much change or difference between the two groups has come from which source? Group differences on the post-test may solely be due to pre-existing group differences. To increase the strength of the design, Analysis of Covariance (ANCOVA), is used (Chapter 13) to reduce the effects of initial group differences statistically by making compensating adjustments to the post-test means of the two groups.

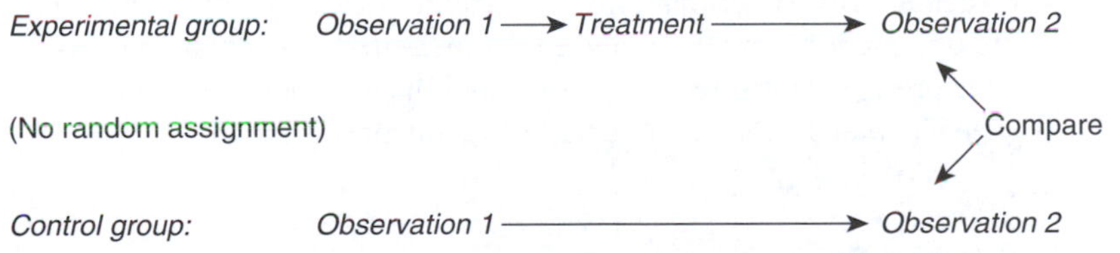

Figure 5.12   Non-equivalent group comparison design.

The difficulty, in quasi-experiments, is trying to find out just how similar the groups were at the very beginning, before any treatment at all began. You may be able to use background information such as test scores, 'personality' or other standardized test results, 'demographic' information such as own or parental education, occupation, or income. But even if we assign groups to treatments based on their known differences, such as high ability and low ability groups, the groups may differ on other unmeasured variables such as motivation or confidence, that caused the outcome differences, instead of the differences in ability you thought was the true independent variable.

Issues with using intact groups

Intact groups are those that existed prior to any treatment or intervention. Normally (say, 75 to 80% of the time) this is true as we study students, employees, customers of a particular company, etc. The important issues are:

1   how subjects were allocated to groups in the first place;
2   what happens in the group; and
3   the length of time groups pre-existed prior to interventions.

If subjects are (i) randomly assigned to groups in the first place (as in school/university classes where there are many equivalent sections), (ii) the tasks and experiences prior to the intervention are virtually identical in each group, and (iii) the pre-intervention time is short (probably a few weeks at most), then if you randomly assign groups to experimental and control conditions, you probably are approximating to a true experiment.

Intact groups created on certain criteria like 'tracking' or 'streaming' systems in schools, sports teams grouped by ability, and enlisted service men versus officers in the military, are examples of non-random assignment. Their curricula and itineraries may be different, providing subjects in different groups with different experiences. Researchers are usually worried whether the employees were selected for employment on some personal bias of the HR manager, or students were assigned to the classroom in a non-random way, or whether certain patients self-selected a hospital for a particular reason. The problem is whether some subtle factors were operating to exert a bias of selection factors in the assignment to groups and that we have often no way of finding out in most cases.

Validity

We have emphasized that the aim of research design is to ensure that changes in the DV are really the result of manipulating the IV. This logic of an experiment is referred to as **internal validity**. Primarily, it asks the question: Does it seem reasonable to assume that the treatment has really produced the measured effect? Extraneous variables which might have produced the effect with or without the treatment are often called 'threats to validity'. (See Chapter 17 for a more detailed treatment of validity).

Blind studies

We pointed out the **Hawthorne effect** in Chapter 1 in referring to the reactive subject, i.e. subjects alter their behaviour by simply being in the centre stage of a study, with a great deal of attention focused on them and their being aware of it. Dealing with this problem is handled by having a control group that is subject to the same conditions as the treatment groups, then administering a placebo to the control group. A placebo is any treatment apart from the experimental one so that the subject wrongly believes that they are being experimented on. It is an analogy of the 'sugar pill' in medical experiments when testing the effect of a real pill. The study is termed a 'blind' experiment as the subject does not know whether they are receiving the treatment or a placebo. The study is termed 'double blind' when neither the subject nor the person administering the treatment/placebo knows who is in the experimental or control group.

What you have learned from this chapter

You need to develop conceptual and theoretical framework out of a theory or a pattern of observations is essential to clarify the elements of the investigation. You are then able to propose testable hypotheses. You also must operationalize the variables involved so that they can be measured.

The major types of variables are independent variables which are manipulated to produce changes in the dependent variable.

You have been presented with a variety of research designs that exist in order to try and control confounding variables that would influence the outcome, preventing us from knowing whether it was the IV that had the effect on the DV that has been shown or some other variable. Random allocation to experimental and control groups is a major technique to achieve control as this balances out unknown influences. Matching subjects in pairs on important relevant variables and then allocating them randomly to each group is another similar procedure.

To remove individual differences entirely a repeated measures design is used but counterbalancing the treatments is essential to control order effects. Quasi-experimental designs lack randomization to control individual differences but are unavoidable when using intact groups.

Review questions and tasks

Qu. 5.1
Operationally define the concepts of:

(a) 'sexual harassment'
(b) 'job involvement'
(c) 'financial performance'
(d) 'stress'
(e) 'productivity'
(f) 'job enrichment'

Discuss the appropriateness and measurability of class members' suggestions.

Qu. 5.2
Draw conceptual and theoretical frameworks for the theory that job enrichment leads to a perception of more meaningful work. Check your response in the website for Chapter 5.

Qu. 5.3
Explain the differences between and purposes of conceptual and theoretical frameworks. Check your response with the material above.

Qu. 5.4
Phil Green, the CEO of **Emblem Hotels**, was wondering how to differentiate among three different types of accommodations offered under the **Emblem flag** in order to attract the appropriate type of client for each. **Deluxe** was meant for business travellers, **Express** aimed to provide inexpensive accommodation for families on holiday, while **Royal** provided high quality services for wealthy international travellers. Phil felt the revenues could be increased if clients and potential clients understood these distinctions better. Keen to develop a strategy

to eliminate brand confusion, he conducted a customer survey of those who had used each type of facility. Most customers were unaware of the differences. Many complained about the age of the buildings and the poor maintenance. The quality of service was rated poor too. Furthermore, rumour was spreading that a name change was likely and franchise owners were becoming angry.

Phil realized he needed to understand how the different classifications would be important to the different customers then he could develop a marketing strategy. He also recognized that unless the franchise owners cooperated his plans would never reach fruition.

For the above case (a) identify the problem, (b) develop a conceptual framework, (c) develop a theoretical framework.

Check your answer on the Web page for this chapter.

Qu. 5.5
Why is the problem definition stage more critical in the research process than the problem solution stage?

Qu. 5.6
Explain briefly and simply why the experimental approach is the only one of the four that provides causal explanations.

Qu. 5.7
In groups, work out the advantages and disadvantages of the between groups, repeated measures and matched samples designs.

Qu. 5.8
Design an experiment that would examine the research question 'does time of day affect employee productivity?' Draw a diagram to illustrate your design. Share your designs and justifications for the design around the class.

Qu. 5.9
What are the essential differences between an experimental and a quasi-experimental design? Discuss in groups.

Qu. 5.10
Explain why intact groups are difficult to involve in experimental studies. Check your response in the material above.

Now access the Chapter 5 website and check your answers. Try the additional questions and activities there.

Part 2
Entering, Describing and Obtaining Data

Chapter 6
How to Enter Data into SPSS and Undertake Initial Screening

'Never display a bar chart at an Alcoholics Anonymous meeting'

(Source unknown)

'Salesman: This computer will cut your research workload by 50%'

'Researcher: That's great, I'll take two of them'

(Source unknown)

Content list

After studying this chapter, you should be able to:

1 Understand and recognize the four different levels of measurement.
2 Enter variable names and characteristics into the SPSS variable view window.
3 Enter raw data into the SPSS data view window.
4 Create composite variables like total scores and means for questionnaire/survey items using SPSS.
5 Use SPSS for data screening and check for data entry errors.

Introduction

The importance of this chapter cannot be underestimated. You will learn about the statistical programme we use in this book that analyzes data. Once you have mastered the basics of entering variables and data you will be prepared for using the programme for statistical analysis in succeeding chapters.

Levels of measurement

You must identify correctly the level of measurement of your data for SPSS in order to:

• set up the variables before entering the data;
• select the correct statistical test for analysis of the data.

A fundamental step in the conduct of research is measurement – the assignment of numbers to objects or events according to rules. Researchers begin with variables, then use rules to determine how these variables will be measured and expressed in numerical form. The variable *holiday preference* may be measured according to the numbers indicated by respondents who are asked to select one among (1) Beach, (2) Cruise (3) Golf, (4) Touring or (5) Other. The variable *employee morale* may be measured by the scores of employees who have taken a particular organizational morale scale.

> **Measurement.** *The process through which observations are translated into numbers.*

Variables can be classified on the basis of their level of measurement. This classification affects how we can use them in statistical analysis and the procedures that can be meaningfully used with them. Variables can be at one of four levels:

1 nominal,
2 ordinal,
3 interval, and
4 ratio.

Nominal scale of measurement

This is the most primitive scale of measurement. Nominal means **to name**; hence a nominal scale does not actually measure but rather names or classifies observations into categories. Measurement at this level only demands that two or more relevant categories can be distinguished (e.g. yes/no to a survey question) and that the criteria for placing individuals or objects into one category or another is known.

The names or labels used to identify the categories of a nominal variable do not represent different magnitudes of the variable. The numbers arbitrarily assigned to the categories serve merely as labels. All the members of a category are assigned the same number and no two categories are assigned the same number. In preparing data for a computer, the numeral 0 might be used to represent a male and the numeral 1 to represent a female. The 1 does not indicate more of something than the 0. The numbers assigned to football players constitute a nominal scale. We would not say that the player with number 9 on his jersey is necessarily three times a better player than the one with 3 on his jersey. Bus route 10 is not twice as long as bus route 5. Types of financial investments would be measured on a nominal scale, with categories such as bonds, property, shares, term deposits, etc. Other common variables measured with nominal scales are religious affiliation, country of residence, ethnic group, occupation, makes of washing machines, lists of postal areas, political party preference and so on. Similarly, when children in a poll are asked to name the television channel they watch most frequently, they might respond '7', '9', or '10'. These numbers serve only to group the responses into categories and carry no numerical significance; mathematical calculations using these codes would be meaningless. One may use only those statistical procedures based on counting, such as reporting the number of observations in each category as in the chi square procedure (see Chapter 14).

Nominal variables are often **qualitative** although **quantitative** variables can be 'reduced' or 'degraded' to the nominal level, e.g. salaries could categorized into high, medium and low groups and labelled (1), (2), and (3) respectively. Age can also be degraded into groups.

> *Nominal measurements. Names or classifications are used to divide data into separate and distinct categories.*

Ordinal scale of measurement

The next highest scale of measurement is ordinal; that is we can place individuals, objects or events in rank order. Ordinal measurement occurs, for example, when supervisors rank staff on certain characteristics, such as their social maturity, leadership abilities, cooperativeness, and so on. If four products are ranked by a consumer, they may be ranked as 1, 2, 3, and 4, where 4 is the best and 1 is the worst on a particular criterion. Employees may be ordered as *general employees, supervisors and managers;* social class may be ranked as *upper, middle and working;* attitudes toward reducing salaries in times of economic slump may be ranked on a five-point scale as *very favourable, favourable, neutral, unfavourable or very unfavourable.*

The values of the numerical scores tell us nothing more than the ranking or order of position. Neither the difference between the numbers nor their ratio has meaning. There is no implication that the difference between rank 1 and rank 2 is the same as the difference between 2 and 3, and so on. The difference in volume of export sales between the company ranking 1 in export sales and the company with a rank of 2 may be the same, less than, or greater than the distance between the companies with rankings of 2 and 3. A product ranked '2' is not twice as poor as one with a ranking of '1'. There is simply no basis for interpreting the magnitude of differences between the ranks.

The major analytic techniques for ordinal data are Wilcoxon, Mann-Whitney and Spearman's rank order correlation (see Chapters 12 and 15).

> *Ordinal measurements. Measurements that rank observations into categories with a meaningful order.*

Interval scale of measurement

Variables on an **interval** scale are measured numerically, but unlike ordinal data, not only carry an inherent ranking or ordering of objects or events according to the amount of the attribute they represent, but also establish equal intervals between the units of measure. Equal differences or intervals between any pair of numbers represent equal differences in the attribute being measured. Thus, the arithmetic operations of addition and subtraction are meaningful. The Centigrade scale for temperatures is an example of an interval scale. The difference between 20C and 25C is equal to the difference between 30C and 35C. We could not say, however, that 30C degrees is twice as hot as 15C. This is because there is no true zero point on an interval scale.

Any statistical procedures based on adding and averaging may be used with this level scale along with the procedures appropriate for the lower level scales. These include most of the common parametric statistical procedures.

Examples of interval variables are the birth rates of various ethnic groups, the population sizes of cities, the number of tourists visiting a region, the number of years of education one has completed, and test scores.

> *Interval measurements. Measurements on a numerical scale in which the value of zero is arbitrary but equal intervals exist between successive points on the scale.*

Ratio scale of measurement

The **ratio scale** is the strongest scale of measurement. This is exactly the same as interval measurement with one important provision. A ratio scale of measurement has an absolute zero point that is measured as 0. Most physical measurements such as distance and weight have zero points that are absolute. With this sort of scale of measurement it is possible to work out ratios between measures. So, for example, a branch office that is 60 kilometres away is three times as far away as a branch that is only 20 kilometres away; a building that is 15 metres high is half the height of a building that is 30 metres high; a salary of $50,000 is twice as large as a salary of $25,000; an item that weighs 100 kilos is one-half as heavy as an item weighing 200 kilos; a firm with a 40% market share has twice as much of the market as a firm with a 20% market share.

Of all four levels of measurement, only the **ratio** scale is based on a numbering system in which zero is meaningful. Therefore, the arithmetic operations of multiplication and division also take on a rational interpretation. A ratio scale is used to measure many types of data found in business analysis. Variables such as costs, profits, and inventory levels are expressed as ratio measures. The value of zero dollars to measure revenues, for example, can be logically interpreted to mean that no sales have occurred.

> *Ratio measurements. Numerical measurements in which zero is a meaningful value and the difference between values is important.*

Relationship between the four levels

The four measurement levels may be viewed as forming a hierarchy increasing in sophistication from the crude nominal scale to the more refined ratio scale. Each measurement level offers more information about a variable than did the previous one. It is always possible to move downward in the hierarchy (degrading the data) with respect to a specific measurement. In other words, any variable measured at the interval level may be treated as if it were ordinal or nominal, and an ordinal variable may be treated as a nominal variable. For example, age is a ratio variable. Since the various ages are also ordered, age of employees could be treated as an ordinal variable, using ordered categories such as 'under 20', '20–29', '30–39', etc. Similarly, since we could artificially assign names to the values, we could even treat age as a nominal variable, with levels such as apprenticeship age, working age and retirement age.

However, by degrading our data to a lower level we fail to use the information provided by it to its fullest. For example, by changing interval data to ordinal, i.e. ranking a set of scores, we lose the information about the intervals between individual items of data. It is not possible to move in the other direction in the measurement hierarchy. If a variable is measured only on a nominal scale, it is not possible to turn it into ordinal level data, as there is no natural ordering of the categories. In general, it is important to try to measure variables at as high a level as possible, because more powerful statistical techniques can be used with higher level variables.

Important note

SPSS does not distinguish between interval and ratio data but treats them together as one measurement level category and calls them *scale* data.

SPSS Activity 6.1: How to enter data into SPSS

The Statistical Package for the Social Sciences, or its acronym SPSS, is the major statistical analysis tool used across a wide variety of academic subject areas as it is completely Windows compatible. The instructional material below will give you a basic familiarity with the SPSS environment that will allow you to explore some of its capabilities later in your own time. Using SPSS is a five stage process:

1 Starting SPSS.
2 Defining variables on Variable View window.
3 Inputting data onto the Data View window.
4 Statistically analysing the data using appropriate statistic and dialogue boxes.
5 Interpreting the print out.

This chapter will deal with the first three stages. Stages 4 and 5 will be studied progressively as you proceed through the book.

Starting SPSS

Open SPSS by using the sequence: **START** > **PROGRAMS** > **SPSS**. SPSS will open and display the *What would you like to do?* Dialog box.

- To create a new file – Select *Type in data* and click on *OK*.
- To open an existing file – Select *Open an existing data source* and click on *OK*. Select the file from the list shown, or select *More Files*.
- When you open an SPSS file on a Web page of this book the data file will be transferred onto the data view window.

In this activity you will be creating a new file, so select *Type in data* and click on *OK*.

The variables and dummy data you will use to practise the input of new data is located in Table 6.1. When you have inserted all the variables and data your data view screen should look like Table 6.1.

SPSS basics

When a new file is opened, a blank SPSS *Data Editor* screen will appear. It looks like a spreadsheet. At the bottom left-hand side there are two labels *data view* and *variable view*. The Data Editor screen opens as the *data view* option. In the *data view* option:

- Each row represents a case/respondent with each case listed numerically down the left-hand side in light grey.
- Each column represents a variable, such as gender, age or question/item on a questionnaire/test and is presently headed *var* until an actual variable is entered via the *variable view*.

Table 6.1 **Variables and data set for practising setting up a data file**

	Gender	Age	Quals	Qu1	Qu2
1	1	22	2	5	4
2	1	36	2	3	1
3	1	27	2	4	3
4	1	31	1	5	4
5	1	28	2	4	5
6	2	26	2	5	4
7	2	32	3	3	2
8	2	25	2	2	3
9	2	30	2	4	1
10	2	23	1	4	3

| Candidate or case number already in left hand column of data view | Male = 1 Female = 2 | | Cert = 1 Degree = 2 Post-Grad = 3 | 5 = Strongly Agree 4 = Agree 3 = Neutral 2 = Disagree 1 = Strongly disagree | |

Data coding scheme for variables

- The data entered into each cell are a datum value. It represents the response to the variable for that case or respondent.
- Ten menus are listed across the top of the sheet. **Analyze** and **Graphs** menus are available in all windows so that new output can be created without returning to the data editor. Briefly the main features of each menu are:

1 **File**: create new files, open existing ones, saves files and prints.
2 **Edit**: modify and copy text.
3 **View**: change characteristics of windows.
4 **Data**: define variables merge files, insert and sort cases and variables, select and weight cases.
5 **Transform**: rank and recode cases, and create new variables from existing data.
6 **Analyze**: holds a selection of statistical procedures for analyzing data.

7 **Graphs**:   create a range of graphs and charts.
8 **Utilities**:   displays file and variable information.
9 **Window**:   arrange select and control attributes of windows.
10 **Help:**   access to information on how to use the many features of SPSS.

Setting up your data file

Defining variables on SPSS variable view screen

1   Before you can enter the data from Table 6.1 into the *data view* spreadsheet of SPSS (the data editor window) you need to define or label the variables being measured by the data. In this case, the variables are gender, age, qualifications and individual question scores from an attitude questionnaire, The variables in this activity are listed across the top of Table 6.1.

2   To insert a variable name you must click on the *variable view* tag at the bottom left of the screen. The new screen will be displayed. Each row now represents a different variable in the vertical plane down the left-hand side as 1, 2, 3, etc. and the row of columns is headed with data attributes such as name, type, label, etc. As this is a new file, there will be no entries yet.

3   Highlight with the black box for variable 1 the cell under '*name*' and type the name of your first variable '*gender*'. A variable name must start with a letter and have no spaces. The remaining characters can be a letter, number, full stop or symbols @, #, $, or _. In our current activity your first two variables '*gender*' and '*age*' do not need to be shortened but we often shorten long variable names for simplicity. For example, '*qualifications*' could be shortened to '*quals*', and individual questions are easily reduced to '*qu1*', '*qu2*', etc. Shorten your variables to something that identifies the variable in your mind, e.g. '*rating of effectiveness of leadership*' could be '*efflead*' while '*monthly shopping bill*' becomes '*shop$pm*', '*customer satisfaction*' is '*custsat*' and '*attitude to supervisor*' is '*supatt*'. The name appears as the column heading when in *Data View*.

4   Move your black box highlight to '*type*' column. Click and this will add information across all the columns in the row. '*type*' will have a default setting of *numeric*. Leave it as the default setting as you are unlikely to use any of the other options.

5   Ignore the next columns '*width*' and '*decimals*' too as the default allows eight numerals with two decimal places, sufficient for most researchers. Move to another setting only when it is more appropriate.

6   Highlight with black box the '*label*' column and give your variable its full name, e.g. '*qualifications*'. This is very useful in case at a much later date you cannot remember what the abbreviated code in the name box actually stands for; e.g. *qu2* can now be written in full as '*working conditions good*', etc.

7   If your variable has discrete levels then complete '*values*' by allocating numbers to levels of your variable using the values label dialogue box brought up by clicking on '*values*' then on the button with three dots on the right. For example, *gender* could be recorded as 1 = male and 2 = female; qualifications can be 1 = Certificate, 2 = Degree, 3 = Post-graduate, etc. For our first variable '*gender*' type '1' in the value box and

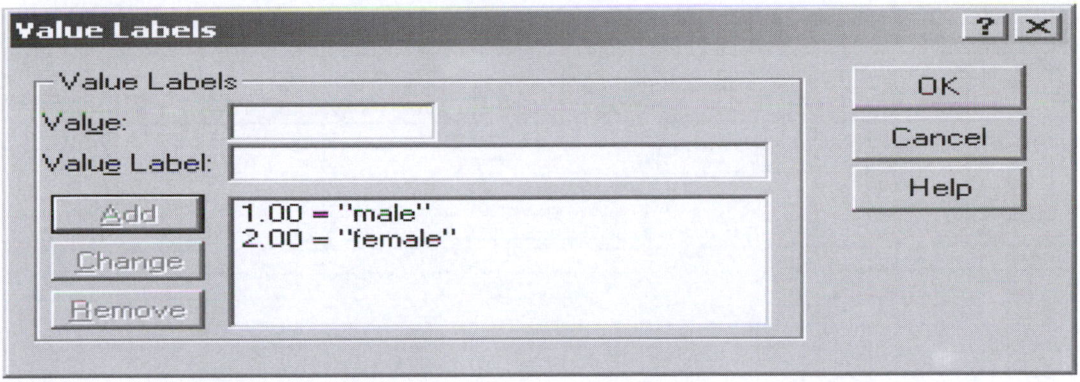

Figure 6.1   Screen shot of value labels box completed for gender.

'*Male*' in the value label box then click on '*add*' button. This places *1 = Male* in the box. Repeat this so that *2 = Female* is also placed in the box then click OK. The value labels box for *gender* is shown in Figure 6.1. If you have more levels than two, continue with successive numbers until you have labelled every level of your variable and they are all in the box. Items from questionnaires and surveys that have (say) five point scales labelled from *strongly agree* to *strongly disagree*, or some other verbal sequence, must also be entered here. When completed, click *OK*. A screen shot of the value labelling for a five-point questionnaire item *qu1.* is also shown in Figure 6.2. The values labels attached to categories of the variables are shown in Figure 6.3 in the values column. The variable label will appear on the analysis output and makes identification of results easier.

8   '*Missing Values*' enables you to indicate gaps in the data table where a participant was unwilling to give information (say on their age) or simply forgot to answer. Click on the three dots and use the discrete missing values box. Put a number that would not be part of your normal range of scores such as 99 or 999 in the first space in the Discrete

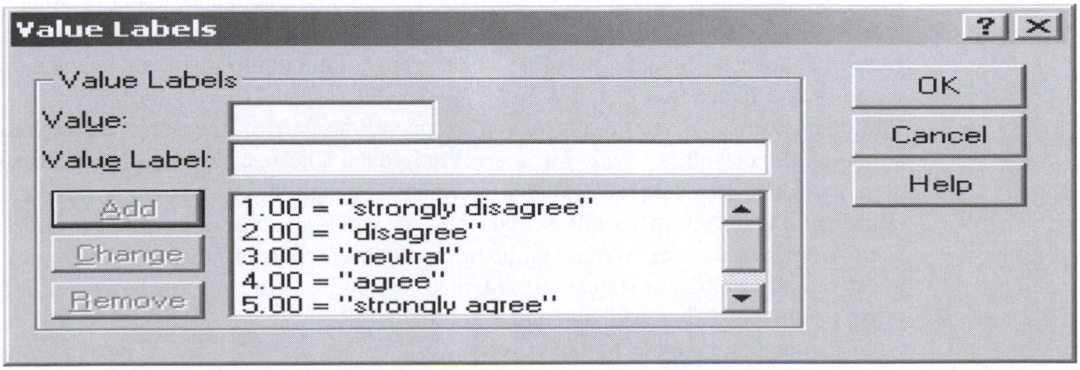

Figure 6.2   Screen shot of value labels box for the five-point scale on qu1.

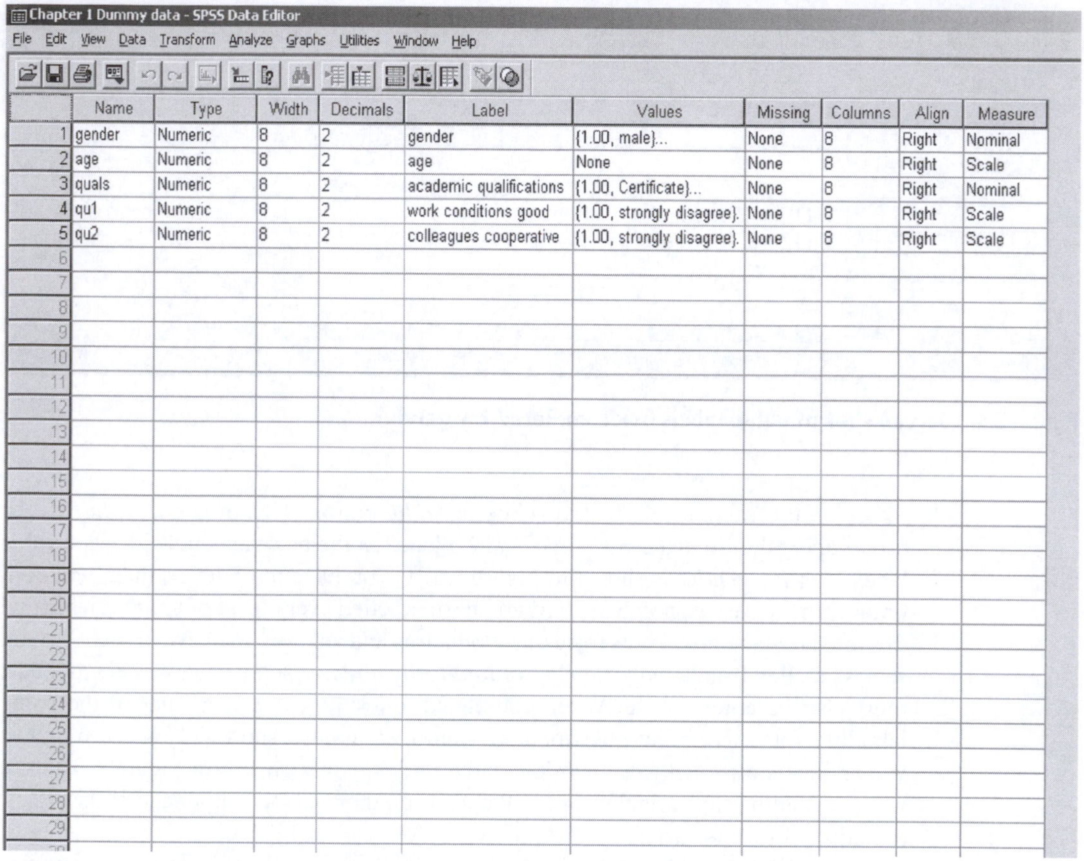

	Name	Type	Width	Decimals	Label	Values	Missing	Columns	Align	Measure
1	gender	Numeric	8	2	gender	{1.00, male}...	None	8	Right	Nominal
2	age	Numeric	8	2	age	None	None	8	Right	Scale
3	quals	Numeric	8	2	academic qualifications	{1.00, Certificate}...	None	8	Right	Nominal
4	qu1	Numeric	8	2	work conditions good	{1.00, strongly disagree}.	None	8	Right	Scale
5	qu2	Numeric	8	2	colleagues cooperative	{1.00, strongly disagree}.	None	8	Right	Scale

Figure 6.3 The completed variable view screen for activity 6.1.

Missing Values option. SPSS will ignore this number in its calculations so that, for example, the mean score calculated by SPSS will reflect the actual number of respondents for that item.

9 Leave '*Column*' as the default. '*Align*' can remain as default too if you are happy with a right-side alignment.

10 The final column '*Measure*' allows you to specify the level of measurement of your variable. The default is '*scale*' for interval/ratio data. Click on the button and choose '*ordinal*' for ranked data and '*nominal*' for category data. In our activity, *gender* and *qualifications* are nominal while *age* and the five-point scale questions can be regarded as providing scale (interval) data (although some researchers argue that they are ordinal data and at other times can be regarded as nominal categories when used in a cross-tabulation analysis (Chapter 14).

11 After completing variable 1 *gender*, repeat for all other variables. If you have a series of variables that have the same value labels, you do not need to repeat the typing. If you administer a questionnaire with a set of five-point scale items, for example,

such as '*strongly agree*', '*agree*', '*neutral*', '*disagree*', '*strongly disagree*' to which you have allocated in the value label column numbers such as *1 = strongly agree*, to *5 = strongly disagree*, it is easy to copy these value labels for all the questions by completing the value labels for the first variable. Select the cell in the values column you have just completed then select *Copy* from the *Edit* menu. Highlight as many cells in the column below as required by the number of similar questions and click *Paste* from the *Edit* menu and your values will be copied to all cells selected. This saves time in filling out the value labels box each time when they are being replicated for each question. The completed variable view table should look like the one shown in Figure 6.4.

Entering data on the data view screen

1   When all the variables have been entered, click on *data view* at the bottom left-hand side to revert to the original horizontal plane that lists variables across the top of the spreadsheet. See the screen shot (Fig. 6.4) of the data view screen with variables just inserted along the top of the spreadsheet.

2   You can now enter your data in the cells below each variable for the cases, participants or respondents. The cases are already numbered down the left-hand side. If you make

Figure 6.4   **Data view screen with variables listed in bold across top ready for data entry.**

an error in entering data in a cell simply highlight the cell, type in a new value and click *Enter*. You can move around, entering values in the cells by using *Enter* then the Arrow keys on your computer, or the mouse to move to the next cell. If you are entering a large data set, it is advisable to save after every 10 completed cases. The completed data view screen is shown in Figure 6.5. As you enter each survey form write the case number on it that corresponds with the case number on the left-hand column of the *Data View* so that if you notice later some data missing or there is an error in typing then you can go straight to the right survey form.

Saving data file

1 Finally, when you have completed the data entry or done as much as you want in one session, you must save your data to a file. Click on '*file*' then '*save as*' option. Type an appropriate name without a suffix for the file in the file name box. SPSS automatically adds the suffix '*.sav*'. Do not alter this as you will be unable to reload your file. Give your file a name relevant to the topic of the data. Save in whatever particular

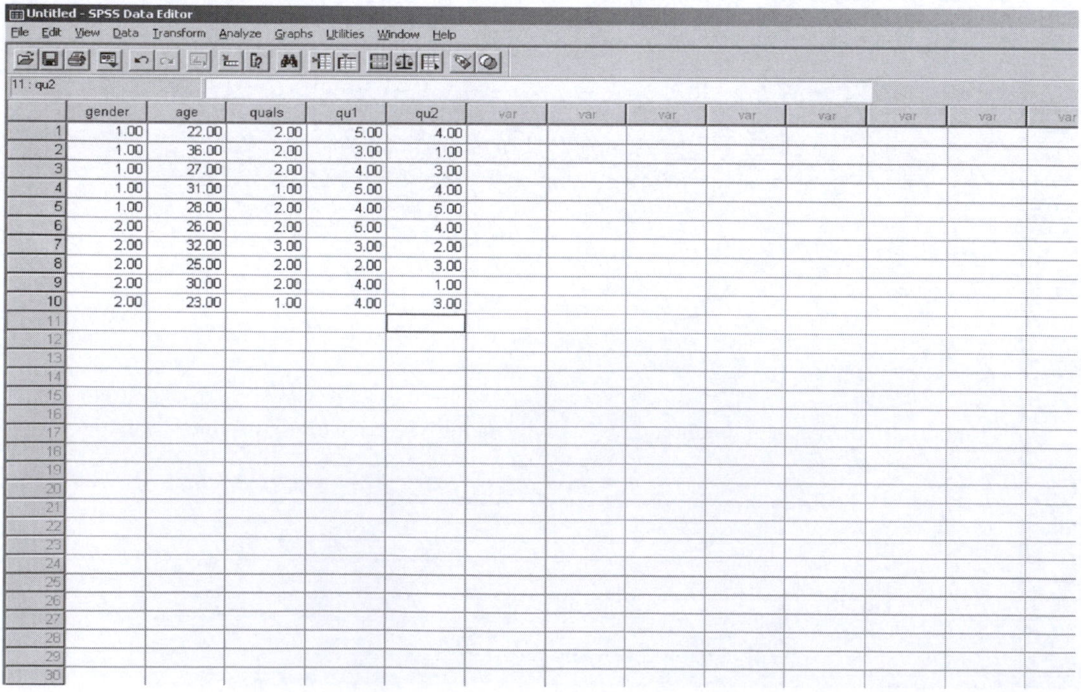

	gender	age	quals	qu1	qu2	var	var	var	var	var	var	var	var
1	1.00	22.00	2.00	5.00	4.00								
2	1.00	36.00	2.00	3.00	1.00								
3	1.00	27.00	2.00	4.00	3.00								
4	1.00	31.00	1.00	5.00	4.00								
5	1.00	28.00	2.00	4.00	5.00								
6	2.00	26.00	2.00	5.00	4.00								
7	2.00	32.00	3.00	3.00	2.00								
8	2.00	25.00	2.00	2.00	3.00								
9	2.00	30.00	2.00	4.00	1.00								
10	2.00	23.00	1.00	4.00	3.00								
11													
12													
13													
14													
15													
16													
17													
18													
19													
20													
21													
22													
23													
24													
25													
26													
27													
28													
29													
30													

Figure 6.5 Completed data view screen for activity 6.1.

drive or directory you wish. The default holder is usually C:\Program Files\SPSS\ (File name).sav. You are urged to make a back-up copy.

Do not get confused.   Remember, in the *data view* window each row represents data from one case (respondent, participant or subject) and each column holds data from one variable. In the *variable view*, each row provides information about one variable. For most variables, you can accept default settings and all you need to do is enter a variable name and if necessary add variable and value labels and ensure you have the correct option under *measure*. If you seek more advice and want to look at other options, use the *Help Menu* on the *data view*

Analyzing data

After all data have been input, SPSS can be used to analyze the information. All analysis options are located under the Analyze menu. Later chapters will deal with various types of statistical analyzes. The analysis produced will appear in the SPSS *Viewer* window.

SPSS viewer window

This window is vitally important as it is the output window that comes up after you have requested SPSS to undertake some activity. It displays the results of your statistical analyzes and depicts the graphs that you have requested. The SPSS viewer is split into two screens or panes. The relative width of the panes can be altered by dragging across the vertical line that separates them.

On the narrower left-hand screen is a list of all the SPSS results, named using the variable labels. It is a list of contents that act as a summary or navigation system. Clicking on an icon there will move you to that part of the detailed output, usually tables and graphical output, in the larger display pane on the right. You can also click on a table or graph in the right pane to select it.

Figure 6.6 is an example of an SPSS Viewer with table and graph on the right-hand side and a contents list on the left. The table has been selected by clicking on the next to bottom item on the contents list and shows up in the right-hand pane with a red arrow and a highlight box around it. This table can be edited and also be copied and pasted to another document. In many later chapters we will be using the viewer to produce statistical and graphical output.

Formatting SPSS output

The output generated by SPSS can be formatted and edited as required. There is often superfluous information. Delete what you do not want; format, save and print the rest.

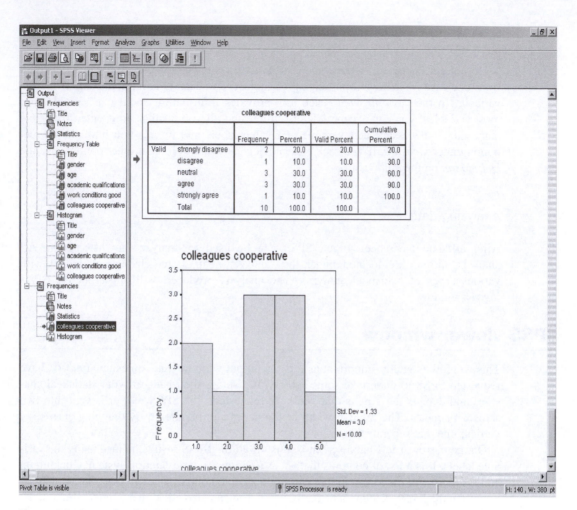

Figure 6.6 Example of SPSS viewer screen.

Formatting tables

1 In the SPSS *Output Viewer*, double click on the table to be adjusted – a hatched border will appear around the table.
2 On the menu bar, select *Format, Table Properties*.
3 In the *Table Properties* dialogue box, adjust the formatting as required.
4 Click on *Apply* to see the changes – when the format is as required, click on *OK*.

Formatting charts

1 In the SPSS *Output Viewer*, double click on the chart to be formatted – the chart will open in the SPSS *Chart Editor*.

2   Select the part of the chart to be changed:
- Use *Format* to alter colour, fill and text attributes.
- Use *Gallery* to alter the chart type.
- Use *Chart* to alter the titles used on the chart.

3   Click on *File, Close* to return to the SPSS Viewer window.

Printing and manipulating output

To print output:

1   Click on *File, Print*.
2   Select whether *All* output, or only the *selected* output is printed.
3   Click on *OK* – the output will be sent to the default printer.

To preview output before sending to the printer:
- Click on the *Print Preview* icon, or select *File, Print Preview* from the menu bar.

Incorporating output in other applications

Results obtained in SPSS may be incorporated in applications such as Microsoft Word by using *Copy* and *Paste*. (Word cannot read SPSS output files.)
In the SPSS *Viewer*:

1   Select the output to be copied.
2   Click on *Edit, Copy* on the menu bar.

In Microsoft Word:

1   Open the document in which the output is to be inserted.
2   Position the cursor where required.
3   Click on *Edit, Paste* on the menu bar.

SPSS tables appear as a Word table, and can be edited. SPSS graphs are pasted as a graphic; these can be resized, but any modifications to colour, font size, etc. must be done prior to pasting into the Word document.

It is vital that SPSS can re-open your saved files. You must save files with the.sav extension; output and chart files must have the .spo extension.

Sources of further information – online help in SPSS

Click on Help, and then select from:

- Topics – In Depth information on SPSS.
- Tutorial – Step by Step guide on SPSS.

- Statistics Coach – Information on statistics.
- SPSS Home Page – information from SPSS website.

Screening for input errors and creating new variables

Once all data have been inserted into the statistical programme there are several important tasks before proceeding with the first step of obtaining summarized descriptive statistics, presented usually in both the form of tables and graphs:

- screen it for input errors (typing in wrong figures, etc.);
- checking for outliers;
- missing values; and
- create new composite variables such as totals and means (arithmetical average), and recoding items where necessary.

We all make typos by hitting the wrong key. I have produced many writing this text (which I hope I have noticed and corrected) and you probably made a few as you tried to input the data for the first time in activity 6.1 above. We also misread things we are copying. As a result, there are likely some errors in every data file you set up. There are several simple but effective ways of screening the data for errors of input to ensure all scores and codes are legitimate. The most common problem is *out of range values* (typing 100 instead of 10) which can be detected quite easily by getting SPSS to produce descriptive statistics such as frequencies and graphical displays like histograms, boxplots, stem and leaf diagrams for the various variables using the *Frequencies, Descriptives* and/or *Explore* commands under the *Analyze* and *Graphs* menus. We are then able to see whether there are any data values that are impossible given the range of values set for the variables. Please load Chapter 7 Data File SPSS A from this book's SPSS data files Web page for the following demonstrations.

To obtain frequencies of a distribution

1 Select *Analyze,* then *Descriptive Statistics* and click on *Frequencies* which opens the *Frequencies Dialogue box.*
2 Select the variables *transpor* and *qu1*. Use the arrow button to move them into the *Variable(s): box.* Ensure *Display frequency tables* is ticked (Fig. 6.7).
3 Click on *OK*.
4 Printout of descriptive statistics as Tables 6.2(a), (b), and (c) will appear.

You can check the number of categories for any variable in the *values* column of the *variable view*. Since *transpor* has four categories and *qu1* has seven categories (a seven-point rating scale) we would check the printout to make sure only these numbers of categories respectively were listed with frequency counts. Normally we would investigate every variable. Reviewing the printout for Table 6.2(b) we can see that the expected four categories are the only ones present. In Table 6.2(c), however, notice a *12* standing out like a sore

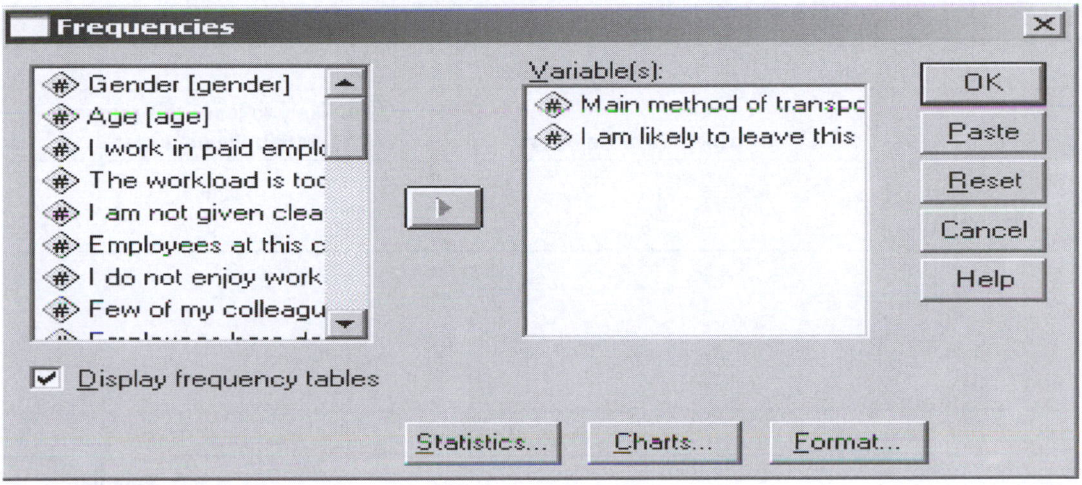

Figure 6.7　**Frequencies box.**

thumb for *qu1* in addition to the expected seven categories. We need to locate this wrong figure in the *data view* and find the case it refers to. Then, using the original questionnaire for that case we can determine whether it should be a 1 or a 2 and insert the correct figure before continuing any further analyzes with that variable. Better still produce some graphs and charts that detect the error and the actual case number as in the examples below.

To obtain histogram, box plot and stem and leaf plot

1　Select *Analyze* menu. Click on *Descriptive Statistics* and then *Explore* to open the *Explore Dialogue box.*
2　Select variables required (*hworkpw*) and click on arrow button to move it into the *Dependent List: box.* Under *display* only check the plots box or else you will get a large of amount of statistics you do not need at this stage.
3　Click on *Plots* to obtain *Explore: Plots subdialogue box*
4　Click on *Histogram* and *Stem and Leaf.* Under *Boxplots* ensure *Factor levels together* is selected (Fig. 6.8).
5　Click on *OK* and the printout shown in Table 6.3 emerges.

Table 6.3 simply indicates that 80 cases were included with no missing data. The histogram for *I work in paid employment for (hrs/pw) below* (Fig. 6.9a) again identifies another suspicious score.

The next chart (Fig. 6.9b) is the stem and leaf diagram which again displays the distribution but along a horizontal axis this time with the stem in 'tens' and the leaf in 'units'. The scores have been grouped into fives so that scores 0–4 form the first group, scores 5–9 the

Table 6.2(a) **Frequencies**

		Statistics	
		Main method of transport	**I am likely to leave this company within the next year**
N	Valid	80	80
	Missing	0	0

Table 6.2(b)

		Main methods of transport			
		Frequency	**Percent**	**Valid-percent**	**Cumulative percent**
Valid	car	45	56.3	56.3	56.3
	bus	17	21.3	21.3	77.5
	walk	16	20.0	20.2	97.5
	bike	2	2.5	2.5	100.0
	Total	80	100.0	100.0	

Table 6.2(c)

		I am likely to leave this company within the next year			
		Frequency	**Percent**	**Valid-percent**	**Cumulative percent**
Valid	Strongly Disagree	33	41.3	41.3	41.3
	Disagree	14	17.5	17.5	58.8
	Tend to Disagree	6	7.5	7.5	66.3
	Unsure	14	17.5	17.5	83.8
	Tend to Agree	4	5.0	5.0	88.8
	Agree	4	5.0	5.0	93.8
	Strongly Agree	4	5.0	5.0	98.8
	12	1	1.3	1.3	100.0
	Total	80	100.0	100.0	

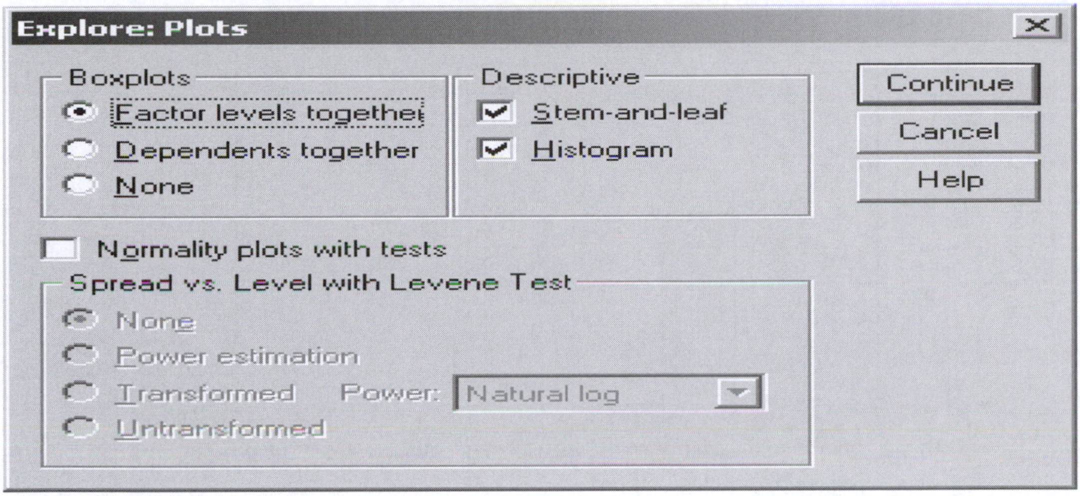

Figure 6.8   Explore: Plots screen.

second and scores 10–14 next, etc. with their associated frequencies on the left. Modes (most frequently occurring value) are easy to detect with this stem and leaf chart.

The final graphic in this set is a box plot (Fig. 6.9c). All these charts suggest an error with one value 100 being quite extreme. It is identified on the box plot as case 1 with a value of 100, which does not seem feasible as a value for hours worked per week. This needs checking on the original questionnaire sheet for case 1 to see if it is a typo.

Once all potential errors are detected, clarified and cleaned up, further analysis can be conducted. You can also obtain histograms, bar charts and pie charts under the *frequencies* menu too.

Checking for outliers

An outlier is a case that is extremely different from the other case values and is often excluded from the analyzes. They are eliminated in most cases because they have an undue influence on calculations like means and squared differences from the mean, as in calculating

Table 6.3   Case processing summary

	Cases					
	Valid		Missing		Total	
	N	Percent	N	Percent	N	Percent
I work in paid employment for (hrs/pw)	80	100.0%	0	.0%	80	100.0%

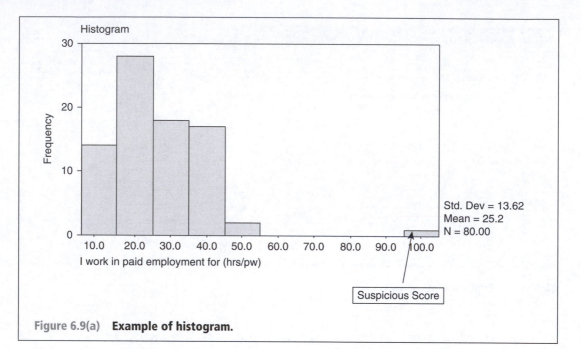

Figure 6.9(a) **Example of histogram.**

I work in paid employment for (hrs/pw) Stem-and-Leaf Plot

Frequency   Stem & Leaf

.00   0.

2.00   0 .   59

12.00   1 .   000000001223 *(i.e. 8 tens,1 eleven, 2 twelves,1 thirteen*

16.00   1 .   5555555566666788

12.00   2 .   000000002344

8.00   2 .   55557888

10.00   3 .   0000044444

10.00   3 .   5556666678

7.00   4 .   0000112

2.00   4 .   56

1.00 Extremes   (>=100) *(a repeat of the suspicious score)*

Stem width: 10

Each leaf: 1 case(s)

Figure 6.9(b) **Example of stem and leaf plot.**

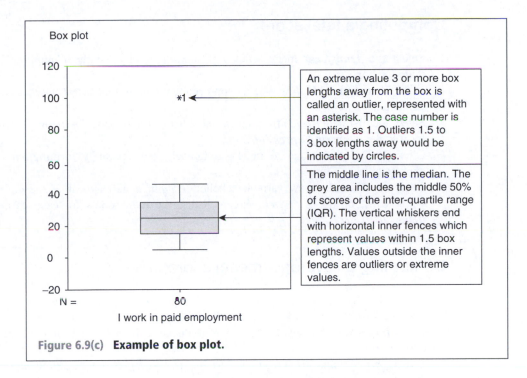

Figure 6.9(c)   Example of box plot.

standard deviations. Many outliers are easily identified on box plots, stem and leaf plots and histograms and on investigation can turn out to be typos.

Creating new variables from existing variables

Obtaining composite or summated scores for a set of items

Very commonly, we often require a total score (summated score) and mean (mathematical average) score for a set of items that form an attitude scale. We tend to analyze data from questionnaires using the total score or the mean rather than the individual items. To perform the operations to obtain a total score and a mean score from a set of items we use the *Compute* command of SPSS.

Load Chapter 7 data file SPSS B from the book's SPSS data files Web page. We are going to create a total score and mean score for every respondent (case) for items *qu13* through to *qu22* inclusive. All these items form a scale that measures employees' percep-tions of their personal competency to overcome difficulties (psychologists would call this 'self-efficacy'). Although the individual items can be analyzed separately, a total score or an average score is an economical way of summarizing each employee's general perception of their self-efficacy.

Computing a total score

1 Select the ***Transform*** menu, click on ***Compute*** and open the ***Compute Variable*** dialogue box.
2 In the ***Target Variable: box*** type an appropriate name. In this case *Tcmptnce* (i.e. total competence).
3 Select the first item (*qu13*) from the variable list box and using the *arrow button* transfer it to the ***Numeric Expression:*** box.
4 Click on the + *button* and continue adding each item separately, forming a numerical expression as in Figure 6.10.
5 Click on ***OK*** and a new variable labelled *Tcmptnce* will appear at the end of the variable list on the *data view* screen, listing the total scores for each case across items *qu13–qu22*.

Computing an average (mean) score

1 Select the ***Transform*** menu, click on ***Compute*** and open the ***Compute Variable*** dialogue box.
2 In the ***Target Variable: box*** type an appropriate name. In this case *Mcmptnce* (i.e. mean competence).
3 Select the first item (*qu13*) from the variable list box and using the *arrow button* transfer it to the ***Numeric Expression:*** box.
4 Click on the + *button* and continue adding each item separately, forming a numerical expression as before in Figure 6.10. Then place a set of brackets around the list and add a slash followed by the number of items, in this case 10 (i.e. /10 is added to the previous numeric expression) as in Figure 6.11, so that the total score is divided by 10.

Computing a percentage

1 Select the ***Transform*** menu, click on ***Compute*** and open the ***Compute Variable*** dialogue box.
2 In the ***Target Variable: box*** type an appropriate name. In this case *percmpte* (i.e. percentage of total competence).
3 Create the numeric expression again as above by clicking on the + *button* and adding each item separately. Then add an asterisk followed by 100/ followed by the maximum possible score, in this case 70 (Fig. 6.12).

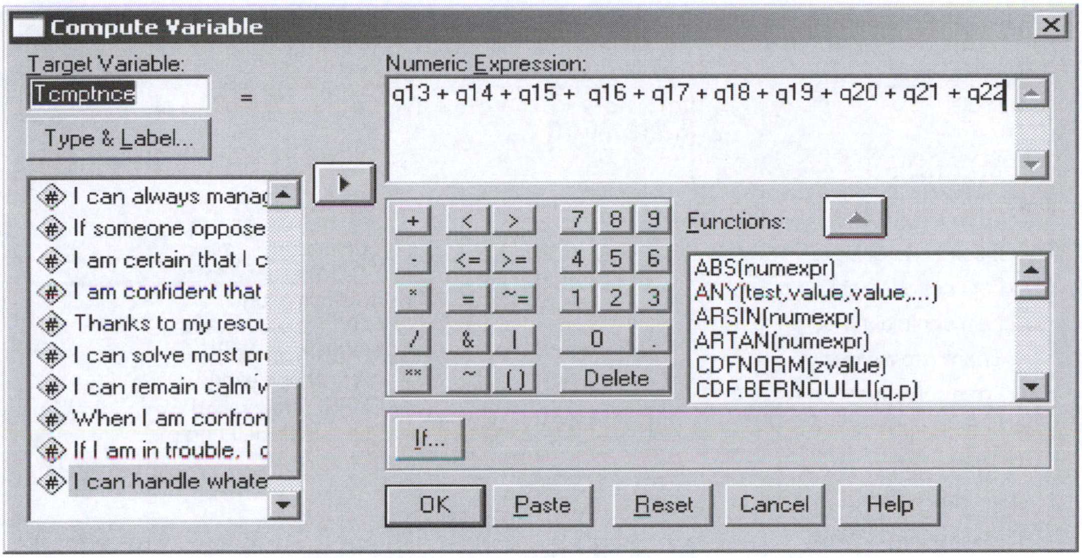

Figure 6.10 **Compute variable box – computing a total score.**

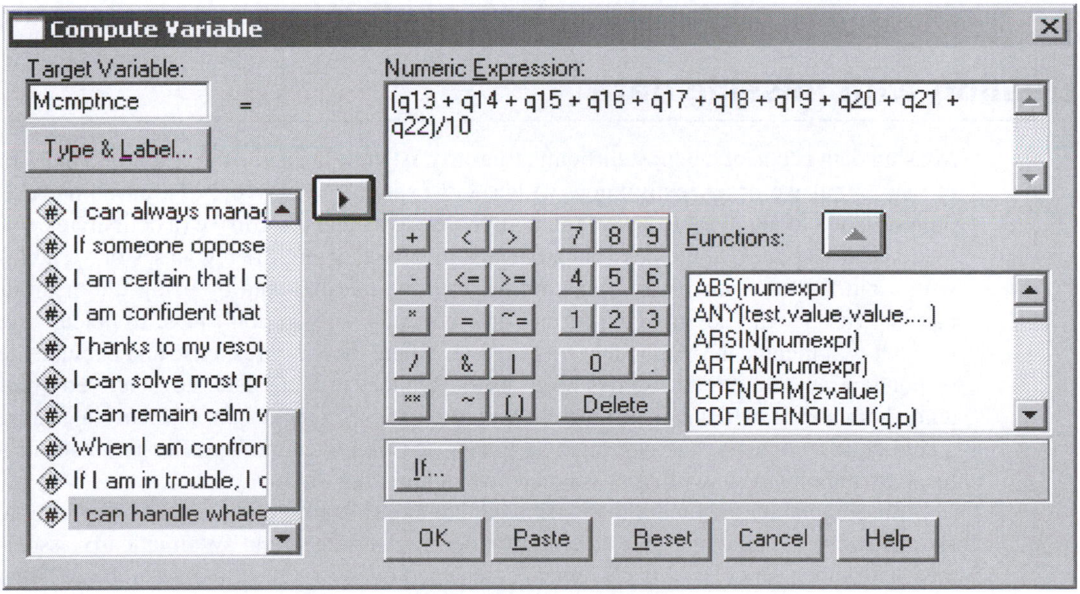

Figure 6.11 **Compute variable box – computing a mean score.**

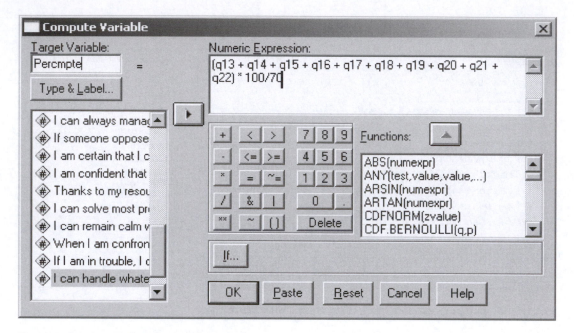

Figure 6.12 Computing a percentage.

Dealing with missing data

Missing data is one of the most difficult issues to deal with. It can be the result of a number of causes but we never really know which. For example, it may only be an unintended omission or a total refusal to answer an item respondents feel is intrusive (a deliberate decision not to respond). Some possible strategies involve deleting the few cases or variables with a number of random omissions, or estimate the missing data by using the mean or median. SPSS will undertake the former automatically, so you don't have to delete anything. It will include the respondent for variables where there is a response and exclude the respondent where no response has been made. Random missing data, i.e. scattered unintended omissions, will not distort results but systematic missing data is serious, suggesting a deliberate avoidance of answering a particular question by a number of respondents or a respondent being an unwilling or coerced one and missing out many items.

If missing values are randomly distributed then the sole problem is reduction of sample size. However, if missing values are non-randomly distributed and systematically associated with other variables, e.g. all female cases aged over 35 refuse to give their age, then this impacts on generalizability to distort results.

What you have learned from this chapter

Measurement is defined as the assignment of numbers to objects or individuals according to some rule. Four different scales of measurement have been presented to you: nominal, ordinal, interval, and ratio. The levels differ in the interpretation that can be made of the numbers used and in the statistical tests that SPSS can carry out on them

This chapter has also introduced you to the SPSS statistical programme and shown you how to set up the variable view screen and enter data into SPSS. The first task after setting up the variable view screen and entering data is to check the accuracy of input using a variety of charts and graphs that would show clearly out of range data.

The creation of some further composite variables, such as totals and means, is usually necessary for later statistical analysis. Appropriate strategies for dealing with missing data were considered.

Review questions and tasks

Qu. 6.1
What level of measurement would you use to investigate the following:

(a) which brands of cigarettes are smoked by students at the university?
(b) among three types of assessment multiple choice, essay, or a mix of both, which is the one preferred by most students?

Qu. 6.2
In what ways is the interval scale more sophisticated than the ordinal or nominal scales?

Now turn to the Chapter 6 Web page and read the additional material there. Carry out the SPSS activity to get some more practice using it and answer the questions.

Chapter 7
Describing and
Presenting Your Data

'A statistician can have his head in the oven, his feet in an icebox and say that on average he feels fine'

'Statisticians do all standard deviations'

'Is it appropriate to use a pie chart in making a presentation at a baker's convention?'

'In what ways are measures of central tendency like valuable real estate – location! location! location!'

'First draw your curves then plot your data'

(Sources unknown)

Content list

After studying this chapter you should be able to:

1 Define the three commonly used measures of central tendency and understand their uses.
2 Understand the guidelines for selecting a measure of central tendency for a particular situation.
3 Define variance and standard deviation, understand their relationships and what they are describing.
4 Present descriptive data in a variety of graphical and tabular forms using SPSS.

Introduction

This chapter introduces you to *the most frequently used* descriptive statistics and how to use SPSS to obtain them. The initial mass of data on the spreadsheet of the data view is unintelligible, disorganized and unusable as it is. The sheer volume of data must be reduced to more manageable proportions that will enable us to analyse, compare, interpret, and visually present them in a meaningful and actionable manner. The characteristics of **frequency of occurrence, central location, spread** and **shape** form the major elements in making a set of data intelligible, since all data observations form a distribution of values.

Descriptive statistics – organizing the data

Making the data intelligible and usable

The business world has become a formidable user of effective visual summarizing devices like tables, diagrams, charts and graphs to impart numerical data on such aspects as performance, quality, product content to clueless customers to increase sales, and to in-house dozing directors to gain support for some project or other. Unfortunately, these visual summarizing devices can be used, intentionally or otherwise, to mislead rather than enlighten, and some of the pitfalls that await the unwary and the unquestioning are included on the Web page for this chapter.

Just as we turn daily rainfall and temperature data into monthly averages, so we can do the same with business data. We don't need to remember every daily maximum temperature for the month – the average gives us a clear indication. Nor do we want to know which particular individuals in our sample rent homes, or have a mortgage or own their homes, but the total number or percentage of the whole in each category. Nor do we want to know each person's weekly salary, but rather the average weekly salary, perhaps on a gender basis, or age group basis, or industry basis. We want to end up with a few summary numbers which provide some kind of representation or profile of the data in a numerical and if possible visual presentation. We have to organize and manipulate the data to reveal the underlying pattern, if any, the data presents to us.

The four most commonly used 'patterning' or 'summary' measures are:

1   The number of items or frequency of occurrence in each given value category or set of values, i.e. the **distribution of frequencies.**
2   The average value of a set of values: this is the measure of **the central tendency of the data.**
3   The spread of the values above and below the average: this is the measure of **dispersion or variability** of the data.
4   The distribution of the values of a variable. What is its shape; is there a tendency to bunch towards lower or higher values, i.e. **skewness.** Or is there an approximation to a normal distribution?

This chapter will introduce the first three characteristics of a distribution of data noted above, together with visual displays that offer concise ways of summarizing information. The next chapter covers another major property of **data** – measures of **skewness,** which tell us whether a distribution is symmetrical or asymmetrical. These properties of data yield a relatively complete summary of the information that can be added to by pictorial displays of charts, frequency distributions and graphs. They are the building blocks on which more sophisticated calculations and comparisons can be based but no particular measure is very meaningful taken on its own. In many cases, knowledge of only two of these – **central tendency** and **dispersion** – is sufficient for research purposes and form the basis of more advanced statistics.

Measures of central tendency

The most commonly used and interesting numerical property of a distribution is usually its **central tendency,** or the general location of scores indexed by some value around which a distribution tends to centre. This value is popularly called the **average,** and implies what is typical, usual, representative, normal, or expected. Because of these different connotations, statisticians prefer more precise terms. The **mode, mean,** and **median** are three different conceptions of central tendency described in this chapter. Each of these interprets the concept of average in a slightly different way.

The mode

The mode is the simplest measure of central tendency and is easily determined in small data sets merely by inspection. In larger data sets, it can be determined by producing a stem and leaf diagram or histogram. The mode is defined as the most frequently occurring score in a group of scores. It is the typical result, a common or fashionable one (à la mode), but unfortunately not a mathematically sophisticated one. In the following set of data, we can identify the mode as the value 8, as it occurs more frequently than any of the other score values.

4, 5, 5, 5, 6, 7, 7, | 8, 8, 8, 8, | 9, 10.

↑

mode

> **The mode.** *The observation that occurs most frequently in a set of data.*

The distribution in the above example would be described as **unimodal,** as there is only one score which occurs with a greater frequency than any other. In some distributions no score occurs with greater frequency than any other. For the set of observations 10, 11, 13, 16, 18, 19 there is no mode at all. In other distributions there may be two or more modes. A distribution with two or more modes is said to be **multimodal**. Multimodal covers a range of possibilities. For example in the following list of data:

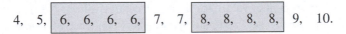

4, 5, | 6, 6, 6, 6, | 7, 7, | 8, 8, 8, 8, | 9, 10.

the distribution is **bimodal** with both 6 and 8 considered as modes. It is customary in such cases to cite the two modes, but then the concept of the mode as the most typical score no longer applies. So, while the mode is easy to obtain, there may be more than one mode or even no mode in a distribution. In a rectangular distribution where every score is the same, every score shares the honour.

We cannot rely on the mode to accurately reflect the centre of a set of scores, since we can have several modes and even in a unimodal distribution the most frequently occurring score may not always occur somewhere near the centre of a distribution. As a result, the mode has limited usefulness as a measure of central tendency. However, the mode is the only measure of central tendency that can be used with qualitative variables such as employment status, blood type, ethnic group, and political party affiliation. For variables that are inherently discrete, such as family size, it is sometimes a far more meaningful measure of central tendency than the mean or the median. Whoever heard of a family with the arithmetically correct mean of 4.2 members? It makes more sense to say that the most typical family size is 4 – the mode. Other than this, the mode has little to recommend it except its ease of estimation.

The median

Median (Mdn) means 'middle item'. The median is the point in a distribution below which 50% of the scores fall. It is determined by placing the scores in rank order and finding the middle score. The size of the measurements themselves does not affect the median. This is an advantage when one or two extreme scores can distort an arithmetical average or mean (see below). The procedure for determining the median is slightly different, depending on whether N, the number of scores, is odd or even.

For example, if we have a series of nine scores, there will be four scores above the median and four below. This is illustrated as follows:

16   6   11   24   17   4   19   9   20

Arranged in order of magnitude these scores become:

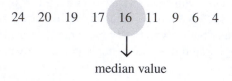

24   20   19   17   16   11   9   6   4

median value

In our example, we had a set of odd numbers which made the calculation of the median easy. Suppose, however, we had been faced with an even set of numbers. This time there would not be a central value, but a pair of central values. No real difficulty is presented here, for the median is to be found halfway between these two values.

If we put the following numbers in rank order and find the median score:

16   29   20   9   34   10   23   12   15   22

these numbers appear as follows:

34   29   23   22   20   16   15   12   10   9

$$\text{median} = \frac{20 + 16}{2} = 18$$

The median. The middle observation after all data have been placed in rank order.

Because the median is not sensitive to extreme scores it may be considered the most typical score in a distribution. However, using the median often severely limits any statistical tests that can be used to analyse the data further, since the median is an ordinal or ranked measure. For example, medians from separate groups cannot be added and averaged. It is therefore not widely used in advanced descriptive and inferential statistical procedures.

The mean

The most widely used and familiar measure of central tendency is the arithmetic mean – the sum of all the scores divided by the number of scores. This is what most people think of as the average. Or in simple mathematical terms, the mean (M) is simply the sum of all the scores for that variable (ΣX) divided by the number of scores (N) or:

$$M = \frac{\Sigma X}{N}$$

The usual symbol for a sample mean is M although some texts use $\overline{X}$ (or 'X bar'). The letter X identifies the variable that has been measured. If we are concerned with the population mean, some texts designate this as μ, the Greek letter mu (pronounced mew). In this text, as we are usually dealing with sample means, we shall be generally using M.

> **The mean.** *The sum of all the scores in a distribution divided by the number of those scores.*

The mean is responsive to every score in the distribution. Change any score and you change the value of the mean. The mean may be thought of as the balance point in a distribution. If we imagine a seesaw consisting of a fulcrum and a board, the scores are like bricks spread along the board. The mean corresponds to the fulcrum when it is in balance. Move one of the bricks to another position and the balance point will change (Fig. 7.1).

The mean is the point in a distribution of scores about which the summed deviations of every score from the mean are equal to zero. When the mean is subtracted from a score, the difference is called a **deviation score.** Those scores above the mean will have positive deviations from it while the scores below the mean have negative deviations from it. The sum of the positive and negative deviations are always zero. This zero sum is the reason why measures other than actual deviations from the mean have to be used to measure the dispersal or spread of scores round the mean.

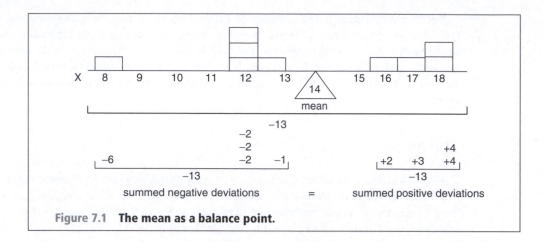

Figure 7.1   The mean as a balance point.

Deviation score. The difference between an individual score and the mean of the distribution.

Characteristics of the mean

Since the mean is determined by the value of every score, it is the preferred measure of central tendency. For example, a corporation contemplating buying a factory and taking over its operation would be interested in the mean salary of the workers in the factory, since the mean multiplied by the number of workers would indicate the total amount of money required to pay all the workers. A sociologist studying the factory's community would probably be more interested in the median salary since the median indicates the pay of the typical worker.

A major advantage of the mean is that it is amenable to arithmetic and algebraic manipulations in ways that the other measures are not. Therefore, if further statistical computations are to be performed, the mean is the measure of choice. This property accounts for the appearance of the mean in the formulas for many important statistics.

Problems with the mean

There are two situations in which the mean is not the preferred measure of central tendency:

- when the distribution is very skewed; and
- when the data are qualitative in character.

Skew

Suppose that the following data were obtained for the number of minutes required to load a company lorry with a day's deliveries: 10.1, 10.3, 10.5, 10.6, 10.7, 10.9, 56.9. The mean is 120/7 = 17.1; the median is 10.6. Which number best represents the time taken? Most of us would agree that it is 10.6, the median. The mean is unduly affected by the lone extreme score of 56.9. If a distribution is extremely asymmetrical the mean is strongly affected by the extreme scores and, as a result, falls further away from what would be considered the distribution's central area, or where most of the values are located and becomes untypical, unrealistic and unrepresentative.

Because the median has the desirable property of being insensitive to extreme scores it is unaffected. In the distribution of scores of 66, 70, 72, 76, 80 and 96, the median of the distribution would remain exactly the same if the lowest score were 6 rather than 66, or the highest score were 1996 rather than 96. The mean, on the other hand, would differ widely with these other scores. Thus the median is preferred in skewed distributions where there are extreme scores as it is not sensitive to the values of the scores above and below it – only to the number of such scores.

Qualitative data

Suppose that the dependent variable is ethnic group membership and we collect the following data: European, Malay, Chinese, Indian, Thai, Korean. There is no meaningful way to represent these data by a mean; we could, however, compute the mode and say the most typical member of the particular organization is Chinese.

Relative merits of the mean, median and mode

Computation of all three measures of central tendency is relatively easy and SPSS produces them without much effort. We will show you how below. Each of the measures of central tendency imparts different information and the three values obtained from one distribution can be very different as they represent different conceptions of the point around which scores cluster. The question then becomes which one should be used in what situation? The choice is based on:

- the level of measurement of the variable;
- the intended use of the statistic; and
- the shape of the distribution.

Level of measurement

The first consideration is the type of scale represented by the data. With a nominal scale, the mode is the only legitimate statistic to use. Recall that the mode is determined only by frequency of occurrence by category and not by the order of the variables or their numerical values. For example, suppose that a city population is divided into three groups on the basis of type of residence: 15% have privately rented accommodation, 60% live in their own accommodation, and 25% live in public housing. We might report that the 'average' person lives in their own accommodation. In this case, we are using the mode because this is the most frequent category and the data are nominal.

If we were talking about the 'average' salary of employees, we would most likely use the median. That is, we would place all the salaries in order (ordinal scale) and then determine the middle value. The median would be preferred over the mean because the salaries of a few highly paid CEOs would distort the mean to a disproportionate extent and it would not be the most typical. The median is an ordinal statistic and is used when data are in the form of an ordinal scale.

With an interval or ratio scale the mean is the recommended measure of central tendency, although the median or mode may also be reported for these types of scales. For example, if we were reporting the number of items produced by a factory on a daily basis and seeking a measure of the average daily production over the month, this data would be assumed to represent an interval scale, and the mean would generally be used.

Purpose

A second consideration in choosing a measure of central tendency is the purpose for which the measure is being used. If we want the value of every single observation to contribute to the average, then the mean is the appropriate measure to use. The median is preferred when one does not want extreme scores at one end or the other to influence the average or when one is concerned with 'typical' values rather than with the value of every single case. If a city wanted to know the average taxable value of all the industrial property and real estate there, then the mean would be used since every type of real estate would be taken into consideration. However, if it wanted to know the cost of the average family dwelling, the median would give a more accurate picture of the typical residence as it would omit several luxury atypical dwellings.

The median is also of value in testing the quality of products. For example, to determine the average life of a torch battery we could select 100 at random from a production run and measure the length of time each can be used continuously before becoming exhausted and then take the mean. However, this mean will not be a good reflection of how batteries as a whole last as a few batteries with lives that grossly exceed the rest or a few dud ones will distort the figures. If the time is noted when half the batteries 'die' this median may be used as a measure of the average life.

If the purpose of the statistic is to provide a measure that can be used in further statistical calculations and for inferential purposes, then the mean is the best measure. The median and mode are essentially 'terminal statistics' as they are not used in more advanced statistical calculations.

Shape of the distribution

The choice between the mean and the median as a measure of central tendency depends very much on the shape of the distribution. The median, as was shown earlier, is not affected by 'extreme' values as it only takes into account the rank order of observations. The mean, on the other hand, is affected by extremely large or small values as it specifically takes the values of the observations into account, not their rank order.

Distributions with extreme values at one end are said to be skewed. A classic example is income, since there are only a few very high incomes but many low ones. Suppose we sample 10 individuals from a neighbourhood, and find their yearly incomes (in thousands of dollars) to be:

25   25   25   25   40   40   40   50   50   1000

The median income for this sample is $40,000, and this value reflects the income of the typical individual. The mean income for this sample however, is 25 + 25 + 25 + 25 + 40 + 40 + 40 + 50 + 50 + 1000 = 130 or $130,000. A politician who wants to demonstrate that their neighbourhood has prospered might, quite honestly, use these data to claim that the average (mean) income is $130,000. If, on the other hand, they wished to plead for financial aid for the local school, they might say, with equal honesty, that the typical (median) income is only $40,000. There is no single 'correct' way to find an 'average' in this situation, but it is obviously important to know which measure of central tendency is being used.

As you can see, the word 'average' can be used fairly loosely and in media reports and political addresses the particular average may not be identified as a mean or a median or even a mode. Measures of central tendency can be misleading and, in the wrong hands, abused. Hopefully you are better informed now.

Measures of dispersal or variability

Close behind central tendency in importance as a descriptive statistic is *dispersion* – the extent to which scores differ from one another – that is, their scatter or spread. Averages or measures of central tendency are a useful way of describing one characteristic of a frequency distribution. But reducing a large set of data to one statistic can lead to a serious loss of information. Consider the three distributions below. Both mean and median are equal for each distribution, i.e. = 10, but a second characteristic differs quite markedly in each:

(a)	8	9	**10**	11	12
(b)	10	10	**10**	10	10
(c)	1	5	**10**	15	19
			mean		
			and median		

As you can see, the variability of scores or spread of scores around the mean appears to be the most prominent candidate, and we need to know how to measure this variability. This concept of variability provides another way of summarizing and comparing different sets of data.

The notion of variability lies at the heart of the study of individual and group differences. It is the variability of individuals, cases, conditions and events that form the focus of research. We can actually derive a mean, median and mode for a set of scores whether they have variability or not. On the other hand, if there is considerable variation, our three measures of central tendency provide no indication of its extent. But they provide us with reference points against which variability can be assessed.

Range

One method of considering variability is to calculate the range between the lowest and the highest scores. This is not a very good method, however, since the range is considerably influenced by extreme scores and in fact only takes into account two scores – those at both extremes.

Variance

A better measure of variability should incorporate every score in the distribution rather than just the two end scores as in the range. One might think that the variability could be measured by the average difference between the various scores and the mean, M:

$$\frac{\sum(\text{score} - M)}{N}$$

This measure is unworkable, however, because some scores are greater than the mean and some are smaller, so that the numerator is a sum of both positive and negative terms. (In fact, it turns out that the sum of the positive terms equals the sum of the negative terms, so that the expression shown above always equals zero.) If you remember, this was the advantage of the mean over other measures of central tendency, in that it was the 'balance point'.

The solution to this problem however is simple. We can square all the terms in the numerator, making them all positive. The resulting measure of variability is called the *variance* or V. It is the sum of the deviation of every score from the mean squared divided by the total number of cases, or as a formula:

$$V = \frac{\sum(\text{every score} - \text{Mean})^2}{\text{Total number of cases}}$$

or

$$V = \frac{\sum(X - M)^2}{N}$$

Variance is the average squared deviation from the mean. Don't worry about this formula as SPSS will calculate it for you and produce all the descriptive statistics you need. You will be shown how to do this later in this chapter. These simple mathematical explanations are provided just so you can understand what these various statistics are.

An example of the calculation of the variance is shown in Table 7.1. As the table shows, the variance is obtained by subtracting the mean (M = 8) from each score, squaring each result, adding all the squared terms, and dividing the resulting sum by the total number of scores (N = 10), to yield a value of 4.4.

Because deviations from the mean are squared, the variance is expressed in units different from the scores themselves. If our dependent variable were costs measured in dollars,

Table 7.1 **Calculating variance**

Score	Score – mean	(Score – mean)²	
8	8 – 8 = 0	$0^2 = 0$	$\dfrac{44}{10} = 4.4$
11	11 – 8 = 3	$3^2 = 9$	
6	6 – 8 = –2	$(-2)^2 = 4$	
7	7 – 8 = –1	$(-1)^2 = 1$	
5	5 – 8 = –3	$(-3)^2 = 9$	
9	9 – 8 = 1	$1^2 = 1$	
5	5 – 8 = 3	$(-3)^2 = 9$	
9	9 – 8 = 1	$1^2 = 1$	
9	9 – 8 = 1	$1^2 = 1$	
1	11 – 8 = 3	$3^2 = 9$	
		$\Sigma = 44$	

the variance would be expressed in square dollars! It is more convenient to have a measure of variability which can be expressed in the same units as the original scores. To accomplish this end, we take the square root of the variance, the standard deviation.

Standard deviation

It is often symbolized as σ when referring to a population and 'SD' when referring to a sample, which in this book, and in most research, it usually is. The standard deviation reflects the amount of spread that the scores exhibit around the mean. The standard deviation is the square root of the variance. Thus:

$$\sigma \text{ or } SD = \sqrt{V} \ \text{ or } \ \sigma = \sqrt{\frac{\Sigma(X-M)^2}{N}}$$

In our example in Table 7.1, the SD is about 2.1, the square root of the variance which we calculated as 4.4.

> **The standard deviation.** *The square root of the mean squared deviation from the mean of the distribution.*

Here is an example of using measures of dispersal:
Paul Lim is the manager of *Golden Value* investments. Paul was interested in the rates of return of two different funds. *Growbucks* showed rates over the last five years of 12, 10, 13,

9, and 11 percent, while *Dollarise* yielded 13, 12, 14, 10, and 6%. Which one should Paul select for his clients? Both funds offer an average return of 11%, therefore the safer investment is the one with the smaller variance and standard deviation, as this indicates a smaller degree of risk.

For *Growbucks* with M = 11: $V = \dfrac{1^2 + 1^2 + 2^2 + 2^2 + 0^2}{5} = 2$ SD = 1.41%

For *Dollarise* with M = 11: $V = \dfrac{2^2 + 1^2 + 3^2 + 1^2 + 5^2}{5} = 8$ SD = 2.38%

Since *Growbucks* shows less variability in its returns and offers the same average return than *Dollarise, Growbucks* represents the safer of the two investments.

Interpreting the SD

Generally, the larger the SD, the greater the dispersal of scores; the smaller the SD, the smaller the spread of scores, i.e. SD increases in proportion to the spread of the scores around M as the marker point. Measures of central tendency tell us nothing about the standard deviation and vice versa. Like the mean, the standard deviation should be used with caution with highly skewed data, since the squaring of an extreme score would carry a disproportionate weight. It is therefore recommended where M is also appropriate. Figure 7.2 shows two different standard deviations: one with a clustered appearance, the other with scores well spread out, illustrating clearly the relationship of spread to standard deviation.

So, in describing an array of data, researchers typically present two descriptive statistics: the mean and the standard deviation. Although there are other measures of central tendency and dispersion, these are the most useful for descriptive purposes.

The quartiles and interquartile range

We have already seen that the median divides a distribution exactly in half. A distribution can also be divided into quarters using **quartiles**. The first quartile (Q1) is the score that separates the lowest 25% of the distribution from the rest. The second quartile (Q2) is the score that has exactly two quarters or 50% of the distribution below it. The third quartile (Q3) is the score that divides the bottom three-fourths of the distribution from the top quarter. The **interquartile** range is the distance between the first and third quartiles, i.e. the mid 50% of the scores, and is the range of the boxplot (an SPSS graph we will produce later) representing all data between Q1 and Q3. Because the interquartile range focuses on the middle 50% of a distribution, it is less influenced by extreme scores and gives a more stable measure of variability than the range. However, it does not take into account actual differences between scores.

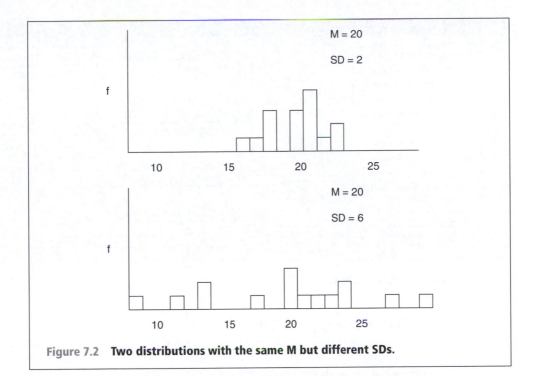

Figure 7.2 **Two distributions with the same M but different SDs.**

Using SPSS to calculate and display descriptive statistics

You will need to access Chapter 7 Data File SPSS B on the book's SPSS Web page.

To obtain descriptive statistics

1 Click on *Analyze >> Descriptive Statistics >> Explore* to obtain the *Explore* dialogue box.
2 Transfer to the *Dependent List* box by clicking and highlighting those variables for which you wish to obtain descriptive statistics. In this example we will transfer *age* (Fig. 7.3).
3 In the *Display* box click on *Statistics* which will bring up the *Explore: Statistics* dialogue box.
4 Ensure *Descriptives* is chosen. Select *Continue >> OK* to produce the output (Table 7.2).

If you wish to compute separate sets of descriptive statistics for a qualitative variable, say for men and women separately, after step 3 above, place the variable, e.g. *gender*, into the *Factor List* box. This is what we have done in our example (Fig. 7.3). This will provide descriptives on *age* for men and women separately.

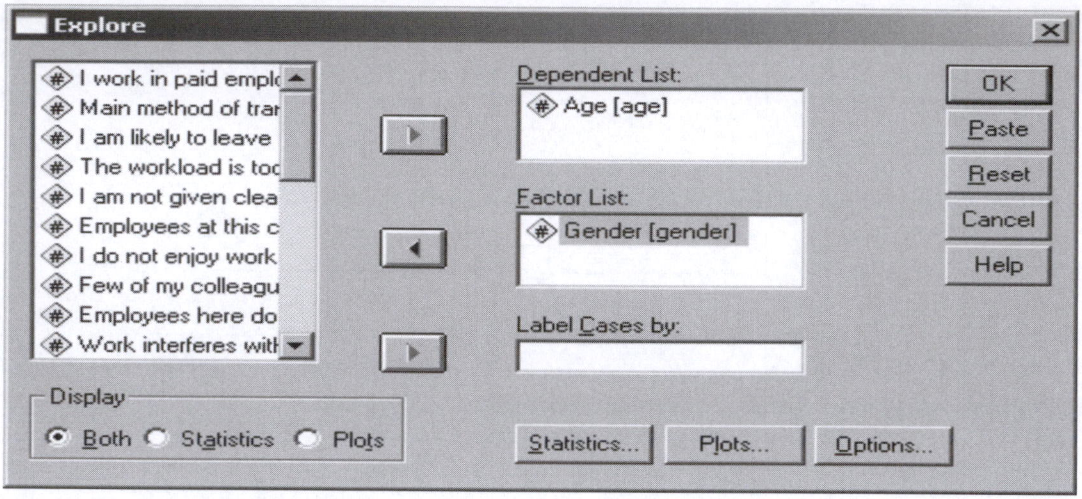

Figure 7.3 **Explore dialogue box.**

How to interpret the output in Table 7.2
- The top sub-table reveals the number of cases and whether there is any missing data. Missing cases are the number of scores which have been disregarded by SPSS for the purposes of the analysis. There are none in this example.
- The important statistics lie in the much larger bottom descriptives table, namely the mean, median, variance and standard deviation. For example, the mean female age was 21.78, the median was 18 and the standard deviation was 8.46 (rounded).
- There are many other statistical values that have been calculated, such as **the inter-quartile range, 95% confidence intervals, skewness, variance, range, maximum and minimum score,** etc. In the next few chapters you will be introduced to those you have not yet met. You would not report all the measures displayed but reproduce those of interest in a more simplified form, omitting some of the clutter of detail. Remember that these descriptive statistics are produced on the *Explore* menu.

As well as using *Explore*, you can also obtain a smorgasbord of descriptive statistics from *Descriptives*. These include the **mean, sum, standard deviation, range, standard error of the mean, maximum and minimum score,** and **skewness.** Try out the descriptives menu in your own time. It is easy to use.

Reporting of values on SPSS

While SPSS reports this data to three decimal places, two decimal places are usually more than enough for most social science and business data. Measurement in these fields does not need to be as sensitively accurate as in the physical sciences, so three decimal places is overkill and infers a precision not warranted.

Table 7.2   Example of descriptive statistics produced by the Explore procedure

Case Processing Summary

		Cases					
		Valid		Missing		Total	
	Gender	N	Percent	N	Percent	N	Percent
Age	Male	29	100.0%	0	.0%	29	100.0%
	Female	51	100.0%	0	.0%	51	100.0%

Descriptives

	Gender			Statistic	Std. Error
Age	Male	Mean		22.62	1.537
		95% Confidence	Lower Bound	19.47	
		Interval for mean	Upper bound	25.77	
		5% Trimmed Mean		21.62	
		Median		18.00	
		Variance		68.530	
		Std. Deviation		8.278	
		Minimum		17	
		Maximum		49	
		Range		32	
		Interquartile Range		6.50	
		Skewness		2.033	.434
		Kurtosis		3.421	.845
	Female	Mean		21.78	1.184
		95% Confidence	Lower Bound	19.41	
		Interval for mean	Upper bound	24.16	
		5% Trimmed Mean		20.51	
		Median		18.00	
		Variance		71.493	
		Std. Deviation		8.455	
		Minimum		17	
		Maximum		55	
		Range		38	
		Interquartile Range		3.00	
		Skewness		2.472	.333
		Kurtosis		5.840	656

Sometimes SPSS will report values with a confusing notation like 7.41E-03. This means move the decimal place 3 steps to the left. So 7.41E-03 becomes a more familiar .00741. In the same way a figure like 7.41E+02 becomes 741.0 since the + sign tells us to move the decimal place 2 steps to the right.

Tabulating and grouping data

While it is important to be able to demonstrate means, and standard deviations, etc. little or no sense can be got out of any series of numbers until they have been set out in some orderly and logical fashion (usually a table or chart like a histogram) that enables comparisons to be made. Never present data to management or clients in a raw form. They need to be grouped in some way and summarized, so that we can extract the underlying pattern or profile, make comparisons and identify significant relationships between the data. What are the figures, given half a chance, trying to tell us? Tabulation is that first critical step in patterning the data.

Tabulation by frequency distributions and cross-tabulation

A frequency distribution table presents data in a concise and orderly form by recording observations or measures in terms of how often each occurred. We have already produced frequency tables in Chapter 3 when dealing with the initial screening of the data for accuracy of input (Tables 3.2(b) and (c)).

Frequency. The number of times an observation occurs.

A frequency distribution. A list of observations with their corresponding frequencies.

A useful extension of the simple frequency table is the cross-tabulation table which tallies the frequencies of two variables together. SPSS possesses the cross-tabulation feature which we will demonstrate using Chapter 7 SPSS data file B. Access that file now on the SPSS data file Web page of this book.

To obtain a cross-tabulation

1 Click on *Analyze >> Descriptive Statistics >> Crosstabs ...*
2 This brings up the **cross-tabulation dialogue box.** Two variables – *types of transport used to work* against *perceptions of spending too much time travelling to work* (Fig. 7.4) are transferred to *row(s)* and the other to *column(s)* box respectively.
3 Click on **OK** and output presented below will appear. These show the cross-tabulated frequencies and suggest that walkers and cyclists do not feel they spend too much time travelling but a fair proportion of car drivers feel they do (Table 7.3).

Explanation of output in Table 7.3
1 The top subtable is a summary of how many cases were involved.
2 The lower subtable reveals the distribution of responses, which tends to suggest that car drivers are divided on whether they spend too much time travelling to work, whereas those who walk are certain they do not spend too much time.

Table 7.3   **Crosstabs tables**

Case Processing Summary

	Cases					
	Valid		**Missing**		**Total**	
	N	**Percent**	**N**	**Percent**	**N**	**Percent**
Main method of transport *I spend too much time travelling to work	80	100.0%	0	.0%	80	100.0%

Main method of transport* I spend too much time travelling to work Crosstabulation

		I spend too much time travelling to work							
Count		**Strongly disagree**	**Disagree**	**Tend to disagree**	**Unsure**	**Tend to agree**	**Agree**	**Strongly agree**	**Total**
Main method of transport	car	8	8	5	3	7	4	10	45
	bus	1	1	7	2	2	2	2	17
	walk	11	3	0	1	0	1	0	16
	bike	1	0	1	0	0	0	0	2
Total		21	12	13	6	9	7	12	80

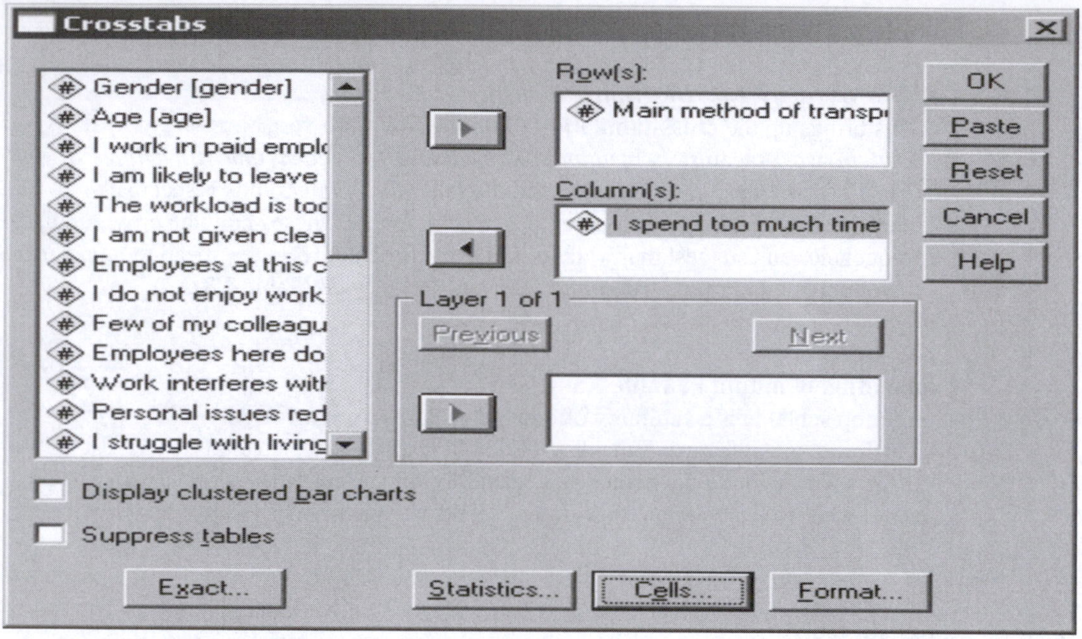

Figure 7.4   **Crosstabs dialogue box.**

Graphs and charts for displaying descriptive statistics

Frequency distributions present the main features of data succinctly, but they are still abstract numerical representations and require effort to interpret. Graphs and charts can impart the same information but speak to us more directly with greater ease of interpretation, making them particularly useful when we want to present data to a conference, or the general public in advertising leaflets or information material. SPSS has a wide range of high-resolution charts and graphs such as bar charts, histograms, pie charts, stem and leaf plots, and box plots which can be produced to clarify the results with eye-catching displays and aid understanding of a mass of figures. These visual aids are located under **Graphs** in the menu bar and basic instructions on how to produce some of these using SPSS now follow. There are many ways to graph data. This presentation is limited to the most commonly used graphs and charts.

Frequency polygon

The most common ways of representing frequency distributions graphically are by numerous variations of the **frequency polygon,** the simplest of which is the **line graph.**

The frequency polygon is preferred to the histogram for distributions in which underlying continuity is explicit or assumed because the continuous line of the polygon suggests continuity more than do the separate bars of the histogram. The histogram is preferred for discrete distributions and is probably a little easier for the general public to interpret. The frequency polygon is also preferred for comparing two or more sets of data on the same graph.

To produce a simple frequency line graph by SPSS

- Click *Graph* >> *Line*.
- In the *Line Charts* dialogue box select *Simple*.
- Choose *Summaries for Groups of cases.*
- Click *Define* to produce the *Define Simple Line: Summaries of Groups of Cases:* dialogue box.
- Select the variable you wish to plot and then click the arrow button to place it into the *Category Axis* box.
- Select *OK*.

Figure 7.5 is a line graph for the frequencies of the variable *age* from Chapter 7 Data File SPSS B. You will probably have noticed that the *Define Simple Line: Summaries of Groups of Cases* dialogue box also enables you to produce cumulative frequency and cumulative percentage line graphs. Cumulative simply means succeeding values are the sum of all preceding values plus the current value so the graph increases by successive additions and always rises.

For a frequency polygon a dot is placed above each score so that:

- the dot is centred above the score; and
- the height corresponds to the frequency or percentage.

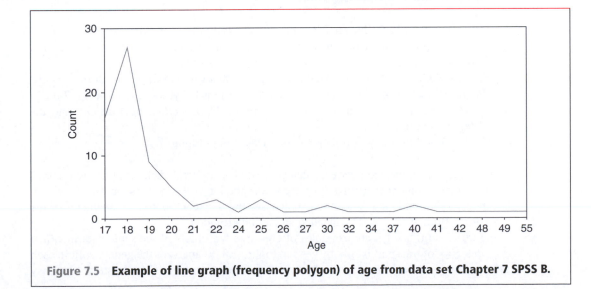

Figure 7.5   **Example of line graph (frequency polygon) of age from data set Chapter 7 SPSS B.**

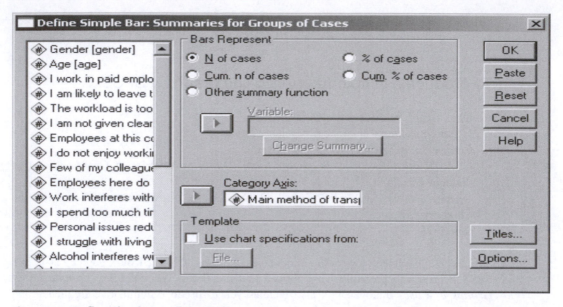

Figure 7.6 **Define Simple Bar dialogue box.**

Bar charts

A common method of presenting categorical data is the bar chart where the height or length of each bar is proportional to the size of the corresponding number.

SPSS instructions for the bar chart

1 Using data file SPSS Chapter 7 B click on **Graphs >>Bar ...** on the drop down menu.
2 The **Bar Chart** dialogue box provides for choice among a number of different bar chart forms. Chosen **Simple** for this demonstration. Then **Define**.
3 The **Define Simple Bar** dialogue box emerges with a variety of options for the display. We have chosen **N of cases** but there are other options for you to explore (Fig. 7.6).
4 Transfer the required variable – in our example *Main method of transport* into the **Category Axis** box.
5 Click **OK** and the output presents the **Bar Chart** as in Figure 7.7.

A vertical bar is erected over each category or class interval such that its height corresponds to the number of occurrences or scores in the interval. The bars can be any width, but they should not touch, since this emphasizes the discrete, qualitative character of the categories. Both axes should be labelled and a title provided.

Figures 7.8 (a) and (b) are examples of clustered bar charts of the same data in which each category of transport is split by gender. Figure 7.8 (a) analyzes the gender split in each category by N while the second displays the data as a percentage. They illustrate how easy

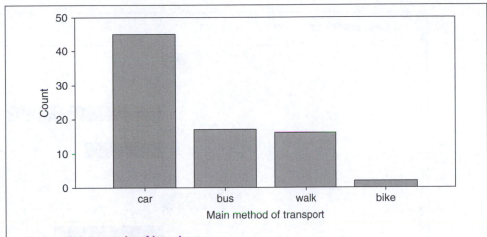

Figure 7.7 **Example of bar chart.**

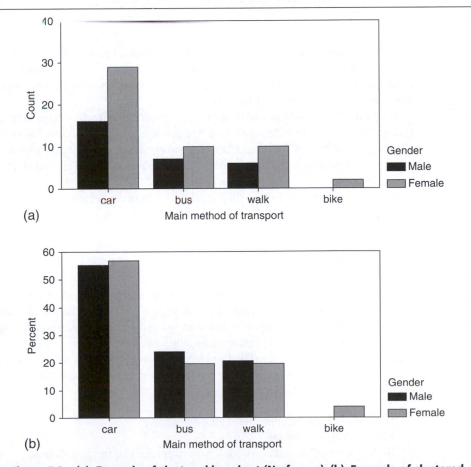

Figure 7.8 **(a) Example of clustered bar chart (N of cases). (b) Example of clustered bar chart (by percentage).**

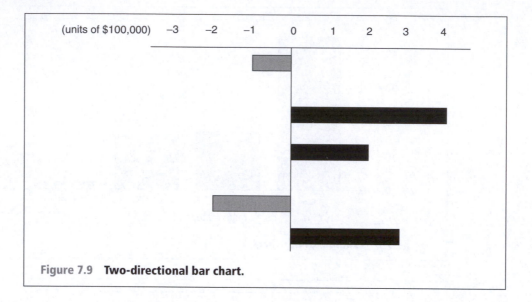

Figure 7.9 **Two-directional bar chart.**

it is to pick up the main features such as the fact that no male cycles and that percentages are very similar for other categories, though this is not apparent in terms of numbers. This illustrates the fact that when displaying data, experiment with different displays to obtain one which is suitable for your purpose.

The **two-directional bar chart** has bars going in opposite directions to indicate positive and negative movements from an assumed average, or norm. Figure 7.9 presents data for annual profitability of five branches of a supermarket chain. This form of bar chart is particularly useful in highlighting differences in movements of a variable between different regions or countries or over different time periods.

The way information can be displayed on a bar chart is limited only by the ingenuity of the person creating the display.

Pie charts

A **pie chart** can be used as an alternative to the bar chart to show the relative size, contribution or importance of the components, as in Figure 7.10. It can be found under **graphs** on the drop down menu. Perhaps this is the most easily visually interpreted graph, merely a circle divided into sectors representing proportionate frequency or percentage frequency of the class intervals/categories. The last stage of construction is labelling the sections of the pie, placing percentages on the slices and providing an appropriate title. Use *Chart Editor* for this. For example, to place percentages on the pie:

- Double-click on the chart to select it for editing.
- Select *Chart >>Options*.
- In the pie chart *Options* box click next to percents in the *Labels* box.

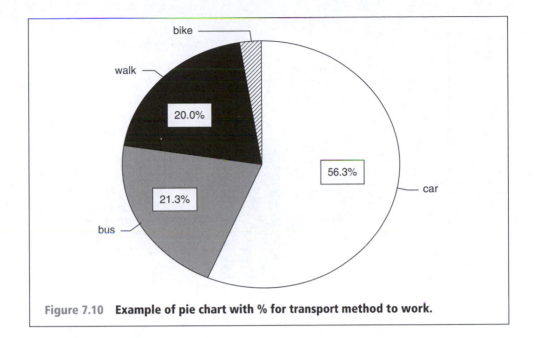

Figure 7.10   Example of pie chart with % for transport method to work.

- Select *Format* then click on the down arrow next to *Position* and select *Numbers inside, Text outside.*
- Choose *Continue >>OK* to display the edited pie chart.

There are two major disadvantages with pie charts. Firstly, comparisons between sectors is difficult as visual relations between sectors that are similar in size is hard without percentages placed on the sectors. Secondly, negative quantities cannot be recorded. For example, in splitting the pie chart into sectors representing the amount of profit each department made in the year, you cannot show the loss made by one department.

Box and whisker plot

We met these very simple displays when checking the data file for errors as the box plot provides a graphical representation of the major elements of the data. The box itself contains the middle 50% of the observations in the distribution (interquartile range) and the horizontal line depicts the median value in the data. Whiskers run vertically from the top and bottom of the box and these lines are terminated by horizontal lines (outer fences) that indicate the maximum and minimum observations of the general data. However, outliers beyond these will be noted by case number as we saw in Chapter 6. Box plots can be obtained in the drop down menu under **Graphs.**

The box plot is useful for detecting skewness of distributions by noticing where the median is located and disparities between the length of the two whiskers. In a symmetrical distribution, the median is centred and the whiskers are of equal length. In Figure 7.11 there is a heavy clustering of observations at the high end of the scale.

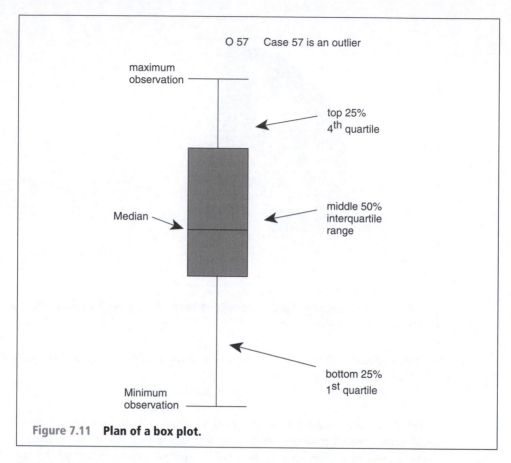

Figure 7.11   Plan of a box plot.

Stem and leaf display

This technique was also used earlier to detect error in the input. It separates data entries into 'leading digits' and 'trailing digit'. The number 62 consists of a leading digit of 6 and a trailing digit of 2. This is no more than the old tens and units split. Figure 7.12 is a display of data shown as a list then in a stem and leaf format to show how it works.

In Figure 7.12 the column of numbers to the left of the vertical line is the 'stem', i.e. in this case the tens column. The list of numbers on the right of the line is the 'leaf' or the units that branch out as trailing digits. A set of ten that has no data is left blank on the 'leaf' side. Should you be dealing with three-figure numbers the system is the same, i.e. for 123, the 12 form the stem and 3 the leaf. The display provides a quick visual impression of the distribution and again is available under **Graphs.**

Frequency histograms

A histogram is similar in appearance and construction to a bar graph, but it is used to display the frequency of quantitative variables rather than qualitative variables. A bar or rectangle

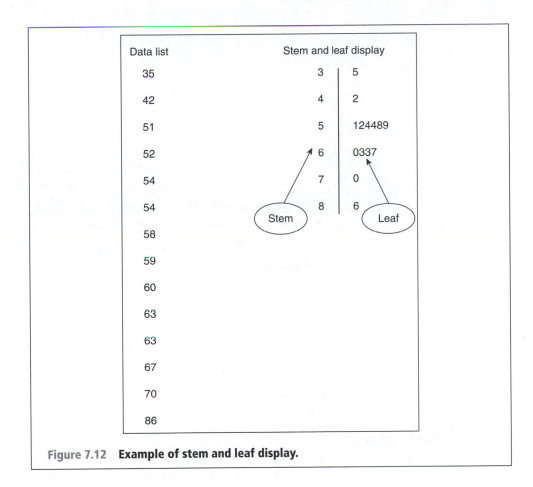

Figure 7.12   Example of stem and leaf display.

is raised above each score interval on the horizontal axis. Successive bars are placed touching each other to show the continuity of the scores in continuous data (unlike bar graphs where there is separation). An empty space should also be left at any interval where there is no data to record.

The vertical axis should be labelled *f*, or frequency, and the horizontal axis labelled to show what is being measured (scores, weight in kg, employee age groups, reaction time in seconds, sales per month and so on). As usual, a descriptive title, indicating what the graph is showing, is always placed with the graph.

A histogram is shown in Figure 7.13 of the variable *age* from Chapter 7 data file SPSS B. Note that the edges of the bars coincide with the limits of the class intervals in blocks of five years, e.g. 17.5–22.5 with 20 as the midpoint. There are no cases that fall in the range 42.5–47.5 years old. Histograms are also located in the drop down menu under **Graphs.**

A histogram has one important characteristic which the bar chart does not possess. A bar chart is in one dimension representing a single magnitude. The height or length of the bar

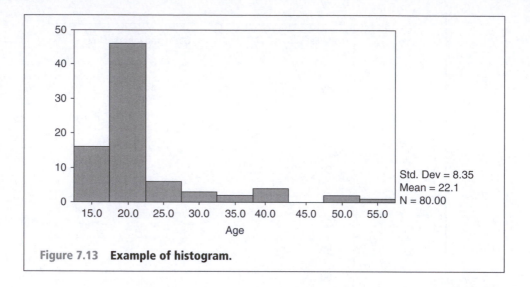

Figure 7.13 **Example of histogram.**

corresponds to the magnitude of the variable, the width of the bar is of no consequence. A histogram, however, has two dimensions, namely, frequency (represented by the height of the bar or rectangle) and width of the class (represented by the width of the bar). It is the area of the bar which is of significance.

Editing charts

Charts can be edited in many ways in the output viewer to enhance them for presentation. Among other 'goodies', you can insert titles, add 3D effects, colour fill, explode sectors of a pie chart, add percentages to pie chart slices, etc. Double-click on the chart to bring up the **Chart Editor**. Play around modifying your output using the various menus on the chart editor.

Writing up your descriptive statistics

As a general rule you would state the number of cases involved and quote the mean and standard deviation of the distributions for each variable for the whole and subgroups. You may also need to present the median and other descriptives obtained from SPSS using both tables and verbal report. You would also, as appropriate, display a variety of graphs and charts, such as histograms and box plots to summarize the data, and indicate the shape of the distributions from these. Don't try to report all of the SPSS output since there is often an excess of detail. Avoid SPSS-specific terms, like 'valid percent', as it has little meaning for those readers not conversant with SPSS.

What you have learned from this chapter

This chapter has introduced you to some basic descriptive statistics, their uses and how they can be obtained and displayed using SPSS. The goal of descriptive statistics is to simplify the organization and presentation of data.

You are now aware of three important measures of central tendency, namely the mean, median and mode, each yielding a somewhat different type of information. The purpose of central tendency is to determine the single value that best represents the entire distribution of scores.

The mean, an interval statistic, is generally the most widely used measure of central tendency. It takes into account every score in the distribution and can be used in computation for more sophisticated statistical analyses, but it is affected by extreme scores. For markedly skewed distributions, the median is preferred. The mode may be more meaningful for inherently discrete variables such as family size.

The other major descriptive statistics you have met are those concerned with variability or the spread of scores in a distribution. The most important are the variance and standard deviation. The standard deviation is the square root of the variance and is the basis of many other statistical operations which you will meet later in the book. The larger the spread of scores round the mean the larger the standard deviation.

Tables of descriptive statistics and cross-tabulations, frequency distributions, graphs and charts such as line graphs, histograms, box plots, pie charts and bar graphs are all useful for ordering data and presenting them in an easily interpreted form. You have been shown how to produce these on SPSS in this chapter.

Review questions

Qu. 7.1

(a) What is the mode in the following set of numbers?
3, 5, 5, 5, 7, 7, 9, 11, 11.

(b) Is the mode in the following set uni, bi or tri-model?
4, 4, 5, 5, 6, 7, 7, 7, 8, 8, 9, 9, 9, 12, 13, 13.

Check your answer on the chapter website.

Qu. 7.2
What is the median of the following set of numbers: 23, 16, 20, 14, 10, 20, 21, 15, 18?
Check your answer on the website.

Qu. 7.3
Explain in what circumstances the median is preferred to the mean.

Qu. 7.4
List the advantages and disadvantages of each of the mean, median and mode.

Check your answers to the following multiple choice items on the Chapter 7 Web page.

1   A figure showing each score and the number of times each score occurred is a:

   (a) histogram
   (b) frequency distribution
   (c) frequency polygon
   (d) frequency polygram

2   The frequency of a particular value plus the frequencies of all lower values is:

   (a) the summated frequency
   (b) the additive frequency
   (c) the cumulative frequency
   (d) the relative frequency

3   A display of raw data which combines the qualities of a frequency distribution and a graphic display of the data is a:

   (a) root and branch
   (b) principal and secondary
   (c) stem and leaf
   (d) pre and post

4   In drawing a pie chart we have total costs of running a factory as $12,000,000. If wages and salaries are $3,000,000 what proportion of the pie is that sector representing this cost element?

   (a) 30%
   (b) 12%
   (c) 25%
   (d) 33%

5   You are told that 6 employees are needed to load the trailer. The figure 6 is the:

   (a) percentage
   (b) proportion
   (c) frequency
   (d) dependent variable

6   As the numbers of observations increase the shape of a frequency polygon:

   (a) remains the same
   (b) becomes smoother
   (c) stays the same
   (d) varies with the size of the distribution

7   If a set of data has several extreme scores, which measure of central tendency is most appropriate?

   (a) mode
   (b) median
   (c) mean
   (d) variance

8   The mode is preferred when:

   (a) there are few values
   (b) the data is in rank order
   (c) a typical value is required
   (d) there is a skewed distribution

9   In a box plot the box represents:

   (a) the data
   (b) the quartile range
   (c) the middle 50% of values
   (d) the median

10   The usual measure of dispersal is:

   (a) the variation
   (b) the standard variance
   (c) the standard difference
   (d) the standard deviation

11   When you have categorical variables and count the frequency of the occurrence of each category your measure of central tendency is:

   (a) the mean
   (b) the mode
   (c) the median
   (d) you would not need one

12 If the standard deviation for a set of scores was 0 (zero) what can you say about the distribution?

(a) the mean is 0
(b) the standard deviation cannot be measured
(c) all the scores are the same
(d) the distribution is multi-modal

13 Four directors of QuikBuild earn $190,000, $195,000, $90,000 and $180,000 respectively. The appropriate measure of central tendency is:

(a) the mode
(b) the median
(c) the mean
(d) the weighted mean

14 If the raw data are in terms of metres, the standard deviation will be in terms of:

(a) metres squared
(b) metres and centimetres
(c) hundreds of metres
(d) metres

Now access the website for Chapter 7 and attempt the additional questions and activities there.

Chapter 8
Normal Distribution, Probability and Statistical Significance

'Statisticians do it with 95% confidence'

'Statisticians probably do it'

'Statisticians do it with only 5% chance of rejection'

'Statisticians do it – after all it is normal'

'Statistics means never having to say you are certain'

'Are statisticians normal?'

(Sources unknown)

Content list

> ## By the end of this chapter, you will:
>
> 1 Be able to distinguish different types of skew distributions.
> 2 Understand the concept of normal distribution and its characteristics.
> 3 Understand the use of Z scores.
> 4 Recognize the relationship between normal distribution and probability levels.
> 5 Understand the concept of statistical significance.
> 6 Learn how to use SPSS to produce Z scores and transform skewed data to normality.

Introduction

This chapter introduces you to the essential statistical concepts underlying all research. In Chapter 7 you were introduced to the measures of central tendency and dispersal as major ways of describing data sets. But all distributions have shape too and frequency distributions were also presented as convenient ways of visually presenting the shape of a distribution. The major distribution of interest is the normal distribution as this allows us to calculate the probability of occurrence of any value in the distribution – the basis of establishing statistical significance.

Distributions

Distributions shown by frequency polygons

The main reason for constructing histograms and frequency polygons is that they reveal the score distribution along the X-axis showing the **form** or **shape** of the distribution. If we plot the data we have obtained from any of our previous observations, we would find a host of differently shaped curves or frequency distributions. A distribution's shape is as important as its spread or central tendency and visual representations are superior to numerical ones for discovering a distribution's shape. The most immediately obvious characteristic of a graphed frequency distribution is its symmetry or lack of symmetry.

Skewed distributions

These many differently shaped frequency distributions can be classified as normal or skewed. An asymmetrical curve characterized by a high point or hump that is off-centre and by tails of distinctly unequal length is called a **skewed curve**. That is, in a skewed curve the observations or scores pile up at one end. Skewed curves are labelled according to the direction in which the longer tail is pointing.

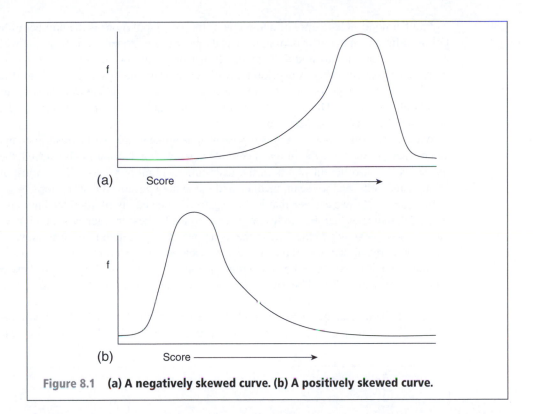

Figure 8.1   (a) A negatively skewed curve. (b) A positively skewed curve.

Skewed frequency distributions – *these distributions are biased by factors that tend to push scores one way more than another.*

For example, Figure 8.1(a) and (b) displays two skewed distributions of scores for two end-of-year statistics examinations. What reasons could you suggest might have caused the skewedness in each case? We are looking for factors that bias scores in one direction rather than another.

Perhaps for Figure 8.1(a) we might guess the examination was too easy; the marking too lenient; the students had worked hard; the students were highly motivated; or the material had been thoroughly taught. With Figure 8.1(b) our thoughts veer the other way and ideas about the paper being difficult, severe marking, poor teaching, or low student motivation come to mind.

Figure 8.1(a) is a negatively skewed curve, the left tail being longer than the right, the low end of the score scale. This means that while the higher frequencies are concentrated toward the high scores, the extreme scores are at the low end.

When the right tail of the distribution is distinctly longer than the left (Fig. 8.1b), we have a positively skewed distribution. The preponderance of scores tend to be at the lower end of the score values, and the fewer extreme scores are at the high end, hence the long tail to the right.

Another noticeable feature of a line graph (frequency polygon) is the number of highest points or humps in the distribution, i.e. has it one or more modes? A distribution with only one highest point is **unimodal**. This means that one score or one score interval contains more cases than any other. A distribution with two or more humps or peaks is **multimodal**, which covers a range of possibilities such as two humps or **bimodal**, three peaks or **trimodal**, and so on. The areas at each end of the graph where the frequencies decrease are called the **tails** of the distribution.

When a frequency distribution is represented as a line graph, an interesting comparison can be made of the three measures of central tendency. If a distribution is skewed, the three measures fall at different points in the distribution. Figures 8.2(a) and (b) illustrate this relationship between the mean, median, and mode in two skewed distributions.

In Figure 8.2(a) we can see that in the negatively skewed distribution the hump is on the right; this indicates that the mode corresponds to the highest frequency – a high numerical value. The tail extends to the left, so the mean, which is sensitive to each score value, will be pulled in the direction of the extreme scores and will have a low value. The median, the middle score, is least affected by the hump and tail and hence will have a value between the other two measures. It will be lower than the mode but higher than the mean.

In a positively skewed distribution (Fig. 8.2b), the mean will have a higher numerical value than the median because extremely high scores of the lengthy tail will pull the mean to the right. A hump usually occurs to the left to give the mode a low numerical value and

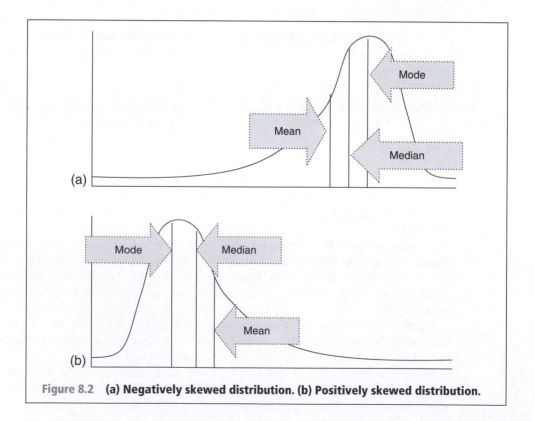

Figure 8.2   **(a) Negatively skewed distribution. (b) Positively skewed distribution.**

again the median will be in the middle. It will be helpful to remember that the mean is always pulled in the direction of the skewed side of the distribution, a fact which demonstrates the influence of extreme scores on the mean.

Normal distribution

When we obtain a distribution that is perfectly symmetrical and unimodal we have a **normal distribution** or **Gaussian curve**. It is affected only by random influences, has no skew and the mean, median, and mode all fall at exactly the same point. The normal distribution is the most important theoretical distribution in statistics. Random influences that are just as likely to make a score larger than the mean as to make it smaller, will tend to balance out, so the most frequently found scores are located in the middle of the range with extreme scores becoming progressively rarer towards the tails of the graph (Fig. 8.3). The normal distribution is a family of distributions (i.e. different means and standard deviations) which have common characteristics. The following are defining characteristics of the family of normal distributions and Figure 8.3 depicts these constants:

(a) The distribution is bilaterally symmetrical and bell shaped. The right side will always be a mirror of the left-hand side.
(b) As a corollary of (a), the mean, median and mode always coincide. This is the only situation where this congruence occurs, because the median (middle score) must be

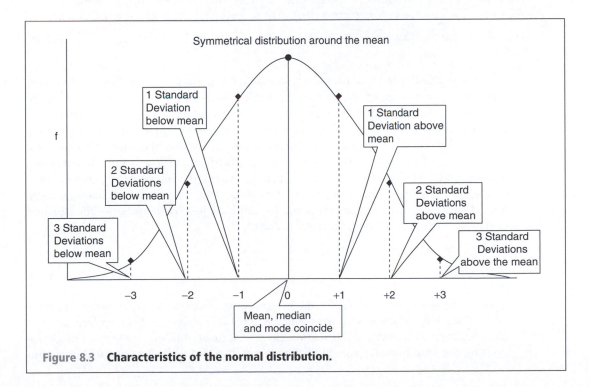

Figure 8.3 **Characteristics of the normal distribution.**

exactly in the centre since exactly half of the scores are on each side of the graph. The mean is also exactly at the centre since there is a corresponding score on each side of the graph so the average of all these pair of values is the middle value. The mode is also in the centre as the most frequently occurring number represented by the apex of the hump.

(c) The tails of the curve never quite reach the X-axis but continue outwards to infinity yet simultaneously get progressively and infinitely closer to the axis.

(d) In practical terms, the range of the distribution is 6 standard deviation units, i.e. 3 on each side of the mean. The proportion of cases beyond ±3 standard deviations is so small that it is common practice to use ±3 as arbitrary limits in illustrative diagrams. Of course the standard deviation value is different for every distribution, so while the range is essentially ±3 standard deviations, the range of scores along the baseline will differ as in Figure 8.4 (a), (b) and (c).

(e) As the standard deviation of the distribution decreases the base becomes shorter with a steeply peaked curve; as the standard deviation increases the base extends and the curve gradually becomes flatter. The degree of peakedness is termed **kurtosis**.

(f) SPSS **Descriptive Statistics** provide values for the **skewness** and **kurtosis** of a distribution. These values should be zero if the distribution is perfectly normal. As these values increase the approximation to normality decreases.

The normal distribution – This is a distribution of chance or randomness. Randomness or chance refers to the property of events that are not predictable.

The normal curve is a mathematical abstraction. It is not associated with any event in the real world, just as circular objects do not exist simply because there is an equation for the area of the circle family. Likewise, the equation for the normal curve defines a family of normal curves which differ in terms of their spread (standard deviations) and central tendency (means). But, in all other respects, members of this family have the same characteristics. Figures 8.4(a), (b), and (c) illustrate several normal distribution curves with different means and standard deviations. Curve (a) has a smallest standard deviation while (c) has the largest standard deviation. The standard deviation units along the baseline of a normal curve are called *Z scores*. Each standard deviation unit increases by the value of the standard deviation of the distribution (Figs. 8.4a, b, and c).

Z scores

The Z score simply re-labels each score in terms of its deviation from the mean. The mean of the Z score distribution is always 0 and the SD of Z is always 1. Z is therefore the standard deviation of the normal distribution. So now, instead of labelling the standard deviations on the base line of a normal distribution as standard deviations, we will now term

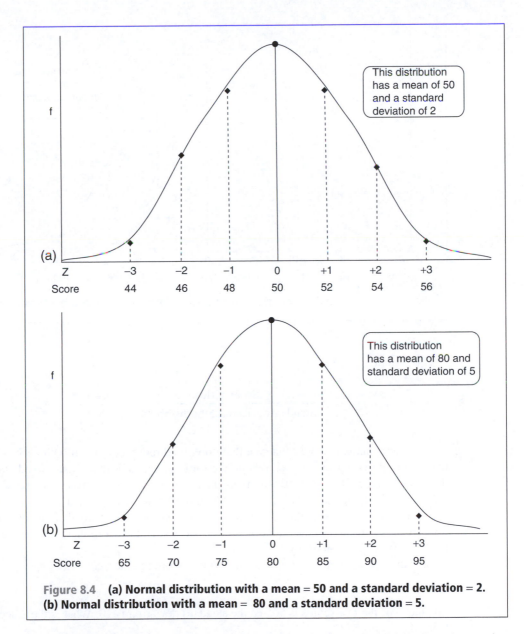

Figure 8.4   (a) Normal distribution with a mean = 50 and a standard deviation = 2. (b) Normal distribution with a mean = 80 and a standard deviation = 5.

them Z scores. Z scores take account of both M and SD of the distribution. A negative Z score indicates the value is below the mean.

Z scores – these are expressed as standard deviation units along the baseline of a normal distribution.

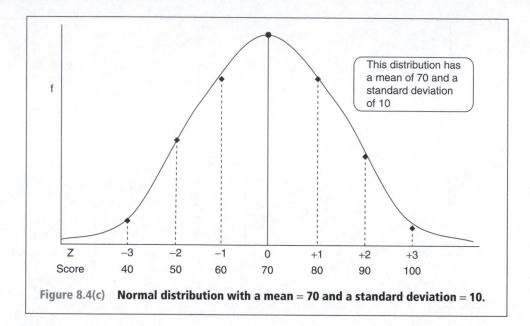

Figure 8.4(c) **Normal distribution with a mean = 70 and a standard deviation = 10.**

The formula is:

$$Z = \frac{\text{Score} - \text{Mean}}{\text{Standard deviation of the distribution}} = \frac{X - M}{SD}$$

Z scores are standard scores and can, therefore, be directly compared with each other as they represent comparative positions on the same scale, even if the means and standard deviations on the different distributions are different. In the three distributions above, while a Z score of +1 represents values of 52, 85, and 80 respectively, each of these scores is equivalent. They represent the same level of performance as they are all 1 standard deviation above the mean. For each unit of Z in Figure 8.4(a), the score increases or decreases by 2, in (b) by 5, and in (c) by 10.

Here are some examples of how to convert raw score to Z scores.

Example 1

The mean of the raw scores is 50 and the standard deviation is 10. What is the Z score for Don who scores 65?

$$Z = \frac{X - M}{SD} = \frac{65 - 50}{10} = +1.5$$

Don's Z score is +1.5 and this means it is 1.5 standard deviations above the mean in the distribution. It can be represented diagrammatically as below. Scores below the mean, of course, have negative Z values and therefore the sign must always be shown with a Z score.

Don's score of 65 is equivalent to a Z score of +1.5

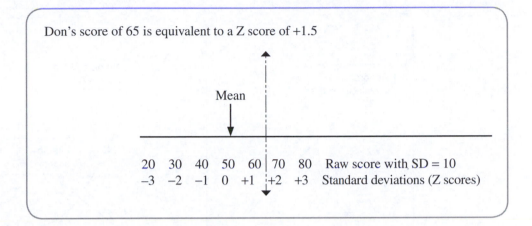

20	30	40	50	60	70	80	Raw score with SD = 10
−3	−2	−1	0	+1	+2	+3	Standard deviations (Z scores)

Example 2

As part of an apprenticeship selection assessment, applicants are required to take three tests, consisting of Test 1 (numeracy), Test 2 (literacy) and Test 3 (general knowledge). Given the following results for Candidate R, on which of the three tests does that individual do best?

	Raw score	Mean	Standard deviation
Test 1. Numeracy	81	75	12
Test 2. Literacy	16	13	2
Test 3. General Knowledge	31	34	10

(a) Calculate Z for numeracy test:

$$Z = \frac{X - M}{SD} = \frac{81 - 75}{12} = +0.5 \text{ above the mean}$$

(b) Calculate Z for literacy test:

$$Z = \frac{X - M}{SD} = \frac{16 - 13}{2} = +1.5 \text{ above the mean}$$

(c) Calculate Z for general knowledge test:

$$Z = \frac{X - M}{SD} = \frac{31 - 34}{10} = -0.3 \text{ below the mean}$$

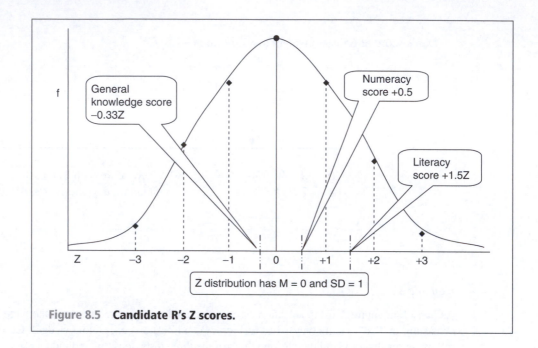

Figure 8.5   Candidate R's Z scores.

Candidate R achieves better results on the literacy test, where his raw score was only 16, than on the numeracy or the general knowledge tests, where his scores were 81 and 31 respectively, as the Z score shows that R is further above average for test 2 than for test 1, while test 3 reveals that the candidate actually scores below average. Candidate R's results can be represented diagrammatically on one distribution now that they are all expressed in terms of one standard scale. In Figure 8.5, the means have all been made equal to zero (the mid point on the Z scale) and the raw scores expressed as Z scores (deviations from the zero point). The three positions can now be compared as they are all on the same scale.

Thus Z scores provide a standard unit of relative worth and enables us to compare across different distributions.

> *Z scores.* The difference between a raw score in a population and the mean of that population measured in standard deviations of that population.

SPSS activity

Using SPSS to compute Z scores

1   Access SPSS Chapter 8 Data File A in website of this text: Click ***Analyze***, >>***Descriptive Statistics***, >>***Descriptives***.
2   Select '*age*' as your chosen variable and move it to the ***Variables Text*** box.

3 Select *Save Standardized values as variable.*

4 Click *OK*

A Z-score equivalent for each raw score will be calculated and placed in a new column in your *variable view* window labelled as z(variable name), in this case '*zage*'. This new 'variable' will be lost unless you save your data before ending the session.

Detecting outliers

Remember that an outlier is a score very different from the rest of the scores. They can be identified by Z scores. Any extremely large Z score stands out when we glance down the column as we expect only 1% to have values of 2.58 or greater. Any over 3.29Z are definite outliers.

Areas under the normal curve

The normal distribution displayed in Figure 8.3 has been so thoroughly studied that the proportion of the area under the curve that lies between the mean and any Z score is well known. It is obvious that 50% of the area lies on each side of the mean (or Z = 0). In particular, there are four areas of interest.

- 68% of the area **approximately** lies between +1Z(SD) and −1Z(SD) from the mean.
- 95% of the area **approximately** lies between + 2Z(SD) and −2Z(SD) from the mean.
- 99% of the area **approximately** lies between +2.57Z(SD) and −2.57Z(SD) from the mean.
- 99.9% of the area **approximately** lies between + 3Z(SD) and −3Z(SD) from the mean.

NB: Please note the 'approximately'

Since the area under the curve represents the total number of cases plotted, then the particular percentages of areas under the curve quoted above can be translated into the percentage of cases lying within the designated areas. Figures 8.6 and 8.7 show these areas and percentages.

These examples using Z and calculating percentages of areas should have made you realize that different events, scores or observations along the baseline of a normal distribution can be said to occur with certain levels of probability. For example, observations located between at +1Z (or 1SD above the mean) and −1Z (or 1SD below the mean) occur on approximately 68% of occasions. That is, there is a probability of .68, or 68/100, or 68% of an event or score occurring between those two limits. Similarly, there is a probability of 2.5%, or .025, or 2.5/100 that an event will occur at or beyond +2Z. Thus events, observations or scores are more likely to occur around the mean of the distribution, i.e. have a high degree of probability. Events, observations or scores that occur near the tails of the distribution are rare and have a low probability. Any point on the baseline can be assigned a probability level of a score occurring there. This leads us into a more detailed

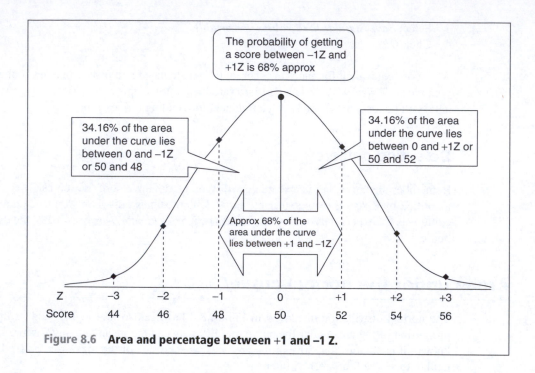

Figure 8.6 **Area and percentage between +1 and −1 Z.**

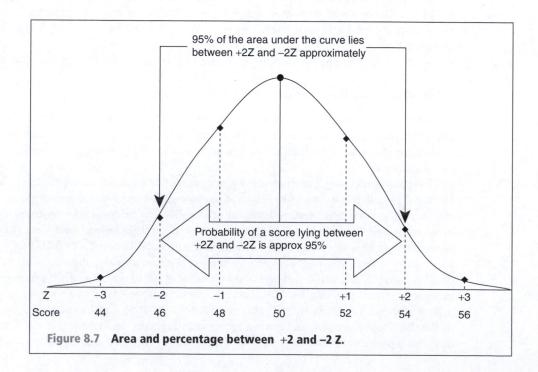

Figure 8.7 **Area and percentage between +2 and −2 Z.**

consideration of probability. Tables exist (provided on the Chapter 8 Web page) that enable us to calculate the areas and therefore probabilities of occurrence between any two Z points along the X-axis.

Testing whether a distribution is normal

We need approximately normal distributions for these areas and probabilities to be approximately correct. More important is the fact that many statistical tests (parametric tests) should only be used when we can assume normality or close approximations to it. We can certainly superimpose normal curves over histograms but it is difficult to determine accurately if the curve deviates more than we would like from normality. We need an objective measure. Skewness and kurtosis do provide one set of objective measures on certain aspects of normality. Another way of assessing the issue is to determine whether the obtained distribution as a whole deviates from a normal deviation distribution with the same mean and standard deviation. The **Kolmogorov-Smirnov** and **Shapiro-Wilk** tests do this. If these tests are non-significant then the distribution in the sample does not differ from a normal distribution. The **Q Q plot** also shows how the obtained scores deviate from the normal distribution with the normal distribution shown as a straight line. Using all the techniques suggested you should be able to make a sensible decision about your distribution.

The Kolmogirov-Smirnov, Shapiro-Wilk tests and Q-Q plot are accessed via:

1   *Analyze >> Descriptive Statistics >> Explore*. Enter any variables of interest into the *Dependents List*
2   *Plots >>Normality Plots with tests*. This will produce all the diagnostics you need.

Probability

The role of uncertainty

Taking risks is not pleasant but business managers must shoulder numerous risks in running their operation – that is partly what they are paid for. But the application of quantitative techniques, for example, has made the problems of estimating future sales and taking sound investment decisions easier.

The key concept enabling uncertainty to be brought into business calculations is probability. Probability is a numerical measure of how likely something will happen or has happened. Sometimes it is possible to put an exact value on a probability, but often probability is only an educated estimate similar to the chance of rain on a particular day. When an exact measure is possible, the situation is usually a simple one in the sense that not many factors affect the outcome. For example, when spinning a coin there are only two possible outcomes and in general only one force affecting how the coin will fall, so that the probability of 'heads' can be given a definite value of 50% or 0.50.

However, the outcome of a World Cup soccer international between Brazil and England is subject to a variety of unknown factors, like weather, pitch conditions, injuries incurred, refereeing judgements and the form of players on the day. Although a specified team is '*very likely*' to win, the probability of the outcome is a guess because of the lack of precise evidence which would make this possible. The predicament of the businessperson predicting the future sales levels or changes in exchange rates is more like this than it is the coin-spinning example.

Measuring probability

Probability is a mathematical way of describing the outcome of an event. For example, the outcome of a coin toss can be expressed in probabilities, i.e. 0.5 (50%) heads and 0.5 (50%) tails. Probability ranges from 0 to 1.

* Zero probability reflects an impossible event. For example it is impossible that the result of a year's trading can be both a profit and a loss.
* An event with a probability of one is absolutely certain. For example, it is absolutely certain that the Pope is an unmarried Roman Catholic.

In practice, most events in business, like those in weather prediction, are neither impossible nor absolutely certain, and hence have a value less than 1 but greater than 0. Probabilities between zero and 1 reflect varying degrees of uncertainty. The more likely the statement is true, the closer it will be to 1.

> **Probability**. The numerical likelihood measured between 1 and 0 that an event will occur.
> The probability value of 1 means absolute certainty of an event or outcome.
> The probability value of 0 implies the absolute impossibility of an event.

There is a second likelihood: that of a thing not occurring, or 'q'. Since only two possibilities exist – an event happens or it does not happen – 'p' + 'q' must equal 100% or 1. In statistics the most common way of expressing probabilities is in decimal form with a base of 1.0, i.e. 1.00 = 100%; .50 = 50%; .05 = 5%.

Probability and normal distribution

If we plot the distribution of heads and tails obtained from tossing many coins simultaneously, on a large number of occasions we find that it approximates to the normal distribution. Figure 8.8 shows this for 10 coins tossed simultaneously, 1,024 times. The approximation to normality increases with more tossings. This distribution and associated probability levels are based on the assumption that only chance factors are operating, i.e. the coins are symmetrical, uniform and not double headed! Thus the coin has no tendency whatsoever to fall on one side more often than another: there are absolutely even chances of heads and tails. In graphical form, the results form a histogram with a close resemblance to a normal distribution with 50/50 head or tails in the centre and each side spreading out with smaller and smaller probabilities. This occurs because most of the coin tossing

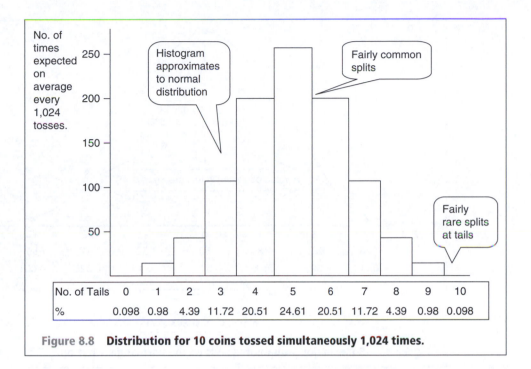

Figure 8.8   Distribution for 10 coins tossed simultaneously 1,024 times.

distributions are on or around the chance expectancy of 50/50, with fewer and fewer recorded splits of heads and tails that are quite different from that towards the extremes of the distribution. For example, in Figure 8.8, we note a split of 1 tail/9 heads only occurs by chance on 10/1,024 occasions, a probability of .0098 (.98%) or just less than 1 in a 100. For 6 tails/4 heads the figures are 210/1,024, a probability of 0.2051 (20.51%) or around 1 in 5. (Of course, the same figures apply to 4 tails/6 heads as the distribution is symmetrical). So again, we can see that chance occurrences distribute themselves normally with frequent events around the middle of the distribution and rarer events located in the tails of the graph.

Moving back to a normal curve from a histogram, look at Figure 8.9. In addition to the marking of three standard deviations above and below the mean, the approximate 'p' level of each point has been added. At the mean there is a probability .5; at +1.0Z and –1Z from M the probability of obtaining a score by chance at that point is .16; a score occurs by chance at –2Z and +2Z with a probability of .023 and so on. In other words, as with our coin tossing, the rarer the combination of H/T – or the rarer the observation or score – the lower the probability level of it occurring and the nearer the tails of the distribution the event is placed. The greater the deviation of the score from the mean, the less frequently it is likely to occur.

Do you notice any similarity between the 'p' values and the areas contained within the curve beyond the point? Since approximately 68% of the area or scores lie between ±1Z from the mean, then the probability of drawing a score at random from the normal distribution at or between these points is approximately 68% or .68. That is why the probability of an event at +1Z and –1Z is .16. If we add both .16s together we obtain .32, which, added to

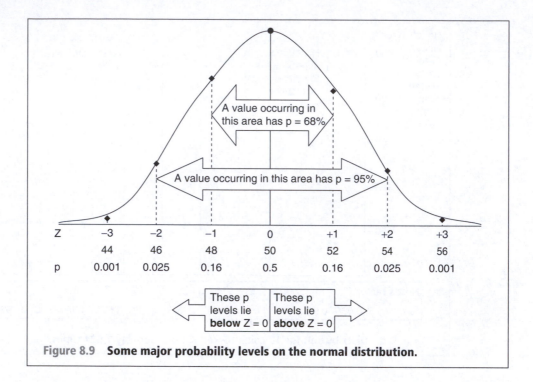

Figure 8.9   Some major probability levels on the normal distribution.

the 68% between +/–1Z gives us 100%. Similar calculations can be done with the other points and areas. For example, approximately 95% of the area under the normal curve lies within +/–2Z, leaving about 2.5% in each tail. So that the probability of a value occurring at or greater than +2Z or less than –2Z is 2.5% or .025 in both cases. So we can:

• provide the probability of a particular value if we know its Z score;
• provide the probability of obtaining a value between specific Z scores or within particular areas under the curve.

From Figure 8.9 we can see that Z scores, raw scores, areas under the curve and probability levels can all be linked in a normal distribution.

Important note on accuracy

The figures we have been using so far are only very close whole number approximations to ease your memory. The accurate figures are that 95.44% lies between +/– 2Z. This leaves 2.3% beyond those points in each tail. The accurate probability of drawing a score at random at +/–2Z is then 0.023. The slight difference between the theoretical probability of .023 and the approximation of .025 we have just worked out exists because the 95% limits are not ±2Z exactly but lie at ±1.96Z. The whole number ±2Z is easier to remember as a major defining point than ±1.96Z. Similarly, the accurate figure for the area between

+ and − 1Z is 68.34%, not our rounded 68%, though as we become more confident in dealing with the normal curve and statistical significance these other less convenient-to-remember numbers will begin to take root.

> **The normal distribution**. *This is a distribution of probability.*

Statistical significance

By now you should have grasped the principles that:

(a) the normal distribution curve depicts the distribution of chance occurrences round a mean;

(b) some occurrences occur more frequently by chance than others; and

(c) each occurrence can be assigned a probability value, i.e. the likelihood of its occurring by chance.

In evaluating research results, what we need to know is whether the results might be expected fairly frequently on a chance basis, or whether it is a rare chance event, with a consequent low probability and therefore a really different result not expected in that distribution. Remember our coin-tossing exploit? You noticed that a gross discrepancy between the number of heads and tails in any particular toss was quite a rare event (Fig. 8. 8). But how far must the outcome be away from the expected, how infrequent must it be, or how far removed from the mean of a normal distribution, before we say that, although the outcome can occur by chance very rarely, the fact that we have obtained this outcome in a one-off study implies that this is probably **not a chance variation**, but due to the systematic manipulation of the independent variable. That is, there is a **real effect** creating a large variation as biased coins would do causing an unlikely split of heads and tails – obviously not chance at work.

Now that we are able to allocate probability levels to all points or scores on the normal distribution curve, the next step is to decide at what level of probability we believe that a result is unlikely to be due to chance, always remembering that **every outcome is possible** on a chance basis, even if the odds are as high as those required for winning lotto. We are looking for cut-off points where we can say it is very unlikely that this observation, score or event is simply one of the chance occurrences round the distribution mean.

We want to know the odds against a chance occurrence. If the odds against occurrence by chance are lower than a certain probability, then we can say that the result is **statistically significant**. In practice, we focus attention on certain conventionally accepted probability levels, which you will repeatedly encounter in research reports. These specify the probability of the chance occurrence of findings.

• The highest probability generally accepted for statistical significance is p = 0.05, that is, this result would only occur 5 times in 100 by chance. It is frequently called the

5% level of significance. The significance level is also often called the **alpha** level and designated α, so that a research report may say the 5% significance level was used or **alpha** was set at .05.

- A lower and more stringent significance or alpha level set is often p = .01 or 1 occurrence by chance in 100. This is termed the **1% level of significance**.
- An even lower more stringent level is p = .001 or 1 occurrence by chance in 1,000.

> *The level of significance or alpha level. The probability value that defines very unlikely outcomes.*

In general, the **lower** the probability of a chance result (low p value), the more confidence the researcher has that the observation or score is not a chance variation around the mean of the distribution but is in fact statistically significantly different from the rest of the distribution, even perhaps part of a different distribution. By defining cut-off probability values, or **levels of significance**, we can designate which values are statistically significant or very unlikely by chance.

So the level of significance is simply a probability value that is used to split the values or results obtained into two sections:

- those that are common and presumably chance or random variations round the mean; and
- those that are so rare, occurring in the tails of the distribution, that they are really different from the rest and are unlikely to be a chance variation round the mean.

Figure 8.10 shows the **accurate** Z scores that distinguish at the 5% and 1% levels those areas that are statistically significant from those that are not. Statistical significance starts from the boundaries of the Z scores designated and are regarded as ones that are probably not chance variations. Values within the +/−1.96Z boundaries are regarded as sufficiently common (i.e. 95% of occurrences are found here – p = .95) to be considered as chance variation only (Fig. 8.10).

The three p values of .05, .01 and .001 are **conventionally accepted** as the major thresholds for decisions about statistical significance. As researchers, we opt for low probability, in order to minimize the possibility of claiming a significant result when the result is likely a chance one. The error of drawing a false conclusion that a relationship exists between variables is more serious than the error of failing to uncover some actual relation. So the minimum level usually acceptable is the .05 or 5% level. But remember that even here results will still occur by chance five times in a hundred. By saying our result is significant at the .05 level, we are saying it is very unlikely to be due to chance, though that suspicion must always be in the back of our minds.

That is why even more rigorous levels of .01 and .001 are also employed, as chance results are even more unlikely at or beyond these points, thus increasing our confidence in rejecting the view that chance has caused the result, but rather assume that the result is statistically significant. Nevertheless, even at very low probability levels, chance does still

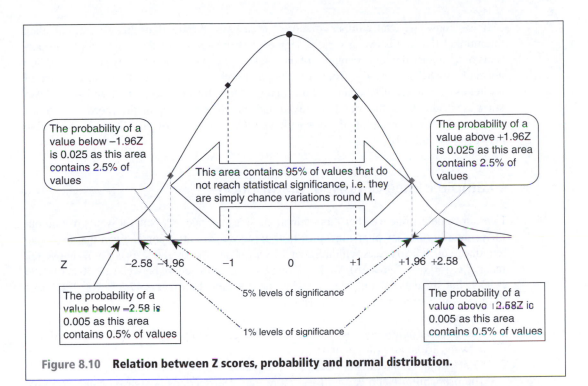

The probability of a value below −1.96Z is 0.025 as this area contains 2.5% of values

The probability of a value above +1.96Z is 0.025 as this area contains 2.5% of values

This area contains 95% of values that do not reach statistical significance, i.e. they are simply chance variations round M.

The probability of a value below −2.58 is 0.005 as this area contains 0.5% of values

The probability of a value above +2.58Z is 0.005 as this area contains 0.5% of values

Z   −2.58 −1.96   −1   0   +1   +1.96 +2.58

5% levels of significance

1% levels of significance

Figure 8.10   **Relation between Z scores, probability and normal distribution.**

operate on rare occasions and we do not know on which! So statistical analysis of data can never definitely prove a hypothesis, only support it at certain levels of probability.

If we now rewrite the previous information in terms of probabilities of occurrence we have:

- The probability of a value between +1Z(SD) and −1Z(SD) from the mean is .6826 or 68.26%.
- The probability of a value between +1.96Z(SD) and −1.96Z(SD) from the mean is .95 or 95%.
- The probability of a value between +2.58Z(SD) and −2.58Z(SD) from the mean is .99 or 99%.
- The probability of a value between +3Z(SD) and −3Z(SD) from the mean is .999 or 99.9%.

The converse of several of these probabilities invoked for the determination of statistical significance are:

- The probability of a value lying beyond +2.58Z(SD) and −2.58Z(SD) from the mean is .01 or 1%.
- The probability of a value lying beyond +1.96Z(SD) and −1.96Z(SD) from the mean is .05 or 5%.

NB: Please remember all these very important figures.

If we know the total number of scores or cases in the distribution, we can calculate the number that fall between various segments of the curve, for these are simply proportions of area turned into percentages of the total number. For example, if we possess 10,000 normally distributed scores from the general public, on a test that measures level of awareness about climate change, how many scores lie between +1 Z and –1 Z? We know that 68.26% of the area is involved and therefore 68.26% of the scores too. Since there are 10,000 scores plotted we must have 6826 scores out of the 10,000 in the region between –1Z and +1Z.

Example of use of normal distribution

In order to determine whether more telephone lines are needed, Nat Tel wants to find out the probability for any phone message lasting more than 180 seconds given that the mean length of call is 150.6 secs with a SD of 15 secs. The time of 180 secs is 1.96Z above the mean, i.e. $150.6 + (1.96 \times 15)$. We know that the area of the curve between +1.96 and –1.96 is 95%, but since we are only dealing with one side here, half that is 47.5%. Nat Tel comes to three conclusions with this information.

1   There is approximately a 47.5 % (or .475) chance that any single telephone call will last between 150.6 and 180 seconds.
2   47.5% of all phone calls last between 150.6 and 180 seconds.
3   The probability that a call will last more than 180 seconds is approximately 2.5% or .025, i.e. 50% – 47.5%.

In summary, the real importance of the normal distribution for us is that it provides a model for the distribution of sample statistics, in particular sample means and differences between means of samples, and links probability, sampling and statistical significance. The beauty of the normal distribution is that there is a known probability associated with any value from the distribution. More specifically, as we have seen, the area under the curve between any specified points represents the probability of obtaining scores within those specified points. SPSS calculates the probabilities for you when you carry out a statistical test. You do no calculations but you must be able to interpret what the probability or significance stated on the printout implies.

Selecting a level of significance

There is still the thorny question of why we would be prepared to risk one level of significance, say the 5%, rather than the 1%. How small should the significance level be – that is, how small should the probability of an event be – before we reject the possibility of it having occurred by chance? There is no simple answer. It is up to you to decide what odds you are prepared to accept when deciding whether the results of your research are statistically significant (i.e. significantly greater than chance). This decision may involve political, social, business, educational, philosophic and economic considerations, as well as statistical ones.

In order to explore this question consider a Russian roulette example. Assume that you are presented with a box of 200 pistols, exactly 10 of which you know to be loaded, and you are allowed to take one of them out. The probability that this pistol is loaded is, thus, 10/200, or 0.05. Would you act as if it were loaded or as if it were not?

In deciding, you would take into account not only the probability that the gun is loaded but also the consequences of your acting as if it were loaded. If you were asked whether you would be willing to hold the gun to your head and pull the trigger, you would act as though it were loaded (wouldn't you – with odds of 1 in 20!?). On the other hand, if you were asked whether you would be willing to use it to defend yourself in a duel, you would act as though it were not loaded. This approach is perfectly rational: though the probability is the same in both cases, the consequences are not. Thus, to answer our question, we must always consider the consequences of accepting or rejecting the hypothesis.

This example suggests that choosing a significance level is always a matter of deciding what odds you are prepared to accept in a particular situation that your results are due to chance. A pharmaceutical company may feel doubtful about introducing a powerful drug with nasty side effects if there was only a 1-in-20 (p = .05) chance that it was doing good, although you might accept these odds if it were the only hope of saving people's lives. But I don't think any of us would fly in a plane with a 1-in-1,000 chance of crashing (p = .001)!

In most aspects of business (possibly because usually nothing too terrible can happen from accepting a result as significant), it is a convention to accept that odds of either 5 in 100 (i.e. 5% significance level) or more rigorously, 1 in 100 (i.e. 1% significance level) are reasonable gambles for most situations.

Note 1: We are solely concerned here with the concept of statistical significance. The term 'significant' in 'statistically significant' means that the result is unlikely due to chance. It does not mean that the result is important! What may be highly significant statistically may be of no significance whatsoever in the business world.

Note 2: When significance lies beyond the 1 in 1,000 level SPSS reports it as .000 in the significance column. It is conventional to change this in reporting results to p < .001.

SPSS activity – assessing normality

Scale variables never conform perfectly to the classical normal distribution. Since we need distributions that are approximately normal in order to apply parametric statistical tests, one task is to assess whether the distribution of each scale variable is so.

Access SPSS Chapter 8 Data File A in the website of this text and select the variable *'I work in paid employment hrs/wk'* which we will assess for normality.

- Select in sequence *Analyze > Descriptive Statistics > Frequencies.*
- Select the variable *'I work in paid employment hrs/wk'* and transfer to the *Variable(s)* box.
- Click on *Statistics* and ensure *skew* and *kurtosis* are checked.
- Click on *Charts, >> histogram* and select *with Normal curve.*
- *OK* and obtain the printout.

Table 8.1 **Descriptive statistics table**

Statistics

Hours per week in paid employment

N	Valid	113
	Missing	0
Mean		13.2566
Std. Deviation		8.42274
Skewness		.967
Std. Error of Skewness		.227
Kurtosis		.892
Std. Error of kurtosis		.451

These two figures form the skew ratio of 4.25

We assess normality by:

(i) the ratio of *skew* to the *standard error of skew*; and
(ii) the ratio of *kurtosis* to the *standard error of kurtosis*.

Using a value of 2.58 (1% significance level) as the cut-off between marginal accept-ability of normality and non-normality. The closer the ratios are to zero the more confident we are that we have a reasonable approximation to normality. Table 8.1 reveals that the ratio of skew to standard error of skew is 4.25 and the kurtosis ratio is 1.98. As the skew ratio is more than 2.58 we can conclude there are moderate levels of skew. Positive values of skew indicate a positive skew while negative ones reveal a negative skew. Positive values of kurtosis indicate more peakedness while negative ones indicate a flatter curve. The kurtosis ratio is acceptable in this example.

The histogram (Fig. 8.11) also displays a superimposed normal curve since we selected '*with Normal Curve*'. The curve reveals a discrepancy between it and the distribution with its positive skew. If we wish to use parametric statistics on this variable we need to 'normalize' it.

SPSS activity – to transform skewed distributions to normality

We can often 'fix' skew by transforming the raw scores into a new variable which is more likely to be normally distributed. Table 8.2 provides some options. This transformed vari-able is then used rather than the original one. Note that a sizeable ceiling or floor effect, where many subjects are obtaining maximum or minimum scores respectively, has limited effect on transformation towards a normal distribution as zero or maximum positions will not alter.

Table 8.2   Transformations to improve normality

Skew type	Transformation type needed		
Moderate +ve skew	square root transformation required		
Substantial +ve skew	log transformation required		
Extreme +ve skew	inverse transformation required		
Moderate −ve skew	1. reflect	2. use square root transformation	3. reflect back
Substantial −ve skew	1. reflect	2. use log transformation	3. reflect back
Extreme −ve skew	1. reflect	2. use inverse transformation	3. reflect back

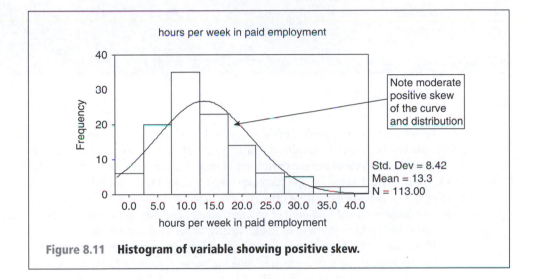

Figure 8.11   Histogram of variable showing positive skew.

We will demonstrate a square root transformation of the distribution of the variable '*I work in paid employment hrs/wk*'. This will produce a new variable named *hrwksqrt* at the end of the variable list on *variable view*.

1 *Transform >>Compute* to raise *Compute Variable* screen (Fig. 8.12).
2 Type a new variable name *hrwksqrt* in the *Target Variable* box.
3 Type the transformation equation *sqrt(paid_emp)* in the *Numeric Expression* box (Fig. 8.12).
4 *OK*
5 A new variable *hrwksqrt* has now been added on the variable view for which the skew ratio must be rechecked.
6 *Analyze >>Descriptive Statistics >>Frequencies*.
7 Select the variable '*hrwksqrt*' and transfer to the *Variable(s)* box.
8 Click on *Statistics* and ensure *skew* and *kurtosis* are checked.
9 Click on *Charts, >>histogram* and select *with Normal curve*.
10 *OK* and obtain the printout.

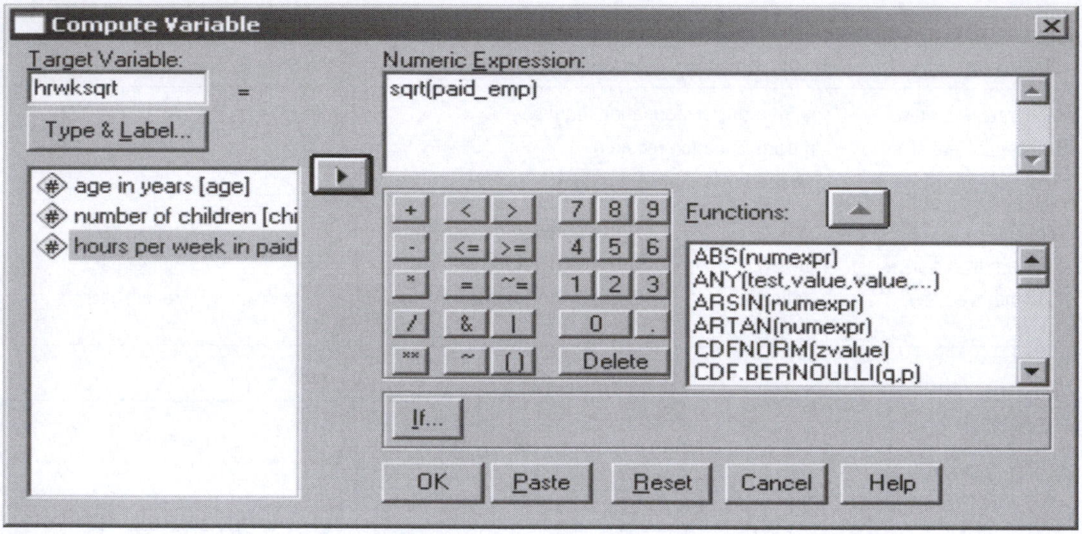

Figure 8.12 **Compute variable screen.**

From the *Statistics table* (Table 8.3) check the value of *skewness* by dividing by the standard error. Visually examine the histogram and superimposed normal curve (Fig. 8.13).

The ratio of skew to the standard error of skew is now –2.10, down from 4.25. The superimposed normal curve on the histogram now shows the distribution to be more normal (Fig. 8.13). Note that the floor effect of a number of respondents not working (zero hours) has an influence on the amount of change feasible and this has made the kurtosis flatter, as revealed by the kurtosis ratio of 2.44, slightly larger than the original figure of 1.98.

If the square root function is not able to correct the skew, we would repeat the process using the natural log transformation, placing *ln(paid_emp)* in the numeric expression box and *hrwkln* as the target variable. Should you have to perform a converse transformation on

Table 8.3 **Descripitive statistics for new variable**

Statistics		
HRWKSQRT		
N	Valid	113
	Missing	0
Mean		3.4102
Std. Deviation		1.28117
Skewness		.447
Std. Error of Skewness		.227
Kurtosis		1.103
Std. Error of kurtosis		.451

These two form a skew ratio of –2.10

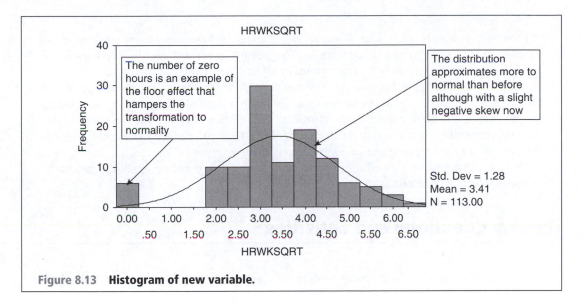

Figure 8.13 Histogram of new variable.

a very extreme skew, place *1/ paid_emp* in the *numeric expression* box and *hrwkinv* in the *target variable* box.

With negatively skewed data, square root, logarithmic and inverse transformations simply make the skew worse. The procedure for correcting a negative skew involves reflecting the distribution to create a positive skew then transform as though it is a positive skew as above. This produces a variable with respondents in reversed rank order, therefore we then reflect the score back to retain the original order. To reflect a distribution you recode by subtracting every score on the original variable from the next whole number greater than the maximum value in the distribution.

When transformations do not work, consider collapsing your scale variable to nominal categories, i.e. age into age groups or house prices into price groups.

What you have learned in this chapter

You have seen that shape is one of the basic characteristics used to describe a distribution. Skewed distributions have values piled up in an assymetrical form. The most important distribution for inferential statistics is the normal distribution which is bilaterally symmetrical around the mean. It is a distribution of chance occurrences in which the mean, median and mode coincide. Areas between points under the curve can be determined and can be converted to proportions of the number of scores plotted.

In order to compare or combine scores from different normal distributions you are now able to standardize the distributions to a single scale, the Z score. Z scores specify an exact location within a normal distribution. The Z score has a mean of 0 and standard deviation of 1. The sign of the Z score indicates whether the score is above or below the mean and the magnitude specifies the number of standard deviations between the score and the mean.

Probability varies between 1 and 0 and all values along the baseline of the normal curve can be assigned a probability level of occurrence. You are now aware that +/–1.96Z and +/– 2.57Z are two conventional cut-off or criterion points or significance levels, the 5% and 1% probability levels, used to indicate that if an event occurs beyond these points in probability terms then the event is most likely not to be due to chance or random fluctuation. As well as designating significance levels these cut-off points also form the end points of confidence intervals that state the probability of an event occurring within them. Thus you can see that normal distribution, probability and significance levels are closely related.

Variables that have a skewed distribution need 'normalizing' before applying parametric statistics which assume normality.

Review questions and activities

Qu. 8.1
Can you explain why the mean, median and mode coincide at 0 on the normal curve?

Qu. 8.2
Which are the three equivalent scores that are represented by –2Z in Figs 8.4a, b, and c?

Qu. 8.3
What is the probability of drawing a value between 50 and 52 in Fig. 8.4a.? If 1,000 respondents' scores are in the distribution, how many lie between 48 and 52?

Qu. 8.4
What is the probability of getting a value between 46 and 54 in Fig. 8.4a? If 2,000 scores are plotted on the distribution, approximately how many lie between 48 and 50?

Qu. 8.5
Approximately what proportion of the total area under the normal curve lies between

(a) 0 and +1Z?
(b) 0 and –2Z?

Qu. 8.6
Referring to Fig. 8.8, what is the probability of

(a) obtaining 7 heads?
(b) obtaining 0 heads?

Qu. 8.7
Referring to Fig. 8.9

(a) What is the probability of a score of 46?
(b) What is the probability of obtaining a value by chance between +1Z and -1Z
(c) At what scores are there a probability of occurrence of 0.025

Qu. 8.8
For normal distribution with M = 80 and SD = 10, find the probability value of obtaining a value

(a) between 80 and 90
(b) between 60 and 100
(c) at exactly 70
(d) at exactly 80

Qu. 8.9
How many values in Fig 8.10

(a) lie below −1.96Z if 1000 scores are plotted in the distribution?
(b) are plotted between −1.96Z and +1.96Z ?

Qu. 8.10
With a normal distribution involving 20,000 values, how many lie beyond +2.65Z?

Qu. 8.11
For a normal distribution with M = 100 and SD = 20,

(a) what score separates the top 50% from the bottom 50%
(b) what is the minimum score needed to be in the top 2.5%
(c) what scores form the boundaries for the middle 68%

Now access the Web page for this chapter and try the questions and activities as well as studying the additional material there.

Chapter 9
Sampling Issues

'You don't have to eat the whole steak to know the meat is tough'

(Source unknown)

Content list

By the end of this chapter you should be able to:

1 Describe the role of sample, population and sampling frame in the sampling process.
2 Understand the concept of standard error of the mean and sampling error.
3 Know how to calculate the standard error of the mean and of a proportion.
4 Understand what the Central Limit Theorem implies.
5 Understand how to use the standard error of the mean to estimate confidence intervals around the population parameter.
6 Understand how to select different forms of probability samples, and under what conditions they are employed.
7 Explain the difference between probability and non-probability samples.
8 Identify and understand the strengths and weaknesses of different forms of probability and non-probability sampling.

Introduction

This chapter deals with the vital issues of why we sample and how we do it, for it is rare that any researcher ever studies the whole population of interest. Thus the researcher has to use a sample to infer the characteristics of the population of interest. This means that choosing the members of the sample and applying the correct sampling techniques are vital so that the sample is representative of the population. You will learn about different forms of sampling and the measurement of the error that surrounds any sample statistic since the sample will never be an exact replica of the population and only estimates characteristics or parameters of the population.

Much of our everyday life is based on sampling – generally inadequate sampling in most cases. We may surreptitiously taste a grape in the supermarket display, test drive a specific make of car, spray a perfume tester, skim through a magazine and using the sample decide whether to buy the product. A lecturer samples the amount of learning among the students by an essay examination, which usually only tests parts of that learning. We expect the next glass of Rockhampton Red to taste exactly like the last one we had. And if we sample too much one evening the police will take other kinds of samples from us – breath, blood and urine. These too will be taken as being representative of the population or universe from which they are drawn. The examples above suggest that sampling occurs in much of our daily lives and that sometimes it is inadequate; we are all guilty of making invalid generalizations and inferences about products, events, or individuals based on very limited experience or knowledge.

But, if we can obtain samples that are truly representative of the population, then generalization from the sample becomes a vital scientific procedure, since it is rarely possible to have access to and study all members or events of a defined population. Because research involves making inferences from samples to populations we term the statistical procedures based on this strategy inferential statistics.

Populations and samples

Populations and parameters

In research, a population is not a demographic population but the entire collection of all observations of interest (people, objects, or events) *as defined by the researcher*. The researcher must specifically define the target population – the entire group about which they want to make judgements. For example:

- all fortnightly paid staff in a particular company is a population;
- all accountancy graduates from a particular university is a population;
- all house mortgages over $300,000 taken out in 2007 in the capital city is a population.

A population is not restricted to people, but can be types of investment, brands of cigarettes, types of industrial accidents, credit card transactions, highway fatalities, and so on. They could be also defined by geographic boundary or time-period such as all electors in the York district, all the cars produced by Mitsubishi during 2006, or all companies going into receivership in the UK in 2007. A population may have relatively few units (e.g. all the students in the business studies faculty of one university or all employees in a single workplace); or a large number of units (e.g. all tourists visiting Singapore in 2006 or the voting population of the EU. The nature of a study or project determines the definition of the population to be considered.

> *Population. A population is the entire collection of all observations of interest to the researcher.*

The **parameters** of a population are its measurable characteristics. Examples of parameters are the mean income of all wage earners in the country, or the total output of all oil fields in the country. The point to remember is that a parameter describes a population.

> *Parameter. A parameter is a descriptive measure of a characteristic of the entire population of all observations of that characteristic.*

Samples and statistics

Although researchers are generally interested in some measure of the defined population, the large size of most defined populations means that it is not usually possible or practical to measure every single person or element. For example, it would not be feasible to measure the attitude of every person in the country towards the banning of cigarette smoking in public places. Obtaining the data on average weekly rent paid for all rental properties in a country would also be an overwhelming task. So we are resigned, on most occasions, to estimate the population parameter with a statistic from the sample we have selected. Accountants who wish to acquire accurate information about a firm's accounts receivable, accounts payable, or goods in process could organize a complete count and spend vast amounts of money, time and effort to get it done. However, they can get the same information at a tiny fraction of the cost if they follow proper procedures of sample selection and data collection.

Importantly, this smaller and more manageable portion, the **sample**, must be selected in such a way that it represents the population, i.e. it is a miniature version.

> *Sample.* A sample is a representative portion of the population which is selected for study.

The basis for creating a representative sample is random sampling so that:

- all members of the population have an equal chance of being selected; and
- all possible samples of the same size have an equal chance of being selected.

Non-random sampling prevents inferences being made about the population.

Why not use the population rather than a sample?

There are numerous reasons why a complete population survey or *census* may be impossible, and we are left with no option but to sample.

Practicality

For example:
- **Management:** To find out how employees feel about practices for promotion, a sample of a large organization's employees is selected and interviewed. This is a quicker and simpler way of gaining a feeling for the issue than attempting a full employee survey.
- **Business:** Royalties for pop tunes played over the radio are calculated on the frequency with which each piece is played. The population is all pop tunes played by all radio stations in the country. A sample of radio stations provide the data on which royalties are calculated.
- **Marketing:** The effectiveness of several different marketing strategies are tested out on a small sample of potential consumers before a national plan is put into operation.
- **Accounting:** Monthly audits of a large organization can involve a sampling of accounts. If these are satisfactory no further auditing is performed that period. Complete audits will only occur on a yearly basis.
- **Advertising:** Television advertising costs are determined mainly by size of audience at different times of the day and different days of the week. It is impossible to investigate the viewing practices of all TV owners, therefore a sample is taken.

- **Quality control:** A manufacturer of lamp bulbs wants to ensure the proportion of defective bulbs is low. The population is all the lamp bulbs made in a particular week. But since the test is very destructive, only a sample of bulbs is used. If all the population of bulbs were tested there would be no product to market.

Costs in money and manpower

Many studies consume materials such as questionnaires, may involve travel expenses and also involve staff time. Complete surveys concerned with large populations entail heavy postal charges or an incredibly large staff of interviewers. Is this sort of thing justified when statistical theory assures us that a certain size of sample provides accuracy within 3% or 1%?

Inaccessible population

Even when the population is well-defined and, in principle, countable, it does not follow that it is possible to get information about every member. People are absent on vacation, ill in hospital, or may have recently moved.

Varying population

Individual members of some populations are varying so rapidly that it is impossible to keep track of them all: e.g. movement between jobs by contract workers. In such circumstances the only statistics with any meaning must be obtained from some sort of sample and they will be interpreted as referring to some 'average' population.

When to take a census

In fact, there is rarely a need to take a census. A well-selected sample can provide information comparable to that of a full census. There are some situations, however, when a census is preferable. A census is preferable to a sample only when:

- the population of interest is small and identifiable;
- sampling might eliminate important cases from the study; and
- credibility requires the consideration of all members of the target population.

For example, a chain of restaurants might have 15 franchisees. A survey of the franchisees' reactions to the chain's new advertising campaign should be a census because:

- a sample from 15 franchisees would be small;
- all franchisees' opinions need to be heard; and

- the study would be more credible than a sample because all the franchisees participated (i.e. no one can say, 'Well, the results are wrong. They didn't ask me or the chap in the next town!').

> *A census.* A complete enumeration of the entire defined population.

A **statistic** is any descriptive measure of a sample. The average income of the sample is a statistic. The statistic is to the sample what the parameter is to the population. More importantly, **a statistic serves as an estimate of the parameter**. Although we are really interested in the value of the parameter of the population, we generally estimate it with a statistic from the sample we have selected.

> *Statistic.* A statistic describes a sample and serves as an estimate of the corresponding population parameter.

The business person is very concerned with adequate sampling; they are not just interested in the consumers chosen for a particular survey, or the quality of several items from a product range, they are interested in consumers in general and in the quality of every item produced on a particular production line. They hope to demonstrate that the results obtained from a small sample would be true for other groups of consumers and for all the items on that production line. Thus, in business research terms, sampling has exactly the same meaning as in our everyday experience.

The usefulness of sampling

Business firms and other organizations spend a great deal of time and money sampling consumer attitudes, consumer preferences, employee satisfaction, on censuses to determine their accounts receivable (or payable) and to take physical inventories of equipment, raw materials, goods in process, and the like. Relatively small samples of the relevant populations, if carefully drawn using any of the random sampling techniques described below, can produce high-quality results.

For example, airlines face the difficulty of settling accounts with each other concerning passengers travelling on several different airlines during a given trip. Each airline picks up thousands of tickets per week that were paid to and issued by competitor airlines. Calculating the revenue allocation for each ticket was extremely time consuming and costly, so three airlines conducted a four-month test by comparing first a census of tickets, and then a stratified sample. The difference in the census and sample results came to less than $700 per $1 million of tickets. They concluded that sampling instead of a census was far more cost effective and virtually as accurate.

The concept of sampling therefore involves:

- taking elements of the defined population according to acceptable procedures;
- making observations/assessments on this smaller group of elements; then
- generalizing findings back to the defined population from which the sample was drawn.

Sampling error

No researcher can get a quart out of a statistical pint pot. If the collected sample data is faulty then no amount of statistical manipulation will improve the accuracy of the findings in respect of the population. Even after using appropriate sampling methods correctly, there will always be sampling error because the sample is never exactly the same as the population. The degree to which it is 'out' is the **sampling error**. The concept of 'error' here does not imply incorrectness but acknowledgement that there is a variation between the parameter and the statistic used to estimate it.

> *Sampling error. Sampling error is the difference between the unknown population parameter and the sample statistic used to estimate the parameter.*

There are at least two possible causes of sampling error:

1 The first source of sampling error is mere chance or random error in the sampling process. Due to the luck of the draw in selecting the sample elements, it is possible to choose, unknowingly, atypical elements that misrepresent the population.

2 A more serious form of sampling error is *sampling bias*. Sampling bias occurs when there is some tendency in the sampling process to select certain sample elements over others. If the sampling procedure is incorrectly designed and tends to promote the selection of too many units with a particular characteristic at the expense of units without that characteristic, the sample is said to be biased. For example, the sampling process may inherently favour the selection of males to the exclusion of females, married persons to the exclusion of singles, or older employees rather than younger ones.

> *Sampling bias. Sampling bias is the tendency to favour the selection of certain sample elements over others.*

Standard error of the mean

Sampling errors

Activity 9.1

Try this activity in class to gain an understanding of what sampling error is and to demonstrate that sampling error occurs even with random sampling. In Table 9.1 there are 10 columns. For each column, you are going to draw 10 numbers from the 10 single numbers 0 to 9 in a random fashion from a container. To draw these random samples, write the numbers 0 through to 9 on separate slips of paper. Alternatively, you could use golf balls or table tennis balls, each marked in black ink with one of these numbers. Place the 10 slips of paper or 10 balls in a box and shuffle them around. The first column has been done for you. Now you draw the remaining nine samples of 10 numbers randomly.

1   Draw out one slip or ball. Record the number.
2   Place the slip or ball back into the container, shuffle, and draw a second time.
3   Continue drawing and replacing it in its box until you have selected all the random numbers you need.
4   When you have drawn the 9 samples of 10 random numbers each, compute the arithmetic mean for each column.

The population mean (a parameter) must be the average of the sum of the numbers 0–9, i.e.

$$\frac{0+1+2+3+4+5+6+7+8+9}{10} = 4.50$$

Now you can see if any sampling error has occurred in your random samples in your version of Table 9.1. Are any of your sample means exactly 4.5? This is not likely, though many will be close to it. When we tried it, our sample means ranged from 3.1 to 6.4, with 4.7 as the sample mean closest to the population mean. In other words, there is not only a variation from the population mean but each sample differs from the others in their accuracy to predict or estimate the population mean. There is always some sampling error. Now, compute the mean of the 10 sample means. This mean of means should be a more accurate reflection of the population mean than any of the individual sample means. In fact, as we drew more and more samples, the average of sample means of the same size becomes closer and closer to the population mean.

So you can see that sampling error is not a mistake; it is a technical term referring to variations caused by chance, the degree to which a random sample or observation differs from the population or expectation. It is the natural variability inherent among same-sized samples from a population. Thus, even random sampling conducted in the approved way will only provide sample statistics that can estimate with varying degrees of confidence the

Table 9.1   Insert your samples of random numbers in the table

	Samples									
	1	2	3	4	5	6	7	8	9	10
	9									
	7									
	6									
	7									
	3									
	8									
	4									
	1									
	3									
	1									
Totals	49									
Sample	M = 4.9									

respective population parameters. A random sample is never the same as the population because it does not contain the whole population and each sample contains a different set of individual pieces of data. But since a range of sample means has variability we can calculate its standard deviation to provide a numerical index of that variability, just as we did with individual scores in Chapter 7.

Most of the statistics you will deal with later are attempts to disentangle sampling error from real differences or relationships so that we know if any real differences or relationships exist. Real differences/relationships are ones that exceed those expected from sampling differences alone. This is why we apply significance levels to the testing of hypotheses. A sample mean that is at or beyond two standards errors from the mean has a 5% or less likelihood of occurring by chance and therefore probably indicates a sample that is significantly different from the population. (Revise Chapter 8 on areas under the normal curve if you have difficulty in understanding this last sentence.)

Standard error of the mean (SE$_M$)

The numerical index of sampling error is the standard error of the mean, which is the standard deviation of the distribution of same-sized sample means (SE$_M$). It measures the variability of the sample means around the population mean. Thus SE$_M$ is a very important statistic because it specifies precisely how well a sample mean estimates the population mean. In most situations, we only possess one sample mean as an estimate of the unknown population mean. Although we don't expect the sample mean to be exactly the same as the population mean, the standard error of the mean will tell us how good an estimate it will be.

- A small SE_M implies that the sample mean is a close approximation to the population mean, while a larger one indicates that the sample mean is less efficient as an estimate of the population mean.
- The larger the size of the sample, the more probable that the sample mean will be close (a good estimate of) to the population mean, for the obvious reason that, as sample size increases, it becomes more like the population because there is more of the population in the sample.

Calculation of the standard error of the mean

It is possible to obtain the estimate of the amount of sampling error for a mean on the basis of only one sample. The formula for the standard error of the mean (SEM) is:

$$SE_M = \frac{sample\ standard\ deviation}{\sqrt{sample\ size}}$$

The SE_M is much smaller than the standard deviation of raw scores because sampling means are not as spread out as the original scores since they are derived from means of sets of raw scores. The equation makes it clear that as n (or sample size) increases so sampling

> **The standard error of the mean.** *This is the standard deviation of the distribution of sample means around the population mean.*

error is reduced. SPSS calculates SE_M as part of the *descriptive statistics menu.*

How can we tell which sample gives us the best estimate of the population parameter or best description of the population? We can't! Fortunately, although we select samples on a random basis and all samples are subject to chance errors, there are three assumptions which aid our cause in using our single sample mean (which is usually the only one we have anyway) as an estimate of the population mean:

1 The errors or deviations of a series of values from their mean value result from a large number of minor deviations.
2 These deviations are just as likely to be above as they are to be below the mean value.
3 These deviations will lie within very narrow limits, i.e. most values will deviate by only a small amount with very few extreme deviations.

These assumptions are captured in the **Central Limit Theorem**.

The Central Limit Theorem

The **Central Limit Theorem** states that when the sample has at least 30 members, the distribution of all sample means of the same sized samples closely approaches a normal distribution without regard to the distribution of the population from which the sample is drawn. So whatever the sample size, once above 30, if we sample a large number of times and compute the mean of each same sized sample, then the mean of our many sample means (the sampling distribution of means) will be the same as the population mean. For sample sizes of 30± one can safely assume that the sampling distribution of means will approximate to a normal distribution.

> **The Central Limit Theorem.** *As n increases, the sampling distribution of same sized sample means approaches a normal distribution with the sampling distribution mean equal to the population mean.*

As the distribution of sample means is a normal distribution, the same proportions and probabilities we met before with the normal distribution in Chapter 8 apply. Here are those important values again, now in terms of the standard error of the mean:

- 68% of means of all same-sized samples lie between +1.00 and −1.00 SE_M (p = 0.68);
- 95% of means of all same-sized samples lie between +1.96 and −1.96 SE_M (p = 0.95);
- 99% of means of all same-sized samples lie between +2.57 and −2.57 SE_M (p = 0.99).

These ranges are the confidence intervals which indicate the probability that the actual population mean lies within a given range around the sample mean. If we restate the probabilities listed above, we can say that there is a 68% probability that the unknown population mean lies within one standard error either side of the known sample mean (a total range of two standard errors). This gives roughly a two in three chance that the difference (deviation) between the mean of the only obtained sample we possess and the true mean of the whole population will not exceed a value of one standard error either side. Similarly, we can argue that in 19 cases out of every 20 (or 95 in 100) that the population mean will not lie outside twice the standard error either side. These ranges of values within which such a population value may lie is termed respectively the 68% or the 95% confidence interval.

The fact that the distribution of sample means tends to normality should not be a surprise. Whenever you take a sample you expect the sample mean to be near to the population mean, and the more samples you take, the greater the number that will be fairly close, while only a few will be grossly different from the population mean. Thus they 'pile up' around the population mean so that their average is equal to the population mean.

Look at the hypothetical graphed examples (Fig. 9.1) and note how the SE_M decreases with increasing sample size. This is because the larger the sample, the more similar it is to the population and as a consequence, the sample mean from such sized samples will all lie closer to the population mean, i.e. the confidence interval is smaller so the estimate will be closer.

By artificially generating a population of 1,000 normally distributed scores so that the mean and standard deviation of the entire population would be known, Horowitz (1974) demonstrated the normal distribution of sample means. These 1,000 scores ranged from

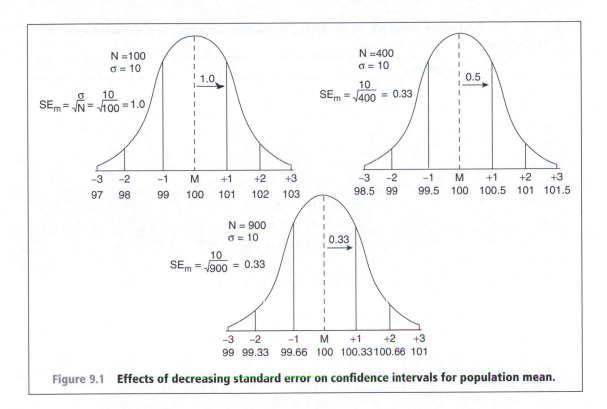

Figure 9.1 **Effects of decreasing standard error on confidence intervals for population mean.**

0 to 100 with a mean of 50 and a standard deviation of 15.8. The scores were listed on 1,000 slips of paper and placed in a container. Ninety-six samples of 10 slips each were drawn and the means calculated. The sampling distribution of these 96 means are shown in Table 9.1 where the intervals between which means might fall are on the left and the number of means falling within each interval is on the right. The distribution is almost perfectly symmetrical, with almost as many in any interval being a certain distance below the true mean of the population (50) as above it. Also, the mean of the 96 sample means (49.99) is quite close to the actual mean of the population (50.00).

But the main thing to note in Table 9.1 is the great variability among the sample means. Although each sample of 10 was randomly selected and not biased in any way, one sample had a mean of 37.8 while another had a mean of 62.3, even though they were sampled from the same population. If you were conducting a study and found two very different sample means like this and were trying to decide whether they came from the same underlying distribution or two different distributions, you might think that such a large difference would indicate that they came from different distributions or populations. Usually, this is a good rule – the larger the difference between means, the more likely they are to be reliably different – but as we have seen here, even random sampling from a known distribution can produce sample means that differ greatly from each other and from the true population mean, which is known in this case. This is a lesson that should be kept in mind while pondering small differences between means in any research study you undertake.

Table 9. 1 **The distribution of sample means for the 96 samples. Each sample mean was based on 10 observations**

Interval	Frequency	
62.0-63.9	1	
60.0-61.9	1	
58.0-59.9	3	
56.0-57.9	7	
54.0-55.9	9	
52.0-53.9	12	
50.0-51.9	15	Population mean = 50.00
48.0-49.9	15	Mean of sample means = 49.99
46.0-47.9	13	Standard deviation of sample means(SE_M = 5.01)
44.0-45.9	9	
42.0-43.9	6	
40.0-41.9	3	
38.0-39.9	1	
36.0-37.9	1	
	96 samples	

After Horowitz (1974), Table 8.1a.

The standard error of a proportion

Up till now we have been concerned with sample means. However, a great deal of sampling in the business world is concerned with the proportion or percentage of a given population possessing particular characteristics, making certain choices, having certain preferences, holding particular opinions, percentage of items not passing quality control or profit margins, for example.

Assume we have been conducting a survey on TV ownership and viewing habits. Information is required on the proportion of TV sets that can receive digital transmissions. We shall assume that the survey of 100 people reveals that 70% of all sets have this facility and that 30% do not. What is the standard error for the 70% that have? This is calculated as follows:

The standard error of a proportion (SE_p) is obtained by means of the formula:

$$SE_p = \sqrt{\frac{pq}{n}}$$

where p represents the proportion of the sample possessing the characteristic in question, q represents the proportion that does not possess that characteristic, and n is the number of people included in the sample.

$$SE_P = \sqrt{\frac{pq}{n}} = \sqrt{\frac{0.7(0.3)}{100}} = 0.0021 = 2.1\%$$

Strictly speaking, a proportion is expressed as a fraction between 0 and 1. However, many researchers prefer to work in percentages and so the standard error of the proportion is converted to its equivalent percentage by multiplying the standard error by 100. We can therefore be 95% certain that the proportion for the population as a whole will be within the limits 70% plus or minus 2.1% (1.96) or approximately between 66% and 74% can receive digital transmissions.

SPSS activity – selecting random samples and standard error

It is very enlightening to discover for yourself how sample means, sample standard deviations and sample standard errors of the mean can vary even when samples are chosen randomly by computer from the same population. This activity enables you to select a number of samples. To use these instructions you will need to use an interval variable '*age*' from the Chapter 7 data set SPSS B provided on the text's SPSS website

1   *Analyze >> Descriptive Statistics >>Descriptives*. Transfer the interval variable '*age*' to the *Variables:* box (Fig. 9.2).
2   Click on the *Options* button and select *Mean, Std deviation, Maximum, Minimum* and *S.E.mean* (Fig. 9.3). These will provide descriptive data for the *age* of the data set population.
3   Click *OK* and print out population descriptives as at Table 9.2.
4   Obtain a random sample by selecting *Data >> Select Cases*. Ensure '*age*' is the selected variable.
5   Choose *Random Sample of cases* and click on the *Sample* button. Select *Approximately* and type in the sample size you want by typing in a percentage such as 20%.
6   Select *Continue* and highlight your chosen variable '*age*' on which you already have obtained the population data at (2) above. Ensure the default *Unselected cases are filtered* button is selected (Fig. 9.4).

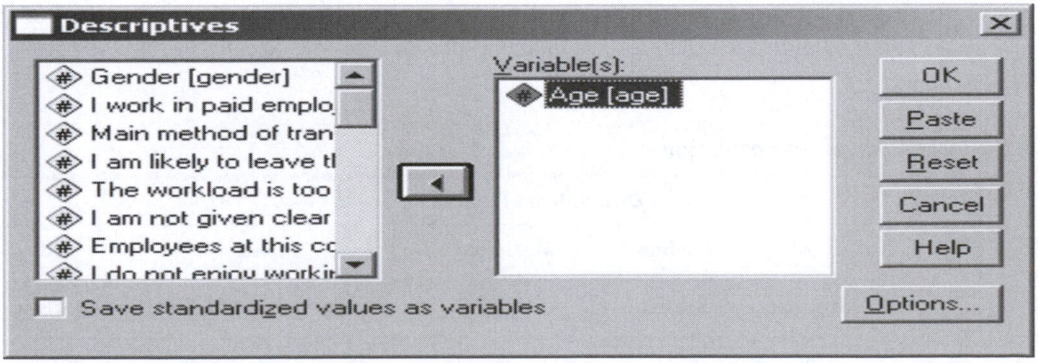

Figure 9.2   Descriptives dialogue box.

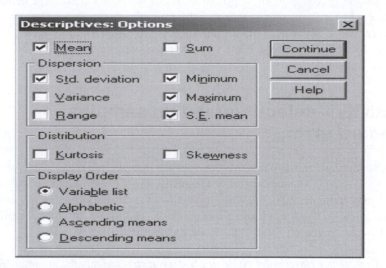

Figure 9.3 **Descriptives options dialogue box.**

7 Click **OK**. You will note that some of your cases on the *data view* now have a 45 degree angle line through them in the left hand column. These are the cases that are NOT selected for your sample.

8 To obtain descriptive results: ***Analyze >>Descriptive Statistics >>Descriptives***. Obtain the printout for this sample (Table 9.3). Notice the differences between the sample statistics and the population data (Table 9.2).

9 Repeat steps 4 to 8 three or four times to obtain the descriptive statistics of other random samples of the same size. The programme will choose different samples each time but you must retain the same percentage for selection so that you can compare the descriptive statistics.

10 After completing step (8), change the percentage selected and either type in a lower or higher figure and select several more samples of that new size.

Table 9.2 **Descriptives for population**

	N	Minimum	Maximum	Mean		Std.
Descriptive Statistics						
	Statistic	Statistic	Statistic	Statistic	Std. Error	Statistic
Age	80	17	55	22.09	.93	8.349
Valid N (listwise)	80					

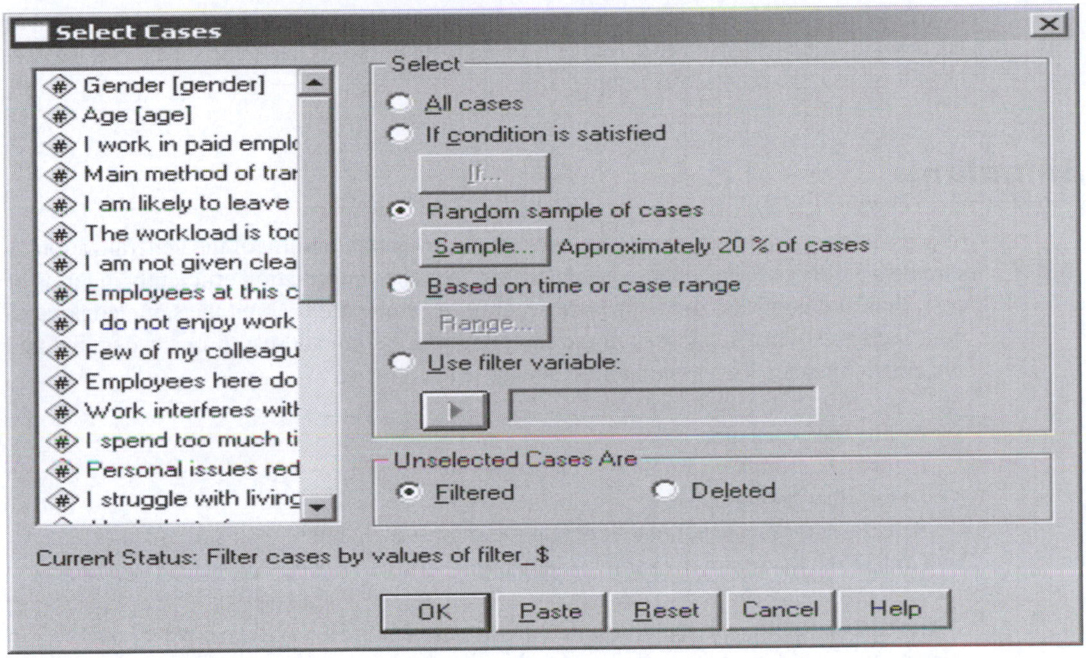

Figure 9.4 **Unselected cases are filtered.**

11 Print out all your tables so that you can compare the statistics from the population of cases produced at step 2 with those derived from the different samples and two size levels.

By now you should be able to see how valuable standard error is. Essentially, it tells us how closely the result we get from a sample reflects the true result for the whole population from which the sample is drawn, and from it we can establish the limits within which we can be confident that the mean lies with a stated level of probability. We are also now aware that the size of sample also affects the size of the standard error and by implication the

Table 9.3 **Descriptive statistics for first sample**

Descriptive Statistics

	N	Minimum	Maximum	Mean		Std.
	Statistic	Statistic	Statistic	Statistic	Std. Error	Statistic
Age	16	17	55	24.63	3.29	13.155
Valid N (list wise)	16					

degree of confidence we can place in the estimate of the population parameter. The level of accuracy considered acceptable for decision-making purposes has to be set against the cost of getting it with increases in sample size.

Sampling

Successful sampling requires a balance of efficiency and reliability of the generalization. A sample's ability to balance these needs, that is, to gather information efficiently in terms of cost, time and numbers, and to provide accurate generalizations about the sampled population, increases when key issues in the sampling process are addressed in a sequential and systematic manner. This systematic sequence is as follows:

1   Define the population.
2   Identify the sampling frame.
3   Determine the sample size.
4   Select a sampling technique to obtain the sample elements.
5   Collect the data from the sample elements.

The first two items and the fourth item in the above sequence will be covered below. The third item is detailed on the Web page for this chapter as it somewhat mathematical and you may not want to tackle it yet. The fifth item involves the use of such methods as surveys, questionnaires and interviews, which will be discussed in later chapters.

1 Defining the population

The first task in sampling is to identify and define precisely the population to be sampled. If we are studying immigrant unemployment, we must define carefully what we mean by '*immigrant*' (all or particular ethnic groups; those not born here or born in the country but of immigrant parents? etc.) and '*unemployed*' (only those registered as looking for work?; both males and females?; between what ages? etc.). Careful attention must be given to the precise limits of the population, whether or not to include individuals whose position is marginal. For example, in defining a population of shop customers, does one include an accompanying spouse, accompanying children without income, browsers who do not buy, or only include the person who fronts up at the till and pays?

If we are trying to locate the population of computer owners, even the innocuous-sounding question '*Do you have a computer at home*' can be qualified in a number of different ways. We must be absolutely clear what it is we require precise information about. Are we concerned with both desktops and laptop computers? With bought or rented computers? With standard word processing types linked to Internet/the office, or those that only play games? Do we include just PCs or Apples as well? Do we want reliable figures in terms of regional/ethnic/socio-economic variations in household computer ownership or just overall? We must be sure that we are sampling the correct population for the study, and select a total sample size that will allow us to have confidence in the accuracy of the figures from the smallest sub-sample for which information is needed (e.g. children with PC in bedroom; wireless laptop owners, etc.). We must also restrict our conclusions only to the defined population.

The adequacy of a target population definition is evaluated in terms of how well the definition (1) unambiguously describes the group of interest, and (2) serves to differentiate those things or individuals who are of interest from those who are not. The following example illustrates the care needed to satisfy these criteria.

Example

Imagine account executives are trying to identify the competitive positioning for their client, a manufacturer of pills that cure male erectile dysfunction. One says: '*Price is the most important factor. Especially when it can be linked to value. Can we claim that our product is the lowest priced name brand erectile dysfunction cure?*' It is agreed that research will be conducted to determine the viability of this claim. The agency researcher says that she will '*obtain a random sample of the prices of the leading brands of pills for curing male erectile dysfunction in stores across the country*'.

Why is this target population definition in the last sentence above inadequate? Here are a few specific issues to consider in each of the key components of the definition (you may raise other concerns in addition):

- *Price* – Which price? The regular selling price, bulk purchase price or a sale price? Is the retail price the manufacturer's recommended price, perhaps as marked on the package, or the actual price at which the outlet is selling the product?
- *Leading brands* – How will these be identified and selected? Is 'leading brand' based on sales, distribution, advertising expenditures, or consumer awareness?
- *Stores* – Which type of stores will be sampled? Any shop that sells male impotence cures? Chemists/pharmacists only?
- *Male erectile dysfunction cures* – Any product designed to relieve this problem or just the pill type?
- *Across the country* – Where? In every city? In major metropolitan areas? In cities over or under a certain size? In rural areas? In each state/province or only in some?

Every combination of answers to the prior questions leads to a different definition of the target population. The 'right' target population definition is the one that all involved in the research agree unambiguously defines the target population and best responds to the informational need motivating the research. In this example, the research team might decide to refine the prior target population definition as follows:

- *Price* refers to the usual selling price as indicated on the item's shelf description.
- *Male erectile dysfunction pills* refer to any product specifically sold to relieve male erectile dysfunction.
- *Leading brands* are defined as the five top selling brands of male erectile dysfunction pills (as defined previously) based on year 2006 unit sales.
- Prices will be sampled in all chemists/pharmacists in the capital city of each state/province where *Chemists/pharmacists* refers to any store which dispenses prescription medicines, whose merchandise primarily consists of medical and health items and where there is a qualified pharmacist on duty. This includes those in major supermarkets as well as independent shops.

- Finally, prices of the following sized packages will be sampled: 100 and 250 regular tablet and 30 tablet gelcap. These are the leading sizes based on unit sales.

As can be seen, this target population definition explicitly and unambiguously (with explanation and justification from external sources) defines the target population. If we are dealing with people, populations of individuals are typically defined in some combination of demographic, geographic, product use, and category relevant behaviours.

- *The demographic* component of the target population definition usually specifies relevant age, gender, income, or other related characteristics of the population of interest.
- *The geographic* component specifies the geographic area(s) in which the target population resides.
- *The behavioural* component specifies relevant category – or product-related behaviours.

For example, a population of interest can be defined in terms of purchase patterns (i.e. 'brand loyal' defined as individuals whose three of the past four purchases were of the same brand), category participation (i.e. have taken three or more holidays in Mexico in the past six years; watched CNN World News at least once a day during the last week), or purchase frequency (i.e. have purchased an imported laptop computer within the past six months).

2 Identifying the sampling frame

The sampling frame is the list of the target population. Suppose the population in which we are interested was the employees of a particular company, a total population of 600 employees. Since the population is clearly defined it can, in principle, be listed, i.e. a list including each employee's name or code number. This population list forms **the sampling frame**. The sampling unit is each single element of the sampling frame.

A perfect sampling frame is identical to the target population, that is, the sample frame contains every population element once and only once, and only population elements are contained in the sampling frame. Additionally, a perfect sample frame contains complete and accurate information on each element in the target population. Electoral lists, membership lists, client bases, and purchasing lists often gleaned from computer and Internet records often function as sampling frames in business research. Perfect sample frames are quite rare in actual practice and, typically, sample frames will either over-register or under-register the target population.

> *Sampling frame. A full list of the target population,*

Perfect registration

A manufacturer of electrical pumps wishes to conduct a survey of attitudes and purchasing behaviours among his current clients. The target population is defined as companies that have purchased at least $1,000 worth of electrical pumps within the past three months. The names of all clients meeting these criteria are selected from the manufacturer's database and are placed on a separate list (the sampling frame) from which study participants will be selected.

Over-registration: Sample frame larger than target population

You have just completed a six-month advertising campaign of a new uni-sex perfume range in Paris and wish to determine levels of advertising and product awareness as well as brand perceptions. You decide to use random digit dialing among prefixes that are identified as Paris. There are two over-registration problems. First, because of the way telephone companies assign telephone prefixes, not all telephones with a Paris prefix actually are in metropolitan Paris. Second, the research should be conducted among individuals who have lived in metropolitan Paris for at least six months, the period of the advertising test. Random digit dialing will not discriminate between those who have and have not resided for the required amount of time.

Under-registration: Sample frame smaller than target population

In a study, you are asked to conduct a survey of the reactions of non-legally qualified real estate conveyancing agents to a new law that prevents them advertising their services. You select a list of members of their national association as the sample frame. This frame suffers from under-registration because not all of them are members.

3 Selecting a sampling method

A sample can be any part of a population regardless of whether it is representative or not. Representativeness is not implicit in the concept of a sample. But if we want to generalize validly from the sample to the population from which it was drawn it must be representative, i.e. reflect in miniature the population characteristics. One of our great concerns in this current chapter will be to distinguish between representative samples and those which are not, and to demonstrate ways of drawing samples that will be representative.

But representative in terms of what variables in the population? The answer is that the sample must be representative of those variables which are known to be related to the characteristics we wish to study. The size of the sample is important too. Usually, the smaller the sample the lower the accuracy, but size is less important than representativeness. There is a famous example of a sample of 10 million voters supposedly representative of the electorate in the USA to poll voting intentions for the presidential election in 1936. The forecast, despite the sample size, was disastrously inaccurate because the sample was contacted by telephone. Telephone ownership biased the sample in favour of the middle class, who were mainly Republican. The Republican candidate went to bed on the eve of polling day contented with the prospects of an overwhelming victory. He awoke to find that his Democratic opponent was to be the new president!

> *A **representative sample***. *Any part or cross-section of a defined population which is selected on a probability basis, and from which information can be obtained and statistical inferences or predictions made about the entire population.*

Probability and non-probability sampling

It is obvious that a sample that will never have exactly the same characteristics as the population from which it is drawn cannot be assumed. The best we can do is say that a sample will be representative within certain limits.

- A **probability sample** is a sample in which each individual, household, event or item (the sample element) has a known chance or probability of being selected for inclusion in the research, i.e. an equal chance, in the case of strict random sampling. Selection or exclusion from the sample is not affected by any factor other than pure chance. The selection is performed, for example, with a table of random numbers, computerized random number selection, or random digit dialing on a telephone survey.
- A **non-probability sample** is a sample that is not selected by chance, but rather selected in some less random and often deliberate way. Inclusion may be made on the basis of purposive selection, opportunity or expert judgement.
- **Probability samples** let a researcher estimate sampling error, statistically determine the sample size required for a specified degree of confidence (see Chapter 9 Web page), and confidently generalize the findings to the population.
- **Non-probability samples** are quick and inexpensive to obtain as well as being relatively easy to design and carry out. However, sampling error or reliability cannot be calculated. It is impossible to know what population is actually being sampled and therefore generalizing to a population is inappropriate.

Probability sampling methods

When we take samples, as opposed to carrying out a complete census, we do so with some loss of accuracy in the results. This is where probability comes to our aid. Probability theory tells us that an unbiased selected sample or cross-section of a particular population (say, car owners) may be, *within measurable limits,* representative of the whole population of car owners.

Generally speaking, the larger the number of items or members in the population and the greater the homogeneity in the market-relevant characteristics of those units, the more likely it is that probability sampling will be effective. The mass markets for many consumer products and services are of this type. Examples of marketing applications of probability sampling techniques include consumer brand preference studies, advertising and promotions research, pricing studies, sales and market estimation and forecasting. The huge number of similar items on a production flow line are also very amenable for sampling for defects.

1 Random sampling

A random sample is a pure lottery system in which all the units or members of the population are listed and numbered consecutively in the sampling frame. Random sampling requires that:

- each member of the population has an equal chance of being selected;
- the selection of one subject is independent of the selection of any other; and
- each possible sample in a given size of samples is equally likely to be obtained.

Random sampling must be done with replacement. This means on the occasion of every selection the same population must be used. Probabilities change on successive selections if there is no replacement. The probability of obtaining an ace of spades on drawing from a pack of cards must be 1/52. If you draw another card but don't replace the first card you drew, the probability of drawing the ace of spades in now 1/51. This is particularly important if the population is small. However, it is less important if the population is large, e.g. if the population is 1,000,000 the probability change is negligible from the first selection of 1/1,000,000 to the next.

For small samples drawn from small populations, like the balls in the Lotto draw, a manual technique is feasible but with larger populations the alternative is to use a random number table or computerized random selection.

You performed an SPSS random selection earlier in this chapter. Because every element of the population has an equal chance of being selected, results may be generalized to the population but even a random selection has some **sampling error**, so generalization is always an inference, not a certainty. Remember, this sampling error enables us to estimate a range around the sampling mean within which it is probable the population mean lies.

> *A random sample.* A sample chosen by a random process that guarantees each unit in the sampling frame an equal chance to be selected.

2 Systematic sampling

In systematic sampling, we take a serially numbered list of units in the population and read off every nth number from a selected starting point in the sampling frame. Thus, to take a 10% sample one could select every tenth number from a complete list of names and/or addresses from the electoral roll or a firm's list of customers.

Systematic sampling can only be performed if the defined population can be listed serially in a sampling frame so that the sample can be drawn at fixed intervals from the list. Imagine that we wanted to select 200 employees from 600, a 1-in-3 ratio. A starting number between 1 and 3 is chosen randomly (for our 1-in-3 ratio) by drawing the number by some random system. Selection continues by taking every third person from that starting number. So, if 3 was randomly chosen as the starting number, successive selections would be 6, 9, 12, 15, etc. The selected starting number fixes which successive numbers are taken or not taken.

The major disadvantage of systematic sampling is that if a periodic cycle exists in the sampling frame, it biases the sample. For example, if a list of 200 employees was in department sequence by alphabetical order and within each department males were listed before females, and in each department there were 20 employees then a sampling interval of 20 would generate a sample all of the same sex. A housing survey that systematically only selects homes/apartments all in a particular position if each housing block is built to the same pattern. But people in the top apartment may always be different from a family in the bottom apartment in each block.

> **A systematic sample**. A sample formed by selecting every nth item from the population.

3 Stratified sampling

The word *strata* indicates divisions of the population. This technique of sampling draws simple random samples from each of several subgroups or strata into which the population has been divided. This reduces sampling error and increases precision without increasing sample size. Sometimes the frame or population to be sampled is known to contain mutually exclusive and clearly distinguishable subgroups or **strata** that differ greatly from one another with respect to some characteristic of interest, e.g. male and female or age group, while the elements within each stratum are homogeneous, e.g. all same gender or same age group. In such circumstances, a **stratified sample** is chosen by taking separate (simple or systematic) random samples from every stratum in the frame or population, often in such a way that the sizes of the separate samples are proportional to the size of the different strata. If you want to emphasize the effect of a strata or one strata is rather small then select a disproportionate stratified sample, of course always justifying why and the proportions chosen.

The characteristics which the researcher uses to define these strata are usually those variables which are known to relate to the characteristics(s) under study. Thus, a population can be divided on the basis of (say) social class membership, sex, level of education, age, ethnic group, salary level, etc., if these are known or believed to be important. Having stratified the population, a simple random or systematic sample is drawn from each stratum following the processes indicated earlier

Reasons for using stratification

1 Separate subpopulation sampling frames require that subsamples be drawn independently, as in a study of Internet service satisfaction which requires sampling frames of businesses and householders who used different Internet providers. Each provider has their own list of subscribers. In this example subscribers can be split into the business or householder strata and provider strata.
2 When one or more subgroups are scheduled for more intensive analysis.

3   Variations in the forms of questions or forced choice answers may be necessary for some items. This would lead to separate analysis of these particular items for each subgroup. Questions on health issues affecting work absence directed to female employees will differ from those directed to male employees (e.g. gynaecological issues). If somewhat different questions are to be asked, sampling frames may need to be separated into strata.

4   Stratified sampling adds an extra ingredient to random sampling by ensuring that each group or strata within the population are sampled randomly. It offers increased possibility of accuracy by ensuring all subgroups of the population are represented in the sample in the same proportions as they are in the population. Even with random sampling there is always a risk of a 'wild' sample of all men or all women, however low the probability, because random sampling can produce any possible combination!!

> **Stratified sample**. *The sample is formed by taking proportions from each strata of the population so that it conforms to the pattern in the population.*

4 Cluster sampling

Cluster sampling is the sampling of entire natural groups rather than individuals. It is the clusters that are randomly sampled. It can be thought of as a procedure in which the population is sampled in chunks or blocks, rather than as separate individuals. It retains the principle of randomness yet allows a research design that is feasible in terms of cost, time and other resources. Furthermore, lists of the whole population are not required but instead required only for the selected clusters. Much business research is predominantly interested in the group rather than the individuals or items composing it. In business contexts many clusters are present, e.g. employees grouped in branch offices, customers at each supermarket branch.

A researcher who wanted to sample the residents or shops of a city, for example, might divide the city into blocks, randomly select a few of these and then interview every resident or shop owner within the chosen blocks. Because of the geographic proximity of those interviewed, this procedure would save considerable transportation expenses and time in comparison to a citywide simple random sample of individual residents or shop owners, who would almost certainly be located in a multitude of different places. Cluster sampling is often used for research with data collection needs that require personal, at-home or at-work interviews.

Quality sampling by business firms often follows a similar route. Imagine a firm that had just received a shipment of 1 million coffee cups. Its warehouse would be filled, perhaps, with 10,000 sealed cartons, each containing 100 cups. An inspector who wanted to determine the quality of the cups by taking a 10,000-cup sample could take a simple or systematic random sample of them but might then have to open and unpack nearly all of the 10,000 cartons in order to find the individual cups selected. It would be much easier to regard each carton as a geographic cluster, to select 100 cartons randomly, and to inspect every single cup in these cartons only. Some 9,900 of the cartons would not have to be opened at all. Cluster sampling shifts data collection to groups of sampling units rather than individual sampling units.

If all of the individuals in all the selected chunks or clusters are taken as the sample of the population, this is termed a 'one-stage cluster random sampling plan'. If a sample of the individuals in each of the selected clusters is taken, this is a 'two-stage cluster random sampling plan'. Any further sampling would be a multi-stage cluster sample. At each stage the principle of **random selection** is maintained.

> *A cluster sample. The sample is formed by identifying clusters or groups in the population and selecting a sample of the clusters.*

Here is an example (Fig. 9.5) of multi-stage cluster sampling where a national chain with 7,000 employees wished to determine the attitudes of its employees to a proposed new pay structure. Rather than take a random sample which may have involved only a few employees in each branch, a cluster sampling in stages was adopted to enable whole groups of employees in one branch at a time to be surveyed.

Sample selection bias in probability samples

The goal of probability sampling is the selection of a group of individuals or objects that represent the population from which they were selected. The elimination of selection bias is important, because only without bias can a researcher confidently generalize the research results to the sampled population.

Sample bias occurs when members of the population of interest are selected in violation of the basic principle of random sampling. Imagine that you wish to select a random sample of students from your university or college. You make a conscientious effort to interview every tenth student who enters the cafeteria over the lunch break. You chose the cafeteria because most students go there at least once during the day. However, because students from different faculties visit the cafeteria at different times of day with different frequencies, and not all visit at least once, the sample would be biased. It would over-represent the type of student who uses the cafeteria. The sampling planning process should therefore include an explicit discussion of what potential sample biases were identified and avoided in the study.

Non-probability sampling methods

In spite of its advantages, not all business research uses probability sampling. Some informational needs do not require the precision and generalizability of probability samples and may not justify the time and expense of probability sampling. Non-probability sampling selects elements in some non-random way. Due to the inability to quantify sampling error this form of sampling should not be used if a probability sample is possible. The major forms of non-probability sampling are convenience, judgement, quota, snowball and purposive.

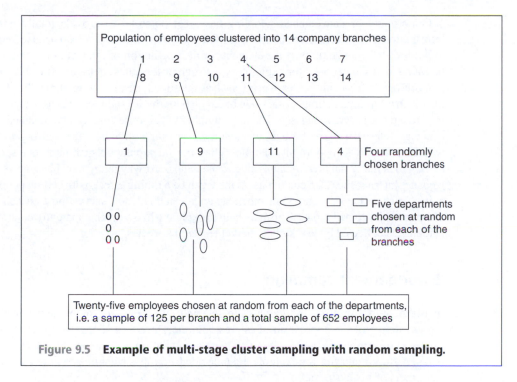

Figure 9.5   **Example of multi-stage cluster sampling with random sampling.**

1 Opportunity sampling

Opportunity sampling, sometimes also called **convenience sampling**, involves selection of participants because they are convenient and accessible. Interviewing friends, associates, members of your sports club, consumers in the local supermarket, people living in your neighbourhood, people passing through the local bus station, individuals walking down the street, workers contacted at their union branch meeting, selecting the last 30 transactions because the records are handy, or using student groups you are teaching, are all forms of this type of sampling. Other convenience or opportunity samples involve asking for volunteers, but we never know whether volunteers differ in some way from those who are not. Convenience sampling, as might be expected, is uncomplicated, quick, and low in cost. However, because the chance of selection is unknown, they are likely biased in some way with no possibility of generalization to a wider population; there is never any assurance that the sample is in any way representative of the defined population. For example, who you interview at the bus station or in the shopping mall may depend on time of day or even the day itself. However, it is often used because no alternative is open. This happens when, due to constraints of finance and even permission, research can only be carried out on conveniently accessible groups.

An opportunity sample. A sample selected from conveniently available participants.

Opportunity or convenience sampling has great potential to provide totally unreliable information and, therefore, should only be used when there is absolutely no need to generalize to the broader population or if the elements of the population of interest in the study cannot be found in any other way, for exploratory research or for quick, non-generalizable information relevant to a specific research need, such as questionnaire pretesting. It may be of interest to note that 'opinion polling' is too often based on opportunity samples such as listener 'phone in's' to a radio programme issue. The large number of responses that can be obtained quickly using an Internet survey through an intentional or unintentional visit to an organization's website is clearly an opportunity sample. What specific population such Internet respondents belong to is really unknown, mainly due to the haphazard way many may have arrived at the website. Internet sites also entail bias, as there can be a timing effect, with certain people only going online at the weekend while others go on late at night, so a survey must give all groups an opportunity to participate. This may help to explain why so much apparently contradictory evidence is collected by less skilled market research agencies.

2 Judgement sampling

In **judgement sampling** individuals are selected on an expert's judgement that they are representative of the population of interest and therefore will serve the research purpose. This sort of sampling is used when you need a population with a specific set of characteristics. A store manager, for example, may decide to sample what he considers the 'typical' customers of his business.

One's confidence in the results of the research conducted with judgement samples is directly proportionate to the expertise used to identify and select the sample. For example, the selection of cities for test marketing a new product is almost always made on judgement. An expert may believe that the most appropriate targets for a student bank account savings scheme are parents with children aged 10 to 17. This age group judgement may be wrong and provide misleading direction as it ignores the fact that grandparents may be as important an influence as parents on grandchildren's savings habits. Judgement samples are recommended only when there is absolute confidence in the expert's opinion or, as with convenience sampling, when only preliminary, exploratory information is required.

> *A judgement sample. A sample based on an expert's identification of who or what should be included in the sample.*

3 Quota sampling

Quota sampling is the most sophisticated form of non-probability sampling. In quota sampling the researcher, instead of being given a list of specific individuals and/or addresses to contact, is free to select, within proportioned quotas, units with pre-determined characteristics (e.g. location, age, socio-economic group, sex and other consumer criteria, or types of business, types of product uses, major use categories and other industrial criteria).

It aims at securing proper representation by splitting the universe down into more homogeneous segments, selecting units from each of the segments or strata and combining them to form a total sample. A quota sample of the retail television trade might specify the exact number of outlets to be contacted in terms of each of the following criteria: TV region, location (e.g. high street or shopping centre), ownership (e.g. chain versus independent), providing or not providing repair services, supplying or not supplying rental facilities, total shop turnover per year, annual value of TV sales and rentals, and so on.

Quota samples are executed through the following five steps:

1 Determine the defining characteristics of the key subgroups.
2 Determine the percent of the total population represented by each defining characteristic.
3 Determine the percent of the total population represented by each quota cell.
4 Translate the percent into a sample size.
5 The interviewer selects individuals in each quota until they have fulfilled their quota requirements.

The fifth stage above is really at the level of an opportunity sample in that people conveniently present in the location or at home and fitting the requirements are included. However, since they are included because they possess particular characteristics and in specifically fixed proportions, then some degree of generalization is feasible which is not possible with true convenience samples. Bias can be introduced into a quota sampling survey as interviewers tend to approach potential interviewees who are similar to themselves, generally middle class, well dressed and literate, and often under-represents the older person or mothers with very young children, and the handicapped of any age.

> *A quota sample*. *A sample composed of freely selected but predefined number or proportion of units of each category of predetermined characteristics.*

4 Purposive sampling

Purposive sampling is explicitly chosen to be non-representative to achieve a specific analytical objective, for example, a survey of households who own a beach house as well as a main residence. Here, similar to quota samples, a researcher divides the universe into a number of segments in which a predefined, but arbitrary, number of interviews will be conducted. This form of sampling entails the following three steps:

1 Determine defining characteristics of the key subgroups.
2 Determine the number of individuals required in each group, from the perspective of data analysis.
3 Sample the population.

> *A purposive sample.* A sample deliberately selected to sample a specific group with a specific purpose in mind.

5 Snowball (or referral) sampling

This uses initial contacts to provide further contacts or cases through referrals. It is a bit like networking. With very specific and small populations it is the easiest way to locate members as new contacts are mentioned by people you are currently surveying. In studying the attitudes of people with a specific type of physical handicap towards changes in government benefits for that group, you may need to use both formal and informal networks to locate such persons.

Tips for sampling

This is a set of suggestions, not rules; a general guide, not a blueprint.

1 Define clearly the population to which you intend to generalize from the results of your sample.
2 Estimate the size of sample required.
3 Consider the possibility of a simple random sample. Often this will not be practicable, due to lack of sampling frame containing whole of the population.
4 If simple random sampling is not practicable, decide if stratification would increase convenience or efficiency. For example, if surveying attitudes to private school funding the sample might be broken down by social class, age group, whether parents or not, household income, etc.
5 If not using 4, then consider clusters selected on a random basis. Use several small clusters rather than a few large ones, or preferably a two-stage or multi-stage design which will cover a wider range of clusters for the same sample size.
6 If 5 is not possible, then consider non-random samples. The crucial problem is that it is not possible to estimate of the sampling error which is always present, or to generalize to a presumed population.
7 Even an opportunity sample may yield information of considerable value, particularly in an exploratory study of an area previously under-researched or in 'case' studies using a small number of individuals. The value of any conclusion from these types of study will depend on an intelligent assessment of how far the conditions have been satisfied for valid scientific generalization.

In conclusion, the choice of actual sampling method to use in a given set of circumstances is best left to the experts but the user is entitled to know why a particular method has been selected. From the standpoint of those commissioning the research, the key consideration will be the importance of the findings in relation to the decision that has to be made on them and the cost of acquiring them. Cost is a function of the degree of accuracy required in the results, since the latter determines the sample size. It is to determining sample size requirements we now turn.

What you have learned in this chapter

You have seen that valid sampling procedures are essential to obtain reliable estimates of population parameters. Sampling is usually cheaper, quicker and as accurate as a census if done properly. The target population must be defined unambiguously and a feasible sampling frame established. The distribution of sample means is normal for samples of around 30 or more. The mean of the distribution of sample means is identical to the mean of the population from which the sample has been drawn. The variability of sample means is measured by the standard error of the mean. A standard error for proportions can also be calculated. These provide confidence intervals within which the population mean can be assumed to lie.

A distinction between probability and non-probability samples has been made. A probability sample is one where every member of the population has a known chance of being included in the sample. Selection is purely by chance. A non-probability sample occurs when the elements are not strictly selected by chance from the population but are selected in a more fortuitous or, alternatively, a more purposeful deliberate way.

Random sampling involves the selection of units in a way that gives every unit an equal chance of selection. Random number tables or computer generation will ensure this requirement is satisfied. Stratified sampling involves selecting every nth unit on the sampling frame. Cluster sampling involves dividing the elements of the population into groups called clusters and a sample of clusters are selected randomly. When all the elements in the selected clusters are included in the sample of the population, it is a one-stage cluster random sampling plan. When a sample of the elements in each of the selected clusters is chosen to be in the final sample of the population, it is a two-stage cluster random sampling plan. Clusters should be similar in composition from cluster to cluster with wide differences among elements in the clusters.

Non-probability sampling includes convenience sampling, quota sampling, purposive, snowball and judgement sampling. The major problem with non-probability sampling is that we never know the population the sample represents, nor can we know what biases exist in the selection process.

Review questions and activities

Qu. 9.1
Why are samples used rather than population censuses?

Qu. 9.2
Define each of the following in one sentence each:
Population, parameter, sample and statistics.

Qu. 9.3
Calculate for each graph in Figure 9.1 within what limits approximately you would expect 95% of sample means to lie.

Qu. 9.4

(a) A random sample survey of 2,000 motorists found that 827 or 41.4% of them had been to their service garage for repairs and for servicing during the previous three months. What is the standard error of this proportion?
(b) Now calculate the standard error of the proportion for samples of 1,000, 4,000 and 8,000 in the above example. What is the relationship between sample size and standard error of the mean and what are the implications of this?

Check your answers on the website.

Qu. 9.5
Look at the variations in Means, SD's and SE_M's that have been generated in samples of the same and different sizes drawn randomly from the same population. Discuss these variations in class and consider why they occur.

Qu. 9.6
Consider the following hypothetical circumstance. Imagine that within the past three months *The Body Builder* magazine has added five additional pages of advertising to its weekly issue. These pages have been added on a test basis and were only included in magazines sent to retail outlets and subscribing homes in the capital city. The magazine now wants to assess perceptions of the advertising, specifically, whether readers believe there is *currently* too much, not enough, or just the right amount of advertising. The opinions of individuals who read the test issues will be compared to those who receive the normal issue. Two population definitions are required, one for the test and one for the non-test (control) conditions. Six researchers each present a different definition of the target population for the test condition.

Sample definition A: Purchasers of the magazine.
Sample definition B: Subscribers to the magazine.
Sample definition C: Readers of the magazine.
Sample definition D: Any individuals who have read the magazine within the past 30 days.

Sample definition E: Any individuals between the ages of 21 and 45 who have read at least the last three issues of the magazine within the past four months.

Sample definition F: Any individuals over the age of 17 who have read at least the last three issues of the magazine within the past four months.

Explain why all six definitions of the population above for the test condition are inadequate and try to formulate one that would be better. Check your answers on this chapter's Web site.

Qu. 9.7
Would a list of bookshops advertising in the *Yellow Pages* be an over-registered, a perfect or under-registered sampling frame?

Qu. 9.8
Determine the population and sampling frame for each of the following:

(a) The local public library wants to conduct a customer satisfaction survey.
(b) A large insurance company wishes to assess staff reaction to a new bonus policy.

Check your answers on the website.

Qu. 9.9
Why can a stratified sample be more representative than a simple random sample?
Check your response in the material above.

Qu. 9.10
In what situation might a multi-stage cluster sample be useful?
Check your answer in the material above.

Qu. 9.11
Identify the relevant population and sampling frame, and indicate an appropriate sampling method for the situations below:

(a) The Human Resources Department wish to determine whether single parent employees have a higher rate of absenteeism than married employees.
(b) A building supply company wants to determine the amount of pilferage from its materials storage warehouses on the east coast.
(c) The State's Industry Ministry wants to determine the relationship between drug abuse and antisocial workplace behaviour.

Check your answers on the website.

Qu. 9.12
An interviewer is asked to obtain answers to a survey on shopping habits from 50 people, 25 of each gender. She positions herself outside a major shop in the town centre at 9 a.m. on a

Monday morning and starts interviewing people one by one. Discuss this approach in class. Can you identify some of the problems this study raises?

Q. 9.13
Probability sampling is not always preferable to non-probability sampling designs. Explain this.

Check your answer in the material above.

Now access Chapter 9 website, undertake the questions and problems there, and study the additional material.

Chapter 10
Hypothesis Formation, Types of Error and Estimation

'Why did the researcher take viagra? He did not want to be associated with a small p value and regarded as not significant'

(Source unknown)

Content list

By the end of this chapter you will:

1 Understand what a hypothesis is and why a hypothesis must be testable and operationally stated.
2 Understand the logic behind testing the null hypothesis.
3 Be able to formulate a testable hypothesis.
4 Understand how statistical significance levels act as criteria in testing null hypotheses.
5 Be able to distinguish between one-tailed and two-tailed tests and the implications of each.
6 Be able to distinguish between the concepts of Type I and Type II error and their implications.
7 Understand the use of sample statistics in point and interval estimation.

Introduction

This chapter will bring together your understandings of material in previous chapters on frameworks, normal distribution, probability, significance, sampling and standard error, and demonstrate how these understandings lead to the formulation and testing of hypotheses, using the concept of standard error and significance to estimate whether the effect is due to chance or is a real one.

What is a hypothesis?

In Chapter 5 we traced the research process down from the broad theory through conceptual and theoretical frameworks so that a precise operational hypothesis(es) can be designed to enable the research to be conducted. That demanding planning stage is a most important part of the process, because we are then able to focus on exactly what specific questions we are trying to answer.

A hypothesis is a hunch, an educated guess, a proposition that is empirically testable. If research were limited simply to gathering facts, knowledge could not advance. Without some guiding idea, every investigation would be fruitless, since we could not determine what is relevant and what is irrelevant. Try this everyday example of hypothesis formulation. Suppose the only light you had on in the bedroom was the bedside table lamp. Suddenly it went off. You would try to work out the reason for it. I hypothesize that it could be one of the following:

- lamp bulb failure;
- plug fuse failure;
- main power fuse failure;
- electricity grid failure.

You probably thought of similar causes but whatever you thought is an implied hypothesis; an educated guess. You can test each potential reason or hypothesis in turn until the cause is located. Let us imagine the cause was a fuse failure in the plug. Because the lights came on after I changed the fuse only lends support to the hypothesis. It does not prove it. The fault could in fact have been caused by a temporary faulty wiring connection, which in turn caused the fuse to blow. In mending the fuse, I corrected the connection by chance as I caught the wire with my screwdriver unbeknown to me. We never 'prove' hypotheses. 'Proved' carries the connotation of finality, and certainty. Hypotheses are not proved by producing evidence that support them; they are simply not disproved, and can therefore be retained as the best possible answer until at some future time later evidence suggests that they are wrong. The scientific process never leads to certainty in explanation; only the rejection of existing hypotheses and the construction of new ones, which may stand up better to the test of empirical evidence.

On the other hand, if the observed facts do not confirm the prediction made on the basis of the hypothesis, then the hypothesis is rejected immediately and conclusively. This distinguishes the scientific hypothesis from everyday speculation. This mode of accounting for problems is the characteristic pattern of scientific thinking. It possesses three essential steps:

1   The proposal of a hypothesis or tentative assumption to account for a phenomenon or test the validity of some situation.

2   The deduction from the hypothesis that certain phenomena should be observed in given circumstances.
3   The checking of this deduction by observation and testing.

An example might be that '*customers prefer influenza relief medicine in tablet rather than liquid form*'. This hypothesis could be investigated by a scientific approach counting the purchasing decisions when both forms are equally available on the same shelf at the same price. Another hypothesis might be that '*younger employees have different opinions from older employees on a number of issues affecting conditions of employment*'. This hypothesis could be assessed by designing a *survey sampling plan* and would require identifying the two populations of employees of interest and then following through with the development of a survey instrument and the actual sampling of employees. Hypothesis testing is an inferential procedure that uses sample data to evaluate the credibility of a hypothesis about a population.

> *A hypothesis.* A tentative assumption that is capable of being tested.

Criteria for judging hypotheses

Hypotheses may derive from theory or from problems, as we saw in Chapter 5. However, regardless of the source of the hypothesis it must meet several criteria:

1   Hypotheses should be stated clearly, in correct terminology, and operationally defined. General terms such as *personality, production glitches, unemployability, job burnout,* etc. should be avoided. More appropriate therefore are: '*anxiety level as measured by 'X's' test*'; '*Workplace bullying as measured by the number of …*' etc. Such hypotheses as '*Creative advertising slogans are a function of a fertile mind*' and '*Democratic practices enhance social integration in the work place*' are too vague. For example, how do we judge *creativity* or define *fertile mind or social integration?* In Chapter 5 we considered how variables can be operationalized by specific definitions or by obtaining responses to specific items or tests. Reread that section of Chapter 5 if necessary.
2   Hypotheses should be testable so that it is capable of being either confirmed or refuted. A hypothesis which cannot be tested does not belong to the realm of science. For example, the following hypothesis is testable: '*Employees who attend voluntarily health and safety talks and demonstrations show significantly higher levels of knowledge on health and safety topics than those who do not attend*', since it is possible to determine who or who did not attend and their levels of knowledge. Additionally, since hypotheses are predictors of the outcome of the investigation, an obvious necessity is that instruments should exist (or can be developed) which will provide valid and reliable measures of the variables involved. Such instruments can be tests, questionnaires, rating scales, interview schedules, scientific/technical measuring devices, etc.

3 Hypotheses should state expected relationships between variables explicitly.

4 Hypotheses should be limited in scope. Hypotheses of global significance are not required; precise, focused and succinct hypotheses are preferable.

5 Hypotheses should be grounded in past knowledge, consistent with most known facts, i.e. the knowledge gained from experience or a review of previous studies. They obviously cannot be consistent with all known facts, since many studies give contradictory results. In these cases, the hypothesis may be formulated to resolve the contradiction. For example, different results in studying the relationship between job satisfaction and salary might be due to some studies using only males while other used females or mixed gender groups, or older workers and not younger workers, or not taking account of the variety of positions employees can hold in an organization. Thus, a new hypothesis could be established linking job satisfaction with position held rather than salary. But the hypothesis should never lead the cynical reader to say '*What ever led you to expect that*' or '*You made this one up after you collected the data*'.

> **An operational definition.** One that specifies or defines unambiguously in measurable terms.

Stating the hypothesis

Hypotheses may be stated either in the form of proposed **relationships** or in terms of **comparisons (differences)**.

(a) For example, a relationship hypothesis would exist if we propose '*that changes in demand for a good are related to changes in price of the same good*'.

(b) An example of a difference or comparison hypothesis is '*that female employees take more sick days than male employees*'.

The statistical tests used for each type of hypothesis are different so we always need to know which type we are stating. A relationship hypothesis will use some type of correlation test (Chapters 14 and 15) whereas a difference hypothesis will use, for example, a **'t' test** or **analysis of variance** (Chapters 12 and 13).

Making hypotheses testable

The following examples illustrate the sort of questions that must be answered in turning a general research question into a hypothesis capable of being tested, involving operationalization of concepts.

1 Do supervisors become more effective with training?

The statement is too broad and needs to be delimited, for example:

- Which supervisors? Younger ones? Older ones? Both? Male or female or both?
- How will effectiveness be measured?

- What kind of training is included?
- What is meant by 'becomes more effective'?

Therefore, a more specific hypothesis might be: '*Male supervisors become statistically significantly more effective in interpersonal skills as measured by the Social Skills Test after a one week training course in social skills than those who have not taken the course*'.

2   *Do new supermarket managers have different opinions from supermarket managers with longer tenure on a number of issues affecting the operation of supermarkets.*

Some of the questions that must be answered before an appropriate hypothesis and survey-sampling plan can be developed are:

- What are the issues of importance that must be included in the survey?
- How are 'new supermarket managers' defined? By age? By years of management experience?
- What is meant by 'longer tenure'? How long?
- Specifically, what is meant by 'have different opinions'? To be different, by how much must opinions disagree?

An examination of the two examples above should lead to a common observation that without specifying all the terms and clarifying all meanings we cannot attempt to test a hypothesis.

Tips for writing good research hypotheses

1   Clear and precise. Meaning of key terms are defined.
2   Feasible. In terms of time, resources, accessibility, etc.
3   Can be tested.
4   Reasonably consistent with known facts.
5   Ethical. No physical or psychological harm will be done.
6   Significant. Will contribute useful knowledge.

Hypothesis testing: null and alternative hypotheses

Hypothesis testing is one of the most important concepts in research. Unfortunately, it is a complicated process and the logic seems to operate backwards. You have an idea that something exists or happened such as:

- Groups are different from each other.
- Some treatment has an effect on an outcome measure.
- One variable relates to or predicts another variable.

This is the basis of your hypothesis, but there are two possibilities:

1 Nothing really exists/happened, or
2 Something important exists/happened.

There are two opposing possibilities:

1 Nothing much happened = **The Null Hypothesis** – symbolized as H_o
  • The hoped for effect was barely apparent.
  • The groups were not all that different.
  • The treatment doesn't seem to help anybody.
  • The variables don't appear to be related.

2 Something exists or happened = **The Alternate Hypothesis** – symbolized as H_1
  • There was a strong effect due to the intervening treatment.
  • There is a great difference between the groups.
  • One variable strongly correlates with or predicts another.

Can you see the logic! When you test a hypothesis statistically, you are trying to see if something happened and comparing against the possibility that very little happened.

The logic of traditional hypothesis testing then requires that we set up two competing statements or hypotheses, the null hypothesis and the alternative hypothesis. These hypotheses are mutually exclusive and exhaustive.

H_o: The finding was simply a chance occurrence (null version) – very little really occurred.
H_1: The finding did not occur by chance but is real (alternative version) – something beyond chance variation did occur.

How do we test or compare these competing hypotheses? This is the counter-intuitive part. We start by trying to **disprove** the null hypothesis.

The null hypothesis is assumed to be true unless we find evidence to the contrary. If we find that the evidence is just too unlikely to support the null hypothesis, we assume the alternative hypothesis is more likely to be correct. In 'traditional statistics' a probability of something occurring equal to or less than .05 (= 5% = 1 chance in 20) is conventionally considered the border line for 'unlikely'. This significance level is the risk of rejecting a null hypothesis when the latter is correct. (If you need to refresh your knowledge about significance levels go back to the last part of Chapter 8.) If the calculated significance level is 5% or less ($p < .05$) then we can reject the null hypothesis that the difference or relationship is simply a chance one. If it is more than 5% ($p > .05$) then we retain the null hypothesis as the result is probably due to chance.

The null hypothesis does not say that there is '*no difference*' or '*no relationship*'. It states the difference or relation is such that it would regularly occur by chance as one of the many sampling differences or relationships that occur close to and around the population mean. Remember from Chapter 9 that there will always be differences as these occur between random samples by chance and are measured by the standard error of the mean. But they are usually quite minimal, distributed around the theoretical sample or population mean.

They only represent sampling mean differences and are not due to anything you did. That is, such differences occur frequently by chance. Remember that approximately 95% of all random sample means are found between ±1.96Z, while 68.32% are located between ±1Z.

That is why we use the words '*no statistically significant difference*' in the null hypothesis statement and not '*no difference*'. There will be differences but they do not reach statistical significance as judged by the level of significance we have chosen (5%, 1% or .01%). Non-significant differences are therefore chance or fairly small differences that occur within the area bounded approximately by ±1.96Z (i.e. 95% occurrence by chance). Statistically significant results occur rarely and should be equal to or less than the 5% level ($p < .05$). Strongly significant results may reach the 1% level ($p < .01$ or 1 in 100 by chance) or even the .01% level ($p < .001$ or 1 in 1,000 by chance). Any significance less than .001 is quoted in SPSS results as .000.

We never test the research or alternative hypothesis as any non-zero difference or relationship could conceivably satisfy it. Suppose we hypothesize that there should be a difference between the lateral thinking scores of advertising executives and accountants with a possible range of marks from a lateral thinking test of 0–20. This hypothesis would be satisfied by any difference in the mean scores from 0–20; the difference might be 3, 5, 17 or 19 marks – any of these would satisfy the hypothesis. We have only to determine that the difference was greater than zero. When we test the null hypothesis, which states that the treatment has not had any significant effect beyond that due to chance or sampling error, we are given a baseline to determine whether there has been any further effect beyond the chance level. We can thus set precise limits – *our significance levels* – for the rejection of a null hypothesis. This is the basic principle on which most statistical tests are based.

So, in order to demonstrate that we have a real effect which implies that our treatment works, that our groups differ, or that there is a real relationship:

1 We firstly try to show that our treatment did work, that our groups do differ, or that there is a real relationship.
2 We can then reject the null hypothesis (H_0) and accept the alternative hypothesis (H_1).
3 If we show that the treatment did not work, that there is no group difference to speak of or that there is no real relationship then we must retain the null hypothesis (H_0) and consequently cannot accept the alternative hypothesis (H_1).

> **The null hypothesis.** *The assumption that any difference or relationship that exists between populations is due to chance.*

> **The alternative hypothesis**. *A restatement of the hypothesis in the same terms as those used in the null hypothesis except that the differences or relationships are assumed to be real and not due to chance.*

Tips for hypothesis testing

1 Set up the null hypothesis, i.e. any observed difference between conditions is entirely attributable to chance fluctuations (random error).

2 Choose an alpha (α) or significance level value at .05 or .01, i.e. outside the 95% area.

3 Calculate the exact probability that the observed difference could have been derived by chance alone (SPSS will do this for you).

4 State you are retaining the null hypothesis if this probability is higher than the selected level of significance. State you are rejecting the experimental or alternate hypothesis if the null hypothesis cannot be rejected and has to be retained.

5 State you are rejecting the null hypothesis if a conventional level of significance or even lower probability is attained. In this latter situation, the probability that random error alone produced a difference as large as the one we observed is so low that we feel confident to reject this possibility.

6 State you are accepting the experimental or alternate hypothesis if the null hypothesis has been rejected.

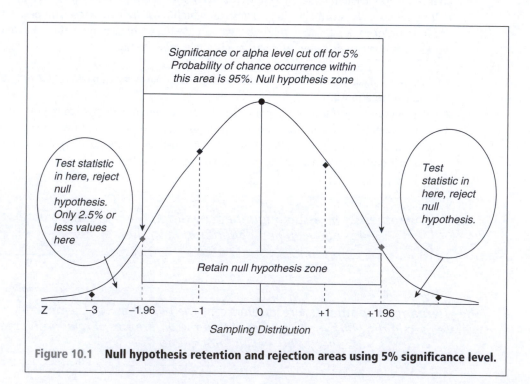

Figure 10.1   Null hypothesis retention and rejection areas using 5% significance level.

If you do not find significance, it does not mean that there is no difference, relationship or effect. It means you did not detect anything that reached the significance level cut-off. The logic is that maybe if you tested more subjects you might have obtained statistical significance, as sample size is important. You probably remember that the larger the sample size the smaller the standard error of the mean. Or you could change the experimental conditions to yield a greater effect.

Figure 10.1 summarizes graphically the null and alternate hypotheses areas on the normal distribution curve.

> **No significant difference**. This statement implies that any differences are within the range of chance or sampling error and do not reach a stated significance level.

Here is another example to help you get your brain round this seemingly illogical argument of testing the converse of what we really want to test. Consider the following hypotheses:

- The **null hypothesis** (H_0): '*That business college students who undertake six-week work experience do not obtain grades that are statistically significant different from those who do not undertake the work experience.*'
- The **alternative hypothesis** (H_1): '*That a six-week work experience results in a statistically significant difference in grades between business college students who undertake it and those who do not.*'

If we find that students with six weeks of work experience perform similarly to those without six weeks of work experience, with only slight variations due to chance, our results therefore show **no significant difference**. Remember, this does not mean they perform exactly the same, i.e. no difference. There are differences, but they are so minimal as to be meaningless and are likely due to chance variations from sampling error (remember no two samples are exactly the same). We would therefore **accept our null hypothesis**. The null hypothesis is in fact this expression of chance variation.

If we find that one group performs significantly different than the other at a defined level of significance, usually $p < .05$ (5% level) or $p < .01$ (1% level), we would then **reject the null hypothesis as these differences are unlikely chance differences**, and by definition, **accept the alternative hypothesis** that there is a real difference in performance since such results would only occur by chance 5% or 1% of the time.

Probability and 'proof' in statistical testing

Statistics can never 'prove' anything. All a statistical test can do is assign a probability value to the results you have, indicating the likelihood (or probability) that they come from random fluctuations in sampling. The lower the probability that they reflect a random fluctuation the more we have confidence that there is a real effect. Remember that different samples from the same population will vary from each other – most only slightly but some quite differently, because the different samples are formed of different subjects.

If the likelihood that these numbers come from random fluctuations is **low**, a better decision might be to conclude that maybe these **aren't random fluctuations that** are being observed. If there is a statistically significant difference or relationship, we reject the initial randomness hypothesis (the null hypothesis) in favour of one that says, 'Yes we do have a **real** relationship here' (the alternative hypothesis) and then go on to discuss or speculate about this difference or relationship.

If our observations would be very unlikely to occur if the null hypothesis were true, it follows that the null hypothesis is **probably false**, and consequently the alternative hypothesis is **probably true**. Notice the nagging use of the word '*probably*'. Unfortunately, that is as far as hypothesis testing can take us. We are dealing with probability and we shroud our conclusions in a proper degree of humility. This is why we never ever talk about '*proving*' a hypothesis; we have simply found support for it at a particular level of probability.

By placing the term **statistically significant** in the statement of the null hypothesis, we are emphasizing the fact that our test of the null hypothesis invokes the test against a stated and conventionally acceptable level of statistical significance. It is because we are using probability levels (levels of significance) we can never prove a hypothesis. Even at these levels a result may occur occasionally by chance. These chances, as you are aware, are 1 in 20 for $p > .05$, 1 in 100 for $p > .01$, and 1 in 1000 for $p > .001$. So if we employ the 1% significance level ($p > .01$), for example, we know that a difference will actually occur at this level once in a hundred occasions over the long run simply by chance. If our result is at or beyond that level, we are hoping and assuming that it is not the one in a hundred result. But we can never know – it may be!!

Uncertainty is present whenever we deal with samples rather than populations in that we can never claim anything about populations with 100% certainty. The goal of the game of statistical inference is to keep the level of uncertainty in our results within acceptable limits. There is no absolute standard. We say this to provide you with a realistic perspective on statistical analysis of behavioural data. All statistical procedures (SPSS) do is 'crunch the numbers' (this is the 'objective' aspect); however, humans must ultimately decide what is to be made of those numbers (this is the 'subjective' part) and choose to make a decision that the results are significantly significant because the results achieve their subjectively chosen level of statistical significance.

Another problem is what to do when your p-value is, say .051. A value of $p = .051$ is technically non-significant, whereas $p = .049$ is significant! Yet, in real terms, the difference between these two probabilities is minimal and indefensible. However, in the former case, you do need to admit that your finding was non-significant. But having done that, you may cautiously talk about the 'trends' in your data. You may have to word your statements with terms such as 'suggests', 'might indicate', 'tends toward'!!! If your p-value comes in 'under .05', then you can claim 'significance', but if $p = .049$ don't get over-enthusiastic!

You need to examine the SPSS output, usually under headings such as '*Sig.*' or '*Two-tailed Sig.*', or '*Prob.*' for the probability (or 'p-value') of your results being a real difference or a real relationship. This is then to be the probability you quote as being the 'level of significance' associated with your results. As a general guide, treat the p-value as a measure of the confidence or faith you can have in your results being **real** (and not being due to chance fluctuations in sampling). Although, remember that when using the 5% level a result at this level will occur 5% of the times by chance. Unfortunately you will never know whether it is or not.

How unlikely is 'unlikely'? What does 5% probability mean?

Imagine someone coming up to you and saying that they could select an Ace on one draw from a standard pack of cards. The chance of doing this would be = .067 (about 7%). Now suppose they actually did it! This seems pretty unlikely! Would you think that this was a trick (e.g., cut corners, slightly thicker cards, more than four Aces in the deck!) or was it just a fluke? In other words, was this likely to be a systematic event with a logical explanation or 'cause', or, 'just one of those things', a random coincidence?

The actual probability of drawing an Ace from 52 cards does not reach a probability of 5% or less. We would therefore have to conclude that this is not a 'statistically significant' event. We would retain the null hypothesis of a fair selection and conclude that the event was just a fluke.

But what if this person did the same thing again!! The chance of this (assuming our null hypothesis to be true) is about $.07 \times .07 = .0049$ (or about .005%). In this case, the probability of this event happening twice in a row (just by chance, or by 'fair selection') is pretty remote (about one chance in 200!). We might be better advised to reject the null hypothesis. In effect, we have decided that *this is such an unlikely event that it could not have occurred randomly!!* Hopefully these examples give you a feel for what a .05 or 5% probability is like.

The unconfirmed research hypothesis

But what if the research hypothesis is not confirmed and the null retained? Then either it is false or some error exists in its conception. Some of the previous information may have been erroneous, other relevant information overlooked, the experimental design might have been incorrect. When the researcher discovers what they think is wrong, a new hypothesis is formulated and a different study conducted. This is the continuous ongoing process of the scientific method. Even if a hypothesis is rejected, knowledge is advanced because the result makes us well aware that the particular hunch postulated does not hold.

Testing hypotheses: directions and tails

Hypotheses can be stated in a **NON-DIRECTIONAL** or **DIRECTIONAL** form.

Non-directional hypotheses

These state that one group differs from another on some characteristic, i.e. it does NOT specify the **DIRECTION** of the difference.

Example

H_0 – *'That there is no statistically significant difference between the number of mistakes made by male and female bank tellers'*.

H_1 – *'That there is a statistically significant difference between the number of mistakes made by male and female bank tellers'*.

We are not prejudging whether it is males or females that make the most errors.

Directional hypotheses

These specify the DIRECTION of the difference or deviation from the null value, i.e. that one group is higher, or lower, than another group on some attribute

Example

H_0 – *'That female bank tellers do not make significantly fewer mistakes than male bank tellers'*.
H_1 – *'That female bank tellers make fewer mistakes than male bank tellers'*.

Here we are making a specific directional claim that females make fewer errors and hope our data will support this.

Non-directional hypotheses use two-tailed tests

This is because we do not specify the direction of difference. Tail refers to the ends of the normal distribution.

- Thus the regions of rejection must lie in both tails of the normal distribution because the difference might be one way or the other.
- Assuming an alpha level (significance level) of .05:
  (a) the rejection region to the right is marked by the critical value of +1.96 and contains .025 of the cases;
  (b) that to the left is at −1.96 and also contains .025 of cases.

Directional hypotheses use one-tailed tests

- Assuming an alpha level of .05: the region of rejection is fixed entirely in the predicted tail of the distribution:
  (a) that tail alone must now contain .05 of the cases;
  (b) the critical value now becomes a Z score of +1.65.
- The size of the region of rejection remains the same (.05), but because it lies only in one tail of the distribution, the cut-off is a smaller critical value: 1.65 < 1.96.
- Hence, a one-tailed test offers a better chance to reject your null hypothesis.

> ***Non-directional or two-tailed hypotheses.*** *These do not predict the direction but simply state that there will be a difference; that is the effect of the independent variable may go in either direction.*

> *A **directional** or **one-tailed hypothesis**. This specifies the direction in which the difference lies.*

We will consider with an example the issue of the implications for the probability levels that can be used to assess whether the null hypothesis is rejected or retained in one and two-tailed situations.

Suppose we have a sample of 83 employees who have experienced self-paced learning methods in developing a new trade skill and we want to find out whether this experience has affected their performance in the skill, as assessed by a standard test for assessing that skill. Suppose, further, that we are in the fortunate position of knowing the general performance norms of all employees on that skills test. We hypothesize that the mean score on the skill test for the sample will be significantly different from the population mean value. We decide to test the null hypothesis at the 5% level of significance (i.e. we seek a p equal to or less than .05).

Our basic data are as follows:

Sample size	-83
Mean for population	$= 24$
Mean for sample	$= 25$
Standard deviation for sample	$= 5$

$$\text{Standard error} = \frac{5}{\sqrt{83}} = 0.55$$

We can test the null hypothesis by seeing how many standard errors our observed sample mean value is from the population mean value. The value we obtain for this difference is:

$$Z = \frac{25 - 24}{0.55} = 1.81$$

We know all values that are equal to, or exceed, 1.96 standard errors from the mean have a probability of occurrence by chance of 5% = .05 or less. As our obtained value is 1.81 standard errors from the population mean and this does not reach the significance level necessary, so the null hypothesis is retained. We have no supportive evidence to suggest that our employees are performing significantly differently from the population (see Fig. 10.2).

In the example above we did not say whether the employees' experience of self-paced learning methods is likely to produce an improvement or a deterioration in their skill level compared to the population. Our hypothesis is **non-directional**. But, supposing we have strong grounds for believing that self-paced learning methods will improve performance. In this case, we have a directional hypothesis and can specify the direction in which rejection of the null hypothesis will occur, by actually stating in our null hypothesis '*that self-paced learning will not produce a significantly better performance as measured by….*' This would reflect an alternative hypothesis '*that self-paced learning will produce a significantly better performance as measured by …*'. Instead of taking into account both tails of the probability distribution, we now have to deal with only one – **the top end**.

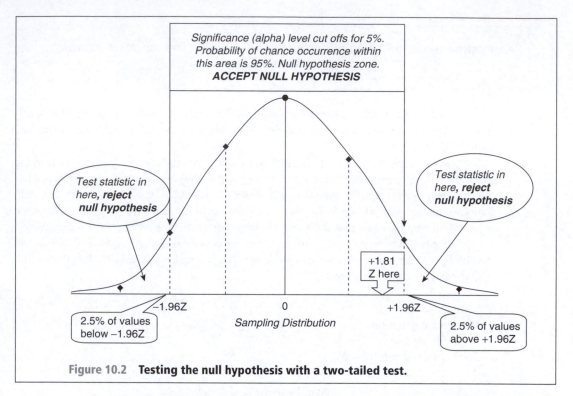

Figure 10.2 **Testing the null hypothesis with a two-tailed test.**

To find out the probabilities for rejection of this one-tailed hypothesis, we mark out the areas in the positive half of the curve equal to probabilities of .05 and .01. These are shown in Figure 10.3.

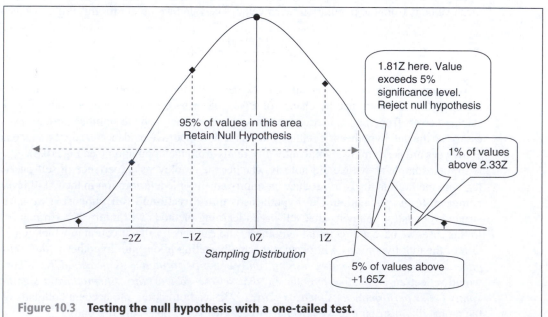

Figure 10.3 **Testing the null hypothesis with a one-tailed test.**

In this case, to reject the null hypothesis at the p < .05 level, we have to find a value that is greater than the population mean value by only 1.65 standard errors. Thus, our directional null hypothesis about the effect of self-paced learning is now strongly supported. In other words, if we can confidently state the direction of a null hypothesis, we do not need such large observed differences to support it at particular significance levels and it becomes 'easier' to accept the alternative hypothesis.

Directional tests should be used with caution because:

* they may allow the rejection of H_0 when the experimental evidence is weak, or
* they may predict in the wrong tail! This has consequences, of not only non-significant findings, but acute embarrassment!

One application in which one-tailed tests are used is in industrial quality control settings. A company making statistical checks on the quality of its products is only interested in whether their product has fallen significantly **below** an acceptable standard. They are not usually interested in whether the product is better than average; this is obviously good, but in terms of legal liabilities and general consumer confidence in their product, they have to watch that their product quality is not worse than it should be.

The size of the critical region for rejection is determined both by the significance level or alpha level chosen and whether we have a directional or non-directional hypothesis. Sample data that fall in the critical region will warrant rejection of the null hypothesis. A summary of the different forms of the hypothesis is located in Table 10.1.

Table 10.1   The relationships between types of hypotheses

Alternative hypothesis	Directional (one-tailed)	Non-directional (two-tailed)
Assessing relationships	The greater the job satisfaction among employees the lower the turnover rate	There is a relationship between job satisfaction and turnover rates
Assessing differences	Male employees report greater job satisfaction levels than female employees	There is difference in the job satisfaction between male and female employees
Null hypothesis	**Directional (one-tailed)**	**Non-directional (two-tailed)**
Assessing relationships	There is not any greater job satisfaction among employees with lower turnover rates	There is no significant relationship between job satisfaction and turnover rates
Assessing differences	Male employees do not report greater job satisfaction levels than female employees	There is no significant difference in job satisfaction between male and female employees

Statistical errors: Type I and Type II

In performing a statistical test you are usually looking for some result such as:

1 A difference between means (as with a t-test or Anova).
2 A difference between proportions (with a chi-square).
3 A relationship (a correlation or regression).

But you can make an error or two.

You might say things are **significantly different when they are not – a Type I error.** You may **miss a significant relationship that really exists – a Type II error.**

What are Type I and Type II errors?

The main aim of statistical testing is to correctly reject a false null hypothesis and correctly retain a true null hypothesis. Since we are accepting some level of error in every study, the possibility that our results are erroneous is directly related to our acceptable level of error. If we set alpha at 0.05 we are saying that we will accept 5% error, which means that if the study were to be conducted 100 times, we would expect significant results in 95 studies, and non-significant results in 5 studies. How do we then know that our study doesn't fall in the 5% error category? We don't. Only through replication can we get a better idea of this.

There are two types of error that researchers are concerned with: **Type I** and **Type II**. (Fig. 10.4).

- A **Type I** error occurs when the results of research show that a significant difference exists but in reality there is no difference. This is directly related to alpha in that alpha was likely set too high and therefore lowering the amount of acceptable error would reduce the chances of a Type I error, i.e. lower alpha from 5% to 1%. Type I errors are determined by the alpha level and are therefore under the investigator's control.
- Lowering the amount of acceptable error to 1%, however, increases the chances of a **Type II** error, which is the retention of the null hypothesis when in fact it should be rejected. In other words, the greater the chances of a Type I error, the less likely a Type II error, and vice versa.

I hope you can detect an analogy between gambling and hypothesis testing. By setting a particular significance level, the researcher is gambling that chance results can be distinguished from genuine ones. If the level is set too high, i.e. a very low probability value, then it may be decided that a difference is a chance result when it is in fact a genuine one. If it is set too low, we may be in danger of accepting a result which is really a chance effect.

The selection of a particular level of significance should be made before the data is analysed, just as anyone who bets on the horses must do so before the race is run. You can't go and place your bet after the race. If we go around manipulating the result after the event to suit our wishful thinking, then there is no reason to gather the data in the first place, and we might just as well believe anything we want to believe.

> **Type I error.** *Rejecting the null when it is true. The probability of rejecting a **true null hypothesis** is equal to the alpha level (significance level).*
> **Type II error.** *The probability of accepting the null hypothesis when it is false.*

Interaction of directional tests and Type I and Type II errors

It should be clear from the above that stating a null hypothesis in a directional form – a one-tailed test – loads the dice in favour of its rejection, i.e. we accept the alternative hypothesis on terms that are less rigorous, a Type I error. Can you see why? Most researchers commendably opt for caution by keeping the null hypothesis non-directional and consequently using a two-tailed significance test. Sometimes this caution may not be as admirable as it seems, for if we set the significance level or α (alpha) at too rigorous a level, say $p < .001$, in a non-directional test, there is the danger we will retain a null hypothesis when it is false and reject the alternative hypothesis when it is in fact true. **This is a Type II error**.

Effects on business decisions

Of course, we don't want to accept null hypotheses when they are false! This Type II error can be costly for business as it can lead to uninterrupted production at a time when the machinery needs adjustment; or the continued use of a supplier whose performance is unsatisfactory; or a government agency to take no action against a company polluting the local river.

On the other hand, by using a 5% level we make it easier to reject a false null hypothesis but at the same time increase the chances of showing erroneous support for a false alternative hypothesis – **the Type I error**. The rejection of a true null hypothesis can be costly in business. It may lead to the interruption of production to adjust a machine that needs no adjustment or switch to a new supplier when the performance of the old one was actually satisfactory; it may lead to a government agency condemning a company for violating pollution standards when it has not done so.

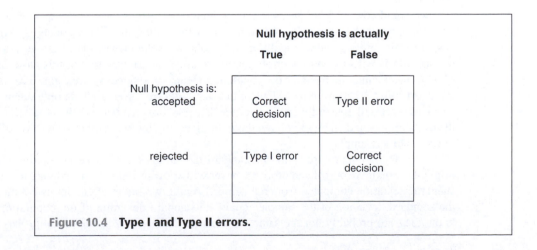

Figure 10.4   Type I and Type II errors.

Point and confidence interval estimation

Hypothesis testing is certainly the major way of determining whether a particular sample mean is significantly different or not from the population parameter. Newspapers often carry headlines like, '60% *of the general public approves this year's budget*' or '71% *of government employees approve of the no smoking rule in the workplace*'. Clearly, these percentages are obtained from samples; not everyone was asked, but the sample statistic is being used as an estimate of the population parameter. We will now examine the procedures used to estimate the true population mean and the true population proportion. There are two major types of estimates: **point estimates and interval estimates**.

Point estimates

A point estimate consists of a single sample statistic that is used to estimate the true population parameter. For example, the average time workers take to complete a given task is estimated at 32 minutes; a product's market share is estimated at 70%. Although in practice only one sample is chosen, we know for example that the average value of all sample means is the population mean. We also know that the sample mean varies from sample to sample.

Suppose we draw a random sample of 100 customers from a population of 1,000. We compute the mean and the standard deviation from an attitude scale towards banning the sale of wine in supermarkets and find these statistics to be M = 110: SD = 10. An important question we must now ask ourselves is 'how well does this mean provide a valid indicator of what the population of our customers think?'

Or, if we were to draw a large number of random samples of 100 customers from this same population, would the means of these samples be 110, below or above 110, and, if they are near 110, how near? What we do, in effect, is to set up **a hypothetical distribution** of sample means, all computed from samples of 100 customers, each drawn from the parent population.

If we could compute the means of this population of means, or if we knew what it was, everything would be simple. But we do not know this value, and we are not able to know it since the possibilities of drawing different samples are so numerous. The best we can do is to **estimate it with the only sample mean we** *have*. We simply say, in this case, let the sample mean equal the mean of the population mean – and hope we are right! **This is our point estimate**. Then we must calculate the standard error around our sample mean. This standard error will give us the measure of the dispersal or spread of sample means if we had the time, money and energy to obtain them. In fact using the standard error we do not need to take another sample.

A similar argument applies to the standard deviation of the whole population (of the original scores). We do not and probably never will know it. But we can estimate it with the standard deviation computed from our sample. Again, we say in effect, let us assume that the standard deviation of the sample equals the standard deviation of the population. We know they are probably not the same value, but we also know, if the sampling has been random, that they are probably close. This is why the SE_M formula employs the standard deviation of the sample and not that of the unknown population.

> **A point estimate.** A single statistic used as the estimate of the population parameter.

So when a random sample is selected, its mean provides a **point estimate** that is a single value estimate of the population mean, and a SD of a sample can be a point estimate of the population σ. The best bet is to estimate that the sample statistic, say the mean, is located in the exact centre of its sampling distribution, and therefore gives a perfect estimation of the population mean. In other words we take the sample statistic to be the same value as the population parameter as it is the only mean we possess – the best we have.

Interval estimates

Because point estimates are not accurate, we also need an estimate derived from the knowledge of the variability of sample means through the concept of sample error. This will estimate what the range of values is within which the population mean likely lies. The interval we construct has a specified confidence or probability of correctly estimating the true value of the population mean. Similar **interval estimates** can be derived for the true population proportion. Thus, with varying degrees of confidence, we can state that with 95% confidence a product's market share lies between 66% and 74% or with 80% confidence it lies within 68% to 72%.

In hypothesis testing you have seen that we focus on values that equal or exceed a chosen significance level or alpha. We tend to emphasize the critical rejection areas and considered the middle 95% of the area of the normal distribution with some disdain. Essentially what happens in this middle ground is 'normal' and 'expected', whereas we are always hoping to find the 'abnormal' and the 'very different' in the tails of the distribution when we undertake research. In estimation, we have a different perspective to that taken generally when we are testing hypotheses. Our perspective in estimation is to home in on the area *between* the significance level criterion points. We are looking at this area as a confidence area bounded by the conventional significance levels which now become the boundaries of the confidence interval. We know that the area within which 95% of all sample means fall is bounded by the 5% significance levels, one on each side of the distribution. We call this range logically the 95% confidence interval, and similarly we know that 99% of sample means fall within the range of the 1% significance levels, thereby defining the 99% confidence interval. SPSS provides the 95% confidence intervals (values of both upper and lower boundaries) of any chosen interval variable on its 'Descriptives >> Explore' menu.

The confidence interval can be interpreted in two different ways. Firstly, when we state that we are 95% confident that the population mean hourly wage is between $24 and $25 we are not saying that there is a 95% probability that the population mean lies between $24 and $25. The 95% is in fact our level of confidence that the population mean is within that interval, not to the level of probability that it is with that range. If we consider the situation carefully, the probability that the population mean is within that that range is either 1 or 0, i.e. either it is or it isn't.

The second interpretation is based on the realization that many different sample sizes can be taken. Each different sample size will produce a slightly different interval range; for example, $24.2 to $24.98, rather than our original $24–$25. Thus the second interpretation states that if all possible confidence intervals are constructed, 95% of them will contain the unknown parameter. In other words, a 95% confidence interval estimate implies that if all possible samples of the same size were taken, 95% of them would include the true population mean somewhere within the interval. With our usual single sample we can say that we have 95% confidence that we have selected a sample whose 95% interval does include the population mean. If we want to be more confident we can use the 99% interval. There is thus a trade-off between the level of confidence and the width of the confidence interval. Increasing confidence can only be achieved by widening the confidence interval, but of course this makes the estimate less precise.

> **Confidence interval.** *The range within which we believe the true population estimate to lie.*

> **Confidence level.** *The probability that the population parameter falls within the confidence interval.*

For the interval estimate your best bet is to predict that the sample statistic, say the mean, is in the middle of its sampling distribution, i.e. make a point estimate, and then by marking off the chosen significance level equidistant on each side of the point estimate, we can estimate that the population mean also lies within that confidence interval (Fig. 10.5).

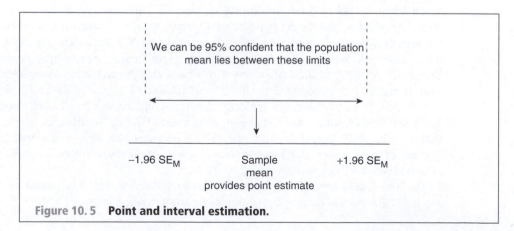

Figure 10.5 **Point and interval estimation.**

Example 1

Suppose that as part of a postal questionnaire survey of Internet use, 435 Internet users are asked to supply details about the length of time they have had wireless connections. Could we confidently expect identical answers from other similar sized samples of householders? From our sample of 435 households, the average length of time wireless Internet has been installed is five years and that the standard deviation is one year (52 weeks). The standard error of the mean in this case will be:

$$SE_M = \frac{52}{\sqrt{435}} = \frac{52}{20.8} = 2.5 \, \text{weeks}$$

For a large number of samples of the same size taken from the same population, approximately 68.26% (two out of every three) of the sample means would be expected to lie within one standard error of the true population mean. However, we have one sample with one sample mean. So, we turn things around and say that, in our example, there is a probability of approximately 2/3 (two in three) that the true figure for the whole population of those with wireless connections in their homes will lie within the range five years ± 2.5 weeks. Further, we are 95% confident that the true mean will lie within 1.96 standard errors of the sample mean (i.e. five years ± five weeks) and 99% confident that it will lie within three standard errors (i.e. five years ± 7.5 weeks). This is the measure of the confidence which can be placed in the accuracy of the sample mean as being true for the whole population from which the sample has been drawn.

Example 2

Imagine the balances of a random sample of 256 accounts have a sample mean of $1,075 and a sample standard deviation of $650. This sample mean can provide a point estimate of the mean balance of all accounts with the bank, i.e. the population mean bank account balance can be estimated as $1,075. The standard error of the mean is:

$$\frac{650}{\sqrt{256}} = \$40.62$$

As this is a large sample we can use the Z distribution and the upper and lower limits of the 95% confidence interval for the population mean is:

$$\$1,075 \pm (1.96 \times 40.62) = \$1,154.61 \text{ to } \$995.39$$

By widening the interval to the .01 level ($1,179.78 to $970.22) we could be almost certain that the population mean would lie within it. Although this latter set of limits increases our confidence that the population mean lies within it, the price paid is a loss of precision in the interval estimate as the interval is larger.

Estimating a proportion

So far we have been concerned with sample means. However, a great deal of sampling in the business world is concerned with the proportion or percentage of a given population possessing particular characteristics, making certain choices, having certain preferences or holding particular opinions, e.g. what proportion of the 20–30 year age group drink coffee rather than tea. The standard error of the sample proportion is

$$SE_p = \sqrt{\frac{pq}{N}}$$

The sample proportion gives a point estimate of the population proportion. To obtain the 95% confidence interval which has limits at ± 1.96 we calculate that the population mean likely lies between +1.96 SE_p and –1.96 SE_p.

Example 1

Our survey of wireless Internet use reveals that 70% have VOIP facility and that 30% do not. What is the estimate for the population of Internet users?

The standard error of a proportion (SE_p) is obtained by means of the formula:

$$SE_p = \sqrt{\frac{pq}{N}}$$

where p represents the proportion of the sample possessing the characteristic in question, q the proportion that does not, and N is the sample size. In this example:

$$SE_p = \frac{0.7(0.30)}{\sqrt{435}} = 0.0219 = 2.19\%$$

While a proportion is expressed as a fraction between 0 and 1, market researchers prefer to work in percentages and convert the standard error of the proportion to its equivalent percentage by multiplying the standard error by 100 as above.

We can therefore say that we can be 95% certain that the proportion for the population as a whole will be within the limits 70% plus or minus 1.96(2.19) or between 65.71% and 74.29%. There are two characteristics of a confidence interval that should be noted.

- To gain more confidence in your estimate you must increase the width. Conversely, to have a smaller width you must give up confidence. This is the basic trade-off between confidence and precision.
- If you have a bigger sample size, you have more information about the population, and this allows you to make a more precise estimate (and use a narrower interval).

By now, you should be able to see how the standard error helps. Essentially, it tells us how closely the result we get from a sample reflects the true result for the whole population from which the sample is drawn, and it establishes the limits within which we can be confident in the sample result. But we are also now aware that the size of sample also affects the size of the standard error and by implication the degree of confidence we can place in the estimate of the population parameter.

What you have learned in this chapter

You are now aware that a hypothesis is a conjecture put forward to explain an observation, but in order to be tested and disproved it must be stated in an operational form. Hypothesis testing is an inferential procedure for using the limited data from a sample to draw a general conclusion about a population. You are deciding whether:

(a) the differences or relationships arise purely by chance or, whether
(b) the differences or relationships are so great as to be unlikely chance differences and are real.

You learnt to distinguish these two mutually exclusive options as the null hypothesis and the alternative or research hypothesis. We set a level of significance that creates a critical level to distinguish chance from a statistically significant effect, usually at .05 (5% level) or .01 (1% level). Sample data that fall beyond the critical point in the critical region in the tails of the distribution imply that the effect is unlikely due to chance as it is a rare event on a chance basis. Consequently we assume that the effect is real and therefore the null hypothesis cannot be retained, and the alternative hypothesis is therefore supported. If the sample data do not fall at or beyond the chosen significance level then we retain the null hypothesis.

You cannot avoid Type I and Type II errors. There is always a probability of making a mistake by rejecting the null hypothesis when it is in fact true. This is a Type I error equal to the level of significance applied. You can reduce the Type I error by being conservative and reducing the significance level say to 1% or even .1%. However, this would result in Type II error, where a null hypothesis would be accepted when it is in fact incorrect. This is why we recommend 5% and 1% as reasonable balance points between the two errors.

Directional tests (one-tailed tests) may be used when the researcher predicts that a treatment effect will be in a particular direction. Directional tests should be used with caution as they may allow the rejection of the null hypothesis when experimental evidence is weak (Type I error).

We can also use sample data to estimate a population parameter. The estimate can be either a point (single value) estimate or an interval estimate. Point estimates are precise but don't provide much confidence. Interval estimates are less precise but provide greater confidence. The width of the confidence interval is an indication of the precision.

Review questions and activities

Qu. 10.1
As more practice in operationalizing variables, in class discuss possible operational definitions for the terms 'popular supervisor', 'employee morale', 'personal relationships', 'anxiety', 'low productivity', 'successful salesperson', 'reliable worker'.

Qu. 10.2
Which of the following hypotheses is a relationship type and which a difference type? Then in groups write some more examples of both types of hypotheses.

(a) that production managers and shop floor workers differ in job satisfaction levels;
(b) that there is a relationship between stress levels and number of days work absence among police officers.

Qu. 10.3
In class groups explain what is wrong with these hypotheses. How would you improve them?

(a) Some types of employees always tend to be late to work whereas others are good timekeepers.
(b) The relationship between economic downturns and social unrest is strong in some countries.

Qu. 10.4
Explain to others in your group why the critical region for rejection differs between directional and non-directional tests.

Qu. 10.5
Within your class groups explain the relationship between directional/non-directional tests and types of error.

Qu. 10.6
An international car rental agency knows from a sample of 225 of its 5,000 cars that the mean km per litre is 10 and that the SD is 1.5. The agency wants to determine the 95% confidence interval for mean km per litre of all its cars.

Check your answer in the Web page for this chapter.

Qu. 10.7
A random sample survey of 1,000 motorists who purchased a brand new Fotoykya car six months ago found that 18% of them had been back to their garage for a repair during the previous three months. What is the standard error of this proportion?

Check your answer in the Web page.

Qu. 10.8
A new product is tested on a random sample of 90. A total of 63 say they will buy the new product. A point estimate of the population proportion who will buy the product is 63/90 or .7 (70%). What is the standard error of the proportion? What are the 95% confidence limits?

Check your answer on the Web page.

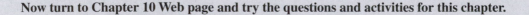

Now turn to Chapter 10 Web page and try the questions and activities for this chapter.

Chapter 11
Effect Size and Power

'Statistics is the art of never having to say you are certain'

(Source unknown)

Content list

By the end of this chapter you will be able to:

1   Understand why statistical power and effect size have become important when interpreting results.
2   Understand how power relates to significance level, sample size and effect size.
3   Calculate statistical power and effect size.
4   Estimate sample sizes needed to achieve desired levels of power and effect size.

Introduction
This chapter reveals another approach to interpreting statistical results. Many researchers have become concerned that probability and significance levels are not the full picture when interpreting statistical results. Effect size in particular is now promoted as a more powerful way of indicating the effect of treatments. This chapter will, therefore, move away from the probability approach and introduce these other procedures.

Why are effect size and power important?

So far we have focused on the concept of statistical significance and probability values as the crucial elements in interpreting results. However, they can lead to misleading interpretations for a number of reasons:

1 Chance sampling variations can make it appear that a worthless treatment really worked and the importance of minor findings are inflated in the investigator's mind if they hit the 'magic' threshold significance figure of .05.

2 Conversely, important information may be overlooked in studies that just fall short of statistical significance. It is almost as if a study that does not quite reach a pre-stated significance level is worthless, and most of these never get published with interesting findings which could be the basis of further investigation lost for ever. Thus, focusing too heavily on a single significance figure as a draconian cut-off between what is acceptable and what is not has a major effect on the development of cumulative knowledge.

3 Dividing research findings into two categories – significant and not significant – is a gross oversimplification, since probability is a continuous scale. A rich data set reduced to a binary accept-reject statement may lead to false conclusions due to naturally occurring sampling error, even when using appropriate sampling methods in a rigorous way.

A vital yet often ignored question in statistical analysis is – are my findings of any real substance. We are usually asking one of three things:

- Is this a theoretically important issue?; or
- Is this issue one of business, economic, political or social relevance?; or
- Will the results of this study actually help people?

While statistics can help to quantify the strength of the findings of the research, none of these questions are essentially statistical. This is due to the word '*significance*' possessing a different meaning within statistics from that in normal daily use. This leads us to believe that even in a statistical context it also has the same implications as the normal sense. Statistical significance means no more than you can be confident that your results are unlikely to be a random variation in samples (sampling error) but signify differences and relationships which rarely occur by chance, with the implication that the findings reflect real differences and relationships.

But a statistically significant result can have **little significance** whatsoever in the everyday sense. If we focus too much on statistical significance it can blind us to the dangers of exaggerating the importance of our findings.

Investigators now realize that there is more to the story of a research result than '$p < .05$'; more than simply avoiding Type I errors, without considering how to avoid Type II errors. This chapter helps you become a little more sophisticated about other ways of interpreting research results. This sophistication means learning a little about the relationships between power, effect size, and types of error.

Type I and Type II errors (again!)

You met these types of error in Chapter 10. They are concerned with how conclusions from hypothesis testing can be incorrect. Error as a statistical concept is *not* about making mistakes. It is about how, even when we do everything properly, we can still be led to the wrong conclusion. The purpose of a hypothesis test is to determine whether or not a particular treatment or condition of a sample has an effect in making it significantly different from another sample. The null hypothesis states that there is no significant effect and the researcher is hoping that the sample data will provide evidence to reject this hypothesis. The hypothesis testing procedure always involves some risk in reaching a wrong conclusion. Let us revise your understanding of Type I and Type II errors as they are vital to understanding why our conclusions about our results can be wrong.

Type I error (or α)

Suppose you conducted a study and set the significance level cut-off at say 5% or p = .05. If you conducted many studies like this, you would often (about 5% of the time) believe you had support for the research hypothesis when you did not. This is a **Type I error**. Type I errors are of serious concern to business persons and social scientists, who might construct entire new production programmes, personnel selection procedures, advertising campaigns, etc. based on a conclusion from hypothesis testing that is in fact mistaken.

Since researchers cannot tell when they have made a Type I error, what they can do is try to ensure the chance of making a Type I error is as small as possible. What is the chance of making a Type I error? It is the same as the significance level or alpha we set. If we set the significance level at $p < .05$, we are saying we will reject the null hypothesis if there is less than a 5% (.05) chance that we could have obtained our result if the null hypothesis were true. When rejecting the null hypothesis in this way, we are still allowing up to 5% chance that the null hypothesis is actually true. That is, we are allowing a 5% chance of a Type I error. The problem is that we never know when our seemingly 'significant' result is simply due to sampling error. Because of this, and the fact that the significance level is the same as the chance of making a Type I error, the lower we set the significance level, the smaller the chance of a Type I error. Researchers who do not want to take a lot of risk set the significance level much lower than .05, such as $p < .01$ or $p < .001$. In this way the result of a study would have to be more extreme to lead to a conclusion to reject the null hypothesis.

Using a significance level like $p < .001$ is like buying insurance against making a Type I error. However, as when buying insurance, the better the protection, the higher the cost. What is the cost in setting the significance level at too extreme a level? It is the Type II error!

Type II error (or β)

If you set a very stringent significance level, such as .001, there is a different kind of risk. You may conduct a study in which in reality the alternative hypothesis is true, but the result does not come out extreme enough to reject the null hypothesis. Thus, you make the error of not rejecting the null hypothesis when in reality the null hypothesis is false (the research hypothesis is true). This is the **Type II error** or **beta**. A Type II error means that the treatment really does have an effect but the hypothesis test failed to discover it because the significance level was too stringent.

Type II errors especially concern those interested in practical applications, as in business, because a Type II error could mean that a useful practical procedure is not implemented. As with a Type I error, we never know when we have made a Type II error; however we can try to conduct our studies so as to reduce the probability of making a Type II error. One way of buying insurance against a Type II error is to set a more lenient significance level, such as $p < .05$. In this way, even if a study results in only a small difference, the results have a good chance of being significant. There is a cost to this insurance policy too – a Type I error. The trade-off between these two conflicting concerns usually is resolved by compromise, hence use either of the standard 5% and 1% significance levels.

More and more researchers are recognizing now that the rigid significance cut-off and the TypeI II errors can be avoided if we change our perspective from hypothesis testing to ways of measuring whether the treatment has had an effect. For this we need to look at effect sizes.

Effect size

What a statistically significant t-test or p does *not* tell us is how large an effect the independent variable had. Measures of effect size are used to determine the strength of the relationship between the independent and dependent variables. Measures of effect size reflect how large the effect of an independent variable was.

We also need something other than an inferential statistics test to measure the size of the effect of an independent variable. What is needed to measure effect size is an indicator that reflects the strength of the relationship between the independent and the dependent variables that is **independent of sample size**. Several measures have been proposed and used.

Measures for estimating effect size

The more frequent effect size measures are:

- the standardized mean difference (d);
- correlation coefficients such as r and phi (Chapter 15); and
- eta^2. This is a type of correlation known as the correlation ratio. It is used for determining the strength of association when there is a curvilinear rather than a linear relationship. For non-linear relationships in which the correlation is not equal to zero, eta^2 squared fits the points by a curved line.

We will consider each in more detail.

Standardized mean difference for two groups (usually experimental and control)

The commonly used measure of effect size is *d*. It is a ratio that measures the difference between the means of the levels of the independent variable relative to the within-group standard deviation. There are several alternative but mathematically equivalent formulae for computing *d*, depending on the original statistic calculated for the significance test. The most common two for the independent t test (Chapter 12) are:

$$d = \frac{M_{experimental} - M_{control}}{\text{pooled within group SD}} \quad \text{or } d = t\sqrt{\frac{N_1 + N_2}{N_1 N_2}}$$

$$\text{The pooled within groups sd} = \sqrt{\frac{(N_1 - 1)SD_1^2 + (N_2 - 1)SD_2^2}{N_1 + N_2 - 2}}$$

Instead of pooling the SD many researchers simply assume that the SD being the population SD is the same for both groups and therefore use the population SD as the denominator.

For the paired or related groups design test (Chapter 12):

$$d = \frac{\text{Mean of the differences between occasion}}{\text{SD of the differences}}$$

As you already know, the standard deviation tells us approximately how far, on the average, scores vary from a group mean – it is a measure of the 'dispersal' of scores around a mean and, in the case of the within-group standard deviation, tells us about the degree of 'error' due to individual differences (i.e. how individuals vary in their responses). The standard deviation serves as a useful measure by which we can assess a difference between means. The 'size' of the effect of the independent variable is always in terms of the average dispersal of scores occurring in an experiment. If there is a lot of within-group variability (i.e. the within-group standard deviation is large) then the difference between two means must be greater to produce the same effect size than when there is little within-group variability (i.e. the standard deviation is small). Because effect sizes are presented in standard deviation units, they can be used to make meaningful comparisons of effect sizes across experiments using different dependent variables (e.g. in meta-analysis – extension Chapter 22).

> *Effect size.* A measure of the effect of the independent variable.

Cohen's effect size conventions

Cohen (1992) has come up with some effect size conventions based on the effects observed in many actual studies. These recommended conventions at least tell us what to consider as small, medium, and large effects.

- A small effect size: d = .2 implies the populations of individuals overlap by about 85%. This small effect size of .2 is, for example, the difference in height between 15- and 16-year-old girls, which is about a ½-inch difference with a standard deviation of about 2.1 inches.
- A medium effect size: d = .5, means an overlap of about 67%. This is about the difference in heights between 14- and 18-year-old girls.
- A large effect size: d = .8. This is only about 53% overlap. It is about the difference in height between 13- and 18-year-old girls.

Assume two population means are 208 and 200 respectively, providing a difference between means of 8 and the standard deviation of the populations of individuals is 24. Thus, the effect size is:

$$d = \frac{\text{Population M}_1 - \text{Population M}_2}{\text{Population SD}} \quad \frac{208 - 200}{48} = \frac{8}{24} = 0.33$$

If the mean difference had been doubled at 16 points and the population standard deviation was still 24, the effect size is doubled: 16/24, or .66. By dividing the difference between means by the standard deviation of the population of individuals, we standardize the difference between means in the same way that a Z score gives a standard for comparison to other scores, even scores on different scales.

As another example, most IQ tests have a standard deviation of 15 points. An experimental training procedure on how to tackle IQ tests that increased performance by 3 IQ points has a small effect size, since a difference of 3.0 IQ points between the mean of the population who go through the experimental procedure and the population that does not, divided by the population standard deviation of 15 produces d = .2. An experimental procedure would have to increase IQ by 8 points for a medium effect size, and by 12 for a large effect size.

We are only concerned with one population's SD, because in hypothesis testing we usually assume that both populations have the same or similar standard deviation, i.e. the concept of homogeneity of variance – evaluated by Levine's test on the SPSS printout for the Independent Groups test (Chapter 12) and ANOVA (Chapter 13).

Correlation coefficient method: r as an effect size

The Pearson product-moment correlation coefficient (Chap. 15) for the two groups or 'r' is an effect size in itself, and if this is not reported, it can be computed quite easily for most other statistical tests basically by turning the statistic into a correlation. Once this is done, it makes it easy to assess the size of the effect.

For a t test

$$r = \sqrt{\frac{t^2}{t^2 + df}} \quad \text{or}$$

$r = \dfrac{Z}{\sqrt{N}}$ where Z is the value of the reported p value and N is the sample size.

We can also turn a d into an r and vice versa :

The relation between r and d is: $r = \dfrac{d}{\sqrt{\dfrac{d^2 + 1}{pq}}}$

where p is the proportion of cases in the first group and q = 1 – p.

Again we use the same conventional interpretation of effect size levels so that when r = 0, there is no difference between the two groups; if near ± .2 is small; near ± .5 is medium; while near ± .8 is large. Large effect sizes obtained under natural (less controlled) situations are more impressive than under strictly controlled situations.

The chi square statistic (Chapter 14)

A two-by-two chi square (see page 338) can be turned into a correlation using r_{phi} in the following formula. r_{phi} is the Pearson r for frequency scores:

$$r_{phi} = \sqrt{\frac{\text{chi square}}{N}} \quad \text{where N is the number of subjects}$$

The result can be interpreted as though a correlation. It is always positive as chi square is always positive. If your chi square is larger than two-by-two then you can use the contingency coefficient instead. Here the formula is:

$$\text{contingency coefficient} = \sqrt{\frac{\text{chi square}}{\text{chi square} + N}}$$

It is feasible to interpret the contingency coefficient as though it were r although they are not exactly parallel.

Eta²

To compute the effect size for analysis of variance (ANOVA – Chapter 13), a correlation measure termed eta² is employed. This is analogous to a correlation but describes a curvilinear relationship rather than a linear one. It is used with the various forms of ANOVA because it is difficult to ascertain which of the independent variables is explaining the most variance.

To calculate eta² for any of the independent variables in an ANOVA the following formula is used, although SPSS provides this eta² statistic in the printout:

$$\text{eta}^2 = \frac{(\text{between groups } df)(\text{F ratio})}{(\text{between groups } df)(\text{F ratio}) + \text{within groups } df}$$

Importance of effect size

• Measures of effect size can be used to summarize a series of experiments that have included the same independent variable and dependent variable (see Chapter 22 on meta-analysis). This allows for a quantitative comparison of the outcomes across the series of experiments. For example, effect size can be used to find out whether a particular independent variable consistently had about the same amount of impact across the experiments, irrespective of sample sizes, different means and variances. This comparison is especially important in applied research examining the effectiveness of treatments, such as new training programmes or new sales techniques.

• Measures of effect size provide information about the *amount* of impact an independent variable has had. Thus, they complement tests of statistical significance, which give only an indication of the presence or absence of an effect of an independent variable. In this way, we can use measures of effect size to rank several independent variables within the same experiment as one indication of the relative importance of the independent variables. Within a particular study, our general knowledge of what is a small or a large effect size helps us evaluate the overall importance of a result. For example, a result may be significant but not possess a large effect size; or a result that is not significant (perhaps due to a small sample) may have just as large an effect size as was found in another study (perhaps one with a larger sample) in which the result was significant.

• Measures of effect size help us calculate the sample size needed for a study with a particular level of power.

An important development in statistics in recent years is a procedure called **meta-analysis** (extension Chapter 22). This is a procedure that combines results from different studies, even results using different methods of measurement, to draw general conclusions. **When combining results, the crucial thing being combined is the effect sizes**. As an example, a social psychologist might be interested in the effects of ethnically mixed workplaces on racial prejudice, a topic on which there has been a large number of surveys. Using meta-analysis, they could combine the results of these surveys. This would provide an overall effect size. It also could tell how effect size differs for studies done in different employment contexts in different countries or about varying prejudice levels towards different ethnic groups in the workplace.

None of the important questions addressed using effect size can be answered using the traditional inferential statistics procedures of significance levels and p values. Nonetheless, measures of effect size and inferential statistics tests are complementary and many studies are now quoting both. Measures of effect size are more informative than are p values in helping researchers determine the substantive importance of experimental outcomes. At times, we want to know just how much of an 'effect' our treatment had, not just whether it reached a conventionally acceptable level of significance. Knowing the answer in terms of effect size may help us decide whether to actually implement this treatment in an applied setting. For example, the original work by Smith *et al.* (1980) on psychotherapy outcome studies found an average effect size of r = 0.32. For those unaware of the meaning of effect size, the finding was viewed as confirmation of the failure of psychotherapy. However, an effect size of this magnitude is equivalent to increasing the success rate from chance to 66%, an effect that is quite large and of course for those undergoing therapy quite important. Table 11.1 provides increases in success rates for corresponding values of effect size 'r'.

Here is another example to show why one should not to discount small effect sizes. Consider the fact that studies have indicated there is a small positive effect of taking exercise to try to prevent stress related illness. Considering the large number of people who are at risk for stress related illness, the small positive effect of taking exercise could still have a beneficial impact on millions of people. In terms of the potential numbers of people who could benefit, a small beneficial effect of taking exercise would not be a small effect at all (particularly in a practical sense of medical fees and costs).

Importance of effect size in evaluating the results of a study

The message here is that, in evaluating a study, you must consider first whether the result is statistically significant. If it is, and if the study has any potential practical implications, you must then *also* consider whether the effect size is sufficiently large to make the result

Table 11.1 **Success rate increases corresponding to 'r'**

| Effect size 'r' | Success rate increased | |
	From	To
0.10	45%	55%
0.20	40%	60%
0.30	35%	65%
0.40	30%	70%
0.50	25%	75%
0.60	20%	80%
0.70	15%	85%
0.80	10%	90%
0.90	5%	95%
1.00	0%	100%

Based on Rosenthal and Rubin (1982) *Journal of Educational Psychology,* 74: 168.

useful or interesting. If the sample was small, you can assume that a significant result is probably also practically significant. If the sample size is very large, you must consider the effect size directly, as it is quite possible in such a case that the effect is too small to be useful.

Note that the implications are a bit of a paradox in light of what most people believe about sample size. Most people assume that the more people in the study, the more important the result. In a sense, just the reverse is the case. All other things being equal, if a study with only a few people manages to be significant, that significance must be due to a large effect size. A study with a large number of people in it that is statistically significant may or may not have a large effect size.

Power of a statistical test

Another aspect that inferential statistics fails to consider is the probability for reaching the correct decision, rather than examining the potential for making an error as we do with p values.

Inferential statistics are designed to help you determine the validity of the null hypothesis. Consequently, you want your statistics to detect differences in your data that are inconsistent with the null hypothesis. **The power of a statistical test is its ability to detect these differences if the research hypothesis is true**. Put in statistical terms, power is a statistic's ability to correctly reject the null hypothesis when it is false. That is minimizing Type I error. (If the research hypothesis is false, we certainly do not want significant results – that would be a Type I error). Up to now little concern has been given by researchers to the concept of power, or reducing Type II errors where we fail to reject the null hypothesis when in fact the null hypothesis is incorrect, which can occur if we set a too rigorous p value like .001.

> *Statistical power. The probability that the test will correctly reject a false null hypothesis.*

However, the issue of the power of your statistical test is an important one. Rejection of the null hypothesis implies that your independent variable affected your dependent variable. Failure to reject the null hypothesis may lead you to abandon a potentially fruitful line of investigation. Consequently, you want to be reasonably sure your failure to reject the null hypothesis is not caused by a lack of power in your statistical test. The more powerful a statistical test the more readily it will detect a treatment effect when one really exists (correctly rejecting the null hypothesis).

Now you may ask, 'If the research hypothesis is true in reality won't the experiment necessarily give a significant result?' Unfortunately no, because the effect of the independent variable on the particular representative sample that happens to be selected from the population may not be large enough to reject the null hypothesis. It might well be more effective on another random sample; this variation in effect is due to sampling error. Because we only usually conduct a study once and accept the result as common for all similar samples, we are blithely unaware of the true state of affairs. This is why meta-analysis (Chapter 22) is becoming so important, as this technique enables us to combine many replications of the same study, some successful and others unsuccessful in refuting the null hypothesis, to find the overall general effect or trend. **The power of a statistical test is the probability of making a correct rejection of the null hypothesis when it is false**.

The concept of power and Type II error (or β) are closely related, since the test can either correctly detect the presence of the treatment effect or it can fail to do so. Thus the probability of correctly rejecting a false null hypothesis must be 1 – β.

> *Statistical power* = 1 – β.

Although we have defined power we have not attempted to compute a value for this probability. The difficulty stems from the fact that power depends both on the size of the treatment effect and sample size. When there is a large effect, i.e. little overlap between the group data distributions, power will be high. Two distributions might have little overlap either because there is a large difference between their means or because they have so little variance (SD²) that even with a small mean difference they do not overlap much.

The extent to which the two populations do not overlap is **the effect size**, because it is the extent to which the experimental manipulation has an effect of separating the two populations. That is, the larger the difference between the two population means, the greater the effect size; the smaller the variance within the two populations, the greater the effect size. The greater the effect size, the greater the power. In any study, the bigger the difference we obtain between the means of the two populations, the more power in the study. Thus there are different values of power associated with different magnitudes of treatment effect size. But there are also other factors that influence power.

Factors that influence power (other than effect size which has been considered above as a special topic)

Increasing sample size

The other major influence on power, besides effect size, is sample size. Basically, the bigger the sample, the more power. There are two reasons for this.

1   Sample size influences power because the larger the sample size, the smaller the standard deviation of the distribution of means. If the distributions have a smaller standard deviation, they are narrower and thus there is less overlap between them. If our two samples in an independent group t test were 200 strong each the power moves up to 95% from 84% if only 100 were in each group. With 500 participants in each group power is 99%. In most practical cases, sample size is the main way to

modify a study to bring it up to sufficient power. However, there is always a limit to what you can handle in terms of time and cost as well as the availability of more subjects.

2   Secondly, the power of your statistical test increases with the size of your sample because larger samples provide more stable estimates of population parameters. In particular, the standard error of the means from your treatments will be lower, so the likely population means fall within narrower confidence limits. Consequently it is easier to detect small differences in population means and thus to reject the null hypothesis when it is false.

Sample size provides a major problem with correlation (Chapter 15). Even a small correlation can be statistically significant given a large enough sample. A correlation of .81 is needed to be statistically significant at the 5% level with a sample size of 6. However, a sample size of 100 requires only a correlation of .20 to be statistically significant at the 5% level. The squared correlation coefficient (the coefficient of determination) indicates the proportion of the total variance shared by two variables (see p. 348). If the correlation is only .20 then $r^2 = .04$, i.e. the two variables only have 4% of their variance in common. This is negligible, yet in a statistical sense is significant, because of the large sample from which it was derived. Thus the coefficient of determination is often a more useful indication of the common variation and the value of the correlation than is the significance level.

What all this indicates is that if you include enough subjects, you could conceivably find statistical significance in even the most minute and trivial of relationships or differences. Consequently, your sample should be large enough to be sensitive to differences or relationships, but not so large as to produce significant but trivial results. Thus, sample size is the major factor researchers can control to affect the power of the statistical analyses they use to analyse their experiments. We have already seen that sample size is also vital in making sound estimations of population parameters from sample statistics in Chapter 9.

Increasing the predicted difference between population means: changing the design of a study

In some cases, it is possible to change the way the study is done so the researcher has reason to expect a larger mean difference. Consider measuring the impact of stress management techniques on an employee's attendance records. One way to increase the expected mean difference might be to make the techniques more elaborate, spending more time on workshop demonstrations and practice, and so forth. A disadvantage of this approach is that it can be difficult or costly.

The design of a study can also increase the power to detect significant differences. For example, using the repeated measures design (Chapter 12) keeps error variation generally smaller than in the independent group design because individual differences have been removed. The smaller error variation leads to an increased ability to detect small treatment effects in an experiment, and that is just what the power of a statistical analysis is – the ability to detect small treatment effects when they are present.

Decreasing the population standard deviation

It is possible to decrease the population standard deviation in a planned study in at least two ways. One way is to do the study using a population that is less diverse than the one originally planned. With the employee stress example above, you might only use employees working shifts within a particular industry rather than a wider national sample of all types of workers. The disadvantage is that the results apply only to the more limited population from which the sample was drawn.

Another way to decrease the population standard deviation is to use conditions of testing that are more stable and measures that are more precise. For example, testing under a standardized situation or in a controlled experimental setting usually produces smaller overall variation among scores in results (meaning a smaller standard deviation). Similarly, using tests with clear instructions and clear procedures for measuring behaviour also reduces variation. When practical, rigour is an excellent way to increase power.

Using a less stringent level of significance

As we discussed earlier, the level of significance used should be the least stringent that reasonably protects against Type I error; normally, this will be .05. It is rare that much can be done to improve power in this way. Less extreme significance levels (such as .10) mean more power, and more extreme significance levels (.01 or .001) mean less power to produce significant differences. Less extreme means more power because when the significance level is not very extreme (such as .10), the rejection area for the null hypothesis is bigger. More extreme means less power because when the significance level is more extreme (such as .001), the rejection region is smaller.

Using a one-tailed test

Whether you use a one- or a two-tailed test depends on the logic of the hypothesis being studied and it is rare that you have much of a choice about this factor. However, a one-tailed test is more powerful than a two-tailed test. This in fact is the counter argument to the criticism made earlier of one-tailed tests (Chapter 10). It is easier to reject the null hypothesis with the one-tailed test than with the two-tailed test because the rejection area is larger since p required for rejection of the null hypothesis is larger (closer in to the mean). Using a two-tailed test makes it harder to get significance on any one tail as the significance boundary moves out to the tail more. Thus, keeping everything else the same, power to detect a significant result is less with a two-tailed test than with a one-tailed test.

Role of power when planning a study

Determining power is very important when planning a study. If the power of a planned study is low, this means that even if the research hypothesis is true, this study is not likely to give significant results in support of it (Type II error). The time and expense of carrying out the study would probably not be worthwhile. What is an acceptable level of power?

Table 11.2   Factors that influence power

Feature of the study	Factor increasing power	Factor decreasing power
Effect size	*Large effect size*	*Small effect size*
Predicted difference between population means	Large differences	Small differences
Population standard deviation	Small population SD	Large population SD
Sample size (N)	Large N	Small N
Significance level (alpha)	Lenient (such as .05 or even .10)	Stringent (such as .01 or even .001)
One-tailed versus two-tailed test	One-tailed	Two-tailed

Cohen (1992) suggests that ordinarily a study should have 80% power to be worth conducting. Obviously, the more power the better but costs of greater power, such increasing sample size often make even 80% power beyond one's reach. The power of a planned study can, in principle, be increased by changing any of the factors summarized above and in Table 11.2.

The relationship between effect size, power and sample size

For any statistical test, power is determined mainly by three factors:

- the p level (the level of risk of drawing a spuriously positive conclusion);
- N or the sample size; and
- r or the effect size.

Table 11.3   Sample sizes needed to detect various effects at p = .05 two-tailed

Power	Effect sizes (r)						
	.10	**.20**	**.30**	**.40**	**.50**	**.60**	**.70**
.15	85	25	10	10	10	10	10
.20	125	35	15	10	10	10	10
.30	200	55	25	15	10	10	10
.40	300	75	35	20	15	10	10
.50	400	100	40	25	15	10	10
.60	500	125	55	30	20	15	10
.70	600	155	65	40	25	15	10
.80	800	195	85	45	30	20	15
.90	1000	260	115	60	40	25	15

Based on Cohen (1988) *Statistical Power Analysis for the Behavioural Sciences,* Lawrence Erlbaum, p. 92).

These three factors are so related that knowing two enables the determination of the third. Thus if you set 'p' and 'r' in advance you can find out how big a sample you need to achieve these levels. Table 11.3 provides some information on determining sample size for various levels of effect with 'p' set at .05. For example, if you anticipate a small effect level based on a review of previous findings, say r = .20, and you set decide to work with power = .8 or better, since this happens to be a strongly recommended level (Cohen 1988), Table 11.3 shows that you need approximately 195 subjects.

What you have learned from this chapter

You now realize that significance testing and probability levels are not the only procedures and criteria that can be used to evaluate the results of investigations. Power analysis and effect size estimation are two further procedures that social science researchers are now finding as valuable as significance testing in assessing effects.

Measures of effect size reflect how large the effect of an independent variable was independent of sample size. The more frequent effect size estimates you have been introduced to are:

- the standardized mean difference (d);
- correlation coefficients such as r and r_{phi}; and
- eta^2 for curvilinear rather than a linear relationship.

Effect size measures are essential for meta-analysis (extension Chapter 22 on website). The power of a statistical test is its ability to correctly reject the null hypothesis when it is false or the probability it will yield a significant result if the research hypothesis is true.

The power of your statistical test is affected by your chosen significance level, the size of your sample, effect size, whether you use a one-tailed or two-tailed test, and whether you use a repeated measure or independent design. The main practical ways to increase the power of a planned experiment are increasing effect size and sample size. Statistical power is important because you can calculate power when planning a study, as it helps determine how many participants or observations you need to get a particular level of effect.

Review questions and activities

Qu. 11.1
Why is 'p' not regarded as the full story when interpreting results? Review your answer in the light of the material above.

Qu. 11.2
Explain why there is always a trade-off between Type I and Type II errors.

Qu. 11.3

(a) Interpret the following two effect sizes: d = .87; d = .18.

(b) Given a mean difference of 6 and population SD of 4 what is the effect size? Interpret your result.

Compare your responses with those on the website.

References

Cohen, J. 1988. *Statistical Power Analysis for the Behavioural Sciences*. Lawrence Erlbaum: New York.

Cohen, J. 1992. A power primer. *Psychological Bulletin*, 112, 155–159.

Keppel, G. 1991. Design and Analysis. Englewood Cliffs: Prentice-Hall.

Smith, M., Glass, G. & Miller, T. 1980 *The Benefits of Psychotherapy*. Baltimore: John Hopkins University.

Additional reading

Harlow, L., Mulaik, S. & Steiger, J. (eds) 1997. *What If There Were No Significance Tests?* Lawrence Erlbaum: New York.
This is a sound discussion and argument about the core issues touched on in this chapter.

Now go to Chapter 11 Web page and try the questions there.

Part 3
Statistically Analyzing Data

Chapter 12
Hypothesis Testing for Differences Between Means and Proportions

'She was only the statistician's daughter but she knew all the standard deviations'
'Lipton's are big on statistics especially t tests'

(Sources unknown)

Content list

> ## By the end of this chapter you will be able to:
>
> 1 Understand the rationale and assumptions underlying difference testing.
> 2 Understand the concept of the standard error of the difference.
> 3 Be able to apply the one sample t test.
> 4 Be able to distinguish between an independent and a related measures approach to testing differences between means.
> 5 Know when to use non-parametric alternatives.
> 6 Be able to carry out parametric and non-parametric tests for independent and related measures designs.
> 7 Know how to test for differences between proportions.
> 8 Be able to evaluate power and effect size for tests of difference.
> 9 Understand how to use SPSS to undertake tests of significant differences.

Introduction

The importance of this chapter is that it starts us on the exciting journey of conducting statistical analyses on our data. Now that you have an understanding of the logic of hypothesis testing, the Z distribution, significance, probability and standard error we shall begin to investigate how a variety of statistical tests can be used, starting with those that test hypotheses of significant differences between two sample means or between proportions.

In many decision-making contexts, we need to know whether a sample is from a particular population or whether two samples or sets of scores are from the same population or from two different populations. For example:

- An organization may want to know whether its male employees are receiving significantly higher salaries than its female employees for the same work.
- The production manager may wish to determine whether the production levels from a particular evening shift are significantly different from the average night shift production level at all the company's factories round the country.
- A drug manufacturer needs to check for possible significant differences in incidences of a particular reaction to a drug between asthmatics and non-asthmatics.
- Are shoes made by Footloose more expensive than similar ones made by Twinkle Toes?
- Do Japanese-made cars have more breakdowns than Korean-made cars?

In each of these examples, decision makers are concerned with the parameters of the populations – in particular the means. They are not as interested in the actual values as they are in the relationship between these values – that is how do these parameters differ? For example, in asking the question – '*do female employees earn less than male employees?*', we are interested in the mean differences, if any, not the actual amounts. The hypotheses in this chapter are obviously stated in terms of *differences between means* and where there are only two means we usually use t tests. There are three main types of t test:

- the one sample t test;
- the independent group t test;
- the repeated (or paired) measures t test.

Before we look at some examples using SPSS, a few design issues and assumptions will be presented and considered in turn.

Design issues and assumptions

Design issues

The one sample t test is used where we have a sample and can test to see if its mean lies within the sampling distribution of the population it is presumed to represent. A two-group comparison situation can take various forms. It can be a clear contrast between two random samples or it can be one sample tested on two occasions, or it can be two groups but with every member of one sample paired with a member in the other sample on relevant variables. Please revise the detailed differences between the independent, repeated and paired groups designs in Chapter 5 if you have forgotten about them. The three boxes below repeat the summary provided in Chapter 5.

> ***Independent groups design.*** *Two independent samples are selected randomly, one for each treatment condition and compared often in a control and experimental contrast.*

> ***Repeated measures design.*** *One sample is measured in both treatment conditions – a before and after approach.*

> ***Paired or matched samples design.*** *Individuals, units or observations are matched as pairs on one or more variables and allocated at random, one of each pair to each sample.*

We will turn now to the second of the two issues before we introduce the particular methods of testing difference hypotheses.

Assumptions: Parametric vs. non-parametric tests

There are parametric and non-parametric test alternatives for the research designs above. While the functions of these tests are the same, that of testing the viability of the null hypothesis, they are used under different conditions and assumptions.

The assumptions for parametric test

1 Equal interval or ratio level data (scale data in SPSS terminology).
2 Normal distribution or closely so.
3 Homogeneity of variance. That is, the variance should be similar in each group. Variance is the standard deviation squared. SPSS will provide a measure of this in Levine's Test in producing the t test output. We will demonstrate this in the SPSS practice activity below.
4 Samples randomly drawn from the population.

If any of assumptions 1, 2, and 4 are not met then non-parametric tests should be used, but because non-parametric tests require ordinal or nominal data they are less powerful and less sensitive to real differences between groups than parametric tests. Most parametric tests are relatively insensitive to slight violations of assumptions 2, 3 and 4 and so tend to be used if possible.

> *Parametric tests. Tests that are based on assumptions about population distributions and parameters.*

Non-parametric test statistics do not depend on the form of the underlying population distribution and use ordinal or nominal level data. Non-parametric procedures are advantageous in that they can be used with data that was originally interval as such data can be down-graded to the ordinal level. They make fewer and less stringent assumptions and therefore are more widely applicable and can be applied when sample sizes are rather small, where assumptions of normality could not be sustained.

> *Non-parametric tests. Tests that make no assumptions about population parameters or distributions.*

The one sample t test: testing hypotheses for single samples

We are now going to introduce a simple test that enables us to draw inferences about a population from a sample.

The statistic t is a variation of Z used when the standard deviation of the population is not known. You remember that the formula for Z is:

$$Z = \frac{\text{Difference between the sample mean and population mean}}{\text{Standard error of the mean}}$$

and is asking '*compared to the standard error (measure of random fluctuation), how far away from the population mean does my sample mean lie?*' It is the ratio of the SE_M to the difference between means.

On most occasions, we do not know the population standard deviation in order to calculate the standard error of the population distribution. Fortunately, a simple solution is available. When the population parameters are unknown, those of the sample are employed to provide estimates of the population parameters. So instead of Z we use t. Its formula is very similar to Z:

$$t = \frac{\text{sample mean } - \text{ population mean}}{\text{estimated standard error of mean (derived from sample)}}$$

The only difference between t and Z is that the sample standard deviation is used to calculate the standard error for t. The t distribution approximates to normality with increasing sample size, so the differences between the t distribution significance levels and those of Z disappear with sample sizes over 120. With smaller sample sizes t has a flatter, more spread out distribution than Z, so the .05 and .01 levels of significance are a little further out. But do not worry about this as SPSS does the necessary calculations.

One sample t test

This test is used when we wish to test the null hypothesis that the mean of a particular sample differs from the mean of the population only by chance, i.e. is a sample mean from a particular population, when determining whether our sample is similar to or significantly different from the general run of samples chosen from that population. This is often the case when we are testing, for example, whether a particular production run is maintaining itself within acceptable tolerance limits.

Example 1

Suppose the mean weight of all widgets produced in a year in a large factory is 167 cm with a SD = 3 cm. On the last production run before the start of the national day weekend holiday a random sample of 144 widgets reveals a mean length of 169 cm. Is this larger mean simply the kind of deviation from a population mean that is an accident of sampling (the null hypothesis)? Or is this departure a reflection of sloppy employee performance just before a holiday and large enough to be a statistically significant departure? We hypothesize a one-tailed test that states '*the last production run produced a mean widget length significantly greater than the population mean'*. The null hypothesis states that '*the last production run did not produce a mean widget length significantly greater than the population mean'*. A one-tailed test is appropriate as we are determining whether a sample with this *greater* mean length is feasible from within the sampling distribution by chance. We start by calculating the standard error then using this to find the t score location of the sample mean (since we have a large sample in this situation t = Z).

$$\text{The standard error of the mean} = \frac{\text{SD}}{\sqrt{\text{N}}} = \frac{3}{\sqrt{144}} = 0.25$$

$$t = \frac{170 - 169}{0.25} = \frac{1}{0.25} = 4$$

Our t ratio of 4 is telling us that our sample mean is 4 standard deviations above the population mean in the sampling distribution of means from that population. The probability of t (or Z) = +4 or more is well beyond the .001 or 1 in a 1,000 level. Hence we must reject the null hypothesis and accept the alternative that the widget is significantly longer than standard. We might conclude that the production run on that last day before the holidays should be scrapped as the workers had their minds elsewhere rather than on the quality of what they were producing.

t Test. *A univariate hypothesis test using the t distribution rather than the Z distribution and used when the population standard deviation is unknown and the sample size is small.*

SPSS activity

The one sample t test

We will test the hypothesis that a sample mean is not significantly different from its presumed population mean. Please access SPSS Chapter 12 Data File A. We will assume that the data for variable '*self concept*' is the population set of data and we will assume we have tested a small sample and obtained a sample mean of 40.3. We want to determine whether this sample mean is simply a chance variation around the population mean.

Procedure

1 *Analyze >> Compare Means >> One Sample T Test*.
2 In the *One Sample T Test* dialogue box place the variable (self concept) using the arrow button into the *Test Variables: box*
3 In the *Test Value: box* type 40.3 which is the mean score of your sample (Fig. 12.1).
4 *OK*

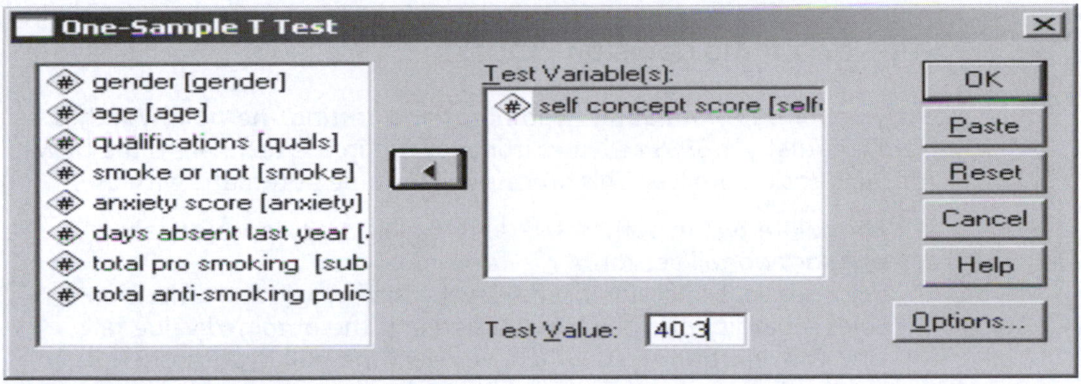

Figure 12.1 **One sample t test dialogue box.**

Interpreting the printout (Table 12.1)

The tables help us to determine whether a sample mean (our test value) is part of the sampling distribution of the population or whether it is unlikely at some level of significance to be part of that distribution.

The top sub-table displays the mean of 39.0388 for the 438 members of this particular population. The sample (the test value) has a mean of 40.3 and with t = 2.01 and p = .045, is just statistically significant at the 5% level. We would thus conclude that the sample is significantly different from the population against which it has been compared. Of course, from our discussion of Type I and Type II errors, we should always remain aware that it could be one of those 4.5% that do occur by chance and we have rejected a null hypothesis when we should not have done so (a Type I error).

Table 12.1 **One sample statistics test**

One-Sample Statistics

	N	Mean	Std. Deviation	Std. Error Mean
self concept score	438	39.0388	13.12921	0.62734

One-Sample Test

Test Value = 40.3

	t	Df	Sig. (2-tailed)	Mean Difference	95% Confidence Interval of the Difference Lower	95% Confidence Interval of the Difference Upper
self concept score	−2.010	437	.045	−1.2612	−2.4942	−.0282

Tips about the decision process

As we will be formulating hypotheses and testing the null hypothesis fairly regularly in SPSS activities from now on in the text here is the flow of the decision process. This process will become automatic with use.

1 Formulate two hypotheses, H_0 and H_1, selecting appropriately a one- or two-tail version.
2 Set a conventional significance level which provides the decision rules regarding the null hypothesis; i.e. if the obtained value falls into the rejection region, then we reject the null hypothesis. If it does not then we retain the null hypothesis.
3 Have SPSS calculate your statistic.
4 Make a decision about H_0 and H_1 by noting the significance or probability level achieved on the printout.
5 Report your result by including both descriptive and inferential statistics in your statement; e.g. 'The mean length of a sample of 136 widgets was 170 cm compared to the population mean of 167 cm ($\sigma = 2$). A one sample t test revealed that the mean length of the sample was not significantly greater than that of the population, $Z = 0.17$ $p > .05$. The null hypothesis was retained.

Degrees of freedom

Degrees of freedom are frequently quoted in statistical printout and are used to evaluate the obtained statistical value rather then N. We often need to know the degrees of freedom for any particular statistic. What are they?

Imagine that you are holding a dinner party for 12 people. You wish to seat them round one large table in a pre-arranged seating plan. When you have labelled the places for 11 guests, the twelfth or final person must sit at the only seat left. So we can say that although $N = 12$, there are only $N - 1$ degrees of freedom. The final place is always fixed. This principle applies with statistics too. Consider 10 individual scores. When we know the mean and every score but one, the value of that score is fixed to give us the already known mean. In fact all but one of the scores can vary. The final score's value is determined by whatever the remaining nine are because of the necessity that their scores sum to $N \times M$. Thus one score in a set is not free to vary. The number of degrees of freedom is therefore $N - 1$. If we have three numbers that sum to 24 and hence a mean of 8, with two numbers known as 10 and 6, the third must be 8. If we alter 10 to 11 and 6 to 7 then the third number is fixed as 6.

When we are using two or more groups each group loses one degree of freedom. Let us return to the dinner party. We try to place men and women in alternate seats round the table. With six men and six women, we would know where the last man and woman had to sit. So with two gender groups each must lose one degree of freedom so we only have five degrees of freedom for each or 10 degrees of freedom in total $(N-1) + (N-1)$. To determine the probability achieved, degrees of freedom are used by SPSS and are often quoted in the printout. As sample size increases probability approaches the normal distribution and degrees of freedom have little impact, but they do when sample sizes are small and have the effect of increasing the probability level needed to achieve significance.

> *Degrees of freedom. The number of values free to vary in a set of values.*

Statistical tests for two independent groups (between-subjects design) – comparing two samples

The aim of all the statistical tests that follow in this chapter is to determine whether two groups differ significantly or not. There are only two possibilities. One is that both groups are samples from the same population and their means only differ by chance sampling variations (i.e. not statistically significantly – maintain null hypothesis). The other is that their means do differ statistically significantly and are likely from different statistical populations. These two options are depicted in Figure 12.2.

The top pair of distributions overlap considerably and therefore the two distributions and their respective means are most likely chance variations, i.e. two random samples from the

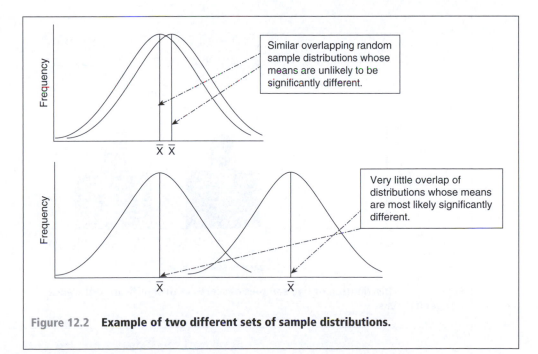

Figure 12.2   Example of two different sets of sample distributions.

same population distribution. The bottom set hardly overlap and this suggests their means are significantly different and represent two different sampling distributions. The top set suggest we retain the null hypothesis; the bottom pair suggest we reject the null hypothesis in favour of the alternative.

For significant differences we need means far apart, small standard deviations and largish samples. If we have small differences between group means, small samples and large standard deviations then it is most likely the means are not significantly different as these features lead to overlap.

One way of looking at the statistical inference of significance in a 'difference' hypothesis is to reason that, if the difference is genuine, then the two groups are each a sample from two different populations. For example, if we take two random samples of employees to test their speed on learning how to use a new piece of equipment, one a sample of females, the other a sample of males, then if there is no significant difference in learning times, they have likely been drawn from the same population. That is males and females have the same learning speed on this particular equipment. If there is a significant difference, then we can infer that female and male employees form different populations as far as their speed of learning this new technique is concerned. The following figures (12.3 and 12.4) illustrate

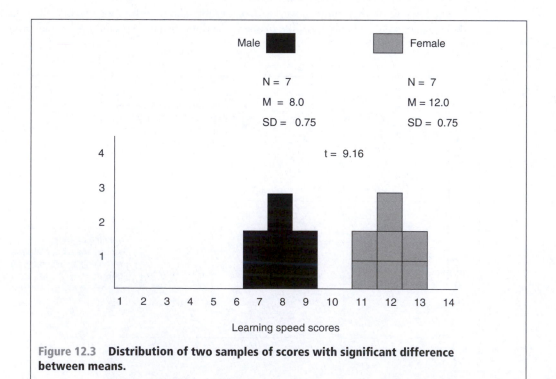

Figure 12.3 Distribution of two samples of scores with significant difference between means.

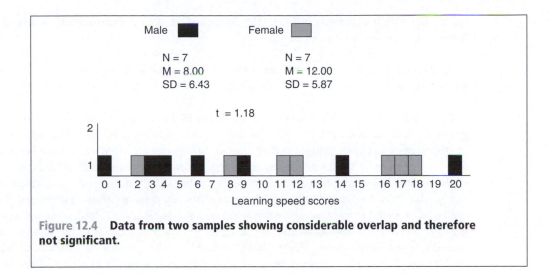

Figure 12.4   **Data from two samples showing considerable overlap and therefore not significant.**

this example and also turn the normal graphs (Fig. 12.2) into another form to ease understanding of what it is we are trying to determine in applying a t test in a two-group situation. Both figures show a sample of seven each from male and female populations with the same sample mean in both. The only difference is variability as shown by their standard deviations

Figure 12.3 shows each sample data clustered around the mean of that sample. Sample variability is small but the means are significantly different (in this case t = 9.16). Our independent variable of gender is having a considerable effect. Figure 12.4 shows that the two samples overlap and it is not easy to see a difference between the two samples. In fact all 14 scores could have come from the same population. In this case t = 1.18 and we conclude that there is not sufficient evidence to reject the null hypothesis and therefore gender differences do not influence mean scores.

The standard error of the difference

The figures above indicate that we are dealing with the distribution of differences between sample means; i.e. does the difference between the two sample means lie within the expected chance distribution of differences between the means of an infinite number of pairs of samples, or does it lie beyond the conventionally accepted levels of statistical significance?

Because we are comparing two samples, not one, the standard error is no longer appropriate. We now need the **sampling distribution of the difference between two sample means**. Consider two distributions of sample means. Now suppose we take a sample mean from population 1 and another sample mean from population 2, then take one away from the other, we are left with a figure that measures the difference between the two sample means, each taken from a different distribution.

- If sample mean 1 is larger than sample mean 2 the value will be positive.
- If sample mean 1 is smaller than sample mean 2 then the difference will be negative.

By taking every possible pairing of sample means from two sample distributions and graphing all these mean differences we will end up with a normal distribution, but this time of **differences between sample means**. Some differences are positive and are balanced over a large number of differences by those that are negative. Most differences are quite slight, hovering around the mean of the differences, with larger differences occurring more rarely. Thus, a normal distribution of differences between pairs of means is produced. This is an exact parallel to what we saw when we drew large numbers of samples when discussing random sampling and standard error (Chapter 9), where the means of the samples of a population distributed themselves normally around the 'true' population mean. In the case of differences between sample means, we have the same principle applying. The SD of this distribution is **the standard error of the difference between means**. It estimates the dispersal of the differences between every possible pairing of means. This is usually symbolized as SE_{diff}. You will never need to calculate this as SPSS calculates all the statistics you will require.

> ***The standard error of the difference between two means.*** *The standard deviation of the distribution of differences between every possible pairings of sample means when each pair is formed from one sample mean taken from each population.*

Suppose, for instance, that a random sample of male advertising executives produces a mean score of 52 on a creativity tests while a random sample of female advertising executives attain, a mean of 54. Does this difference of 2 points reveal a real superiority on the part of females on this particular task? The answer depends on how this obtained difference of 2 in mean score would vary if further pairs of random samples were tested. Our obtained difference of 2 is only one difference in a sampling distribution of the difference between means, where the standard deviation is **the standard error of the difference between means**.

The t statistic – the measure of difference between two means

The t statistic now forms a critical ratio following the basic structure we used earlier:

$$t = \frac{\text{obtained difference between means}}{\text{difference expected by chance (standard error of the difference)}}$$

We are testing the difference between the sample means against the standard error of the difference as the denominator, since we wish to determine whether the difference between the sample means (the numerator in the ratio) is one that would occur by chance or would occur so unlikely by chance that it reaches one of our conventional significance levels.

The null hypothesis usually states that there is no significant difference between the two sample means. The alternative hypothesis states that there is a significant difference (two-tailed) or that one mean is greater (or less) than the other (one-tailed). The usual significance levels apply. If the difference between the two sample means lies outside the null hypothesis acceptance region of ±1.96, we reject the null and accept the alternative hypothesis.

Effect size for the t test for independent groups (means)

Effect size for the t test for independent means is the difference between the population means divided by the standard deviation of the population of individuals. When using data from a completed study, the effect size is estimated as the difference between the sample means divided by the pooled estimate of the population standard deviation (the square root of the pooled estimate of the population variance). Stated as formulas:

$$\text{Effect size (d)} = \frac{\text{Population M}_1 - \text{Population M}_2}{\text{Population SD}}$$

$$\text{Estimated effect size (d)} = \frac{\text{M}_1 - \text{M}_2}{\text{SD pooled}}$$

The mean difference is reported in the SPSS output, but the pooled standard deviation has to be calculated from the reported standard deviations for the two groups. However, it is easier to compute d using the following equation:

$$d = t\sqrt{\frac{\text{N}_1 + \text{N}_2}{\text{N}_1\text{N}_2}}$$

A d can range in value from negative infinity to positive infinity. The value of 0 for d indicates that there are no differences in the means. As d diverges from 0, the effect size becomes larger. Regardless of sign, d values of .2, .5, and .8 traditionally represent small, medium, and large effect sizes, respectively.

SPSS activity – independent t test to compare two independent groups

You need two variables to calculate an independent t test. One represents the independent variable (or grouping variable) which must be a nominal variable usually represented on data view as 1's and 2's. The second variable consists of the scores of the dependent variable

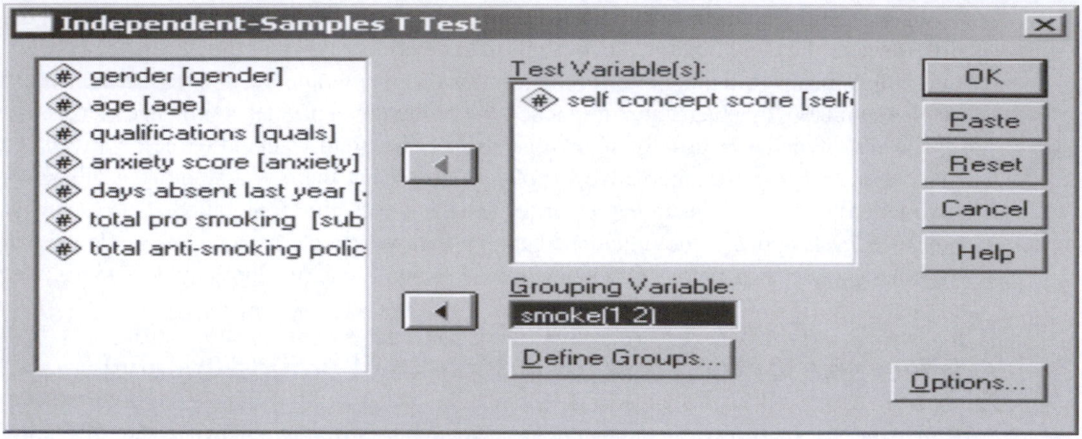

Figure 12.5 **Independent samples t test box.**

for both groups. Each row then (individual, case, item) contains a code to designate which group they are in, and a score on the independent variable. In this example we will hypothesize that there is a significant difference in self concept between those who smoke and those who do not. Access SPSS Chapter 12 Data File A.

1 *Analyze >> Compare Means >> Independent-Samples t Test* to open *the Independent Samples t Test* dialogue box.
2 Select your dependent variable (*self concept score*) and click on the arrow button to place it into the *Test variables* box.
3 Select your grouping (independent) variable (must be categorical and a dichotomy) and move it to the *Grouping Variable* area (in this example *smoke or not*) (Fig. 12.5).
4 Choose *Define Groups* and enter the two category codes you have used in your data entry, e.g. beside Group 1 enter 1 and beside Group 2 enter 2 (Fig. 12.6). These will then appear in the main t test box (Fig. 12.5).
5 *Continue >> OK* to produce the output.

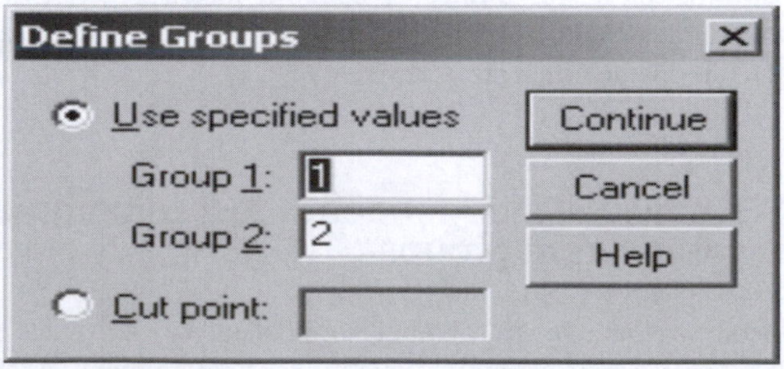

Figure 12.6 **Define groups box.**

How to interpret the output in Table 12.2

- The printout consists of two subtables. The top one summarizes the descriptive statistics for the two groups (smoke or no smoke) on the dependent variable of self-concept. The mean self-concept score for non-smokers is 46.61 while that for smokers is 28.28. Is this difference of 18.33 sufficiently large for us to say that the two groups are significantly different in terms of self-concept level? The bottom table reveals this.
- In the bottom table, the output for the independent groups t-test on SPSS is somewhat confusing because there are two versions of the independent samples t-test. Which one you should use depends on whether the estimated variances for the two groups of scores are significantly different or not.

Table 12.2   Printout of independent samples t test

Group Statistics					
	Smoke or not	N	Mean	Std. Deviation	Std. Error Mean
self concept score	non-smoker	257	46.6148	11.16826	.69666
	smoker	181	28.2818	6.54159	.48623

Independent Samples Test									
		Levene's Test for Equality of Variances		t-test for Equality of Means					
								95% Confidence Interval of the Difference	
		F	Sig.	t	df	Sig. (2-tailed)	Mean Difference	Std. Error Difference	Lower	Upper
self concept score	Equal variances assumed	43.592	.000	19.816	436	.000	18.3330	.92516	16.51468	20.15136
	Equal variances not assumed			21.579	423.301	.000	18.3330	.84956	16.66314	20.00290

Use this bottom line if F is significant

F is significant so equal variances cannot be assumed

P > .0001 so highly significant difference between means

- Read the columns under Levene's Test for Equality of Variances. This test tells you whether you have satisfied the homogeneity of variance assumption. If the probability value is statistically significant then your variances are *unequal and you must use the lower line of figures.* Non-significance indicates that *variances* are approximately equal so use the upper line.
- Levene's test for equality of variances in this case tells us that the variances for non-smokers and smokers are significantly different (sig = .000). Therefore, in this case we must use the row for 'Equal variances not assumed'.
- The t value, its degrees of freedom and its probability are displayed in the output. The t value is 21.579, which with 423.3 degrees of freedom has a two-tailed significance level of .000. The 95% confidence limits are also provided.

An additional piece of information is shown in Figure 12.7 where error bar charts are displayed showing the high degree of separation of the 95% confidence intervals of the smokers and non-smokers on self-concept score. This is not normally obtained but is a useful visual demonstration of the distribution of scores on the DV. It was obtained by clicking on **Graphs** then **Error bar** and inserting *self-concept* as the variable and *smoke or not* as the category entry.

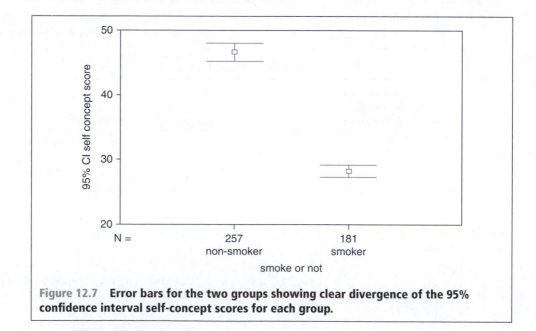

Figure 12.7 Error bars for the two groups showing clear divergence of the 95% confidence interval self-concept scores for each group.

How to report the results in Table 12.2

An independent-samples t test was conducted to evaluate the hypotheses that smokers and non-smokers differ significantly in their self-concept levels. The mean self-concept score of non-smokers (M = 46.61, sd = 11.17) was statistically significantly different (t = 21.579, df = 423.3, two-tailed p = .000) from that of smokers (M = 28.28, sd = 6.54). The effect size d = 2.09 implies a very strong effect.

Many researchers are probably unaware of the existence of Levine's unequal variance t test. If you have to use it, you should write as we should in this case: 'Because the variances for the two groups were significantly unequal (F = 43.59, p < .000), the output line for unequal variances was used'.

Mann-Whitney U test (non-parametric independent groups test)

The Mann-Whitney U test is used when testing for differences between two independent groups when the assumptions for the parametric t test cannot be met. This means that the data may be ordinal and/or that the variances are quite dissimilar and/or that the samples are small, and/or that the distribution is not close to normal. The test does not require equal numbers in the two conditions. It must, however, be possible to rank the scores produced by the subjects, i.e. the scale of measurement must be at least ordinal. The Mann-Whitney U test is less likely than the t test to show a significant difference between groups if one really exists. This is because the t test makes full use of the information from interval data, while the Mann-Whitney test considers only the ranking of the subjects (i.e. uses ordinal data). Remember you can downgrade your data from interval to ordinal by using the rank data facility on SPSS (see activity below).

The logic of this test is based on the simple observation that if there is a real difference between scores in two samples then the scores in one sample should be generally larger than the scores in the other sample. Thus, if all scores are ranked in order, the ranks of one sample should be mainly concentrated at one end while the ranks from the other sample are concentrated for the most part at the other end. If no treatment effect exists, then the ranks will be randomly mixed because the scores from the two samples overlap considerably (Fig. 12.8). Thus, instead of comparing mean scores, as in the t test, we are comparing mean ranks.

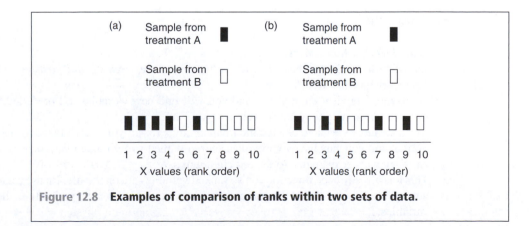

Figure 12.8   **Examples of comparison of ranks within two sets of data.**

> **The Mann-Whitney test** *ranks scores from the two samples into one set of ranks and then tests to determine whether there is a systematic clustering into two groups paralleling the samples.*

SPSS presents evidence as to whether our mean rank difference is one that would occur less than 5% or 1% of the time.

Computing an effect size statistic for the Mann-Whitney test

SPSS does not report an effect size index for the Mann-Whitney test, but simple indices can be computed to communicate the size of the effect. For example, the difference in mean ranks between the two groups can serve as an effect size index.

SPSS activity: the Mann-Whitney test (non-parametric) – two independent samples

We will use SPSS Chapter 12 data set B for this demonstration and test whether there is a significant difference between males and females in number of days absence in 2006. Remember that Mann-Whitney requires ordinal (ranked) data. Prior analysis, like that carried out in Chapter 8, where we assessed the degree of normality or skewness, revealed that the variables *days absent, self-concept, starting salary, current salary and subtest 'a'* were positively skewed and therefore could be better analyzed by a non-parametric test, especially as there are only 22 and 18 persons in each group. To degrade scale data into ordinal is relatively easy.

Ranking data

1 *Transform* >> *Rank cases*.
2 Transfer the variables, e.g. *startsal, salnow, absence, pretest, and post-test* into the *Variables* box and hit *OK*.
3 Go to the data view on your file and you will find new variables, all preceded by the letter 'r', indicating they are ranked.
4 Go to variable view and change the final columns for all your new ranked variables to ordinal and you may have to provide a shorter name to your ranked variables as adding an 'r' may cause the name to exceed eight items.
5 This has already been done for you so ranked variables are on the file. Please remember whenever you undertake this procedure, save your file so that you retain the new variables.

Conducting a Mann-Whitney test

1 **Analyze** >> *Nonparametric Tests*.
2 Choose *2 Independent Samples* which opens the ***Two-Independent Samples Tests***
   dialogue box.
3 Select your dependent variable and move it using the arrow button to the ***Test Variable***
   List box.
4 Select your independent or group variable and place it in the ***Grouping Variable box***.
5 Select ***Define Groups***.
6 Type whatever codes you have used to define your categories of the independent
   variable into the Group boxes, e.g. '1' in the ***Group 1 box*** and '2' in the ***Group 2 box***.
7 Select ***Continue*** and make sure that ***Mann-Whitney U*** is selected in the ***Test Type*** area
   (Fig. 12.9).
8 ***OK*** to produce your output.

Interpreting the printout in Table 12.3

The table displays data comparing males and females on the variable *Rank of Absence*.

The top table provides the mean rank given to each group on each variable. For example,
female absence rank mean is 18.83 while the average rank given to male absence is 21.86.
This means that the absences for males tend to be slightly larger than those for females as
the ranking is done from lowest number of absences = rank 1 to most = rank 40. The lower
table displays the Mann-Whitney U value and the significance level. These are 168.0 with a
two-tailed significance of .413. This value is therefore not significant and we must retain the
null hypothesis that the difference in mean rank between genders is only a chance one.

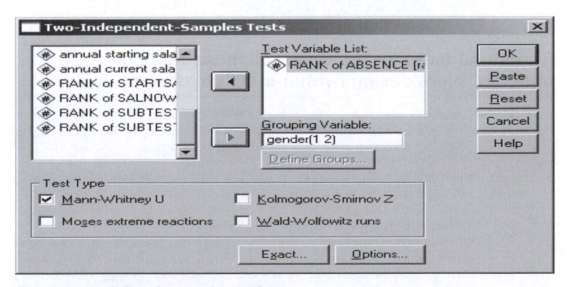

Figure 12.9 Two independent samples tests box.

Table 12.3   **Output for Mann-Whitney test**

Ranks

	Gender	N	Mean Rank	Sum of Ranks
RANK of ABSENCE	male	22	21.86	481.00
	female	18	18.83	339.00
	Total	40		

Test Statistics[b]

	RANK of ABSENCE
Mann-Whitney U	168.000
Wilcoxon W	339.000
Z	.819
Asymp. Sig. (2-tailed)	.413
Exact Sig. [2*(1-tailed Sig.)]	.427[a]

[a] Not corrected for ties.
[b] Grouping variable: gender.

> Ranks not too different so significance not achieved

How to report the results in Table 12.3

We could report the results of this analysis as follows: '*The Mann-Whitney U-test showed that there was no significant differences in absence rates in 2006 between male and female employees (U = 168.0, p = .413)*'.

Statistical tests for the repeated measures and matched pairs design (within-subjects design)

The repeated measures and matched pairs t test are used when testing for significant differences between two samples which are 'related' – that is, the results of the first group are not independent of the second group. Examples of related samples are:

1   When the same subjects are tested under two different conditions, e.g. undertaking a task with two different sets of instructions; or
2   In a before-and-after type of study where changes after an intervention are compared with the performance level before the intervention; or
3   When subjects in two groups are paired by selecting individuals who are as similar as possible with respect to other external variables, which may all influence the outcome of the research. Subjects might, for example, be matched for learning ability, sex, age and IQ.

The first two options above are often termed repeated measures design. The third situation above, the matched pairs design, is often used to circumvent some of the problems that can arise in the course of performing test and retest procedures on the same set of participants, as in the second repeated measures design above. For example, many psychological tests and questionnaires can only be administered once to any participant as performance on a retest may be affected by familiarity with the test items and memory of previous responses. This is known as the practice effect, and the improvement in scores from this can mask any changes due to the treatment effect that has been applied between the two occasions of testing. By using two matched pairs groups, one, designated the experimental group, can be compared with the control group on the second testing, as only the experimental group has had the intervening treatment as shown below:

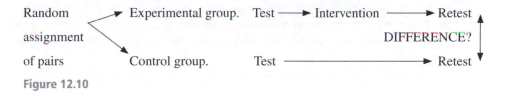

Figure 12.10

This matched pairs design looks similar to the independent groups design, but because of the deliberate pairing, the logic of the calculations are different. Any difference on the retest between the two can be attributed to the intervention (or lack of it) (Fig. 12.10).

The repeated measures or matched pairs design (parametric test)

In the previous section, we were dealing with two samples chosen independently from two populations. In the examples of the effect of noise on performance we compared two groups and in the personal skills example we compared two training programmes. However, there are numerous occasions when it makes more sense to take two samples that are not independent of each other. The use of paired samples permits a more precise analysis because there is greater control of sources of error stemming from individual differences. For example, the head of a government department wants to determine whether typing speed depends on the word processing software used. If 20 administrative officers use the Write software package and 20 use the Input software package and the results compared, this would be an independent groups design. But differences in results might be due to individual typing skill anyway and not the packages. But if 20 administrative officers were each tested on both packages using counterbalancing then the design is **the related** or **repeated measures design**. In this latter design the individual differences in typing skill between the two sets of officers are removed and differences in typing speed are solely related to the two different word processing packages.

For convenience, in the description of the test below, it will be assumed that the scores are obtained from the same subjects. However, if they were produced by different but matched subjects, this has no effect on the procedure.

Assumptions of the test

The assumptions of the test are that:

(a) the measurements are made on an interval scale;
(b) the subjects have been randomly selected from the defined population;
(c) the variances of the scores for the two samples or occasions should be approximately equal;
(d) the population from which the samples have been drawn is normally distributed. (This means, in practice, that the distribution of the scores for the subjects in each condition must be normally distributed.)

Within reasonable limits, the assumptions can be broken without invalidating the test. However, when the assumptions of the test are broken, the power of the test is reduced so that the non-parametric Wilcoxon test (see below) may well be as or more powerful.

In the t test for the repeated measures design, one compares the actual difference that has been observed between the two sets of data with the estimate of the difference that could be expected by chance alone, i.e. the standard error of the difference. The standard error of the difference between the means for the repeated measures test is symbolized SD to distinguish it from the symbol SEdiff (used with the independent groups t test).

Computing the effect size statistic for the parametric paired-samples t test

SPSS supplies all the information necessary to compute d.

$$d = \frac{mean}{sd} \quad \text{or} \quad d = \frac{t}{N}$$

where the mean and standard deviation are reported in the output under Paired Differences.

The d statistic evaluates the degree that the mean of the difference scores deviates from 0 in standard deviation units. If d equals 0, the mean of the difference scores is equal to zero. As d diverges from 0, the effect size becomes larger. The value of d can range from negative infinity to positive infinity. Regardless of sign, d values of 0.2, 0.5, and 0.8 traditionally represent small, medium and large effect sizes, respectively,

SPSS activity – the parametric related groups or paired samples t test

We will illustrate the computation of a Related Groups or Paired Samples t test with SPSS Chapter 12 Data File B. We will test the hypothesis that there is a significant difference between starting salary and current salary of the employees.

How to proceed

1 *Analyze >> Compare Means >> Paired Sample t Test*.
2 In the *Paired-Samples t Test* dialogue box click on your first dependent variable (*starting salary*) which moves it to the **Current Selections** box as Variable 1.
3 Select your other variable (*current salary*) which puts it beside Variable 2: in the **Current Selections** box.
4 Click on the arrow button to move both variables into the **Paired Variables** box (Fig. 12.11).
5 *OK* to produce the output.

How to interpret the output in Table 12.4

- Three subtables are produced. The top one provides descriptive statistics. The average starting salary was $24,225 with an SD of $7.64 while the mean current salary was $52,287 with an SD of 14.1.
- The second subtable displays a Pearson correlation between the two sets of scores.
- In the bottom subtable the paired difference between these two mean scores is presented along with t, the significance level, and the standard error of this mean. The difference between the two means is $28,062 and the standard error of means for this sample size is 1.614.
- The t-value of the difference between the sample means is 17.385 (the sign does not matter) which has an exact two-tailed significance level of 0.00 with 39 degrees of freedom.
- The effect size was $17.385/ \sqrt{40} = 2.75$.

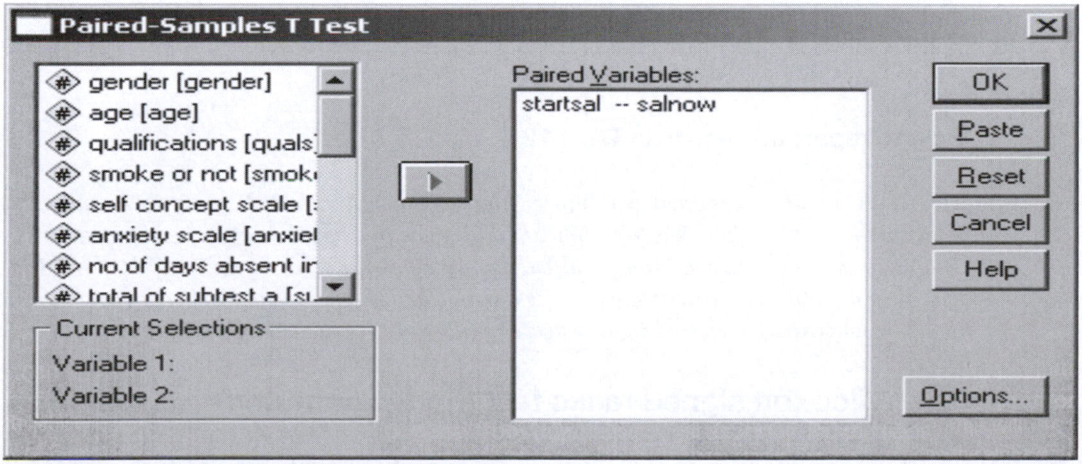

Figure 12.11   Paired samples t test box.

Table 12.4 **Paired samples t test output**

Paired Samples Statistics

		Mean	N	Std. Deviation	Std. Error Mean
Pair 1	annual starting salary in $1000's	24.2250	40	7.64010	1.20801
	annual current salary in $1000's	52.2875	40	14.41549	2.27929

> Before and after difference large and reveals significance

Paired Samples Correlations

		N	Correlation	Sig.
Pair 1	annual starting salary in $1000's & annual current salary in $1000's	40	.735	.000

Paired Samples Test

		Paired Differences			95% Confidence Interval of the Difference				
		Mean	Std. Deviation	Std. Error Mean	Lower	Upper	t	df	Sig. (2 -tailed)
Pair 1	annual starting salary in $1000's –annual current salary in $1000's	−28.0625	10.20884	1.61416	−31.3274	−24.7976	−17.385	39	.000

How to report the results in Table 12.4

The results could be reported as follows: '*A paired samples t test (N = 40) was conducted to evaluate whether there was a significant difference between initial and current salaries. The mean scores between initial and current salaries differed significantly (t = 17.385, df = 39, p < .000) with current salary having a significantly higher mean than the starting salary*' (as we would expect!). *The calculated effect size (d) was 2.75, indicating a large effect.*

The Wilcoxon signed ranks test (non-parametric)

The Wilcoxon two related samples test is used instead of a related groups or paired t test if the differences between treatments can only be ranked in size, or if the data are quite skewed, or if there is clearly a difference in the variance of the groups, i.e. assumptions for the 'related' t test do not apply. The aim of the Wilcoxon signed ranks test is to compare observations across two occasions or conditions in a repeated measures or matched pairs context to determine whether there are significant differences between the observations from the two sets of data.

The test considers the rankings of differences in score between occasions 1 and 2. If there are only random differences, as stated by the null hypothesis, then there should be roughly equal numbers of high and low ranks for the plus and minus differences. If there is a preponderance of high ranks for one sign, this means that there are larger differences in one direction than would be expected by chance.

Computing an effect size statistic for Wilcoxon

For the Wilcoxon test, the mean positive ranked difference score and the mean negative ranked difference score could be reported.

SPSS activity – the repeated groups and paired groups non-parametric Wilcoxon test

For this test we will use paired data that are already ranked in SPSS Chapter 12 Data File B and determine whether there was significant improvement in performance score from pretest to posttest after a week's intervening training period.

How to proceed

1   *Analyze >> Non-parametric Tests*
2   Click on *2 Related Samples Test* in the second drop down window.
3   Highlight your two variables (in this case *rpretest* and *rposttest)* and place them in the **Current Selections** box.
4   Using the arrow button transfer them to the **Test Pairs List** box.
5   Make sure **Wilcoxon** is selected in the **Test Type** area (Fig. 12.12).
6   *OK* to display the output.

Interpreting the printout in Table 12.5

This table displays results comparing the before-and-after performance of 40 persons in one organization who had been sent on a training course.

- Two subtables are produced. The top one lists the mean ranks of employees who took the two tests: 21 employees performed more poorly on the posttest than they did on the pretest while 19 did better.
- The bottom subtable produces a standardized Z value of –0.303 which has a two-tailed probability of .762. This negative Z supports the data from the top table that the training course was ineffective and no significant difference emerged. The difference was simply chance variation. Note that we used a two-tail test because we did not want to assume the course would produce improvements.

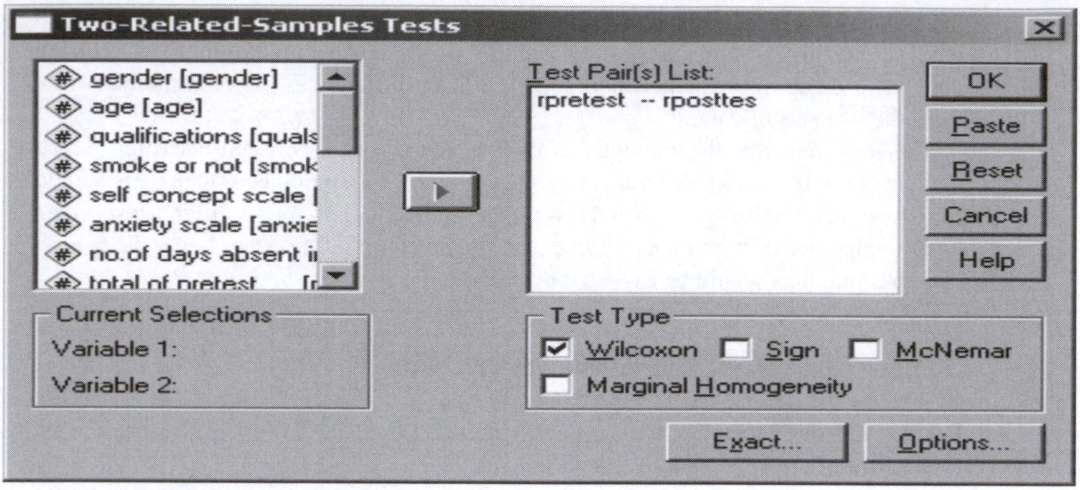

Figure 12.12 Two related samples tests.

Table 12.5 **Wilcoxon test output**

Ranks

		N	Mean Rank	Sum of Ranks
RANK of POSTTEST – RANK of PRETEST	Negative Ranks	21(a)	18.45	387.50
	Positive Ranks	19(b)	22.76	432.50
	Ties	0(c)		
	Total	40		

[a] RANK of POSTTEST < RANK of PRETEST.
[b] RANK of POSTTEST > RANK of PRETEST.
[c] RANK of POSTTEST = RANK of PRETEST.

Test Statistics (b)

	RANK of POSTTEST - RANK of PRETEST
Z	−.303(a)
Asymp. Sig. (2-tailed)	.762

[a] Based on negative ranks.
[b] Wilcoxon Signed Ranks Test.

How to report the results in Table 12.5

'A Wilcoxon test was conducted to evaluate whether undertaking a training course would alter the performance levels of 40 employees The results indicated that there was no statistical significant difference in performance levels after the training course (Wilcoxon, Z = −.303, p = .762)'. It is recommended that this course be abandoned or rewritten.

Choosing the correct test

You have just used four different tests for similar purposes but meeting different assumptions and design requirements. We will be meeting a number of other tests in the next few chapters that also assess differences between two or more groups. All these tests are included in the following table to show what considerations determine their use. It would be useful to try to remember these so you not only choose the correct test but can justify the choice is challenged.

Tips for choosing correct tests of difference

Independent Samples Tests		
Level of measurement	*Two independent groups*	*More than two independent groups*
Scale (interval and ratio)	Independent samples t test	One way ANOVA
Ordinal	Mann-Whitney	Kruskal-Wallis
Nominal	Chi square	Chi square
Related Samples tests		
Scale (interval and ratio)	Paired samples t test	Repeated measures ANOVA
Ordinal	Wilcoxon Signed Ranks	Friedman
Nominal	Chi square	Chi square

Testing for differences between proportions

As well as looking at mean differences, we often need to compare proportions such as the proportion of defects produced by one method compared to another method; or the proportion of successful house mortgage applications granted in one bank compared to another; or the proportion of persons under 30 years of age buying a particular product compared to persons over 30 years of age. The approach is very similar to comparing means in independent samples except we need to compute an estimate of the standard error of a difference between two sample proportions.

Example: A two-tailed test

We test two similar drugs to prevent travel sickness to determine which is more effective. In one sample of travellers, 71 out of 100 claimed drug 1 was effective while drug 2 was claimed to be effective by 58 out of 90 travellers in a second sample. We want to test at the 5% level of significance whether there is a significant difference in perceived effectiveness. The null hypothesis states that there is no significant difference between the two sets of percentages. This is a two-tailed test.

We need firstly to calculate the various proportions:

$$p_1 = .71; \qquad q_1 = .29 \qquad N_1 = 100$$
$$p_2 = .644; \qquad q_2 = .356 \qquad N_2 = 90$$

Both samples are large enough to use the normal distribution. The confidence interval of Z for 95% of the area under the curve is ±1.96Z.

$$\text{The standard error for proportions} = \sqrt{\frac{pq}{N}}$$

The estimated standard error of the difference is:

$$SE(p_1 - p_2) = \sqrt{\frac{p_1 q_1}{N_1} + \frac{p_2 q_2}{N_2}}$$

$$= \sqrt{\frac{(.71)(.29)}{100} + \frac{(.644)(.356)}{90}} = \sqrt{.004459} = .0668$$

$$Z = \frac{p_1 - p_2}{.0668} = \frac{0.71 - .644}{.0668} = .988$$

The standardized value lies within the acceptance area of the null hypothesis since it does not exceed the tabled value of Z (i.e. ±1.96). Therefore we conclude that the two proportions do not differ in their preferences.

Example: One-tailed test of difference between proportions

Conceptually, the one-tailed test is no different to a one-tailed test for the differences between two means. Suppose, for income tax purposes, the national government has started using two methods for personal assessment of tax. The first requires the normal mail-in form but the second allows the taxpayer to complete an eform on the computer and directly email back to the tax office. The tax office believes that the normal handwritten mail-in form will have fewer mistakes than the newer email version. A random sample of 50 mail-in forms and 75 computer-completed forms are examined: 10% mail-in forms have errors while 13.3% of email forms contain errors. The tax office wish to test with alpha set as .01 and a null hypothesis stating that the mail in forms do not have significantly fewer errors than the eforms.

The summary data is:

Mail-in forms: $p_1 = .10$; $q_1 = .90$; $n_1 = 50$

Eform: $p_2 = .113$; $q_2 = .867$; $n_2 = 75$

With samples of this size we can use the normal distribution and Z. The critical value for Z for 95% of the curve in a one-tail test is approximately 2.33. This we can use as the boundary of the null hypothesis acceptance region.

The estimated standard error of the difference is:

$$SE(p_1 - p_2) = \sqrt{\frac{p_1 q_1}{N_1} + \frac{p_2 q_2}{N_2}} = .0556$$

We now test this standard error against the difference between the two proportions.

$$Z = \frac{.10 - .133}{.0556} = -.593$$

This figure of −.593 lies well within the null hypothesis acceptance region (Fig. 12.13). The taxation department should accept the null hypothesis that there is no statistically significant difference between the two methods of personal income tax submission.

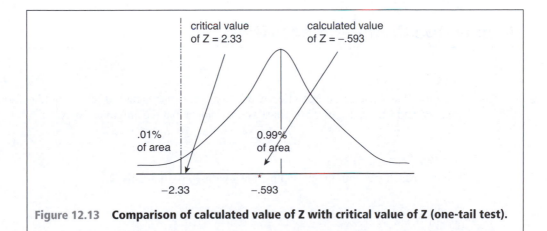

Figure 12.13 Comparison of calculated value of Z with critical value of Z (one-tail test).

Important things you have learned from this chapter

You have learned rationale and the SPSS procedures for analysing differences between two sample means or proportions as well as knowing how to determine whether a single sample comes from a particular population. You have also seen how the research designs affect the particular statistical test used.

The independent measures t test is used to draw inferences about differences between two treatment conditions. Two independent samples are randomly drawn, one for each treatment condition. The null hypothesis states that there is no significant difference between sample means. This often takes the form of an experimental and control group approach.

In repeated or related measures design a single sample of subjects is randomly selected and measurements repeated on this sample for both treatment conditions. This often takes the form of a before-and-after study. The null hypothesis states that there is no significant difference between conditions. The matched-pairs design employs two groups which are matched on a pair-by-pair basis, which can then be regarded as the same group tested twice. The repeated measures design has the advantage of reducing error variance due to the removal of individual differences. This increases the possibility of detecting real effects from the experimental treatment.

The Mann-Whitney test and Wilcoxon tests are non-parametric alternatives to the independent group and repeated measures t test respectively. These tests do not require normal distributions or homogeneity of variance. Both employ ordinal data. The rationale is that if differences between conditions are random then there should be roughly equal sum of ranks in the two conditions.

You are now able to use SPSS to analyse data employing the various forms of difference tests, and methods for testing for differences between proportions are provided too

Review questions and activities

SPSS Activity 12.1
Use the SPSS Chapter 12 Data File A and conduct a one sample t test using the variable 'anxiety' and a test value of 22.0. Make a conclusion about the null hypothesis.

Qu. 12.1
The degrees of freedom in one sample t test with 30 participants is:

(a) 30
(b) 29
(c) 28
(d) 1

Qu. 12.2
The independent t test assesses:

(a) the difference between median values;
(b) the differences between the standard errors;
(c) the differences between mean scores;
(d) the differences between standard deviations.

Check your answer in the material above.

Qu. 12.3
The degrees of freedom in an independent t test with 30 participants in each group is:

(a) 60
(b) 59
(c) 58
(d) 56

Check your answer in the earlier discussion of df.

SPSS Activity 12.2 Using Chapter 12 Data File B
Conduct a Mann-Whitney test to determine whether significant differences occur between gender and current salary.

Discuss your results in class.

SPSS Activity 12.3 Using Chapter 12 data File A
Using the same data set conduct the following t tests:

1 Test the hypothesis that there is a significant difference between smokers and non-smokers in level of anxiety.
2 Test the hypothesis that there is a significant difference between males and females in level of anxiety.
3 Test the hypothesis that there is a significant difference between males and females in level of self-concept.

Discuss your results in class.

Now access the Chapter 12 Web page and try the SPSS activities and further questions there.

Chapter 13
Analysis of Variance Techniques (ANOVA)

Content list

By the end of this chapter you will be able to:

1. Understand the rationale and logic behind ANOVA.
2. Differentiate 'between group variance' from 'within group variance'.
3. Use and interpret a simple one way ANOVA.
4. Use and interpret a related measures ANOVA.
5. Use and interpret a factorial ANOVA.
6. Use and understand ANCOVA.
7. Understand the purpose of *post hoc* tests.
8. Use a Kruskal-Wallis test and a Freidman test.
9. Compute various types of ANOVA on SPSS and understand the printout.

Introduction

This chapter is important because it shows you how to test for significant differences when there are more than two groups. In Chapter 12 you learned how to test for significant differences between two groups. But on many occasions we have more than two groups. Analysis of variance (ANOVA) enables us to test for significant differences between two or more groups as well as look at the interaction of two independent variables on the dependent variable.

Why ANOVA is important

Analysis of variance (ANOVA) and t tests are two different ways of testing for mean differences. ANOVA has the tremendous advantage in that it can compare two or more treatment conditions and several DVs, whereas t tests are limited to two treatment conditions. When we are looking at a complex situation with more than two conditions of the IV and sometimes more than one IV, the methodology for dealing with this situation is classified under the general family of **analysis of variance (ANOVA)** techniques. Variance is a statistic that measures variability of values within a data set. It is closely related to standard deviation as **variance = SD²** or **√variance = SD**. We saw how to measure variance in Chapter 8. Since variance is the sum of squared deviations of each value from the mean divided by N, the name often given to variance in ANOVA is the **mean squared deviation**, or for short, **mean square** or **MS**.

> **ANOVA**. *This is a hypothesis testing procedure used to determine if mean differences exist for two or more samples or treatments.*

Like t tests, the purpose of ANOVA is to decide whether the differences between means of observations is simply due to chance (random sampling error) or whether there are systematic effects that have caused scores of observations in one or more groups to be statistically significantly different from those in other groups. That is, treatment effects are greater than those differences due to sampling error. The types of questions that ANOVA can answer include:

- a car manufacturer needs to determine which of four types of engine oil provides the best engine protection;
- the Ministry of Agriculture wants to compare yields from three varieties of rice under four different water irrigation patterns;
- an organizational psychologist wishes to explore whether male and female employees differ in motivation levels under three different working arrangements;
- a production manager wishes to know whether the average lifetime of an essential component is the same irrespective which of three suppliers provide it;

- an advertising manager needs to consider the sales effectiveness of various forms of advertising a particular product.

In all these examples a t test is not feasible since there are more than two groups, and while it is possible to conduct t tests between every pair of variables, we increase the chances that any significant finding might be one of the few due to chance. (Remember, at the p = .05 level, 1 in 20 results reach significance level by chance.)

The logic of ANOVA

ANOVA is built on comparing variances from two sources. These two estimates are:

- The Between Group variance – a measure of the effect of the independent variable plus the error variance.
- The Within Groups variance – the error variance alone.

The ratio between them is called the F ratio. The ratio is interpreted in association with the degrees of freedom associated with sample sizes. The basic procedure is to derive two different estimates of the population variance from the data and then calculate a statistic from the ratio of these two estimates. A significant F ratio informs us that the group means are not all equal. When the variance between groups relative to within groups is large then the F ratio is large. The larger the F ratio the more likely it is significant and that there are significant differences between some or all group means. A small F ratio close to 1 implies that the two variance estimates are very similar and therefore there are no significant differences between means; in other words, variations between the groups are no different from variations within the groups.

If you are familiar with signal detection theory, you may find it convenient to think of Between Group variance in terms of signal or information, and Within Group variance (error) in terms of noise. In signal detection theory, every observation consists of a signal that is meaningful plus noise which tends to hide or obscure the signal. If your TV aerial is not working properly, you may not be able to hear the programme for the noise or static. If the signal strength is sufficiently greater than the static then you can hear the broadcast. In the context of ANOVA, the signal is the difference between sample means and noise is the variation within each sample. If the variation between means is large enough to emerge from the noise generated by the variation within samples then the ANOVA will yield a significant F ratio, that is the group mean differences are far greater than random sample error differences that occur anyway.

Assumptions of ANOVA

The three major assumptions are:

- Normality. However, ANOVA is fairly robust for departures from normality as long as they are not extreme.
- Homogeneity of variance. This similarity of variance in each group is needed in order to 'pool' the variances into one Within Group source of variance.

- Independence of errors. Error here refers to the difference between each observation or score from its own group mean. In other words each score should be independent of any other score.

ANOVA reduces Type I and Type II errors

ANOVA is not only more economical than conducting multiple t tests, it also reduces the chances of producing both Type I and Type II errors.

Type I errors

We already know that if alpha is set at 5% this carries with it the burden of a probability of .05 of being wrong. If a scientific journal made it a practice to publish findings that all reached the .05 level of significance and each article contained one significance test, then in the long run 1 in 20 articles would be unjustified in reaching its conclusions about the null hypothesis. Extension of this reasoning would imply that if each article contained 20 t tests at the .05 level then one would be likely due to chance.

This problem is minimized by wrapping up a series of t tests into one ANOVA to produce a single level of significance, whose probability of pointing to an unjustified conclusion remains fixed at 5% or whatever significance level is chosen.

Type II errors

The virtues of ANOVA also extend to enhancing the probabilities of finding a result that might otherwise have been missed. ANOVA is more powerful than a series of t tests to detect significant differences because of the increased number of scores involved (i.e. larger N). With four groups of 15 observations, each t test is only comparing two means derived from two samples of 15 or 30 observations. In ANOVA all groups are involved, thus N increases to 60.

One way between groups ANOVA (independent groups ANOVA)

A one way ANOVA has only one IV which splits into two or more categories and seeks to demonstrate significant differences between the categories of the IV on the DV. For example, we may have a study comparing supervisor ratings of work task performance under three different noise conditions. The three noise groups are selected randomly and initially tested on work performance to ensure comparability. They work under the three noise conditions for a week and their week's performance is compared.

IV Noise conditions　　　　　　　　　　　　*DV performance*
(Nominal level)　　　　　　　　　　　　　　*(Scale level)*

No background music

Gentle quiet music　　　　　　　　　　→　　Measure of work performance

Loud cacophonous rock.

Obviously, there will be some differences in average performance scores, but are they sufficiently different to be significant or simply random sampling error variations around the mean? Our aim in ANOVA is to measure this variability and to explain its source.

> **One way analysis of variance**. *A analysis of variance in which there is only one independent variable.*

F ratio and comparison of sources of variance – a short theoretical diversion

While SPSS will undertake all the statistical manipulations it is useful to have a basic understanding of what is happening. The first step is to determine total variability or variance for the entire set of data. To do this we combine all scores from all samples to compute one general measure of variability or variance. Having done this, we break it apart into its separate components.

There are two basic components of this general variability between all subjects or observations in the one way ANOVA.

1 Between groups or treatments (conditions) variability. This variability is due to the differences between groups and is reflected in variability between sample means. The sources of this variability are:

   • treatment effects, i.e. the different music noise conditions in our hypothetical study;
   • individual differences, i.e. the uniqueness of people – in this case their differential responses to music noise; and
   • experimental error, i.e. uncontrolled and unknown causes.

2 Within groups or treatments (conditions) variability. There is variability within each sample as each person within a sample produced different results from others in that sample. This is due to:

   • individual differences; and
   • experimental error.

Once we have analysed the total variability into its basic components we simply compare them by computing **the F ratio**. For the independent measures ANOVA that we are considering here:

$$F = \frac{\text{variability between treatments}}{\text{variability within treatments}} \quad \text{or} \quad \frac{\text{between treatment variance}}{\text{within treatment variance}}$$

or

$$F = \frac{\text{treatment effect} + \text{individual differences} + \text{experimental error}}{\text{individual differences} + \text{experimental error}}$$

The single yet vital difference between the numerator and the denominator is variability caused by the treatment effect. If the null hypothesis is true then the numerator and the denominator are very similar because there is little or no treatment effect, i.e. different music noise levels had no effect – the samples are very similar with their slightly different means simply random variations around the sampling mean. The F ratio then equals 1 or close to 1.

If the null hypothesis is false the treatments, i.e. various noise levels, have had some effect and the F ratio must be much greater than 1. This is because the treatment variable is having an effect over and above that of the chance sampling variations of means, creating quite dissimilar sample means.

The F ratio. *This is the ratio of the variation between samples to the variation within samples.*

The structure of the t and F statistic are very similar; in fact $F = t^2$. t compares the actual differences between sample means with the differences expected by chance between sample means as measured by the standard error of the mean. In the same way F measures differences between samples, as measured by the variability between them and differences expected by chance, as measured by the within group variability. Because the denominator in the F ratio measures only uncontrolled and unexplained variability it is often called *the error term or residual*. Since the numerator contains treatment effects as well as the same unsystematic variability of the error term, the difference in variability must be due to the treatment.

$$F = \frac{\text{Magnitude of variation between groups}}{\text{Magnitude of variation within groups}}$$

$$= \frac{\text{Between group variance}}{\text{Within group variance}}$$

So the bigger the value for F, the more likely that the difference is significant and will also be found in the population means.

Something else is also important when calculating the probability – **the larger the samples**, the more likely the differences also exist in the population (reflected in the 'degrees of freedom').

Figures 13.1a and b illustrate in a simple way small and large treatment effects. In Figure 13.1a the clear differentiation between the groups suggests a strong treatment effect which is greater than the within treatment variability. If the between treatment effect is small compared to the within treatment effect, this would lead to a non-significant F ratio, since the effect of the treatments does not really change the variations within the groups, as in Figure 13.1b. That is, irrespective of the treatments there is still little difference between the ranges within each group. In general, where scores from two treatment samples are intermixed randomly with no clear distinction between treatments, the F value will not be statistically significant, as in Figure 13.1b.

This is a very simple example but it does help you to realize what is happening when you perform an analysis of variance.

> **MS**. *The variance or mean square deviation.*

> **MS**$_{between}$. *A measure of the variance between sample means.*

> **MS**$_{within}$. *A measure of the variance within samples often called the error term as it measures unexplained variance.*

If this is getting difficult just remember that SPSS will calculate F and report its probability.

Post hoc tests

When you reject the null hypothesis because you have a statistically significant result, this is not closure for ANOVA and a time to rejoice. It creates more questions. With a t test there are only two treatments or groups and the rejection of the null hypothesis provides a straightforward conclusion that the two means are significantly different. When you have more than two treatments or groups, the situation becomes more complex. Rejecting the null hypothesis indicates that at least one significant difference exists between the means. With three or more means, the issue is to find where those differences are. Are they all significantly different from each other or are only two different from each other with the third not significantly different? To answer these questions we need to perform a ***post hoc*** analysis (*post hoc* is Latin for after the event). The major *post hoc* tests are Tukey's HSD, Scheffe, Bonferroni and the Games-Howell procedure. We will use Tukey in our examples,

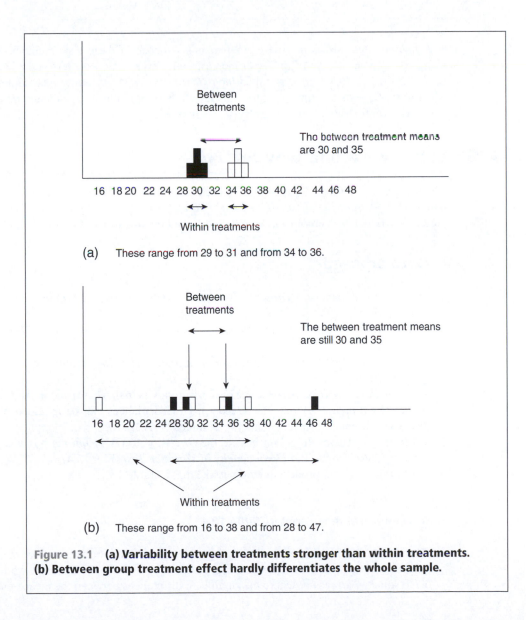

Figure 13.1   (a) Variability between treatments stronger than within treatments. (b) Between group treatment effect hardly differentiates the whole sample.

but all the tests may be accessed on SPSS. The Bonferroni is best when there are only a few comparisons, the Tukey is more powerful when there are a number of comparisons with samples that are very similar in size, but both are useful to control Type I error when variances are approximately equal. When variances differ use the Games-Howell or Dunnett.

> **A post hoc *test*.** *The test is conducted **after a significant F test** in order to identify where significant differences lie among three or more treatments.*

A *post hoc* test makes pair-wise comparisons. As each of these tests includes the risk of a Type I error, the risk of this error increases with every pair-wise test you make. This accumulation of Type I error is called the experimenter-wise or family-wise alpha level. Most *post hoc* tests attempt to control this family-wise alpha level by demanding a more rigorous level for significance on every successive test.

SPSS activity – a one way ANOVA

The computation of a one-way independent groups analysis of variance will be illustrated using *SPSS Chapter 12 data file B* for a study on whether there are significant differences in current salary between employees who hold different qualifications. Access this file now.

How to proceed

1 *Analyze >> Compare Means >> One-Way ANOVA* to open the *One-Way ANOVA* dialogue box.
2 Choose your dependent variable '*annual current salary*' and move it to the *Dependent List*: box.
3 Select the IV (grouping variable) '*qualifications*' and move it into the *Factor* box (Fig. 13.2).
4 Click on *Post Hoc* (if you have three or more groups as in this case) and in the *Post Hoc Multiple Comparison* box select *Tukey* if equal variances can be assumed. Choose *Dunnet C* if equal variances cannot be assumed (Fig. 13.3).
5 *Continue >> Option* to gain access to the *One Way ANOVA Options* box where you click on *Descriptives* and *Homogeneity of Variance Test* (Fig. 13.4).
6 *Continue >> OK* to produce the output like that in Table 13.1.

How to interpret the output in Table 13.1

- The top subtable provides the descriptive statistics. The important ones are the salary means for each qualification type since once we have a significant result we need to have some awareness of where the significant differences between the means may lie.

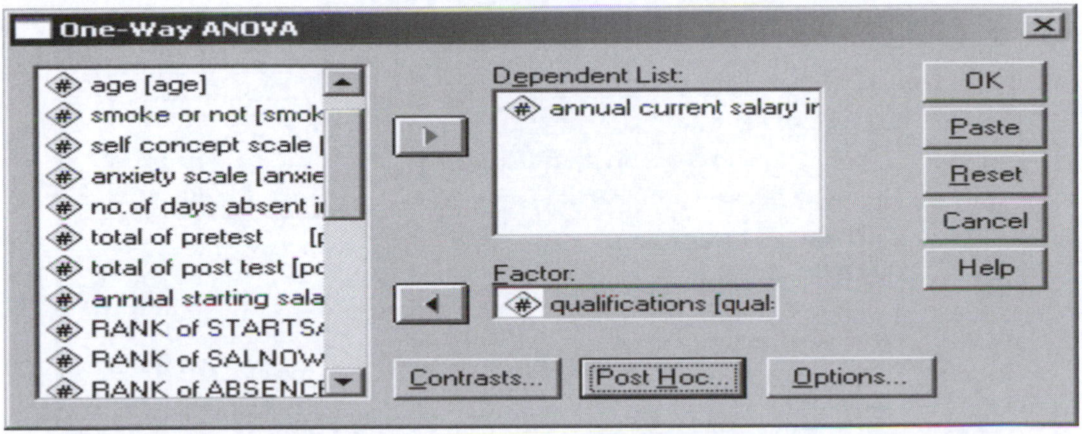

Figure 13.2   **One way ANOVA box.**

- The second subtable enables us to check that the homogeneity assumption has not been violated. Levene's Test suggests that there is a non-significant difference of 0.163 between the group variances, therefore homogeneity of variance can be accepted.
- The main ANOVA subtable appears next. This shows an F (2,37) = 17.85, p = .001. It is strongly statistically significant. The (2,37) are the degrees of freedom.
- The final subtable reports the Tukey *post hoc* test, which determines where significant differences lie. These tests indicate that the significant difference in current salaries lies between the Bachelor degree holders and both the Master and Ph.D.s, but that there is no significant difference between Masters and Ph.D. holders in mean salary. The homogeneous subsets table reveals the same pattern with Masters and Ph.D.s in the same subset and Bachelors in a different subset.

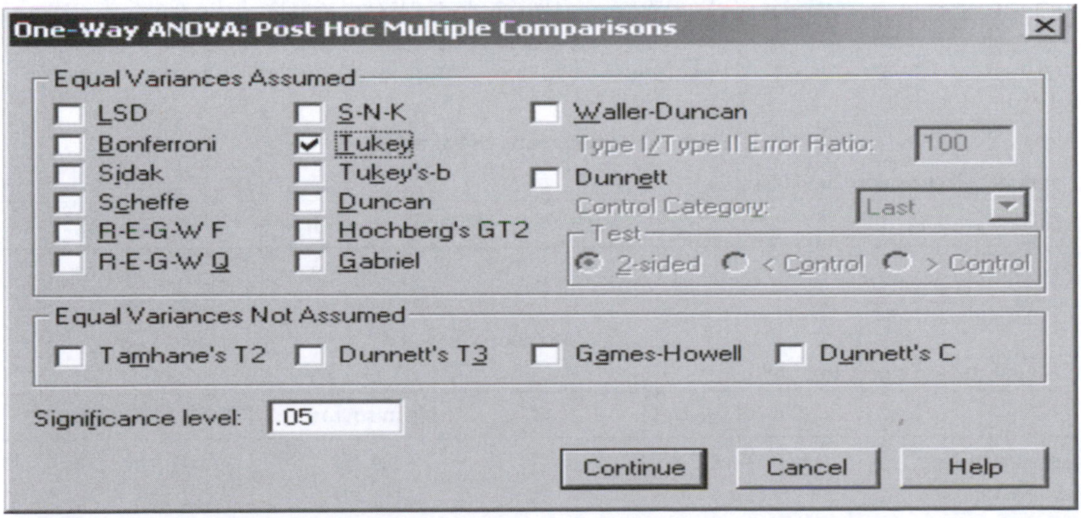

Figure 13.3   **Post hoc multiple comparison box.**

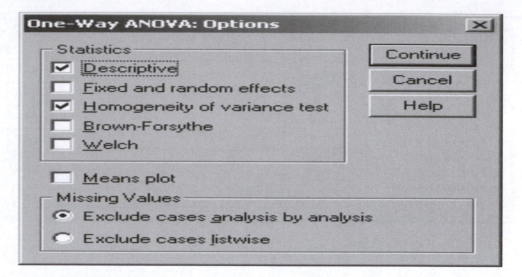

Figure 13.4   Options box.

Table 13.1   One-way ANOVA output

Descriptives

annual current salary in $1000's

	N	Mean	Std. deviation	Std. error	95% confidence interval for mean		Minimum	Maximum
					Lower bound	Upper bound		
bachelor degree	24	44.5833	8.04426	1.64203	41.1865	47.9801	34.00	67.00
masters degree	9	59.3333	14.67992	4.89331	48.0493	70.6173	35.00	84.00
Doctorate	7	69.6429	12.33124	4.66077	58.2384	81.0474	56.00	90.00
Total	40	52.2875	14.41549	2.27929	47.6772	56.8978	34.00	90.00

Test of Homogeneity of Variances

annual current salary in $1000's

Levene statistic	df1	df2	Sig.
1.904	2	37	.163

ANOVA

annual current salary in $1000's

	Sum of squares	df	Mean square	F	Sig.
Between Groups	3979.753	2	1989.877	17.850	.000
Within Groups	4124.690	37	111.478		
Total	8104.444	39			

Table 13.1 —cont'd

Post hoc tests

Multiple Comparisons

Dependent Variable: annual current salary in $1000's

Tukey HSD

(I) qualifications	(J) qualifications	Mean difference (I–J)	Std. error	Sig.	95% confidence interval Lower bound	Upper bound
bachelor degree	masters degree	−14.7500*	4.12691	.003	−24.8258	−4.6742
Doctorate		−25.0595*	4.53546	.000	−36.1328	−13.9863
masters degree	bachelor degree	14.7500*	4.12691	.003	4.6742	24.8258
Doctorate		−10.3095	5.32089	.142	−23.3004	2.6814
Doctorate	bachelor degree	25.0595*	4.53546	.000	13.9863	36.1328
masters degree		10.3095	5.32089	.142	−2.6814	23.3004

* The mean difference is significant at the .05 level.

Homogeneous subsets

Annual current salary in $1000's

Tukey HSD[a,b]

qualifications	N	Subset for alpha = .05 1	2
bachelor degree	24	44.5833	
masters degree	9		59.3333
Doctorate	7		69.6429
Sig.		1.000	.085

Means for groups in homogeneous subsets are displayed.

[a] Uses Harmonic Mean Sample Size = 10.148.

[b] The group sizes are unequal. The harmonic mean of the group sizes is used. Type 1 error levels are not guaranteed.

- The overall interpretation is that a qualification above Bachelor brings significant salary increases. The null hypothesis that there is no significant difference in salary level between holders of different academic qualifications is rejected.

Computing effect size

Generally partial Eta^2 is used in this form of ANOVA. It is interpreted as the proportion of the dependent variable that is related to the factor. This can be calculated using the formula:

$$\text{Partial Eta}^2 = \frac{\text{Sum of squares main or interaction source}}{\text{Sum of squares main or interaction source} + \text{Sum of squares error}}$$

In our case 'main' is the main effect or between groups effect while 'error' is the within groups effect:

$$\frac{3979.753}{8104.444} = 0.491$$

This is a moderate effect size suggesting 49% of the variation in the DV can be explained by the IV.

How to report the results in Table 13.1

We could report the results of the output as follows:

'The effect of qualification level on current salary was significant overall (F(2,37) = 17.85, p < 0.001) and the effect size was strong at 0.419. However, post hoc tests indicate that the means for Masters and Ph.D. holder groups did not differ significantly but both differed significantly from the mean of the Bachelor group. This suggests that possession of a higher degree is an important factor in determining salary levels but it does not matter which higher degree you possess'.

> **Now access the website for Chapter 13 and try the SPSS activity for the one way ANOVA.**

Repeated measures ANOVA

The ANOVA we have just considered was an independent group measure. The within group or repeated measures ANOVA is similar, although the denominator in the F ratio does not include individual differences as the same subjects undertake all levels of the treatment factor and only reflect experimental error.

$$\text{You will remember that the F ratio} = \frac{\text{variance between treatments}}{\text{variance within treatments}}$$

The error term is intended to produce a balanced equation if the treatment has had no effect, so in the repeated measures ANOVA the F ratio is:

$$F = \frac{\text{treatment effect} + \text{experimental error}}{\text{experimental error}}$$

> *Repeated measures analysis of variance. Analysis of variance in which each individual is measured more than once so that the levels of the independent variable are the different times or types of observations for the same people.*

When individual differences are large a repeated measures ANOVA is more sensitive to treatment effects. Let's suppose we know how much the variability is accounted for by the different components. For example:

treatment effect	10 units of variance
individual differences	1,000 units of variance
experimental error	1 unit of variance

For the independent measures we get:

$$F = \frac{\text{treatment effect} + \text{individual differences} + \text{experimental error}}{\text{individual differences} + \text{experimental error}}$$

$$F = \frac{10 + 1000 + 1}{1000 + 1} = \frac{1011}{1001} = 1.01$$

For the repeated measures we get:

$$F = \frac{\text{treatment effect} + \text{experimental error}}{\text{experimental error}}$$

$$F = \frac{10 + 1}{1} = 11$$

The repeated measures F is much larger because we have removed individual differences and so we are more likely to detect significant treatment effects which are no longer confused with individual differences.

SPSS activity – one way repeated measures ANOVA

We will illustrate the computation of a one-way repeated measures analysis of variance with dummy data relating to 40 employees who undertook a three-month training programme. Their performance of the work skills being developed on the programme was tested on three occasions: at the start (train1), midway (train2) and at the end of the programme (train3). Thus, we have a situation in which the same group produced three sets of scores. We want to know if there has been a significant improvement in skills and during what phase that improvement if any occurred. The data can be accessed on SPSS Chapter 13 Data File A. Please access it now.

Before we calculate ANOVA we must ensure that the homogeneity of variance assumption has not been violated. With repeated measures we have to compare the largest variance of the three occasions with the smallest variance of the three occasions. If the ratio is less than 3 we assume the assumption has not been violated. The check is performed by entering *Analyze > Descriptives > Descriptive Statistics* on SPSS and obtaining the variances for each occasion. In our case the ratio is 1.91.

How to analyze the data

1 *Analyze >> General Linear Model >> Repeated Measures* to open **the *Repeated Measures Define Factor(s)* dialogue box.**
2 In the ***Within Subject Factor Name*** text box type the factor name '*train*'.
3 Type the number of levels of the within subject variable in the ***Number of Levels*** box. In our case this is 3. Click ***Add*** to move to the box below.
4 ***Define >> Repeated Measures*** dialogue box.
5 Click on the 3 within subject variables, i.e. *occasions of testing (train1, train2 and train3)* and move them to the ***Within-Subjects Variables*** box (Fig. 13.5).
6 Choose ***Options*** and select ***Descriptive Statistics, Estimates of Effect Size***, and ***Observed Power*** (Fig. 13.6).
7 ***Continue >> OK*** to produce the output.

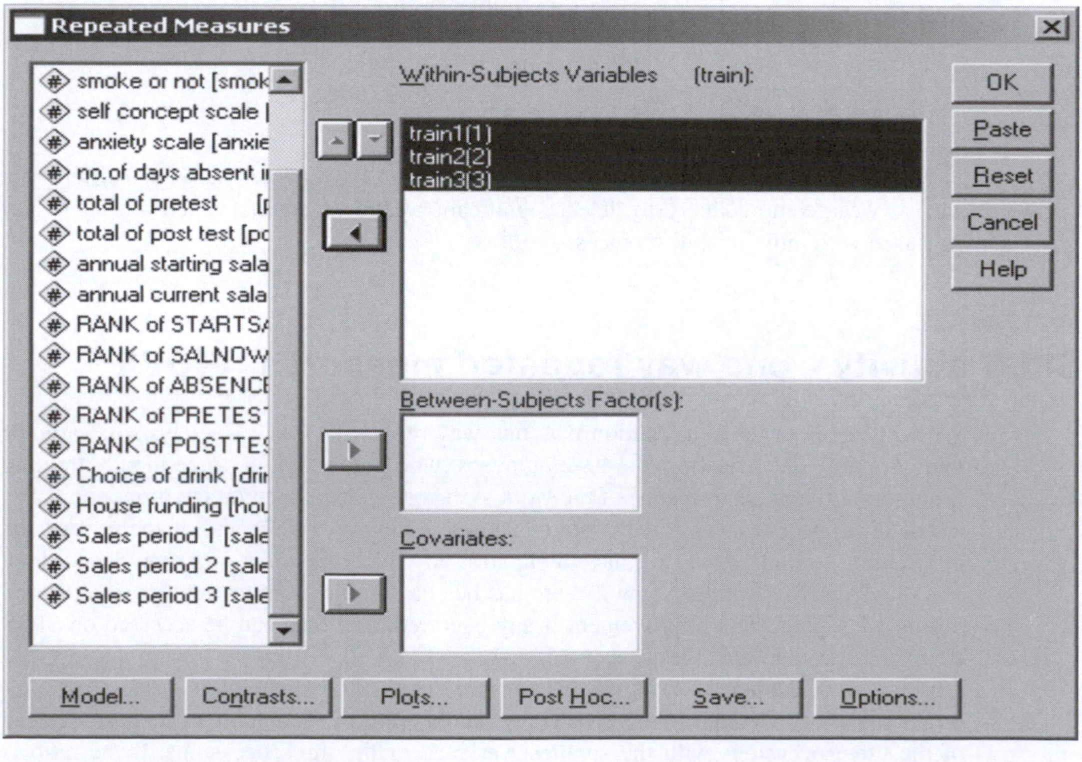

Figure 13.5 Repeated measures box.

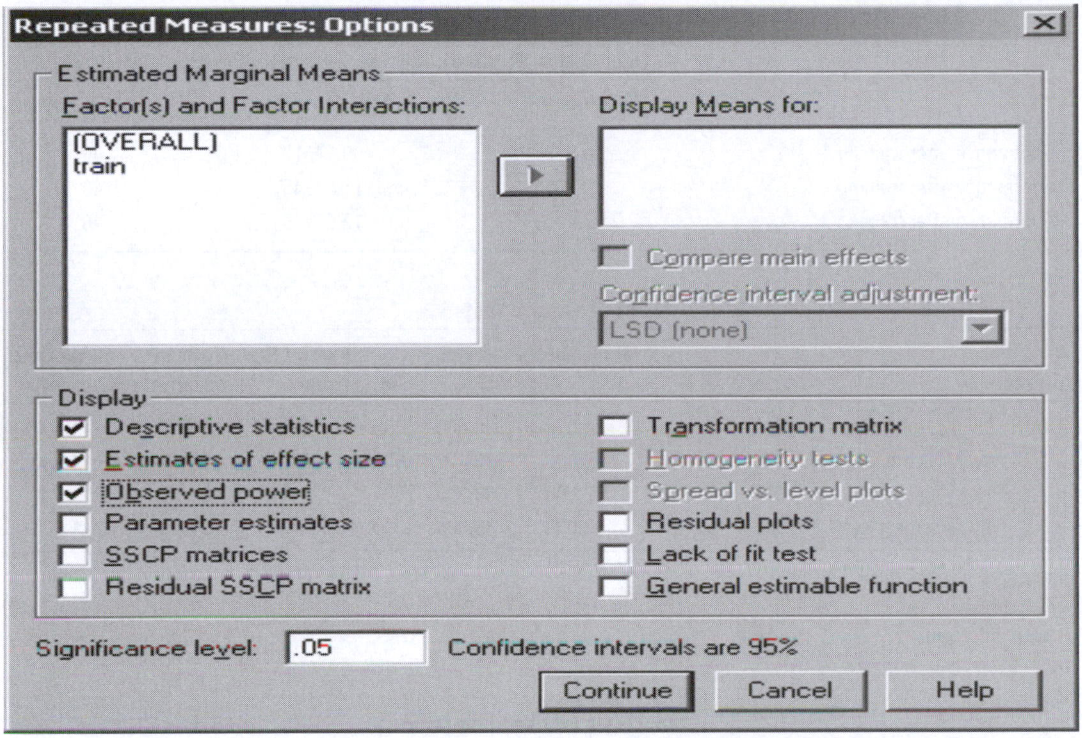

Figure 13.6   Repeated measures: Options box.

As it is essential to know the mean of each condition when you interpret the ANOVA output, included in the instructions above is the process to obtain the means and standard deviations for the three occasions of testing.

You will find SPSS produces a mountain of output for the Repeated Measures procedure. The output which is of most interest to us and reproduced here is the Descriptive Statistics subtable, the Multivariate Tests, Mauchley's Test and Tests of Within Subjects Effects subtables.

How to interpret the output in Table 13.2

- The three means and SDs are quoted in the top table. There appears to be improvement throughout the training period.
- Before we can interpret the ANOVA results we must consider the assumption of **sphericity**. This is that the variance of the population difference scores for any two conditions should be the same as the variance for the population difference scores of any other two conditions. Forget the complications and inspect the table labelled

Table 13.2   **Repeated Measures ANOVA output**

Descriptive Statistics			
	Mean	**Std. deviation**	**N**
Performance after training 1	26.9125	9.14617	40
Performance after training 2	49.1500	11.14945	40
Performance after training 3	57.4000	12.67756	40

Multivariate Tests[c]									
Effect		**Value**	**F**	**Hypothesis df**	**Error df**	**Sig.**	**Partial Eta squared**	**Noncent. parameter**	**Observed power[a]**
TRAIN	Pillai's Trace	.910	191.451[b]	2.000	38.000	.000	.910	382.903	1.000
	Wilks' Lambda	.090	191.451[b]	2.000	38.000	.000	.910	382.903	1.000
	Hotelling's Trace	10.076	191.451[b]	2.000	38.000	.000	.910	382.903	1.000
	Roy's Largest Root	10.076	191.451[b]	2.000	38.000	.000	.910	382.903	1.000

[a] Computed using alpha = .05.
[b] Exact statistic.
[c] Design: Intercept.
Within Subjects Design: TRAIN.

Mauchly's Test of Sphericity[b]

Measure: MEASURE 1

					Epsilon[a]		
Within subjects effect	**Mauchly's W**	**Approx. chi-square**	**df**	**Sig.**	**Green house-Geisser**	**Huynh-Feldt**	**Lower-bound**
TRAIN	.795	8.717	2	.013	.830	862	.600

Tests the null hypothesis that the error covariance matrix of the orthonormalized transformed dependent variables is proportional to an identity matrix.
[a] May be used to adjust the degrees of freedom for the averaged tests of significance. Corrected tests are displayed in the Tests of Within-Subjects Effects table.
[b] Design: Intercept.
Within Subjects Design: TRAIN.

Tests of Within-Subjects Effects

Measure: MEASURE 1

Source		**Type III sum of squares**	**df**	**Mean square**	**F**	**Sig.**	**Partial Eta squared**	**Noncent. parameter**	**Observed power[a]**
TRAIN	Sphericity Assumed	19894.088	2	9947.044	225.549	.000	.853	451.098	1.000
	Greenhouse-Geisser	19894.088	1.660	11986.043	225.549	.000	.853	374.360	1.000

Table 13.2—cont'd

Tests of Within-Subjects Effects—cont'd

Measure: MEASURE 1

Source		Type III sum of squares	df	Mean square	F	Sig.	Partial Eta squared	Noncent. parameter	Observed power[a]
	Huynh-Feldt	19894.088	1.724	11536.575	225.549	.000	.853	388.945	1.000
	Lower-bound	19894.088	1.000	19894.088	225.549	.000	.853	225.549	1.000
Error (TRAIN	Sphericity Assumed	3439.913	78	44.101					
	Greenhouse-Geisser	3439.913	64.731	53.142					
	Huynh-Feldt	3439.913	67.253	51.149					
	Lower-bound	3439.913	39.000	88.203					

[a] Computed using alpha = .05.

Mauchley's Test of Sphericity. If this is non-significant we can report the values for df and F along the Sphericity assumed line. If it is significant, as here, use the same table but use the Greenhouse-Geisser values for df and F in the second line.

- Since the F value is highly significant, and a large effect size, we would conclude that there is a significant difference in the mean scores on the three occasions and that the programme had produced a significant improvement with $F(2, 1.66) = 225.549$, $p = .001$. Effect size of Eta^2 is .853 and observed power 1.000.

- In order to interpret the meaning of the ANOVA, you always need to consider the means of each of the three groups of scores. If you have three or more groups, you need to check where the significant differences lie between the pairs of groups. This can be done by conducting *post hoc* pairwise comparisons.

Performing pairwise comparisons

You can do this by conducting a paired sample t test for every pairing (Chapter 12).
Table 13.3 details the paired sample results.

How to interpret Table 13.3

All the comparisons were highly significant with $p < .001$.

Table 13.3   **Paired sample t test**

			Std. deviation	Std. error mean	95% confidence interval of the difference		t	df	Sig. (2-tailed)
		Mean			Lower	Upper			
			Paired Samples Test						
			Paired differences						
Pair 1	Performance after training 1 – Performance after training 2	−22.2375	7.66359	1.21172	−24.6884	−19.7866	−18.352	39	.000
Pair 2	Performance after training 1 – Performance after training 3	−30.4875	11.23724	1.77676	−34.0813	−26.8937	−17.159	39	.000
Pair 3	Performance after training 2 – Performance after training 3	−8.2500	8.92203	1.41070	−11.1034	−5.3966	−5.848	39	.000

How to report the results in the output

We could describe the results of this analysis in the following way:

'A one-way repeated measures ANOVA showed a significant treatment effect from the training programme for the three occasions of testing. ($F(2,1.66) = 225.549$, $p < .001$. Eta squared is .853 and observed power 1.000). The start mean was 26.91, the train2 mean was 49.15, and the end of programme train3 mean was 57.4. Post hoc paired t tests between all three pairs suggested that there were highly significant differences between all pairings ($p = .001$). The results can be regarded as quite robust support for the effectiveness of the training programme.'

> **Now access the Chapter 13 website and try the SPSS activity on the repeated measure ANOVA.**

Two factor ANOVA or two way ANOVA or factorial ANOVA

In some experiments there are two variables or factors that may interact. For example, the effect of anxiety on performance may depend on level of self-esteem with anxiety only having an effect when self-esteem is low. Again verbal reinforcement may work well to produce a specified behaviour with professionally qualified employees but not so well with

> **Factorial analysis.** *When two factors of interest are to be examined at the same time.*

unskilled and semi-skilled employees, who respond better to tangible tokens of reinforcement such as a financial inducement.

In factorial ANOVA we can test a null hypothesis for each of the independent variables and also one for their interaction, the interaction effect. An interaction occurs when the effect of one independent variable on the dependent variable is not the same under all the conditions of the other independent variable. We have become familiar with the term interaction in the context of health where drugs or medicines can interact. Consider two drugs A and B and their effect on blood pressure. Drug A may lower blood pressure significantly but if drug B is also taken blood pressure increases. Thus there is an interaction in their joint effect. The same often occurs between variables in human behaviour. For example, we may be exploring the effects of different payment regimes on motivation levels of employees. We may find that males have higher motivation levels when working under payment regime A rather than B, while females register higher motivation levels when working under payment regime B than under A. In other words there is an interaction between gender and payment regime that impacts on motivation level, as the effect of the payment regimes is not the same for both genders.

Since the between treatments variability is split between the two factors and the interaction, the two factor or two way ANOVA has three distinct hypotheses.

1   The main effect of factor A (Independent Variable A). The null hypothesis states that there are no statistically significant mean differences between levels of factor A.
2   The main effect for factor B (Independent Variable B). There is a similar null hypothesis for factor B.
3   The A × B interaction. The null hypothesis states that there is no statistically significant interaction. That is, the effect of either factor is independent of the levels of the other factor.

An interaction is better seen when depicted in a graph, as in Figure 13.7. However, it is only possible to assess whether they are statistically significant by testing them with ANOVA. An interaction is indicated when the graphed lines are not parallel. The dependent variable is usually placed on the vertical axis while one of the independent variables forms the horizontal axis. The second independent variable is graphed. The following four graphs plot production figures produced under two different production methods by younger and older employees. In Figure 13.7(a) there is no main effect for production method as the means are both the same. However, there is a main effect for age as younger employees do better under both methods. There is no interaction as the lines are parallel.

In Figure 13.7(b) there is a main effect for age as the younger employees' mean is above the older employees' mean in both methods. There is also an interaction as the younger employees score higher with A while older employees do better on B.

In Figure 13.7(c) there is a main effect for age as younger employees' mean is higher than that of the older employees in each method. There is also an effect for production

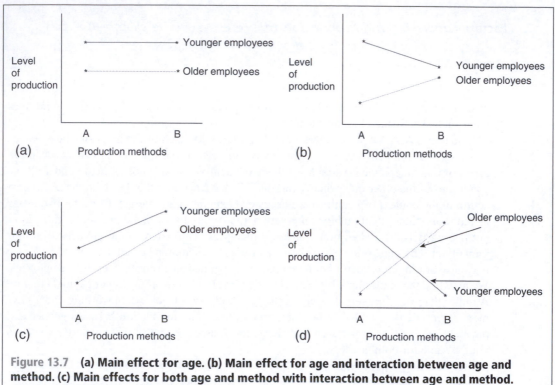

Figure 13.7 **(a) Main effect for age. (b) Main effect for age and interaction between age and method. (c) Main effects for both age and method with interaction between age and method. (d) No main effects but an interaction effect.**

method with method B producing better results than method A for both age groups. There is also an interaction with older employees improving their performance more on B than younger employees.

In Figure 13.7(d) there is neither age nor method effects as older employees' mean equals younger employees' mean and methods means are also equal. However, there is a strong interaction as older employees do much better on B while younger employees do much better on A. Remember that in cases where lines are not parallel only a statistical test will show whether there is a significant interaction present. Visual inspection is not adequate.

Interaction. *This occurs when the effect of one independent variable on the dependent variable is not the same under all the conditions of the other dependent variable.*

Main effect. *The effect of a single factor on the scores in a factorial data set.*

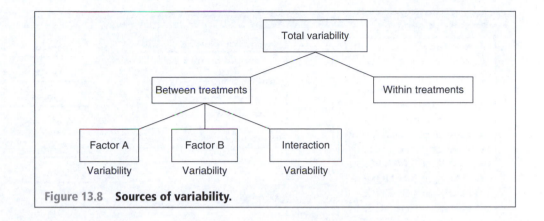

Figure 13.8   Sources of variability.

SPSS activity – two way (factorial) ANOVA

This procedure will be explained by investigating whether differences in current salary at a business company are affected by qualifications and gender, and whether there is an interaction effect between qualifications and gender in determining salary. Access SPSS Chapter 13 Data File A.

How to proceed

1 *Analyze >> General Linear Model >> Univariate*
2 Select dependent variable, e.g. *'current salary'* and move it to *Dependent Variable* box with arrow button.
3 Click on the IV's (grouping variables) *'qualifications'* and *'gender'* and move them to the *Fixed Factor(s)* box (Fig. 13.9).
4 Click *Options* and select *Descriptive Statistics, Estimates of Effect Size, Observed Power* and *Homogeneity Tests* (Fig. 13.10).
5 *Continue >> Post Hoc*. Select any factors that have more than two groups and place in *Post Hoc Tests For* box.
6 Select *Tukey*.
7 *Continue >> OK*.

How to interpret the output in Table 13.4

- The descriptive statistics suggest that, while the salary means between the qualification levels for males are different and increase with level of degree, the salary means for different qualification levels for females really only differ between bachelor and both the higher degrees which are very similar.
- Levine's test is satisfactory, showing homogeneity of variance (p = .372).
- The tests between subject effects subtable reveals a main effect for qualification (F = 16.853, p < .001) and for interaction (F = 4.364, p = .021) but none for gender.

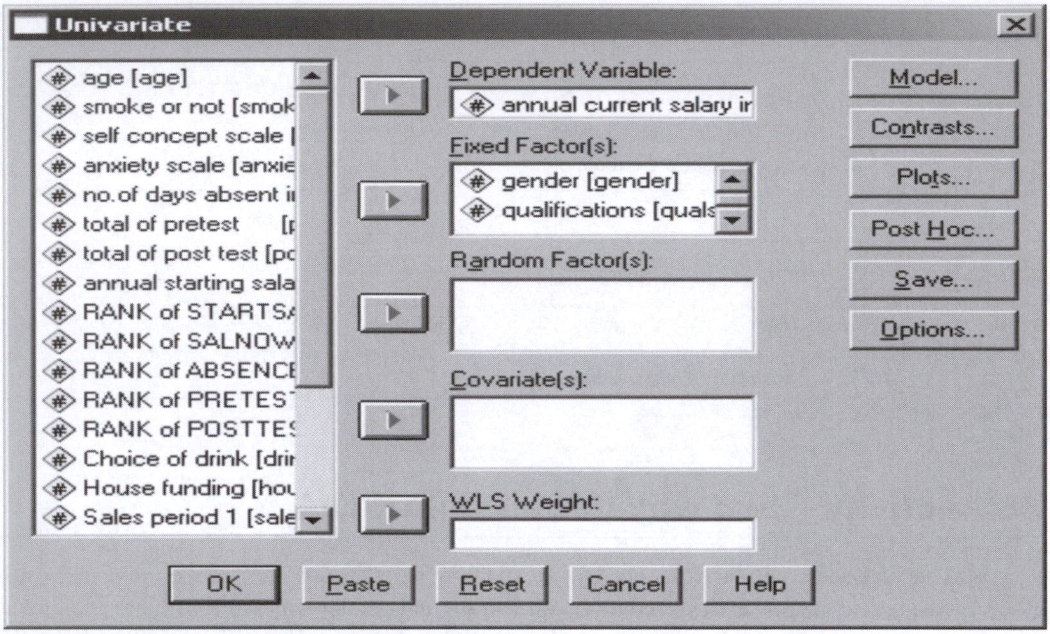

Figure 13.9   Univariate box.

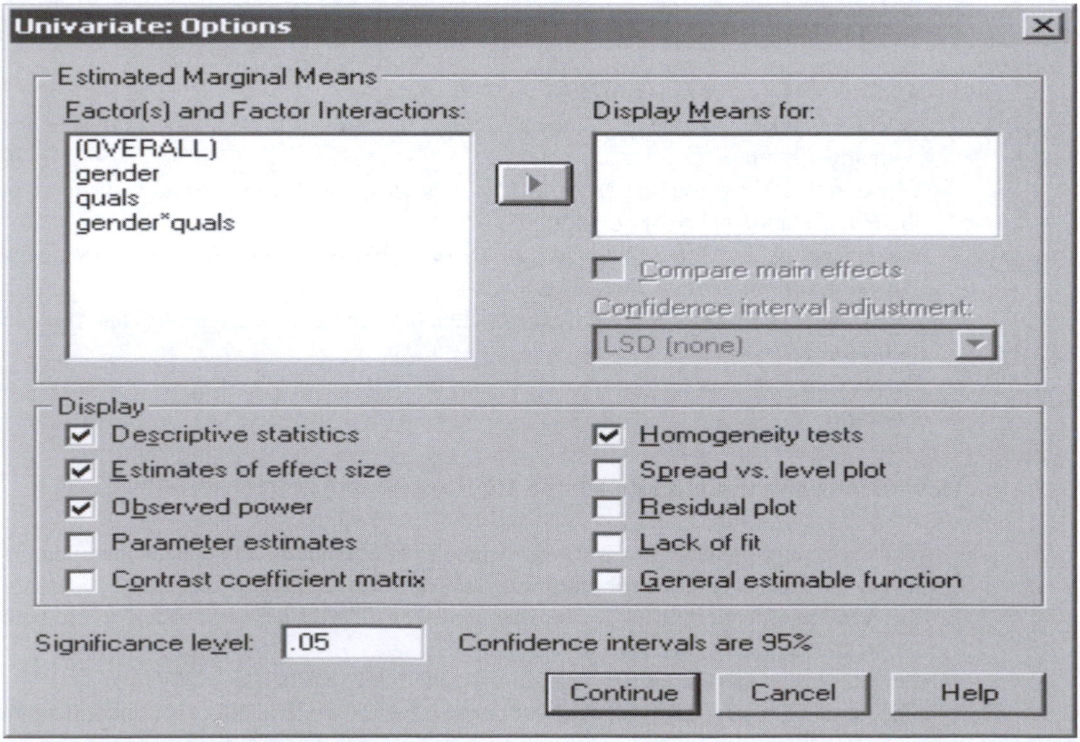

Figure 13.10   Univariate: Options box.

Table 13.4   Two way ANOVA output

Univariate Analysis of Variance

Warnings

Post hoc tests are not performed for gender because there are fewer than three groups.

Between-Subjects Factors

		Value label	N
gender	1.00	male	22
	2.00	female	18
qualifications	1.00	bachelor degree	24
	2.00	masters degree	9
	3.00	Doctorate	7

Descriptive Statistics

Dependent Variable: annual current salary in $1000's

Gender	Qualifications	Mean	Std. deviation	N
male	bachelor degree	45.1923	8.68557	13
	masters degree	48.5000	10.44829	4
	Doctorate	71.3000	13.96245	5
	Total	51.7273	14.67889	22
female	bachelor degree	43.8636	7.56667	11
	masters degree	68.0000	11.74202	5
	Doctorate	65.5000	9.19239	2
	Total	52.9722	14.47967	18
Total	bachelor degree	44.5833	8.04426	24
	masters degree	59.3333	14.67992	9
	Doctorate	69.6429	12.33124	7
	Total	52.2875	14.41549	40

Levene's Test of Equality of Error Variances[a]

Dependent Variable: annual current salary in $1000's

F	df1	df2	Sig.
1.113	5	34	.372

Tests the null hypothesis that the error variance of the dependent variable is equal across groups.

[a] Design: Intercept+GENDER+QUALS+GENDER.

* QUALS.

(Continued)

Table 13.4—cont'd

Tests of Between–Subjects Effects

Dependent Variable: annual current salary in $1000's

Source	Type III sum of squares	df	Mean square	F	Sig.	Partial Eta squared	Noncent. parameter	Observed power[a]
Corrected Model	4883.329[b]	5	976.666	10.309	.000	.603	51.545	1.000
Intercept	88939.696	1	88939.696	938.790	000	.965	938.790	1.000
GENDER	116.138	1	116.138	1.226	276	.035	1.226	.190
QUALS	3193.180	2	1596.590	16.853	000	.498	33.705	.999
GENDER * QUALS	826.973	2	413.486	4.364	.021	.204	8.729	.717
Error	3221.115	34	94.739					
Total	117463.750	40						
Corrected Total	8104.444	39						

[a] Computed using alpha = .05.
[b] R Squared = .603 (Adjusted R Squared = .544).

Post Hoc Tests – qualifications

Multiple Comparisons

Dependent Variable: annual current salary in $1000's

Tukey HSD

(I) qualifications	(J) qualifications	Mean difference (I–J)	Std. error	Sig.	95% confidence interval Lower bound	Upper bound
bachelor degree	masters degree	− 14.7500*	3.80447	.001	− 24.0726	− 5.4274
	Doctorate	− 25.0595*	4.18109	.000	− 35.3050	− 14.8140
masters degree	bachelor degree	14.7500*	3.80447	.001	5.4274	24.0726
	Doctorate	−10.3095	4.90516	.104	− 22.3293	1.7103
Doctorate	bachelor degree	25.0595*	4.18109	.000	14.8140	35.3050
	masters degree	10.3095	4.90516	.104	− 1.7103	22.3293

Based on observed means.
* The mean difference is significant at the .05 level.

Table 13.4—cont'd

Homogeneous Subsets			

Annual current salary in $1000's

Tukey HSD[a,b,c]

		Subset	
Qualifications	N	1	2
bachelor degree	24	44.5833	
masters degree	9		59.3333
Doctorate	7		69.6429
Sig.		1.000	.058

Means for groups in homogeneous subsets are displayed.
Based on Type III Sum of Squares.
The error term is Mean Square(Error) = 94.739.
[a] Uses Harmonic Mean Sample Size = 10.148.
[b] The group sizes are unequal. The harmonic mean of the group sizes is used. Type I error levels are not guaranteed.
[c] Alpha = .05.

These results were also reflected in the eta squared effect sizes and observed power, which were only strong for the qualification main effect and the interaction effect.

- The significant interaction effect is best interpreted by a graph (Fig. 13.11). This significant interaction effect shows that, for females, possession of a master's degree is the vital step, whereas for males a Ph.D. is the qualification that really brings a higher salary. The large difference at master's level, between male and female current salaries, is the cause of the significant difference. Males also receive a slightly higher salary at the lowest and highest qualification levels. The descriptives subtable also reveals this pattern but it is less easy to detect.

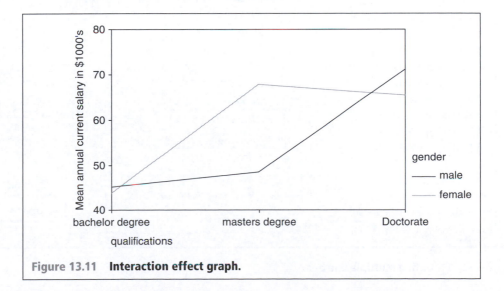

Figure 13.11   Interaction effect graph.

- The *post hoc* test is necessary only for the significant main effect of qualification and reveals that the significance lies between the mean salary for bachelor holders and the mean salaries for both higher degrees. No significance was noted between the two higher degree mean salaries.

Procedure to draw interaction effect graphs

1 *Graphs >> Line >> Multiple >> Define.*
2 In the *Define Multiple Line: Summaries for Groups of Cases* box, select *Other summary function* and transfer the DV there (in this case *current salary*).
3 Into *category axis* place the IV you want on the X axis (here *qualifications*) and into *Define Lines* By place the other IV (in this case *gender*) (Fig. 13.12).
4 *OK*.

You can place either the IV in either *Category axis* or *Define Lines By* selection boxes. It just reveals the interaction in a different way but does not change the interpretation. If you switch them around in this example, the differential effect of having a master's degree is really emphasized.

Now access the website and tackle the SPSS activity on factorial ANOVA.

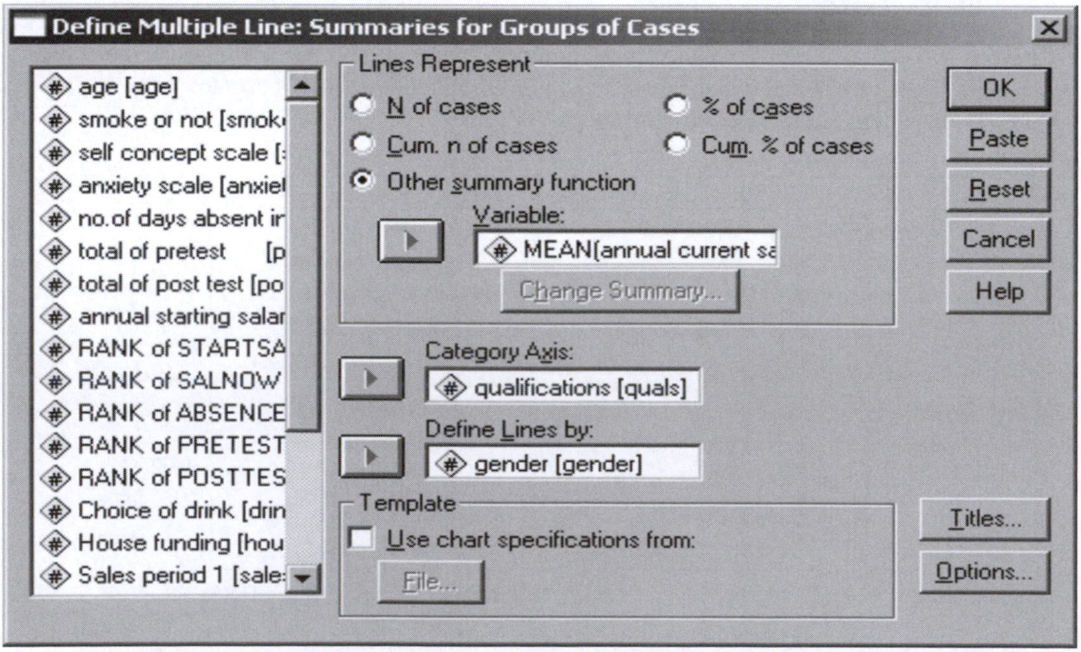

Figure 13.12 **Define multiple line box.**

Analysis of covariance or ANCOVA

An ANCOVA is a form of analysis that is based on a combination of regression (Chapter 16) and ANOVA. It tells you whether your groups differ on a dependent variable when you have partialled out (removed the effects of) another variable called the covariate that has a relationship with the dependent variable. ANCOVA therefore adjusts the means on the covariate so that the mean covariate score is the same for all groups and therefore any changes in the DV are solely due to the treatment variable.

For example, skilled task performance increases with age between 20 and 40 years old but length of experience is a covariate that would mask the effects of age since age and experience would have some reasonable correlation. ANCOVA then answers the question, **'What would the means of each group be on the DV if the means of the three groups had the same mean on experience?'**, i.e. it adjusts the DV means so that we can investigate the mean differences for age only. It is mostly used in pretest–post-test designs where researchers want to partial out (remove or hold constant) the effect of a confounding variable. Using simple difference scores between pre and post-test does not achieve this.

As another example, imagine we want to test whether alcohol affects driving performance. Three levels of alcohol (placebo, low alcohol, high alcohol groups) were tested to determine if there were differences in driving errors made on a simulator. Of course, while alcohol may have an effect, length of driving experience of subjects would also have some influence. We could show this variation in driving error by using number of years driving experience on a one way ANOVA. But our real interest is the effects of alcohol levels so these differences will get totally mixed up with the experience factor. Clearly an ANCOVA is needed to remove (partial out) the effect of years of driving experience.

A common use of ANCOVA is in the pretest–post-test design. In this situation the pretest scores are used as the covariate as it is normally correlated with the post-test scores, disguising the true effect of the intervening treatment. We want to ensure that we are measuring the effects of the treatment on the post-test only.

> *ANCOVA. A technique that adjusts the means on the covariate so that the mean covariate score is the same for all groups.*

SPSS activity – ANCOVA analysis

Imagine a sales manager wants to determine whether her male or female staff were statistically significantly more successful salespersons, basing her research on her 40 sales staff. However, she felt that age would also contribute and might mask the gender effect and that a better picture would emerge if she controlled the age factor. Load SPSS Chapter 13 Data File B.

How to proceed

1 *Analyze >> General Linear Model >> Univariate* to open the **Univariate** box.
2 Move the *DV* (*sales in period 2*) to the **Dependent variable** box.

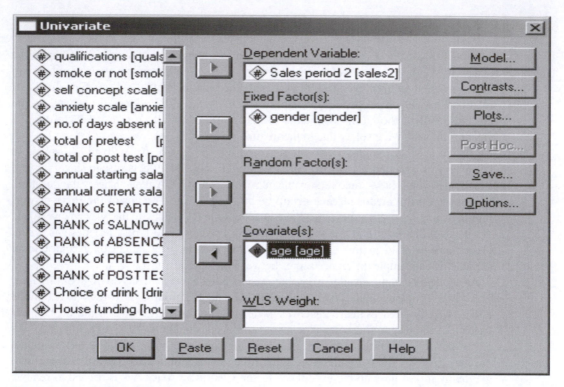

Figure 13.13 **Univariate box.**

3 Move the *IV* (*gender*) to the **Factor box**.
4 Move the *covariate* (*age*) to the **Covariate** box (Fig. 13.13).
5 Click on **Options** to open **Univariate:Options** subdialogue box.
6 Check for **Descriptive statistics, Estimates of Effect Size, Observed power** and **Homogeneity tests.**
7 **Continue >> OK**.

Interpreting output in Table 13.5

- The first two subtables provide the basic descriptive data.
- Levine's test is not significant (p = .213) therefore we have not violated assumptions of homogeneity.
- The output indicates no significant effect for gender even when there is a statistical control for age. There is a significant main effect for age (F = 5.947, p = .02), suggesting that it is age, reflecting years of experience, that is most important for sales success.
- Effect size is not large and only explains 13.8% of the variation in sales. Observed power for age is also fairly average. Effect size and power for gender are minimal.

Table 13.5   Output for ANCOVA

Between-Subjects Factors

		Value label	N
gender	1.00	male	22
	2.00	female	18

Descriptive Statistics

Dependent Variable: Sales period 2

gender	Mean	Std. deviation	N
male	42.7500	17.93092	22
female	46.2778	17.31985	18
Total	44.3375	17.52265	40

Levene's Test of Equality of Error Variances[a]

Dependent Variable: Sales period 2

F	df1	df2	Sig.
1.607	1	38	.213

Tests the null hypothesis that the error variance of the dependent variable is equal across groups.

[a] Design: Intercept+AGE+GENDER.

Tests of Between-Subjects Effects

Dependent Variable: Sales period 2

Source	Type III sum of squares	df	Mean square	F	Sig.	Partial Eta squared	Noncent. parameter	Observed power[a]
Corrected Mod	1764.242[b]	2	882.121	3.197	.052	.147	6.393	.576
Intercept	10646.432	1	10646.432	38.580	.000	.510	38.580	1.000
AGE	1641.034	1	1641.034	5.947	.020	.138	5.947	.661
GENDER	370.839	1	370.839	1.344	.254	.035	1.344	.204
Error	10210.452	37	275.958					
Total	90607.250	40						
Corrected Total	11974.694	39						

[a] Computed using alpha = .05.

[b] R Squared = .147 (Adjusted R Squared = .101).

Using SPSS with a before–after design or pretest–post-test design

Access SPSS Chapter 13 Data File B and we will see if, by holding the sales level prior to training constant, there is a significant effect on the post-training level sales between those who trained and those who did not. That is, did training have an effect on post-test sales? The instructions are the same as those already given above. Note the pretest level is the covariate, the group factor is whether the person attended training or not and the DV is post-test sales. The printout is displayed below.

Interpretation of Table 13.6

We will focus on the last two tables.

- Levine's test is non-significant and therefore satisfactory (p = .380)
- Training has a significant effect ((F = 7.636, p = .01, and effect size .22) independent of initial sales performance. But initial sales performance has a much stronger effect. Thus prior sales performance is a better predictor of later sales performance (82.3%) than training (22%) but the latter does add to performance significantly.

Table 13.6   **Ancova output**

Between-Subjects Factors			
		Value label	N
employee training	1.00	been on training course	17
	2.00	not attended training course	13

Descriptive Statistics			
Dependent Variable: end of training sales performance			
Employee training	**Mean**	**Std. deviation**	**N**
been on training course	27.5882	4.28746	17
not attended training course	19.2308	6.17999	13
Total	23.9667	6.60973	30

Table 13.6—cont'd

Levene's Test of Equality of Error Variances[a]

Dependent Variable: end of training sales performance

F	df1	df2	Sig.
.795	1	28	.380

Tests the null hypothesis that the error variance of the dependent variable is equal across groups.

[a] Design: Intercept+SALES1+TRAINED.

Tests of Between-Subjects Effects

Dependent Variable: end of training sales performance

Source	Type III sum of squares	df	Mean square	F	Sig.	Partial Eta squared	Noncent. parameter	Observed power[a]
Corrected Mode	1133.552[b]	2	566.776	114.702	.000	.895	229.404	1.000
Intercept	273.211	1	273.211	55.291	.000	.672	55.291	1.000
SALES1	619.011	1	619.011	125.273	.000	.823	125.273	1.000
TRAINED	37.729	1	37.729	7.636	.010	.220	7.636	.759
Error	133.415	27	4.941					
Total	18499.000	30						
Corrected Total	1266.967	29						

[a] Computed using alpha = .05.

[b] R Squared = .895 (Adjusted R Squared = .887).

> Now access the website and try the SPSS ANCOVA activity.

Non-parametric alternatives of ANOVA

Kruskal-Wallis one way non-parametric ANOVA

The Kruskal-Wallis test is a non-parametric alternative to the one way between groups ANOVA and an extension of the Mann-Whitney test to situations where more than two samples are involved. It determines whether independent samples are from different populations and uses ordinal data. Therefore all scores must be transformed into ranks by combining all scores from all samples into one series. When this is completed, the sum of ranks in each condition is found. The test determines whether these sums of ranks are distributed randomly, indicating that they are likely to have come from samples all drawn from the same population (null hypothesis) by comparing mean ranks of each group.

> *Kruskal-Wallis. Non-parametric equivalent of a one way between groups ANOVA using ranked data.*

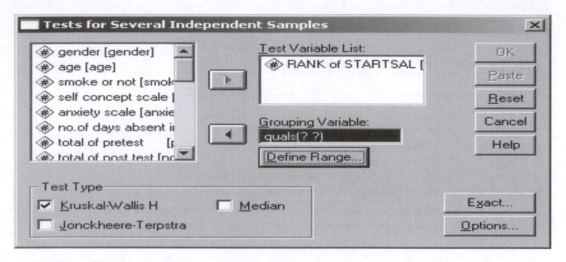

Figure 13.14   **Test for several independent samples box.**

SPSS activity – Kruskal-Wallis test

A personnel manager of a large multi-national is interested in seeing whether 40 new employees with different qualification levels are being rewarded with an appropriate starting salary. The data appears to violate the assumptions of ANOVA so a non-parametric test using rank (ordinal) data is prescribed. Access SPSS Chapter 13 Data File A.

How to proceed

1   *Analyze >> Non-parametrics >> K-independent samples*.
2   Ensure only the *Kruskal-Wallis* option is selected in the *Test Type* box.
3   Click the treatment variable (in our example *Rank StartSal*) and move it to the *Test Variable* list box (Fig. 13.14).
4   Select *Group* (*in our case qualifications*) and move that to the *Grouping Variable* box.
5   Choose *Define Range*. Type 1 as the minimum value; type as maximum value the total number of groups (in our case this is 3) (Fig. 13.15).
6   *Continue >> OK*.

Figure 13.15   **Define range box.**

Table 13.7   Kruskal-Wallis test output

Ranks			
	Qualifications	**N**	**Mean rank**
RANK of STARTSAL	bachelor degree	24	15.31
	masters degree	9	24.22
	Doctorate	7	33.50
	Total	40	

Test Statistics[a,b]	
	RANK of STARTSAL
Chi-Square	14.318
df	2
Asymp. Sig.	.001

[a] Kruskal-Wallis Test.
[b] Grouping Variable: qualifications.

How to interpret output in Table 13.7

- The top subtable lists the mean ranks on starting salary for each group.
- The test statistics subtable offers a chi square (14.318, p = .001) which indicates a significant difference between median ranks.
- If there are significant differences, pairwise comparisons among the groups need to be conducted using the Mann-Whitney test (Chapter 12) to determine between which pairs the significant difference lies. We did this and found that the significance lies between groups 1 and 2, 1 and 3, but not between 2 and 3.

How to report results in printout

'A Kruskal-Wallis test was conducted to evaluate differences among the three qualification groups on mean starting salary. The test was significant (chi square = 26.92, p = .001). Post hoc pairwise comparisons using Mann-Whitney demonstrated a significant difference between the bachelor holder salary level and both the higher degree holders' salaries. There was no significant difference between the Masters and Ph.D. salary levels'.

Friedman two way non-parametric ANOVA

This test is a non-parametric repeated measures ANOVA on ranked data that can be applied when measurements are made at several points in time and when assumptions of normality are not met. Imagine we want to find out whether significant differences in performance of

40 employees occur over three training periods and between which training periods but we are aware that assumptions for ANOVA are not met, then Freidman would be the appropriate test. Access SPSS Chapter 13 Data File A.

SPSS activity – Friedman test

How to proceed

1 *Analyze >> Non-parametric tests >> K Related samples.*
2 Transfer the variables (train1; train2; and train3) to the *Test Variables* box.
3 Choose *Friedman* and *Kendall's W* in the *Test Type* area (Fig. 13.16).
4 *OK*.

How to interpret the results in Table 13.8

- The test statistics subtable reveals a statistically significant result (chi square = 71.250, p = .001).
- Kendall's W .891 can be used as an effect size index; in this case a large effect size suggesting 89% of the variation between occasions is accounted for.
- If significance is reached, a follow-up test must be applied to determine where the differences lie. For this we use Wilcoxon (see Chapter 12), to test each pair in turn. We did this and all pairings are significantly different, suggesting that improvement is continuous throughout the programme.

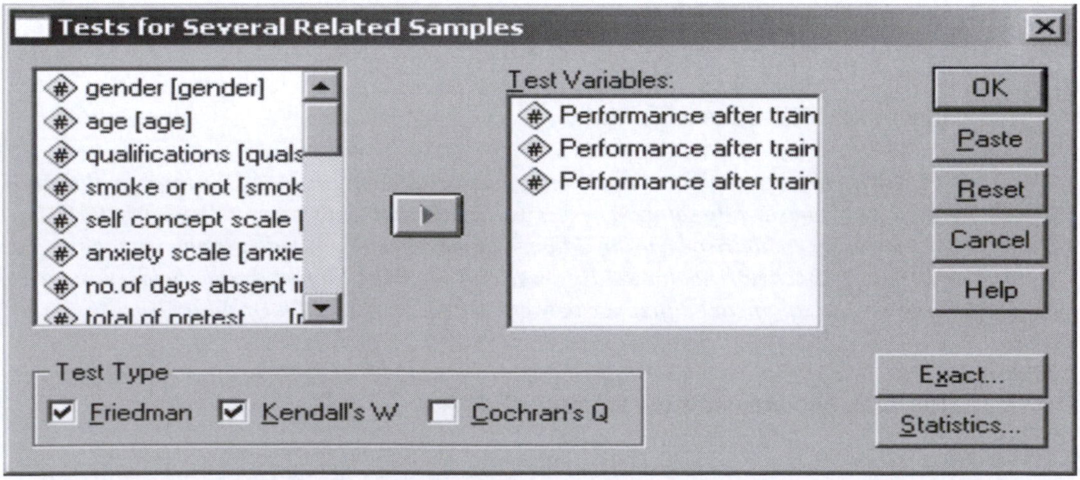

Figure 13.16 **Test for several related samples.**

Table 13.8   **Friedman test output**

Ranks	
	Mean rank
Performance after training 1	1.00
Performance after training 2	2.13
Performance after training 3	2.88

How to report results of the printout

'A Friedman test was conducted to evaluate mean rank differences between 40 employees in their performance after periods of training. Significant differences were obtained at the end of each training period (chi square = 71.250, p = .001). Kendall's W of .891 indicated fairly strong effects for the differences. Follow-up pairwise comparisons conducted using a Wilcoxon test revealed that significant differences were present between the three possible pairings of mean ranks'.

Now access the website and attempt the SPSS activities on Kruskal-Wallis and the Friedman test.

Tips for writing a results section for ANOVA

As ANOVA procedures are more involved than most of the previous statistical procedures discussed, here are some guidelines for writing a results section for statistical procedures that may require follow-up tests, such as one-way ANOVA and factorial ANOVA.

Steps
1   Describe the statistical test(s), the variables, and the purpose of the statistical test(s).
   For example: *'A one-way analysis of variance was conducted to evaluate whether different multi vitamin treatments had a significant effect on the number of days absence from work over a year'.*
   • Describe the factor or factors. Describe each factor as a between-subjects or a within-subjects factor.
   • Indicate the number of levels for each factor and describe them if necessary, e.g. the three levels of instruction for the task were oral, written and trial and error. It is not necessary to report the number of levels and describe levels for obvious factors like gender.
   • Describe the dependent variable(s).

(Continued)

2 Report the results of the overall test(s).
- Explain why the particular test was chosen based on assumptions and design.
- Report the F value and significance level (e.g. $F_{(2, 27)} = 4.84$, V .016). For p-values of .000 quote $p < .001$. For multifactor designs, report the statistics for each of the main and interaction effects. State whether the test(s) are significant or not.
- Report effect size to allow a judgement about the magnitude of the effect for each overall test.

3 Report the descriptive statistics, usually by reference to a table or figure that presents the means and standard deviations.

4 Describe and summarize the general conclusions of the analysis. An example: *'The results of the one-way ANOVA supported the alternative hypothesis that three types of stress management treatment each had a differential effect on the reduction of absence for city bus drivers'.*

5 Report the results of the follow-up tests:
- Describe the follow-up tests.
- Summarize the results by presenting the results of the significance tests among pairwise comparisons with a table of means and standard deviations.
- Describe and summarize the general conclusions of the follow-up analyses. Make sure to include in your description the directionality of the test.

6 Report the distributions of the dependent variable for levels of the factor(s) in a graph. Graph interactions if you have a factorial ANOVA.

What you have learned from this chapter

You have seen that ANOVA is a very important family of statistical techniques used to test for mean differences among two or more treatment conditions or populations in both independent and repeated measures designs, as well as complex factorial designs. The null hypothesis states that there are no significant differences between any of the means while the alternative hypothesis only requires at least one mean to be significantly different from the others.

The test statistic is the F ratio. Where the numerator and denominator measure approximately the same variance the null hypothesis is true and F will be 1 or close to it. If the treatment effect is having any influence on the group means the between group variance will be larger than the within group variance and thus F will be larger than 1.

When a significant F is found and there are three or more groups (treatments) then a *post hoc* test like Tukey must be applied to determine between which pair(s) the significance lies.

A factorial ANOVA investigates the effects of two independent variables identified as A and B. Within each factor there can be two or more levels. A factorial ANOVA will determine effects produced by different levels of factor A, effects produced by different levels of factor B, and differences that are produced by unique combinations of A and B. This enables interactions to be assessed where the effect of one factor depends on the levels of the others. A two-factor analysis of variance produces three F ratios – one for A, one for B and one for the interaction of A × B.

ANCOVA enables covariates of the dependent variable to be controlled so the effect of the IV is uncontaminated.

Non-parametric alternatives such as the Kruskall-Wallis and Friedman test are available for you to use when the assumptions of ANOVA cannot be met.

Review questions

Ou, 13.1
In groups explain how the F ratio works.

Qu. 13.2
When there are two treatment conditions, is a *post hoc* test necessary? Explain your answer.

Qu. 13.3
What is a covariate? Can you think up some situations where a covariate might be involved?

Check your answers in the material above.

Now access the website and try the multiple choice questions. You should also tackle the SPSS activities and other questions located there.

Chapter 14
Chi Square

Content list

By the end of this chapter you should be able to:

1 Understand the situations in which chi square is the appropriate statistic.
2 Use chi square in a goodness-of-fit test.
3 Use chi square to determine the degree of relationship between nominal variables in a cross-tabulation (contingency) format.
4 Use SPSS to calculate and interpret chi square goodness-of-fit and cross-tabulation printouts.

Introduction

In the previous two chapters we considered the testing of hypotheses that stated differences between groups. But testing for significant relationships is equally important. In this and the next chapter, we will look at how we test hypotheses that state relationships. The chi square test is a non-parametric test used when the variables are nominal.

What is chi square used for?

The chi square distribution uses nominal data such as counts or frequencies within categories. Many real world business situations produce a collection of count or frequency data and as a result chi square analysis is very common and useful.

For example, the nominal data may be:

- the number of people who indicate which one of three brands of toothpaste they prefer;
- membership or not of a trade union among full-time and part-time employees;
- number of investments by investment categories;
- different categories of responses made to a market research survey question by persons classified by age, sex, job classification or income age group;
- vehicles registered by the Department of Transport, classified and counted under headings such as cars, buses, commercial vehicles, motor bicycles;
- Immigration Department counts of the different type of immigrants, such as residents returning home, foreign work permit holders, business visitors and tourists.

For the chi square test, categories of responses are set up, such as Brands A, B and C of toothpaste, or 'member' and 'non-member' of the union, and the number of individuals, observations or events falling into each category of response.

Response distributions may be like those below:

1   Association between preferences for toothpaste brand and respondent gender:

Brand	Male	Female
Minty	21	46
Pegsave	83	14
Dentcool	27	63

2   The relationship between union membership and type of employment in the company:

Union member	Full time	Part time
Yes	68	13
No	10	74

In each of the above examples, both variables consist of a small number of categories containing the number or frequency of the sample found in each. This constitutes nominal data. With such data, the only analysis possible is to determine whether the frequencies observed in the sample differ significantly from hypothesized or expected frequencies.

Tables like those above are often called **cross-tabulation or contingency tables**. Each cell of the table is the intersection of a row and column and contains the frequency of individuals in that intersection. In Example 1 above, 46 females prefer Minty, while 27 males choose Dentcool. In Example 2, 13 out of 87 part-time employees are union members.

> **Contingency table.** *A two-dimensional table showing frequencies in each combination of categories for two dichotomous nominal variables, i.e. four cells.* **Cross-tabulation** *has more than four cells.*

Chi square is therefore the most common and simple non-parametric test of significance suitable for nominal data where observations can be classified into discrete categories and treated as frequencies. The symbol for this statistic is the Greek letter chi, which is pronounced 'ky' to rhyme with 'sky', and usually written as:

$$\chi^2$$

Chi square tests hypotheses about the independence (or alternatively the association) of frequency counts in various categories. The hypotheses for the chi square test are:

H_0 where the variables are statistically independent or no statistical association, and
H_1 where the variables are statistically dependent or associated.

In our examples above the null hypothesis would state that there is no significant association between your gender and which toothpaste you prefer; or that union membership is independent of (not associated with) type of employment, i.e. that the cross-categories from each variable are independent of each other.

The formula for chi square is the summation **for each cell** of:

$$\frac{(\text{observed frequency} - \text{expected frequency})^2}{\text{expected frequency}}$$

The mathematical formula is chi square $= \sum \dfrac{(O - E)^2}{E}$ where

O = observed frequency – the data observed in our research/survey
E = expected frequency, and
Σ = the summation over all the cells in the table

There are two major uses of chi square:

1   As a *goodness-of-fit test* when it tells us how well an observed distribution fits a hypothesized or theoretical distribution. For example:
   (a) Are some brands of frozen peas chosen by consumers more than others?

(b) Is absence through sickness regularly distributed through the working week or is 'sick leave' more frequent on some days than other days?

(c) Are choices on an item with a three-point response scale of '*yes*', '*no opinion*', '*no*', equally divided, or is there a significant preference for one choice to the item?

2   As a *cross-tabulation* between two categories, each of which can be divided into two or more sub-categories; for example, preference for type of music (classical, jazz, country and western, rock) against age group (below 21; 21–45; above 45); length of service in year groupings against position level.

But to whichever of these uses chi square is put, the general principle remains the same.

One compares the observed frequencies in a sample with the expected (chance) frequencies and applies the chi square test to determine whether a difference between observed and expected frequencies is likely to be a function of sampling error (non-significant – retaining the null hypothesis H0) or unlikely to be a function of sampling error (significant association – reject the null hypothesis and support alternative hypothesis – H1).

> **The observed frequency.** *The number of observations classified in a particular category.*

> **The expected frequency.** *The frequency value that is predicted from the null hypothesis and sample size, and is often the ideal sample distribution.*

Goodness-of-fit chi square

The whole idea of non-parametric tests is that they can be used when we do not know the distribution. In these situations, we often test any assumption we have about the shape of the distribution. Any test that compares the observations with the assumed or expected frequencies to see how well the latter 'fit' the observed frequencies, is called a **goodness-of-fit test**. Two major statistical assumptions are that the distribution is (i) uniform (equally split), or (ii) normally distributed.

The null hypothesis for the goodness-of-fit test states that the frequency distribution of one population does not differ from the known frequency distribution of another population or from chance expectancy. For example, it may be known that 60% of England's population favour the government's water conservation policy and 40% are in opposition. Does this same pattern exist in Scotland and Wales? The null hypothesis states that there is no difference between the populations, i.e. that the distribution in Scotland and Wales fits the national picture.

Because the null hypothesis in a goodness-of-fit test specifies an exact distribution, the alternative hypothesis simply states that the distribution is a different shape from that specified in the null hypothesis. For example, if a fair dice is rolled, we expect each of the six numbers to occur approximately one sixth of the time (H_0). If there is a significant deviation from this then we are entitled to conclude that the dice is biased (H_1). Or we may wish to determine whether the proportion of defective units produced on each of four parallel assembly lines producing computer boards would be the same for each of four different assembly line speeds. The defect rate is known to be 5%. Thus, by having the assembly lines run at different speeds the defect rates could be compared with the known uniform rate to determine whether it would be possible to run the system at some faster speed without sacrificing quality.

> *Goodness-of-fit test. This measures how closely observed sample data fit a particular hypothesized distribution.*

Testing the assumption of uniform distribution

Example 1

Here is an example of a goodness-of-fit chi square using the assumption of a uniform distribution. Consider the question: *'Is more staff sick leave recorded on some days of the week rather than on other days?'* Here is some dummy observed data on number of staff off sick per day.

Monday	Tuesday	Wednesday	Thursday	Friday	Total
64	29	15	20	72	200

What sort of distribution would you expect if day of the week did not in fact have any influence? We would expect an even distribution. That is, one-fifth, or 20%, or 40 each day. The question is now:

'Is the fact that the observed frequencies are different from what we expected more likely due to chance, or does it more likely represent *actual differences* in absences on different days of the week?'

That is: is there an association between days of the week and sick leave? The null hypothesis claims that there is no such significant association and that the observed frequency distribution is simply due to chance. The chi square test permits us to estimate the probability that observed frequencies differ from expected frequencies through chance alone.

But how far can a departure from these frequencies go before we can say that such a discrepancy would occur so infrequently on a chance basis that our observations are significantly different from those expected and that there is relationship? Well, of course SPSS calculates this for us and produces the significance of the result.

Moreover, for small numbers, chi square can actually be easily calculated by hand; we need to enter our observed and expected data into a table of cells on the lines of the following model:

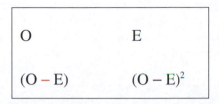

where O = Observed data and E = Expected data

We will now fill in the cells in our example by placing the observed and expected data into their respective cells and calculate $(O - E)$ and $(O - E)^2$. Since we have observed 200 sick leave absences the expected uniform or equal frequency in each cell must be 40, i.e. 20% of the sample size for each of five days.

Monday		Tuesday		Wednesday		Thursday		Friday	
64	40	29	40	15	40	20	40	72	40
24	576	11	121	25	625	20	400	32	1024

$$\text{Chi square} = \sum \frac{(O - E)^2}{E} = \frac{576}{40} + \frac{121}{40} + \frac{625}{40} + \frac{400}{40} + \frac{1024}{40}$$

Chi square = 68.65

A relatively large chi square like this suggests that the 'O's' differed more from the 'E's' than is likely by chance. The raw data was inputed into SPSS and it calculated chi square as 68.65 as above and this is strongly significant $(p < .01)$.

We can reject the null hypothesis with confidence, and accept the alternative hypothesis that sick leave is not randomly distributed through the week. To specify how it is distributed, you must return to inspect the original data where you can readily appreciate that absences are much higher on Mondays and Fridays and much lower on other days of the week. I leave the interpretation and speculation of why to you!

A chi square of zero indicates that the observed and expected frequencies match exactly. Chi square can never be negative since differences between the observed and expected are always squared.

Degrees of freedom in a goodness-of-fit chi square

SPSS uses degree of freedom (df) in its interpretation of the calculated chi square. For the goodness-of-fit chi square df = (number of categories – 1). The number of observations free to vary in our example is 4 because, once we have fixed the frequency of four days, the fifth day has to make the total 200. So the fifth category is fixed and the degree of freedom for that category is lost. The same principle holds true for any number of categories.

> The **degrees of freedom** in a **goodness-of-fit test** is one less than the number of categories.

Example 2

The TEL-MOB company that sells mobile phones wants to make sure they have sufficient inventory level of their four types of phone to guard against the possibility of lost sales because one type of stock is exhausted. The company decides to test the null hypothesis of uniform demand. The alternative hypothesis is that demand is not uniform for all types of mobile phone.

The null hypothesis of uniform demand presumes purchase of an equal number of each type of phone over a fixed period, say of a month. The average number of phones sold each month over the last year was 480. If demand is uniform the company can expect 120 of each phone to be sold each month. This expectation, with the actual distribution of observed sales for the month just past, is shown below.

Phone type

type 1		type 2		type 3		type 4	
140	120	110	120	100	120	120	120
20	400	10	100	20	400	0	0

$$\text{Chi square} = \frac{400}{120} + \frac{100}{120} + \frac{400}{120} + \frac{0}{120}$$
$$= 7.49$$

Again, I put the data on SPSS and found with 3 df that our calculated value is not significant, therefore the null hypothesis that demand is uniform cannot be rejected and the company knows that it should maintain equal numbers of the four types of phone. The minor differences between observed and expected are attributed to chance variation in sales.

Testing for a specific pattern

In this goodness-of-fit approach, the distribution assumption has been fixed in advance, usually the result of a policy decision by a company, and the test is used to determine if policy is being followed.

Example 3

The PacAsia Bank wanted to ensure that it had a particular mix of loans in order to minimize the default rate from local business customers. They set a policy of 60% to business firms, 30% to individuals and 10% to foreign borrowers. One year later, to determine if this policy was being adhered to, the marketing manager randomly selected 85 loans approved in the last month. He finds 62 were extended to businesses, 10 to foreign borrowers and 13 to individuals. Is the bank's portfolio policy intact or in tatters?

If the null hypothesis that the pattern of loans is being maintained correctly, 60% of the 85 loans in the sample should be business loans (i.e. $85 \times .60 = 51$ loans), 30% would be individual loans (i.e. 25.5 loans) and loans to foreign customers would be 10% or 8.5 loans. The following are the expected frequencies:

Loan	observed	expected
Business	62	51
Individual	13	25.5
Foreign	10	8.5

$$\text{Chi square} = \frac{(62-51)^2}{51} + \frac{(13-25.5)^2}{25.5} + \frac{(10-8.5)^2}{8.5}$$
$$= 8.76$$

We placed the original data into chi square and with $df = 2$ and a 5% level of significance, this value of chi square is significant. In this situation, the null hypothesis should be rejected and the pattern of loans does not conform with established policy. There is only a 5% chance that the pattern observed would be produced if the policy was being observed.

> **Goodness-of-fit chi square.** *This measures how closely observed sample data fit a particular hypothesized distribution.*

SPSS activity – goodness-of-fit chi square

We will illustrate the computation of a goodness-of-fit chi square using SPSS Chapter 12 Data File B. We will test the hypothesis that the distribution of choices for soft drink is random, i.e. there is no significant preference for any specific drink.

How to proceed

1 *Analyze >> Non-parametric Tests >> Chi square ...* which opens the **Chi Square Test dialogue** box.
2 Select the variable '*drink*' then click on the arrow button which transfers this variable to *the* **Test Variable List** box (Fig. 14.1).
3 *OK*. The results of the analysis are then displayed as in Table 14.1.

How to interpret the output

• In the top box the four possible outcomes of the drink choice are listed vertically in the first column.
• The observed frequencies are presented in the second column.
• The expected frequencies of cases are displayed in the third column. These are all 10 since the expected frequency for each of the four drinks with 40 personal choices is 40/4.

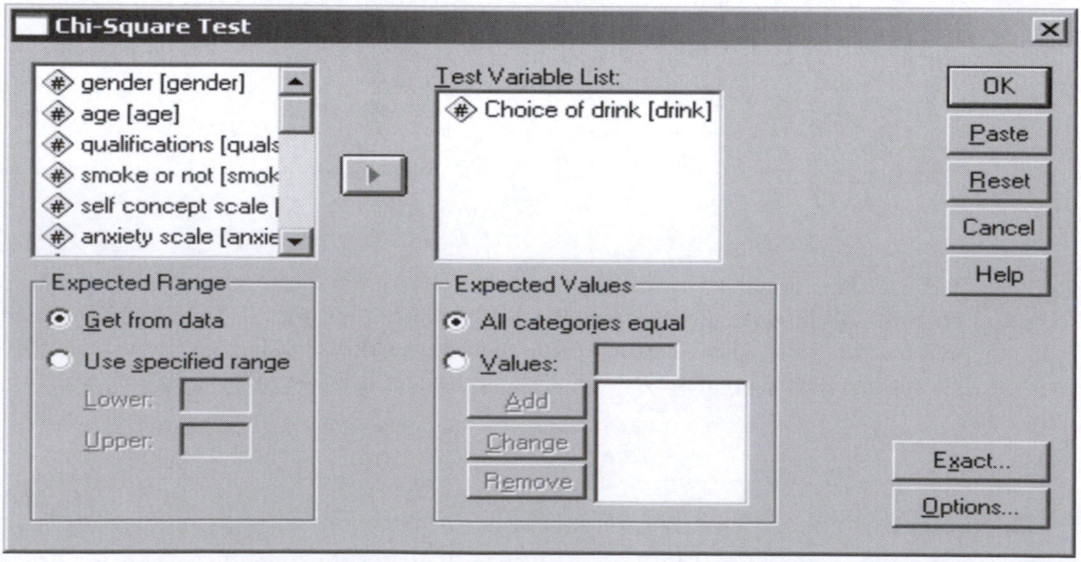

Figure 14.1   Chi square test.

Table 14.1   Chi square goodness-of-fit output

Choice of drink			
	Observed N	Expected N	Residual
Coke	17	10.0	7.0
Pepsi	11	10.0	1.0
Sprite	7	10.0	−3.0
Solo	5	10.0	−5.0
Total	40		

Test Statistics	
	Choice of drink
Chi-Square(a)	8.400
df	3
Asymp. Sig.	.038

ª 0 cells (0%) have expected frequencies less than 5. The minimum expected cell frequency is 10.0.

- The residual column displays the differences between the observed and expected frequencies.
- The value of chi square, its degrees of freedom and its significance are presented in the second box. Chi square is 8.4, its degrees of freedom are 3 (i.e. 4–1) and its significance level is .038. This latter figure indicates that there is a statistically significant deviation from the expected distribution of equality beyond $p < .05$. Coke is most popular while Solo and Sprite are much less preferred, i.e. not all drinks are equally preferred.
- Note the comment below the lower subtable. Chi square requires expected cell frequencies of at least 5.

Effect size

This is computed as

$$\text{Effect size} = \frac{\text{Chi square}}{(\text{Total sample size across all categories})(\text{number of categories} - 1)}$$

$$= \frac{8.4}{(40)(3)} = .07$$

This is obviously minimal and in part due to the small sample.

How to report the results

'A goodness-of-fit chi square was conducted to determine whether free choice of four drinks by 40 persons would produce a distribution not significantly different from that expected by chance, i.e equality. There was a statistically significant difference between the observed and expected frequencies (chi square = 8.4, df = 3, p = .038). This suggests that Coke was the most popular choice while Solo was the least chosen. Effect size of .007 indicates that the observed frequencies deviated minimally from the expected frequencies and a stronger effect size would probably emerge if a larger sample was involved'.

Chi square test of the independence of categorical variables (cross-classification or cross-tabulation or contingency)

Another widely used application of the chi square procedure involves its use with data that are in the form of observations on two variables. For example, a sample of subjects is classified into categories on each of two variables and the question concerns the presence or absence of a relationship between the variables. One might ask:

- Is there a relationship between ethnic background and preference for watching different sports?
- Is there a relationship between income level and number of cars owned?
- Is there an association between consumers' age group and their preference or not for a product?
- Does the support of a strike call depend on national political voting intention?
- Do men and women prefer different levels of risk in making investment decisions?
- Does each factory in the company produce the same level of defective products?

Comparison of the independence of two variables is achieved as before by comparing observed frequencies with expected frequencies. When data of this type is gathered, they are recorded in a **contingency** *or* **cross-tabulation table**. The responses are categorized into cells organized by rows and columns.

Contingency tables

2 × 2 contingency table

One of the most common uses of the chi square test of the independence of categorical variables is with the 2 × 2 contingency table, in which there are two variables each divided into two categories only. Let use imagine our two categories are (i) adult/adolescent and (ii) approve of abortion/don't approve. The data is located in Table 14.2. The calculation produces:

Chi square = 122.78. *df* = 1 (always in a 2 × 2 table!)

Table 14.2 **Example of a two by two table**

	Adolescent	Adult	Total
Approve of abortion	120	18	138
Don't approve of abortion	20	98	118
Total	140	116	256

The result is extremely significant well beyond the .01 level. Hence the null hypothesis that there is only a chance association between age group and attitude to abortion is rejected for this sample. There is a significant relationship between the age group and its approval or disapproval of abortion. The two categories are not independent of each other for these samples, with adolescents approving more strongly and adults disapproving more strongly, from consideration of the raw data in Table 14.2.

N × N cross-tabulation

Cross-tabulation tables can have more than two rows and two columns, though as we increase each the interpretation of results becomes more complex and sample sizes need to be large so that sufficient observed counts occur in each cell.

As an example, consider whether there is an association between number of children in family and number of computers owned. Here is the observed data from our survey placed in a contingency or cross-tabulation format in a 3 × 3 table (Table 14.3).

We hypothesize that there is no significant association between number of computers owned and number of children. SPSS calculates the expected frequency values for each of the cells in the contingency table. Chi square in this example is 38.05, which far exceeds the .01 level. We are well justified in claiming that there is a significant association between family size and computer ownership, with a tendency for larger families to own more computers. We reject the null hypothesis that there is only a chance relationship between number of children in family and computer ownership, i.e. that both categories are independent.

The 'natural' application of the contingency table analysis is for cases in which each observation is measured by two categorical variables. However, quantitative variables may also be used to classify the observations into rows, or columns, or both, by recoding each quantitative variable arbitrarily into intervals so that each interval represents one row or

Table 14.3 **Example of a cross-tabulation table**

No. of computers	Number of children in family		
	One child	Two children	Three or more
Two	20	16	8
One	40	22	10
None	12	36	42

one column. If the quantitative variable is salary, the intervals may be set at *$10,000* with a final category that includes all salaries above a certain value. Age can be converted to a number of age group categories in this way too.

Computing effect size

SPSS provides a number of indices that assess the strength of the relationship between row and column variables. They include the contingency coefficient, phi, Cramer's V, and lambda. The two indices usually used are phi and Cramer's V. The phi coefficient for a 2×2 table is a special case of the Pearson product-moment correlation coefficient for a 2×2 contingency table. Because most social scientists have a reasonable understanding of the Pearson product-moment correlation coefficient (next chapter), they are likely to feel comfortable using its derivative, the phi coefficient. However, if both the row and the column variables have more than two levels, phi can exceed 1 and, therefore, is hard to interpret. Cramer's V rescales phi in these circumstances so that it ranges between 0 and 1.

SPSS activity – chi square for the independence of categorical variables (contingency tables)

Please access SPSS Chapter 12 Data File B. If you wish to calculate chi square with more than two categories in at least one variable then the procedure is the same. In this example, we will examine the null hypothesis that there is no significant relationship between gender and whether the person smokes or not. The procedure is as follows:

1 *Analyze >> Descriptive Statistics >> Crosstabs*. This opens the *Crosstabs: dialogue* box.
2 Click on '*gender*' and then the arrow button beside Row[s]: which transfers it into the *Rows box*.
3 Select '*smoke or not*' and then the arrow button beside Column[s] which moves it to the *Columns box* (Fig. 14.2). It does not matter which variable goes in row or columns.
4 If you wish to display bar charts check the box.
5 Choose *Statistics* at the bottom of the *Crosstabs:* **dialogue** box. This opens the *Crosstabs: Statistics* **dialogue** box.
6 Select *Chi-square*, then *phi* and *Cramer's V* in the *Nominal* data box (Fig. 14.3).
7 *Continue >> Cells*. This produces the *Crosstabs: Cell Display* **dialogue** box.
8 Choose *Expected* in the *Counts* box. (Observed should already be selected).
9 Click on *Row, Column and Total* in the *Percentages* box (Fig. 14.4).
10 *Continue >> OK*.

Interpreting the output in Table 14.4

- Four subtables are produced. The top subtable lists the number of cases processed.
- The second subtable shows the observed and expected frequency of cases in each cell. The observed frequency (called *Count*) is presented first and the expected frequency (called *Expected count*) second.

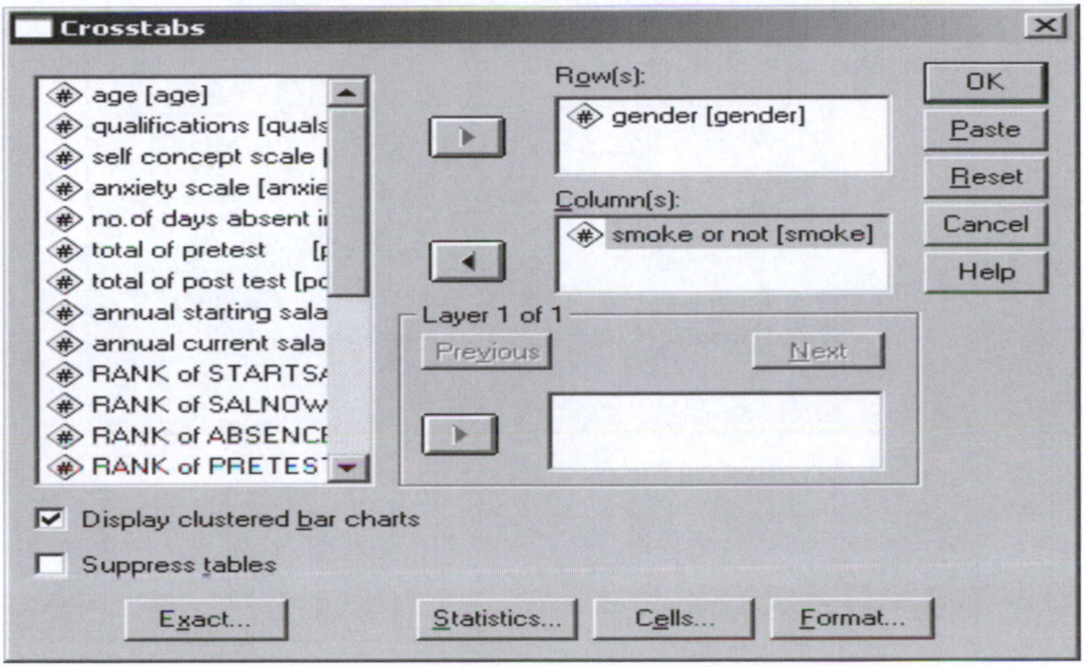

Figure 14.2   Crosstabs.

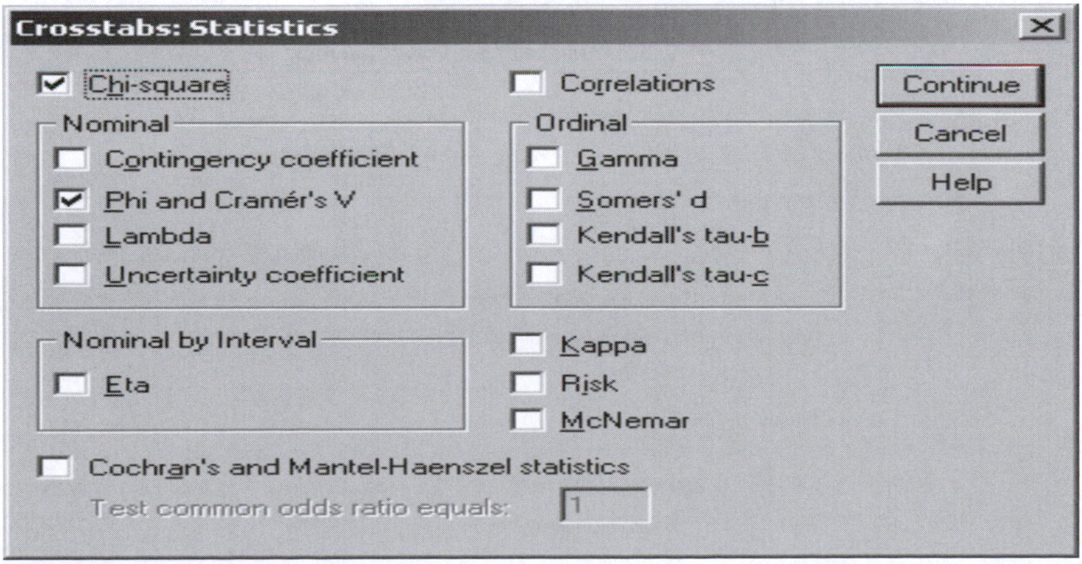

Figure 14.3   Crosstabs: Statistics.

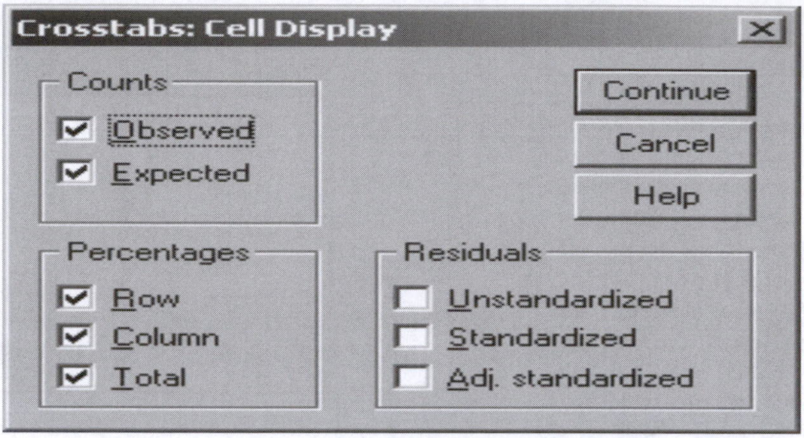

Figure 14.4 **Crosstabs cell display.**

Table 14.4 **Crosstabulation output**

Case Processing Summary

	Cases					
	Valid		Missing		Total	
	N	Percent	N	Percent	N	Percent
Gender* smoke or not	40	100.0%	0	.0%	40	100.0%

Gender* smoke or not Crosstabulation

			Smoke or not		
			Does not smoke	Smokes	Total
gender	male	Count	10	12	22
		Expected count	11.6	10.5	22.0
		% within gender	45.5%	54.5%	100.0%
		% within smoke or not	47.6%	63.2%	55.0%
		% of Total	25.0%	30.0%	55.0%
	female	Count	11	7	18
		Expected count	9.5	8.6	18.0
		% within gender	61.1%	38.9%	100.0%
		% within smoke or not	52.4%	36.8%	45.0%
		% of Total	27.5%	17.5%	45.0%

Table 14.4—cont'd

| | | Smoke or not | | |
		Does not smoke	Smokes	Total
Total	Count	21	19	40
	Expected Count	21.0	19.0	40.0
	% within gender	52.5%	47.5%	100.0%
	% within smoke or not	100.0%	100.0%	100.0%
	% of Total	52.5%	47.5%	100.0%

Chi Square Tests

	Value	df	Asymp. sig. (2-sided)	Exact sig. (2-sided)	Exact sig. (1-sided)
Pearson Chi-Square	.973(b)	1	.324		
Continuity Correction(a)	.447	1	.504		
Likelihood Ratio	.978	1	.323		
Fisher's Exact Test				.360	.252
Linear-by-Linear Association	.949	1	.330		
N of Valid Cases	40				

[a] Computed only for a 2×2 table.
[b] 0 cells (.0%) have expected count less than 5. The minimum expected count is 8.55.

Symmetric Measures

		Value	Approx. Sig.
Nominal by Nominal	Phi	−.156	.324
	Cramer's V	.156	.324
N of Valid Cases		40	

[a] Not assuming the null hypothesis.
[b] Using the asymptotic standard error assuming the null hypothesis.

- The observed frequencies are always whole numbers so they should be easy to spot. The expected frequencies are always expressed to one decimal place so they are easily identified. Thus the first cell of the table (defined as '*male*' and '*does not smoke*') has an observed frequency of 10 but an expected frequency of 11.6. The rest of the table is also easily interpretable.
- The next subtable displays the chi square value, its degrees of freedom and its significance level. Chi square is on the line labelled '*Pearson*', after the person who developed this test. The chi square value is .973. Its degrees of freedom are 1 and its two-tailed probability is .324. There is no significant association between whether a person smokes or not and their gender. The null hypothesis is retained.

- The likelihood ratio test has similar properties to chi square and is an alternative. The linear-by-linear association test is inappropriate for qualitative variables.
- The final table reports phi and Cramer's V as measures of effect size, namely, 0.324.
- Also shown in the output is the warning about the Minimum Expected Frequency of any cell in the table. If there are cells with a minimum expected frequency of 5.0 or less then we should be wary of using chi square and use Fisher's Exact test result instead, which will be produced by SPSS in such cases.
- The clustered bar chart (Fig. 14.5) provides a visual impression of the distribution of the frequencies.

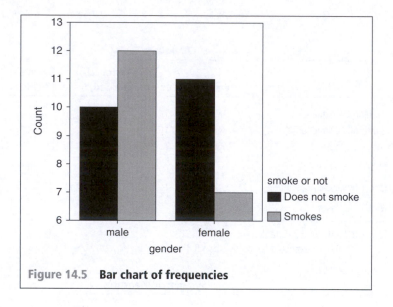

Figure 14.5   Bar chart of frequencies

How to report the results

You could write: '*A 2 × 2 contingency table analysis was conducted to determine whether there was an association between gender and whether the person smokes or not. A non-significant relationship was present with chi square = .973, df = 1, p = .324. The null hypothesis that there is no association between gender and smoking must be retained. The effect of .324 squared suggests that only around 11% of the variation in smoking can be explained by gender*'.

Restrictions in the use of the chi square

1   It is important to remember that chi square is only appropriate for the analysis of data that are classified as frequency of occurrence (counts) within categories (nominal data). When the data are ordinal or interval, other tests of significance are usually preferred. It must only be used on frequencies, *never on percentages*.

2   Categories for a chi square analysis must be mutually exclusive, which means that each response can be classified into only one cell. This is true because a fundamental assumption in the use of the chi square test is that each observation or frequency is independent of all others. For example, a person can only be in one age group and in one salary class.

3   Another restriction in the use of the chi square test is that when there are many categories within each variable, larger samples are needed. If N is small and consequently the expected frequency in any cell is small, the sample statistic may not approximate the theoretical chi square distribution very closely. A rule-of-thumb which one may follow is that in a two-by-two chi square analysis the expected frequency in all cells should at least equal or be greater than 5. With more than a two-by-two table, the expected frequency should be equal to or greater than 5 in at least 80% of the cells. If this condition is not fulfilled, it may be necessary to code together several low frequency categories so we have the larger expected frequencies in each cell or use Fisher's Exact Test result. The fusing of categories is not really desirable, since it involves a reduction in the amount of information available. If practically possible, we might obtain a larger sample so that the conditions are fulfilled for the original classification.

4   The chi square test is sensitive to difference but not direction of difference; it is therefore inherently two-tailed. Only by visual inspection of the obtained data can the direction of association in a significant test be determined.

Alternatives to chi square

If you have small frequencies in a two-by-two or two-by-three table the Fisher Exact Probability Test should be used. The chi square procedure computes Fisher's Exact Test for two-by-two tables when one or more of the four cells have an expected frequency of less than 5. SPSS output automatically provides the significance level for both a one- and two-tail test. These are placed near the bottom of the normal chi square output window as the last two significance levels quoted.

Summary of steps in chi square

- State the null and alternate hypotheses about the proposed relationship.
- Note the observed counts of data falling into different cells.
- Compute frequencies of occurrence of events that we expect under the null hypothesis to provide the expected frequencies for each cell.
- Evaluate the difference between the observed and expected to produce the chi square statistic.
- Observe the computed chi square in the SPSS printout and determine whether statistical significance is achieved.
- Inspect our original data to determine the direction of association if a significant result is obtained.

What you have learned in this chapter

Chi square tests are a non-parametric technique of testing hypotheses of association using nominal data. The two types of chi square tests are:

- the goodness-of-fit test; and
- the test for independence of two nominal variables.

   The former compares how well the frequency distribution for a sample fits with the expected frequency distribution predicted by the null hypothesis. The latter assesses association between two variables, with the null hypothesis stating that there is no significant association between the two variables. Rejecting the null hypothesis implies a significant association between the two variables. Both tests are based on the assumption that each observation is independent of the others, and that one observation cannot be classified in more than one category.

   The chi square statistic is distorted when there are less than five observations in a cell and the Fisher Exact test should be performed if this situation exists.

Review activities

SPSS Activity 14.1
Using SPSS Chapter 12 Data File B conduct a goodness-of-fit chi square on the variable 'house funding' to determine whether there is approximate equality in the types of funding used.

SPSS Activity 14.2
Access SPSS Chapter 12 Data File B. Test the null hypothesis that there is no significant association between qualifications held and type of house funding.

Now access Chapter 14 Web page and attempt the SPSS activities and other questions located there.

Chapter 15
Methods of Correlation: Testing Hypotheses of Relationships

Content list

By the end of this chapter you will be able to:

1 Understand the concept of correlation.
2 Understand the use of Pearson's Product Moment Correlation and Spearman's Rank Order Correlation.
3 Understand the use of a variety of non-parametric correlation tests.
4 Assess the power and effect size of a correlation.
5 Assess the strength of a correlation through the coefficient of determination.
6 Use SPSS to calculate a variety of correlation tests and interpret the printout.

Introduction

In the previous chapter, we studied chi square which tests relationships for nominal data. But much of our data is ordinal or interval. It is therefore important that you acquaint yourselves with methods of testing hypotheses of relationships that are appropriate for interval and ordinal data and for combinations of different levels of data.

What is correlation?

Correlation is the degree of correspondence between variables. This implies the *relationship* is mutual or reciprocating, but we do not include in our concept of correlation any proposition that one thing is the cause and the other the effect. We play safe. We merely say that we have discovered that two things are systematically connected. Now, it may well be that one thing is a cause of another but correlation does not delve that far down on its own.

> **Correlation**. *A measure of the degree of correspondence between variables.*

Correlation is different from the inferential statistics you have so far studied, because those techniques like t tests and ANOVA compare groups as groups, and not the individuals who compose them as we do in correlation. In investigating relationships, we are examining the strength of a connection between two characteristics both belonging to the same individual/ event/equipment. There must be at least two variables with a common basis to them.

Many variables and events are related to each other:

- They can be **positively correlated**, i.e. an increase in one variable coincides with an increase in another variable. As the sun sets the temperature decreases; as car engine size increases so does petrol consumption; income tends to rise with age.
- A **negative correlation** exists when one variable increases as the other decreases. For example, an increase in altitude is associated with a decrease in air pressure; as prices rise demand will fall; there is an increase in consumer spending as unemployment falls.
- A **zero or random correlation** exists when variations in two variables occur randomly, such as time spent on the Internet is not related to income; length of car driving experience bears minimal relationship to engine size of car currently driven.

> **A positive correlation**. *This occurs when an increase (or decrease) in one variable coincides with an increase (or decrease) in another variable.*

> **A negative correlation**. *This occurs when one variable increases (or decreases) as the other variable decreases (or increases).*

> *A random correlation*. *This occurs when there is no real relationship between the two variables.*

The correlation coefficient

Research into relationships between variables demands that we have two sets of observations arising from the same source. We can then examine the extent to which observations on one variable are related to observations on another. Given data from one sample of subjects on two variables such as job satisfaction and self-esteem, how can we describe the extent of their relationship? The simplest method is to plot the two sets of scores against one another in the form of a scattergraph (also called scatterplot or scattergram). Consider a number of possibilities represented by the five scattergraphs forming Figure 15.1. Notice that each point on these graphs represents the intersection of observations derived from 10 respondents on two variables.

> *Scattergraph (scatterplot)*. *A graph of pairings of scores.*

In Figure 15.1(a) and (b), all the points lie on a straight line. Each score is perfectly predictable from every other score because any change in one variable is accompanied by a proportional change in the other variable. In the first case (a), increases in one variable are accompanied by proportional increases in the other variable. This is the **perfect positive correlation**. A numerical index, the **correlation coefficient**, expresses the degree or magnitude of the relationship. In this case, the numerical index is +1.00, the highest possible value that the correlation coefficient assumes and indicates a perfect relationship between the variables.

The general symbol for the correlation coefficient is '*r*'. So a perfect positive relationship (r = +1.00) indicates a direct relationship, where each individual or object is as high or as low on one variable as they are on the other. In other words, each subject has the same Z score on variable X as their Z score on variable Y. In a perfect correlation, all the dots in the scattergram can be connected with a single straight line, e.g. 12 monthly sales revenue figures measured in Taiwanese dollars and measured in Thai Baht. There is also a perfect relationship between the radius and circumference of a circle.

In the second case, Figure 15.1(b), increases in one variable are accompanied by proportional decreases in the other variable. This is a **perfect negative correlation**. An r of –1.00 indicates a perfect negative relationship. This means that the two variables bear an inverse relationship to each other, so that the highest Z score on one variable is associated with the lowest Z score on the other, and so forth. A perfect negative relationship exists between sales and stocks in a supermarket, assuming that the shelves are not refilled from warehouse stock. Another example of a perfect negative relationship is that between the volume of a gas and the pressure applied when temperature is held constant. As pressure increases, the volume of the gas decreases. While perfect positive (+1.00) and negative correlations

(–1.00) can be found in nature, they are rarely found among social, economic, business, educational and psychological variables.

Since perfect positive and negative correlations are unlikely to be met, the sort of picture we are most likely to find is that of Figure 15.1(c), (d) and (e). In (c) and (d) the points are scattered about a straight line in a roughly elliptical shape. Although there is a tendency for pairs of observations to go together, the prediction of one observation from another is no longer perfect. We describe (c) as showing a **positive** correlation and (d) as a **negative** correlation, but they are certainly far from being perfect positive or negative correlations respectively.

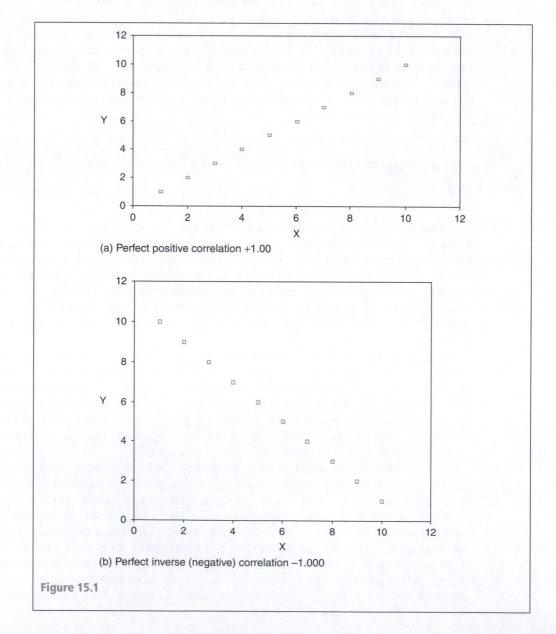

(a) Perfect positive correlation +1.00

(b) Perfect inverse (negative) correlation –1.000

Figure 15.1

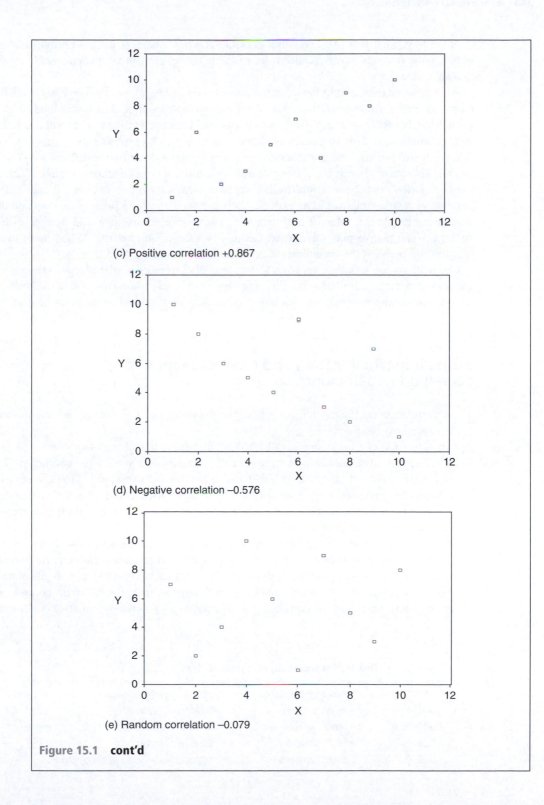

(c) Positive correlation +0.867

(d) Negative correlation −0.576

(e) Random correlation −0.079

Figure 15.1   cont'd

Now, look finally at (e), a random correlation where there is no discernible relation between the two sets of observations, for example the relationship between weekly salary and shoe size.

As a positive relationship between variables becomes less close, the correlation coefficient assumes a value smaller than +1.00. Employees with high skill levels tend to gain promotion, but there are many exceptions because of factors other than skill level that influence promotion, such as vacancies available, selection bias by promotions committee, etc. Although still positive, the correlation coefficient between these two variables is less than +1.00. Other variables may show a negative relationship that is less than perfect; in such cases the correlation coefficient would have a negative sign somewhere between 0 and −1.00. A negative relationship would be expected between the increasing price of an item and the decreasing number of sales of that item. The negative relationship would not be perfect because some people may have to buy even when the price is rising. When there is no relationship between the variables, the coefficient is 0.0 or close to it.

Correlations are usually expressed to two and often three decimal places. There are a number of different correlation coefficients which can be calculated to express the strength of the relationship between two variables, depending on the level of measurement of the data. We will introduce some of these below.

Some important issues and characteristics of correlation coefficients

1   A correlation coefficient indicates both the direction and the strength of relationship between two variables.
2   The direction of relationship is indicated by the mathematical sign + or −.
3   The strength of relationship is represented by the absolute size of the coefficient, i.e. how close it is to +1.00 or −1.00. Table 15.1 is a rough but useful guide to the degree of relationship indicated by the size of the coefficients (irrespective of whether they are positive or negative). If they were negative, we would include the word 'inverse' or 'negative' in describing the relationship.
4   Never confuse negative correlation with zero correlation. The latter simply means no correlation or relationship between two sets of data, whereas a negative correlation is a definite relationship, the strength of which is indicated by its size. It is absolutely necessary to place the algebraic sign (+ or −) before the numerical value of the correlation, as the interpretation of the correlation is affected by its positive or negative condition.

Table 15.1   **Tips for interpreting correlation size**

0.90–1.00	Very high correlation	Very strong relationship
0.70–0.90	High correlation	Substantial relationship
0.40–0.70	Moderate correlation	Moderate relationship
0.20–0.40	Low correlation	Weak relationship
0.00–0.20	Slight correlation	Relationship so small as to be random

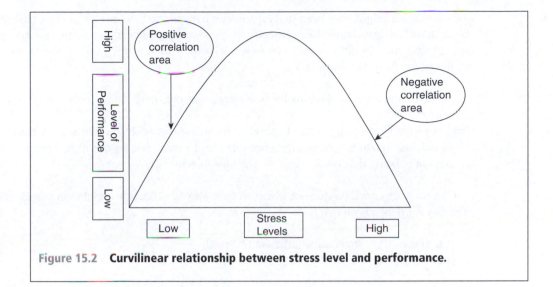

Figure 15.2   Curvilinear relationship between stress level and performance.

5   One major limitation in using the correlation coefficient is that it only measures linear relationships, that is, relationships that produce a straight line of plots, or a close approximation, on a scattergraph. Curvilinear relationships require special techniques beyond the scope of this introductory text. It is essential as a first step before applying an SPSS correlational analysis to plot a scattergraph to check that there is an approximate linear relationship and not a curvilinear one.

There are important variables that do not follow a simple linear relationship. For instance, a well-known pattern within the organizational stress literature is that the relationship between employee performance and workload stress is curvilinear. As Figure 15.2 shows, both low and high levels of stress result in low performance, whilst better performance is associated with moderate levels of stress. If we correlated such data we would probably report negligible or zero correlations as the curve possesses both positive and negative relationships. In fact the relationship is quite complex.

Interpreting the correlation coefficient

Let us imagine that you have followed the tortuous path of correlation without getting lost and are now the proud owner of a shiny new statistically significant 'r' of +0.80 between monthly advertising costs and sales revenues over the last 12 months in your company. Wonderful – but what then?

You have demonstrated a correlation that pertains to only 12 months; you have 12 pairs of observations only. Even assuming that the 12 chosen were typical months, can we feel secure in concluding that a correlation between monthly advertising revenue and sales revenues exists in general? After all, you did not attempt to use data from sales and advertising revenue for your company over a number of years. It is conceivable that, if you had, the correlation might have been 0. Accidents do happen, and the last 12 months observed might have displayed their correlation as a long-shot coincidence, not as an indication of any general rule. In other words, you have a choice: you must pick one of the following explanations for your obtained 'r'.

(a) It happened because there really is a correlation out there, and it showed up in your sample; or,
(b) There really isn't any general overall relationship between the two sets of data, but accidents do happen, especially when one tries to formulate a general rule about many sets of existing data on the basis of a sample of only 12.

Can we ever conclude that our obtained (sample) 'r' reflects a population correlation? The answer depends on two factors:

1   the size of the correlation coefficient obtained;
2   the size of the sample.

Also we must as always assume, with good reason, that the sample is a random one. The need for these two factors should be clear. A small correlation coefficient could be merely an accident of sampling, though if either the correlation coefficient or the sample is very large, the probability of such an accident is reduced. Now, in any population of X and Y scores, there is always going to be some degree of relationship between X and Y, even if the relationship is 0, simply because it is a mathematical calculation. And for every population correlation coefficient, there will be a range of sample correlation coefficients, which will fall into a sampling distribution. For any obtained sample value of 'r', we can ask:

'Assuming that population r = 0, what is the probability that this sample r came from the sampling distribution?'

As usual, if the probability is too small, less than 5% or 1%, we reject the null hypothesis and adopt instead the alternative hypothesis that the population itself contains a correlation greater than zero between X and Y. The critical values of 'r', whether for the 1% or 5% level, are related to the size of sample, so it is not possible to interpret any correlation coefficient unless the value of N is known. As N increases in size, the correlation value required to reach significance is reduced. For example, if N = 30 you need an 'r' of .349 to reach the 5% level of significance, but when N = 100 you only need an 'r' of .194. This is why most researchers prefer to use the **coefficient of determination** (see below) as the way to interpret a correlation rather than significance level alone. After all an 'r' of .194 is quite minimal.

Coefficient of determination

A correlation coefficient or 'r' is not a direct measure of the percentage of relationship between two variables, however, its square is (r^2 – **the coefficient of determination**). Nor can one say that a correlation of +0.90 is three times as close as a relationship of +.30,

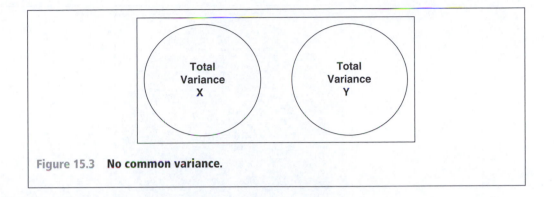

Figure 15.3   **No common variance.**

but merely that it indicates a much stronger degree of relationship. The correlation coefficient is a number that has no connection with the units in which the variables are measured. To define the strength of a relationship in a more precise way we use the coefficient of determination or r^2 (multiplied by 100). This coefficient ($r^2 \times 100$) determines what percentage of the total variance of variable X is due to the variance of variable Y.

Examples

(a) If the correlation (r) between variable X and variable Y = 0, then the coefficient of determination = $0^2 = 0$ or 0%. There is no comma variability (Fig. 15.3).

(b) If the correlation (r) between variable X and variable Y = .8, then the coefficient of determination = $.8^2(100) = .64(100)$ or 64%. 64% of the variance in one variable is predictable from the variance in the other (Fig. 15.4).

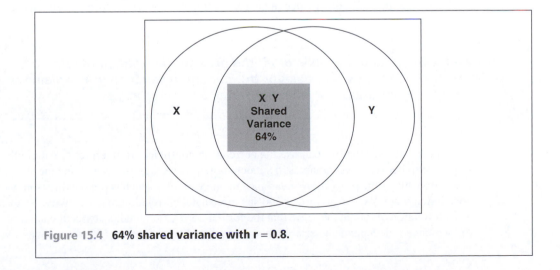

Figure 15.4   **64% shared variance with r = 0.8.**

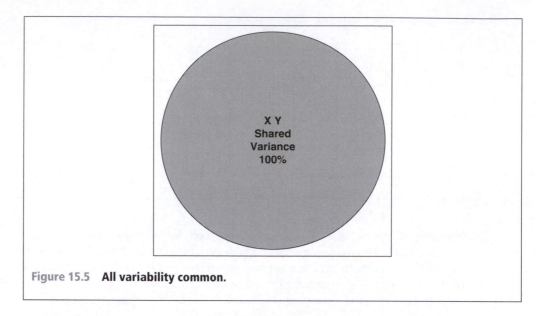

Figure 15.5 **All variability common.**

(c) If the correlation (r) between variable X and variable Y = 1, then the coefficient of determination = 1^2 = 1 × 100 = 100%: 100% of the variability is common to both variables (Fig. 15.5).

Example

Consider the relationship between the number of customer calls made by a particular salesman and the number of orders obtained during the course of a 10-day journey cycle. Suppose the correlation is +.85. This shows a fairly high positive correlation between the number of calls a salesman makes and the number of orders received. The coefficient of determination is 72.25%, i.e. that 72% of variance in orders is explained by the number of calls made.

The coefficient of determination or r². This provides the amount of common variation between the two variables or the amount of variation in Y explained by variation in X when converted to a percentage.

You can now see that we can use the correlation coefficient to interpret the strength of relationship between two variables in a much more precise way. We can define the strength of relationship as the proportion of variance in one variable, which is predictable from variance in the other. We can go further and say now that a correlation of .71 is twice as strong as a correlation of .50, in the sense that the former correlation predicts twice the amount of the variance in a dependent variable than is predicted by the latter (50% as against 25%).

The variance interpretation of correlation emphasizes the point that even with strongly correlated measures a substantial amount of variance in the dependent variable remains unaccounted for, e.g. r = +.80 means that 36% of the variation (over a third) between the two variables is unaccounted for. It is well to bear this in mind when looking at correlations reported in studies and reports. Many researchers set their sights at finding statistically significant correlations, which simply means that the correlation is unlikely to have occurred by chance. When they come to draw inferences from their findings, however, the amount of variance they have actually explained by a significant correlation may be very small indeed.

Assumptions of correlational analysis

The main assumptions are:

- Data must be obtained from related pairs, so that if you have score on X there must also be a score on Y from the same person.
- The scale of measurement must be interval or ratio.
- Each set of scores should be approximately normal.
- The relationship between the two sets of scores should be linear or approximately so.
- The variability of scores for one variable should be roughly similar at all values of the other variable. (This is the concept of homoscedasticity)

SPSS activity – the Pearson correlation coefficient

Several correlation indexes have been developed. The most widely used is the Pearson Product Moment Correlation or 'r'. The Pearson correlation coefficient is employed when both variables are expressed as Scale data (interval or ratio). While an inspection of a scattergraph furnishes some visual impression of the relationship between two sets of measures, a numerical index indicating precisely the degree of relationship is essential.

Calculating Pearson's 'r'

We will illustrate the computation of Pearson's correlation coefficient with SPSS Chapter 13 Data File A that lists a variety of variables for 40 employees. We shall test whether there are significant relationships between starting salary and current salary, current salary and age, and age and number of days absent. The null hypothesis for each of these three correlation tests is that there is no statistically significant relation between each pair of variables. SPSS can carry out a number of correlation test at the same time, although, as the number increases the output table of intercorrelations becomes quite large and unwieldy on the computer screen, as it provides intercorrelations between every variable entered. Now access SPSS Chapter 13 Data File A.

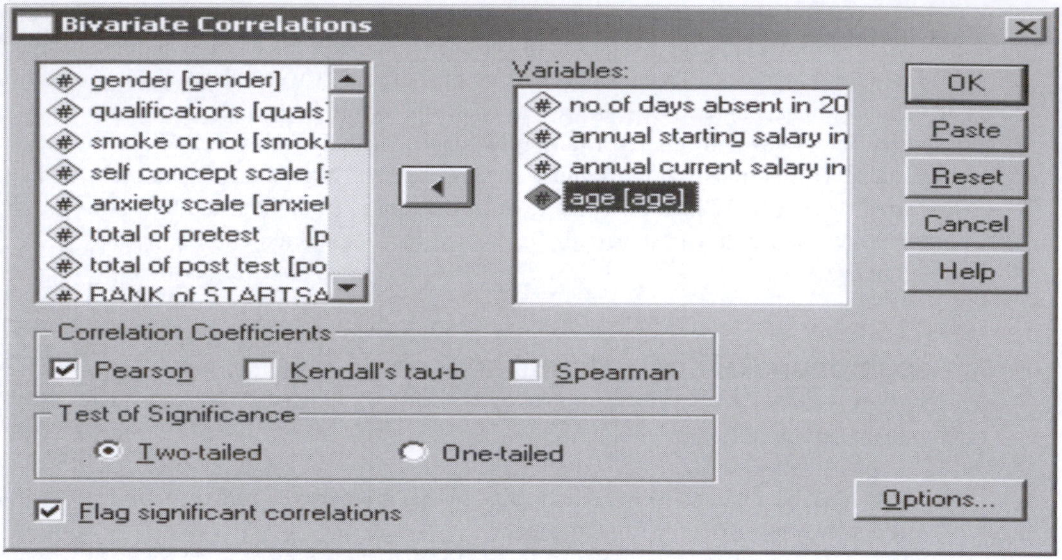

Figure 15.6 Bivariate correlations box.

How to proceed

1 *Analyze >> Correlate >> Bivariate*.
2 Select your variables *(current salary, start salary, age and number of days absent in 2006)* and click the arrow button which places them in the *Variables* box.
3 The Pearson option is the default (Fig. 15.6) so select *OK* to close the *Bivariate Correlations* dialogue box and produce the output (Table 15.2).
4 Ensure *Flag Significant Correlations* is checked.
5 Should you wish, you can also obtain Means and Standard Deviations by clicking *Options* then selecting these items in the *Statistics* box.

Additionally, you should create a scattergraph to display the relationship visually. It lets you see whether you have a linear or non-linear relationship. Correlation assumes a linear or closely linear relationship. If the scattergraph shows a curvilinear shape then you cannot use Pearson.

To produce a scattergraph

1 *Graph >> Scatter*.
2 The *Simple* is the default mode and will provide a single scattergraph for one pair of variables. Click *Define*. (If you wish to obtain a number of scattergraphs simultaneously click on **Matrix >> Define**.)

Table 15.2   Intercorrelation table

		no. of days absent in 2006	annual starting salary in $1000's	annual current salary in $1000's	age
no. of days absent in 2006	Pearson Correlation	1	.070	.027	−.148
	Sig. (2-tailed)	.	.666	.866	.364
	N	40	40	40	40
annual starting salary in $1000's	Pearson Correlation	.070	1	.735(**)	.056
	Sig. (2-tailed)	.666	.	.000	.733
	N	40	40	40	40
annual current salary in $1000's	Pearson Correlation	.027	.735(**)	1	.354(*)
	Sig. (2-tailed)	.866	.000	.	.025
	N	40	40	40	40
age	Pearson Correlation	−.148	.056	.354(*)	1
	Sig. (2-tailed)	.364	.733	.025	.
	N	40	40	40	40

** Correlation is significant at the 0.01 level (2-tailed).
* Correlation is significant at the 0.05 level (2-tailed).

3   Move the two variables (e.g. *current and starting salary*) into the box with the arrow button, then select **OK** to produce the scattergraph (Fig. 15.7).
4   With a correlation it does not really matter which variable you place on which axis.

This scattergraph depicts the plots starting and current salary and reveals a generally positive correlation, in that the plot is bottom left to top right with a linear trend. When we consider the actual calculated correlation in Table 15.2, it will support this visual impression.

How to interpret the output in Table 15.2

- Only one table, a correlation matrix, is produced. The diagonal of this matrix (from top left to bottom right) consists of each variable correlated with itself, obviously giving a perfect correlation of 1,000. No significance level is quoted for this value.
- Each result is tabulated twice at the intersections of both variables. The exact significance level is given to three decimal places.
- The correlation between starting and current salary is +.735; this is significant at the .01 level.

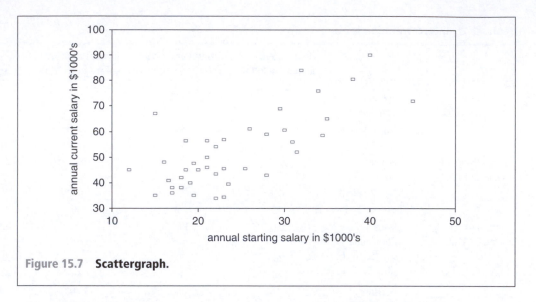

Figure 15.7 **Scattergraph.**

- The correlation between current salary and age is +.354; this is significant at the .05 level.
- The correlation between age and absence is −.148; this is not significant and indicates a random relationship.
- Forty pairs of scores were used to obtain the correlation coefficient.

How to report the output in Table 15.2

'A set of Pearson correlations were computed to determine if there were any significant relationships between a number of employee variables. The correlation between starting and current salary is +.735; this is significant at the .01 level. The null hypothesis can be rejected. Starting salary appears to provide a moderate guide to current salary as it pre-dicts around 54% of current salary level. The remainder of the unexplained variance may involve inter alia qualifications/skills developed over the time period and differential opportunities for promotion.

The correlation between current salary and age is +.354; this is significant at the .05 level and the null hypothesis can be rejected. This relationship is not strong with a coefficient of determination only of around 12.5%, suggesting the existence of a number of other factors that influence the relationship, such as skill level and experience. The correlation between age and absence is −.148; this is not significant and indicates a random relationship. There is no evidence to suggest that absence is more frequent at one age rather than another'.

Rank order correlation (Spearman's rho)

This correlation is typically used when there are only a few cases (or subjects) involved and the data are already ordinal or can be changed into ranks. This correlation is usually designated as '*rho*' to distinguish it from Pearson's 'r'. It is based on the differences in ranks between each of the pairs of ranks. For example, if a subject is ranked first on one measure but only fifth on another the difference (d) = 1 – 5 = 4.

Rank order correlation follows the same principles as outlined earlier and ranges from +1 to –1. While rho is only suitable for ranked (or ordinal) data, interval data can also be used **provided it is first ranked**. However, rho will always provide a lower estimate of correlation than r because the data is degraded, i.e. rho throws away information in that the actual differences in values are not involved in the calculations, only the rank orders, and differences between successive ranks may reflect a variety of real interval differences.

> *Spearman rank order correlation is used where both sets of data are at ordinal level.*

SPSS activity – Spearman's rank order correlation

To demonstrate this statistic, a sample of 40 employees provided data on the relationship between their sales figures and current salary. Access SPSS Chapter 13 Data File A.

How to proceed

If scores are not already in ranks you need to transform them into ordinal data. To do this:

1   **Transform >> Rank Cases**.
2   Select the arrow button to move the variable (*sales 3*) into the **Variables: text** box.
3   Select the **Largest** value button in the **Assign Rank 1 to** area (Fig. 15.8).

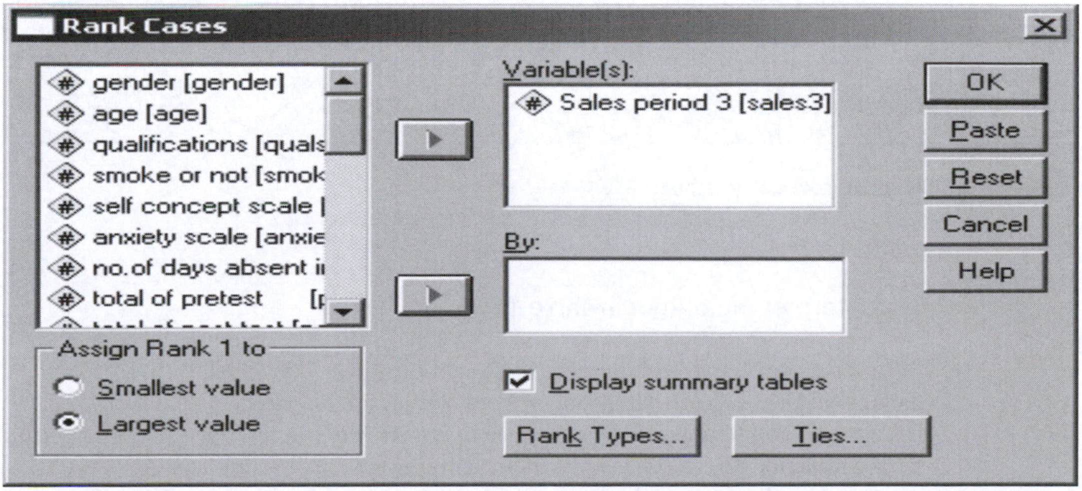

Figure 15.8   **Rank cases box.**

4 Click *OK* and a new variable is created on the data view screen reflecting the ranking of the original variable. This new variable will carry the same name as the original but be preceded by a letter 'r' to designate it as a ranked variable (e.g. '*sales3* will become *rsales3*', '*age*' will become '*rage*' etc.). Rank all interval or scale variables to be used with Spearman this way.

To produce Spearman's correlation:

1 *Analyze >> Correlate >> Bivariate*.
2 Select your variables (in this case *rank of sales3* and *rank of SalNow*) and move them to the *Variables* box.
3 Select *Spearman* in the *Bivariate Correlations* dialogue box and de-select *Pearson*, the default statistic (Fig. 15.9).
4 *OK* and display the output like that shown in Table 15.3.

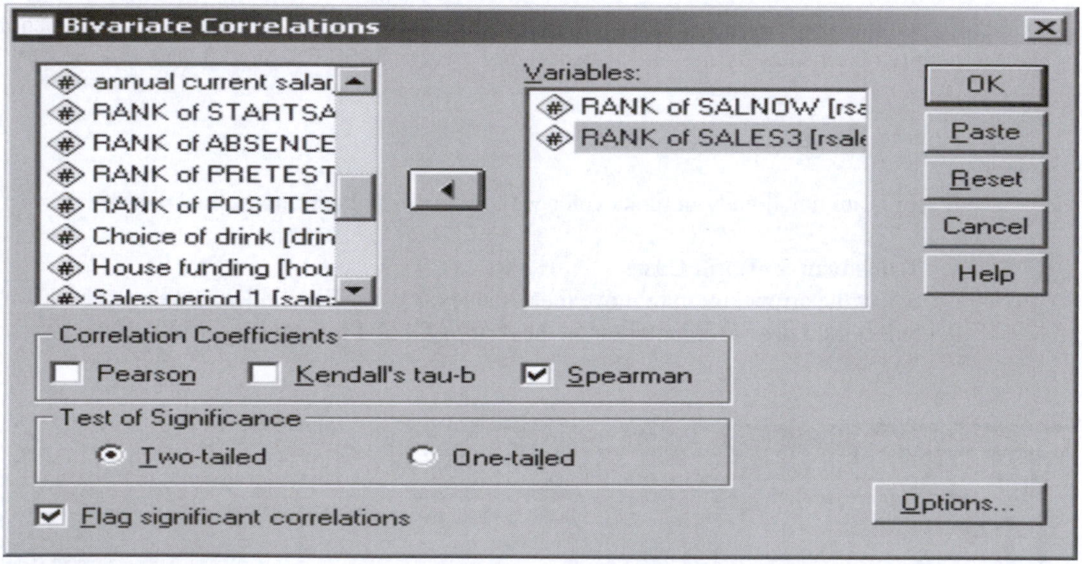

Figure 15.9   Bivariate correlations box.

How to interpret the output in Table 15.3

- Spearman's rho is printed in a matrix like that for Pearson with 1 in the top right diagonal and the results replicated in the top right to bottom left diagonal.
- Spearman's correlation of +.010 between the ranks for current salary and sales performance at period three is close to random and not statistically significant.
- The number of cases on which that correlation was based is 40.

Table 15.3   Correlations

			RANK of SALNOW	RANK of SALES3
		Correlations		
Spearman's rho	RANK of SALNOW	Correlation Coefficient	1.000	.010
		Sig. (2-tailed)	.	.953
		N	40	40
	RANK of SALES3	Correlation Coefficient	.010	1.000
		Sig. (2-tailed)	.953	.
		N	40	40

How to report the results

'A Spearman rho of +.10 was recorded between current salary and sales performance at the end of period three. This was not statistically significant and therefore the null hypothesis must be retained. Given that there is no statistically significant relationship, sales performance is no guide to current salary. The relationship is so low as to be random, and other variables not measured in this study must have a greater influence in determining salary level'.

Effect size and power for correlation – computing an effect size statistic

SPSS calculates the Pearson correlation coefficient, itself a measure of effect size. As with all effect size indices, there is no single acceptable answer to the question, 'What value indicates a strong relationship between two variables?' Cohen's (1988) conventions for the correlation coefficient are usually accepted: .10 for a small effect size, .30 for a medium effect size, and .50 for a large effect size irrespective of sign.

Calculating power

Table 15.4. gives approximate power while Table 15.5 provides minimum sample size for 80% power.

The *Bivariate Correlations* procedure allows you also to obtain Kendall's tau (see below) and one-tailed tests of significance. There are a variety of scatterplots available. These can be edited in many ways. You should explore these.

Problems and errors in interpreting a correlation coefficient

There are a number of problems and likely errors that must be avoided if the interpretation of the correlation is to be meaningful.

Table 15.4   **Approximate power of studies using the correlation coefficient 'r' for testing hypotheses at the .05 level of significance**

	Effect size		
	Small (r = .10)	**Medium (r = .30)**	**Large (r = .50)**
Two-tailed			
Total N: 10	.06	.13	.33
20	.07	.25	.64
30	.08	.37	.83
40	.09	.48	.92
50	.11	.57	.97
100	.17	.86	1.00
One-tailed			
Total N: 10	.08	.22	.46
20	.11	.37	.75
30	.13	.50	.90
40	.15	.60	.96
50	.17	.69	.98
100	.26	.92	1.00

(a) The inherent relationship of variables may differ from population to population. For example, among children between the ages of 10 and 16, physical prowess and chronological age are positively correlated. Among adults between the ages of 20 and 40, these two variables are not correlated. During old age, there is a negative correlation between age and physical prowess.

(b) Whenever a correlation is computed from values that do not represent the full range of the distribution caution must be used in interpreting the correlation. For example, correlating the IQ scores of a group of university professors with their scores on creativity would produce a very different correlation than if a sample of the full IQ range of the population were used. A highly positive correlation obtained from a full range of scores can be obscured when data are limited to a range, as in Figure 15.10. When a population is heterogeneous in the variables of concern, we expect a higher

Table 15.5   **Approximate number of participants needed for 80% power for a study, using the correlation coefficient (r) for testing a hypothesis at the .05 significance level**

	Effect size		
	Small (r = .10)	**Medium (r = .30)**	**Large (r = .50)**
Two-tailed	783	85	28
One-tailed	617	68	22

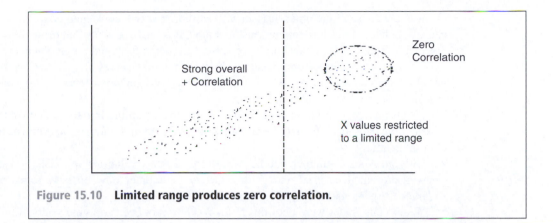

Figure 15.10   **Limited range produces zero correlation.**

correlation than when a population is homogeneous in these variables. For example, in a general population of male college students, we expect a positive correlation between height and success in basketball in the general youth population because the taller boys will tend to do better at the game. In a professional basketball team, we would not expect such a relationship. The members of a professional team are all tall and all very good at the game. In a group that is very homogeneous, we would not observe the high correlation that exists in the population at large because we do not have the range from very poor to very good at the game. This effect derived from restriction in the sample is termed **attenuation**.

In a reverse situation, an overall zero correlation can be inflated to a positive one by restricting the range too, as in Figure 15.11.

(a) We may also find a correlation between two variables, not because there is an intrinsic relationship between these variables, but because they are both related to a third variable. If there is a high positive correlation between drownings at the holiday beach and the sale of tickets for an evening dinner cruise and karaoke, we can predict that if ticket sales increase, so too will the number of drowning accidents. But, while we can predict the likely occurrence of one event from another event, we cannot say that one

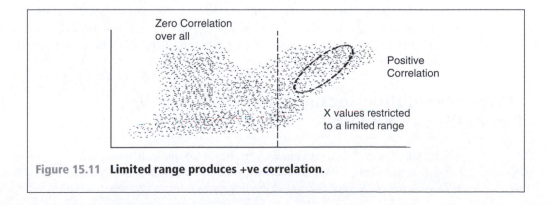

Figure 15.11   **Limited range produces +ve correlation.**

event is the cause of the other. It is easy to assume that two correlated conditions are causally related. Look back at our seaside drama. It is fairly obvious that drownings do not increase the sale of tickets nor vice versa (unless the food and singing acts are so poor the patrons prefer to commit suicide by throwing themselves into the sea). A third variable, such as holiday periods or the occurrence of heatwaves, encouraging more seaside trips, are behind the relationship.

(b) This leads on to a fourth problem hinted at above, that of falling into the seductive trap of assigning causality, i.e. that one variable causes the other. Examine these persuasive communications:

- 'Buy an Apex Computer. Studies have proved that a relationship exists between well-presented material and grades. Get our computer now on easy terms and improve your marks'.

- 'Juan, your grades were poor this term. You have not been applying yourself, have you? The most successful students study at least three hours a day. Now, if you do three hours a day, you will do much better by the end of the school year'.

Can you detect the flaws in the arguments?

(c) Illegitimate inferences of causation are often very subtle; they also become socially important when, for example, a high correlation is noted between poverty and delinquent behaviour. If the conclusion is drawn that poor people naturally tend toward delinquency (which has often been drawn), the existence of the correlation does not support that conclusion. Many other possible explanations besides poverty could be found for delinquent behaviour. Similarly, motor cycling and membership of criminal biker gangs may induce some naive observers to presume the correlation between biker gangs and crime means that those who own a Harley Davidson are more likely to be criminals. The ludicrous nature of such a suggestion, despite a high correlation, could equally well be extended to eating habits. Most Mafia members probably eat spaghetti while Triad members eat noodles, but who would assert that eating either of these two foods induces criminal activity?

(d) A final source of erroneous thinking about correlations lies in the fact that, since correlations are only a mathematical index and therefore can be calculated between any two sets of data, it is apparent that some very high correlations, while mathematically correct, are in reality meaningless. In the West, there is a very high positive correlation between the increase in attendance at church on Sundays and the increase in illegitimate pregnancies in areas of rapid population growth in metropolitan areas over the last 10 years, or between the increase in the immigration rates from African countries and the increase in the divorce rate over a 20-year period, but it would take unusual theories or a rather warped mind to relate either of these examples in a causal manner!

Other correlation techniques: Cramer's V, Kendall's tau and phi

A number of useful non-parametric correlation coefficients exist, such as Cramer's V, Kendall's tau and phi. These are accessed via SPSS cross tabs and were produced when we undertook the analysis of chi square contingency tables in Chapter 14. If a hypothesis test is desired using Cramer, the test should be conducted using chi square as a test statistic. Since V is a function of chi square, any conclusions or p-values obtained using chi square may be equally applied to V.

The phi coefficient is used when the two variables are both true dichotomies. It is appropriate when correlation of responses is made between correct and incorrect answers to two test items or between two yes/no or agree/disagree response type items on a test. Kendall's tau can be used to correlate ranks like rho but has the advantage that it has a more normal sampling distribution than rho for samples under 10. The disadvantages are that it is harder to calculate than rho and yields lower correlation coefficients than rho from the same data. As rho approximates closely to Pearson's r calculated from the same data, it is preferable to tau.

Partial correlation

This is a valuable technique when you wish to eliminate the influence of a third variable on the correlation between two other variables. Partialling out a variable simply means controlling the influence of that variable. As the manager of a government agency responsible for developing and monitoring ethnic harmony between the different ethnic groups in your country, you may be investigating the relationships between a person's age, their ethnic attitudes and their authoritarianism. The results show that age is strongly related to the other two such that the older a person is, the more intolerant they become of others, the more they feel threatened by others. Similarly, the older the person, the more they believe in coercive controls to protect the way they want the society in which they were raised and feel secure to be organized. By partialling out age a 'truer' sense of the relationship between racial intolerance and authoritarianism is obtained.

Here is another example. Suppose the manager of a marriage guidance service wants to know if stress people experience in married life is related to how long they have been married. However, she is aware that part of what causes an association between marital stress and marriage length is the fact that people who have been married longer are likely to have more children, and having children is likely to create or contribute to stress. Simply calculating the correlation between marital stress and marriage length would be misleading. It needs to be determined what the relationship between stress and length of marriage would be if everyone had the same number of children. To put it another way, the researcher wants somehow to subtract the information provided by number of children from the information provided by marital stress and length. Partial correlation accomplishes this.

Other synonymous terms for **partialing out** in research papers, are **'holding constant'**, and **'controlling for'**. The actual statistic for partial correlation is called the partial correlation coefficient which, like other correlations, takes values between −1 to +1 and is essentially an ordinary bivariate correlation, except that some third variable is being controlled for.

SPSS activity – partial correlation

We will illustrate this using data from 40 employees on their *age, their current salary,* and *their starting salary*. A previous study had shown a significant Pearson's 'r' between *starting salary* and *current salary* but this could be an art fact of their *age* since this acts as a base impacting on both. A partial correlation was computed to 'hold constant' the variable of *age* in the relationship between *starting* and *current salary* to check whether this assumption is correct. Access SPSS Chapter 13 Data File A.

How to proceed

1 *Analyze >> Correlate >> Partial* which brings the *Partial Correlations* box into view.
3 Select the variables that represent *starting salary* and *current salary* and move them into the variables box.
4 Select the *age* variable and move it into the *Controlling for* box.
5 Click the *two-tail option* in the *Test of Significance* box (Fig. 15.12).
6 To obtain the correlation between *starting salary* and *current salary* without holding *age* constant click *Options* and select *Zero order correlations*.
7 *Continue >> OK*.

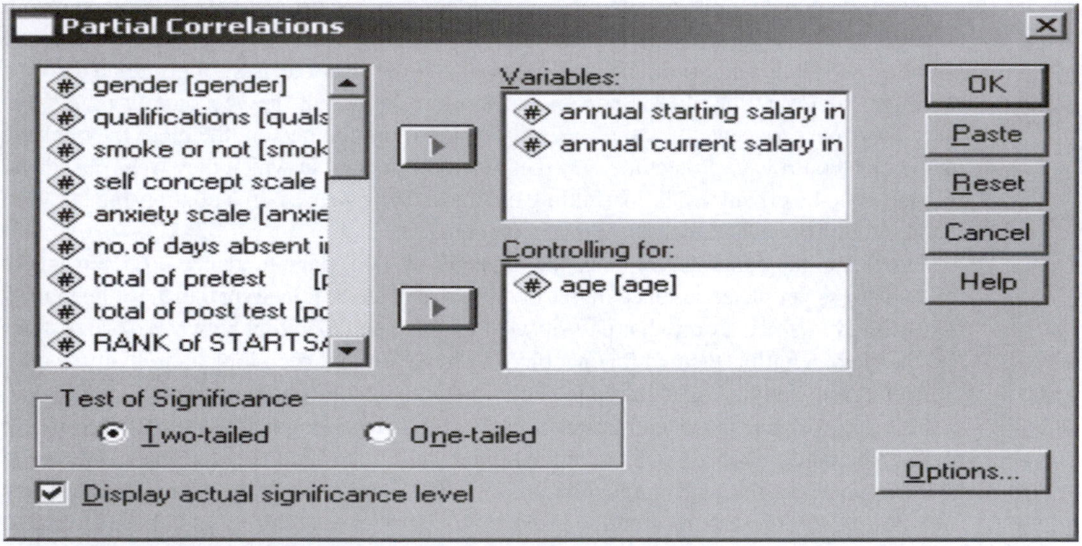

Figure 15.12 **Partial correlation box.**

How to interpret Table 15.6

- The top subtable provides usual bivariate correlations between *staring salary* and *current salary* now **without** *age* held constant. This displays a correlation of +.7353, p < .001.
- Each cell of the bottom table includes the partial correlation coefficient, and the p value on a diagonal format as usual.

Table 15.6 **Example of partial correlation printout**

--PARTIAL CORRELATION COEFFICIENTS--

Zero Order Partials

	STARTSAL	SALNOW	AGE
STARTSAL	1.0000	.7353	.0556
	(0)	(38)	(38)
	P = .	P = .000	P = .733
SALNOW	.7353	1.0000	.3535
	(38)	(0)	(38)
	P = .000	P = .	P = .025
AGE	.0556	.3535	1.0000
	(38)	(38)	(0)
	P = .733	P = .025	P = .

(Coefficient / (D.F.) / 2-tailed Significance)

" . " is printed if a coefficient cannot be computed

--PARTIAL CORRELATION COEFFICIENTS--

Controlling for ..   AGE

	STARTSAL	SALNOW
STARTSAL	1.0000	.7662
	(0)	(37)
	P = .	P = .000
SALNOW	.7662	1.0000
	(37)	(0)
	P = .000	P = .

(Coefficient / (D.F.) / 2-tailed Significance)

" . " is printed if a coefficient cannot be computed

- The partial correlation between *starting salary* and *current salary* with *age* held constant is +.7662, with p < .001, which indicates a stronger significant relationship than the zero order one. *Age* has a small but important effect in moderating the correlation between *starting salary* and *current salary*.
- The null hypothesis that there is no significant relationship between *starting salary* and *current salary* with *age* partialled out must be rejected.

How to report the results

'The partial correlation between current salary and starting salary was computed holding age constant. The significant partial correlation of +.7662 indicates that current salary and starting salary are strongly related. It also indicates that the original significant zero order correlation of .7353 was underestimated by the effect of age, which impacts on both variables'.

What you have learned from this chapter

This chapter has explained to you another set of correlational statistics which can be used for measuring relationships between variables but which do not indicate cause and effect. The correlation coefficient varies between +1, a perfect relationship, and –1 a perfect inverse relationship. The more random the relationship the closer the coefficient is to zero.

The relationship is described by three characteristics:

- Direction. A relationship can be either positive or negative.
- Degree or strength. This is the magnitude of the correlation irrespective of its sign.
- Form. Most correlations form a straight line relationship but others may be curvilinear.

The most common correlation is the Pearson correlation and is used for interval data. The Spearman correlation is used for ordinal data.

To evaluate the strength of the relationship the correlation of determination is calculated by squaring the correlation and calling it a percentage. This indicates the proportion of one variable that can be predicted by using the relationship with the second variable, or the degree of common variation.

When the X and Y values are limited in range caution should be exercised, as a limited range may obscure a strong relationship or exaggerate a weak one. Correlations can be spurious as the calculations for correlation can be conducted on any combination of variables, many of which bear no logical relationship with each other.

When a variable correlates with two other variables of interest it is possible to partial out or control this variable so that the correlation between the two variables of interest reflect their uncontaminated relationship.

Review questions and tasks

Qu. 15.1
Which of the following are positive and which negative correlations?

(a) The rise of lung cancer with the increase in smoking.
(b) The rise in monthly mortgage payments as interest rates rise.
(c) The decrease in dam levels as rainfall decreases.
(d) The increase in the cost of domestic water as dam levels fall.
(e) The fall in weekly income as overtime hours fall.
(f) Children from larger families tend to have poorer health records than those from smaller families.

Qu. 15.2
If we find a straight line graph running from the top left-hand corner to the bottom right-hand corner which correlation does this represent?

Qu. 15.3
Is – .87 a weaker correlation than +.87?

(a) Yes
(b) No
(c) depends on N
(d) depends on p

Qu. 15.4
Jules came bottom in the statistics test and the correlation between the statistics test and the accountancy test was +1. What position did Jules come in the accountancy test?

Qu. 15.5
Which of the following correlations is the strongest?

(a) +.50
(b) –.60
(c) + 65
(d) –.67

Qu. 15.6
If we find a correlation of +.50 between desired age for retirement and current age, how much of the variance in desired age of retirement is predicted from current age. How much variance is left unexplained?

Qu. 15.7
The Coefficient of Determination is always positive and is often reported as a percentage.

(a) false
(b) true
(c) sometimes
(d) depends on the value of r

Qu. 15.8
Draw the scatter graphs for the other pairings in Table 15.2 and come to a decision whether the relationships are linear. Note the pattern–data link.

Check your answers on the Chapter 15 Web page.

Now access the chapter Web page and carry out the SPSS activities there and answer the additional questions.

Chapter 16
Prediction and Regression

'Statistics involve drawing a mathematically precise line from unwarranted assumptions to a foregone conclusion'

(Frank Friday)

'Experimental confirmation of a prediction is merely a measurement. An experiment disproving a prediction is a discovery'

(Enrico Fermi)

Content list

> **By the end of this chapter you will understand:**
>
> 1 The purpose of regression.
> 2 What is meant by a line of best fit.
> 3 The components of the regression formula.
> 4 The purposes of simple linear regression.
> 5 The purposes of multiple regression.
> 6 The difference between hierarchical and stepwise multiple regression.
> 7 The use of dummy variables.
> 8 How to use SPSS for simple and multiple regression and interpret the printout.

Introduction

This chapter extends the work on correlation to the prediction of DV values from a knowledge of the value(s) of the IV(s). The accuracy of prediction depends on the strength of the relationship. By developing regression equations, we can make predictions of the value of the DV from known values of one or more variables in combination. Regression is a widely used technique and links to Pearson's 'r', sharing many of its assumptions, including linearity and the use of scale data.

What is regression?

In the business world the desired effect is typically driven by the impact of multiple independent variables working together rather than by a single variable. We often would like to know or predict:

- the relationship between a battery of selection tests and future job performance by job applicants;
- the relationship of sales revenue to amount of advertising expenditure and number of salespersons;
- the relationship between decrease in pollutant emissions and a factory's annual expenditure on pollution abatement devices;
- how demand varies with price;
- how investment varies with interest rates and disposable income;
- how unemployment varies with inflation;

and many other similar issues that would improve the efficiency and effectiveness of business and management. Whilst all these questions are similar to correlational questions as they seek to determine relationships between variables, regression permits prediction.

The technique of regression allows the researcher to make **predictions** of the likely values of the dependent variable Y from known values of independent variable X in a simple linear regression, or from known values of a combination of independent variables D, E, and F in multiple linear regression.

The accuracy of the prediction depends on the strength of the correlation between the variables. In Chapter 15 on correlation, you learned that correlation enables us to estimate the common variance (variation) between two factors/variables. At $r = \pm1.00$ it is possible to predict exactly the values on one variable from a knowledge of values on another variable. Prediction is increasingly less accurate as 'r' declines in value but, by using regression, it is possible to obtain the best possible estimate of the value of second variable for values of the first variable

Simple linear regression (SLR)

> *Simple regression. A technique for estimating a score or observation in one variable based on a score or observation in another variable, i.e. it enables estimates to be made of Y values from known values of X.*

Line of best fit

Simple linear regression is based on finding the straight line on a scattergraph that 'fits' the scatter points best, i.e. as closely possible. The straight line summarizing the relationship between two continuous variables in a scattergraph is known as **the regression line** or **the line of best fit**. Only one straight line, this line of best fit, will minimize the sum of the square of the vertical distances (squared deviations) between the actual data points and the line, and therefore make errors of prediction as small as possible or the minimum of all possible alternative lines. Some points will be above and some below the line of best fit, and a small proportion may actually be on it.

It is impossible to draw this line by hand or estimate it by eye. This is where regression comes in. Mathematical regression procedures permit the precise line of best fit to be calculated. The equation describing this line is the **regression equation** and is used to predict likely values of the dependent variable Y for particular values of the independent variable X. Even so, the best estimate may not be a good estimate. It can be a poor one if the correlation between the predictor variable and the criterion variable is low.

> *Line of best fit. This line minimizes the sum of the squared deviations from the line to the dots on the scattergraph, thus errors of prediction will be at a minimum.*

The regression formula

The line of best fit is defined by the linear equation:

$$Y = b_0 + b_1 X \text{ or}$$

Y [*predicted score on DV*] $= b_0$ (*constant*) $+ [b_1$ (*slope*) $\times X$ (*known score on IV*)].

For example, suppose $b_0 = 3$ and $b_1 = 2$ and we want to know what Y is when X $= 5$. By substituting in we get:

$$Y = 3 + 2(5) = 13.$$

We will explain below what these symbols in the formula stand for. It is important for you to note that predicted Y will be written in italics to distinguish it from 'real' Y from which it will deviate, usually by some slight degree of error, since the correlations between X and Y with which we deal are never perfect. Y is sometimes called the criterion variable and X is the predictor variable.

Only two lines of best fit flow perfectly through all the dots on a scattergraph, and these are when $r = +1.00$ and $r = -1.00$. In these cases, we are able to make a perfect prediction of the dependent variable value if we know the independent variable value. For example, height in inches is perfectly correlated with height in centimetres. If we know a person's height in inches, we can perfectly predict their height in centimetres.

When correlations between variables are less than perfect, predictions are good estimates rather than exact predictions, because there are exceptions to a consistent orderly relationship between the scores so that the regression line will not pass through all the coordinate values used to determine the slope. But if we have a line of best fit, we know that we can predict fairly closely with only a small range of error.

> **Predictor variable**. *A variable (the IV) from which a value is to be used to estimate a value on another variable (the DV).*

> **Criterion variable**. *A variable (the DV) a value of which is to be estimated from a value of the predictor variable (the IV).*

The slope of the regression line (b_1) is a geometric representation of the coefficient of correlation and is expressed as a ratio of the magnitude of the rise (if r is +) to the run, or as a ratio of the fall (if r is −) to the run, expressed in standard deviation units or in formula terms:

$$\frac{\text{Vertical change}}{\text{horizontal change}}$$

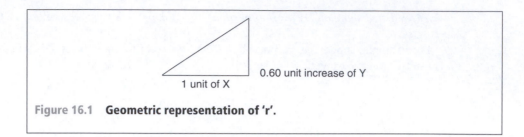

Figure 16.1 Geometric representation of 'r'.

In the above example, if r = + .60, for every X unit increase (run) in X there is a .60X unit increase in Y.

Here is an example

Assume that research has shown that a simple test of manual dexterity is capable of distinguishing between the good and poor employees in a word processing end of course test. Manual dexterity is a **predictor** variable (X) and input accuracy on the computer the **criterion** variable (Y). It should be possible to predict which job applicants are likely to be the more accurate data input personnel from scores on this test of manual dexterity. Using the test might be a lot more effective and cheaper than training all applicants, some of whom are unlikely to make the grade. Imaginary data for such a study are shown in Table 16.1.

Table 16.1 **Manual dexterity and data input accuracy**

Manual dexterity score	Accuracy score
56	17
19	6
78	23
92	22
16	9
23	10
29	13
60	20
50	16
35	19

The scattergraph (Fig. 16.2) depicts the data above. Notice that the scores on the manual dexterity test lie on the horizontal dimension (X-axis) and the accuracy score which we want to predict is on the vertical dimension (Y-axis). In regression:

- the horizontal dimension (X-axis) should always be used to represent the variable from which the prediction is being made (the independent or predictor variable); and

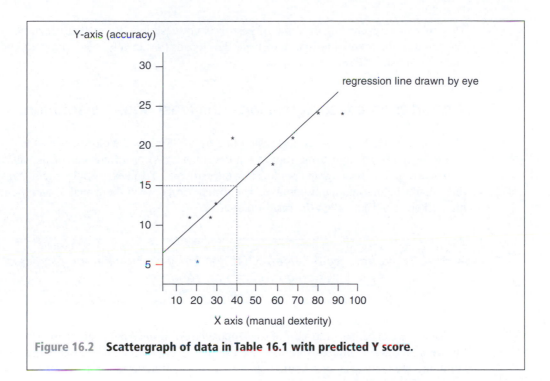

Figure 16.2 Scattergraph of data in Table 16.1 with predicted Y score.

- the vertical dimension (Y-axis) should always represent what is being predicted (the dependent or criterion variable).

It is clear from the scattergraph that accuracy is fairly closely related to scores on the manual dexterity test. If we draw a straight line, **the regression line,** or the **line of best fit,** as best we can through the points on the scattergraph, this line could be used as a basis for making predictions about the most likely score on accuracy from the manual dexterity aptitude test score. In order to predict the likeliest accuracy score corresponding to a score of 40 on the manual dexterity test, we can simply draw:

(i)   a right angle from the score 40 on the horizontal axis (manual dexterity test score) to the regression line; and then

(ii) a right angle from the vertical axis to meet this point. In this way we can find the accuracy score which best corresponds to a particular manual dexterity score (dotted lines on Figure 16.2).

Estimating from this scattergraph and regression line, it appears that the best prediction from a manual dexterity score of 40 is an accuracy test score of about 15.

There is only one major problem with this procedure – the prediction depends on the particular line drawn through the points on the scattergraph. Many different lines could be drawn.

This subjective eyeballing of a line of best fit is not desirable. So mathematical ways of determining the regression line have been developed. Fortunately, the computations are undertaken using SPSS.

A short theoretical digression – the least squares solution

The mathematically calculated regression line by SPSS gives the closest fit to the points on the scattergraph, so that the sum of the deviations (d's) or differences of the actual Y values denoted by scattergraph points from the estimated Y values given by the regression line should be the minimum possible. The difference between the actual Y and the estimated Y (or $Y - Y$) is called **the residual** or error.

> *The residual. The difference between what Y actually is and what we predict it to be using our regression equation.*

The precise criterion – the **sum of the squared deviations from each of the points** – is known as the **least squares solution.** We use the square of each deviation, since simply summing the raw deviations would not stress the magnitude of error. It seems reasonable that the further away a real Y value point is from the estimating line then the more serious the error. In fact we prefer several small errors or deviations than one large one, as this suggests that our line of best fit is a better 'fit' to all the points. Therefore, to penalize large absolute deviations or errors, we square the differences before adding them together. The least squares solution minimizes the sum of the squared errors. Look at Figure 16.3 with its two graphs.

> *The least squares solution. This minimizes the sum of the squared deviations from each point to the regression line.*

In order to specify the regression line for any scattergraph, you need to quantify two things:

1   The point at which the regression line cuts the vertical or Y axis – this is a number of units of measurement from the zero point of the vertical axis. It can take a positive or negative value, denoting whether the vertical axis is cut above or below its zero point. It is normally denoted in the regression formula as b_0 or the **Constant**.
2   The **slope** of the regression line or, in other words, the gradient of the best-fitting line through the points on the scattergraph. Just as with the correlation coefficient, this slope may be positive in the sense that it goes up from bottom left to top right or it can be

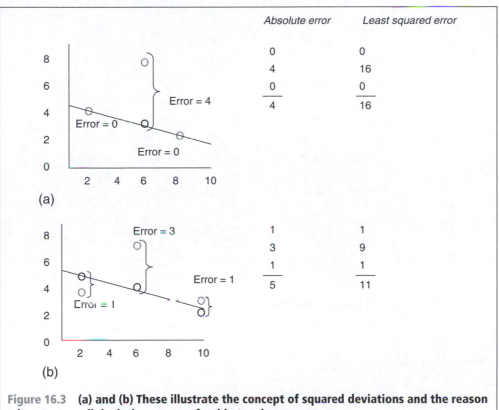

Figure 16.3 **(a) and (b) These illustrate the concept of squared deviations and the reason why many small deviations are preferable to a large one.**

negative in that it goes downwards from top left to bottom right. The slope is designated in the regression formula as b_1.

The intercept and slope are both shown in Figure 16.4. To work out the slope, we have drawn a horizontal dashed line from $X = 0$ to $X = 40$ (length 40) and a vertical dashed line up to the regression line (length about 9 up the Y-axis). The slope b is the increase (+) or decrease (–) of the units produced (in this case +9) divided by the increase in the manual dexterity score (in this case 40), i.e. $+ .225$. The intercept or constant is 5 (where the Y axis is crossed).

In our example, for every increase of 1 in the manual dexterity score, there is an increase of .225 in the accuracy performance measure. We have estimated this value from the scattergraph – it may not be exactly the answer that we would have obtained had we used mathematically more precise methods.

To increase your familiarity with the concept of a regression line, regression equation and the meaning of the symbols in the regression equation, let's look at a well-known perfect correlation in Figure 16.5. Here you can see the relationship between two temperature scales, with X representing degrees Centigrade and Y representing degrees Fahrenheit.

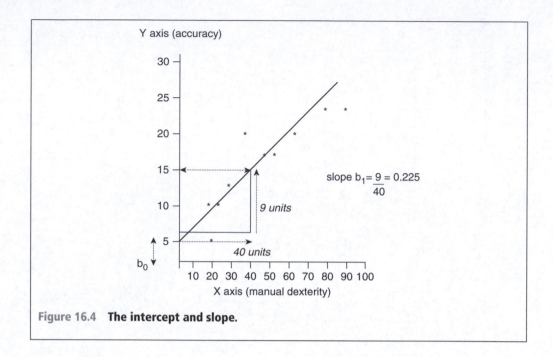

Figure 16.4   The intercept and slope.

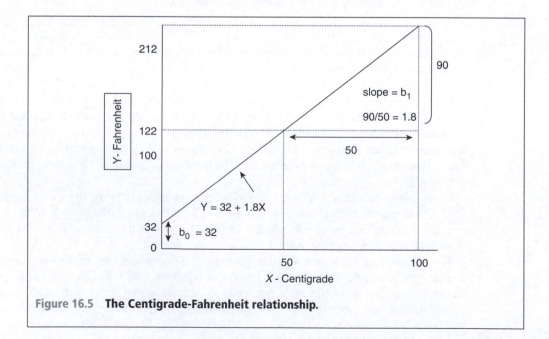

Figure 16.5   The Centigrade-Fahrenheit relationship.

The intercept b_0 crosses the Y axis at 32F. As you know, 32F = 0C. The slope represents the ratio of 50C/90F, or every 1C rise in temperature is equivalent to 1.8F rise in temperature. Thus b_1 = 1.8. The regression equation is therefore:

$$Y = 32 + 1.8X$$

When using a regression equation for prediction we can interpolate within the range of the given X's but we should be careful in extrapolating beyond the range, since we do not know what happens to X beyond its highest and lowest points graphed or what other variables may impinge on the relationship. Always remember that our regression equation is only based on known data.

Regression equations

The regression line involves one awkward feature. All values really should be expressed in Z scores or standard deviation units so that they are comparable. However, it is more practical to use actual scores to determine the slope of the regression line. But because raw scores do not have the same means and standard deviations like Z scores, the prediction procedure employs a **raw score regression coefficient** or b_1.

> b_1. The raw score regression coefficient.

> b_0. The Constant or Intercept where the regression line cuts the Y axis.

When the correlation is negative, the regression equation for the line of best fit is:

$$Y = b_0 - b_1X.$$

This implies that for every increment of X there will be a decrease in Y.

When the line of best fit cuts the horizontal axis and extends to intercept, the vertical axis at a negative point, i.e. below the horizontal axis, the constant will be negative. In this situation:

$$Y = -b_0 + b_1X.$$

You will never have to calculate the various components of the regression equation as SPSS will undertake this.

How accurate is the predicted Y value?

Y values are assumed to be normally distributed

The point to remember is that a value of X may occur several times, but we could very well get a slightly different Y value each time. Regression analysis assumes that this distribution of Y values is normally distributed. This distribution is centred at the mean of these Y values, as illustrated in Figure 16.6. The best our regression model or SPSS can do is estimate the **average** value for Y given any X value.

Standard error of Y

Because Y is assumed to be normally distributed, it is possible to calculate a standard error for the estimated Y value, which tells us how accurate our prediction is and what the range of error round it is. The same confidence intervals (or significance levels) we have used before are employed. The 95% confidence interval indicates the range of values within which the true value will fall 95% of the time. That is, we are likely to be wrong only 5% of times, whereas the 99% confidence interval decreases our likely error to 1%. The mean of the distribution represents the predicted Y score for that value of X. This is displayed in Figure 16.7.

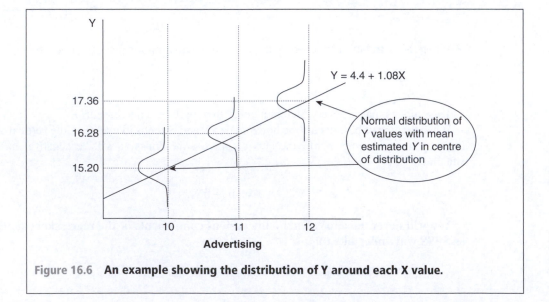

Figure 16.6 An example showing the distribution of Y around each X value.

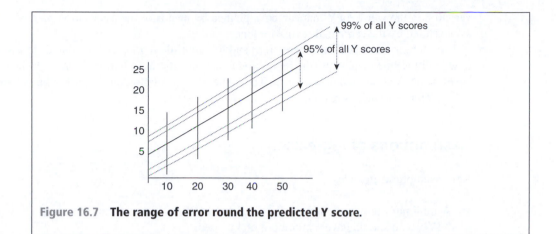

Figure 16.7   The range of error round the predicted Y score.

The variability of the Y distribution reflects error and it is this error that is measured by the standard error of the estimate, which can be used as a measure of the accuracy of prediction. The standard error of the estimate (SE_{est}) to estimate the prediction error of Y is:

$$SE_{estY} = SD_Y \sqrt{1 - r^2}$$

> *The standard error of the estimate of Y* measures the dispersal of the values of Y observed in the sample around the least squares regression line established for the sample.

If the estimated value of the criterion (Y variable) is 6.00 and the standard error of this estimate is .26, then the 95% confidence interval is:

6.00 plus or minus (1.96 × .26) = a 95% confidence interval of 5.49 to 6.51.

Thus it is almost certain that the person's score will actually fall in the range of 5.49 to 6.51 although the most likely value is 6.00. Assuming that the observed points are all normally distributed around the regression line, we can expect to find 95% of the points within $\pm 1.96\ SE_{est}$.

The coefficient of determination

We met the concept of r^2 in Chapter 15. It represents the amount of variance in Y that was common to X. This also means that it can be interpreted as the proportion of the total variation in the values of Y that can be explained by means of the association of Y with X as measured by the estimated regression line.

Therefore, r^2 (simple linear regression) and R^2 (multiple regression), enable us to assess how well the line of best fit (the regression equation) fits the actual data. It might be our best line but it still could be a poor fit. The higher the correlation the better the line fits the data as more variance is explained.

Assumptions of regression

Key assumptions include:

1   A minimum requirement is to have at least 15 times more cases than IV's, i.e. with 3 IV's, you should have a minimum of 45 cases.
2   Outliers can have considerable influence on the regression solution and should be identified and removed as they affect the accuracy of prediction. One extremely low or high value well away from the run of the other values distorts the prediction by changing the angle of slope of the regression line. This is parallel to the effect on a mean by a single outlier pulling it away from the general run of scores. Serious consideration has to be given to omitting any outlier from the calculation. Outlier identification was illustrated in Chapter 8 using box plots and stem and leaf diagrams. SPSS will also identify outliers using the Mahalanobis distance measure.
3   Differences between obtained and predicted DV values should normally be distributed and variance of residuals the same for all predicted scores (*homoscedasticity*). These assumptions can be tested by inspecting residual scattergraphs and histograms.
4   Regression procedures assume that the dispersion of points is linear. Where the amount of scatter around the line varies markedly at different points and forms a pattern then the use of regression is questionable.

Other issues include:

- In order to make predictions, it is assumed that the new individual or new group and the old group are both samples from the same population since we are predicting the Y score for the new individual/group on the basis of the data gathered from the original group.
- Regression is less accurate where one variable has a small range and the other a large range.
- There are always two regression lines between two variables: that from which Variable Y is predicted from Variable X, and that from which Variable X is predicted from Variable Y. They almost invariably have different slopes. However, life is made simpler if we always have the predictor on the horizontal axis and the criterion to be predicted on the vertical axis. You need to be careful what you are trying to predict and from what.
- There is no implication that an increase in X *causes an* increase in Y. Although it may appear, for example, that additional advertising caused more people to purchase their holidays from Holidays R Us, we can only conclude that X and Y move together. The simultaneous increase in X and Y may have been caused by an unknown third variable

excluded from the study. You will remember that we discussed this issue when explaining correlation in the previous chapter.

SPSS activity – simple linear regression

Simple linear regression and a regression plot are illustrated below. We want to determine if we can predict the value of sales per month by the floor area for 14 branches of a multiple chain store. The management is interested in whether by increasing floor area sales can be increased. Access SPSS Chapter 16 Data File A.

How to proceed

1 *Analyze >> Regression >> Linear* to open the **Linear Regression** dialogue box.
2 Click on the dependent variable (*value of sales per month*) and place it in the **Dependent:** box.
3 Select the independent variable (*floor area in sq mts*) and move it into **Independent [s]:** box.
4 In **Method** box ensure **Enter** is selected (Fig. 16.8).
5 Select **Statistics** to obtain **the Linear Regression: Descriptives** dialogue box.

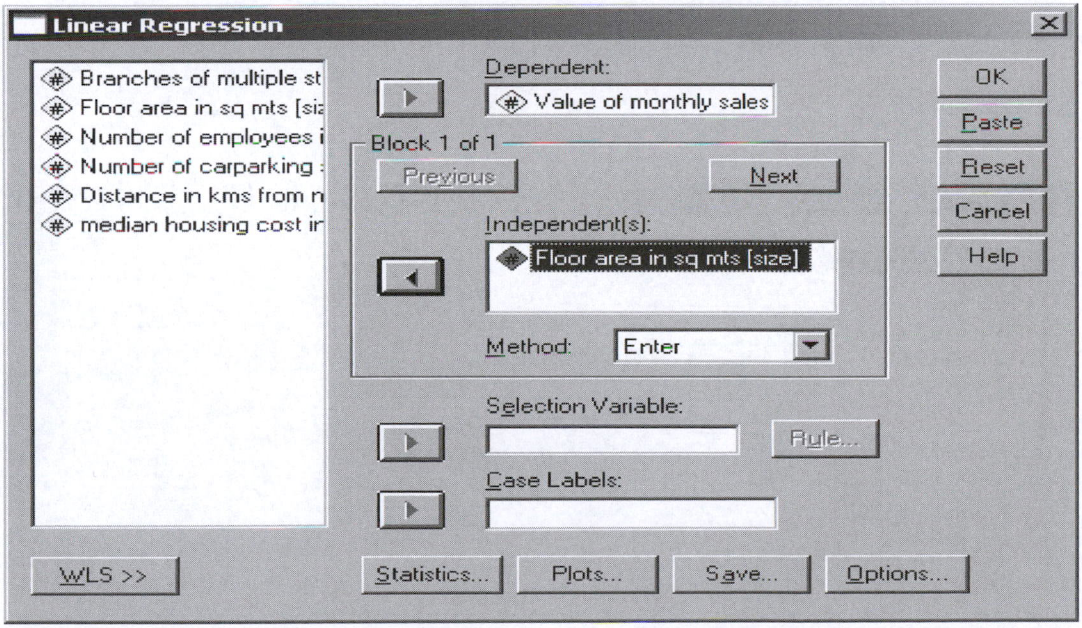

Figure 16.8   Linear regression box.

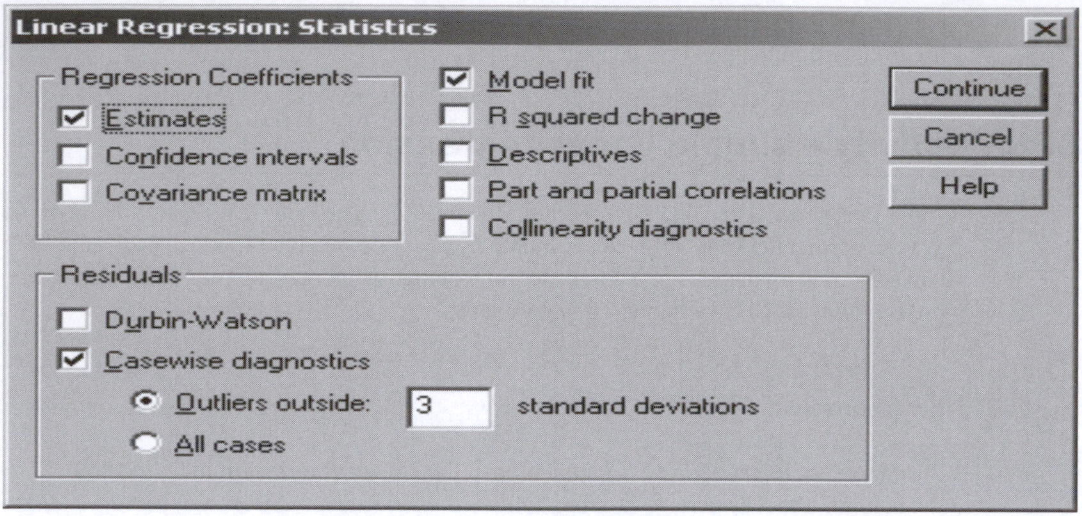

Figure 16.9 **Linear regression statistics box.**

6 Choose *Estimates*, and *Model fit*. Check *Casewise diagnostics* box and accept default value of *3* sd's (Fig. 16.9).
7 Next, click *Plots*. Place *ZRESID* into *Y* box and *ZPRED* into *X* box, finally select *histogram* (Fig. 16.10).
8 *Continue >> OK*.

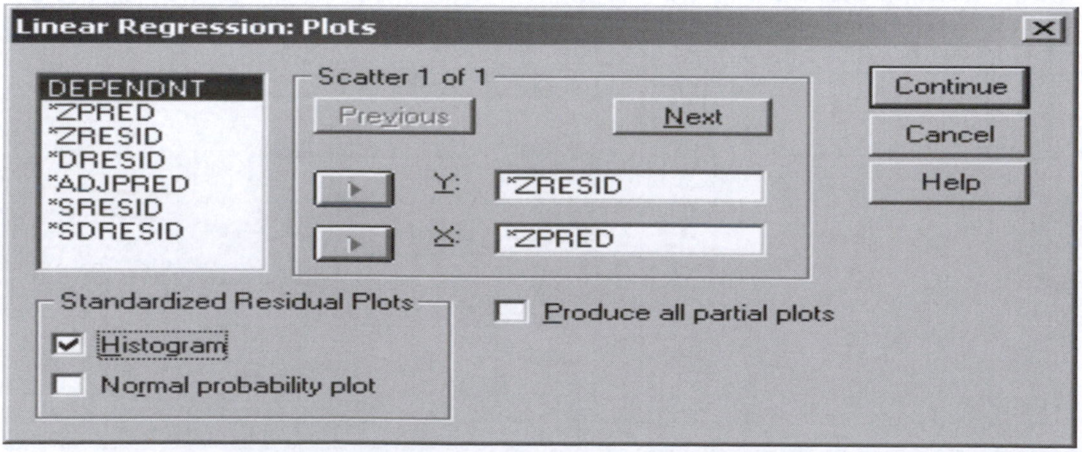

Figure 16.10 **Linear regression plots box.**

How to interpret the output in Table 16.2 and Figure 16.11

With simple regression it is conventional to report the regression equation, quantifying the slope (b_0) and an intercept (b_1). SPSS does not quite follow this terminology but all of the relevant information is located in the third subtable above. The output is far more complex and detailed than you need but the following is what you should take note of:

- The top subtable displays 'R' as +0.954 and adjusted R^2 as .902, which are very high: 90.2% of the variance in monthly sales value is explained by the variance in floor area. Adjusted R^2 is used as this refers to sample data.
- The next subtable indicates that the regression equation is highly significant with an $F = 121.009$, $p < .001$. So, in terms of variance explained and significance the regression equation (often called 'model') is excellent. Should F not be significant then the regression as a whole has failed and no more interpretation is necessary.

Table 16.2   Output for simple linear regression

Model summary[b]

Model	R	R square	Adjusted R square	Std. error of the estimate
1	.954[a]	.910	.902	936.85001

[a] Predictors: (Constant), Floor area in sq mts.
[b] Dependent Variable: Value of monthly sales in $k in 2007.

> 90.2% of variance in DV explained by variance in IV

ANOVA[b]

Model		Sum of squares	df	Mean square	F	Sig.
1	Regression	1.06E+08	1	106208119.7	121.009	.000[a]
	Residual	10532255	12	877687.937		
	Total	1.17E+08	13			

[a] Predictors: (Constant), Floor area in sq mts.
[b] Dependent Variable: Value of monthly sales in $k in 2007.

> Highly significant regression model

b_1

b_0

Coefficients[a]

Model		Unstandardized coefficients		Standardized coefficients	t	Sig.
		B	Std. error	Beta		
1	(Constant)	901.247	513.023		1.757	.104
	Floor area in sq mts	1.686	.153	.954	11.000	.000

[a] Dependent Variable: Value of monthly sales in $k in 2007.

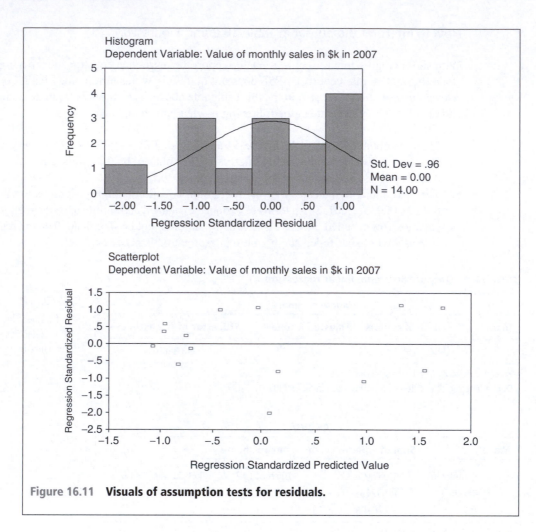

Figure 16.11   Visuals of assumption tests for residuals.

- The coefficients subtable is also crucial and displays the values for constant and beta from which the regression equation can be derived. The constant or intercept, b_0 in our regression formula, is referred to as the Constant in SPSS and has a value of 901.247. The unstandardized or raw score regression coefficient or slope (b_1) is displayed in SPSS under B as the second line and is 1.686. The t value for B was significant and implies that this variable (floor area) is a significant predictor. It is useful to think of B (or b_1 in our symbols) as the change in outcome associated with a unit change in the predictor. This means for every one unit rise (1 sq metre increase in floor space) in B, sales (the outcome) rise by $1,686. Management can now determine whether the cost of increasing floor area (e.g. building, rental, staffing, etc.) will bring sufficient returns over a defined time span.

- The column headed Beta gives a value of 0.954. This is the Pearson correlation between the two variables. In other words, if you turn your scores into standard scores (Z-scores) the slope and the correlation coefficient are the same thing.
- The histogram and standardized residual scattergraph (Fig. 16.11) are essential and address the issue of whether the assumptions for linear regression were met. The histogram assesses normality and reveals no definite skewness or extreme outliers. There appears to be a very slight skew but with only 14 cases this is not severe.
- The residual plot shows a reference line where residuals are 0. The line is produced by double clicking on the plot then:

  Chart > Reference Line
  Y scale > OK
  Position of Lines: 0
  Add > OK

This is a near perfect plot and very acceptable with data spread reasonably equally around the line with no apparent pattern, i.e. it is homoscedastistic. If there is a pattern such as a curve or funnel distribution rather than randomness then we have heteroscedasticity, which suggests that there is no homogeneity of variance.

Regression scattergraph

The production and inspection of a scattergraph of your two variables is warranted when doing regression. The provision of this scattergraph in a report is also of benefit as it provides a clear visual presentation of what may seem to be mathematical diarrhoea:

1. *Graphs >> Scatter*.
2. Accept *Simple option* default, then select *Define*.
3. Move dependent variable (*value of monthly sales*) into the *Y Axis*: box.
4. Transfer the independent variable (*floor area in sq mts*) to the *X Axis*: box.
5. *OK* and the scattergraph will be displayed (Fig. 16.12).

To draw the regression line on the displayed chart:

1. Double click on the chart to select it for editing.
2. In the *Chart Dialogue* box choose *Chart >> Options*.
3. Select Total in the *Fit Line* box.
4. *OK* and the regression line is now displayed on the scattergraph (Fig. 16.12).

How to interpret the scatterplot with regression line

- The regression line sloping from bottom right to top left indicates a positive relationship between the two variables.

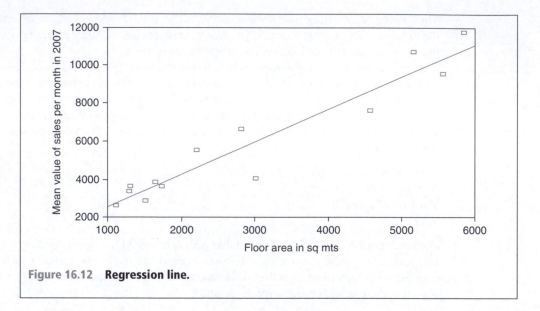

Figure 16.12   Regression line.

• The points seem relatively close to this line, which suggests that the correlation should be a high positive one, and therefore prediction estimates will be close to true values. This is confirmed in the previous tables.

How to report the results

'A linear regression analysis was conducted to evaluate the prediction of monthly sales value from floor area of a set of 14 branches of a large multiple store. The scattergraph indicates that they are positively and strongly linearly related such that as floor area increases so does monthly sales income, in fact by $1,686 per sq mt. A histogram and residual plots indicate that linear regression assumptions are met.

The strong relationship between the two variables was reflected in an R of +0.954 and adjusted R^2 of 0.902. Approximately 90% of the variance of monthly sales value was accounted for by its linear relationship with floor space. The overall regression was highly significant with F = 121.009, p > .001. The regression equation for predicting monthly sales value is: Predicted monthly sales value = 901.247 + 1.686 (floor area in sq mts)'.

Multiple regression

So far, we have focused on a model of simple linear regression in which one independent or predictor variable was used to predict the value of a dependent or criterion variable. But, on other occasions, there can be many other potential predictors that might establish a better or more meaningful prediction. With more than one predictor variable we use multiple regression.

For example, while there is clearly some association between consumer sales of washing machines over a given period and the sale of specified industrial components which go into the making of the machines over the same period of time, the true picture of component sales to washing machine manufacturers, and thus the ability to forecast future component sales to this industry needs to take account of other factors (e.g. average stocks of unsold machines in outlets, manufacturers' own average stocks of machines and unassembled components). The addition of one or more other relevant independent variables will almost certainly improve the understanding of the relationship between consumer sales of washing machines and sales of components to washing machine manufacturers.

Other examples would include:

- the prediction of individual income may depend on a combination of education, job experience, gender, age, etc.
- the demand for a good may depend on a combination of price, consumers' income, price of substitutes or competitors' prices, unemployment rate, population size, advertising expenditure, number of outlets, etc.
- the prediction of the consumption of individual household domestic water based on daily temperature, number of people in the household, size of garden, and cost per kilolitre.

The regression equation in multiple regression quantifies the impact each of the independent variables has on the Y variable.

Using the regression equation, management is able to run 'what-if' scenarios with different values inserted, say for price, advertising dollars invested, number of salespersons, and outlet numbers to see the effect on sales. Changing of different options would predict the combination of the independent variables that would maximize sales. An extremely useful piece of knowledge!!

Multiple regression employs the same rationale as simple regression and the formula is a logical extension of that for linear regression:

$$Y = b_0 + b_1 X_1 + b_2 X_2 + b_3 X_3 + \ldots\ldots\ldots \text{ etc.}$$

The various b's (unstandardized regression coefficients or regression weights) and X's refer to the variables being included in the equation.

When working with Z scores so that all the variables are on a comparable scale, the regression coefficients or weights are standardized regression coefficients, as in simple linear regression, and are called beta weights (β). The regression equation simply substitutes β for b_1.

Multiple regression. A technique for estimating the value on the criterion variable from values on two or more other variables.

Multiple correlation

Multiple correlation (designated R) is a measure of the correlation of one dependent variable with a combination of two or more predictor variables. In multiple regression, researchers can determine the statistical significance of both the overall multiple correlation coefficient, R, as well as for each b or beta individually. In most cases, however, if the overall R is not significant, the individual b's and betas will not be tested for significance. Yet, it is possible for overall R to be significant but for some of the individual b's or betas not to be significant. For example, the overall significant correlation might be due to the strong influence of only one predictor variable, while the others have minimal contributions.

Squaring R, we obtain R^2, the coefficient of multiple determination, analogous to the squared correlation coefficient r^2 or coefficient of determination. R^2 describes the degree to which the predictor variables as a whole (X_1, X_2 ...... etc.) account for variations in the criterion variable Y. For example, an R^2 of .779 implies that all the predictor variables taken together explain 77.9% of the variation in the criterion variable. We usually report **adjusted R^2** since R^2 is often too optimistic as the line of best fit is based on a sample not the population. **Adjusted R^2** gives a more realistic estimate for generalization to the population.

> **The coefficient of multiple determination**. This measures the strength of the relationship between Y and the independent variables.

Assumptions of multiple regression

In addition to the assumptions noted above in simple linear regression, one further major assumption applies in multiple regression, namely, very high correlations between IV's should be avoided. This is **multicollinearity**. Inspect the correlation matrix (Chapter 15) for high correlations of .90 and above as this implies the two variables are measuring the same variance and will over-inflate R. Therefore only one of the two is needed. The Variance Inflation Factor (VIF) measures the impact of collinearity among the IV's in a multiple regression model on the precision of estimation. It expresses the degree to which collinearity among the predictors degrades the precision of an estimate. Typically a VIF value greater than 10.0 is of concern.

SPSS activity – standard multiple regression analysis

We will determine whether mean ratings of 44 employees for four Likert type subscales taken together (*rating of supervisor; facilities at work; relationships with colleagues; and opportunities for promotion and development*) significantly predict mean scores on a scale to measure *overall job satisfaction*. Access SPSS Chapter 16 Data File C.

The first task before starting a multiple regression is to assess **multicollinearity,** the presence of high correlations between independent variables, by inspecting a correlation matrix of the IV's, as in Table 16.3. None of the intercorrelations are sufficiently high to cause concern.

How to proceed (as the procedure is the same as that for simple linear regression the screen shots are not repeated).

1   *Analyze >> Regression >> Linear* to open the *Linear Regression* dialogue box.
2   Click on the dependent variable (*overall job satisfaction*) and place in the *Dependent:* box.

Table 16.3   Correlation matrix

		Overall job satisfaction	Rating of supervisor	Facilities at work	Relationships with colleagues	Opportunities for promotion and development
				Correlations		
overall job satisfaction	Pearson Correlation	1	.350(*)	.042	.601(**)	.621(**)
	Sig. (2-tailed)	.	.020	.784	.000	.000
	N	44	44	44	44	44
rating of supervisor	Pearson Correlation	.350(*)	1	−.066	.085	.267
	Sig. (2-tailed)	.020	.	.668	.584	.080
	N	44	44	44	44	44
facilities at work	Pearson Correlation	.042	−.066	1	−.010	.001
	Sig. (2-tailed)	.784	.668	.	.948	.993
	N	44	44	44	44	44
relationships with colleagues	Pearson Correlation	.601(**)	.085	−.010	1	.635(**)
	Sig. (2-tailed)	.000	.584	.948	.	.000
	N	44	44	44	44	44
opportunities for promotion and development	Pearson Correlation	.621(**)	.267	.001	.635(**)	1
	Sig. (2-tailed)	.000	.080	.993	.000	.
	N	44	44	44	44	44

* Correlation is significant at the .05 level (2-tailed). ** Correlation is significant at the .01 level (2-tailed).

3   Select the four independent variables and move them into **Independent** [*s*]: box.
4   In **Method** box ensure **Enter** is selected.
5   Select **Statistics** to obtain **the Linear Regression: Statistics** dialogue box.
6   Ensure **Estimates, Part and Partial Correlations, collinearity diagnostics** and **Model Fit** are selected and check **Casewise diagnostics** box accepting default value of **3** sd's.
7   Click **Plots**. Place **ZRESID** into **Y** box and **ZPRED** into **X** box, then select **histogram**.
8   **Continue >> OK**.

How to interpret the output in Table 16.4 and Figure 16.13

1   The first important subtable is Model Summary. Multiple correlation R of +0.715 represents the combined correlation of all the independent variables. Adjusted R^2 tells us that 46.1% of the variation in job satisfaction can be explained by variation in the four IV's taken together. This leaves 53.9% unexplained.
2   In the ANOVA subtable we have the F value of 10.186 which is significant with $p > .001$. This informs us that the four independent variables taken together as a set are significantly related to the dependent variable. The chance of obtaining these results assuming the null hypothesis to be correct is less than 1 in 1,000. The multiple correlation is therefore highly significant.
3   The Coefficients subtable reveals the significant regression coefficients, namely, *ratings of supervisor* at $p = .049$; *relationships with colleagues* at $p = .013$ and *opportunities for promotion and development* at $p = .043$. *Facilities at work* was not significant. These significance levels tell us that three variables uniquely contribute to the regression equation, thereby making a significant contribution to the prediction, but that *facilities at work* does not. The magnitude of the unique contributions is given by the relevant part correlation squared (sr^2). We can interpret the B's as indicating that for one unit increase in the IV the DV will increase by that amount. For example, for one unit increase in the rating of supervisor, job satisfaction will increase by 1.026 units. The VIF data suggests that collinearity is no problem as the figures are well below 10.0 for each variable.
4   The standardized beta weights can also be used to compare the relative contributions of each predictor. They display the same rank order in size as do the part correlations squared. The value of the Constant is 7.072. From this information we can now produce the regression equation. *Overall job satisfaction = 7.072 + 1.026 (rating of supervisor) + 0.301 (facilities at work) + 1.21 (relationships with colleagues) + 0.966 (opportunities for promotion and development)*.
5   As no case diagnostics table was produced no outliers had been detected by SPSS.
6   The histogram and scattergraph of residuals showed very acceptable distributions given only 44 cases.

How to report the results

'*A standard multiple regression was performed between overall job satisfaction as the DV and rating of supervisor, facilities at work, relationships with colleagues and opportunities*

Table 16.4   **Standard multiple regression printout**

Variables Entered/Removed[b]

Model	Variables entered	Variables removed	Method
1	Opportunities for promotion and development, facilities at work, rating of supervisor, relationships with colleagues[a]		Enter

[a] All requested variables entered.
[b] Dependent Variable: overall job satisfaction.

Model Summary[b]

Model	R	R square	Adjusted R square	Std. error of the estimate
1	.715[a]	.511	.461	4.476

[a] Predictors: (Constant), opportunities for promotion and development, facilities at work, rating of supervisor, relationships with colleagues.
[b] Dependent Variable: overall job satisfaction.

ANOVA[b]

Model		Sum of squares	df	Mean square	F	Sig.
1	Regression	816.260	4	204.065	10.186	.000[a]
	Residual	781.286	39	20.033		
	Total	1597.545	43			

[a] Predictors: (Constant), opportunities for promotion and development, facilities at work, rating of supervisor, relationships with colleagues.
[b] Dependent Variable: overall job satisfaction.

Coefficient[a]

Model		Unstandardized coefficients		Standardized coefficients			correlations			Collinearity statistics	
		B	Std. error	Beta	t	Sig	Zero-order	Partial	Part	Tolerance	VIF
1	(Constant)	7.072	3.160		2.238	.031					
	rating of supervisor	1.026	.506	.238	2.028	.049	.350	.309	.227	.912	1.096
	facilities at work	.301	.548	.062	.550	.586	.042	.088	.062	.995	1.005
	relationships with colleagues	1.211	.464	.381	2.608	.013	.601	.385	.292	.589	1.699
	opportunities for promotion and development	.966	.461	.316	2.094	.043	.621	.318	.234	.551	1.816

[a] Dependent Variable: overall job satisfaction.

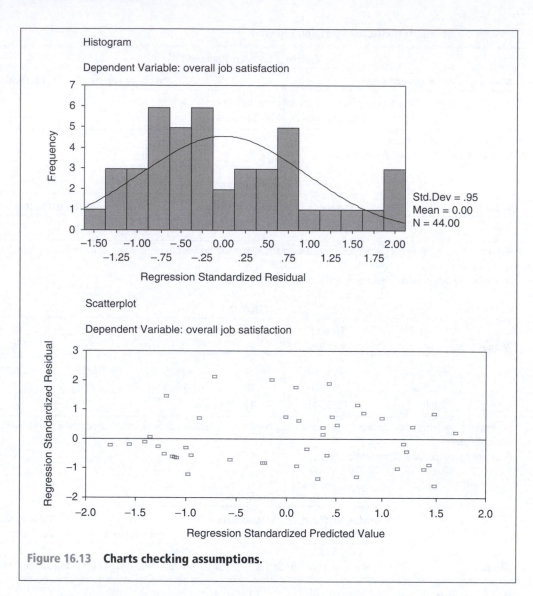

Figure 16.13 Charts checking assumptions.

for promotion and development as IV's. The adjusted squared multiple correlation was significantly different from zero (F = 10.186, p > .001) and 46.1% of the variation in the DV was explained by the set of IV's. All the IV's except facilities at work were found to uniquely and significantly contribute to the prediction of job satisfaction, namely, rating of supervisor (sr² = .051, t = 2.028, p = .049), relationships with colleagues (sr² = .085, t = 2.608, p = .013) and opportunities for promotion and development (sr² = .054, t = 2.094, p = .043).

The data satisfied the assumptions of multicollinearity, normality of residuals, and homosce-dasticity while no outliers were identified.'

Hierarchical and stepwise multiple regression

In the standard form of multiple regression above all the IV's are entered together to provide a single prediction and estimates of the unique contribution of each of the IV's. There are two other forms of multiple regression to be used when we have some basis on which to decide which predictors we enter and in what order. Standard multiple regression we illustrated above throws all predictors in the melting pot at once.

Hierarchical multiple regression

Sometimes researchers are interested in looking at the influence of several predictor variables in a sequential way. That is, they want to know what the prediction will be for the first predictor variable, and then how much is added to the overall prediction by including a second predictor variable, and then perhaps how much more is added by including a third predictor variable, and so on. This is known as **hierarchical multiple regression**. The amount that each successive variable adds to the overall prediction is described in terms of an increase in R^2, the proportion of variance accounted for or explained. The selection process or sequence of adding variables is controlled by the researcher, usually based on consideration of previous research or theory that points to important correlates and predictors. Thus, known and important predictors from previous theory or studies are entered first in order of their possible prediction potential.

Variables that have only a small correlation with the DV cannot account for much of the variance in it and should be added at the end. These variables will probably not improve the prediction. A look at the correlation matrix helps in this choice.

> *Hierarchical multiple regression. The researcher determines the order of entry of the IV's into the equation based on theoretical knowledge.*

SPSS activity – hierarchical multiple regression

We will rerun the previous study. We will assume that theory suggests that opportunities for bettering oneself, such as promotion, plus skill and personal development courses, is the most important predictor of job satisfaction; next we assume that relationships among workmates is important. The task and personal skills of the supervisor are less important as are facilities such as child care, sports teams, and dining room, etc. We will therefore place these predictors into the regression equation successively. Access SPSS Chapter 16 Data File C.

How to proceed

1   *Analyze >> Regression >> Linear* to open the *Linear Regression* dialogue box.
2   Click on the dependent variable (*job satisfaction*) and place it in the *Dependent*: box.
3   Select the first independent variable (*opportunities for promotion and development*) and move it into *Independent* [*s*]: box *Block 1 of 1.*
4   Click *Next* and select the second independent variable (*relationships with colleagues*) and move it into *Independent* [*s*]: box *Block 2 of 2.*
5   Click **Next** and select the third independent variable (*rating of supervisor*) and move it into *Independent* [*s*]: box *Block 3 of 3.* Continue with this process until all IV's are entered (Fig. 16.14).

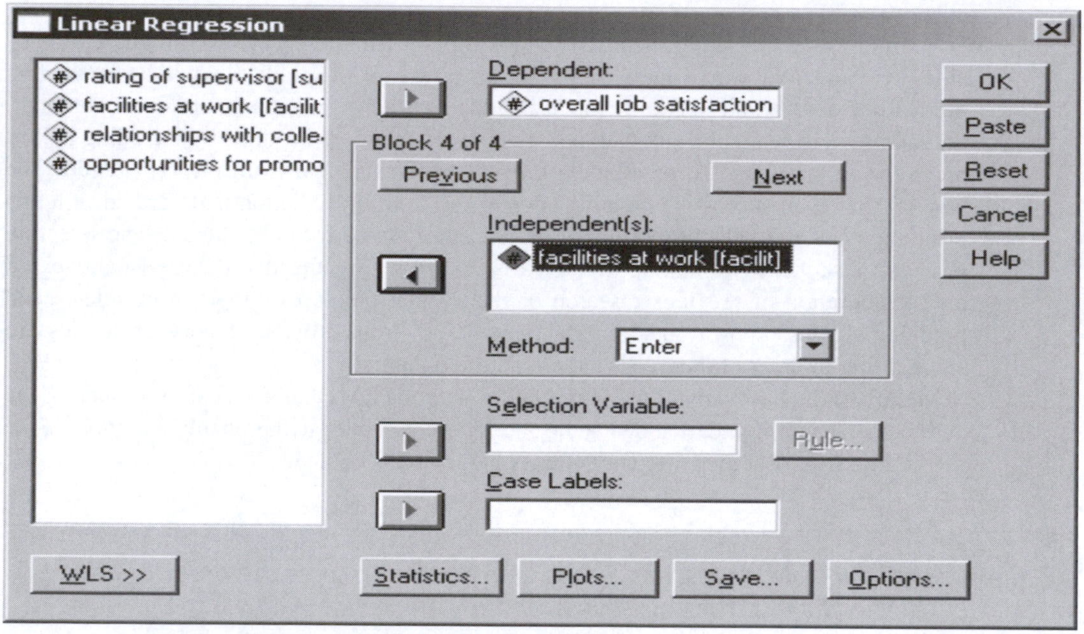

Figure 16.14   **Example entering variables successively in blocks.**

6   Select *Statistics* to obtain *the Linear Regression: Statistics* dialogue box.
7   Ensure *Estimates, Model Fit, Part and Partial Correlations and R Squared change*, are selected.
8   *Continue >> OK.*

As we know from our previous example that collinearity, residuals and outliers are not a problem, we will not repeat any statistics for these.

How to interpret the output in Table 16.5

1 The first subtable reveals the sequence in which we entered the variables, thereby producing four models.

2 The second subtable, Model Summary, provides the R, and adjusted R^2 values for the four models, as well as the change statistics as each model takes in another IV. Whereas with standard multiple regression only one model (equation) is produced, the hierarchical version produces a model for each step, each additional predictor producing a new model, as shown in the model summary subtable.

3 R and adjusted R^2 reveal changes to reflect the addition of each variable. The pattern of adjusted R^2 reveals that model 4 (the addition of the IV *facilities at work*) resulted in a lowering of the predictive ability of the model (46.1%) from model 3 (47%). This points

Table 16.5   Printout of hierarchical regression

Variables Entered/Removed[b]

Model	Variables entered	Variables removed	Method
1	opporturtities for promotion and development[a]	.	Enter
2	relationships with colleagues[a]	.	Enter
3	rating of supervisor[a]	.	Enter
4	facilites at work[a]	.	Enter

[a] All requested variables entered.
[b] Dependent Variable: overall job satisfaction.

Model Summary

Model	R	R square	Adjusted R square	Std. error of the estimate	Change statistics				
					R square change	F change	df1	df2	Sig. F change
1	.621[a]	.386	.371	4.833	.386	26.398	1	42	.000
2	.676[b]	.457	.431	4.598	.071	5.391	1	41	.025
3	.712[c]	.507	.470	4.437	.050	4.047	1	40	.051
4	.715[d]	.511	.461	4.476	.004	.302	1	39	.586

[a] Predictors: (Constant), opportunities for promotion and development.
[b] Predictors: (Constant), opportunities for promotion and development, relationships with colleagues.
[c] Predictors: (Constant), opportunities for promotion and development, relationships with colleagues, rating of supervisor.
[d] Predictors: (Constant), opportunities for promotion and development, relationships with colleagues, rating of supervisor facilities at work.

(Continued)

Table 16.5—cont'd

Model		Sum of squares	df	Mean square	F	Sig.
			ANOVA[e]			
1	Regression	616.563	1	616.563	26.398	.000[a]
	Residual	980.982	42	23.357		
	Total	1597.545	43			
2	Regression	730.558	2	365.279	17.274	.000[b]
	Residual	866.988	41	21.146		
	Total	1597.545	43			
3	Regression	810.207	3	270.069	13.721	.000[c]
	Residual	787.338	40	19.683		
	Total	1597.545	43			
4	Regression	816.260	4	204.065	10.186	.000[d]
	Residual	781.286	39	20.033		
	Total	1597.545	43			

[a] Predictors: (Constant), opportunities for promotion and development.
[b] Predictors: (Constant), opportunities for promotion and development, relationships with colleagues.
[c] Predictors: (Constant), opportunities for promotion and development, relationships with colleagues, rating of supervisor.
[d] Predictors: (Constant), opportunities for promotion and development, relationships with colleagues, rating of supervisor, facilities at work.
[e] Dependent Variable: overall job satisfaction.

Coefficients[a]

Model		Unstandardized coefficients		Standardized coefficients			Correlations		
		B	Std. error	Beta	t	Sig.	Zero-order	Partial	Part
1	(Constant)	12.331	2.326		5.301	.000			
	opportunities for promotion and development	1.899	.370	.621	5.138	.000	.621	.621	.621
2	(Constant)	10.469	2.354		4.447	.000			
	opportunities for promotion and development	1.228	.455	.402	2.697	.010	.621	.388	.310
	relationships with colleagues	1.100	.474	.346	2.322	.025	.601	.341	.267

Table 16.5—cont'd

Coefficientsᵃ—cont'd

Model		Unstandardized coefficients		Standardized coefficients	t	Sig.	Correlations		
		B	Std. error	Beta			Zero-order	Partial	Part
3	(Constant)	8.068	2.566		3.144	.003			
	opportunities for promotion and development	.973	.457	.318	2.129	.039	.621	.319	.236
	relationships with colleagues	1.205	.460	.379	2.620	.012	.601	.383	.291
	rating of supervisor	1.006	.500	.233	2.012	.051	.350	.303	.223
4	(Constant)	7.072	3.160		2.238	.031			
	opportunities for promotion and development	.966	.461	.316	2.094	.043	.621	.318	.234
	relationships with colleagues	1.211	.464	.381	2.608	.013	.601	.385	.292
	rating of supervisor	1.026	.506	.238	2.028	.049	.350	.309	.227
	facilities at work	.301	.548	.062	.550	.586	.042	.088	.062

[a] Dependent Variable: overall job satisfaction.

Excluded Variablesᵈ

Model		Beta in	t	Sig.	Partial correlation	Collinearity statistics
						Tolerance
1	relationships with colleagues	.346[a]	2.322	.025	.341	.597
	rating of supervisor	.199[a]	1.614	.114	.244	.929
	facilities at work	.042[a]	.341	.735	.053	1.000
2	rating of supervisor	.233[b]	2.012	.051	.303	.917
	facilities at work	.045[b]	.391	.698	.062	1.000
3	facilities at work	.062[c]	.550	.586	.088	.995

[a] Predictors in the Model: (Constant), opportunities for promotion and development.
[b] Predictors in the Model: (Constant), opportunities for promotion and development, relationships with colleagues.
[c] Predictors in the Model: (Constant), opportunities for promotion and development, relationships with colleagues, rating of supervisor.
[d] Dependent Variable: overall job satisfaction.

to Model 3 possessing the best predictive function for explaining variance in the DV. The Change statistics inform about the difference made by adding new predictors. F Change represents the increases due to the addition of each variable. The significance of F Change indicates whether the change was a significant improvement or not in prediction. The fourth F Change was not significant (p = .586). R^2 Change expresses the amount of variation in the DV that can be explained by variation in the IV's at each step. This can also be expressed as a percentage. For example, the addition of the fourth IV only manifested a 0.4% change. Evidence is pointing the addition of the fourth variable (*facilities at work*) in the sequence in Model 4 as not adding to the predictive value of the modelling at all. Model 3 appears to offer the ultimate solution in terms of the variables and sample involved

4   In the ANOVA subtable, we have the F values for each model. This informs us that the independent variables used together in all models as a set are significantly related to the dependent variable even those containing the poorest predictor *facilities at work*. This is because the other three variables as a set are good predictors.

5   The unstandardized b coefficients provide evidence of the unique individual contributions of each IV and reveal congruently with the other evidence that *facilities at work* does not contribute significantly in Model 4 and that the other three variables are the important ones, even though in Model 3 rating of supervisor is only on the margins of significance. We can produce the regression equation from Model 3, namely:

Job satisfaction = 8.068 + .973 (opportunities for promotion and development) + 1.205 (relationships with colleagues) + 1.006 (rating of supervisor).

How to report the results

'*A hierarchical multiple regression was performed to determine whether the addition of relationships with colleagues, ratings of supervisor and facilities at work provide improvement in predicting job satisfaction over opportunities for promotion and development alone. Only three models were evaluated as facilities at work added at Model 4 did not improve the prediction. Model 3 produced an adjusted R^2 = 47% and this was significantly different from zero (F = 13.721, p = .001). The three IV's opportunities for promotion and development, relationships with colleagues, and ratings of supervisor were found to uniquely and significantly contribute to the prediction of job satisfaction*'.

Stepwise multiple regression

Decisions about the order of entry for predictors are made solely on statistical decision in stepwise regression. The computer (SPSS programme) goes through a step-by-step procedure with a number of predictors to discover the best combination of predictors. This procedure is useful to identify important variables that can be used later in a more rigorous study. Entry method can be forward or backward.

Forward entry involves the entry of the IV's one at a time. Order of entry and whether IV is accepted are decided by SPSS on whether an F test and a p value exceed certain critical values. The process generally starts with the variable that has the highest correlation with the dependent variable. If this correlation is not significant, the process stops, since even the best predictor is not of any use. If this correlation is significant, the process goes on to the next step, adding the predictor variable which, in combination with this first one, has the highest multiple R. If it is a significant improvement, the programme repeats the process until either all the predictor variables are included or adding any of the remaining ones fails to generate a significant improvement. This method allows us to judge the relative importance of each variable, even if they all end up in the equation, particularly the R^2 change at each step.

Backward selection is the reverse of the forward entry, as it commences with inserting all IV's with SPSS deleting successively those that fail to meet certain critical significance values. This is the preferred method of many researchers especially when they are exploring a new topic.

SPSS allows you to choose any of these methods. The regression equation that is obtained is the optimal group of variables for predicting the dependent variable, *based on the sample studied*. However, when the same variables are studied with a new sample, a somewhat different combination of variables may turn out better predictors. Sometimes this stepwise technique is derided as a fishing expedition which will hopefully trawl up some useful predictors and is often avoided except in exploratory studies.

> *Step-wise multiple correlation*. The number of IV's entered and their order of entry is determined by statistical criteria to produce the smallest set of predictors that will explain the largest proportion of variance in the DV.

SPSS activity- stepwise multiple regression with backward entry

We will use SPSS Chapter 16 Data File C again. We would normally produce the correlation matrix, as in the other forms of multiple correlation, as the first step to check the inter-correlations and remove any variable that correlates very highly with another as both are measuring the same thing (collineararity). SPSS will control the selection criteria for successive models in a backward entry method.

How to proceed

1   *Analyze >> Regression >>* Linear to open the ***Linear Regression*** dialogue box.
2   Click on the dependent variable (*job satisfaction*) and place it in the ***Dependent:*** box.
3   Select all the predictors and move them into ***Independent [s]:*** box ***Block 1***.
4   In ***Method*** box ensure ***Backward*** is selected (Fig. 16.15).

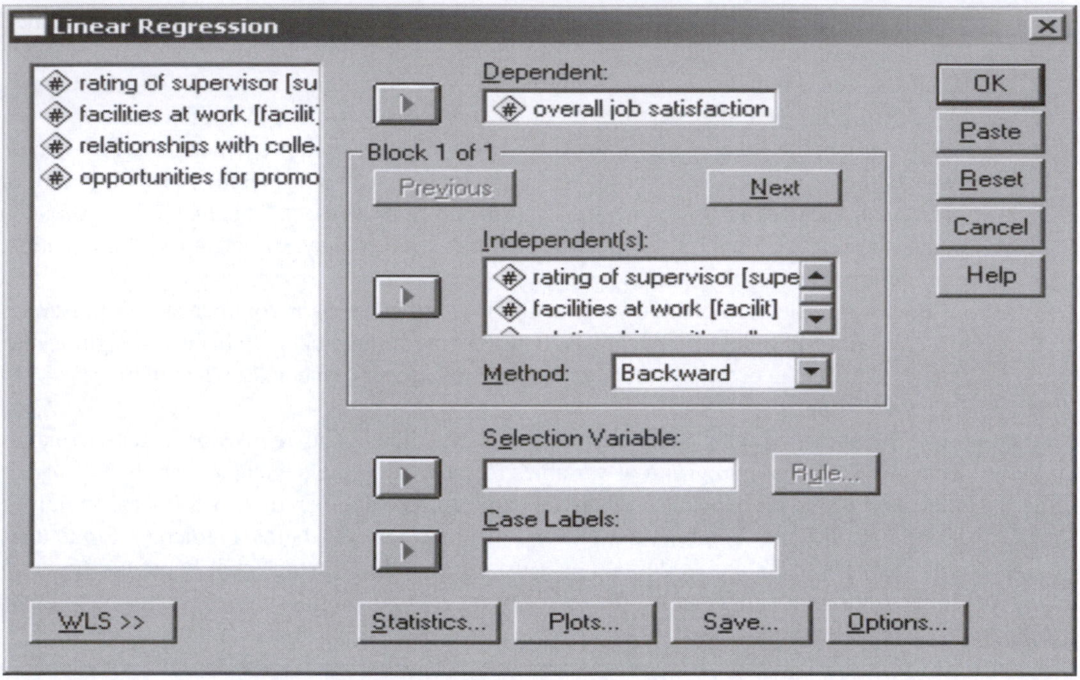

Figure 16.15 **Linear regression dialogue box.**

5 Select ***Statistics*** to obtain ***the Linear Regression: Statistics*** dialogue box.
6 Ensure ***Estimates, Model Fit, Part and Partial Correlations*** and ***R Squared change,*** are selected.
7 ***Continue >> OK.***

How to interpret the output in Table 16.6

1 The first subtable indicates which variables were included in each model. All four variables were included in Model 1. At the Model 2 stage *facilities at work* was removed as it did not meet the statistical criteria used by SPSS and was therefore not aiding the prediction (the final subtable indicates this). No further models were produced, indicating that Model 2 was the best combination that could be derived using backward stepwise regression.
2 The Model Summary subtable reveals again that two steps were taken before the programme was concluded. Therefore the best prediction of the DV requires only three IV's, *opportunities for promotion and development, relationships with colleagues,* and *ratings of supervisor.* Each model produces evidence of the effect of the combination of predictors.

Table 16.6   Stepwise regression output

Variables Entered/Removed[b]

Model	Variables entered	Variables removed	Method
1	opportunities for promotion and development facilities at work, rating of supervisor, relationships with colleagues[a]	.	Enter
2	.	facilities at work	Backward (criterion Probability of 1-to-remove > = .100).

[a] All requested variables entered.
[b] Dependent Variable: overall job satisfaction.

Model Summary

Model	R	R square	Adjusted R square	Std. error of the estimate	Change statistics				
					R square change	F change	df1	df2	Sig. F change
1	.715[a]	.511	.461	4.476	.511	10.186	4	39	.000
2	.712[b]	.507	.470	4.437	−.004	.302	1	39	.586

[a] Predictors: (Constant), opportunities for promotion and development, facilities at work, rating of supervisor, relationship with colleagues.
[b] Predictors: (Constant), opportunities for promotion and development, rating of supervisor, relationship with colleagues.

ANOVA[c]

Model		Sum of squares	df	Mean square	F	Sig.
1	Regression	816.260	4	204.065	10.186	.000[a]
	Residual	781.286	39	20.033		
	Total	1597.545	43			
2	Regression	810.207	3	270.069	13.721	.000[b]
	Residual	787.338	40	19.683		
	Total	1597.545	43			

[a] Predictors: (Constant), opportunities for promotion and development, facilities at work, rating of supervisor, relationships with colleagues.
[b] Predictors: (Constant), opportunities for promotion and development, rating of supervisor, relationships with colleagues.
[c] Dependent Variable: overall job satisfaction.

(Continued)

Table 16.6—cont'd

		Unstandardized coefficients		Standardized coefficients			Correlation		
Model		B	Std. error	Beta	t	Sig.	Zero-order	Partial	Part
1	(Constant)	7.072	3.160		2.238	.031			
	rating of supervisor	1.026	.506	.238	2.028	.049	.350	.309	.227
	facilities at work	.301	.548	.062	.550	.586	.042	.088	.062
	relationships with colleagues	1.211	.464	.381	2.608	.013	.601	.385	.292
	opportunities for promotion and development	.966	.461	.316	2.094	.043	.621	.318	.234
2	(Constant)	8.068	2.566		3.144	.003			
	rating of supervisor	1.006	.500	.233	2.012	.051	.350	.303	.223
	relationships with colleagues	1.205	.460	.379	2.620	.012	.601	.383	.291
	opportunities for promotion and development	.973	.457	.318	2.129	.039	.621	.319	.236

Coefficients[a]

[a] Dependent Variable: overall job satisfaction.

Excluded Variables[b]

					Partial	Collinearity statistics
Model		Beta in	t	Sig.	correlation	Tolerance
2	facilities at work	.062[a]	.550	.586	.088	.995

[a] Predictors in the Model: (Constant), opportunities for promotion and development, rating of supervisor, relationships with colleagues.
[b] Dependent Variable: overall job satisfaction.

Adjusted R^2 at 47% for model 2 is slightly higher than that for model 1 and therefore explains more variance in the DV.

3   In the ANOVA subtable, we have the F values for each step. The final step produces a significant F of 13.721, p = .001. This indicates that the three predictors together significantly predict the DV at a slightly better F level than step 1.

4   The unstandardized B coefficients in the Coefficients subtable reveal t values that are all significant for Model 2 although one is marginal. From the unstandardized b coefficients

in the last step of the Coefficients subtable we can produce the regression equation, namely:

Job satisfaction = 8.068 + .973 (opportunities for promotion and development) + 1.205 (relationships with colleagues) + 1.006 (rating of supervisor).

How to report the results

'*A stepwise regression was conducted to find the best combination of predictors of job satisfaction among the four IV's, namely, opportunities for promotion and development, relationships with colleagues, ratings of supervisor and facilities at work. Only two steps were concluded with opportunities for promotion and development, relationships with colleagues, and rating of supervisor providing the best combination with adjusted R^2 = 47%, and a significant F = 13.721, p = .001. Facilities at work do not appear to be of any importance in determining job satisfaction*'.

Hierarchical and stepwise regression compared

Hierarchical and stepwise regression are similar in that you are adding one variable at a time and checking whether the addition makes a significant improvement in the prediction. But there is an important difference. In hierarchical regression, the order of adding the predictor variables is based on some theory or plan, decided in advance by the researcher. In stepwise regression, there is no initial plan. SPSS simply figures out the best variables to add or delete until no additional contribution occurs.

Dummy variables

The type of regression analyses we have conducted so far requires that all variables are quantitative, but, on occasions, a qualitative variable such as male/female, urban/rural, homeowner/renter may have an important influence on Y. In these circumstances we can incorporate the qualitative variable in the regression analysis by creating dummy variables, i.e. coding a dichotomous variable 0 and 1 and using these values to indicate presence or absence of a particular characteristic. The multiple regression equation is:

$$Y = b_0 + b_1 X_1 + b_2 D$$

When D is coded 0 the formula becomes: $Y = a + b_1 X_1$ (since $b_2 D = 0$)
When D is coded 1 the formula is $Y = a + b_1 X_1 + b_2$ (since $b_2(1) = b_2$)

That is, there are two regression formulae; one for each of the categories in the dichotomous dummy variable.

Imagine you wished to study the relationship between income and weekly spending on entertainment as you feel income has a strong influence on spending. You believe that gender may have some influence on entertainment spending. Assume the calculations have been done to provide us with the regression equations.

The regression equation is:

$$Y = a + b_1X_1 + b_2X_2 \text{ where } X_2 = D$$
$$= 12.21 + 0.791X_1 + 5.11X_2$$

The use of the dummy variable will produce two regression lines, one each for males and females. Although these lines have the same slope, they have different intercepts, thus producing two parallel regression lines that commence at different points on the Y axis. Since we coded males as 0 the equation becomes:

$$Y = a + b_1X_1 + b_2X_2$$
$$= 12.21 + 0.791X_1 + 5.11(0)$$
$$= 12.21 + 0.791X_1$$

This regression line for males has an intercept of 12.21 and a slope of 0.791.

For females the code of 1 produces:

$$= 12.21 + 0.791X_1 + 5.11(1)$$
$$= 17.32 + 0.791X_1$$

This regression line has the same slope but the intercept is now 17.32 (12.21 + 5.11). This means that for any level of income women spend $5.11 more on average than do males.

For example, if we select an income = $40,000 (coded as 40k in the data view) then:

For men $Y = 12.21 + .791(40) + 5.11(0) = \$43.85$
For women $Y = 17.32 + .791(40) = \$48.96$

The difference of $5.11 reflects the fact that the coefficient of 0 for males cancels out the b_2 coefficient. The dummy variable acts like a 'toggle switch'. It is 'on' when the income of females is being estimated but 'off' when the income of males is being estimated. A qualitative variable could have more than two categories, e.g. the first/second/third/fourth quarters of the year; or mortgage holders, renters, and house owners.

A dummy variable. A variable that accounts for the qualitative nature of a variable and incorporates its explanatory power into the regression model.

SPSS activity – hierarchical multiple regression with dummy variable

Bank officials are interested in determining the predictors of how much money is withdrawn from their ATM's in different types of locations each weekend so that they can ensure that sufficient money is placed in the ATM's on Friday afternoon. They believe that the house values in the area, whether the ATM is in a shopping centre or outside the bank and number of people living nearby the ATM are the important IV's in that order. The location of the ATM is a nominal variable and SPSS treats it as a dummy variable using values of 0 and 1 that have been used to classify the location in the variable view. Access SPSS Chapter 16 Data File B, which we will use to conduct a hierarchical multiple regression. As a hierarchical multiple regression has been demonstrated above, no screen shots or instructions will be provided. Output is displayed in Table 16.7.

Table 16.7   Output for hierarchical multiple regression with a dummy variable

Variables Entered/Removed[b]

Model	Variables entered	Variables removed	Method
1	median value of homes in $k with in 10 kms of atm[a]	.	Enter
2	atm location[a]	.	Enter
3	number of people in '000s living within 10 kms of atm[a]	.	Enter

[a] All requested variables entered.
[b] Dependent Variable: mean amount withdrawn over 26 weekends.

Model Summary

Model	R	R square	Adjusted R square	Std. error of the estimate	R square change	F change	df1	dt2	Sig. F change
1	.997[a]	.995	.994	1.144	.995	2499.234	1	13	.000
2	.998[b]	.995	.995	1.115	.001	1.685	1	12	.219
3	.998[c]	.996	.995	1.104	.000	1.253	1	11	.287

[a] Predictors: (Constant), median value of homes in $k within 10 kms of atm.
[b] Predictors: (Constant), median value of homes in $k within 10 kms of atm, atm location.
[c] Predictors: (Constant), median value of homes in $k within 10 kms of atm, atm location, number of people in '000s living within 10 kms of atm.

(Continued)

Table 16.7   —cont'd

	ANOVA[d]				
Model	Sum of squares	df	Mean square	F	Sig.
1 Regression	3273.373	1	3273.373	2499.234	.000[a]
Residual	17.027	13	1.310		
Total	3290.400	14			
2 Regression	3275.470	2	1637.735	1316.337	.000[b]
Residual	14.930	12	1.244		
Total	3290.400	14			
3 Regression	3276.997	3	1092.332	896.473	.000[c]
Residual	13.403	11	1.218		
Total	3290.400	14			

[a] Predictors: (Constant), median value of homes in $k within 10 kms of atm.
[b] Predictors: {Constant}, median value of homes in $k within 10 kms of atm, atm location.
[c] Predictors: (Constant), median value of homes in $k within 10 kms of atm, atm location, number of people in '000s living within 10 kms of atm.
[d] Dependent Variable: mean amount withdrawn over 26 weekends.

	Coefficients[a]					
	Unstandardized coefficients		Standardized coefficients			
Model	B	Std. error	Beta	t	Sig.
1 (Constant)	29.346	1.518		19.328	.000
median value of homes in $k within 10kms of atm	.398	.008	.997	49.992	.000
2 (Constant)	30.525	1.736		17.580	.000
median value of homes in $k within 10kms of atm	.389	.011	.974	37.006	.000
atm location	1.015	.782	.034	1.298	.219
3 (Constant)	29.342	2.018		14.544	.000
median value of homes in $k within 10 kms of atm	.392	.011	.980	36.848	.000
atm location	.884	.782	.030	1.130	.283
number of people in '000s living within 10 kms of atm	.015	.013	.022	1.119	.287

[a] Dependent Variable: mean amount withdrawn over 26 weekends.

How to interpret output in Table 16.7

1   The first subtable indicates the sequence in which the predictors were entered to create the three models. Model 1 included only the median value of home within 10 kms. Model 2 added location of ATM's while Model 3 included all three predictors.
2   The Model Summary subtable reveals adjusted R2 for all three models is extremely high and virtually the same, explaining around 99.4% of the variance in amount of money drawn each weekend by the various combinations of predictors in the models. The fact that Model 1 containing the single variable of the median value of homes within 10 km is essentially as good as the other models suggest that this is a most par-simonious model and, given the minimal R change statistics and F change significances for Models 2 and 3, the implication is that we really only need that single predictor. This is supported in the ANOVA subtable, where there is a very large F value which is highly significant for Model 1 and therefore a considerably high degree of prediction. The F values for the other models are less although again quite significant
3   The Coefficients subtable reveals the individual contributions of each variable and repeats the pattern already noted. Model 1 displays the highest t value of 49.992, p = .001, and the t values of the other variables added in successive models are not significant. Therefore we are confident in claiming that the amount drawn from ATM's over the weekend is best predicted by the median value of homes within 10 kms radius. The other two predictors do not significantly improve the prediction. The regression equation is therefore:

Mean amount withdrawn over 26 weekends = 29.364 + .398 (median value of homes within 10 kms of ATM).

The limited addition to prediction of ATM location can be judged if we use Model 2 to produce the two regressions equations each involving one of the two values of that variable. These Model 2 regression equations are:

(a)   *Mean amount withdrawn over 26 weekends = 30.525 + .389 (median value of homes within 10 kms of ATM) + 1.015 (0).*
(b)   *Mean amount withdrawn over 26 weekends = 30.525 + .389 (median value of homes within 10 kms of ATM) + 1.015 (1) = 31.540 + .389 (median value of homes within 10 kms of ATM).*

Model 2 equation (a) does not in fact alter the predictive value beyond that offered by using only median home value as the predictor and thus hardly differs from Model 1, taking into account the changes in the Constants and B values. Equation (b) only produces a mar-ginal difference in the prediction. Insert some median home value figure into the equations and see for yourself. This explains why ATM location is not a significant contributor in terms of the t value for its B in the coefficient subtable.

How to write up your results

'A hierarchical multiple regression was carried out to determine the best combination of predictors of mean amounts drawn over 26 weekends among house values in the area, ATM

location in shopping centre or outside bank and number of people living nearby the ATM.
Model 1 containing the single predictor house values in the area was found to be the best,
offering an R^2 of 99.4%, while models 2 and 3 did not provide any improvement in prediction
when the F change significances and the t values of the b coefficients were considered'.

What you have learned from this chapter

You are now aware that if two variables are correlated, knowledge of a value in one can be used
to predict a value in the other. The more scatter there is in a scatter diagram the less accurate
the prediction with prediction improving as the correlation coefficient approaches +1 and −1.
The line of best fit or regression line provides the best possible prediction as it minimizes the
error between the predicted and real values of Y. The relationship between the two variables
must be linear.

The regression line equation is $Y = b_0 + b_1X$ where b_0 is the intercept on the Y axis and b_1 the
slope of the regression line. This regression equation will only provide a prediction or estimate
of likely Y values. The confidence interval round the prediction can be gauged using the standard error of the estimate.

In multiple regressions two or more predictor variables are involved in predicting the score
of a dependent variable. Not only can we have SPSS use all predictor variables at one time in
a standard multiple regression, but we can also use two other approaches:

(a) Hierarchical regression is used in research that is based on theory or some substantial previous knowledge and which provides a basis for the sequence of adding each variable into
the model.
(b) Stepwise regression is useful in exploratory research where we do not know what to expect
or in applied research where we are looking for the best prediction formula without caring
about its theoretical meaning. SPSS will enter variables in sequence according to their
predictive ability.

Qualitative variables can also be used as part of a regression equation by using dummy variables.

Review questions

Qu. 16.1
By squaring individual errors the least squares regression line method ensures large
deviations from the estimated regression line have a greater impact:

(a) false
(b) true
(c) sometimes
(d) depends on the correlation

Qu. 16.2
Using the equation $Y = -7 + 2X$ determine the values of Y for the following values of X: 1, 3, 5, 10.

Qu. 16.3
Given the regression equation $Y = 2.6 + .02X$ the constant or intercept is:

(a) .02X
(b) 2.6 above zero on the X axis
(c) 2.6 above zero on the Y axis
(d) not calculable from the information given

Qu. 16.4
The regression equation below shows the relationship between dollars spent on weekly advertising and value of weekly sales in hundreds of dollars for a small swimming pool supplies company.
$Y = 30 + 3X$

(a) If no money is spent on advertising one week, what value of sales can be predicted?
(b) If $200 is spent on advertising, what estimate of sales can be made?

Qu. 16.5
Given the following data what is the range of values within which we can be 95% certain Y falls.
$SD_Y = 12; r = .7; Y = 40$

Qu. 16.6
If $r^2 = .75$, how much of the variation in Y can be explained by the association of Y with X as estimated by the regression line. How much is unexplained and due to other causes. Review the material above and in Chapter 15 to determine if you are correct.

Qu. 16.7
Two regression equations have been developed for different predictions based on different samples of equal size. In one, $r = .79$ while in the other $r = .58$. In which situation will the more accurate predictions be made?

Qu. 16.8
The coefficient of determination explains

(a) the amount of variation in the independent variable explained by the dependent variable;
(b) the amount of variation of the observed values round the regression equation;

(c) the amount of variation in the dependent variable that is explained by the independent variable;

(d) how much error there is in the Standard Error of the estimate.

Qu. 16.9

The statistics lecturer wanted to find out the relationship between the number of hours spent by students studying for his end of semester exam and their examination results. His calculated constant was 31.78, b_1 was 1.67 and $r = +.9586$.

(a) Write out the regression equation.

(b) What is the coefficient of determination and interpret it?

(c) Predict the exam result of a student who studied a total of 24 hours.

(d) Predict the exam result of a student who studied a total of 20 hours and compare it with an actual example of a student who did 20 hours and obtained a real score of 66. Can you explain why the real Y and the estimated Y differ?

Now access the Chapter 16 Web page and attempt the SPSS activities, further questions for this chapter and additional material on path analysis.

Chapter 17
Reliability and Validity

Content list

By the end of this chapter you will:

1   Understand the concept of reliability and its importance.
2   Be able to differentiate different forms of reliability.
3   Understand how to measure reliability.
4   Understand the concept of validity and its importance.
5   Be able to differentiate various types of validity.
6   Understand how validity is assessed.
7   Be able to use SPSS to assess reliability and validity.

Introduction

The material in this chapter is vital for all research studies. When measurements are obtained from human subjects, an instrument like a questionnaire, or technique like interviewing, we need to know what faith we can put in the data. Are they indicating correct or true values of the observations, performance or behaviour? Reliability and validity are the two concepts that we are therefore considering here. This chapter shows you how you can ensure high reliability and validity for your data and instruments, and the sorts of reliability and validity you should seek depending on the particulars of your study.

Reliability

Reliability refers to the consistency and stability of findings that enables findings to be replicated. For instance, a reliable employee is one whose work productivity is of a consistent standard. This consistency can be used to predict the standard of their future work patterns. An unreliable piece of equipment unpredictably produces work of a quality ranging from mediocre to exceptional. Clearly, consistency and stability in the standard of work are poor in this case. Equipment, tests, and surveys must produce an accurate, stable and predictable standard. If people, events and equipment are reliable, we can depend on them, such as salaries always paid correctly at the end of each month. If they are unreliable, like a computer system that keeps going down, we cannot depend on them.

There is a similar need for accurate and stable measures within research. For instance, questionnaires which do not accurately predict consumer attitudes to a product or business are of little worth, since their unreliability of measurement does not allow businesses to accurately assess future consumer behaviour. Psychometric tests that are unreliable predictors for success on the job will inconsistently indicate high scores for some who are really not competent for the job. The Human Resources Dept then have an impossible task of trying to figure out when the tests were accurate and when they were off beam so the wrong persons do not get job offers.

Approaches to understanding reliability

The following approaches delineate subtle differences between the types of reliability within research methodology:

1   One approach asks, 'Is the data/observation which I have just obtained for employee J, Material K, product L, or equipment M, consistent with data if the test was repeated tomorrow, the next day, and then the next day?' This concept of reliability considers whether the obtained value or observation really is a stable indication of the employee's, product's, material's or equipment's performance. This question implies a definition of reliability in terms of stability, dependability and predictability and is the definition most often given in discussions of reliability.

2   Another approach may ask, 'Is this value which I have just obtained on employee J, material K, product L, or equipment M, an accurate indication of their "true" performance/quality/ability?' This question really asks whether the measurements are accurate. This links to (1) above, for if performance or measurement is stable and predictable across occasions then it is most likely an accurate reflection of performance. If there are changes in performance values across occasions then accuracy is unlikely – how do we ever know which value is the 'correct' one?

3   A third approach, which helps in the understanding of the theory of reliability, also implies the previous two approaches. This approach asks how much error there is in the values obtained. A personality scale of employability, a survey of customer preferences or a measurement of the accuracy of a sophisticated piece of technology is done usually only once. Our goal, of course, is to hit the 'true' value(s) on this one occasion. To the extent that we miss the 'true' scores, our measuring instrument is unreliable and contains error. In determining the level of accuracy or stability in a measure, a researcher really needs to identify the amount of error that exists, and the causes for that error.

The theory of reliability

There are two sources of variability in measurement:

(a)   variability induced by real actual differences between individual employees or pieces of parallel equipment in the ability to perform the requirements;

(b)   error variability which is a combination or error from two sources:

(i)   *random fluctuation error*. Subtle variations in individual and equipment performance from day-to-day such as an unreliable worker who may produce exceptional work on one day but follows up with a day of poor quality work. Alternatively, think of your favourite team that backs up a fantastic win against the competition leaders one week, with a loss to the bottom of the table team next week. They are the result of ordinary random or chance elements present in all measures due to unknown causes, to subtle and temporary variations in health levels, to mood, motivation and interest in the subjects, to fortuitous conditions at a particular time that temporarily affect equipment performance or the measuring instrument, and other factors that are temporary and shifting. These random fluctuations sometimes push up performance and at other times pull it down like variations in personal tiredness (good night's sleep vs. baby cried most of the night), health fluctuations (feeling on top of the world vs. sudden onset of hay fever), emotional level (won lottery vs. upset with spouse before leaving for work), etc.

(ii)   *systematic or constant error*. This is the result of one or more variables continually influencing a performance level or measurement in a particular direction, a constant bias pushing values up all the time or pulling them down all the time. For example, practice effect occurs in those employees who improve simply by performing the skills, irrespective of whether they were in the training group or not; or one vehicle tyre wearing more than another because it is always under-inflated compared to other tyres of the same make and type.

> *Random fluctuation error. The extent to which a score has been influenced by irrelevant or chance factors.*

> *Systematic error. The effect of an unwanted variable biasing values in one direction only.*

The greater amount of error in a piece of datum the more unreliability there is in the datum. The less error, the more reliable the datum, since the datum then represents more closely the 'true' value, or correct level.

Reliability can be defined as the relative absence of errors of measurement in a measuring instrument. Error and reliability are opposite sides of the same coin. The more error, the less stable, and less accurate is the data. Our three approaches above recognize that reliability is the accuracy, stability and relative lack of error in a measuring instrument.

Relationships between components of a value or score

There exist three components of a score/value: the true observation or score, the actual observed/obtained score, and the error score. A simple equation can be written which links these three scores.

Observed score (what we got) = true score (what we are after) ± error score, or more simply:

$$X_{obs} = X_{true} \pm error.$$

The error score may, of course, be positive or negative, depending on whether the value(s) are 'over' or 'under' with reference to the true level. The smaller the error score, the closer the observed score approximates the true score and the greater the reliability. Where there is no error component $X_{obs} = X_{true} + 0$, i.e. perfect reliability.

As the error component increases, the true score component decreases and the observed X will increase in difference from the true score. In parallel fashion to the individual score formula, the total variance in obtained data is equal to the sum of the 'true' variance and the error variance, namely:

$$SD^2_{obs} = SD^2_{true} + SD^2_{error}$$

We can now define the reliability of any set of measurements as the proportion of their variance which is true variance, in other words, the ratio of true variance to observed variance. When the true variance is equal to the observed variance, i.e. when there is no error variance, this ratio has a value of +1.0. This is the 'perfect reliability' value:

$$\frac{SD^2_{true}}{SD^2_{obs}} = 1 \quad r_{tt} = +1.0$$ (r_{tt} symbolizes reliability and is in fact the correlation coefficient – in this case a perfect positive relationship between true and observed variances for each case.)

When there is no true variance present, i.e. when the observed variance is entirely error, the ratio has a value of zero. This is the 'nil reliability' value: $r_{tt} = 0$:

$$\frac{SD^2_{true}}{SD^2_{obs}} = \frac{0}{1} = 0$$

Manipulating the above formulae, reliability equals 1 minus the error variance divided by the obtained variance.

$$r_{tt} = 1 - \frac{SD^2_{error}}{SD^2_{obs}}$$

Reliability. The degree to which there is an absence of measurement error.

Determining reliability

A number of approaches to determining reliability exist, all based on the assumption that sets of scores can be correlated to determine the strength of an association.

Test-retest reliability method

When reliability is measured by the test-retest method, a coefficient of temporal stability is obtained since the observations are made twice with an intervening time period. The two sets of results are correlated. A high correlation obviously indicates a very similar pattern of results on both occasions. The lower the correlation is, the less consistent the results between occasions. This reliability coefficient measures error variance due to temporal variations in characteristics of the equipment/event/item/individual measured, e.g. health or emotional tension in persons, as well as variation in conditions of the context in which the observations are made, e.g. temperature change affecting equipment.

There is no standard duration of time that should separate the two administrations of a test. In general, a two-to-three-month period is best If the period is too short, human respondents may remember the answers they gave or their behaviour on the first occasion, spuriously increasing the consistency of scores. On the other hand, boredom, decreased motivation, etc. may influence the values of the second set of observations, thus reducing the congruence of results between the two occasions of testing. If the period is too long, maturational factors – for example, learning experience, ageing of materials, equipment or persons – will influence changes of score on the second occasion and cause an underestimation of the reliability.

If measuring a relatively stable human trait or characteristic and the individual is not subjected, during the intervening time, to experiences that may, in some way, affect the particular characteristic involved, then the intervening period can be over a number of months. However, when measuring a trait, which is influenced by the individual's intervening experiences, the time should be shorter, but not short enough to allow memory or practice effects to artificially inflate the relationship between the two performances. The retesting of equipment can be done frequently with short time lapses if necessary. Thus, an appropriate period of intervening time can only be decided on in the next context of the situation.

The rationale of the test-retest method implies that the same context, equipment quality, human cognitive, intellectual, motivational and personality variables are demonstrated on each occasion so that any changes are due solely to the instability of the test itself being the essential source of error in the test-retest reliability estimate.

Problems also arise on the second testing in ensuring attendance. Those who drop out may have different characteristics from those who return.

> **Test-retest reliability.** *An index of a measure's temporal reliability (stability over time) obtained by correlating the results from two occasions of assessment.*

Alternate or parallel forms method

Because ability, skills, knowledge and motivation may change differentially among respondents from test to retest, and materials and technological equipment alter through use and innovation, the test-retest approach is not always satisfactory. The alternate forms method can be used instead, provided there are equivalent forms of measurement or observation. For example, some standardized tests, rating and attitude scales, have two or more equivalent forms that have been designed to be comparable in content, length, difficulty level and variance. When two equivalent forms of an assessment are administered to respondents on the same occasion, these are correlated and a coefficient of equivalence is obtained, which measures the consistency of performance from one specific sampling of content or behaviour to another. This method cannot take into account temporal fluctuations in performance.

This procedure has two advantages over the previous method. First, one need not be as concerned about memory and practice effect, or changes in materials or equipment, since the two forms of the test are composed of slightly different items and can be applied with a very minimal time lapse between them. Second, a more accurate estimate of reliability is likely to be obtained because the estimate is based on a larger sampling of the universe of items, observations or events. However, these advantages are gained at the price of further time and effort involved in the construction of two parallel forms of the same measuring device. In addition, there are problems of ensuring that they are indeed equivalent.

This estimate is still influenced by fluctuating and temporary factors in the environment, since they cannot be undertaken simultaneously. For example, with people, boredom or fatigue may result; with equipment, slight variations in operating conditions such as heat and humidity can occur.

> *Parallel or alternate forms reliability. A measure of the similarity of results from two parallel forms of the same measuring device.*

Split-half or inter-item reliability method

This is based on the proposition that many temporary factors, which influence the test-retest and alternate forms methods, could be eliminated if a reliability coefficient could be determined from the values of a single assessment, performance or observation. Two values can be obtained simply by splitting the assessment into halves. The values obtained in one half are correlated with values on the other half. The two halves must be equivalent and on this basis it is assumed that a score high in one half will be replicated by a high one in the other half; similarly a low score will occur in both halves. But how to split in half?

A commonly accepted way of splitting a test into two halves is to divide it into odd-numbered items and even-numbered items rather than first half and second half. If a measuring device is constructed so that adjacent items tend to be similar in difficulty level, discriminatory power and content, this is not an unreasonable procedure. However, one might ask what difference in the computed coefficient there would have been if the test had been split in some other way. Consider, a test of only 20 items may be divided into two equal parts in exactly 184,756 different ways. Unless the 20 items are exactly equivalent there would probably be some variation in the reliability estimates obtained by splitting the test in so many different ways.

It is not good practice to correlate the first half of the test with the second half, as this provides scope for error – some participants may run out of time and not finish answering all items; some subjects produce careless responses as boredom, apathy or tiredness increase in the second half of the test and answers in the second half of the test may not accurately reflect the participant's real performance level.

> **Split half reliability**. *A measure of reliability derived from correlating usually the odd-even items on a test.*

The split-half method does reduce the potential for both random and systematic error typical with the retest and alternate methods by using a single measure on one occasion with one set of subjects, but when a measuring device is divided into two parts and the scores are correlated the result is a correlation between values on an assessment that is only one half as long as the original. To counter this, the Spearman-Brown formula is used to estimate the reliability of the assessment in its original length. SPSS undertakes this. To access go to *Analyze > Scale > Reliability Analysis*. Place your test items into the *Item* box as usual then in *Model* select *Split Half*. The printout for the test you have split will include the Spearman-Brown correction. The general formula for the reliability of an assessment N times as long as the given test if you want to do this by hand is:

$$r_{tt} = \frac{N\,r_{tt}}{1+(N-1)r_{tt}}$$

'N' is the ratio of the length of the desired assessment to the length of the present assessment (length is defined as number of items), and r_{tt} is the already obtained reliability. If the correlation between the values on the odd items and even items were .50, this correlation based on 10 items would be substituted into the Spearman-Brown formula as follows:

$$r_{tt} = \frac{(2)(.50)}{1+(2-1)(.50)} = \frac{1.0}{1.5} = .67$$

The value 2 has been substituted for N because it was necessary to determine the reliability of the test twice as long as the two 10-item assessments (20 item split in two halves) used to obtain the original reliability coefficient. The formula indicates that the split half reliability of the 20-item test is actually 0.67.

Any time the split-half method of reliability estimate is utilized, the Spearman-Brown formula must be obtained to provide a reliability estimate that is appropriate for the original length.

> **The Spearman-Brown formula**. *A formula that calculates the reliability of tests N times as long as the original test.*

Internal consistency method

Similar to the split-half method, the internal consistency method is frequently used to determine a scale's reliability by assessing the commonness of a set of items that measure a particular construct. However, it differs in an important way by computing a correlation coefficient for every conceivable way of dividing the test in two. These coefficients are then averaged out to provide an overall coefficient. Two popular internal reliability coefficients are Kuder-Richardson 20 (KR-20) which is used for dichotomous data, and Cronbach's Alpha which is used for scale data. Both can be interpreted as correlations.

This method, like the equivalent-forms method, takes into account variance due to the specificity of the test items and fails to measure temporal instability. It measures the consistency of performance between test items. The more the test items intercorrelate, the higher the internal reliability, i.e. all the items in the test are measuring the same characteristic. The greater the diversity of test items, in terms of the skills required to determine the correct answers, the lower the correlations of the performance on the various test items. This decrease in the inter-item correlations reduces the obtained internal-consistency reliability estimate.

Cronbach's Alpha is very useful in developing attitude scales and questionnaires as the alpha level (or reliability) indicates if the items are measuring the same construct. Items that are not measuring what the rest are can be identified and deleted. It is also very useful in identifying coherent subscales on a long questionnaire and is often used to divide a longer scale into subscales, based on those items that hold together in groups or homogeneous subsets when the totality of all the items do not reveal homogeneity. An alpha of 0.8 or above is regarded as highly acceptable for assuming homogeneity of items, while 0.7 is the limit of acceptability.

> *Cronbach's Alpha (α). A measure of reliability that is equivalent to the average of all the split half correlations from all possible splits into halves of the items in the measuring instrument.*

SPSS activity – assessing internal reliability

The test-retest reliability and parallel forms reliability are no more than our old friend the correlation coefficient between the two occasions of testing and will not be demonstrated here. Refer back to Chapter 15. We will demonstrate a Cronbach Alpha test to assess internal reliability, essentially assessing whether all the items in a scale are measuring the same 'thing'.

Internal reliability using Cronbach's Alpha

Access SPSS Chapter 17 Data File A. This contains responses to 10 items on a 5 point Likert scale provided by 98 employees.

How to proceed

1 *Analyze >> Scale >> Reliability Analysis* to open the *Reliability Analysis dialogue* box.
2 Transfer all the scale or test items to the *Items* box.
3 Ensure *Alpha* is chosen in the *Model* box (Fig. 17.1).
4 Click on *Statistics* to open the *Reliability Analysis Statistics dialogue* box.
5 In the *Descriptives* for area, select *Item, Scale* and *Scale if item deleted*.
6 In the *Inter-item* area choose *Correlations* (Fig. 17.2).
7 *Continue >> OK*.

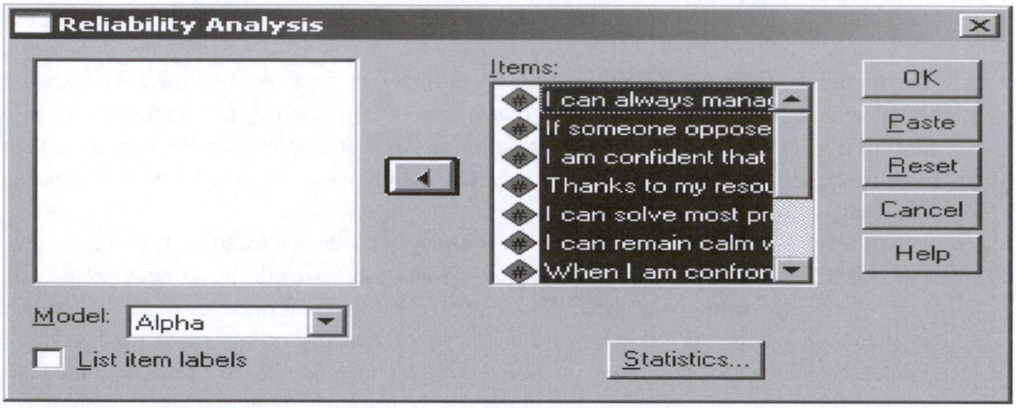

Figure 17.1   **Reliability analysis box.**

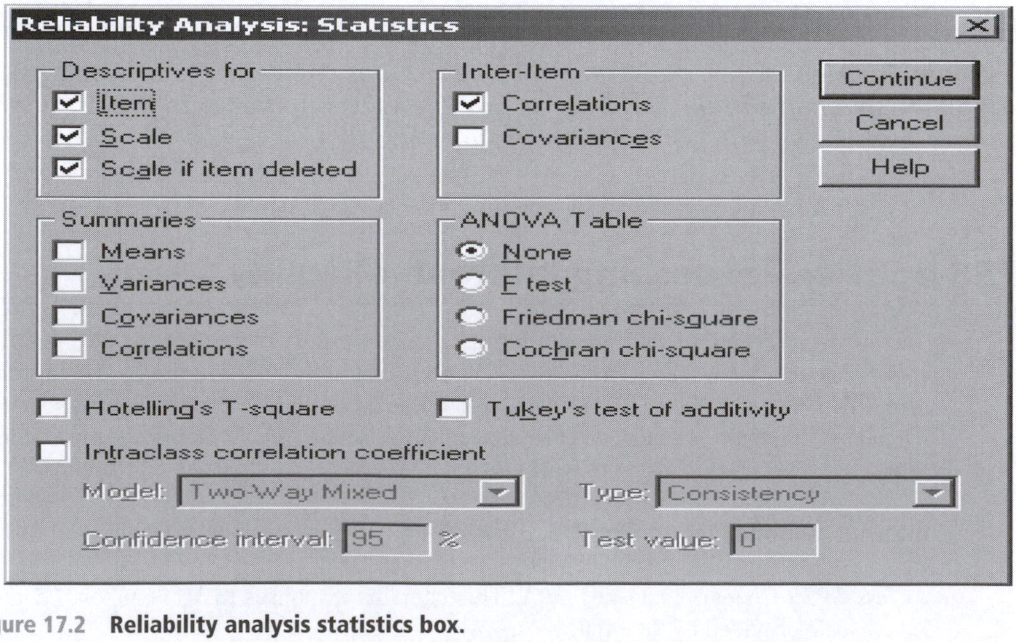

Figure 17.2   **Reliability analysis statistics box.**

At step 2, if you wish to determine the alpha of a subscale (subset of the whole test) then transfer only those items you require.

How to interpret Table 17.1

Table 17.1 shows the inter-item statistics for a 10-item scale completed by 98 employees. The two columns to focus on are the last two.

- The Corrected Item-Total Correlation reveals those items that have low correlations with the test or scale as a whole. Here item 10 stands out as the correlation is not only considerably lower than the rest, which are all in the .5 and .6 area, but it is also negative.
- The last column shows the overall scale alpha or internal reliability if that item is removed. You can discern that if item 10 is removed the overall scale alpha rises to .9175, much higher than the current alpha and indicative of a scale with very high internal consistency, i.e. all items measuring the same concept.
- The overall alpha is .8647, printed below the bottom subtable. This is quite acceptable but by eliminating item 10 we do have the option of an even higher value.

Table 17.1 *Cronbach Alpha printout* **(This is the essential table. A large amount of other descriptive and correlation matrices will also be produced)**

Method 1 (space saver) will be used for this analysis

RELIABILITY ANALYSIS – SCALE (ALPHA)

Statistics for	Mean	Variance	Std dev	N of variables
SCALE	38.1837	40.0690	6.3300	10

Item-total Statistics

	Scale mean if item deleted	Scale variance if item deleted	Corrected item-total correlation	Alpha if item deleted
Q1	34.1939	32.3228	.6455	.8462
Q2	34.2755	33.1914	.5686	.8525
Q3	34.2653	31.4959	.7414	.8383
Q4	34.1531	32.6258	.6756	.8445
Q5	34.3878	32.1368	.7492	.8392
Q6	34.2347	32.1196	.7459	.8393
Q7	34.2245	31.9903	.6860	.8429
Q8	34.1837	31.7391	.7225	.8400
Q9	34.1735	31.0727	.7082	.8402
Q10	35.5612	40.7436	−.1369	.9175

Reliability Coefficients

N of Cases = 98.0   N of Items = 10

Alpha = .8647

This item stands out

This will be the alpha if we leave this item out

Table 17.2   New Cronbach Alpha data for the revised nine item scale

Method 1 (space saver) will be used for this analysis				
Statistics for	**Mean**	**Variance**	**Std dev**	**N of variables**
SCALE	35.5612	40.7436	6.3831	9

Item-total Statistics				
	Scale mean if item deleted	**Scale variance if item deleted**	**Corrected item-total correlation**	**Alpha if item deleted**
Q1	31.5714	32.6804	.6716	.9107
Q2	31.6531	33.4660	.6039	.9152
Q3	31.6429	31.9227	.7601	.9046
Q4	31.5306	32.9733	.7049	.9085
Q5	31.7653	32.6763	.7569	.9052
Q6	31.6122	32.6935	.7496	.9057
Q7	31.6020	32.5101	.6951	.9091
Q8	31.5612	32.0632	.7525	.9051
Q9	31.5510	31.7345	.7019	.9090

Reliability Coefficients
N of Cases = 98.0   N of Items = 9
Alpha = .9175

So we plan to remove item 10 and reassess the internal reliability again on the remaining nine item scale. We rerun the SPSS analysis as above but first remove item 10 by highlighting it and using the arrow button to return it to the variable list.

Table 17.2 reveals clearly that the internal reliability has been improved and the items correlate well together as a set.

For this test, SPSS also produces a table of intercorrelations and a set of descriptive statistics for each item (these have not been shown here). Note that an item eliminated because of low correlation with the test as a whole may not be poorly worded or ambiguous, but may measure some other dimension very well and could be assessed for reliability within another set of items. In fact, if you have to remove five or more items from a large initial set, they should be subjected to a Cronbach Alpha on their own, as they may well form a separate subset measuring another concept or dimension of the overall concept. A more sophisticated way of determining the structure of a test or scale in terms of its sub-groupings of items (factors) is to submit it to factor analysis (Chapter 18). We will meet Cronbach Alpha again in Chapter 23 on attitude testing.

Reverse scoring for negative items

Warning: Before conducting a Cronbach Alpha, make sure all the items are scored in the same direction. Positively and negatively worded items are often randomly distributed in a questionnaire to make respondents really read and understand the item before they respond.

This will require you to reverse score negatively phrased items should you find any, so the scoring is consistent with positively phrased items. That is, agreement with a positive item and disagreement with a negative item result in the same score value. To reverse score, take the maximum value of the response range (usually 5) and add 1 to it. Then take this new value and deduct the score each respondent recorded. For example, someone who obtained 5 originally now gets $6 - 5 = 1$ (the reverse score). However, it is quicker to do this for a large sample using SPSS and the ***Transform > Recode*** process. Retain as 'same variable' and insert 1 in old value box and 5 in new value box, click add and continue with this reversal for the entire score range. The variable will now appear in the data view with its data scored in a congruent direction with the other items. Remember that reverse phrased items are useful to stop response bias as respondents actually have to read the question and think about their opinion. So don't avoid them simply because of this little problem with scoring and assessing internal reliability.

How to report this result

'Internal reliability of a 10 item scale was assessed using the Cronbach alpha technique. The scale produced an alpha of .8647. Inspection of the table suggested that item 10 should be eliminated because of its low and negative correlation with the test as a whole and the indication that its removal would increase internal reliability. A repeat Cronbach Alpha test minus item 10 then produced an alpha of .9175, which is highly acceptable for an attitude scale'.

Factors that influence reliability

Other things being equal, an investigator will choose the method/ test/questionnaire/survey/ equipment with the highest reliability. One with a reliability of +.90 is surely better than one with a reliability of +.60!

A number of factors may influence the reliability of any test. The basic methods for computing a reliability coefficient that have been presented often lead to differing estimates of the reliability of data. The various conditions which can influence the outcome of the computation of a reliability coefficient further emphasize the notion that no assessment or technique has a single reliability coefficient.

Length of assessment

One of the major factors which will affect the reliability of any assessment procedure is the length of that procedure. On an intuitive basis, one can see that as the number of items or measures in any particular assessment is increased, the chance factors which might enter into the data are greatly reduced or balanced out. For example, assessment of the performance of an employee on making three items could be greatly influenced by various chance factors. But, if the three item assessment were lengthened to 10 or 20 items, the error sources would have a greater tendency to cancel each other out, and a better estimate of the true performance would be achieved.

You may already have noted that increasing the length of an assessment increases its reliability. This assumption is inherent in the use of the Spearman-Brown formula. Although this formula is used most often in the computation of the split-half reliability coefficient, it may also be used to compute the increased reliability due to tripling or adding 10 times as many items to a test. The Spearman-Brown formula may also be used to determine the number of items which must be added to an already existing assessment in order to increase its reliability to some desired level. However, a law of diminishing returns sets in so that, as reliability increases, it requires a tremendous extension in length to improve reliability a little. For example, if an assessment with a reliability coefficient of .82 is doubled in length, the estimated reliability coefficient of the longer test would be .90; if it were tripled in length, the estimated reliability coefficient would only be increased to .93. The downside is that increases in the length of a test introduce other problems, including increasing the time needed to complete the test.

Methods of estimating reliability

Methods that take into account both stability and equivalence will tend to give lower coefficients than the other methods because all major types of error variance are included. The Kuder-Richardson and Cronbach alpha methods will tend to yield lower coefficients than the split-halves method because the former reflects test homogeneity, as reflected in all inter-item relationships, rather than merely the consistency of two scores from the halves of a subdivided assessment. With any method involving two assessment occasions, the longer the interval of time between two occasions, the lower the coefficient will tend to be.

Type of measurement

Another factor affecting the reliability of a test is the type of measurement used. Rating scales, observation techniques and interviews are subjective in response and scoring, and more likely influenced by individual opinion, tending to provide low reliability coefficients. Objective measures, such as physiological measures, or equipment performance produce higher reliability coefficients simply because interpretation is not involved so fuel consumption rates, wear on tyres, and income levels produce high reliabilities because the data can be assessed objectively.

Standardization and administration

To increase the chances of high reliability, the administration of the test from occasion to occasion, or between different groups, must be standardized, particularly in terms of time limit, instructions, freedom from distraction, etc. These factors must remain constant or else the results from different measurements will reflect variations in these, as well as expected individual performance variations.

Reliability values need interpretation: in terms of the method chosen to estimate reliability data, in terms of the situation in which the particular data were gained, and in terms of the sources of error they control (or don't control). An interesting way of differentiating between these kinds of reliabilities is to consider some of the causes of error variance in observed scores, as in Qu. 17.6.

Clearly, we can never be certain that no error variance will be present. For example, if an immediate test-retest method is used, it is possible that error variance associated with the subjects will still be present, since, for example, they may be a little more tired on the retest. But it is unlikely to be as great as the error variance associated with subjects if a delayed test-retest method is used, with a long time interval between retests. And the longer the interval, the lower the reliability figures obtained will be. So, the important point is not the exact specification of the source of error variance, but that a reliability coefficient must be interpreted according to the method used to calculate it.

Standard error of measurement

We have seen that standard errors of the mean (Chapter 9) and of the difference (Chapter 12), allow us to measure variation around a hypothetical population parameter. There also exists a statistic which allows us to determine the degree of error around a value using a reliability coefficient. A series of data obtained by an individual or piece of equipment, etc. on the repeated administration of a single test, will approximate to a normal distribution. The spread of this distribution is another way of conceptualizing the reliability of the assessment. The smaller the spread, the greater the confidence with which any one observed score can be taken to represent the 'true' score. We use the SD of this distribution as the index of its spread. This SD of the error distribution is known as the standard error of measurement, or SE_{meas}.

The formula is:

$$SE_{meas} = SD\sqrt{1 - r_{tt}}$$

where SD is the standard deviation of the assessment data and r_{tt} is the reliability coefficient of the assessment.

The interpretation of the standard error of measurement is similar to that of the SD of a set of raw values. For example, there is a probability of .68 that the obtained datum does not deviate from the 'true' score by more than ± 1 SE_{meas}. The other probabilities are of course:

$$.95 \text{ for } X_{obs} \pm 1.96 \ SE_{meas},$$

and

$$.99 \text{ for } X_{obs} \pm 2.57 \ SE_{meas}.$$

This interpretation of the SE_{meas} assumes that errors in measurement be equally distributed throughout the range of test scores. If a person produces a score of 20 on an attitude scale with an SD of 4 and $r_{tt} = .96$, what are the limits within which 95% of this person's attitude score from an infinite number of assessments with the same scale would lie? Here we need to know the SE_{meas} since $1.96 \times SE_{meas}$ will define the 95% limits. Substituting, we obtain:

$$SE_{meas} = 4\sqrt{1 - .96}$$

$$= 4(.2) = .8$$

i.e. the scores obtained from an infinite number of tests would have a SD = .8. The 95% limits are therefore 1.96 × .8 above and below the only real score we know the person has. So the range of error using the 95% confidence limits are 20 ± 1.57, i.e. 21.57 to 18.43. This range is quite revealing for it shows that even with a highly reliable test, there is still a considerable band of error round an obtained score.

If the reliability is lower, this range increases dramatically. For example, with an r_{tt} of .75 and SD = 4, the 95% limits are ± 1.96 × 2 marks on each side of the obtained score, i.e. 23.92 to 16.08. The limiting cases are when $r_{tt} = 0$ or $r_{tt} = 1$. In the former case SE_{meas} is the same as the SD of the scores; in the latter case SE_{meas} is zero, for there is no error. This reveals that a form of assessment or observation needs to have a very high reliability for us to have confidence that the values we have obtained for individual persons or equipment are quite close to their 'real' value.

> **Standard error of the measurement.** *A measure of the range of error around any known score or value.*

Inter-observer reliability

One area where reliability is important lies in the measurement of agreement between judges, observers, or raters, as in interviewing situations or observation of work perform-ance where more than one 'judge' in involved. If judges agree to a considerable extent, then obviously reliability is high; where judges disagree the reliability of the assessment will be low. We can only have faith in the assessment where judges are closely similar in agreement. Again, we are looking at correlations.

Suppose we have three interviewers who have rated five candidates for a job on a scale of 1 to 7, with 1 being 'do not consider' to 7 'excellent'. The intercorrelations of their ratings (Spearman rank order) are depicted in Table 17.3.

Table 17.3   **Ratings of candidates by three interviewers**

Candidates	Interviewer 1	Interviewer 2	Interviewer 3
A	5	6	7
B	3	6	4
C	3	5	6
D	2	2	3
E	1	5	4

Interjudge correlations are: 1 v 2 = .645
2 v 3 = .582
3 v 1 = .800
The mean correlation = .676.

The interjudge correlations only provide a measure of the agreement of pairs of judges. The mean correlation is simply the average and does not tell us the reliability of all three judges taken together. To assess the overall reliability we use the Spearman-Brown formula:

$$R = \frac{N(\text{mean}\,r)}{1+(N-1)(\text{mean}\,r)}$$

Substituting in,

$$R = \frac{3(.676)}{1+(3-1)(.676)} = .862$$

Thus the aggregate reliability of .862 provides a better reflection of their joint agreement.

Validity

The subject of validity is complex, controversial, and here perhaps more than anywhere else, is the nature of reality questioned. It is possible to study reliability without inquiring into the meaning of the variables. It is not possible to study validity, however, without sooner or later inquiring into the nature and meaning of one's variables.

A measurement or assessment technique which is perfectly reliable would seem to be quite valuable, but: 'How valid is it? Does the measurement, assessment or observation technique measure what I want it to measure?' A perfectly reliable assessment may not measure anything of value. Validity information gives some indication of how well a test or other assessment instrument measures a given characteristic, under certain circumstances and with a given set of subjects or objects. It is for this reason that any one assessment technique or test may have many types of validity, and a unique validity for each circumstance and group or items assessed.

Distinguishing between validity and reliability

It is easy to confuse reliability with validity but understanding their distinction is important. Whilst reliability relates to the accuracy and stability of a measure, validity relates to the appropriateness of the measure to assess the construct it purports to measure. A homely example to differentiate these constructs is the production of faulty school rulers. Let us imagine that the quality control in a factory manufacturing 30 cm (12 inch) wooden rulers failed and some rulers were retailed which were inaccurate. The inaccuracy lay in the fact that each cm division was slightly longer than one cm; in fact each was 1.1 cm long. Hence, when we thought we were drawing a line 30 cm long, we were in fact drawing a line 33 cm long (30 cm + [30 × .1 cm]).

Surprisingly, **the ruler is quite reliable, because it produces consistent results, even though the measurements are not what we think they are.** Every time we draw what we assume to be a line 30 cm long, we produce a line 33 cm long consistently. The ruler produces a reliable measurement **but it is not a valid measure of 30 cm**. It is a valid measure of 33 cm, but since we bought it on the presumption that it measured 30 cm it cannot be measuring what it purports to measure. Similarly, test instruments, performance measures, observation techniques and the like can be very reliable, producing consistent results from occasion to occasion, but may not be valid as measures of what we think they are measuring. On the other hand, if an instrument is unreliable it cannot be valid. A dodgy thermometer is another example, consistently wrong (invalid) but consistent in its error (reliable). However, the converse is not true.

So validity relates to the questions: 'what does the assessment device measure?' or 'Is it measuring what it is supposed to measure?' The importance of these questions would seem obvious; yet research literature contains many examples of tests or techniques being used without proper consideration of their validity for the user's purpose.

> *Validity*. To what extent does the testing instrument actually measure the construct/concept/variable it purports to measure?

Types of validity

There are a number of ways of classifying validity. Two main types of validity which most research must take account of include **external** and **internal** validity.

External validity

External validity refers to the extent to which the results of a sample are transferable to a population. Few researchers are interested in observations that do not extend beyond a particular restricted set of sample data and so we usually need to generalize from a limited set of observations. Generalizability depends on whether the observed measurement is representative of the statistical population, the surrounding conditions and the treatments to which we now wish to extend it. Relevant questions include:

- Were the subjects a representative random sample of the general population to which it is desired to extend the research findings?
- Was there something specific in that particular research setting that would cause or influence the measurement?
- Was the treatment accompanied by any personal interaction that may be somewhat peculiar to the research or to the subjects or the experimenter involved?

Of importance is to clarify those instrances where the results of your observations may be legitimately extended, and those instances where they cannot. Providing a comprehensive description of the demographic/biographic/psychological characteristics of the subjects of the research and a complete and comprehensive description of the methodology used, enables some assessment on whether the results can be generalized beyond the sample(s) involved. The generalizability of a study's findings relates to two types of external validity: **population validity** and **ecological validity**.

Population validity

Population validity relates to whether a sample of participants responses are an accurate assessment of the target population. Chapter 9 discussed the importance of a sample's representativeness, with the random selection and random assignment to groups being crucial. Therefore, population validity asks the question: 'To what extent is the sample really representative of the target population?' Clearly, samples obtained by convenience or opportunity and in-tact group membership, are less likely to provide population validity.

Ecological validity

Ecological validity questions the generalizability of a study's findings to other environmental contexts. A considerable weakness to experimental studies, especially those undertaken under laboratory conditions, is that they do not reflect reality. For instance, the superior performance of a brand of washing powder over competitors may exist in controlled conditions within the manufacturer's laboratories, but this may not be reflected when used in a typical household, with a typical well-used household appliance, and rough measures of how much is used (guessing what a cupful or 10 gms is, etc.).

> *External validity*. The degree to which the sample results are validly generalizable to a particular population or context.

Internal validity

Internal validity is concerned with the degree to which the conditions within the experiment are controlled, so that any differences or relationships can be ascribed to the independent variable, and not other factors. Internal validity can be affected by a number of factors, including the study's design to control for unwanted variables, the administration of the study and the extent to which researchers take into account alternative explanations for any causal relationships. Several types of internal validity are identified and include:

1. Content validity

Content validity reflects the extent to which the content of a measurement reflects the intended content to be investigated. For instance, a multiple-choice test item in Management Styles would have no content validity for measuring achievement in a multiple-choice test in Statistics. Furthermore, simply because a test had content validity at one moment in time does not necessarily mean the same test will have content validity in another instance as the definition of the topic under investigation may change. For example, educational success has shifted focus from test performance to skills development.

When students criticize an assessment as not fairly representing the actual content of the course, they are condemning the content validity of the assessment. Content validity then is the representativeness or sampling adequacy of the content (the substance, the matter, the topics) of a measuring instrument, and is most often determined on the basis of expert judgement.

> **Content validity.** *The extent to which an assessment truly samples the universe of content.*

2. Face validity

Face validity is concerned with how a measure or procedure appears and is of particular importance for lay participants who, knowing little about measurement, reliability and validity, are reassured of a test's validity simply on its design and on how professional it looks. It is 'public relations validity'. The high face validity will, hopefully, motivate the subjects to tackle the assessment in a serious way. If the naive subjects looked at a test and starting thinking that the items were ridiculous and seemed (to them) unrelated to the aim of the tests, then motivation would be considerably reduced. Up to a few years ago, we often chuckled over abusive letters in national newspapers from parents asking how on earth some particular (quoted) question could ever measure IQ. Obviously, face validity had failed in instances like this, yet the items probably had high construct, predictive and concurrent validity.

There will be instances where you may wish to underplay the seriousness of a test so that the naive participant remains naive. In some attitude scales, there are sometimes large differences between what a test purports to measure (face validity in terms of title, etc.) and what it actually is measuring (content validity). Researchers often require 'high face validity' for tests or techniques for use in research programmes for industry, the military and schools. However, it is usually impossible to measure a validity of this type.

It is possible to hide the true aim of a measuring device or scale and at the same time increase its face validity by including filler items that are not going to be marked. In this way, a false face validity is created; subjects believe it is measuring one thing when in fact it is measuring another, but consider the ethical implications of this!

> **Face validity.** *A validity of appearances that disguises the real intent of the assessment.*

3. Predictive validity

Predictive validity seeks to determine the extent by which it is possible to predict future performance by some current measure. For example, performance on an apprenticeship course reasonably predicts later performance in the workplace. Predictive validity can be easily determined by correlating the first measure (the predictor) with the outcome measure (criterion) at a later date. However, as with all correlations, a strong relationship does not indicate causation. For instance, success on an apprenticeship could also be highly correlated with a range of personal characteristics, including self-esteem and intrinsic motivation, as well as environmental characteristics, including a highly supportive workplace mentor and home background.

Predictive validity is obviously important for vocational selection, because a person responsible for the selection of those likely to succeed in a given job is concerned with using valid assessment techniques, such as in-tray exercises, as aids in improving selection than simply using subjective judgement.

Predictive validity can only be assessed by comparing a later performance (perhaps several years later) with the original performance scores. It is usual to express predictive validity in terms of the correlation coefficient between the predicted status and the outcome criterion. Many criteria are unfortunately very remote in time and difficult to define. For example, with 'success on the job', should one consider income or self-ratings of ability, or happiness on one's profession, or supervisor's ratings, or perhaps some combination of a number of these individual criteria? Perhaps multiple regression (Chapter 16), would help us choose the best combination?

Although there is no simple answer to the problem of how best to choose a criterion measure, a few suggestions follow:

(a) One should be sure that performance on the criterion measure is a result of the same individual characteristics and external environmental conditions which affected performance on the original predictive measure that you are attempting to validate.
(b) The criterion measure should be reliable, i.e. it should be stable or consistent from day to day or from time to time. Obviously, it is very difficult to predict something that fluctuates markedly over short periods of time.
(c) In choosing a criterion measure, one should consider such factors as the time and the expense required in obtaining the measure.

> *Predictive validity.* The extent to which the measurement will predict future performance.

4. Concurrent validity

Concurrent and predictive validity are very much alike, differing only in time dimension. For predictive validity, we would require an answer to the question, 'Will a high scorer on this test become a neurotic at some time in the future?', whilst for concurrent validity, an answer to the question, 'Is the high scorer a neurotic now?'. Predictive and concurrent validity are both characterized by prediction to an outside criterion and by checking a measuring instrument, either now or in the future, against some outcome.

Concurrent validity correlation coefficients, in which we relate present assessment scores to present performance, can be obtained with less expense and delay than predictive validity coefficients (involving future performance). But high concurrent validity is no guide to high predictive validity in the future as many other variables may impact over time on the criterion performance level.

> **Concurrent validity.** *The extent to which the measurement truly represents the current status of performance.*

5. Construct validity

Construct validity involves relating a theoretical concept to a specific measuring device or procedure. Does the measuring instrument tap the concept as theorized? For instance, a researcher inventing a personality test to measure extroversion will firstly spend time attempting to define extroversion and indicate operational ways of measuring it in order to reach an acceptable level of construct validity. However, there are some constructs like self-concept and intelligence that are hypothetical constructs and we can only infer their construct validity through processes such as Cronbach reliability coefficients (the items must be internally consistent, i.e. show good agreement, one with another), and factor analysis that shows one underlying construct is being measured (a large common factor). Internal consistency between items and also between items and composite variables formed from them is essential for supporting the construct validity of a set of items on a scale. Rule of thumb claims that item-total correlations should exceed .50 while inter-item correlations should exceed .30.

Of course, while Cronbach internal reliability correlations and derivation of strong factors imply that items and tests are measuring the same thing to a certain degree, they do not indicate *what* they were measuring. And we are left with a subjective naming of what the commonness is among the items or tests. Evidence of a test's construct validity may also be provided by its correlations with other tests, particularly those that are already accepted measures of the same construct.

So, in designing a test to measure a construct (for example, authoritarian leadership style, empathy, neuroticism), we are concerned with all types of evidence which make the interpretation of test scores more meaningful and which help us to understand what the scores signify.

The significant point about construct validity, which sets it apart from other types of validity, is its preoccupation with theory, theoretical constructs and scientific empirical inquiry involving the testing of hypothesized relations. Construct validation in measurement contrasts sharply with empiric approaches that define the validity of a measure purely by its success in predicting a criterion.

> **Construct validity**. This indicates the qualities an assessment measures, i.e. the concepts or constructs that account for variability on the assessment.

Without internal validity, an experiment cannot possibly be externally valid, but the converse does not necessarily follow; an internally valid experiment may or may not have external validity. Thus, the most carefully designed consumer survey of food purchases involving a sample of Western persons is not necessarily generalizable to a national population that includes sizeable Hindu and Islamic subgroups. It follows, then, that the way to good investigations in business and industry lies in maximizing both internal and external validity.

> **Internal validity**. The degree to which the results are valid within the confines of the study.

Threats to validity

A number of common threats to validity exist and relate to the validity of the statistical conclusions themselves, and the design of the experiment.

Threats to external validity

Threats to external validity are likely to limit the degree to which generalizations can be made from the particular experimental conditions to other populations or settings.

Failure to describe and operationalize independent and dependent variables explicitly

Unless variables and methodologies are adequately described, future replications of the experimental conditions are virtually impossible.

Selection bias and lack of representativeness

Selection bias is a common problem and relates to the process by which the researcher procures a sample. The use of convenience or opportunity sampling is unlikely to include participants that are representative of the population, unlike random sampling techniques. Even when those persons, events, items, etc. participating in the experiment are representative of an available population, they may not be representative of the population to which the investigator seeks to generalize their findings.

Reactive bias

This is a problem where participants display different behaviours simply because they are participating and no longer represent the population from which they were drawn, thus limiting any generalization (e.g. the Hawthorne effect). Reactive bias also threatens to contaminate experimental treatments in studies when subjects realize their role as guinea pigs compared to those in a control group. It is usually obvious that some investigation is ongoing in the workplace and consumer contexts as employees and consumers are observed and/or interviewed. Medical research has long recognized the psychological effects that arise out of mere participation in drug experiments, and placebos and double-blind designs are commonly employed to counteract the biasing effects of participation.

Inadequate operationalizing of dependent variables

Dependent variables that the experimenter operationalizes must have validity in the non-experimental setting to which the generalization is directed. A paper-and-pencil questionnaire on career choice, for example, may have little validity in respect of the actual employment decisions made by undergraduates on leaving university.

Threats to internal validity

When researchers conduct research they will often measure the outcome of such research with statistical tests to determine whether these observed relationship or difference patterns are statistically significant. Apart from the variables being investigated, other factors may influence the possibility of committing a Type I or Type II error. These extraneous factors can include the sample size, the measures used and experimental design employed.

Low statistical power

Small sample sizes limit the power of statistical test. The larger the sample size, the greater the power to detect differences or relationships between variables. Often, low statistical power will lead to a type II error whereby a test fails to identify an association when one actually does exist.

Violated assumptions of statistical tests

Inferential statistics are based on a number of mathematical assumptions. The major ones include homogeneity of variance (distributions have very similar variances) and normality of score distribution. Violation of some of these assumptions of statistical tests can lead to researchers drawing conclusions that are invalid, increasing the possibility of committing either a Type I or Type II error. Increasingly, however, it is becoming common practice to 'turn a blind eye' to minor violations of the assumptions of statistical tests.

Fishing

Especially when undertaking exploratory research in new areas of investigation, researchers often 'fish' around with all possible associations between variables in order to identify statistically significant findings. However, there is a significant weakness to this approach as the more significance we undertake the more likely a false significant result will occur, supporting our conclusions. You will remember from earlier chapters that if you performed 100 correlations, which were all statistically significant with a 95% confidence interval, 5 out of those 100 correlations (or 1 in 20) would be statistically significant by chance alone and we commit a Type I error, asserting a statistically significant relationship exists when in fact it doesn't. Thus, fishing expeditions increase the likelihood of obtaining a significant result when in fact it is one of the 5 in 100 chance results, but we would never know.

'So', some of you will be thinking, 'what if we were to raise the level of probability to the 99% level?' Unfortunately, this increase also increases the likelihood of committing a Type II error, asserting that a statistically significant relationship doesn't exist when in fact it does.

Unreliable measures

Unreliable measures can also affect statistical validity. The larger the amount of random measurement error, the greater the likelihood of a Type II error.

Heterogeneity of subjects

When participants vary considerably on factors other than those being measured, an increase in the amount of variance is produced. Higher level of error reduces the ability to identify the effects of those factors under investigation, increasing the likelihood of Type II errors.

History

In most research, events other than the experimental treatments will occur naturally during the time between pretest and post-test measurements/observations. Such events, which are often impossible to eliminate or prevent happening, produce effects that can be mistakenly attributed to differences in treatment. For instance, in attempting to address a growing obesity and well-being problem amongst its employees, a company promotes lunch-time activities for its employees and assesses its impact by comparing various health indices over a six-month period. However, unbeknownst to the company, a number of employees also group together to form their own sporting team to compete in an amateur league, involving a match and two practice sessions each week in the last three months of the six-month period of the company's own activity programme. Company officials may attribute any changes to their own activity, and not to the employee's out-of-work activity or quite possibly even a combination of the two activities.

This demonstrates the benefit to repeated testing, especially to gain numerous baseline and post-intervention levels, in order to attain an accurate picture of change in the construct you are measuring. However, you then run the risks associated with maturation and repeated testing.

Maturation

Maturation refers to the psychological or physical changes that occur naturally within the participant or equipment over time. A person often improves in performance with experience and the equipment runs less well with age. Such changes can produce differences that are independent of the experimental treatments. The problem of maturation is obviously more acute in longitudinal studies than in brief experimental studies.

Statistical regression to the mean

Statistical regression occurs due to the unreliability of measuring instruments and to extraneous factors unique to each experimental group and, like maturation effects, increase systematically with the time interval between pretests and post-tests. This regression to the mean simply refers to those instances when subjects or equipment scoring highest on a pretest are likely to score relatively lower on a post-test; conversely, those scoring lowest on a pretest are likely to score relatively higher on a post-test. In a word, in pretest/post-test situations, there is regression to the mean and regression effects can lead the researcher to mistakenly attribute post-test gains and losses to low scoring and high scoring respectively.

To conceptualize this, think about the normal distribution. To obtain a score smaller than the original one in a post-test, is less probable than to get one slightly higher, i.e. closer to the mean. Similarly, if a high score is obtained on the original test, the probability is that the post-test score is likely to be slightly lower. So, there is a general tendency, particularly for initially extreme scores, for regression to the mean to occur on a second testing.

Repeated testing

Repeated testing of the same participants with the same or similar measure of a construct, or when using pretests, can bring about a change in test score. This is due to sensitizing subjects to the true purposes of the experiment and practice effects, which produce higher scores on post-test measures.

Instrumentation

Unreliable tests or instruments can introduce serious errors. With human observers or judges, error can result from changes in their skills and levels of concentration over the course of the period of observations and judgements.

Dropout

The loss of subjects through dropout often occurs in longitudinal studies and may result in confounding the effects of the experimental variables, for whereas the groups may have initially been randomly selected, the residue that stays the course is likely to be different from the unbiased sample that began it. In particular, differential attrition, that is the unequal dropout of participants from the treatment and control groups, is of particular concern by reducing equivalence between groups.

Diffusion of treatment effects

Diffusion relates to those instances where treatment effects may spread from a treatment group to a control group. In assessing the effectiveness of a nicotine patch in a 'stop smoking' programme, those smokers in a control group may see the benefits and success of others in the experimental group and may start the patch themselves, without the experimenter's knowledge. When making comparisons in the rate of cigarettes smoked between groups post-intervention, the ability to detect differences between the treatment and control group is reduced by those members of the control group who have experienced the treatment.

Placebo

Placebo is a well-known process which involves the participants believing that they are receiving an intervention, when in fact they are not. Research in a number of areas of research demonstrates that the effectiveness of an intervention is in part explained by a placebo effect. The fact that the individual expects a change will usually bring about that change to a degree.

What you have learned from this chapter

This chapter has shown you why reliability and validity are crucial aspects of any study. Reliability refers to the stability, accuracy and dependability of data. Methods of measuring reliability include the test-retest, parallel forms, internal consistency and split-half methods. Cronbach alpha analysis is a useful way of determining internal consistency and homogeneity of groups of items in tests and questionnaires. The SE_{meas} interprets the range of error around any value and depends on the reliability. Reliability is affected by a number of factors, including the length of the assessment instrument and the degree of objectivity in the scoring.

Validity assesses whether the test measures what it claims to measure. The major types of validity are content, construct, concurrent and predictive validity. Some researchers distinguish between internal validity, which is the extent that within its own boundary its results are credible; but for those results to be useful, they must be generalizable beyond the confines of the particular context, i.e. they must be externally valid also, capable of being applied to the population from which the sample was drawn.

You are now aware of the numerous threats to validity that exist and how these can be eliminated or managed as far as possible to maximize validity.

Review questions and activities

Qu. 17.1
Which of the following are random or systematic sources of error?

(a) power failure during equipment test
(b) interview candidate has a bout of hiccups during interview
(c) employee's error rate on production line due to playing in a rock band at night club every evening until early morning

Qu. 17.2
Why does a two to three month time gap seem appropriate for human subjects but equipment could be re-tested sooner?

Qu. 17.3
If reliability is 0 what does this mean?

Qu. 17.4
What sort of reliability is used when different forms of the same test are administered on two occasions?

Qu. 17.5
On how many administrations of a test is internal consistency reliability based?

Qu. 17.6
Indicate with a yes or no whether a particular type of reliability is affected by a particular source of error.

	Type of reliability coefficient			
Source of Error variance	Test-retest immediate	Test-retest delayed	Parallel form	Split half
The procedure/method				
The person/event/equipment				
The conditions				

Qu. 17.7
To have confidence in an obtained value would you want a small or large SEmeas ?

Qu. 17.8
In what situations in a business context would low face validity of an assessment instrument be valuable?

Qu. 17.9
Which of the following requires a test with predictive validity?

(a) an engineer wants to assess the defect rate of a machine
(b) an employer wants an estimate of success for his new batch of apprentices before he starts their training
(c) new employee is given a personality test on their first day at work.

Qu. 17.10
Criticize the following criteria:

(a) ratings by employees as an index of supervisor's leadership ability
(b) success at university studies as a criterion of performance as a salesperson

Qu. 17.11
Which one of the following properties of a test would be taken as evidence of its validity.?

(a) Scores on the test correlated highly with scores on another test designed to measure the same ability
(b) Scores on a test at the beginning of a customer relations training programme predicted a supervisor's rating after one year on the job.

(c) Kilometres per litre of petrol used by a prototype test car varied over a series of standardized consumption tests by 10%

Qu. 17.12
Explain why it is important to minimize threats to external validity
Check your responses in the chapter above

Now access the Chapter 17 Web page and tackle the additional questions there.

Chapter 18
Factor Analysis

'Factor analysis is, in principle, nothing more than asking what the common elements are when one knows the correlations'

(Cattell)

Content list

By the end of this chapter you will:

1 Understand the purposes of factor analysis.
2 Know how to carry out a factor analysis using SPSS.
3 Be able to interpret the results of the analysis.

Introduction

Factor analysis is a major technique in multivariate statistics and has a vital task in demonstrating which variables clump together to form super-ordinate variables. It reverses the usual thinking for developing theoretical frameworks and operational variables where we are trying to generate numerous items that measure a particular variable. Factor analysis reverses this by attempting to place together closely related individual items to form a theoretical concept or construct or factor, to detect simple patterns in a more complex pattern of relationships among variables. In particular, it seeks to discover if the observed variables can be explained largely or entirely in terms of a much smaller number of super-variables or underlying factors.

The purpose of factor analysis

The aim of factor analysis is simplification, to make order out of chaos, by identifying basic underlying factors that explain a larger number of other related variables in a parsimonious way. The other day, when I got home from work I switched the light on in the kitchen but it did not come on, neither would the TV, the electric kettle was not heating the water for my cup of tea, and the dish washer I had programmed to wash the dishes while I was at work had not operated. I realized that not all the equipment was faulty; the underlying cause was that the electricity supply was off. A visit to the fuse box confirmed my suspicions and a new piece of fuse wire soon had the electricity back on. This was a situation where a cluster of related variables (the failure of a set of electrical appliances) were underlain by one factor – a blown fuse.

Similar consistently related variables are also common in medical situations. The doctor notes that runny noses, increased body temperature, aching limbs and sore throats seem to occur together. These clusters of symptoms are an indication of a particular illness – influenza. Car breakdowns are generally underlain by two factors – either fuel feed problems (such as the fuel pump or fuel line) or electrical problems (such as problems with battery, condenser, or alternator). These examples illustrate the fact that if a bunch of things are correlated with each other, they must have something in common. That thing in common is called a **factor**. Some writers may use the terms **dimension** or **construct** as a synonym of factor. A factor is a sort of super-variable with its commonness expressed by the group of variables having high intercorrelations but low correlations with any other group.

Another useful analogy is that of the geographical coordinates of latitude and longitude. Early European explorers could describe a large number of events, such as increasing length of winter days, increasing temperature of sea water, proximity of pole star to horizon, etc., that indicated they were essentially travelling south. These variables were obviously related. The concept of latitude encapsulates them all and explains the common component of their relationship.

Our area of interest is not the geographical world, but the world of human behaviour and activity. Management and business activities involve super-ordinate concepts or factors such as leadership, stress, product quality, each containing groupings of highly related individual items of behaviour. Latitude does not actually exist as a line on the earth, but is useful as a way of providing unique descriptions that explain the grouping of phenomena parsimoniously. Similarly, factors do not exist. They are convenient abstractions or super-ordinate constructs that bind together a number of behaviours, events or qualities. We cannot demonstrate their existence; we can only infer them from the pattern of correlations between items. The close correlations between a person's ability to plan and organize, to build up sound personal relationships with employees, to have empathy with employees, to be trusted by employees, fall under the banner of the leadership factor. This factor explains these relationships in a simple and parsimonious way.

Correlations and common-ness

Your study of correlation (Chapter 15) and regression (Chapter 16) indicated that a strong correlation implies that the variables share something in common. The coefficients of determination and multiple determination both indexed this commonness, interpreted as the proportion of variance that is common to both measures.

In Figure 18.1, there are four different relationships between two variables:

- In A there is no correlation and therefore no common variance. Performance in one will give us no idea of performance in the other.
- B corresponds to a small correlation of +0.3. This indicates 9% common variance.
- C corresponds to a high correlation of +0.7 which indicates 49% common variance.
- D corresponds to an extremely high correlation of +0.95 which indicates about 90% common variance.

Factor analysis extends this approach so that a large array of intercorrelations, in which complex interactions between variables, impossible to discern by eye, can be analyzed. The purpose is to find out how much of the variation in all the variables can be accounted for by a very much smaller number of factors or underlying dimensions. The statistical approach involves finding a way of condensing the information contained in a number of original variables into a smaller set of dimensions (factors) with a minimum loss of information.

Many statistical methods, like ANOVA and regression, study the relation between independent and dependent variables. Factor analysis is different; it is used to study the patterns of relationship (correlations) between many variables, with the goal of discovering some underlying constructs or factors that binds groups of them together. Each clump of correlated variables is a factor and the relative connection of each of the original variables to a factor is called the variable's factor loading on that factor. Each factor loading can be

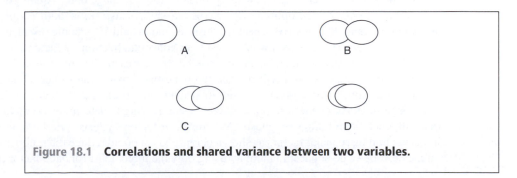

Figure 18.1   Correlations and shared variance between two variables.

thought of as the correlation of that variable with the factor and a variable is considered to contribute meaningfully to a factor if it has a loading of at least +.3 or −.3.

Origins of factor analysis

The initial use of factor analysis was in psychology. It was invented around 100 years ago by Charles Spearman, who hypothesized that the enormous variety of tests of mental ability – measures of mathematical skill, vocabulary, other verbal skills, artistic skills, logical reasoning ability, etc. – could all be explained by one underlying hypothetical 'factor' of general intelligence that he called g. It was an interesting idea, but it turned out to be wrong. Today we accept that there are a number of additional factors, such as creativity and spatial aptitude, that underlie performance across the canvas of intellectual abilities.

Another early use of factor analysis was in the study of personality by Cattell in the USA and Eysenck in the UK. What are the smallest number of words or factors needed to explain the whole gamut of personality? This is a question that job selection panels and business company interviewers would like answered. We have thousands of adjectives and adjectival phrases that describe our personality but many of them are synonyms. The number of fine distinctions we can make between people is considerable, but the aim of factor analysis is to find a basic set of personality factors that will pick up the essential differences. Those people who respond to an item on a questionnaire that they are '*usually sad*' are most likely to indicate on other items that they are '*usually unhappy*', '*usually miserable*', '*usually feeling depressed*' and '*often in tears*'. In other words, there will be very high correlations between admitting to one characteristic and to the others.

Factor analysis enables such synonymous or near synonymous personality descriptors such as *sad, glum, unhappy, miserable, depressed, tearful* to be replaced by a single term such as the factor of *melancholia*. We only need one item in the questionnaire that closely represents the factor; all the other items are redundant. Thus, we could reduce the huge number of personality descriptors and replace them by a few that cover the major dimensions while still preserving most of the individual variations involved. This is what Cattell and Eysenck did, with the former claiming that there are only 16 basic personality factors while Eysenck's research reduced the number to only three. Many personality tests used by job selection agencies measure a few basic underlying factors of personality such as extraversion, neuroticism, group dependency and tough mindedness by small sets of items that reflect each of these underlying factors.

Imagine you are developing a new questionnaire about management. You might want to determine whether it is composed of two types of skills, 'task skills' and 'people skills', and so you create 20 items, 10 reflecting 'task' elements and 10 'people' elements. Since this is a new questionnaire, you want to test your conceptualization by factor analysis that there are in fact really two factors, and if those factors represent the dimensions of task and people skills. If they do, you will be able to create two separate sub-scales, and sum the items on each dimension to obtain two sub-total scores to represent each factor or dimension of management. As another example, imagine we are trying to determine the major factors that influence hotel ratings by guests. As a result of factor analysis on a large number of items we find three major factors as shown below and we could reduce the number of items on the attitude scale or questionnaire by using only the three items for each factor that load heaviest on each of the three factors, since all others are redundant and in effect only repeating the information.

Variables	Factors
Friendly Courteous Competent	Employee Quality
Room size Bed size View Cost	Hotel Room Quality
Extensive menu choice Service and attention Cleanliness	Hotel Catering Quality

Remember, answers obtained by factor analysis are hypothetical and tentative, based simply on the analysis of complex relationship in a matrix of correlations derived from a specific sample to determine what goes with what. A typical factor analysis suggests answers to several major questions:

- Variables that significantly correlate with each other do so because they are measuring the same 'thing'. What is the 'thing' that these correlated variables are measuring in common?
- How many different factors are needed to explain the pattern of relationships among the variables?
- What is the nature of those factors? Can we name these factors in a way that represents and reflects the included variables?

Types of factor analysis

Factor analysis is a generic term. There are basically two very closely related types of factor analysis: Explanatory Factor Analysis (EFA) and Confirmatory Factor Analysis (CFA).

- EFA aims to reduce data sets comprising a large number of variables into a smaller number of factors and thereby identify the underlying factor structure or model. EFA is therefore exploratory in nature. *Example: Given the multiple items of information gathered on why customers buy a particular brand, how many independent factors are actually being measured by these items?*
- CFA aims to confirm theoretical predictions, testing whether a specified set of constructs is influencing responses in a predicted way, i.e. hypothesis testing. CFA provides a way of confirming that the factor structure or model obtained in an EFA study is robust and is not simply a consequence of one set of data. A theoretical model is set up based on the exploratory factor analysis and then tested using a new set of data. *Given a theory*

with four concepts that purport to explain some behaviour, do multiple measures of the behaviour reduce to these four factors? Example: Given a theory that attributes customer purchasing decisions to four independent factors, do multiple measures of customer purchasing decisions reduce to these four factors? Is there support for pre-established theory? CFA has been somewhat overtaken by Structural Equation Modelling, an advanced technique not dealt with in this book. CFA cannot be performed in SPSS. However, SPSS does produce another software package called AMOS, which performs CFA. CFA is also analysed using the LISREL software package.

Principal component analysis

There are an infinite number of equally accurate factor solutions for a given set of correlations. This then leads to the obvious question:

If there are an infinite number of sets of theoretical underlying factors which can describe a set of correlations – how do we choose the most appropriate amongst them?

The route followed by most researchers to solve this problem is to select the solution which is mathematically the simplest, and that is Principal Component Analysis (PCA). PCA derives a linear combination of variables such that maximum variance is extracted from the variables. It then removes this variance and derives another linear combination, which explains the maximum proportion of remaining variance and so on through successive iterations. We will focus on applying PCA in an EFA context in this chapter.

We use PCA in an EFA when we want to:

- discover the nature of the constructs or factors influencing a set of responses and reduce the data set to a small number of factors. The purpose of PCA is to derive a relatively small number of components that can account for the variability found in a relatively large number of measures. This procedure, called data reduction, is typically performed when a researcher does not want to include all of the original measures in analyses but still wants to work with the information that they contain.
- identify the nature of the constructs underlying responses in a specific content area. This is the basis of construct validity.
- determine what sets of items 'hang together' in a questionnaire.
- demonstrate the dimensionality of a measurement scale. Researchers often wish to develop scales that reflect single characteristics. These may form a single questionnaire or separate subscales in a questionnaire may be formed from subsets of items that are each underlain by a different factor.
- generate 'factor scores' representing values of the underlying constructs for use in other analyses.

In all these situations, factor analysis helps the researcher to select a few benchmark items, chosen from many items used in a pilot study, on the basis that they 'load' heavily on the underlying factor(s). Factor loadings are correlations between the factor and the variable (item). High loadings represent surface attributes which are influenced strongly by the factor. By convention, the factor loading must be at least 0.30, but for a variable to unambiguously represent a factor the loading should be 0.60 and above. Any loading below 0.4 is weak and between 0.4 and 0.6 only moderate. Inspection of the variables or items that load heavily on a factor will enable the researcher to 'name' or interpret the factor, i.e. indicate what the factor means or is measuring. Thus you can get the information you need from fewer items on a more reliable and valid scale.

The original variables or items are surface attributes, whereas factors are internal attributes or latent variables. (Latent means hidden and unobservable, and cannot be measured directly.) The latter are hypothetical constructs, which enable us to account for observed phenomena. This is common and routine in many fields. For instance, just as physicists use constructs of gravity and magnetism based on observed events; psychologists infer a factor of intelligence, sociologists infer false consciousness, and business researchers infer organizational climate as major latent variables or factors from observed behaviour and environmental events.

Assumptions for performing a PCA

- Large enough sample to yield reliable estimates of the correlations among the variables, i.e. large ratio of N / variables usually at least 5:1, preferably 10:1.
- Statistical inference is improved if the variables are at least approximately normal.
- Presence of linear relationships among the pairs of variables.
- Absence of outliers among the cases.
- Interval data.

Principal components analysis – basic concepts and principles

A factor analysis usually begins with a correlation matrix. If we find a pattern in a real correlation matrix, what exactly would we have shown?

Table 18.1 displays a dummy correlation matrix revealing the intercorrelations of 6 variables covering a range of activities. By eye, we can detect two distinct clusters of high correlations, namely, chess, bridge and sudoku, and discus, hammer and shot put. These two clusters are

Table 18.1   **Correlation matrix**

	Chess	**Bridge**	**Sudoku**	**Discus**	**Hammer throw**	**Shot Put**
Chess	1.00	*0.89*	*0.85*	0.03	0.01	0.04
Bridge	*0.89*	1.00	*0.80*	−0.05	0.02	−0.03
Sudoku	*0.85*	*0.80*	1.00	−0.04	−0.07	0.02
Discus	0.03	−0.05	−0.04	1.00	*0.76*	*0.71*
Hammer throw	0.01	0.02	−0.07	*0.76*	1.00	*0.85*
Shot Put	0.04	−0.03	0.02	*0.71*	*0.85*	1.00

Table 18.2 Factor loadings derived from correlation matrix in Table 18.1

Variable	Factor 1	Factor 2	Communality
Chess	**0.91**	0.08	0.8345
Bridge	**0.88**	−0.03	0.7753
Sudoku	**0.90**	−0.07	0.8149
Discus	−0.11	**0.87**	0.7670
Hammer throw	−0.06	**0.89**	0.7957
Shot put	0.04	**0.92**	0.8480
Eigen values	2.4298	2.4076	4.8374
% variance extracted	40.49	40.12	80.61

highlighted in bold italic. Each of these groups correlates poorly with the other group. The meaning of these correlation clusters seems fairly apparent. One involves logical thinking while the other involves physical strength.

If we factor analyzed the correlation matrix in Table 18.1, it would produce a factor loading table like Table 18.2. The high factor loading groups are highlighted in bold. Chess correlates 0.91 with factor 1, for example, while discus correlates 0.87 with factor 2.

What is a factor loading?

A factor loading is the correlation between a variable and a factor that has been extracted from the data. The factor loadings are in the Factor I and Factor II columns in Table 18.2. Like correlations, they range between +1.00 and −1.00. As an example, note in Table 18.3 the factor loadings for variable chess.

Chess is highly correlated with Factor I, but negligibly correlated with Factor II.

Table 18.3 Factor loadings for variable chess

Variable	Factor I	Factor II	Communality
Chess	0.91	0.08	0.8345

Communality

The final column is labelled communality. Each observed variable's communality is the proportion of variance in that variable that can be explained by the common factors. It is calculated by summing the squared factor loadings for each variable. How much of the variance in the variable chess is measured or accounted for by the two factors that were extracted in the example above? Simply square the factor loadings and add them together.

$$(.91^2 + .08^2) = .8345$$

This is called the communality of the variable and for chess these two factors explain most of the variations in the variable. Low communalities are not interpreted as evidence that the data fail to fit the hypothesis, but merely as evidence that other as yet unknown factors underlie the variation in that variable.

Eigenvalues and % of variance extracted

These form the two bottom lines on Table 18.2. The SPSS PCA programme extracts factors in order of their magnitude in terms of the amount of common variance explained by that factor. The common variance of all the variables is, by definition, fully explained by the factors. The amount of common variance explained by a factor is termed the eigenvalue. The eigenvalue is the sum of the squared factor loadings of a particular factor. Thus the eigenvalue for factor 1 is $.91^2 + .88^2 + .90^2 + - .11^2 + - .06^2 + .04^2 = 2.4298$.

An eigenvalue corresponds to the equivalent number of variables which the factor represents. In our example, factor 1 associated with an eigenvalue of 2.4298, indicating that the factor accounts for as much variance in the data as would 2.43 variables, on average. Since we are dealing with a 6 variable problem, each variable would account for 16.66% (100% divided by 6 = 16.66%) on average. A 2.4298 eigenvalue factor accounts therefore for 2.4298 × 16.66% or 40.49% of the total variance explained by Factor I.

Now you can see that Factor II has a similar eigenvalue and explains 40.12% of the variance. Since we have now accounted for around 80% of the total variance we can be certain that these two factors are the essential underlying dimensions or factors that explain the differential performance in the two areas of activity. This way of expressing an eigenvalue as percentage of variance extracted is more meaningful than the original eigenvalue. These percentage variances give some idea of the contribution of each factor to total variance. The sum of the eigenvalues is identical to the sum of the communalities.

Naming the factors

We can see that the two factors are like super-variables. The factors represent the clusters detected in the correlation matrix and as we can determine which variables they load on, we could appropriately name factor I '*logical thinking*' and factor II '*physical strength*'. Remember, while it was easy to label these factors, in more complex conditions the naming operation is more difficult and quite subjective, *but generally a* factor should be named on the basis of the variables which contribute the most to that factor (usually variables with loadings greater than 5). Factors are only as good as the variable or item list that produced them, i.e. factors that emerge can only be based on the variables that went in.

Selecting the factors

Most factor analyses will produce a large number of factors. PCA initially produces as many theoretical underlying dimensions as there were original variables. This would not help our cause, which is to explain as much variation as possible in scores across the items (variables) with a few underlying factors.

There are a number of ways to determine how many dimensions to retain for further analysis. We limit the number of factors to those that are important by choosing factors with the largest eigenvalues, as those that are small are measuring little else than error. The simplest method is to choose those dimensions with eigenvalues that are 1 or greater on the basis that a component with an eigenvalue which is less than 1 explains less variance than did an individual item in the original data set. Components with eigenvalues greater than 1 are components which explain more variation than did an original item.

Luckily SPSS produces factors in order of their eigenvalue size working from left to right in the printed out factor table. The selection of factors for interpretation with eigenvalues greater than 1 is known as **Kaiser's rule**.

> ***Kaiser's rule.*** *Only factors having eigenvalues (latent roots) greater than 1 are considered as common factors.*

An alternative method called the **scree test** was suggested by Cattell. In this method, you plot the successive eigenvalues on a graph, and look for a spot where the plot abruptly levels out. Cattell named this test after the tapering 'scree' or rock-pile rubbish at the bottom of a landslide. At the point that the plot begins to level off, the additional factors explain less variance than a single variable, i.e. these factors are factorial scree, inconsequential rubbish, contributing negligibly to the analysis. Therefore, only those factors that occur on and above where the plot levels out are accepted. The dummy scree plot example (Fig. 18.2)

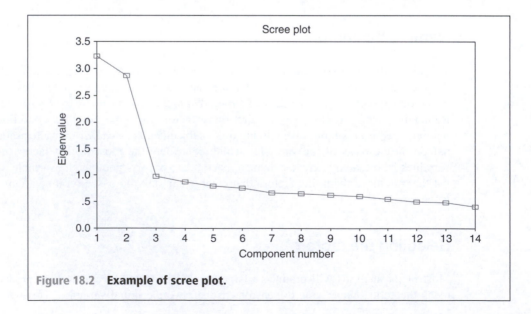

Figure 18.2   Example of scree plot.

suggests that only the first three factors be considered. Some researchers might even eliminate the third one as it is borderline on 1.00 and is very little different in the amount of variance it explains from the subsequent factors that follow.

Rotation

It is usually not easy to identify factors from the initial solution, and rotation is the step in factor analysis that allows you better to identify meaningful factors. By rotating your factors, you attempt to find a factor solution that is equal to that obtained in the initial extraction but which has the simplest interpretation. There are two major categories of rotations, **orthogonal rotations**, which produce uncorrelated factors, and **oblique rotations**, which produce correlated factors. The best and most commonly used orthogonal rotation is **Varimax**. Oblique rotations are less common, with the three most used being **Direct Quartimin**, **Promax**, and **Oblimin**.

Rotation (usually Varimax) increases interpretability by rotating factors so that there is more discrimination between high and low loading variables (high loadings move closer to 1 and low loadings move closer to 0), i.e. maximizing the number of high factor loadings on a factor and minimizing the number of low loadings. The process is called rotation because it involves the rotating of axes on a series of scattergraphs until a more easily interpretable factor structure is obtained (see Fig. 18.4). A Varimax rotation often makes it possible to identify each variable with a single factor.

Imagine in Figure 18.3 the loadings of a test A on the first (F1) and second factors (F2) are 0.58 and 0.74 respectively. These two factors are orthogonal (at right angles). If we put a pin in the origin O and swing the factor axes around to a new position (marked with bold lines) as shown in Figure 18.4, with point A stationary, we obtain new values for the factor loadings which emphasize the differences between the factor loadings. They are now .86 for F1 and .39 for F2 (marked with dotted lines).

This modification does not affect the total common variance of the test which before was $(.58)^2 + (.74)^2 = .8840$ and is now $(.86)^2 + (.39)^2 = .8840$. Rotation has redistributed the common variance and made a sharper distinction between the loadings. If you find rotation

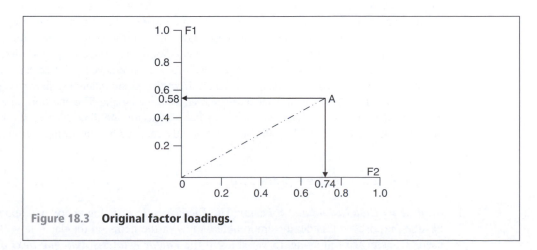

Figure 18.3 **Original factor loadings.**

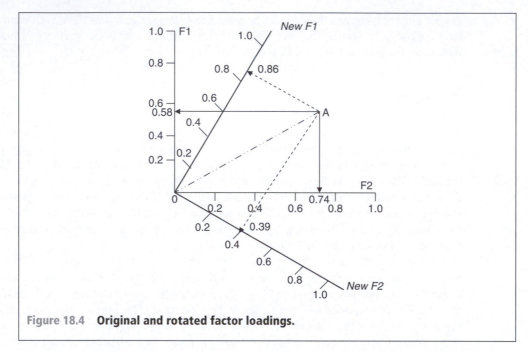

Figure 18.4   Original and rotated factor loadings.

hard to understand, imagine the sort of coordinates used to locate towns on maps. Each town can be uniquely located by two coordinates – latitude and longitude. If we rotate these coordinates of latitude and longitude through, say, 40 degrees, this would mean we have new coordinates to locate our towns with but the relative positions of the towns would not change. Rotation in factor analysis aims to place the coordinates through or as close to as many variables (items) as possible.

SPSS activity – principal component analysis

Select and load SPSS Chapter 18 Data File A from the SPSS web page. This file has data related to a study investigating the reasons why some business faculty students drop out of university. Numerous variables were identified which influence this decision and formed into a questionnaire designed to solicit students' opinions concerning study issues, reasons for attendance, university life, and personal coping on a seven-point scale, where 1 = not important and 7 = very important. The results from the questionnaire are shown on this data set. Only 15 of the questionnaire items will be used for this example. The question we want to answer is 'Does the survey data from these 15 items measure one dimension or several?' The responses may tell us about 15 different things or only one, or any number in between.

Running the factor analysis procedure

1   *Analyse >> Data Reduction >> Factor*. The *Factor Analysis* dialogue box will appear.
2   For the purposes of this demonstration only a few of the items on the data file will be used. Transfer the following 15 variables to the *Factor Analysis dialogue box: q13,*

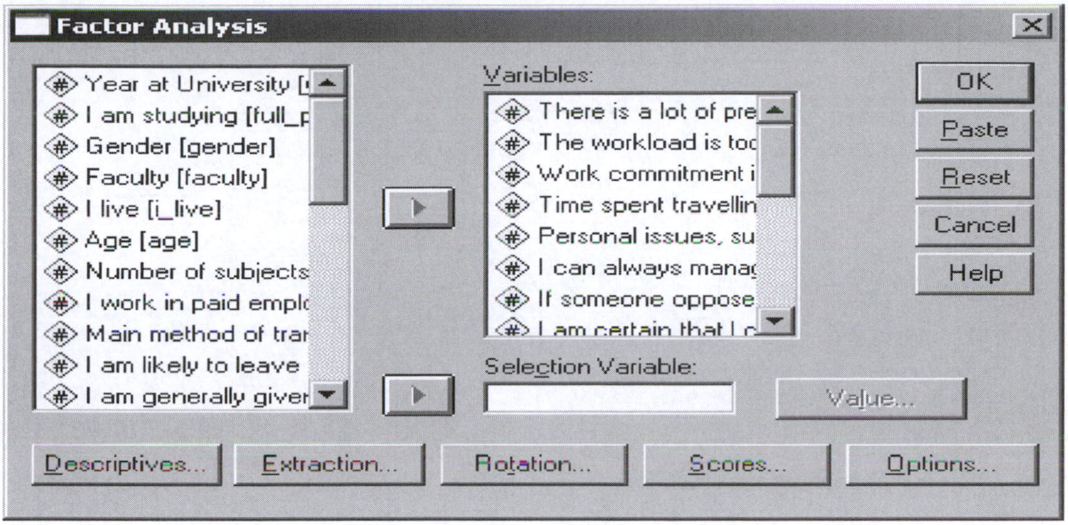

Figure 18.5   Factor analysis dialogue box.

q14, q34, q35, q36, q39 to q48 inclusive. The completed dialogue box is shown in Figure 18.5.

3   Click on the *Descriptives* button and on its dialogue box select the following check boxes: *Univariate Descriptives, Initial Solution, Coefficients, KMO and Bartlett's test of sphericity* (Fig. 18.6).

4   Click on *Continue* to return to the *Factor Analysis* dialogue box. Next click on the *Extraction* button and select the check box for *Scree Plot* (Fig. 18.7).

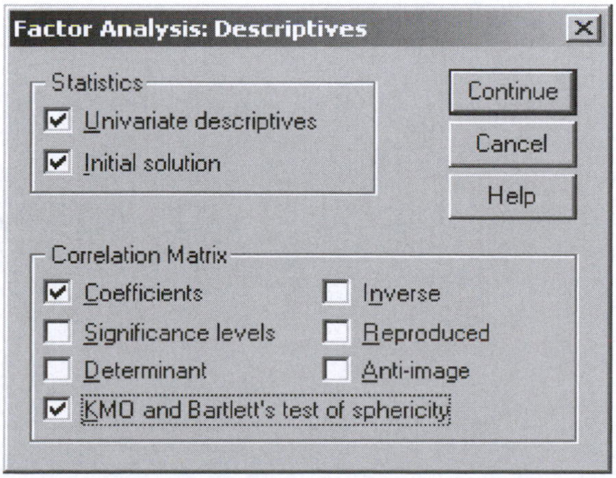

Figure 18.6   Factor analysis descriptives box.

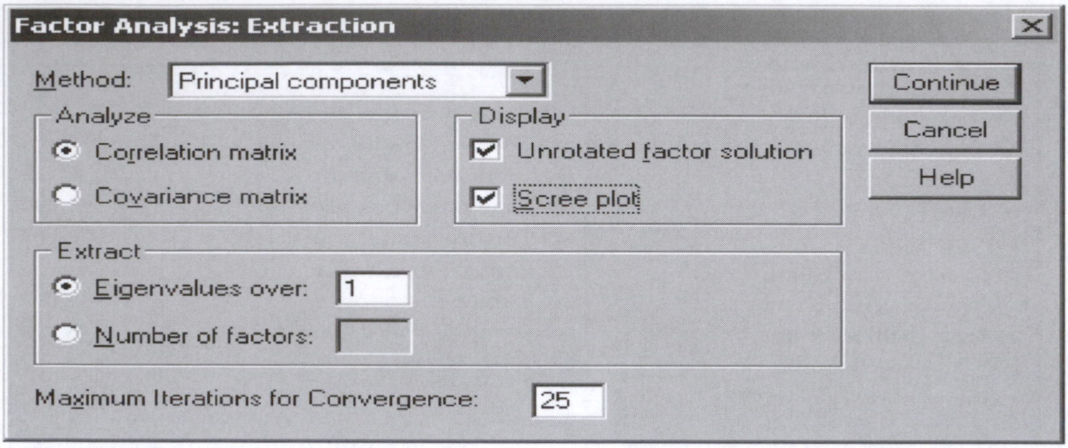

Figure 18.7   Factor analysis extraction box.

5   Click on **Continue** to return to the **Factor Analysis** dialogue box. Click on the **Rotation** button and select the radio button next to **Varimax**. Ensure **Rotated solution** is ticked and at least **25** iterations are shown (Fig. 18.8).

6   Click on **Continue** to return to the **Factor Analysis** dialogue box. Next click on the **Options** button and select the check box of **Suppress absolute values less than**. Type .30 in the text box (Fig. 18.9).

7   Click **Continue** then on **Scores**. If you wish to save each person's factor scores to use in further analyses tick the **Save as variables** check box, retaining **regression** as the default method (Fig. 18.10). This will place the factor scores for each factor as new variables on the *data view screen*.

8   **Continue >> OK** to run the procedure.

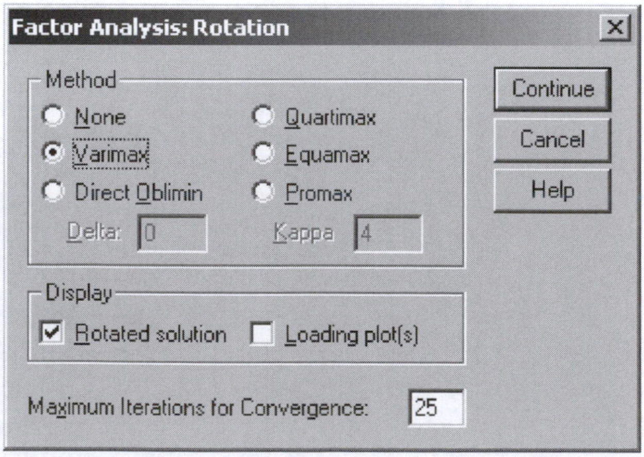

Figure 18.8   Factor analysis rotation box.

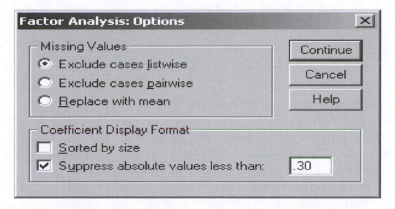

Figure 18.9   **Factor analysis options box.**

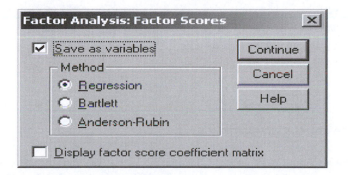

Figure 18.10   **Factor analysis factor scores box.**

Printout and interpretation of the output in Tables 18.4 to 18.9

SPSS produces a large amount of printout material. We will walk you through the many tables one by one.

Descriptive statistics: Table 18.4

The first output from the above analysis is a table of descriptive statistics for all the variables under investigation. Typically, the **mean, standard deviation** and **number of respondents** (N) who participated in the survey are given. Looking at the **means**, one can generally conclude that the personal coping statements were all strongly agreed to and the more specific day-to-day issues were not as strongly agreed to. The standard deviations also suggest that there was more agreement among the respondents over the general coping statements than over the specific issues.

Table 18.4 Descriptive statistics

	Mean	Std. deviation	Analysis N
There is a lot of pressure on me as a student in this degree course	4.46	1.604	113
The workload is too heavy	4.18	1.416	113
Work commitment interferes with my academic performance	3.74	1.995	113
Time spent travelling to uni is excessive	3.58	2.145	113
Personal issues, such as family or friends, adversely affect my uni studies	4.30	1.762	113
I can always manage to solve difficult problems if I try hard enough	5.34	1.131	113
If someone opposes me, I can find the ways and means to get what I want	4.65	1.302	113
I am certain that I can accomplish my goals	5.68	1.120	113
I am confident that I could deal efficiently with unexpected events	5.33	1.137	113
Thanks to my resourcefulness, I can handle unforeseen situations	5.19	1.187	113
I can solve most problems if I invest the necessary effort	5.50	1.196	113
I can remain calm when facing difficulties because I can rely on my coping abilities	4.98	1.363	113
When I am confronted with a problem, I can find several solutions	5.20	1.036	113
If I am in trouble, I can think of a good solution	5.20	1.001	113
I can handle whatever comes my way	5.38	1.291	113

The correlation matrix

The next major output from the analysis is the correlation matrix, which provides the correlation coefficients between every variable in the investigation. The correlation coefficient between a variable and itself is always 1, hence the principal diagonal of the correlation matrix contains '1's. The correlation coefficients above and below the principal diagonal are the same. As the correlation matrix is quite large it is not reproduced here. It is usually large from a factor analytic study and it is impossible to interpret or determine patterns by eye as we did in the simple example earlier in this chapter.

The correlation matrix is examined by eye to see whether the PCA is worth attempting at all. There must be some large correlations present as, if there are no correlations between variables exceeding .30, there is nothing to explain. PCA works by analysing relationships so the matrix must contain them in the first place.

Kaiser-Meyer-Olkin (KMO) and Bartlett's Test Table 18.5

The next valuable item from the output is the Kaiser-Meyer-Olkin (KMO) and Bartlett's test. The KMO measures the sampling adequacy, which should be greater than .5 for a satisfactory factor analysis to proceed. Table 18.5 shows the KMO measure is 0.856 and therefore satisfactory. From the same table, we can see that Bartlett's test is significant. That is, its associated probability is less than .05. This means that the variables do have some correlation to each other, which is what we need if we are trying to find an underlying

Table 18.5   **KMO and Bartlett's test**

Kaiser-Meyer-Olkin Measure of Sampling Adequacy.		.856
Bartlett's Test of Sphericity	Approx. Chi-Square	707.150
	df	105
	Sig.	.000

factor that represents a grouping of variables. Thus again we can proceed with the analysis. If both or one of these indicators is unsatisfactory, it is unwise to continue with the factor analysis.

Communalities (Table 18.6)

The table of communalities (Table 18.6) shows how much of the variance in each variable has been accounted for by the extracted factors. For instance, over 76% of the variance in 'the workload is too heavy' is accounted for, while only 38% of the variance in 'If someone opposes me, I can find the ways and means to get what I want' is accounted for.

Table 18.6   **Communalities**

	Initial	Extraction
There is a lot of pressure on me as a student in this degree course	1.000	.751
The workload is too heavy	1.000	.767
Personal issues, such as family or friends, adversely affect my uni studies	1.000	.353
Time spent travelling to uni is excessive	1.000	.736
Work commitment interferes with my academic performance	1.000	.553
I can always manage to solve difficult problems if I try hard enough	1.000	.494
If someone opposes me, I can find the ways and means to get what I want	1.000	.381
I am certain that I can accomplish my goals	1.000	.564
I am confident that I could deal efficiently with unexpected events	1.000	.713
Thanks to my resourcefulness, I can handle unforeseen situations	1.000	.574
I can solve most problems if I invest the necessary effort	1.000	.534
I can remain calm when facing difficulties because I can rely on my coping abilities	1.000	.568
When I am confronted with a problem, I can find several solutions	1.000	.664
If I am in trouble, I can think of a good solution	1.000	.582
I can handle whatever comes my way	1.000	.547

Extraction Method: Principal Component Analysis.

Total variance explained (Table 18.7)

Table 18.7 shows all the factors extractable from the analysis along with their eigenvalues, the percent of variance attributable to each factor, and the cumulative variance of the factor and the previous factors. Notice that the first factor accounts for 38.11% of the variance, the second 12.53% and the third 7.9%, a total of 58.55% of the total variance. All the remaining factors each control only small amounts of variance and are not significant but between them account for the remaining 41.45%.

Table 18.7   Total variance explained

Component	Initial eigenvalues			Extraction sums of squared loadings			Rotation sums of squared loadings		
	Total	% of Variance	Cumulative %	Total	% of Variance	Cumulative %	Total	% of Variance	Cumulative %
1	5.717	38.111	38.111	5.717	38.111	38.111	5.480	36.532	36.532
2	1.879	12.530	50.641	1.879	12.530	50.641	1.662	11.081	47.613
3	1.186	7.906	58.547	1.186	7.906	58.547	1.640	10.934	58.547
4	.961	6.404	64.951						
5	.863	5.756	70.707						
6	.843	5.618	76.326						
7	.616	4.107	80.432						
8	.498	3.317	83.749						
9	.470	3.130	86.879						
10	.441	2.942	89.822						
11	.396	2.637	92.458						
12	.351	2.340	94.798						
13	.334	2.225	97.023						
14	.255	1.699	98.722						
15	.192	1.278	100.000						

Extraction Method: Principal Component Analysis.

Scree plot

Remember that the scree plot is useful for determining how many factors to retain. The point of interest is where the curve starts to flatten. It can be seen (Fig. 18.11) that the curve begins to flatten between factors 3 and 4. Note also that factor 4 has an eigenvalue of less than 1, so only three factors have been retained. This is consistent with Kaiser's Rule.

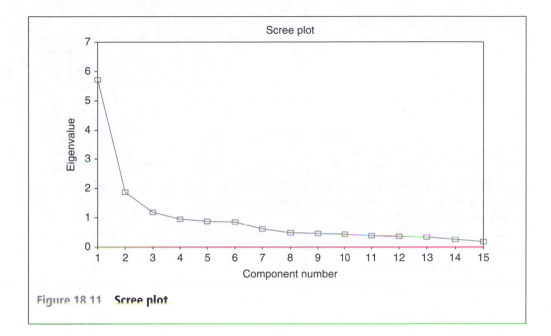

Figure 18.11   **Scree plot**

Component (factor) matrix (Table 18.8)

This table shows the loadings of the 15 variables on the three factors extracted. The higher the absolute value of the loading, the more the factor contributes to the variable. The empty spaces on the table represent loadings that are less than .3, this makes reading the table easier. We suppressed all loadings less than .3. This table produces a reasonably clear factor 1 but the other two factors are less clear with variables loading on both. This is where rotation will help.

Rotated component (factor) matrix Table 18.9

The idea of rotation is to reduce the number of factors on which the variables under investigation have high loadings. Rotation does not actually change anything but makes the interpretation of the analysis easier. Looking at Table 18.9, we can see that the factor loadings are clearer and more differentiated so that three factors stand out. Variables concerned with non-university pressures are substantially loaded on Factor (Component) 3 while academic pressures are substantially loaded on Factor 2. All the remaining variables concerning personal coping beliefs are substantially loaded on Factor 1. These factors can be used as variables for further analysis.

Summary of results

*   The 15 variables were reduced to three major factors using Kaiser's Rule and scree test.
*   These three rotated factors account for 58.55% of the covariance among the variables.

Table 18.8 **Component matrix**[a]

	Component		
	1	2	3
There is a lot of pressure on me as a student in this degree course	−.329	.566	.568
The workload is too heavy	−.373	.599	.518
Personal issues, such as family or friends, adversely affect my uni studies		.456	
Time spent travelling to uni is excessive		.611	−.594
Work commitment interferes with my academic performance		.708	
I can always manage to solve difficult problems if I try hard enough	.701		
If someone opposes me, I can find the ways and means to get what I want	.588		
I am certain that I can accomplish my goals	.744		
I am confident that I could deal efficiently with unexpected events	.838		
Thanks to my resourcefulness, I can handle unforeseen situations	.710		
I can solve most problems if I invest the necessary effort	.725		
I can remain calm when facing difficulties because I can rely on my coping abilities	.733		
When I am confronted with a problem, I can find several solutions	.797		
If I am in trouble, I can think of a good solution	.739		
I can handle whatever comes my way	.730		

Extraction Method: Principal Component Analysis.
[a] 3 components extracted.

Table 18.9 **Rotated component matrix**[a]

	Component		
	1	2	3
There is a lot of pressure on me as a student in this degree course		.849	
The workload is too heavy		.841	
Work commitment interferes with my academic performance			.681
Time spent travelling to uni is excessive			.855
Personal issues, such as family or friends, adversely affect my uni studies			.538
I can always manage to solve difficult problems if I try hard enough	.671		
If someone opposes me, I can find the ways and means to get what I want	.578		
I am certain that I can accomplish my goals	.713		
I am confident that I could deal efficiently with unexpected events	.838		
Thanks to my resourcefulness, I can handle unforeseen situations	.737		
I can solve most problems if I invest the necessary effort	.723		
I can remain calm when facing difficulties because I can rely on my coping abilities	.748		
When I am confronted with a problem, I can find several solutions	.798		
If I am in trouble, I can think of a good solution	.746		
I can handle whatever comes my way	.737		

Extraction Method: Principal Component Analysis. Rotation Method: Varimax with Kaiser Normalization.
[a] Rotation converged in 5 iterations.

- Factor I appears to measure personal coping (36.5% of variance).
- Factor II appears to measure academic workload pressure (11.0% of variance).
- Factor III appears to measure non-university pressures (10.9% of variance).

Computing factor scores

A useful by-product of factor analysis are factor scores. Factor scores are composite measures that can be computed for each subject on each factor. They are standardized measures with a mean = .0 and a standard deviation of 1.0, computed from the factor score coefficient matrix. An orthogonal rotation is necessary if subscale scores are to be used in another analysis such as regression, since it maintains the independence of factors. The factor scores are selected in the **Factor Scores** box on SPSS, which then produces new variables in the data view screen listing the factor scores for each case on the selected factors.

Suppose the 15 variables in this case study were to be used in a multiple regression equation to predict the likelihood of completing the degree course, Instead, the computed factor scores for each of the three factors can be used as the predictor variables as these are not correlated with each other as the initial 15 variables were.

How to write up the results

'*A PCA with subsequent rotation (Varimax) was conducted on 15 items of a questionnaire completed by Business Faculty students concerning selected personal and study problems, and coping ability. Many correlations were in excess of .30 and both the KMO and Bartlett's tests produced criteria that supported the application of PCA. Communalities varied from .751 to .353. Applying Kaiser's Rule and the scree test, three factors were deemed important. Following rotation, factor 1 was loaded on 10 items that reflected general coping ability and accounted for 36.5% of the variance exemplified by the two highest loading items, "I am confident that I could deal efficiently with unexpected events" and "When I am confronted with a problem, I can find several solutions". Factor 2 was loaded on 2 items and accounted for 11% of the variance. It was labelled academic workload pressure and was represented by "There is a lot of pressure on me as a student in this degree course" and "The workload is too heavy". The third factor accounted for 10.9% of the variance and was loaded on 3 items suggesting it was measuring non-university problems, namely, "Work commitment interferes with my academic performance", "Time spent travelling to uni is excessive", and "Personal issues, such as family or friends, adversely affect my uni studies".*

Problems with factor analysis

1   Although it is reasonable to interpret statistical factors as existing qualities which we conveniently label with a name that designates the item content it reflects, such factors are really only evidence of co-variation between a number of variables and their common properties. The big jump from the mathematical answer to naming provides

a superficial aura of objectivity. The naming is quite subjective and reflects a hypothetical concept that cannot be seen or touched, similar to intelligence, consumer confidence, job satisfaction, empathy, etc.

2 Factor analysis can only analyze what is there. The initial choice of tests or items govern the final outcome of the factor structure that emerges.

3 Factor analysis cannot conclusively demonstrate that a particular set of factors is the only valid one. Given alternative orthogonal and oblique solutions as well as rotational solutions, a different structure with another assigned nomenclature can be derived. Different factor analytic methods will provide alternative but mathematically equivalent answers. Several researchers may apply factor analysis to similar or even identical sets of measures, and one may come up with three factors, while another comes up with six and another comes up with 10. This lack of agreement has tended to discredit all uses of factor analysis. But if three travel writers wrote travel guides to Europe and one divided the continent into three regions, another into six, and another into 10, would we say that they contradicted each other? Of course not; the various writers are just using convenient ways of organizing a topic, not claiming to represent the only correct way of doing so. The fewer factors, the simpler the theory; the more factors, the better the theory fits the data. Different workers may make different choices in balancing simplicity against fit.

4 A similar issue arises in identifying the nature of the factors. Two workers may each identify six factors, but the two sets of factors may differ. The travel-writer analogy is useful here too; two writers might each divide Europe into six regions, but each defines a different six regions. When reading a research article using factor analysis, consider carefully whether the name the researcher gives to a factor really does capture the essence of the items, qualities or opinions that load on it.

What you have learned from this chapter

You have seen that factor analysis attempts to identify underlying factors (or dimensions or constructs) that explain patterns of correlations in a set of variables. Factor analysis is often used in data reduction to identify a smaller number of factors that explain most of the variance contained in a much larger set of variables, and to create construct validity for scales.

You have a four-stage sequence to follow in conducting a factor analysis:

- First, descriptives and a correlation matrix are generated for all the variables.
- Second, Principal Components Analysis derives estimates of loadings between each factor and the variables. The loading is a correlation coefficient. A high loading suggests

that the variable represents the factor. The eigenvalue represents the amount of variance accounted for by the factor. The selection of important factors is based on several criteria such as Kaiser's Rule (a minimum eigenvalue of 1) and the scree test.

- Third, the factors are rotated in order to aid interpretation by maximizing the relationship between them and the variables, thus simplifying the factor structure. Orthogonal rotation maintains factor axes at 90 degrees while oblique rotation creates correlated factors.
- Finally, the factors are interpreted. Remember that naming of factors is a subjective act by the researcher and should reflect the variables that load heavily on that factor. Factor analysis will always produce factors so you must retain a 'garbage in garbage out' awareness.

Review questions and activities

Qu. 18.1
A factor is:

(a) a raw score on a test item
(b) a measurement of behavioural activity
(c) a hypothetical entity
(d) a positive correlation

Qu. 18.2
If two measures correlate +.8 what proportion of the variance is shared?

(a) 16%
(b) 1.6%
(c) 64%
(d) +64%

Qu. 18.3
What does the squared factor loading indicate?

(a) What does the eigenvalue explain?
(b) What is the communality?

Qu. 18.4
Why do we usually only retain factors with an eigenvalue of at least 1.00?

Qu. 18.5
What is the purpose of rotation?

Qu. 18.6
Total variance explained

Component	Initial eigenvalues			Rotation sums of squared loadings		
	Total	% of variance	Cumulative %	Total	% of variance	Cumulative %
1	6.824	56.660	56.660	6.710	55.693	55.693
2	2.879	23.890	80.550	2.990	24.906	80.599
3	1.134	9.446	89.996	1.128	9.397	89.996
4	.961					
5	.863					
6	.843					
7	.616					
8	.498					
9	.410					
10	.341					
11	.296					
12	.251					

Extraction Method: Principal Component Analysis.

Using the table above, answer the following questions:

(a) How many variables were there in this analysis?
(b) How many components have an eigenvalue above 1.00?
(c) How much variance has been accounted for in a three factor solution?

Qu. 18.7
In order to name factors that have been extracted researchers should look at:

(a) table of eigenvalues
(b) table of unrotated factor loadings
(c) table of rotated factor loadings
(d) previous research

Check your answers to the items above in the chapter material.

SPSS Activity

Access data file SPSS Chapter 18 data file B on the Web site and conduct a factor analysis on the data from the questionnaire. It consists of 12 5-point scale items focused on self-assessment of management behaviour. Write an interpretation of your printout like the one in the text above and discuss the results in class.

Now access the Web page for Chapter 18 and answer the questions and the SPSS activity there.

Part 4
Survey Methods for Research in Business and Management

Chapter 19
Attitude Questionnaires and Measurement

'There is no limit to the topics about which people may have attitudes ... It would be possible to argue persuasively that in the final analysis everything in life depends on people's attitudes'

(A. N. Oppenheim)

Content list

By the end of this chapter you will understand:

1. What an attitude is and how attitudes are measured.
2. The Thurstone techniques of attitude measurement.
3. The Likert method of attitude measurement.
4. The Semantic Differential method.
5. The Rep Grid approach.
6. Reliability and validity problems of attitude scales.

Introduction

Attitudes have been a key concept in explaining and understanding human behaviour for more than a century. The attitude scale has therefore become a major technique for obtaining data for use in management and business and has been used in many situations. For example, it is of particular value for assessing consumer perspectives and preferences with regard to existing products, new products, packaging, and advertising. It is also important as a way of investigating employee perspectives in the workplace, etc.

What is an attitude?

Like many concepts in social science, an attitude is an abstraction that has no single absolute and correct meaning or definition. Our simple definition is:

A learned predisposition to respond in a consistently favourable or unfavourable way to some aspect of the individual's environment.

In other words, attitudes are beliefs which predispose the individual to respond **positively or negatively to some social object**. This definition states or implies the following three major components:

1 **The belief component**. The belief component involves what a person believes about the object, whether true or not. For example, we may believe that the local supermarket is expensive, has a wide range of stock, has polite courteous staff, has only limited car-parking. Some of these need not be true; their importance lies in the fact they exist in our thoughts and thereby influence our behaviour. Cognitive beliefs are the product of experience, expectation, learning, information, conditioning or irrational prejudice.

2 **The affective component**. The affective or emotional component embodies the person's evaluative positive or negative feelings about the belief. For example, '*I am pleased that the local supermarket has polite and courteous staff; I dislike the limited car parking*'. The consumer who says, '*I like X brand*'; or '*I hate the voice of the person who does the Y ads*' is expressing evaluative beliefs about an object which will influence purchasing behaviour. All cognitive beliefs are evaluative to some degree or other. Even seemingly neutral beliefs like '*the staff are courteous here*' or '*Zippy computers are reliable*' involve an evaluation (in these cases positive ones). The evaluation of a belief can change according to circumstance and mood. If you believe that coffee has a lot of caffeine and that caffeine keeps you alert then you are positively disposed towards it when taking a long drive across the country. You will be less than positive towards it when choosing a drink at bedtime when you want to have a good sleep.

3 **The behavioural component**. This component embodies a tendency to behave in a certain way. '*I will only shop at the local supermarket at times when the shop is not crowded so that I can park.*' '*I only shop at the local supermarket when I am in a rush to get a meal and have run out of an essential item because it is more expensive there.*' This behavioural tendency does not mean that a certain behaviour will occur but that it is **likely** to occur if conditions are right and the opportunity presents itself. Therefore the behavioural component can often be a rather unreliable indication of an attitude.

Attitudes are vitally important to business and commerce for the simple reason that a *consumer with a positive attitude towards a product or service is more likely to buy that product/service.* Attitudes are the crucial link between what consumers think about a product, service, company, supermarket, or advertisements and where and what they buy in the marketplace.

Every year, marketing managers spend large amounts of money researching consumers' attitudes towards products and brands, and millions more attempting to influence (usually strengthen or change) attitudes through advertisements, sales promotions, and other types of persuasion. The attitudes, beliefs and values held by individuals have a direct influence on their purchasing decisions, and these decisions, in turn, may reinforce or strengthen a particular attitude or lead to its modification (Fig. 19.1).

Similarly, an employee with a positive attitude towards their job, or career, or company vision will likely prove to be a more productive, motivated and reliable employee than one harbouring negative attitudes.

An understanding of the way in which consumer attitudes can be measured is therefore of prime importance to the market. If the organization is able to identify the attitudes held by different market segments towards a product or service and also to measure changes in those attitudes, they will be well placed to plan an effective marketing strategy. Attitude research can also provide a useful basis for the identification of new product opportunities and forecasting changes in the pattern of purchasing behaviour. Similarly, measurement of employee attitudes that leads to understanding of what motivates employees, is a valuable tool in enhancing productivity and commitment.

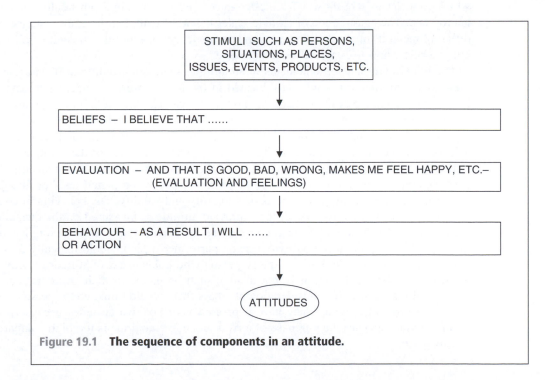

Figure 19.1   The sequence of components in an attitude.

Attitude measurement

Measuring and understanding consumer and employee attitudes allows businesses to maximize their productive potential, but since attitudes are hypothetical concepts they are not directly observable, and their strength and direction can only be inferred from what people say and do. The only way to uncover a person's attitudes is to ask them in an interview or survey, or by completion of an attitude scale. Some attempt at quantification of attitudes is necessary if we are to compare individuals and groups, and also to chart behavioural changes in individuals to determine what factors, processes and procedures best promote attitude change. But it is important to remember that attitude measurement is essentially based on subjective self-report and therefore fraught with problems of reliability and validity.

The most widely used approach to attitude measurement has been the application of standardized questionnaires, which can be completed either by the person themselves or which can be part of an interview/survey approach when the interviewer will ask questions and record the responses. An attitude scale usually consists of sets of statements or words relating to an attitude item. They are usually concerned with measuring the degree of positive or negative feeling (evaluation), that is, degree of favourability, towards the person, object or event. The best-known rating scale techniques are described below.

Despite the existence of many reliable and valid published attitude scales, the business researcher often finds that they wish to assess attitudes to a specific object or event for which no scales exist or for which scales produced and validated in another culture are not appropriate. The construction of attitude scales is not difficult, but there are a number of differing methods of construction, of response mode and of score interpretation. We will tell you below how to establish an attitude scale.

The individual items of statements in an attitude scale are usually not of interest in themselves; the interest is normally located in the total score or sub-scores to sets of items grouped on the basis of factor analysis or Cronbach alpha reliability. An attitude scale usually consists of statements, i.e. the belief components of the theoretical attitude. These statements could therefore all be preceded by '*I believe that* .....' and are rated on a 3, 5, 7 (or even more) point scale. This rating provides an index of the emotive value of the affective component of each statement. Of course, the third element of an attitude, the behavioural act, is not assessed by this form of paper and pencil test but through observation, which again poses issues of reliability and validity. The behavioural component may not be congruent with the expressed attitude as measured on the questionnaire, since other factors like social convention, social constraints, expectation, lack of money, etc. may prevent the behaviour being performed which should logically follow from holding the attitude. For example, a person who holds negative attitudes to ethnic groups other than their own may not display such prejudice in their overt behaviour because of fear of the law, consideration of what others would think, etc. A person may not buy a product to which they have expressed very positive attitudes because peer group pressure dictates the purchase of a rival brand, or the price is too high compared to competitors.

Methods of attitude scale construction

The following section briefly outlines the major types of attitude scales and their construction.

A. Differential scales (Thurstone type)

The method Thurstone and Chave (1929) devised represents attempts to facilitate interval scale measurement.

Step 1

The approach commences with the researcher's selection of a large number of evaluatively tinged statements about a particular object or topic, such as those listed below concerning accountancy as a career. These items are usually selected from a much larger collection gleaned from newspapers, texts, conversations, and direct questioning of people who have relevant experience or knowledge. The initial array of statements may come from any source, so long as they cover a full range of attitudes of extremely favourable to extremely unfavourable towards the object/topic in question, are brief, simple, unambiguous, and capable of distinguishing across the range of different attitudes that people may hold towards the issue.

Example of Thurstone type attitude items
Attitudes towards accountancy as a career

1   Accounting is merely a routine job.
2   Accounting requires more intelligence than other professions.
3   Accounting is a dull boring job.
4   Accountants are the nation's leaders.
5   Accounting is a lazy man's job.
6   The importance of accounting is overestimated.
7   Accounting offers few avenues for advancement.
8   Accounting furnishes a chance for self-expression.
9   Accounting has more influence on a nation than any other profession.
10   Accounting is a rewarding job.

Step 2

The next step is to ask a number of individuals to judge the degree to which each statement expresses a positive or negative attitude towards the object on an 11-point scale. Thurstone originally used several hundred judges in developing each attitude scale, but a much smaller number is adequate, as long as they have some knowledge of the attitude object and are themselves not heavily biased either for or against it.

Each statement is presented on a small card and each judge's task is essentially to sort out the small cards into 11 piles so that they seem to be fairly evenly spaced or graded. Only the two ends and the middle pile are labelled. The middle pile is indicated for neutral opinions. One end is for belief statements about the topic that are judged strongly positive; the other end for those judged strongly negative. The 11 piles then represent a scale from an extremely favourable attitude towards the issue to an extremely unfavourable attitude towards it. The judges are asked not to express their own attitudes, but to be as objective as possible in indicating the extent to which the statement is favourable or unfavourable towards the issue in question.

Step 3

After all judges have sorted the statements into the positions on the 11-point scale a calculation is made of the median score for each item (the position on the 11-point scale which equally divides the judges, with half ranking the item above that point and half below). This median score is subsequently used as the scale value for that item. Calculations are also made as to how ambiguous each item is. This is measured by how widely judgements of the item are spread out across the entire scale. Good items should have a small range; those high in ambiguity will tend to have a wide spread and are discarded.

Step 4

The scale values indicate the degree to which it represents a favourable or unfavourable attitude. A limited number of statements, possibly 20, that show good agreement among the judges and whose scale values assigned by judges have approximately equal intervals between them, which cover the full range of the 11-point scale are then chosen to form the attitude scale.

The questionnaire can now be given to any group of subjects whose attitudes are to be measured, with the instructions that they indicate the three items with which they most strongly agree. An individual's score on the questionnaire is the average (mean) scale score on all the items with which they agree. The scale values, of course, are not shown on the questionnaire, and the items are listed in random order, not in order of their scale value.

In examining attitudes to the Savemor supermarket chain, the attitude scale of 12 items may contain the following items with their scale values.

Scale value statement

0.5 I believe Savemor provides the best value of any supermarket chain in the country.
2.4 I believe Savemor has the consumers' needs at heart.
5.2 I believe Savemor is as good as any other supermarket.
8.7 I believe Savemor sacrifices quality for cheapness.
10.3 I believe Savemor should be boycotted because of its policy towards unionization.

The scale values represent the degree of positive or negative attitudes to the supermarket chain, 1 being the most favourable, 11 being the least favourable, and 6 being neutral. Thus, an individual agreeing with statements scoring an average of 4.2 could be described as holding an attitude slightly favourable to the supermarket, and one with an average of 9.1 as being unfavourably disposed.

An obvious criticism of Thurstone's scales is that the subjects are normally asked to endorse only a small number of items. For this reason, Thurstone's scales need to be longer than Likert's scales to obtain the same reliability. Although many survey researchers will use means, t tests, ANOVA's and other parametric tests to evaluate differences between groups of people in their attitudes, there is no guarantee that the scale values are equal interval data.

Another problem is that the construction of a Thurstone scale is cumbersome and time-consuming; and though its results have been shown to be reliable, the technique is no longer in wide use. The Thurstone scale has the advantage that statements are ascribed numerical values based on the agreement of judges prior to the actual use of the scale. They are based, therefore, on the social perceptions of the society in which the testing occurs.

B. The Likert scale

Soon after Thurstone's first scales were published, Likert (1932) proposed a simpler method of attitude measurement. The procedure involves the researcher selecting a set of attitude statements, again derived from sources such as newspapers, conversations, etc. Subjects are then asked to what extent they agree or disagree with each statement by choosing one of five categories: *Strongly Agree; Agree; Neutral/Don't Know; Disagree; and Strongly Disagree*. Some attitude scales have more and others less than five categories though five is the most common.

No judges are used to rank the scale statements. Respondents answer all items. It is assumed that all subjects will perceive 'strongly agree' as being more favourable towards the attitude statement than 'moderately agree' and 'strongly disagree'. A subject's score is calculated by assigning a numerical value to each of the answers, ranging from 1 for the alternative at one end of the scale to 5 (or whatever the total number of possible choices is) for the alternative at the other, and then summing the numerical values of the answers to all questions to produce a total score.

Items are placed in the scale at random and may be positive or negative towards the topic. Scoring is then reversed for the negative topics so that scoring is always in the same direction. Thus a high overall score can be interpreted as a positive attitude to a topic and a low overall score as a negative attitude. It must be realized, however, that the same overall score can be obtained from different patterns of responses. Again, as with the Thurstone scale, the Likert technique cannot produce equal intervals and, thus, a score of 4 does not represent an attitude twice that of a score of 2. Thus non-parametric analysis should be applied, although most researchers using large samples will apply parametric statistics that really require interval data.

Example items of a Likert scale

'We are interested in your feelings about the following statements. Read each statement carefully and decide how you feel about it. Please respond to each item whether or not you have had direct experience with a trade union'.

- *If you strongly agree (SA), circle I*
- *If you agree (A), circle 2*
- *If you are undecided or uncertain, (?) circle 3*
- *If you disagree (D), circle 4*
- *If you strongly disagree (SD), circle 5*

		SA	A	?	D	SD
1*	*Trade unions hold back progress.*	1	2	3	4	5
2	*1 regard my union subscription as a good investment.*	1	2	3	4	5
3	*Every employee should be compelled by law to join their union.*	1	2	3	4	5

*Reverse scoring on this item, so that all items marked favourably towards trade unions will be scored in the same direction. Items worded in a reverse direction are placed at random to stop people filling in the scale carelessly by going down in one column. This is known as a response set. Forcing people to read and judge the statements carefully by randomly changing the direction of favourability increases reliability and validity.

Two additional steps are recommended in questionnaire development to ensure reliability and validity are acceptable:

- Reliability: The initial set of items should be piloted on a sample of subjects similar to those to be studied later, with Cronbach Alpha (Chapter 17) or factor analysis (Chapter 18) conducted on their responses. There may be subsets of items within the questionnaire that can be identified by the Cronbach Alpha method that permit the measurement of separate aspects of the overall attitude. The major criterion is that the items 'hold together' and produce high internal reliability, and where it has been possible to retest, a high test retest reliability for the whole questionnaire and any identified subsets should be obtained.
- Validity: The presentation of the revised questionnaire should be presented to another two groups known to differ on the attitude being measured. There should be a significant difference in means (using a t test or ANOVA) between the two groups if the attitude scale is really measuring that attitude. This is a measure of its concurrent and predictive validities. Factor analysis can be used to assess construct validity. However, the Cronbach Alpha process of assessing internal reliability is in a sense demonstrating construct validity when it shows items all loaded together as one coherent scale or groups of items clumped together measuring different aspects.

The result is a revised questionnaire that more precisely measures the attitude.

(a) Advantages of Likert method

These include:

 (i) greater ease of preparation than the Thurstone technique;
 (ii) the method is based entirely on empirical data regarding subject's responses rather than subjective opinions of judges; and
 (iii) this method produces more homogeneous scales and increases the probability that a unitary attitude is being measured, increasing validity (construct and concurrent) and reliability.

   As a result, most attitude researchers have relied on some version of the more efficient and easier to construct Likert scaling procedure to measure attitudes.

(b) Disadvantages of Likert scales

These include:

 (i) The Likert-type scale does not claim to be more than an ordinal scale, i.e. it makes possible the ranking of individuals in terms of the favourableness of their attitude toward a given object, but it does not provide a basis for saying *how much more favourable* one is than another. Whether this constitutes a disadvantage of the Likert scale in comparison with the Thurstone scale depends on one's judgement of whether Thurstone scales really meet the criteria for interval scales! Many attitude investigators do assume Likert scales to provide interval data, particularly if their sample is large and randomly selected.
 (ii) The total score of an individual has little clear meaning, since many patterns of response to the various items may produce the same score. We have already noted that Thurstone-type scales are also subject to this criticism, but it applies even more strongly to the Likert scales, since they provide a greater number of response possibilities and combinations.
 (iii) The midpoint suffers from problems of definition. Should we name it 'don't know' or 'no opinion' or 'neutral', etc. All these have slightly different meanings. We return to this issue in the next chapter.

C. The semantic differential

The semantic differential is based on research conducted by Osgood and several collaborators, who were concerned with the 'measurement of meaning' (Osgood *et al.*, 1957). Osgood asked thousands of people to rate an array of objects or concepts in terms of many different attributes, then compared these ratings through factor analysis to locate the major dimensions or factors underlying the data. The semantic differential requires a list of bipolar scales with usually seven rating points lying between each end of the scale. They are termed bipolar since each end of the scale is denoted by the antonym of the other end.

Thus it is common to use adjectives like '*happy-sad*' to characterize the opposite poles of the scale. It is also popular to use descriptive phrases such as 'staff are courteous – staff are not courteous' as end points if for example it was an attitude scale assessing attitudes towards a supermarket chain.

Factor analysis of the ratings given by respondents to the bipolar scales generally produces three major rating factors (i.e. three main dimensions of judgement):

- an **evaluative** factor, in which the object or concept is rated on a good–bad dimension or something similar, such as kind-to-cruel;
- a **potency** factor, involving ratings of strong-to-weak or such related qualities as hard-to-soft; and
- an **activity** factor, where the main concern is active-to-passive, but also includes such qualities as fast-to-slow and hot-to-cold.

The evaluative factor represents the most important of these judgemental dimensions, according to Osgood's statistical analyses. It also happens to be the dimension that most other kinds of attitude scales utilize, as you can see from our examples of Thurstone and Likert scales; and it is the dimension that many definitions of attitude stress as being the key distinction between an attitude and a simple belief. Scales which are loaded on the evaluative dimension are, for instance: *good-bad, successful-unsuccessful, beautiful-ugly, cruel-kind, clean-dirty, wise-foolish, honest-dishonest, happy-sad, nice-awful*. The same set of scales can be used to rate a variety of different objects (persons, items, events, etc, so that it is possible to make direct comparisons among a person's attitudes towards smoking, towards politicians, particular products or towards any other set of items whose attitude ratings the researcher is interested in comparing. Different concepts may require slightly different sets of scales for maximum rating precision; 'kind-cruel', for example, would probably not work as well as 'beautiful-ugly' in measuring attitudes toward modern painting, while we would tend not to use 'beautiful-ugly' when rating a political leader although 'kind-cruel' might well be a relevant dimension to include. Azjen and Fishbein (1980) use the semantic differential as a means of measuring different parts of an attitude in their theory of reasoned action about consumer behaviour.

The reliability and validity of the semantic differential is well documented. A typical layout and instructions for the semantic differential techniques is as follows.

Semantic differential scale

'The purpose of this study is to measure the meanings which certain concepts have for you. This is done by having you judge them against a set of descriptive scales which consist of adjectives and their opposites. You are asked to make your judgements on the basis of what these things mean to you. On each page of this booklet, you will find a different concept to be judged and beneath it a set of scales. You are asked to rate the concept on each of the scales in order'.

Important

1   *Place a circle round the figure that represents your opinion for that scale.*
2   *Be sure you check every scale for every concept; do not omit any.*
3   *Never put more than one circle on a single scale.*

4   *Do not look back and forth through the items. Do not try to remember how you checked similar items earlier in the test. Make each item a separate and independent judgement.*
5   *Work fairly quickly through the items.*
6   *Do not worry or puzzle over individual items. It is your first impression, the immediate 'feelings' about the items that is wanted. On the other hand, do not be careless, for it is your true impression that is wanted.*

Concept to be rated (e.g. Company A, or TV programme or a well-known model of car)

	+3	+2	+1	0	-1	-2	-3	
Good		X						Bad
Modern								Old fashioned
Unknown					X			Known
Responsible	X							Irresponsible
Unimportant				X				Important
Reliable								Unreliable
Exciting								Dull
Unpopular								Popular
Significant								Insignificant
Expensive								Cheap

In this example respondents are asked to show the degree to which they feel the bipolar adjectival scales best describe company A (or product B, etc.) by placing a cross on each line. The result can be expressed as a profile and then compared with other competitors. How the public perceive a product or organization influences what they will buy, how much they trust it, etc and advertising campaigns can be structured around such attitudes. The scoring in the example above runs from +3 to –3 but other surveys often use 7 through to 1.

The particular scales included are those the investigator wishes to include – usually on the grounds of relevance to the attitude under investigation. To prevent the acquiescence response set (always agreeing to positive aspects), scale polarity is reversed for scales at random, and for these the scoring is reversed. In the example above, in order for a high to represent positive attitudes to the product, the scoring on unpopular–popular for example has to be reversed. For individuals, a total score reflecting level of self-evaluation can be obtained on the dubious assumption – as with most other instruments – that all items are equal in their contribution and that the data are interval. With groups, such totals would be averaged, or an average response computed for each of the dimensions, or an average response could be computed for each scale and comparisons made between total scores, dimension scores and individual scales between groups based on some independent variable such as age, income or gender.

Using Osgood's Semantic Differential, it is possible to compare competing brands of the same product or compare consumers' evaluation of a product with their mythical ideal product. The closer the ideal to the real then the product is meeting what the consumers desire. For example, in comparing two products or a real with an ideal the layout would look something like that shown in Figure 19.3. Of course there would be far more attributes measured in a survey than four.

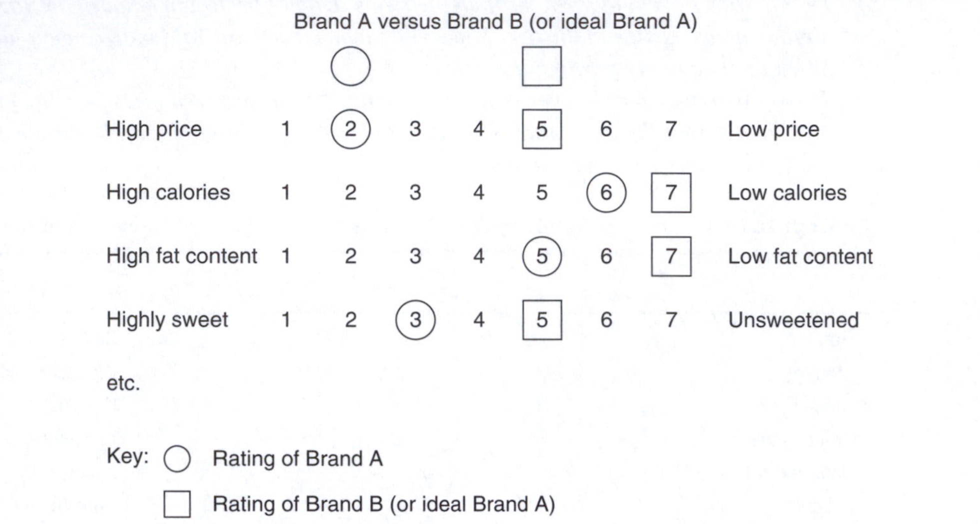

Figure 19.2 **Using the semantic differential to assess attitudes to two products.**

	Brand A	Brand B (or ideal)
Price	2	5
Calories	6	7
Fat	5	7
Sweetness	3	5
Total	16	24

This small comparison (Fig. 19.2) suggests that this particular consumer would purchase Brand B rather than A or demonstrates that their ideal is somewhat different from the existing characteristics of brand A. These comparisons could be group comparisons using variables like age group, income group, gender. Another way of visually depicting the results from a semantic differential is to produce a profile using means. This is illustrated in Figure 19.3.

Advantages

(a) In most uses of the Thurstone and Likert techniques, measurement of an attitude's affective aspects is stressed, though cognitive qualities are often intermingled with the affective judgement. The semantic differential allows these aspects to be separated. The individual's beliefs about an object's potency, activity, and at times other less important dimensions of meaning, may also be crucial to their overall attitude, determining whether their behaviour toward an object is similar to or very different from the

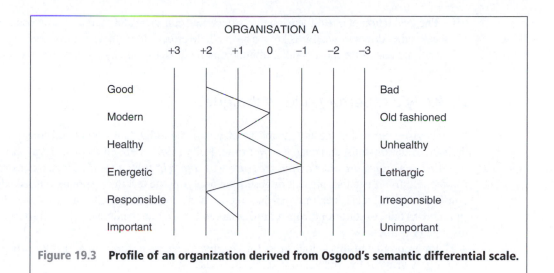

Figure 19.3 **Profile of an organization derived from Osgood's semantic differential scale.**

behaviour of other individuals whose evaluative ratings resemble their own. As an example, one subject might rate the concept MY DEPARTMENT MANAGER as *unfavourable, strong and active*; another subject might rate MY DEPARTMENT MANAGER as equally *unfavourable*, but also *as weak and passive*. The first subject might regard the manager as someone to obey and follow; the second might ignore or attempt to exploit their manager.

(b)   A semantic differential is relatively easy to construct. Bi-polar adjective or adjective phrases are chosen as items on the basis of relevance. Test retest reliabilities can be obtained from testing a pilot group twice. A factor analysis is required if separate dimensions within the overall set of scales are to be identified.

Disadvantages

(a)   The assumption of equal interval data may not be sound, and, like the Likert approach, ordinal data is certainly a more valid assumption.

(b)   Scales weighted heavily on the evaluative dimension for one concept may not be strongly evaluative when applied to another concept. It would seem necessary for a factor analysis to be undertaken to ensure that presumed evaluative scales actually do index the evaluative dimension when referring to a particular attitude object. The marker scale 'good-bad', which is consistently evaluative, will help identify the other evaluative scales.

(c)   Different semantic meanings may be attached to an adjective; 'fast', for example, may mean 50 m.p.h. to one person and 150 m.p.h. to another. So too obviously 'cheap' and 'useful', etc.

(d) The evaluation of one dimension may affect how you view and therefore how you evaluate other dimensions; this is known as the 'halo effect'. Nonetheless, the technique has become one of the most popular attitude scaling devices used by market researchers.

D. Kelly's repertory grid technique

Kelly devised this technique as a means of 'mapping' the individual's 'personal constructs', their interrelationships, and changes over time. Kelly (1955) defined a construct as '*a way in which two things are alike and in the same way different from a third*'. Thus, a construct is a dichotomy; it is either present or absent. In applying the test the respondent is asked to consider three objects, persons, products, etc., and to say in which way two are alike (marked A) but also different from a third (marked D). The respondent can be left to supply his own constructs.

Having completed this initial task, further items can be introduced and the third grid built up. A grid for five brands of beer might be as shown in Figure 19.4.

Constructs	Brand A	Brand B	Brand C	Brand D	Brand E
Strong	A		A	D	
Man's drink	A		A		D
Reasonably priced	A	A			D
Real ale	A	D	A		
Good taste	A		A		D
Artificial taste		A		D	A
Good colour	A		A		D

Figure 19.4   Repertory grid for brands of beer.

Figure 19.4 reveals that Brand A is seen very positively and is a competitor to Brand C though C is more pricey. Brand E is negatively evaluated with poor taste, poor colour, pricey, and not a man's drink. If the same grid is applied to a number of respondents the results, when analysed, can be an invaluable indicator of brand positioning. Successive applications over time can be used to study changes in attitudes as a result of advertising or sales promotion. The Repertory grid is a very powerful tool in that it indicates individuals' subjective perceptions and has a great advantage in its flexibility since it can be used for various types of investigation.

The reliability and validity of attitude scales

The reliability of attitude scales. This is usually assessed via the test-retest method. It would be impossible to split a Likert attitude scale or a semantic differential into two

Alpha coefficient range	Strength of association
<.6	Poor
.6 to <.7	Moderate
.7 to <.8	Good
.8 to <.9	Very good
.9	Excellent

Figure 19.5   Rules of thumb for Cronbach's Alpha.

comparable halves for a split half reliability. It would be feasible but difficult in a Thurstone scale, provided items of the same scale value were included in each half. This would be akin to parallel forms of the scale. Measures of internal consistency are usually used with Likert scales by applying Cronbach Alpha analysis (Chapter 17 with SPSS activity). An item score that is not related to the whole scale may well be measuring some other attitude. Acceptable levels of Cronbach Alpha for attitude scales is 0.7 and above (Fig. 19.5). Refer to Chapter 17 if you need to revise Cronbach Alpha and how to perform one using SPSS.

The validity of attitude scales. This is often checked by concurrent validity using known criterion groups, i.e. sets of individuals who are known in advance to hold different attitudes to the relevant object. For example, random samples of employees who smoke and do not smoke could act as criterion groups for the concurrent validation of an attitude scale towards the banning of smoking in the workplace. If the scale differentiated statistically significantly between these two groups, then it could be said to have concurrent validity.

Predictive validity is also possible by selecting some criterion in the future such as product purchasing behaviour – does the person with the favourable attitude buy the product while the person with the negative attitude does not? Content validity can be gauged by requesting judges to indicate whether the items are relevant to the assessment of that particular attitude. Finally, of course, construct validity using factor analysis of the intercorrelations of item responses will demonstrate homogeneity or heterogeneity of Likert and semantic differential scales. Many attitude scales are multifactorial or multi-dimensional in that they do not measure one unitary attitude but groups of items, each measuring different dimensions of the attitude. For example, a 40 item *Attitude Scale to Your Organization* after analysis by Cronbach Alpha could be split into four separate sub-groups of 10 items each that cluster together strongly, such as *attitudes to the management, to the working conditions, to peer group relationships* and to *training and advancement opportunities.*

In terms of face validity the statements are often fairly obviously related to the attitude object in question. It is extremely difficult to disguise the purpose of the scale in most cases. This of course makes it easy for individuals, deliberately or unconsciously, to bias responses in the direction they think will best suit their own purposes.

General criticisms of attitude scales

The chief criticism that might be levelled at all attitude scales is concerned with the indirectness of measurement, i.e. verbal statements are used as a basis for inferences about 'real' attitudes. Moreover, attitude scales can be easily faked. Although administering the scales anonymously may increase the validity of results, anonymity makes it difficult to correlate the findings with related data about the individuals, unless such data are obtained at the same time. It seems that we must limit our inferences from attitude-scale scores, recognizing that such scores merely summarize the verbalized attitudes that the subjects are willing to express in a specific test situation at a specific time.

Attitude scales are self-report measures and they suffer from the same problems as all other self-report techniques. What a subject is willing to reveal about themselves would seem to depend on such factors as willingness to cooperate, social expectancy, feelings of personal adequacy, feelings of freedom from threat, dishonesty, carelessness, ulterior motivation, interpretation of verbal stimuli, etc. The study of human emotions, feelings and values about objects in the environment is clouded by those very same variables.

Response sets too, such as acquiescence (the tendency to agree with items irrespective of their content) and social desirability (the tendency to agree to statements which social consensus would, it is believed, indicate those that are socially desirable and reject those that are socially undesirable) fog the data derived from attitude scales. The best way of eliminating acquiescence is to order positive and negative items randomly to prevent a subject ticking madly away down the same column.

What you have learned from this chapter

You are now aware of the importance of individual attitudes on behaviour. An attitude predisposes an individual to behave in a certain way towards a person or object, but the relationship between attitudes and behaviour is not always strong as attitude is not the sole determining factor in behaviour. Attitudes are hypothetical constructs that have three main components: belief, affect, and behaviour.

Attitude measurement techniques usually concentrate on determining the affective component of attitude. You have been shown how to construct some of the best known attitude measuring techniques such as the Thurstone scale, Likert scale, Osgood's semantic differential scale, and Kelly's repertory grid.

Whilst showing good internal reliability, the question of their validity is open to doubt. They may often have low re-test reliability and low validity as they are self-report measures and subjects may *inter alia* lie, give socially acceptable answers and misinterpret verbal statements.

Review questions and activities

Qu. 19.1
Briefly explain within your group how this sequence works. Make up some examples.
BELIEF (true or untrue) $\longrightarrow$ EVALUATION (+ve/-ve) $\longrightarrow$ RESPONSE

Qu. 19.2
Discuss in your groups what types of reliability and validity pose problems in the assessment of attitude and why they do so.

References

Ajzen, I. & Fishbein, M. 1980. *Understanding Attitudes and Predicting Social Behaviour*. Englewood Cliffs: Prentice-Hall.

Kelly, G.A. 1955. *The Psychology of Personal Constructs*. New York: W W Norton.

Likert, R. 1932. A technique for the measurement of attitudes, *Archives of Psychology, 140*.

Osgood, C.E., Suci, G.J. & Tannenbaum, P.H. 1957. *The Measurement of Meaning*. Urbana, Illinois: University of Illinois Press.

Thurstone, L.L. & Chave, E.J. 1929. *The Measurement of Attitudes*. Chicago: University of Chicago Press.

Additional reading

Bearden, W. & Netemeyer, R. 1998. *Handbook of Marketing Scales* (2nd edn). Sage Publications: Thousand Oaks, California. This is a useful compendium of attitude scales.

Bruner, G. 1993. *Marketing Scales Handbook*. American Marketing Association: Chicago. Six hundred scales are included covering main areas of consumer behaviour, advertising and sales.

Peterson, R. 2000. *Constructing Effective Questionnaires*. Sage Publications: Thousand Oaks, California. This text provides very detailed instructions on attitude measurement techniques.

Price, J.L. 1997. *Handbook of Organisational Measurement*. www.mcb.co.uk. This a reference book and research tool that provides measures of a wide variety of work behaviours.

> **Now access Chapter 19 Web page and carry out the activities there and answer the further questions.**

Chapter 20
Structured Interviewing and Questionnaire Surveys

Content list

> ## By the end of this chapter you will understand:
>
> 1 The different forms and characteristics that interviews and questionnaire surveys can take.
> 2 Standard ways for asking questions and instrument design for questionnaires and interviews.
> 3 The relative advantages and disadvantages of group self-completion, face-to-face interviews, mailed, Internet and telephone surveys.
> 4 The importance of sampling, response rate, reliability and validity in surveying.
> 5 How to code and analyse responses for computer analysis.

Introduction

Interview and questionnaire surveys are the most commonly used descriptive methods in business research and data collection. The survey gathers data at a particular point in time, which can then be displayed by descriptive statistics and/or analysed appropriately by inferential statistical techniques to which you have been introduced in previous chapters. Surveys provide accurate and usable information if properly designed, valuable for making sensible and effective business decisions.

Major forms and characteristics of surveys

Descriptive and explanatory surveys

1 The **descriptive** survey seeks to estimate as precisely as possible the nature of existing conditions or the attributes of a population; for example, demographic composition, weekly spending on particular goods or services, levels of unemployment, its religious beliefs, voting intentions, its investment patterns, range and costs of drugs and medicines on prescriptions, etc.
2 The **explanatory** survey seeks to establish cause and effect relationships, but without experimental manipulation; for example, the effects of merit schemes on employee motivation, the effects of peer group behaviour, group norms and role modelling on taking days off sick, the effects on purchasing habits of increasing excise duty on cigarettes and petrol. Sometimes, of course, both descriptive and explanatory studies can be carried out in the same inquiry.

Surveys may vary in their levels of complexity from those which provide simple frequency counts of number of employees in different employment categories, to those which can involve correlational analysis, say between increasing interest rates and changes in household spending. For descriptive surveys, representative sampling of the population is crucial, since without representation estimates of population, statistics will be inaccurate, and cannot be generalized to the population. In explanatory studies, control is also crucial, for failure here enables potentially confounding variables to invalidate the findings. All the problems inherent in the obtaining of reliable and valid measures are applicable and are as important in surveys as in more controlled experimental methods.

> ***A survey.*** *A process of collecting information from a sample of people who have been selected to represent a defined population.*

The chief characteristics of the survey are:

(a) A sample of respondents from a defined population reply to a number of standard questions under comparable conditions.
(b) Administration can be by a face-to face interview, group self-completion, by mailing the respondent a form for self-completion, using internet or by telephone.
(c) Results of the properly selected sample survey can be generalized to the defined population.
(d) Use of standard questions enabling comparisons to be made between individuals and between strata or subsets of the sample.

Cross-sectional and longitudinal survey designs

There are two basic survey designs.

The cross-sectional approach

This method involves taking a cross-section of the population, selecting, for example, different age groups or ethnic groups, and measuring the value of one or more variables, such as motivation level, stress level, weekly spending patterns, etc. These data can then be used to calculate norms for each group. It is a point in time snapshot. Cross-sections of other age or ethnic groups can be taken at the same time and differences statistically assessed to index differences between one age group or ethnic group and another (ANOVA test). See Figure 20.1.

There are often difficulties in interpreting cross-sectional data. There may be changes from year to year in the variable being studied. For example, if one were interested in using a cross-sectional approach to examine the decline in ability to remember complex instructions on how to operate a new piece of equipment between the ages of 20 and 55, one might assess these skills in two samples of 100 at each of the two ages. It might then be found that the norms showed increases in memory ability for some types of information (e.g. verbal) but decrements in the memory ability for diagrammatic instructions. Moreover, the actual

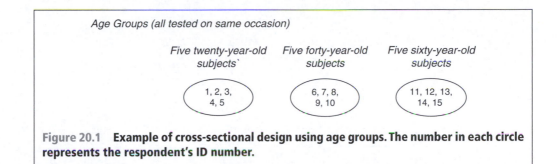

Figure 20.1   Example of cross-sectional design using age groups. The number in each circle represents the respondent's ID number.

sample of 20-year-olds might, if followed up after 35 years, turn out to be much better in all skills than the original 55-year-olds in the sample. The reason for this could be that environmental conditions relevant to the development of those memory skills had changed during this period, though there are other equally likely explanations.

> *A cross-sectional survey*. A survey conducted once at a particular time across a range of groups.

The longitudinal approach

The alternative approach for studying large samples of individuals is a *longitudinal study*, i.e. collecting observations and measurements through repeated contact with the same individuals over a period of years. 'Before-and-after' studies come into this category where there is an attempt to establish the effect of some event on the experimental group which has occurred between the two phases of the survey; for example, the effect of a television programme on attitudes to a particular product or government economic policy. (Repeated measures ANOVA or ANCOVA.) The before snapshot is the baseline.

   Although a much more valuable way of studying development than the cross-sectional method, because the same groups are traced over a number of years, rather than comparing different groups at the same time, the longitudinal approach is extremely time-consuming, costly, organizationally complex, difficult to maintain and slow in producing results. Studies become increasing difficult as the years pass, because people move house or emigrate, marry and change names, and changes in research personnel may introduce error into the data collection. There is also a common tendency for the sample to become biased towards those who are more cooperative in informing the investigators of change of address, and in addition, bias can occur because, for example, different social class groups may be affected by differential illness and death rates (see Fig. 20.2).

> *A longitudinal survey.* A survey repeated on a number of occasions on the same group(s).

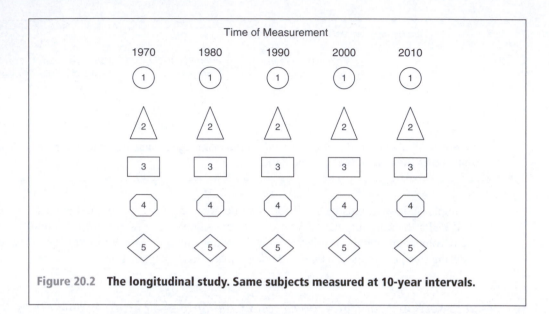

Figure 20.2 **The longitudinal study. Same subjects measured at 10-year intervals.**

The strength of the survey method would appear to be that:

(a) it is often the only way to obtain information about certain subject behaviours, personal information and work context issues;

(b) it is one of the few techniques available to provide information on individual characteristics, beliefs, behaviours and motives;

(c) it can be used on most human populations except young children;

(d) it is an efficient way of collecting data in large amounts at low cost in a short period of time; and

(e) structured surveys are amenable to statistical analysis, using t tests, correlation, ANOVA, chi square, etc.

Selecting the survey method

The selection of method is affected by the following considerations, among others:

(a) Nature of population; such as age, reading or writing skills, wide or localized geographical dispersal.

(b) Nature of information sought; for example, degree of complexity, degree of sensitivity, whether emotive, unimportant, boring, or politically dangerous.

(c) Length of questionnaire/interview.

(d) Financial and other resources; for example, time, and number of interviewers available.

The aim is to select an approach that will generate reliable and valid data from a high proportion of the sample within a reasonable time period at minimal cost. An interviewer-administered face-to-face survey is more accurate and obtains more returns than a postal self-completion survey and is essential where:

(a) the population is inexperienced in filling in forms, is only partially literate, or poorly motivated to respond;
(b) the information required is complicated or highly sensitive; and
(c) the schedule is mainly open-ended, requiring individualized phrasing of subsequent questions in response to the respondent's previous answers.

The least expensive method, self-administered group completion, is the obvious one to adopt if the opposite conditions listed to those above hold, especially if the population is geographically compact, e.g. university students in a large lecture theatre. Where the population is scattered, a self-completion mailed questionnaire or interview with scripted questions over the phone is used. By using random digit dialling, in which a list of phone numbers is generated by computer so that all numbers have equal probability of being selected, a random sample for telephoning is obtained. However, it is only a random sample of those listed in the telephone system. Internet surveys are also becoming more common but what the population you are tapping into is maybe unknown and problematic.

The advantage of the survey is that it can elicit information from a respondent in a few minutes, and with comparable information for a number of respondents, can go beyond description to looking for patterns in data. But the attempt to produce comparable information by standard questions can lead to the obscuring of subtle individual differences. Simplification of behaviour is the price paid to find patterns and regularities in behaviour by standard measures. Interview schedules and postal questionnaires should be tried out in 'pilot studies' to remove ambiguity, test the adequacy of the range of response categories, and trial instructions and administration. One of the most difficult issues is selecting and maintaining a sample size that will provide a desired level of accuracy at a particular confidence level, e.g. ±3% at the 95% level (if you need to refresh your memory of this reread the information on the Web page for Chapter 9).

Mailed and group self-completion surveys

Group self-completion

Group self-completion surveys are used where a large sample can be gathered together as in student classes and employee contexts. This mode is the easiest to manage as dropout is usually nil apart from those who are absent at the time. Cost and time factors are low and standardized context and instructions are ensured. Queries can be dealt with on the spot and several hundred survey completed forms are available in under an hour.

Mailed self-completion

Obtaining a high return on mailed self-completion questionnaires can be challenging. The sample chosen, no matter how representative, is rarely the sample that completes the survey.

When returns are low serious questions can be asked about the representativeness of the sample. Mail surveys tend to have the lowest return rate of all the survey methods. Some effective ways of increasing the rate of return are:

1   Providing stamped, addressed, return envelopes for respondents to use for returning the completed survey forms result in a higher return rate than providing nothing.
2   Follow-up cards or letters in which the investigator politely requests the respondent to cooperate, complete the questionnaire and return it, often stimulate those who have forgotten.
3   A suggested deadline can be helpful if used skilfully, but avoid creating the idea that if not returned by a certain date, it would be worthless to return the questionnaire. Use a return date as a guide.
4   Personally, addressed, signed, typed or written letters with official letterhead tend to increase returns.

A part example of a covering letter for a mailed survey form is presented below.

*'This is a scientific study being conducted by the Business Effectiveness Unit of the Ministry of Economic Entrepreneurial Enterprise. We wish to find out what you think about the subject of **Government provision of courses for would-be entrepreneurs and content for such courses**.*

Your viewpoint will assist in helping others succeed in developing entrepreneurial activities. We would be grateful if you would complete the questionnaire, fold it and place it in the attached postage paid (or stamped) envelope and return by (date) or "as soon as possible". Please answer the following questions honestly. Your responses will remain strictly confidential. Do not sign your name'.

Advantages of mailed questionnaires

1   *Cost.* Less expensive to administer than face-to-face interviews, particularly when responses from a large, dispersed population are desired. In addition, funds are not required for the training of interviewers.
2   Useful when the instructions and questions asked are simple and the *purpose of the survey can be explained clearly in print.*
3   *Each respondent receives the identical set of questions, phrased in exactly the same way.* The absence of an interviewer, or third party, contributes to the standardization of responses, as variations in voice inflections, word emphasis or the use of probes are eliminated. Better standardization, particularly through the use of a structured instrument, means higher reliability.
4   *Errors resulting from the recording of responses by interviewers are reduced.*
5   *The respondent is free to answer in their own time and at their own pace.*
6   *Anxiety and embarrassment, which may result from direct contact, are avoided.*
7   *The problem of the respondent being unavailable when the interviewer is available is overcome.*

8   When a questionnaire is designed for self-administration and mailed, it is *possible to include a larger number of subjects as well as subjects in more diverse locations* than is practical with an interview procedure.

9   A mailed questionnaire that can guarantee *confidentiality* may elicit more *truthful responses* than would be obtained with a personal interview.

10   The *personal appearance, mood or conduct of the interviewer* that may influence the results of an interview, *is not present* when a mail questionnaire is completed.

Disadvantages of a mailed questionnaire

1   *Difficulty of securing an adequate response.* Response rates tend to be much lower than when the group self-completion or the interview method is used. While certain strategies, including follow-up mailings and careful attention to questionnaire design, may result in a response rate as high as 80%, response rates to mail questionnaires seldom exceed 50% and rates between 15 and 30% are common if sound follow-up strategies are not used.

2   *Sampling problems.* Biased sampling likely exists as non-respondents may differ significantly from respondents. Usually, the investigator is unable to learn the reason for non-responses. There are statistical formula for compensating with non-response (Chapter 9 Web site).

3   *Possibility of misinterpretation of the questions by the respondents.* It is extremely difficult to formulate a series of questions whose meanings are crystal clear to every reader. Because of poor wording or differential meaning of terms, significantly different interpretations can be made by respondents. Ambiguous, incomplete or inaccurate information cannot be followed up and will lower reliability and validity. You have no control over how respondents interpret a question. Responses must be accepted as given.

4   The *method is unsuitable when probing is desirable.*

5   *There is no opportunity to acquire supplementary observational data.*

6   *Self-administered questionnaires are inappropriate for very young, illiterate or some disabled people.*

Interviewing

Conducting an interview

The interviewer's main job is to ask the questions in such a way as to obtain valid responses and to record the responses accurately and completely. The initial task is to create an atmosphere that will put the respondent at ease. After introducing themselves in a friendly way, the interviewer should briefly state the purpose of the interview, but should avoid giving too much information about the study which could bias the respondent's responses. The interviewer also has the responsibility of keeping the respondent's attention focused on the task and for keeping the interview moving along smoothly. This can best be done if the interviewer is thoroughly familiar with the questions and their sequence so that the questions can be asked in a conversational tone, without constantly pausing to find what question is coming next. The interviewer must refrain from expressing approval, surprise or shock at any of the respondent's answers.

If comparable data are to be obtained, it is important that the same questions be asked in the same order and with the same wording for all respondents. If the respondent starts to hedge, digress or give an irrelevant response, or if he or she has obviously misinterpreted the question, then the interviewer may probe by saying, *'Can you explain your answer a little further'* or *'Can you tell me a little more than that?'* Of course, the interviewer must be careful not to suggest or give hints about possible responses. A complete and accurate recording of the respondent's answers must be made. On the open-ended questions, the respondent's exact words must be recorded verbatim while they are responding. This can be facilitated by using a tape recorder with the subject's permission. Taping has the obvious advantage of recording the subject's responses verbatim, along with the added advantage of freeing the interviewer to participate in the dialogue rather than having to concentrate on note-taking. However, many people feel uncomfortable about having their answers taped and may become inhibited and excessively cautious about what they say.

Interviews can take place in a number of contexts. In household surveys people are selected usually by some random technique on the basis of where they live and interviewed at home. These can involve a lengthy interview, which may be conducted on a longitudinal basis with regular visits. Intercept surveys involve stopping people as they visit a site, such as a supermarket, bus station, in the main street, holiday resort, etc. These samples will be quota based usually and the interview will generally be short, to the point, and focused on one issue.

Advantages of the interview

1. *Flexibility.* One of the most important aspects of the interview is its flexibility. The interviewer has the opportunity to observe the subject and the total situation. Questions can be repeated or their meanings explained where they are not understood by the respondents. More complex questions can be asked. The interviewer can also probe for additional information when a response seems incomplete or not entirely relevant.

2. *Response rate.* More people are more willing to talk and react verbally than write responses to questions. A key benefit is therefore the high response rate, which makes the data more representative than data solicited through a mail questionnaire. Properly designed and executed interview surveys should yield response rates of at least 80–85%. As fewer participants are needed than for a mail survey, this method is particularly suited to studies in which the size of the representative sample is small.

3. *A face-to-face interaction assists in the establishment of rapport and a higher level of motivation* among respondents.

4. *A useful method when extensive data is required on a small number of complex topics.*

5. *Probing may be used to elicit more complete responses* and the presence of the interviewer generally reduces the number of 'don't know' and non-responses to questions as explanation and clarification are readily available.

6. *Observation of the respondent's non-verbal communication and environment are possible.* Such observations may provide added dimensions to data collection.

7   The *interviewer is able to control the sequence of the items* as the respondent cannot look ahead and anticipate trends in the enquiries.
8   *This approach is useful in obtaining responses from people who would find a written response impossible,* such as very young children, the elderly, illiterate and some disabled groups.
9   Individualized appreciation can be shown to the respondents.

Disadvantages of the interview

1   They are *more expensive and time-consuming* than questionnaires. Scheduling of interviews becomes a problem. Thus a smaller number of respondents may be interviewed due to time and financial considerations.
2   *Finding skilled and trained interviewers with appropriate interpersonal skills may be difficult.* High inter-rater reliability is difficult to achieve.
3   *Interviewer effects may bias result from interaction between the interviewer and respondent.* These include personal characteristics of the interviewer (such as age, gender, educational level, social status, ethnicity, language (first or second), authority (white coat effect), stranger effect, and experience at interviewing). Variations in the use of interview techniques, including tone of voice and the inconsistent use of probes, also reduce standardization.
4   *Respondent effects* also bias answers and include deference or acquiescence (informant agrees all the time): expectancy (informant answers the way they think the interviewer wants them to); errors of memory; self-insight; social desirability (desire to provide good socially approved answers). Validity and reliability are seriously affected by all these factors.
5   Respondents may feel that they are being put on the spot.
6   *Flexibility afforded by unstructured interviews may generate* coding difficulties later when attempts are made to categorize and evaluate responses.

Telephone interviews

Telephone surveys were very popular over the last decade, especially as computer controlled random digit dialling was possible to obtain random samples. However, the recent flood of selling over the telephone by often aggressive salespersons at inappropriate times has sullied the approach and few surveys are conducted by phone these days. Phone surveys can be based on business directories, professional associations lists, credit lists, etc. Because people at home or work have limited time to speak over the phone these surveys tended to be brief, simple and well focused on a very specific topic. It is a low cost method with high penetration as nearly all homes in developed countries have phones.

Disadvantages include a high degree of outright refusal to take part, a limitation to simple questions without many options, contact is not guaranteed as people are often out and many people are suspicious of unknown callers.

Table 20.1 summarizes the comparative merits of three approaches to surveying. A quick look reveals why the telephone interview became so prominent up to recently. They are

Table 20.1   **Methods of data collection compared**

Mailed questionnaire	Telephone interview	Personal interview
Assumes the most of the respondent	Can reach the unreachable	Assumes the least of the respondent – least demanding
Cheapest method of collecting data	More economical than personal interview	Most expensive method
Can reach widely distributed population	Speedy and efficient	Slowest method
Difficult to obtain adequate response rate	Response rate is generally high	Response rate is high
No interviewer bias/ no distribution bias	Interviewer's voice may be biasing	Interviewer's presence may be biasing
Difficult to maintain standardization	Interviewer maintains standardization	Interviewer maintains standardization
Respondent is not always known	Can control participation of other household members	Difficult to control the participation of other household members
No third party bias	Monitoring presents biasing	Monitoring can be biasing
Questionnaire should be short	Questionnaire can be longer than mail	Longer questionnaire justifies the cost
Unlimited answer choices	Limited answer choices	Unlimited answer choices
Appearance of questionnaire is important	Appearance of the questionnaire is not important	Appearance of the questionnaire is not important
Questionnaire must be simple	Questionnaire can be more complex than mail but easy enough for interviewers	Questionnaire can be more complex than telephone
Informant cannot be observed	Informant cannot be observed	Informant can be observed
Difficult to get information to open-ended questions	Interviewer edits open-ended responses	Easier to ask open-ended question-behavioural cues

relatively inexpensive, provide representative sampling, may be completed quickly and for non-sensitive issues provide valid data. But face-to face interviews are the method of choice when sensitive issues, in depth probing and clarification of responses in needed. The wide availability of mailing lists makes mail surveys, although least desirable on many counts, feasible when cost is an overriding factor and a dispersed special interest population is the target. In terms of cost and ease of administration, the group self-completion method is best if the topic is non-controversial and the sample is conveniently located.

Internet-based surveys

Internet-based surveys are becoming increasingly popular because they appear more economical in time and cost, and easier to conduct than surveys using more traditional methods. They also facilitate access to large populations and samples, world wide if necessary. You can specifically target your sample or population by sending an invitational email directing your chosen sample available from a list (e.g. professional association, university staff, etc.) to your website on which your survey lies. Large representative samples for specific professional or interest groups are possible if you place your survey on professional association or interest group sites (with permission of course).

Internet surveys are far preferable to mail or telephone surveys when a list of e-mail addresses for the target population is available, eliminating mail or phone invitations to potential respondents. A clear and compelling email message invites potential respondents to your website to take the survey.

Tips for turning potential respondents into actual respondents

1 Address messages to a single person when possible.
2 Always use the blind carbon copy (BCC) field in contacting an entire group. Never list more than one address in the 'TO' or 'CC' fields since all recipients will see the entire list.
3 Include a valid email address in the 'FROM' field, or recipients will consider your message 'spam'.
4 Provide the URL that will take people directly to your survey (if you are inviting them to your website).
5 Tell recipients how to contact you if they have a problem or concern.
6 Identify the source of purchased email address lists so recipients know whom to contact if they want to be removed from the list.
7 Ignore 'flame' or 'hate' messages received in response to your email invitation. A few in any group always take offence to something, and email makes it far too easy for these people to 'speak' before they think!
8 Ensure you have the right to use the email list of a professional group, company's customers, employees, etc.

However, if you seek a general population, you could simply place your survey on your website and wait. Surfers may find your website and complete the survey. You will rarely know what the characteristics are of this population who found your survey. Uninvited visitors to your website are haphazard, unintentional and provide only an opportunity sample.

Sample size requirements may be no problem but the only thing we can say about the sample with justification is that it is a population of persons who have access to the Internet, but what it represents in terms of age, ethnicity, employment groups, etc. is impossible to say. The sample is worldwide too and therefore language and cultural nuances may come into play, affecting how people interpret the items and respond. For example, questions on interest rates would not generate responses from Islamic respondents, and human rights issues would be ignored by respondents in China for fear of persecution. Respondents to Internet surveys tend to be younger, middle class and more affluent than the general population. There is a day of the week effect as some people only surf at weekends so you must leave your survey available for these as well as for different time zones. In other words, don't get too excited and cut off after the first 400 respondents on day one as there will certainly be some sort of bias.

Develop a questionnaire for the web

Questionnaire development for Web surveys differ dramatically from their traditional brethren. Web surveys permit a full range of question formats (single select, multiple select, sliding scale, and open-ended questions) and additionally, a drop down list format that enhances the look of your Web survey for questions with long lists of alternative answers. They also offer better support than their paper counterparts for skip patterns (the ability to skip automatically over entire blocks of questions based on previous answers), and can provide multi-lingual formats.

Do not distribute your survey as an attachment to an email. This might overstretch their mail box capacity, and it is difficult to return as it has to be printed off, completed and mailed back. If you are distributing your survey from a website, pay attention to the amount of time it takes to display the survey on a remote browser. Don't overdo graphics and embedded components as it adds to the time taken to download your survey and increases the probability that potential respondents will abandon your survey before it is fully displayed in their browser.

Encouraging completion

At the beginning of your Web survey write an enticing introduction that clearly states the purpose of your research. Because Web surveys are self-selecting (i.e. you have no control over who decides to participate), it is important that your introduction grabs the attention of those who you want as potential respondents and encourages their participation. It is easy for online survey participants to abandon a survey, so you must communicate up-front why they should help you with your survey. The introduction should also include instructions on how to complete the survey, an estimate of how much time it will take and a submit button at the end. Therefore keep your survey short, simple, and to the point. Finish with a place for participants to add comments and thank them for their assistance. If you plan to publish the results, include instructions on how and when participants can get a copy.

If your website has heavy traffic, place a hypertext link on your home page, through which visitors can reach your survey. Once you have sent out invitational emails, responses should come in fairly immediately. Surveys that rely on passive participation (clicking on

Table 20.2   **Some advantages and disadvantages of internet surveying**

Advantages	Disadvantages
Continuous collection of data as long as you want to run it	Potential for multiple submission from individuals
Specific sample from lists	General invitations can lead to biased samples
Economical	Technical issues can lead to loss of data, and responder frustration, e.g. network speeds
Highly motivated voluntary participants	Little control of experimental settings or sampling
Increased generalizability of findings (not just university students)	Considerable time and cost expenditure on designing, developing the survey and its layout, and maintaining website
Drop out decreased	Ethical issues such as informed consent, withdrawal buttons, and debriefing
Expense and time saved on entering data as already electronic record	Data storage issues
Cross cultural research facilitated	

web site links or responding to indirect advertising) generally take much longer. In either case, you need to decide how long to keep your survey active based on your target audience. If you are surveying a known group of people (e.g. customers, employees, etc.) you might need to send out email reminders to prompt some people to participate.

You can analyse results as soon as responses are received. Unlike traditional survey techniques, the online nature of Web surveys makes it possible to process results without incurring virtually any coding or data-entry costs because the data are captured electronically, but the costs for design and programming can be high.

Questionnaire and interview schedule construction

General suggestions

The construction of a new survey requires decisions on how information is to be gathered in terms of types of questions, and response format. The main consideration for the choice of response format is the data analysis method you wish to employ, namely, *open ended* where content analysis will be required and *closed* where a variety of parametric and non-parametric techniques are available. The appearance and arrangement of the survey form itself is also vital to a successful study. A well-planned and carefully constructed questionnaire will increase the response rate and also will greatly facilitate the coding and analysis of the collected data. The model questionnaire and interview survey schedule is designed in four parts:

1   Introduction.
2   Demographic questions.

3   Body of study with sensitive items near end.
4   Expression of thanks and contact address/details of researcher.

Many survey designers find it most suitable to place demographic questions concerned with the gender of the respondent, age, ethnic group, socio-economic status, qualifications and the like, on the first page following the initial polite request to complete the survey and the general instructions.

Sensitive questions come last as, if one of the early questions offends it would lead to refusal to complete the questionnaire, whereas the general demographic questions do not usually offend and lead the respondent well into the questionnaire, thereby making it more difficult to withdraw later.

Tips for constructing a mail questionnaire

Because the response rate to mail questionnaires is affected by the visual appearance of the questionnaire, particular attention should be paid to the following format suggestions:

1   Make the questionnaire as 'appealing to the eye' and easy to complete as possible.
2   Include brief but clear instructions. Construct questions so they do not require extensive instructions or examples. Print all instructions in bold type or italics.
3   Avoid constructing sections of the form to be answered only by a sub-set of respondents; such sections may lead respondents to believe the form is not appropriate for them or it may cause frustration and result in fewer completed forms.
4   If you have sections that consist of long checklists, skip a line after every third item to help the respondent place answers in the appropriate places.
5   Avoid the temptation to overcrowd the pages of your questionnaire with too many questions. Many people squeeze every possible question onto a page, which can cause respondents to mark answers in the wrong place. Leave plenty of 'white space'.
6   Arrange the questionnaire so that the place where respondents mark their answers is close to the question. This encourages fewer mistakes.
7   Avoid using the words *questionnaire or checklist* on the form itself. Some people may be prejudiced against these words after receiving many forms not designed with the care of yours.
8   Place the name and address of the person to whom the completed questionnaire is to be returned even if you have included a self-addressed return envelope.

Questionnaires used for mail surveys differ in many ways from those used for interviewing. For example, questions that ask people to rank 10 things by assigning each of them a number from 1 to 10 work better on mail surveys because the respondent can see all 10 at once. They do not work as well on an interview because the respondent sees no list and would have to remember all 10 items to be ranked, unless a separate sheet is provided with the list printed on it. Also, some questions that read well on a mail survey can be tongue-twisters for interviewers.

The physical appearance of mail surveys is more important than that of interview forms because the respondent sees the actual questionnaire. The survey needs to be set out clearly and unambiguously. Respondents need to know what is being asked of them. You need to take into account the amount of time you are asking people to spend on your survey.

Thinking up questions for a questionnaire is not a problem; coming up with the right questions is. Usually, a literature review, preliminary interviews with potential respondents, and discussions with experts provide a multitude of possible questionnaire items. The difficult task is selecting only those items that are really needed to accomplish the purpose of the study and for which the respondent can actually answer or be willing to answer. For example, a member of the household may not know what the household expenditure is per week or may feel it is too sensitive a question to answer.

The following are format considerations unique to interview schedules.

1   Print questions on one side of the page only because it is cumbersome for interviewers to turn to the reverse side during an interview.
2   Clearly distinguish between what the interviewer should read aloud and other instructions that are for the interviewer only. Use different fonts for this.
3   Skip questions should be clearly indicated. Skip questions are those not to be asked if respondents have made a particular answer to a previous question.
4   Arrange questions so that interviewers do not have to refer back to earlier parts.
5   Limit the number of response options so that the interviewee can remember them all.
6   Leave enough space on each page so that the interviewer can note any additional important information.

Types of questions

One broad division of the types of questions is the distinction between '*demographic*' questions and questions that focus on the topic. Demographic items ask for factual information such as gender, age, income, number of dependants, occupation, qualifications, smoker or non-smoker. The responses to these items can be evaluated against some objective truth. These demographic items are variables which can be used to form subgroups or IV's for the testing of difference hypotheses, where the DV is some measure from the topic items. For example, do different age groups produce significant differences in their overall beliefs that the current government's economic policies are causing inflation. Topic items are mainly of three types: open-ended items, closed items and scale items.

Format for open-ended questions

Open-ended items simply supply a frame of reference for respondents' answers, coupled with a minimum of restraint on their expression. There is a freewheeling quality with only enough direction given to stimulate a respondent to cover the required area of interest in depth while having freedom of expression. This usually ensures a richness and intensity of response. Open-ended items form the essential ingredient of unstructured interviewing and exploratory research. Open-ended items promote a feeling of contribution by the informant, but they take far more time for analysis and are difficult to code due to their idiosyncratic nature. A question like '*What do you think about the government's policy on the environment?*' can evoke a plethora of different answers. Open-ended questions should be used sparingly in self-completion surveys.

Examples

(a)   *What aspects of your work activities do you most enjoy?...............*
      Can you tell me why ?.......................
(b)   *Which subject in your B.Bus. degree do you believe has best prepared you for the position you have applied for?..................... Can you explain why?.................*

A particular kind of open-ended question is the funnel. This starts with a broad question or statement and then narrows down to more specific ones. An example would run like this:

(a)   *Many young people smoke these days. Is this so at your office?*
(b)   *Do any of your friends at work smoke?*
(c)   *Have you ever smoked?*

Open-ended questions are flexible. In interviews, they allow the interviewer:

• to probe so that they may go into more depth if they choose, or clear up any misunderstandings;
• to test the limits of the respondent's knowledge;
• encourage cooperation and help establish rapport; and
• make a truer assessment of what the respondent really believes.

Open-ended situations can also result in unexpected or unanticipated answers which may suggest hitherto un-thought of relationships or hypotheses. The major problem is coding or content analysing the responses, and specialized programmes like NVivo, Leximancer and NUDIST are required to undertake content and theme analysis.

Coding open-ended questions provides problems as a multitude of different responses can be given. An open-ended question might ask, '*What is your occupation?*'. First you could code every different occupation with a different number. This would work but provide a stupendous number of categories not amenable to analysis. A better approach would be to group occupations according to some dimension. It might be socio-economic status (SES) for example. So we might have three levels of SES: low, middle, high (and code 1, 2, and 3 respectively). Then when you come across 'truck driver' you decide to put this in 'Low' and give it a 1. A response of 'doctor' might be put into 'High' and be given a 3. You can see that this is very arbitrary and open to quite different results, depending upon who is doing the coding. So obviously you need to find standardized ways or unambiguous ways of doing the coding. A good option is to get a number of people to do the coding and see how well they agree (inter-rater or inter-coder reliability). If the coding system you have is clear and consistent you will get a high correlation and if it is poor you will get a low correlation.

> **Open-ended questions.** *Questions that permit the respondent to supply their individualized response.*

Format for closed questions

Using *closed questions*, a highly standardized survey provides pre-written response options for each question, which must be responded to in the same order, with the same wording and even the same voice tone if used in a structured interview to ensure each subject is responding to the same instrument. They are fast to administer, easy to score and code but they may omit important responses. For example: '*Do you check your email everyday?* ___ *Yes* ___*No*'. What about 'sometimes' or only on workdays, etc.

Closed items restrict the respondent to choose from two or more fixed alternatives. The most frequently used is the dichotomous item: *yes/no* or *agree/disagree*, for instance. Sometimes a third alternative such as '*Undecided*' or '*Don't know*' is also offered. The alternatives offered must be exhaustive, i.e. cover every possibility. You must be careful with the interpretation of the midpoint '*don't know*' option. Does it really mean a lack of knowledge or any of the following: unwilling to answer, have no opinion, indecision, or don't understand question. The label '*Undecided*', has a very different meaning from a mid-point labelled '*Neutral*' or '*don't know*'. Therefore, label the mid-point according to the 'exact' meaning the scale requires. However, a '*don't know*' response option can be useful. When surveys find that many people do not know about a given issue, that information alone is very valuable.

Here are some examples of closed items.

Example 1
Do you feel that contributions to a pension fund should be compulsory for everyone in full-time employment? Please tick box.

☐   *Yes*
☐   *No*
☐   *Don't know*

The categorical response mode is similar but simpler in that it offers respondents only two possibilities.

Example 2
   Paying for education increases motivation to study   *True*   *False*

   Or

   In the event of war, would you be prepared to give
   up your job and fight for your country?   *Yes*   *No*

Summing the numbers of responses to each option in examples 1 and 2 yields nominal measures, suitable for chi square.

A combination of closed and open questions can be included in the same question where the initial response will be to a closed set of alternatives but subsequent probes elicit the reasons for the choice. This is useful in face-to-face interviews. Other open-ended items might ask a supplementary question to a closed item, e.g. 'can you explain why you chose ....?' Closed items have the advantage of achieving greater reliability and being more easily coded, but can be superficial, annoy respondents who find none of the alternatives suitable and force responses that are inappropriate. These weaknesses can be overcome, however, if the items are written with care, mixed with open-ended ones, and used in conjunction with probes if part of an interview.

Closed questions. Questions that have a preset range of response options.

Format for scale questions

Scale questions are the ones that interest us most. These items ask for respondent's opinion, such as what you would do in a certain situation, or what you have done in the past, or how strongly you agree or disagree with a series of statements. They cannot be so readily gauged against objective truth or there is no right or wrong answer and they are usually combined into a total score.

Many scales use the Likert type rating technique or the semantic differential (Chapter 19). But you still have to decide how many anchor points to provide (as low as two – e.g. *'Yes/ No'* or *'True of me/Not True of me'* to five, ranging from *'strongly agree to strongly disagree'*, or seven, eight or nine points). You have to decide whether to measure frequency (*'How often in the past 3 months have you …?'*) or intensity (e.g. *'How strongly do you agree or disagree with the following statements?'*). When several items are used to measure the same variable or construct, we have a scale or index. For example, if we want to measure a person's sociability, there would be numerous items asking things about enjoying parties, entertaining people, telling jokes, etc. which can be added up to form a total score for sociability.

Another consideration when constructing scales is whether to include some reverse-worded items to combat some people's tendency to respond to the items in the same way. Some people tend to agree with statements that are put to them, so that if you have all the items worded positively a bias might develop. A few reverse worded items ensure that each person stops to think about what the item is actually asking for.

Example
How would you rate your current supervisor? (Circle number.)

1   Very poor
2   Less than adequate
3   Adequate
4   Good
5   Excellent
6   Have no supervisor

Ranking questions ask respondents to indicate the order of their preference among a number of options. Rankings should not involve more than five or six options because it becomes too difficult for respondents to make the comparisons. An example of a ranking item follows.

Example
Which ice creams do you find most tasty? Please rank the following ice creams, with 1 being the most tasty to 5 the least tasty.

Ranks

Delight
Extra
Creamy
Happyway
Golden Milk

Ranked data can be analyzed by adding up the rank of each response across the respondents, thus resulting in an overall rank order of alternatives. Rank orders for different groups can be compared by Spearman's correlation and non-parametric difference tests can assess differences in mean ranks for a brand between groups.

A checklist response requires that the respondent selects one of the presented alternatives. In that they do not represent points on a continuum, they are nominal categories.

Example
Which languages do you speak? (Tick as many as apply):
English
French
Spanish
Bahasa Malay
Mandarin
Thai
Korean
Japanese
Other (please specify)

This kind of response tends to yield less information than the other kinds considered.

The response options offered to respondents can affect their answers. Confusing options lead to unreliable results and, usually, low response rates. Ensure a response category is listed for every conceivable answer. Omitting an option forces people either to answer in a way that does not accurately reflect reality or not to answer at all.

Example

How many years have you worked for this company?

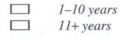 1–10 years

☐ 11+ years

In this case, people who have under 1 year's service are unable to answer the question.

Scales must be balanced around a mid-point in the response answer:

		1. Strongly agree
		2. Agree
1. Strongly agree ⟶	SHOULD BE ⟶	3. Neutral
2. Agree		4. Disagree
3. Disagree		5. Strongly disagree

Frequently some items are not relevant to all respondents. In these situations you should use filter questions to ensure the respondents take an appropriate route through the survey.

Example

Section F

Q 15. *Do you have any children?*

    (Circle ONE number)

Yes	*1*	*Go to Q 16*
No	*2*	*Go to Section G,*
		Page 18

Q 16. *How many children do you have?*

    (Circle ONE number)

One	*1*
Two	*2*
Three	*3*
Four	*4*
Five or more	*5*

Notice that the respondent who answers 'No' to Q 1 in Section F will move directly to Section G, omitting all questions which are not of relevance to them. As well as saving the respondent a lot of time, it will also enable you, at the time of the analysis, to identify those respondents who have children and those who haven't, and then perform analyses on this subset of the data.

Respondents generally find it easier to deal with vertical response options:

☐ Yes
☐ No

rather than horizontally:

☐ Yes   ☐ No

This also helps reduce errors that occur when people mark the blank after the intended response rather than before it.

Make certain the respondent knows exactly what information should be put in 'fill-in-the-blank' items.

Example

Incorrect	*What is your age?*	....
Correct	*What is your age?*	.... *years*
		.... *months*

How do I express a question?

1   The most effective questions are worded simply and specifically, so do not try to impress with 'big' words which may confuse respondents. Avoid jargon and stuffy bureaucratic words, e.g. 'downsizing'. Use language levels that are familiar and appropriate to the sample for whom the questions are intended.

2   Avoid writing 'double' questions that ask for more than one piece of information per question. This will make the question impossible to answer. Consider the following example: '*Do you like Crunch Bars and Delicious Melts?*' This question asks whether respondents like both. Suppose they like one but not the other? Again don't ask, '*What do you think of proposed changes to benefits and hours?*' In both examples, ask two questions instead.

3   Avoid words that can have a variety of interpretations. What do *value, liberal, conservative, population, environment, satisfactory, regularly, welfare, typical, community* or *green solutions* mean to different people. You will not know which meaning respondents had in mind when they answered; for example, '*Do you drink alcohol regularly?*' Here regularly could mean anything from '*with every meal*' to '*every Christmas at lunchtime*'. If a question asked, '*Do you believe the country's population should be less passive about maintaining the environment?*', it certainly would be an ambiguous question. Which part of the population – adults of working age, retirees as well, or all over, say, 12 years old? What does 'passive' mean here? What aspects of the environment? A simple question like '*how often do you visit the doctor*' can be ambiguous.

Are chiropractors and physios counted? What about community clinics when you only see the nurse?

In essence make sure your respondents understand the question posed. A fictitious international survey on world health posed the following question. '*Would you please give your personal opinion about how to alleviate the shortage of clean drinking water in country X*'. The survey was a huge failure. For example,

- In S.E. Asia and Africa they did not know what *clean drinking water* meant.
- In Europe they did not know what *shortage* meant.
- In China and the Middle East they did not know what *personal opinion* meant.
- In the USA they did not know where *country X* was.

This humorous example does make an important point.

4   Avoid using double negatives. Instead of asking questions like (a) below, ask questions directly and concisely as shown in (b):

(a)   *Don't you believe tertiary students should not pay tuition fees?*

☐   *Yes*

☐   *No*

(b)   *Do you believe tertiary students should pay tuition fees?*

☐   *Yes*

☐   *No*

5   Be careful if you use abbreviations or acronyms. Ensure respondents know what your abbreviations mean. Did you know what 'SPSS' meant before you started this course?

6   Avoid using, '*if yes, then...*' questions on mail surveys. Usually these questions can be asked in an alternative manner. Consider the following example:

Are you married?

☐   *Yes*

☐   *No*

If yes, is your wife employed?

☐   *Yes*

☐   *No*

The same information can be obtained by asking the better question:

Is your wife employed?

☐   *Yes*

☐   *No*

☐   *I'm not married*

7   Avoid loaded questions which may reflect your own biases. For example, '*what do you see as the main benefits of the government cutting income tax?*' This is only one side of the issue. You must also ask about the disadvantages too in the next question. Avoid emotional stands like '*should government raise the drinking age to 21 to reduce the carnage among teen drivers?*' It suggests the direction respondents are expected to answer. Bias resulting from loaded questions is a particularly serious problem in interviews because respondents find it more difficult to disagree with an interviewer than with a self-complete questionnaire.

8   Do not be overly enthusiastic about asking people to rank various things by 'assigning a number from 1 to 10 with 1 being the most important and 10 being the least important'. This type of question assumes people do not feel the same about two or more of the things ranked, and this is usually not true. These questions also assume people can rank a long list of items, and often they cannot.

9   With very controversial issues specify referent situations. For example, instead of '*do you approve of abortion?*' ask '*under what conditions do you approve of abortions?*' And provide an exhaustive range of options.

10 If you want general information from respondents, include an open-ended question at the end of the form. Although such questions are more difficult than objective questions to analyse and score, they can be a useful supplement. Furthermore, the free-answer questions provide quotable quotes, which may add sparkle and credibility to the final report.

11 An important factor often forgotten is the order in which questions are placed. A question about the logging of equatorial forests for timber might receive a different response if immediately preceded by an item eliciting agreement or otherwise to environmental protection than if the preceding question had been on the economic situation and unemployment. Similarly, a social survey might need to consider the order of questions when using one requesting the respondent to indicate their level of agreement with a pregnant woman obtaining an abortion on demand and a general one on women's rights. The general one can sensitize attitudes to the specific question immediately following.

12 In closed questions ensure all options are covered by including the option '*others, please specify*' but make sure you have no more than seven options. Any more and the list becomes unwieldy.

13 Use specific time frames. Instead of '*are you often late for work?*' ask '*how many times have you been late for work in the last four weeks?*'

14 In phone surveys, avoid words that sound alike but have different meanings like *profits* (*prophets*) or *fare* (*fair*).

15 Avoid leading questions. Don't ask '*do you think that more women should be promoted to executive positions?*' This will evoke an obvious '*yes*'.

16 Place positively worded and negatively worded items at random within a rating scale so that respondents do not mechanically answer them without much mental engagement.

Concluding the survey

Finally, a brief note at the very end of the questionnaire can:

(a)   ask respondents to check that no answer has been inadvertently missed out;
(b)   solicit an early return of the completed schedule;

(c)   thank respondents for their participation; and

(d)   offer to send a short abstract of the major findings when the analysis is completed.

Tips for writing survey questionnaire items

1   Questions must be unambiguous.
2   Vocabulary must be appropriate for sample.
3   Each question must have clear purpose.
4   Scales and instructions must be clear.
5   Avoid jargon.
6   Avoid double-barrelled questions.
7   Avoid loaded questions.
8   Avoid threatening questions.
9   Lay out questions and response areas so that there is plenty of white space.

Pretesting

Once a survey has journeyed through to a draft, a pretest or pilot of the questionnaire is essential to reveal confusing, badly written and other problematic questions. Pretesting involves administering the questionnaire to a sample as similar as possible to your target group. Pretesting also enables interviewers to practise and open-ended response coding schemes to be developed. Sometimes you may be able to adapt an existing questionnaire, but if it is being applied to a different population or culture you will also need to pretest due subtle language or context differences to check that it is meaningful. For example, 'How much do you pay for gas' on an American survey would have be altered to 'How much do you pay for petrol' on a UK survey.

A change in the wording of a question can bring wildly different answers. In one survey, male university students were asked if they thought it was important whether or not their marriage partner was a virgin when they were married: 80% said NO. Another sample was asked if it was acceptable for the person they would marry would have engaged in premarital sex: 80% said NO.

Why was there such a difference? It turned out that 'premarital sex' meant many partners to the sample men, while 'virgin' implied that the woman would have had premarital sex only with them. The latter was OK.

Anonymity and confidentiality

The issues of anonymity and confidentiality of respondents may affect your response rate. An anonymous study is one in which nobody can identify who provided data on completed questionnaires. For interviews, anonymity is usually impossible, and for mail surveys, anonymity is not practical because of the need to send follow-ups to non-respondents. It is usually possible to guarantee confidentiality to people in surveys and interviews, as data can be entered into the computer in a way that the ID code cannot be linked up to the original survey form, except by the project director. If you guarantee confidentiality, do not call it 'anonymity'.

It helps to use identifying numbers on questionnaires instead of names. In mail surveys, be sure to mention the fact that this number is being used and exactly why it is being used.

Validity and reliability

Some attention must be given to the validity question, i.e. whether the interview or questionnaire is really measuring what it is supposed to measure. The most obvious type of validity is content validity, which may be assessed by having some competent colleagues who are familiar with the purpose of the survey examine the items to judge whether their content is adequate for measuring what they are supposed to measure, or whether they are a representative sample of the behaviour domain under investigation.

Some studies have used direct observation of behaviour to assess concurrent or predictive criterion related validity of responses. After responses were obtained, observations were made to see whether the actual behaviour of the subjects agreed with their expressed attitudes, opinions, or other answers, such as making purchases of items they had indicated they would. Other data sources, such as third parties, may also be used as criteria.

Some variables that influence the validity of a questionnaire are as follows:

(a) How important is the topic to the respondent? We can assume more valid responses from individuals who are interested in and motivated about the survey topic and/or are knowledgeable about it.

(b) Does the questionnaire protect the respondent's anonymity? It is reasonable to assume that greater truthfulness will be obtained if the respondents could remain anonymous, especially when sensitive or personal questions are asked.

Having two different interviewers interview the same individuals to check on the consistency of the results is one procedure for assessing reliability of interviews. Internal consistency may be checked by building some redundancy into the instrument. That is, items on the same topic may be rephrased and repeated in the questionnaire or interview to enable consistency of response to be noted.

It is usually not possible to undertake a test-re-test reliability of a questionnaire or interview with the same individuals after a period of time or to administer two different forms of the questionnaire to the same individuals. Other factors influencing the reliability and validity of a subject's responses involve such issues as self-insight, acquiescence, social desirability. The interaction of interviewer and respondent such as gender, age, dress, race, social class and attractiveness of the interviewer are all known to influence the responses and rapport.

Response rate

Another important consideration is response rate. If you give out 300 surveys and only get 50 back, you have a poor response rate (16.7%). You then have the major problem of how representative of the population of interest is your 50 returned questionnaires? Are the characteristics of the 50 who returned the survey somehow different to the 250 who did not return the survey? We discussed the statistical method used to deal with this issue in Chapter 9 website.

You need to maximize response rate. The most important principle is to maximize the rewards or benefits for the person responding while minimizing the costs for them. So, issues like including stamped addressed envelopes for the return of the survey and making the survey short and interesting, with clear instructions, need to be considered. Also, the survey should not look formidable, with small print, many arrows and boxes, and verbose instructions. Many researchers include small tokens or payments for completing the survey.

Data preparation for computer analysis

To facilitate analysis of survey data by computer, the questionnaire/interview must be written and formatted so that responses can easily be coded. Refer back to Chapter 3 on how to set up a data file and insert variables into the variable view screen. As you know by now, you must decide whether to allocate a numerical coding (usually 1, 2, 3, ….n) to each respondent's response to or position on every variable. For example '*Yes/No*' responses to a question may be categorized as 1 and 2, while job level held may be represented by seven categories labelled 1 through to 7. We need therefore to allocate these numerical codings in advance and keep a record of them. The survey form should permit a 'scoring' of the responses in terms of these codes, which then have to be entered in the correct cell on the data view screen. Figure 20.3 is an example, but of course you can design your own to suit the content and response categories of any survey you design.

You should also make coding provision for omissions – those items the respondent has failed to answer refer to Chapter 6.

Suggestions to ease coding and input

1   It is not a good idea to ask respondents to place a mark over the number they select as this can obliterate the number which cannot be read clearly by whoever is entering the coding. It is far better to ask respondents or interviewers to tick in a box or circle the number. For example:

    Sex (Circle ONE number)

                                  Male   *1*

                                  Female   (2)

	Value labels			Variable	
I Ref No.		079		ID	079
II Sex	Male	X		Gender	①
	Female				2
III Age	20–24			Age	1
	25–29				2
	30–34	X			③
	35–39				4
	40+				5
IV Ethnic group	Malay			Ethnic	1
	Chinese	X			②
	Indian				3
V Educational level	Postgraduate			Education	1
	Graduate	X			②
	Diploma				3
	Certificate				4
	Completed secondary school				5
	Did not complete secondary school				6
VI Reasons for applying for business management course					
	Interest in management			Reason	1
	Desires promotion	X			②
	Rigor mortis setting in				3
	Girl friend has also applied				4
	No particular reason				5
etc.				*(This side only exists on your master coding sheet)*	

Figure 20.3   An example of simple coding for part of an interview record for respondent 79.

2 Asking a respondent to fill in numbers is often unavoidable; for example, if you need to know the number of years worked, money values, etc. However, if it is not necessary (depending on the data required), then avoid it because problems often arise with legibility of entries. Clear instructions may help overcome such problems. Ensure that where respondents or interviewers must fill in numbers or write words they are instructed to do this legibly – perhaps print the words.

3 'Open-ended' questions require extensive work on the part of the coder (often yourself!) before the interview data can be handed in for data entry. For open-ended questions (e.g. *'Why did you choose to invest with this particular bank rather than with XYX bank?'*), a coding frame has to be devised after the completion of the questionnaire. This is best done by taking a random sample of the questionnaires (10% or more, time permitting) and generating a frequency tally of the different responses as a preliminary to coding classification. Having devised the coding frame, the researcher can make a further check on its validity by using it to code a further sample of the questionnaires. It is vital to get coding frames right from the outset; extending them or making alterations at a later point in the study is both expensive and wearisome.

4 If possible, the answers should be on the right-hand side. This is not always feasible and other layouts are acceptable as long as the coding and column numbers are clear and in a logical order.

5 The first variable (column) on the data file should be the ID no., which is also placed on the questionnaire in case you have to return to it should a coding error be noted when running descriptives to check input accuracy (refer to Chapter 3).

6 Don't assume that each question on the survey only has one column on the data file. If the question contains a list of options where more than one can be chosen then there must be as many columns as there are options. For example, 'which of the following holiday destinations would interest you?', given seven destinations to which a dichotomous yes/no must be provided to each would require seven columns.

Content analysis

Content analysis is the systematic quantification of characteristics the investigator may be interested in, in terms of their frequency of occurrence within a selected context. The theme is the most useful unit of analysis. A theme is often a sentence, or statement. An open-ended question about the complaints of customers may be analysed for the types of complaint (a super-ordinate theme) which breaks down into subthemes – is it to do with slow checkout counters, lack of certain brands on the shelves, appliances breaking on initial use, food past used by date, rude staff, etc. exemplified by quoted examples.

Content analysis is laborious, time-consuming and expensive. It should be used when the nature of a research problem is such as to require it. It should not be used when an easier method is available and appropriate. The use of software for content analysis is recommended (e.g. NUD*IST; Leximancer; NVIVO).

This chapter has been a brief review of some aspects of survey research. You should now be able to determine which method would be most appropriate for any survey you would conduct and also possess a facility for writing unambiguous well-formatted questions of a variety of types. From many of the previous chapters you will have gained information and skills in coding, data input and appropriate statistical techniques. It is a big area and if you wish to know more and envisage that your future career in business will involve conducting surveys then you should read some of the texts listed below.

Tips in sequencing survey research

1   Define what exactly is to be investigated, i.e. clarify the research problem, research questions and hypotheses, and determine the population which is to be studied.
2   Decide on the collection methods and procedures that will be used to gather the data, taking into account characteristics of the population chosen, the complexity and sensitivity of topic of interest, and the resources (staff, money and time) available.
3   Sample from the population of interest to yield a representative sample selected by a random technique providing a sample of sufficient size to generate reliable and valid results (Chapter 9). The most common sampling deficiency in surveys is to use an opportunity sample that does not represent a known population. For example, surveys on the spread of AIDS have been found deficient as they tend to use limited groups, such as readers of certain magazines, or only those who are willing to discuss their sex lives. Similar situations arise in the ubiquitous radio talk programmes in which mainly the cynical, angry, intolerant and frustrated ring in to register their 'vote' on some issue.
4   Construct the data-gathering instrument using content, question types, and sequencing to suit the method of delivery.
5   Carry out a pretest (piloting) of the instrument and determine whether it will obtain the desired data, wording and format are appropriate, and that it is reliable. At this stage, training other interviewers is essential.
6   Conduct the survey, code of the data, process the data, interpret results, and report findings.

What you have learned in this chapter

You are now aware that interviews and questionnaire surveys are frequently used in the business field. The descriptive survey provides information while the explanatory survey seeks to establish cause and effect. Survey data is usually obtained by means of a questionnaire, a series of predetermined questions that can be either self-administered, administered by mail, placed on the Internet, or presented by interviewers in a face-to-face or telephonic context. When the questionnaire is to be administered by interview, it is often called an interview schedule.

The group self-completion and interview methods are more reliable and valid, producing more usable returns than a telephone, mailed or Internet survey. Web based and email surveys are well-suited for larger survey efforts and for some target populations that are difficult to reach by traditional survey methods, and can be conducted more quickly than mail or phone surveys. Longitudinal and cross-sectional surveys are undertaken to assess changes over time. The use of questionnaires in research is based on one basic underlying assumption: that the respondent will be both willing and able to give truthful answers.

Two kinds of items generally are used in the construction of schedules and questionnaires: closed highly structured items which involve scales, ranking, matching and listing, and open-ended items. The former are easy to score and code; the latter require detailed content analysis to derive classes of responses. Questions should be written clearly and concisely, with a layout for responses that enables the respondent to complete the form without difficulty. A pilot study will enable problems to be removed before the full survey. Reliability is difficult to assess as it is not usually possible to undertake a test retest procedure. Content, concurrent and predictive validity are more easily assessable. With computerized data analysis precoding the question items is essential.

Review questions and activities

Qu. 20.1
Discuss, in groups, the ways bias may be introduced into survey results when (a) interviewing and (b) using a mailed questionnaire.

Qu. 20.2
Discuss, in groups, the major advantages of using personal interviews over mailed interviews.

Qu. 20.3
Under what conditions might you wish to conduct a survey by telephone?

Qu. 20.4
In a survey to assess the adequacy of parking facilities at a shopping precinct a questionnaire was given to local motorists and included the following questions. (a) have you ever driven a car? (b) what is your income group? (c) where do you park? In groups, comment on these questions and formulate other questions which you believe should be in the questionnaire. Would a postal questionnaire within the postal code (zip code) of the supermarket be adequate for the parking survey above? Share your answers.

Qu. 20.5

A well-known Sunday newspaper contains a questionnaire seeking the opinions of its readers concerning an important question on whether shops should be open until midnight seven nights a week. In groups, consider objections would you make to this method of determining opinions of people in general? How might such opinions be best obtained? Share your responses.

Qu. 20.6

In groups, discuss the problems of Internet surveys. Consider ways of mitigating (removing or reducing) the problems you detect. Share your responses.

Qu. 20.7

What are the advantages and disadvantages of open-ended questions compared to closed questions?

Qu. 20.8

Discuss in groups what you perceive to be the main factors which would affect reliability and validity in (a) face-to-face interviews, and (b) a mail questionnaire.

Qu. 20.9

A researcher has received back 52% of questionnaires sent out to three companies. In groups, consider what methods you could suggest to contact non-responders to request they complete and return the questionnaire.

Qu. 20.10

A researcher has been requested by a national day care provider to survey a sample of parents who use their centres to determine their satisfaction/dissatisfaction with the provision of day care. The following questions are included:

1   How many children have you?
2   What are their ages?
3   How long have they attended these centre(s)?
4   Do you get a government rebate to help with the cost?
5   What do you like best about the centre(s) your children attend?
6   Which day care centre(s) do they attend?
7   What do you like least about the centre(s) they attend?
8   What contact have you had with their carers?
9   How much per week does it cost, less any government rebate?
    (a)   Do these questions constitute a structured interview, a semi-structured interview or an unstructured interview?
    (b)   Is the sequence arranged correctly?

(c) *Should the interview schedule be mailed out, conducted over the telephone in the early evening when both parents are at home, or face-face at the centre as parents pick up their children? In relation to this you may wish to determine what sampling strategy to adopt.*

(d) *Which questions may require probing by open-ended questions. Design some probing questions.*

Share your answers

Activity 20.1

Complete several surveys on the following sites to get more insight on how to set questions, layout, instructions and answer formats, etc.

www.survey.net

www.dssresearch.com/mainsite/surveys.htm

www.hermes.bus..umich.edu/cgi-gin/spsurvey/questi.pl

Additional reading

All these books extend the material of this chapter.

Fink, A. & Kosecoff, J. 1998. *How to Conduct Surveys*. London: Sage.

Peterson, R. 2000. *Constructing Effective Questionnaires*. Thousand Oaks, CA: Sage.

Sapsford, R. 1999. *Survey Research*. London: Sage.

Schonlau, M., Fricker, R.D. & Elliott, M.N. 2004. *Conducting Research Surveys via E-mail and the Web*. New York: Rand.

> **Now access the Chapter 20 Web page and try the questions, activities and SPSS activity**

Part 5
Reporting and Presenting Research

Chapter 21
Writing Up and Communicating Research

Interpreting research paper reports!!

'It has been known for some time ...' ('I couldn't be bothered to look up original references')

'While the results do not provide definite answers to the original question posed ...' ('The experiment did not work — but with deft glossing and massaging I might get a publication out of it')

'Two of the subsamples were selected for more in-depth analysis ...'('I ignored the others as they did not make any sense')

'Typical results are ...' ('I will focus on what supports my original hypothesis')

'More additional work is required for a complete understanding ... ...' ('I don't really understand the results')

'Thanks go to A. Kando for help with the design and analysis, and also to A.N. Other for valuable comments and discussion' ('A.Kando did the work and A.N. Other explained to me what it meant.')

(Sources unknown)

Content list

By the end of this chapter you will:

1   be aware of the sequence of a research report;
2   understand the essential contents and purpose of each part of a report;
3   be able to write a research report in a conventional and acceptable style;
4   understand how to prepare and deliver an effective oral presentation.

Introduction

Most of the chapters in this text have focused on designing a research study, developing the statistical skills necessary to code data into SPSS and analyse it, the ability to determine the correct statistical test to use, and finally to understand the output of these results. However, while you may have developed the ability to address these skills, you still need to be able to write up and present your findings concisely for others to understand as written and oral presentations. While your use of language and statistical concepts will be determined by the characteristics of the target audience and their ability to read and understand reports, the format for writing and presenting a research report generally follows a consistent sequence, as described in Table 21.1.

The sequence of a research report

This sequence is developed below and summarized in Table 21.1. Some of the issues mentioned may not be applicable to all research studies but the general principles will apply.

Title and authorship

The first item in any report is the front page that presents the title of the report, who wrote it and often the author's place of employment with an email contact. The title should be precise, as short as possible yet provide a potential reader with a clear idea of the topic of the research. Redundant phrases such as 'A Study of ......' should be omitted. For example instead of 'A Study Of The Relationships Between Supervisor Self Esteem And Supervisor

Table 21.1 Summary of the sequential constituent parts of a research report

Section	Role
Title and authorship	A short but informative title plus the names of those involved with place of employment.
Abstract	A brief summary of the research undertaken.
Introduction	A justification for the research to be undertaken, based usually on a review of the literature.
Method	A description of the design, sample, materials and procedures used.
Results	A presentation of the results with statistical analysis and implications for hypotheses.
Discussion and conclusion	A discussion of the results in the light of previous research introduced in the introduction, with suggestions for future research.
References	An alphabetical and chronological list of all references cited throughout the report.
Appendices	A collection of relevant supplementary information, e.g. scripted interview instructions, coded copy of questionnaire.

Competence Among Supervisors On Production Lines In The Automobile Manufacturing Industry In Britain', a more succinct form would be '*Production Line Supervisors' Self Esteem and Competence in the British Automobile Industry*'.

The abstract or executive summary

Although placed at the front of a research paper, the abstract is usually the last section to be written. It comprises a brief summary, between 100 and 150 words, of the study and provides readers an overview of the purpose, the sample, design and procedure, and the main findings – the highlights of the report in a nutshell. It should be able to stand on its own as a clear succinct summary. It is not an introduction to the report. You will remember from your literature searches that the number of studies that relate to an area of interest can be too numerous too read. So your abstract must enable readers to determine whether your study is worthy of reading in its entirety or relevant to their interests. Scan-reading abstracts is an excellent way to 'identify junk', but abstracts are often written with a bias towards highlighting the positive aspects of the research.

Introduction

There are three primary aims in writing an introduction. These include:

1 Stating the purpose of the study and identifying the area to be investigated.
2 Reviewing studies relevant to the topic.
3 Stating the hypothesis or hypotheses to be tested.

While the opening section of the introduction should introduce the reader to the general topic to be discussed, with a general and broad-based discussion of the topic, the focus of the introduction should be on developing a framework of past research on which to form the hypothesis of the current study (Chapter 5). A common mistake by inexperienced report writers is to assume that all 'related' research must be included in the introduction. An exhaustive review is in itself a monumental task and is more suited to a review article, textbook, or chapter in a textbook. Instead, a more limited literature review, focused on the specific area of interest, is more appropriate. An easy concept to understand this process is the flipped pyramid model (Fig. 21.1) whereby the introduction starts off with a broader introduction to the topic and research question, funnelling to the apex by narrowing the review of the literature to a particular reference of the topic to be studied, and ending at the apex with a clear statement of the hypothesis/es. Overall you are channelling down to answer the questions, 'Why was this particular research done?', and 'What was the specific focus of the study?'.

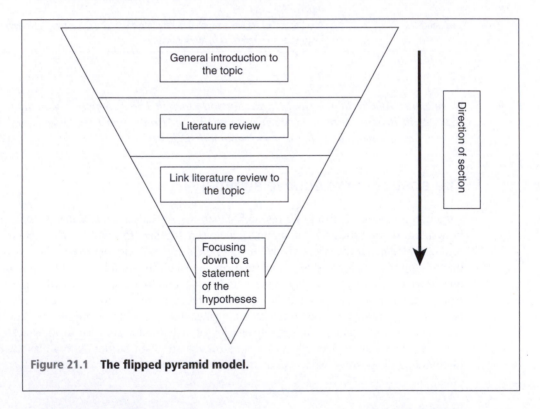

Figure 21.1   The flipped pyramid model.

The method section

The purpose of the method section is to inform readers of the details of the study undertaken, with information relating to the design and procedures, participants, sampling method and the materials used. It basically answers the question, 'How was the research done?'.

Design and procedure

This section should include a detailed step-by-step description of how the study was undertaken. This allows others to fully replicate the procedures undertaken in your study. The section should detail the experimental design undertaken, such as a 'between' or 'within subjects' or correlational design, with the treatment of each condition being described in full detail. For example, was a blind condition used for the experimental condition?

Participants

Information about the participants who are sampled is extremely important. Who are they – students, employees, adult consumers? What sort of sampling was used? How large were the samples? The sampling obviously affects the generalizability of the results. Often the differences in findings between studies can be attributed to the different characteristics of the samples drawn. As such, many characteristics of sample should be reported as possible. Relevant information should include:

- Age
- Gender
- Salary level
- Social economic status

- Highest level of education
- Nationality
- Married status
- Length of work experience

In addition, the sampling procedure should be identified and if subjects were assigned to different experimental conditions, then the process determining the allocation to groups should be described.

Materials

The details of all test instruments used should be stated. This includes the name and source of a test with information about its reliability and validity. If you have constructed a test specifically for this study, then evidence of reliability and validity is needed. Copies of test instruments, especially those that are self-developed, and other apparatus, which can include equipment such as CD ROM, videos, products, photographic stimuli, etc. should be appended to the completed report. As with the design/procedural section, provision of all test materials allows for full replication by others. The adequacy and appropriateness of the methods used for collecting data should be made clear.

Reporting results

The primary purpose of the results section is to present the data, and a standard way to structure the results section involves addressing each hypothesis in order. The normal format is for the results of the research, often statements about the outcomes of each test, to be reported factually and formally without detailed or penetrating analysis. Results should be presented both verbally and with figures and tables to aid understanding. The expounding of the meaning of the results should be left to the Discussion section.

There are conventions to adhere to when reporting statistics. Start by providing descriptive statistics, such as central tendency and standard deviation/variance indices. These can then be followed by the more complex inferential statistics, such as ANOVA or correlations. When reporting the results of the findings from inferential tests make sure to include the obtained value of the test statistic, degrees of freedom, and level of probability with the implications for the null and alternative hypotheses. In addition, there is an increasing trend for effect sizes to also be reported.

For example, an independent t-test revealed that males and females differ in their attitudes to single gender health clubs. It was hypothesized that males have positive attitudes to mixed health clubs, whilst females have negative attitudes to mixed health clubs and are positive towards uni-sex health clubs. The results for this one-tailed test were reported as shown in Figure 21.2.

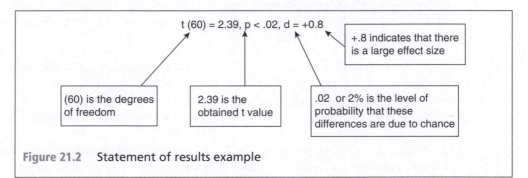

Figure 21.2   Statement of results example

The implications for the null hypothesis would be stated as: 'The null hypothesis is rejected and the alternative hypothesis that there is significant gender difference in mean attitude to uni-sex and mixed health clubs with males preferring mixed and females the uni-sex clubs'.

The use of tables and figures, which includes charts, graphs, pictures and diagrams, allows you to present large quantities of data in a concise and easy to follow form, enabling readers to process and absorb information much more quickly. Conventions for the use of tables and figures include:

- being numbered chronologically;
- a heading for tables;
- a caption for figures;
- being preceded by a written statement of the table's/figure's contents;
- clear labelling.

Discussion and conclusion

This section is to allow you the opportunity to provide a more detailed analysis of your results, to relate your findings to the previous research findings identified in your introduction, to indicate the relevance and implications of your findings, and to suggest directions for future research. Any failings or weaknesses to your methodology need to be identified and addressed here. You should not make any statements here which are not supported by the facts found. Some speculation is acceptable, but only if it is described as such and relates logically to the data or theoretical basis of the study.

The structure of the section can be thought as being opposite to that described in the introduction section. Remember that the flipped-pyramid model details starting the introduction with a broad general statement of the topic and then finishing with a specific statement of the hypothesis. In the conclusion, we place the pyramid right side up, and reverse the structure by starting with a restatement of the hypotheses and the main findings of this study, next indicating any limitations of the study, then relating these findings to previous research and theory, and finally detailing broad implications of this study, including implications for future research (Fig. 21.3).

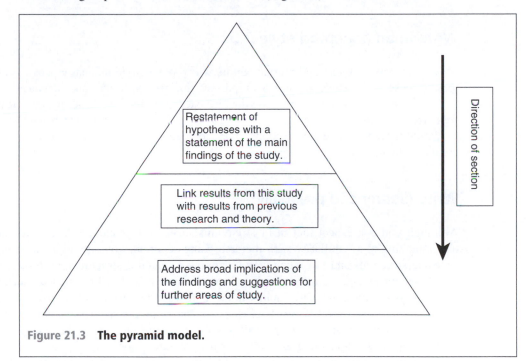

Figure 21.3   The pyramid model.

The discussion section usually includes a strong concluding paragraph that pulls all main conclusions and implications together.

Reference list

All references that are mentioned in your report need to be fully identified and listed. It is important to remember that a reference list differs markedly from a bibliography. The separation of citations into References (i.e. papers actually referred to in the text) and Bibliography (other material read to support the research but not directly cited or quoted) is acceptable. The process of citing and the standard format for referencing has already been discussed in Chapter 4.

Appendices

At the end of the report, an appendix is included to provide supplementary material, such as the questionnaires used, test material, raw data, etc. Each appendix should be labelled with a capital letter and a short heading to easily identify it.

Other important issues

Aside from the structure of the report, there are several other elements which should be borne in mind.

Write in an accepted style

Most university lecturers and journal editors will provide style manual guides to adhere to, and these will include guidelines on presentation issues, format and language usage. For instance, many require work to be double spaced, a minimum Arial or Times Roman font size of 12 point to allow for ease of reading, and with a large right-handed margin to allow for comments and corrections to be included. Arty fonts and unusual formatting are not welcome.

Write clearly and precisely

Although you can expect that in most circumstances your readers will have a general understanding and familiarity with the area being reported, you should avoid complex sentence structures and too much jargon. Complex sentence structures, with paragraph length sentences, are far too difficult for most to understand at first glance. Academic posturing is not unknown and results can be submerged in a welter of statistics comprehensible only to an expert. Overuse of statistics can cloud the real issues. However, it is reasonable to assume most of your readers will have some background knowledge of the area and of statistical procedures to follow what you have done.

Remember from your own experiences of what is was like when you were performing a literature search for your own paper; the more informative papers were those which were easy to read and understand, and rarely required a second or third look to understand the meaning of what has just been read.

Acknowledge the work of others

Never pass off others' work as your own or plagiarize. In Chapter 5 we presented procedures for citing the work of others within the body of your report, and how to list these within the confines of a reference list.

Avoid sexist language

It is increasingly common practice to rephrase sentences so that they do not imply gender implications. For example, replacing 'the bank teller completed *her* questionnaire', with 'the bank teller completed *the* questionnaire', prevents the development of unnecessary bias or prejudice. Exceptions may exist when undertaking a more detailed case analysis.

False accuracy

Do not use two or more decimal places for a small sample as it implies more accuracy than warranted. Do not hide reality behind percentages. If profit increased 50% this might only be from $100 to $200. Graphical material should have appropriate scales too so that a small increase is not magnified out of proportion.

In summary:

A good paper will be clearly and precisely written and readable, with a sound structure, presentation and a logical sequence. Overall it should have an appropriate intellectual level and provide evidence of at least some originality.

Checklist

Here is a checklist you may like to use to ensure you have covered the essentials in any report you write:

	Yes	Maybe	No
Have you been unbiased in presenting different perspectives?	☐	☐	☐
Does the literature review cite credible references?	☐	☐	☐
Does the research paper contain a literature review that summarizes current knowledge?	☐	☐	☐
Does the literature review provide a comprehensive and balanced overview?	☐	☐	☐
Is the hypothesis or research question clearly defined?	☐	☐	☐
Is the hypothesis or research question linked to the issues identified in the literature review?	☐	☐	☐
Is the research design employed, clearly identified?	☐	☐	☐
Are important characteristics of the participants provided?	☐	☐	☐
Does the procedural section provide enough detail to allow for a full replication?	☐	☐	☐
Is the test instrument clearly identified and appropriate to the research question?	☐	☐	☐
Have you presented your results in a structured and logical manner?	☐	☐	☐
Is the presentation and analysis of the data accurate?	☐	☐	☐
Does your discussion describe the limitations to the methodologies and results, as well as the strengths?	☐	☐	☐
Is the reference list cited in an appropriate way?	☐	☐	☐
Do you identify the source of funding for the study (if any)?	☐	☐	☐

Oral research presentations

Presenting your research findings orally can be a challenge as it means:

- reducing the breadth of content included in a written report; and
- focusing on particular aspects which are most interesting and appealing to a particular audience for a one-off presentation.

It is important to keep in mind that, unlike a written article, audience members lack the opportunity to reread material and so presentations must be simple and interesting enough to keep an audience attentive, yet remain informative. Two key principles that can aid your developing an effective presentation include the '*KISS*' and the '*Tell*' em' principles.

KISS (Keep It Simple Stupid) involves trying to keep your presentation simple and straight-forward to maintain audience interest. Steps include:

- shortening the amount of a written report to be included in the presentation;
- focusing on the main findings;
- clearly drawing conclusions from the findings;
- effective use of audio and visual aids;
- using cue cards rather than reading a written speech verbatim;
- effective verbal and non-verbal communication skills such as varying speed, tone and volume accompanied by eye contact round the room and effective gestures;
- where feasible include a few questions during or at the end to involve audience.

The '*tell*' em' principle reflects a repetitive structure by which to organize your presentation. This will usually involve firstly introducing the topic of discussion and presenting a brief synopsis of the key issues (tell them what you are going to say), followed by a thorough discussion of the main points, which in effect repeats the main message with detail, then concluding with a summary of what has been presented, leading again to the main point(s) (tell them what you said), i.e several repetitions in slightly different ways.

Preparing your presentation

- Consider your audience: Their level of background knowledge will influence the presentation style and the extent to which you go into detail.
- The time available will determine the scope your presentation can cover. It's important not to try and cram too much into too short a space of time.
- Outline a structure to your presentation that clearly identifies and explains your main points with adequate use of examples.
- Write notes using keywords and phrases rather than sentences. This will prevent you simply reading your notes.
- Practise your delivery.

- Try to anticipate the possible questions audience members may ask, in order that you can prepare your responses.
- Whilst practice is extremely important be careful not to come across as a recording.

Develop visual aids such as PowerPoint. It is important to use the following conventions when developing visual aids:

- Use an easy-to-read font style with a size of no less than 20 points.
- Don't use sentences if possible; try to limit contents of each slide to key words and phrases.
- Ensure slides are in order.
- Whilst slides should be colourful, be careful not to use too many distracting colours and sound effects which clash with essential material.
- Tables and figures should be simple to follow.

Delivering your presentation

- Greet your audience in a relaxed and confident manner.
- Ensure you have the attention of all the audience before starting.
- Use effective non-verbal communication by maintaining eye contact with all members of the audience, and facing the audience as you speak.
- Varying vocal tone and intonation to emphasize and elaborate key ideas will enhance audience engagement.
- Adhere to time restrictions. If you find yourself running out of time, pass over sections which are less important or ask for questions to be kept to the end of the presentation.
- As your presentation progresses it is important to relate the main ideas with your main hypothesis or problem.
- Identifying the appropriate time to distribute handouts is tricky as there are pros and cons to handing them out before, during or after your presentation. Handing them out beforehand is time-saving, but may result in the audience reading through them whilst you really want them to be fully listening to you. Handing out during the presentation can take time, but allows you to hand out supplementary material only when they are needed. Handing out materials after the presentation means that the audience does not have handouts during the presentation when they need it.
- In conclusion, summarize the main points at the end, relating them to your thesis statement, and suggest areas for further investigation and possible future trends.
- After your presentation, take time to consider how well your presentation went in order that you can learn from your experience. Feedback from audience members can aid your critical reflection.

In summary: Create an effective presentation by:

- sounding spontaneous, conversational, and enthusiastic;
- using body language effectively;
- using visual aids to enhance the message.

Characteristics of ethical research reporting

Good ethical research reports:

- involve judgement, carefully evaluating all major sources of information and providing a comprehensive overview of the aspects to an issue that may provide the in-depth background necessary in order that readers fully appreciate the area of investigation;
- identify possible limitations or contradictions, and do not ignore or deceive;
- detail the research design, particularly with reference to sampling, instruments, methods and justifies statistical techniques;
- attempt to determine what is supported by using appropriate hypothesis testing procedures. It is very easy to obtain findings that support your research hypothesis with a carefully selected sample that you know will only produce the results you want to find. For instance, if you wanted to demonstrate that employee satisfaction in a specific company was high, it would be possible to identify those sections of the company that are well-paid, have high productivity, and historically have been positive about their experiences of working within the company. Such a sample could be used unethically to justify satisfaction amongst the overall company population.
- make conclusions with an air of caution. Remember that research does not 'prove' anything, rather we can only provide support for our hypothesis within a degree of probability. Conclusions should avoid exaggerating claims, and identify possible weaknesses or uncertainties in design and findings.

What you have learned from this chapter

You have been shown the conventional sequential parts to a research report accompanied with detailed explanation. A checklist for determining whether your report is covering all the bases is provided. The essence of composing and delivering an effective oral report is offered. There is a final reminder that ethical issues also pervade the writing and presentation of a study.

Now access the Web page for this chapter and try the activities there.

Index

Page references followed by f indicate an illustrative figure; t indicates a table